W9-COY-069

Treat this book with care and respect.

*It should become part of your personal
and professional library. It will
serve you well at any number
of points during your
professional career.*

STRATEGY, POLICY, AND CENTRAL MANAGEMENT

Seventh Edition

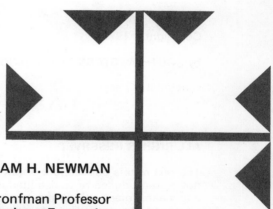

WILLIAM H. NEWMAN

Samuel Bronfman Professor
of Democratic Business Enterprise
Graduate School of Business
Columbia University

JAMES P. LOGAN

Professor of Management
College of Business and Public Administration
University of Arizona

Published by

SOUTH-WESTERN PUBLISHING CO.

G48

CINCINNATI   WEST CHICAGO, ILL.   DALLAS   PELHAM MANOR, N.Y.
PALO ALTO, CALIF.   BRIGHTON, ENGLAND

To the memory of

SAMUEL BRONFMAN

and his belief in

the creative capacity

of independent

business enterprise

PREFACE

Social reforms, material shortages, inflation, local wars, international politics, and new technology are all adding to the complexity of company management. Today the tasks of central management extend well beyond finding or creating new markets. Company managers must adjust to all sorts of changes to assure a sustained inflow of resources and a continuing outward flow of services.

Companies inevitably perform social as well as economic functions as they convert resources into services. And under today's pressures, executives charged with overall management must be alert to an increasing diversity of impacts that result from the strategy, policy, and management design they select.

This book confronts this highly dynamic environment in two ways: (1) It lays out a model or approach for executives—and students—to employ in tying their enterprise into the opportunities and challenges created. (2) It uses many of these active forces in the text and the cases to illustrate the application of the model to realistic, tough, demanding situations. These two distinctive features of the book make it relevant to a turbulent world. More specifically—

(1) To deal with the baffling array of influences and opportunities, managers need an approach—or model—to help them sort, interrelate, and evaluate. Such a model should suggest what to watch and how to put the pieces together into a meaningful analysis. At the same time, the model must be sufficiently simple, and easily related to concrete events, so that practicing managers can apply it to the situations they face.

The framework of this book is such a model. Students familiar with it will have a penetrating tool to analyze new businesses and to interpret threats and opportunities for companies they already know. Like any general model, the framework must be thoughtfully adapted to specific cases—dropping irrelevant points and expanding others. Nevertheless, successful use of this model in diverse industries attests to its general usefulness.

Very briefly, the model sets forth typical relationships between environment→company→strategy→policy→organization→execution, with feedback loops. Each Part in this book, while focusing on one of these facets, builds upon the other Parts.

(2) The new environment for business offers a stimulating array of challenges in formulating company strategy. Examples of these challenges are

introduced throughout this revision of *Strategy, Policy, and Central Management*. Readers will be particularly interested in:

New cases (21) that involve hospitals, retail stores, publishing, agriculture, education, professional service, and public utilities as well as large and small manufacturing firms. Forty percent of all cases in the book deal with relatively small, growing enterprises having fewer than one hundred employees.

The "resource-converter" viewpoint on social responsibility of private firms, introduced in Chapter 1.

The four-stage growth treatment of organization design, developed in Chapter 16.

Additional focus on the interaction between strategy, policy, and management design, especially in chapters on research and development, allocating capital, and a concluding discussion on the integrating role of central managers.

The three-tier arrangement of cases, so successful in previous editions, has been continued. This provides:

1. End-of-chapter cases.
2. Integrating cases for groups of chapters.
3. Comprehensive cases covering the entire range of the book.

This scheme gives instructors wide flexibility in blending the cases and the text to fit their particular needs.

Acknowledgements cover a wide span. The model is a lineal descendant of a diagnostic approach to company-wide problems used by James O. McKinsey, founder of the preeminent consulting firm. The cases come directly or indirectly from a large number of business executives who are willing to share their knowledge and experience with tomorrow's prospective leaders. And many educators have contributed ideas both to the development of the model and to cases. No comprehensive book such as this is possible without the help of numerous other people.

We want specifically to acknowledge permission from the Executive Programs of the Graduate School of Business, Columbia University, for permission to reproduce cases first written for their use. Professors J. E. Schnee, of Rutgers University, and R. S. Alexander and E. K. Warren, of Columbia University, also contributed cases. The actual drawing together of the manuscript and making it intelligible to the publisher was ably performed by Camilla Koch. For all this assistance we are most grateful.

William H. Newman
James P. Logan

CONTENTS

LIST OF CASES / END OF CHAPTER INTEGRATING COMPREHENSIVE

Firm Name	Nature of Case	Page

SOCIAL RESPONSIBILITY AND CENTRAL MANAGEMENT

Vital role of enterprises

Western nations, and especially the United States, rely on thousands of independent enterprises to convert resources into desired goods and services. Moreover, these enterprises provide most of the initiative for improving and adapting this flow of goods and services to new wants. Consequently, successful management of these enterprises is vital to many people, and in fact to the survival of our pluralistic society.

This book examines the way a single enterprise can select and pursue its particular role in the complex overall process of converting resources. We will be concerned with devising favorable relationships between the enterprise and its many outside contributors, and also with designing an internal system for effectively utilizing the resources received.

The external relationships and the internal system are interdependent because the terms necessary to attract resources place restraints on the internal system, and the output of the internal system restrains the rewards that the enterprise can offer to outsiders for their cooperation.

This interdependence requires the managers of an enterprise to think in terms of a total, interacting set of forces. The central managers[1] of each enterprise must fit a whole array of activities together into an integrated whole. It is this need for both external and internal integration that makes central management unique and challenging.

Although we shall deal mostly with private, profit-seeking companies, the same approach and many of the same factors apply to not-for-profit ventures. The key tasks of central managers in both types of enterprises are alike. Management problems are affected more by the kind of services provided and by the size of operations—as we shall frequently note throughout the

---

[1] Central managers (or central management) include all the senior executives who concentrate on running the enterprise as an integrated whole. We prefer the term "central management" rather than "top management" because it is more descriptive and also because it carries less connotation of social status and use of power.

book—than by the form of ownership. The critical task for each firm is to find a unique niche where it can render distinctive service.

Conceptual framework

To set the stage, this first chapter explains three related viewpoints that we shall use throughout the book:

1. Socially responsible action for a business enterprise, we shall argue, is that course which enables the enterprise to function as a dynamic resource converter on a continuing basis.
2. Central management is the group within each enterprise that designs a particular course which enables the firm to perform in such a socially responsible fashion.
3. To assist central management to fulfill this role, an analytical framework is presented. This framework—which also forms the structure of our book—aids in sorting numerous influences and issues into a related sequence of thought and in building a coherent view of total company activities. In other words, the framework assists central management to act in a socially responsible manner.

Each of these viewpoints needs elaboration because their application is much more complex than this simple, abstract statement suggests.

ACTING IN A SOCIALLY RESPONSIBLE MANNER

A business firm, like any other social institution, can endure only if it continues to contribute to the needs of society. And in our current topsy-turvy world all facets of "the establishment" are being challenged. It is important, then, that central managers understand the mission of the enterprise they direct.

The concept of social responsibility is far from clear. Some idealists would like to include every reform that is socially desirable. But a business executive has neither the competence nor the means to undertake improvements in prisons, churches, classrooms, and other areas remote from his normal activity. So, to give practical meaning to the idea, we need an approach to social responsibility that relates to actions and outcomes directly affected by executive decisions.

A useful approach is to think of a manager as a *resource converter*. From the viewpoint of society, an enterprise justifies its existence by converting resources into desired outputs. (a) Resource inputs of labor, materials, ideas, government support, capital, and the like are converted by a firm into (b) outputs of goods, services, employment, stimulating experiences, markets, and other conditions desired by those who provide the inputs. The job of central managers is to design and maintain a converting mechanism that will generate continuing flows of these inputs and outputs.

An auto garage, for instance, converts labor, parts, machinery, and capital into auto repair services, jobs, rent, etc. Likewise, a poultry farmer converts chicks, feed, labor, equipment, and other resources into outputs of eggs, meat, jobs, a market for grain, and a profit on capital. Civilized society depends on a continuing flow of such conversions. And when we talk of the social responsibility of businessmen, we are mainly concerned about the effectiveness and the side effects of resource conversions.

This concept of central managers dealing primarily with resource conversion puts the emphasis on constructive action. Three basic elements are involved: (1) building continuing exchange flows with resource suppliers, (2) designing an internal conversion technology, and (3) integrating and balancing the external and internal flows.

Building continuing exchange flows with resource suppliers

The relationship with each resource supplier always involves a two-way exchange. The diagram below shows these flows for five typical outside groups. For a specific company there will be a wider variety of subgroups, but the underlying concept is the same. Each group of contributors provides a needed resource and receives in exchange part of the output flow of the enterprise.

Much more than money is involved. Typically, an array of conditions provides the basis for continuing cooperation. Employees, for instance, are

ENTERPRISE = RESOURCE CONVERTER

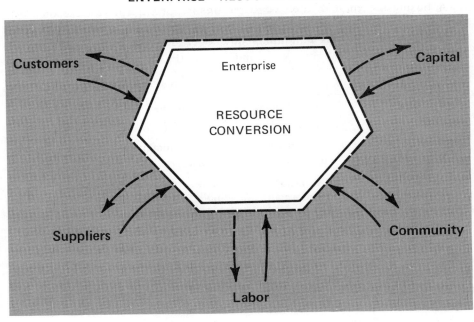

Enterprise

RESOURCE
CONVERSION

Customers

Capital

Suppliers

Community

Labor

→ Resource inputs

←--- Need satisfaction outputs

concerned about meaningful work, stability of employment, reasonable supervision, future opportunities, and a whole array of fringe benefits in addition to their paychecks. Suppliers of materials want a continuing market, sure and prompt payment, convenient delivery times, quality standards suited to their facilities, minimum returns, and the like. Investors are concerned about uncertainty of repayment, security, negotiability of their claims, veto of major changes, and perhaps some share in the management. For each resource contributor, mutual agreement about the conditions under which the exchange will continue is subject to evolution and periodic renegotiation.

Because a steady flow of resources is necessary, wise central managers will:

1. *Predict changes* in conditions under which each resource group will be willing and able to continue its cooperation.
2. Conceive and promote *revised exchange* of inputs and outputs that will (1) be attractive to the resource group and (2) be viable for the enterprise.
3. Start discussions of changes *early* to allow time for psychological as well as technical adjustments.
4. Assist and work with *other agencies* concerned with the change.

Central managers devote a substantial part of their efforts to negotiating—or guiding their subordinates in negotiating—these agreements covering the bases of cooperation. It is a never-ending process because in our dynamic world the needs of resource suppliers shift, their power to insist on fulfilling their needs changes, and the value of their contributions to the enterprise varies. In fact, most of the widely discussed "social responsibility" issues deal with some modification of previous conditions of cooperation, such as:

Input Group	Reason Prompting a Change
Labor	"Equal opportunity" for women and minorities.
Investors	Inflation protection; public disclosure of information.
Community	Environmental protection; uninterrupted supply of energy.
Suppliers of materials	Predictable, long-run markets.
Customers	"Consumerism" pressures for quality guarantees, informative labeling.

The real core of social responsibility of a business executive is the maintenance of resource flows on mutually acceptable terms. And this is a very difficult assignment in terms of rapidly changing values and expectations—as the succession of crude oil crises illustrates. But note that social responsibility, at least in our view, is not something new, tacked onto an executive's job. Rather, it is reflected in the recognition of shifting social needs and the approach an executive takes in adapting to them. Thus, when we examine adjustments to environmental changes, in Parts 1 and 2, we shall repeatedly deal with socially responsible action.

Designing an internal conversion technology

Each enterprise, large or small, must maintain a balance between the outputs it generates and the satisfaction it has agreed to provide its suppliers of resources. For instance, promises of stable employment must be compatible with protection promised to suppliers of capital. Such ability to make ends meet depends, partly, on the skill of executives in devising a *conversion technology* suited to their particular company. The way the resources are converted strongly affects the outputs available. So, in addition to negotiating agreements assuring the continuing availability of resources, central managers must design internal systems to effectively utilize the resources.

Every enterprise has its technology for converting resources into outputs. For example, a school has its teaching technology, an insurance company has its technology for policy risks, and a beauty shop has its technology for shaping unruly hair.

This internal conversion technology involves much more than mechanical efficiency. The desired outputs, as we have already noted, include interesting jobs, low capital risks, minimum pollution of the environment, improved job opportunities for women and minorities, and a host of other features. Consequently, devising a good internal conversion technology is a very complex task.[2] This selection of an internal conversion technology is one of the key elements in each company's strategy—as will be illustrated in Chapter 4.

Integrating and balancing the external and internal flows

Important as attracting resources and designing conversion technologies may be, it is the *combination* of (a) responding to new "needs" of resource contributors and (b) restricting total responses to what total output permits that poses the final challenge to central management. Socially responsible executives must be sufficiently responsive to the ever-changing desires of resource contributors to maintain a continuing flow of needed resources, and at the same time they must maintain the life of their enterprise by generating the right quantity and mix of outputs to fulfill commitments. If they do not, some key resource will be withdrawn and the enterprise will collapse.

---

[2] In abstract symbols, the technology should meet the following conditions:
With each resource contributor designated by subscripts $1, i, e, s, c, \ldots n$ and
S = satisfactions required by a resource contributor
C = contributions by a resource contributor
CT = conversion technology
O = total output of satisfactions
then:

$$O => (S_1 + S_i + S_e + S_s + S_c \ldots . S_n)$$
$$O = f\, CT\, (C_1 + C_i + C_e + C_s + C_c \ldots . C_n)$$

And as viewed by each resource contributor:
$$S_x => C_x$$

Throughout this book we shall be exploring ways in which companies can effectively cope with a dynamic environment—partly by adjusting the exchanges of inputs and outputs with resource groups, and partly by reshaping their conversion technology to generate desired outputs. A recurring theme will be anticipating pressures for change. By adjusting promptly to new conditions, a company usually increases its "output" and thereby makes a greater social contribution.

Considering a company as a resource converter uses a broad social viewpoint. We suggest that this is a better way to conceive of "the purpose of a company" than the more common cliche "to make a profit." Every successful resource converter must indeed make a profit in order to continue to attract capital. But this is a narrow oversimplification. To survive, a company must also provide attractive employment, be a good customer, earn continuing support of governments and the community, and serve customers well. The task for central management is to find a way to do all these things simultaneously while keeping abreast of changes in each field.

An approach to this complex task is outlined at the close of this chapter and is then elaborated throughout the book.

THE ROLE OF CENTRAL MANAGEMENT

Central management viewpoint

Central management is concerned with the total enterprise—the "whole business." As already noted, an array of interactions with external groups must be negotiated, and internal systems that utilize available resources to best advantage must be designed. When dealing with such matters, central management takes its own unique perspective. Other executives will be confronted with the same problems, but with a more specialized viewpoint.

Central managers give particular attention to interdependence. Commitments to customers must be reconciled with vacation schedules for employees; automated production must not generate air pollution; high-risk research and price competition may cause an unbearable cash squeeze—these examples only suggest the many *interrelationships* between different aspects of a company's operations. Somehow, someone must develop an *integrated* course of action.

Specialized attention to segments of a firm's activities is also necessary, of course. With the knowledge explosion, specialists are essential. But as specialists deal with ever-narrower scopes, the task of integration becomes more difficult and more vital. A major distinctive characteristic of the central management viewpoint is this relating of parts to the whole, integrating them into a *balanced, workable* plan.

A second distinctive concern of central management is setting *priorities* for the enterprise. A robust firm in our volatile environment has many different options, yet only a few can be pursued. People in marketing, finance, research, and other functional fields naturally differ in their recommendation of the best path to follow. Also, some persons are more sensitive to social needs than others, and eagerness to take risks will vary. So, to achieve concerted, unified action, one or two objectives must be singled out and plans for achieving these goals must be specified. This process clarifies the *mission* to be sought. Optimum results are obtained only when such guidance is clearly accepted throughout the organization.

Central management, then, focuses on missions and priorities on the one hand, and on interrelationships, functional integration, and a balanced plan of action on the other.

But being aware of central management's point of view still leaves us with a practical question: How can we (and central managers) proceed to "analyze" such intricately involved situations?

Need for analytical framework

Even the preceding terse description indicates that the task of central management is complex. And, as with any complex situation, a tested approach that divides the complicated mass into simpler elements can be very helpful. The approach outlined in this book is basically a framework for thinking about central management issues. It expedites analysis, and it assists in forming a synthesis of action to be taken.

Of course, any single approach must be adapted and amplified to fit the peculiarities of a specific company. In a small importing firm, for instance, organization may be relatively unimportant, whereas political outlook is crucial. On the other hand, the senior executives in a young electronics company may be predominantly concerned about technology and additional sources of capital.

Most useful is an approach that draws attention to a limited (comprehensible) number of basic issues in a systematic arrangement and that at the same time is reasonably complete in the potential opportunities for improvement it flags or suggests. Such a way of thinking about central management problems is more important than an exhaustive listing of all possible difficulties.

FUTURE-ORIENTED APPROACH

To maintain a forward-looking view of the central management job, the following approach is very useful:

1. Design company *strategy* on the basis of continuous matching of (a) anticipated opportunities and problems in the industry with (b) distinctive company strengths—and limitations.
2. Amplify and clarify this strategy in *policy*, which serves as a more specific guide to executives in the various functional divisions of the company.
3. Set up an *organization* to carry out the strategy and policy. This involves making clear who does what, and also developing key personnel who can push forward in the direction singled out in the strategy.
4. Guide the *execution* of the strategy and policy through the organization. This calls for programming, activating, and controlling the operations.

Since this division of tasks of central management will be used throughout the book, the nature of each section should be recognized from the start. So let us take a closer look at what is involved.

Analyzing the outlook for the company

Many factors impinge on the future development of any enterprise. Changes in population—its age, location, occupation—affect the kinds of services people want; their income limits what they can actually buy. Government is a big customer, but its purchases shift from spacecraft to housing to wheat for foreign relief. New ways to control insect pests may obsolete chemical plants; new social mores may obsolete college dormitories. Inflation distorts cost structures; international travel upsets foreign exchange rates; war in the Middle East creates new shortages of petroleum supply—this list of opportunities and problems could go on and on.

A practical way to bring some kind of order out of this array of environmental changes is to concentrate on an industry. This industry may be one the company is already in or one that it is thinking about entering. The aim of these industry analyses is to predict growth, profitability, and especially the key factors for future success.

Turning to the specific company, its strengths and limitations relative to its competitors should be carefully assessed. Then, by matching the company strengths with key factors for success in the industry, the outlook for the company can be predicted. This sequence of analysis is elaborated in Chapters 2 and 3.

Of course, the company need not stand still. It can take steps to alter its strengths, and it may by its actions modify the services or the prices of the entire industry. Similarly, an industry occasionally makes a dent on the environment. For instance, business representatives participate in debates on national priorities and help shape guidelines for protection of our natural environment. On balance, however, the company must adapt to its environment. Central management should, therefore, continuously monitor those factors that are likely to aid or complicate its development.

Designing company strategy

Armed with the forecast of the world in which the company will operate, central management shifts to active, positive thinking: "What are we going to do about it?" "What should be the mission of our unique enterprise, and what steps do we have to take to fulfill that goal?"

Picking the right target obviously is crucial. It is also difficult. To be most useful, this master strategy should (a) identify the particular services—that is, the product-market scope—which the company will promote; (b) select the basic resource conversion technology by which these services will be created—a technology that hopefully will give the company some relative advantage as a supplier; (c) with this concept of its economic and social mission, determine the major steps necessary to move the company from its present course to the desired one; and finally, (d) establish the criteria and the standards that will be used to measure achievement. No strategy is complete without all four of these dimensions being clarified.

A critical judgment in designing strategy is what to accept as unchangeable. Every company possesses (or can attract) only limited resources, and it has to be careful that the goals it sets are doable. In addition to sensing a future opportunity, central management must realistically assess the cost of grasping the opportunity in terms of people, outside help, money, and other resources. It must then decide whether "that is something we can do." This issue, along with other aspects of strategy formulation, is explored in Chapter 4.

Establishing policy

Strategy concentrates on basic directions, major thrusts, and overriding priorities. The full implication of the strategy, however, is clarified by thinking through the more detailed policy that guides execution of the strategy. Central management must actively participate in shaping policy (a) partly because working through the policy implications is an excellent way to check the practicality of a basic concept and (b) especially to make sure that the intent of strategy is correctly interpreted into the work of the various departments of the company.

Almost all companies need policy guidance on product lines, customers, pricing, and sales promotion. Likewise, the implication of strategy on research and development, production, and procurement should be expressed in policy. In the personnel area, policy on selection, development, compensation, and industrial relations helps build the desired manpower resources; and financial policy regarding allocation and sources of capital shape money resources. Each of these fields is examined in Part 2. A significant role of policy is to indicate the direction and degree of emphasis these and other sensitive fields should receive in order to effectively project company strategy.

Most attention in this book is directed toward change—adapting to new opportunities and pressures. Nevertheless, during the time any given strategy is in effect, consistent integrated action is highly important. Policy is a major tool of central management for securing such consistent behavior. Policy permeates the numerous daily activities of a firm and helps establish a normal, predictable pattern of behavior.

Building an organization

Strategy and policy are carried out by an organization. Unless this organization is well designed for its tasks, the plans, however sound, may lead to mediocre results. In fact, if the strategy relies on, say, pioneering in a new field, an ineffective organization that failed in such leadership could bring disaster.

The way in which activities are combined together into sections and departments will affect the choice of problems to receive first attention, the speed of coordination, and the cost of performing the service. Decentralization is well suited to a strategy stressing local service, but it encounters difficulty with computerized production scheduling. A strategic decision to expand internationally alters the optimum power and location of staff units. Product diversification usually modifies the range of decisions that can be made wisely in the senior corporate office. As these examples indicate, central management must appraise the company organization in terms of where tasks critical to the success of its strategy can be performed most effectively.

Also vital are executives with qualities and experience that fit the organization design. These and related organization issues are examined in Part 3.

TASKS OF CENTRAL MANAGEMENT

Guiding execution

With strategy, policy, and organization decided, the stage is set. Actual achievement, however, awaits the action. Central management necessarily relies heavily on junior executives for immediate supervision of operations. But central management can never fully divest itself of leadership in the execution phase of purposeful endeavor. As explained in Part 4, this phase includes specific programming of nonrepetitive work, communicating and motivating, and exercising control over the rate and the quality of performance.

Substantial amounts of time are necessary for this make-happen effort. Many people, inside the company and out, have to be contacted personally. And, unexpected difficulties inevitably call for on-the-spot adjustments. But during the process the executives are accumulating both information and a subjective feel for the actual performance of company services that are immensely valuable in planning the following cycles of activity.

Interaction and evolution

The chart at the right depicts the broad division of central management tasks that we have briefly described

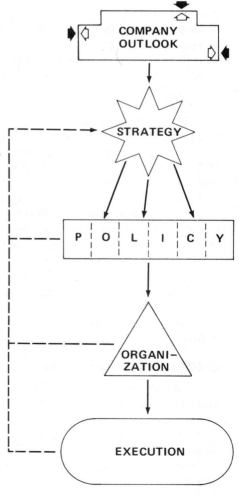

—analyzing company outlook, designing strategy, establishing policy, setting up organization, and guiding execution.

Two qualifications to the simple sequence shown in the chart should be made explicit. First, in a going concern each phase influences all the others to some degree. Firmly established policy or organization, for instance, may make a proposed strategy easy (or difficult) to put into action; in that case, policy or organization influences the choice of strategy. Such a "reverse flow" is suggested by the light line on the side of the chart. The same effect is implicit when we analyze the strengths and the limitations of a company as part of the background data for designing a strategy: the historical momentum and the existing policy, organization, and controls contribute to the strengths and the weaknesses of the present company. Nevertheless, while some of this "reverse flow" is always present, the primary sequence for a dynamic service enterprise is the one emphasized on the chart and used as the structure of this book.

Second, a neatly integrated package of strategy, policy, organization, and execution does not stay neat. The environment changes. Even the company's own success creates the need for revision. Consequently, the broad process described must be repeated and repeated again. Minor adjustments and refinements will be occurring most of the time. Major reshuffling, however, is expensive in both financial and human terms; so, like tooling-up for a new automobile model, a particular design should be followed long enough to learn how to use it well and to recoup the investment. But, it is recognized that sooner or later retooling will be necessary.

These qualifications—the interaction between parts and the need for successive revisions—do not diminish the usefulness of the basic model proposed. Quite the opposite, these added complexities make an analytical framework even more valuable as an aid to orderly thinking.

The versatility of the model is further developed in Chapter 23 where it aids in the examination of managing multinational enterprises. Coming at the end of the book, Chapter 23 also serves as a review of the step-by-step breakdown in Parts 1 through 4.

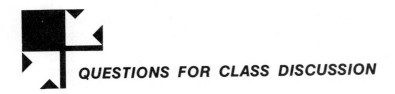

QUESTIONS FOR CLASS DISCUSSION

1. (a) What is the social responsibility of an electric utility company? Consider air and water pollution, uninterrupted consumer service, conservation of energy resources, stable employment, prices charged for services, effect of transmission lines on the landscape, adequate profits to attract investment for expansion,

aiding rural and community development, and support of good government. (b) What do you consider to be the chief task of central management of an electric utility?

2. Social standards change. We praised pioneers for clearing land and draining swamps, but now similar action is illegal. Likewise, legislation and company practice protecting women workers was hailed as a social advance fifty years ago; now such practice is unfair discrimination. And so forth. (a) Is it the responsibility of company central managements to decide what social standards should be? (b) Since a new standard often affects previous jobs, markets, financial returns, and other prevailing resource conversion patterns, should central management take an entirely passive position on changes in standards?

3. Much agricultural production and food processing is inherently seasonal. The resulting seasonal demand for labor was met over many years by using (a) young people (the school term avoided harvest season) and (b) migrant labor. In today's society, what social responsibility does the operator of a fruit company have for people who work in the orchards and in the canneries?

4. The John Smith Shoe Company decided to move to Missouri from upstate New York because its taxes would be reduced; a modern, low-cost plant was available; and there was a plentiful supply of unskilled and semiskilled labor. Sales of the company's rather old-fashioned women's walking shoes had been declining and a line of children's shoes was proposed. What basic problems of administration did the executive committee need to face in connection with the move? Are social responsibility issues involved?

5. Apply the concept of an enterprise being a resource converter to (a) a hospital and (b) a university. From a social viewpoint, is alertness to social and technological changes by hospital and university managers as significant as such alertness by soap and soup manufacturers? What means are available to encourage changes by hospital and university managers?

6. The leading life insurance companies in the United States are "mutuals"—owned and ultimately controlled by policyholders rather than by profit-seeking stockholders. Do you think the social mission of the mutual companies differs significantly from that of the stock companies in the insurance industry? Is the task of their respective central managements different? Does "the purpose of business is to make a profit" fit either type of company?

7. The future-oriented approach to central management problems outlined in this chapter has been effectively applied to numerous medium- and large-sized enterprises. Do you think it fits a small enterprise such as an automatic car-wash station or a building contractor?

8. Both *concepts,* explained in a textbook and in discussion, and *cases* are used to develop managerial competence in company training programs and in university courses. Both concepts and cases are presented in this book. What advantages and limitations do you see in using (a) concepts and (b) cases for education about central management?

CASE 1 / Advanced Developments, Inc.

A long series of investigations and tests had led the geologists of Advanced Developments, Inc. (a Delaware-chartered firm) to two copper-bearing ore bodies that appeared to have considerable promise for future development as large, open-pit mines. A preliminary drilling program to test out the suspected ore bodies aroused considerable protests from nearby residents and some of the press. Executives of the firm took these protests seriously, for they were determined that the firm would be "an ecologically good neighbor." But the promise of a substantial copper find was important to the firm's strategy of being in the forefront of geological exploration and of diversifying its operations.

Before the major decision was made to commit financial resources to the objective of proving out a substantial ore body, the company economists, market researchers, mining engineers, and geologists studied world markets thoroughly in an attempt to understand demand for copper, the prospects for future supply, and potential price movements. While many of these studies were highly technical, their conclusions can be summarized fairly simply in a few paragraphs and tables.

Demand. The usefulness of the red metal and the desire for end products made from it are attributable to its relative efficiency in conducting electricity and conducting heat and to its physical properties of malleability and resistance to corrosion (especially when alloyed). These inherent properties of copper provide total combined values that substitutes cannot completely duplicate.

While aluminum has replaced copper in use in the long-distance, ultra-high-voltage transmission of electric power, copper is expected to maintain its preeminent position in other aspects of electrical generation, transmission, and use. This includes the extensive use of copper in products ranging from computers to mass transit systems to a multitude of household appliances.

Copper's use in construction has grown at substantial rates exceeding 10% per year as the result of the metal's importance in air-conditioning units, desalination plants, and drain, waste, and vent piping.

In fact, it is only within the past 15 years that the industry has done much systematic work on copper's technical qualities and its potential uses. The Copper Development Association and the International Copper Research Association have, since the middle 1960's, underwritten and monitored research projects in copper metallurgy and aggressively brought the use of copper-base alloy systems and copper-clad alloy systems to producers and consumers.

Per capita consumption in the United States in 1975 was about 24.7 lbs., up from 18.8 lbs. in 1964 and the highest consumption rate in the world. Total consumption in 1975 was about 2.5 million tons compared with domestic production of 1.9 million tons, leaving a deficit of 0.6 million tons—most of which had to be imported.

Copper—Selected Statistics and Forecasts

	Mine Production (short tons)			*Forecasts—U.S.*[1] (in millions of short tons)				
Year	*United States*	*World*	*U.S. Price Cents/lb.*	A_L	A_M	A_H	*B*	*C*
1912	624,500	1,125,700	16.3					
1920	612,300	1,056,000	17.5					
1930	705,100	1,775,800	13.0					
1940	878,100	2,668,500	11.3					
1950	909,300	2,760,000	21.2					
1960	1,080,200	4,650,000	32.0					
1965	1,351,700	5,549,000	35.0					
1970	1,719,700	6,638,000	57.7	1.06	1.44	1.78		
1973	1,717,900	7,940,000	59.5					
1974	1,870,000	8,600,000	70.5					
1975	1,900,000	8,800,000	63.1	1.07	1.68	2.19		
1980				1.08	1.85	2.70	2.20	2.43
1990				1.05	2.40	4.10	2.81	3.77
2000				1.13	3.24	7.10		

A = Forecasts by Landsberg, H. H., Fischman, L. L., and Fisher, J. L., *Resources in America's Future,* Baltimore: The Johns Hopkins Press, 1963. A_L = lowest predicted projection; A_M = middle-range projection; A_H = highest predicted projection.
B = Forecast by United States Department of Commerce.
C = Forecast by a private consulting firm.

[1] These are forecasts of mine output needed (copper supply). They were each derived from forecasts of consumption and assume that new mines will be brought into production to meet the increased demand.

Supply. The best estimate available is that U.S. mines, in total, operated at 70% of feasible capacity in 1975. Since modern mining technology is similar around the world, this capacity percentage probably reasonably represented the world situation.

Old mines are, however, taken out of production every year and new mines have to be opened to continue the available supply. Finding a new mine requires knowing in general where copper is located and then doing extensive searching, geological analysis, and test-drilling to pinpoint an ore body.

Major copper-bearing regions important in the world market occur in Canada, the western United States, Chili, Peru, Zaire, Zambia, the Philippines, Australia, and Papua, New Guinea. U.S.-owned mines were nationalized in the South American countries some years ago (with compensation arranged eventually), while Chile, Peru, Zambia, and Zaire—which, among them, control about 38% of the Free World's output—belong to the Intergovernmental Council of Copper Exporting Countries. This Council attempts to gain for its members the benefits which the OPEC has brought to the Arabian countries and to imitate the success of the International Bauxite Association as well as the cartels formed by six phosphate-producing countries, the tin producers, and the mercury producers (Algeria, Italy, and Spain).

In commenting on the world supply of copper, Dr. C. Fred Bergsten, Senior Fellow of the Brookings Institution, once cited a number of effective cartel arrangements.

"Thus the Third World directly threatens the interests of the United States in obtaining assured supplies of primary products at reasonable prices and in avoiding losses of jobs and exports.

"It threatens relations among the United States, Western Europe, and Japan, by triggering scrambles among them for special deals with commodity suppliers . . ." [1]

The industry in the United States. Although data with which to calculate concentration ratios is hard to come by, it is generally known that four large companies own or control by far the largest portion of the copper mining, smelting, and refining facilities in the United States. High concentration in this industry of primary production is attributable in part to the difficulty of entry. To newly locate, prove out, and begin mining and first-stage milling operations on an extensive low-grade ore body requires an investment of up to $350 million and 7 years as a minimum span of time. In full operation the mine and mill would provide about 1,200 jobs. Thus increased competition, which ordinarily is of benefit to the nation, is not a simple matter in the copper business.

Preliminary geological surveys and consultation with well-known industry experts indicated two areas of high promise in the boomerang-shaped copper-bearing region that runs from western New Mexico through eastern and southern Arizona into the state of Sonora in Mexico. The first of these areas is located in the Organ Pipe Cactus National Monument in southern Arizona;[2] the second is in an exurb of one of Arizona's major cities and abuts another National Monument and a well-used state park. Both areas appeared suitable for open-pit mining and had slopes suitable for slag heaps and waste ponds. The exurban land lies 6 miles beyond the present city limits.

According to the Mining Act of 1872 and all recent amendments to it, and in accordance with all applicable state laws, Advanced Developments, Inc., or its parent company, Mineral Resources, Inc., needed to obtain the permission of the Secretary of the Interior to build roads into the Organ Pipe Cactus National Monument so that drilling rigs could be moved in and test-drilling begun. This permission was granted, upon application, and Advanced Developments notified the chief ranger of the Monument—as the law required—of its intention to begin a program of test-drilling.

No approval from any government official or agency was needed to begin test-drilling in the exurban area. Under the law, the land had been sold to private owners with the mineral rights reserved to the federal government. Thus, it was perfectly legal for the company to begin a test-drilling program, lay roads, and move equipment about. Indeed, the firm was encouraged to do so by the intent of the law. No permit was required. The firm might have to buy out a claim if some other person had staked out and maintained drilling operations consistently over a period of years. However, there was no evidence of this activity on or near the ore body in which Advanced Developments, Inc. was interested. About 2,000 persons lived on or near the sections under consideration.

The firm began drilling operations on land that was obviously not built upon. However, the rigs were close enough to some houses to be immediately noticed and the householders began to ask what was going on.

---

[1] "The Response to the Third World," *Foreign Policy*, Winter 1974-75, pp. 3-34.

[2] Organ Pipe Cactus National Monument is being preserved in its natural state because of its distinctive flora. Many different species of cactus grow within the 516 square miles of the Monument. Over 300,000 tourists visited last year to camp and enjoy its scenic splendor.

In its first public announcement, Advanced Developments, Inc. stated that it would act as "an ecologically good neighbor during the exploration and use no explosives near homes." Despite this announcement, a group of homeowners formed an organization called STOMP (Stop Mines and Pollution) and wired the governor of the state requesting his aid and the calling of a special session of the state legislature to consider the development of mining claims on private land.

The governor's answering telegram said that previous commitments prevented his meeting with the group and that he had no indication that the legislature had authority to act in the matter of the mines. The state senator from the legislative district in which the drilling was taking place stressed that Arizona probably could not legally interfere with mining on federal land anywhere. However, he planned to introduce legislation in the next regular session of the state legislature to restrict mining exploration and development on state-owned land.

Some weeks later the state attorney general's office issued a memorandum giving a legal opinion requested by the governor on what alternatives those opposed to the mining might pursue. The opinion stated, in part, ". . . almost universal agreement that nothing can be done to prevent mining activity in the 3½ sections of land in question . . ." The governor then stated that a mine would provide jobs in an area that continually needed new jobs as the result of a high rate of immigration from other states.

Investigations by Advanced Developments, Inc. indicated richer ore bodies than had originally been suspected. An investigation by STOMP revealed that Mineral Resources, Inc. was a wholly-owned subsidiary of The Standard Company, an integrated, multinational oil company, which did not market gasoline in Arizona.

While these investigations were proceeding, STOMP acquainted Arizona's two senators and one representative with its view of the situation. One senator voted in committee against an amendment to a bill to prohibit new surface mining in national parks and federal recreation areas. The other introduced a federal bill to allow property owners to acquire the mineral rights to their land upon application to the Secretary of the Interior. This senator and the U.S. representative introduced twin bills to ban mining in Organ Pipe, Coronado, and four other national monuments and parks. But the representative said higher-priority bills would delay consideration of a mining ban for as long as eighteen months. Both bills have been referred to the respective interior committees. Even if legislation were passed, the federal government would have to buy out existing claims to stop the exploration. The representative said the expense "would be considerable" if the government acquired a claim after a rich copper lode was found.

One of the major local newspapers commented: "Organ Pipe is one of the few remaining untouched areas in Arizona. Such areas must be protected from the ravages of strip mining."

Following a statement by a lawyer for the Phelps-Dodge Corporation, "You can move the town, but you can't move the ore body," a delegation from the city's Chamber of Commerce visited Advanced Developments, Inc. to attempt to persuade its management to cease the drilling and exploration activities that were embarrassing and causing the condemnation of the general business community.

Required: (a) What social responsibilities has the management of Advanced Developments, Inc. or Mineral Resources, Inc. in this case?

(b) In your opinion, should the firm proceed with its test-drilling program in the two promising areas it has found? Explain.

Part 1

DETERMINING COMPANY STRATEGY

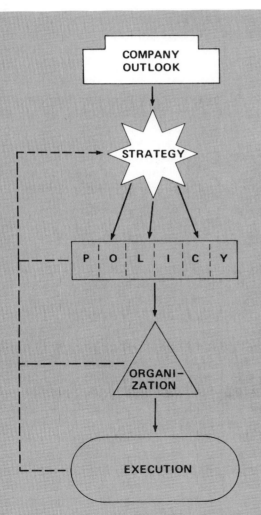

Chapter

PREDICTING THE DYNAMIC ENVIRONMENT

Change

A sharp cutback in gasoline supplies would upset our economy. People could not get to work, vacation resorts would close, railroads would be rejuvenated, social relations would become more provincial—to mention only a few of the ramifications.

Similarly, the rise of independent nations in Africa is much more than a local political matter. World sources of raw materials are jeopardized; potential new markets for such items as radios and pharmaceuticals are created; fair-employment practices in, say, Detroit, become even more crucial in foreign diplomacy; added strain is placed on satellite communication.

These examples of change illustrate a major problem for modern executives: adapting the direction and the operation of their enterprises to shifts in the technological, social, political, and economic environment of the United States and the world. Change is the one thing business managers know will occur.

This chapter highlights the nature of changes that are taking place and the manager's task in forecasting them. As pointed out in Chapter 1, anticipating environmental shifts is crucial to formulating strategy and setting wise policy.

DYNAMIC SETTING OF BUSINESS

For the central manager, predicting *both* (a) a major change and (b) its impact on operations is necessary. Note in the following examples—which convey only an impression of the changes affecting business rather than a full description—how this dual purpose of analysis recurs.

Technological changes

Electronic computers. The dramatic development of computers has become the classic example of a new generation of technology. Computer capabilities have been increasing tenfold every three or four years. Meanwhile the minimum size has dropped from that of a freight car to a golf ball. Clearly, the physical capabilities have outrun our knowledge of how to use this electronic wonder.

Most commercial (as contrasted with scientific) computers today merely perform clerical operations that can be done more slowly on other machines. On balance, they have increased rather than decreased employment because they are turning out vast quantities of data that previously had not been compiled. But the outpouring of numbers is hardly a revolution.

The new uses that will have the most influence on business strategy still lie in the future. Banks, for example, may maintain a whole set of books for a depositor, pay his bills, and provide subtotals for use on the annual income tax return. And these changes may contribute to a rearrangement of our financial institutions. Medical diagnosis, traffic control, and chemical analysis are among the many other possibilities. Computers will enable libraries to cope with the vast knowledge explosion, and eventually the postal clerk sorting mail may be as obsolete as a telegraph operator.

Computers will assist in automating production. However, automation—which has been with us a long while—requires process standardization and probably will develop somewhat more slowly than the application of computers to new services.

In the management field, computers are already performing "programmed" tasks such as reordering inventory. If it wishes, management can be informed daily whether Joe Jones is meeting his sales quota; but with all the talk about a computer being able to learn, it will be a long time before the machine decides when to fire Joe. More helpful is the computer's ability to stimulate parts of a complex business decision; here again, the bottleneck is program design and useful input data rather than machine capacity.

Transportation and communication. New technology permits greater speed and versatility in the movement of goods and people—a vital factor in industrial growth. Thus, from 1940 to 1975 the proportion of total freight moved by trucks increased from less than 10% to over 23%; oil pipelines rose similarly. At the same time, the share going to railroads declined from 63% to 41%. Air passenger traffic, which was nil in 1940, has moved up to about 9% of passenger traffic miles traveled, mostly at the expense of buses and rails.

The effect of growth in motor transportation can be seen in the increased consumption of oil, from less than 25 billion gallons in 1940 to over 100 billion gallons in 1975. Future growth will be tempered, however, by the world supply of crude oil and air pollution controls.

Communication is making similar strides. The number of telephone calls has doubled in the last twenty years, and new technology for sending multiple messages over the same line suggest accelerated growth in the future. Radio and more recently worldwide television via satellites have removed great barriers to intellectual isolation.

Energy and resources. Maintaining a balance between the accelerating use and the supply of natural resources is both a technological and an economic problem. Our insatiable appetite for electrical energy may outstrip the supply that can be economically produced. For Europe and Japan especially, the uncertain supply of oil from the Middle East has stepped up construction of nuclear power plants. But the required investment is tremendous. As a result, manufacture of products requiring high energy inputs is moving out of our traditional industrial centers. Nevertheless, nuclear energy by the fusion process is within our grasp and will probably be especially important to developing nations that lack other energy sources.

Perhaps the supply of fresh pure water, rather than energy, will become the bottleneck expansion. Most large metropolitan areas in the country face serious water shortages, and the decline in water tables suggests that the problem may be more than lack of adequate facilities. Clearly, we are going to need new technologies to help us use water more effectively.

At the same time, control of water pollution is essential. Both communities and plants will have to use new techniques to hold down contamination.

One of our greatest potential resources is the ocean. It contains vast mineral resources and has a capacity to support both animal and plant life that is virtually untapped.

New processes. From time to time some great scientist predicts that the rate of discovery and invention will decline. Up to date, these predictions have been very wrong, and the talent being devoted to scientific research suggests that just the opposite will occur. Consider the laser beam, a recently discovered high-frequency ray that has vastly greater potential than the x-ray. In military usage, laser scanning systems promise much greater accuracy than radar. The possible civilian applications are numerous. For example, a highly focused laser beam can produce temperatures above 10,000° C., and a machine using such a beam might greatly expedite drilling tunnels for highways, water, or similar uses. Other possibilities lie in sending laser beams through glass "wires," a development that would speed up conversion of telephone lines into TV cables. The laser beam is basically a single discovery that opens up a whole array of possibilities.

In the field of medicine almost daily announcements are made of advances in diagnostic techniques, control, or treatment for virus infections, mental disease, abnormal weight, and many other aspects of health.

We do not know just where dramatic changes in technology will occur. The very small sample of possibilities briefly mentioned above suggests that substantial changes are already in the making.

Social and political changes

Like technology, the social-political environment of a company presents both opportunities and obstacles. Also like technology, part of the changes can be foreseen—the forces that will generate them are already known. The nature, magnitude, and timing of other social changes are shrouded in uncertainty.

Population. The United States now has over 210 million people, an increase of over 60 million since the end of World War II. Population growth, looked at in total, means more consumers and more workers—more people who buy and more people who can turn out goods and services needed.

A few years ago estimates of population growth to 300 million by the turn of the century were common. These estimates were based on a high birth rate in the 1950's and early 1960's. Recently, attitudes toward family formation, birth control, and responsibility of rearing children have contributed to a sharp drop in the birth rate. Now the century-end population is often predicted at 265 million, with a stable population shortly thereafter. Clearly, the population pressure for economic growth is dropping.

Our population is highly mobile. They move from farm to city and from city to suburb. They also move from East to West and from South to North. The drift from rural to urban centers of population has been going on for a long time. During the current century, the proportion of people living in rural territory (places of 2,500 or less) has dropped from 60% to 30%. No longer can we assume that our labor force will have attitudes toward work and self-reliance engendered by a farm background.

More striking in recent years has been the move from downtown areas to the suburbs. In fact, in the largest population centers (those with over 2 million people) the population of the central cities actually decreased in the period 1950-1970. Only Los Angeles with its exuberant city limits reported a growth. Declines occurred in Boston, Chicago, New York, Philadelphia, Pittsburgh, San Francisco, and Washington. At the same time, the suburbs of most of these cities grew 50%-90%.

This move to the outskirts has not only helped boom housing and the construction industry, it has also revolutionized retail selling. Concurrently, it has created mass need for urban renewal. The older areas in the central cities typically house our lowest income group; this leads to overcrowding and poor maintenance. And such conditions foster social deterioration—frustration, indifference, drug addiction, crime. Slums are not new. Those of the 19th century were far worse physically, but usually they had more social resilience.

Compounding the urgency for urban renewal is the fact that a high proportion of recent migrants from the farm to the city centers are black. The whole array of issues connected with racial injustice is intermingled with the consequences of urban decay. Here then is a part of the total business environment calling for a type of imagination and skill quite different from that needed in a laboratory generating new technology.

Workforce. Women are the most dynamic element in our workforce. Not only are they 42% of all entries into the workplace, but also they are moving into many jobs previously held only by men—from bank tellers to corporate directors. Only a generation ago "progressive" labor laws sought to protect women (and children); now *any* differentiation is illegal. This shift in social and legal values greatly enlarges the supply of able people for key posts.

More people are spending more time in school. Only 9% of the 20-24 year old group went to school in 1950; by 1970 this figure had rocketed to 22%. The number of college graduates grew from 49,000 in 1920 to 925,000 in 1975.

These educational changes affect business in several ways. A better educated population means better skills available in the work force. Many of these skills are needed for modern sophisticated operations; but people with college educations can no longer be regarded as exceptional individuals, and problems arise in matching skills and aspirations to the work available. The corollary is that workers for dirty, boring, backbreaking jobs will become more difficult to find and more restive about their assigned tasks.

Managers must also learn to deal with a significant number of potentially productive employees who feel "alienated" toward all parts of "the establishment," including successful business firms. Whatever may be the psychological and social causes of disenchantment, employment of such men and women will never be satisfactory to either the individual or the company until some concurrence on worthwhile goals is achieved.

The role of unions is also changing. Originally a blue-collar institution, union action has extended to teachers and numerous other government groups, salespeople, engineers, and supervisors. Our labor laws foster monopoly power of various classifications of workers, and society has not yet learned how to cope with the pressures they can exert. For the business manager, collective pressure in a bargaining atmosphere calls for a basic change in the process by which a large number of policy decisions are made.

Government policy. Government action impinges on business in a variety of ways. Most obvious is an increasing array of direct regulation—dealing with such issues as antitrust, fair trade (advertising, pricing, and the like), sale of securities, labor relations, minimum wages, or air pollution. Taxes take a larger bite of gross revenues than do profits, and the way they are levied sharply influences company behavior.

On the other hand, nearly every kind of business benefits, at least indirectly, from import restrictions, subsidies, research grants, financial aids, or other forms of assistance. Moreover, government is a tremendous customer; all levels of governement combine to buy 21% of the total goods and services produced (more in wartime). For some industries, such as aerospace, the federal government is virtually the only customer. Of course, the level of these supports and purchases responds to a variety of political forces.

Overriding partisan politics is war. Apart from the question of sheer survival, a major war drastically alters allocation of resources and the activities companies are permitted to perform. Consequently, one of the elements in every company strategy is what provision, if any, should be made for the possibility of war.

International development. The birth of a new nation or a new government in power occurs almost monthly. Especially in Africa, we are witnessing the formation of many new states, and throughout the world feelings of nationalism are strong. At the same time, radio, movies, magazines, and travel have greatly expanded the aspirations of "have not" nations. This inherently unstable situation is complicated by the "have" nations in their jockeying for influence and for economic or military advantage.

In this milieu the businessman faces contradictory factors. Great human need and perhaps incentive for local investment are countered by occasional confiscation of mines and oilwells, import quotas, and similar acts. The result is widely fluctuating risk in dealing with developing countries.

Nevertheless, international trade for the world as a whole is growing significantly. New technology and increased productive capacity make trade highly desirable. The problem is that any expansion will hurt someone someplace, even though the net effect is a gain, and national leaders cannot ignore local political pressures. So adjustments in tariffs and import quotas are hard to predict.

Basic to all foreign trade and aid are international monetary arrangements. Settlement of trade balances in gold—the orthodox method— has been virtually abandoned. Therefore, a variety of devices is administered by the Bank for International Settlements, such as currency reserves and borrowing rights. But these devices are only adjuncts to fiscal stability and control of inflation in the respective countries. Few governments, even in the so-called advanced countries, are strong enough internally to resist the pressures for inflation.

Economic changes

Total output. The preceding discussion of technology and of social and political forces concerns business executives because they are examples of changes in the methods they might use and the environment in which they operate. But what of the overall results, the total flow of goods and services?

U.S. business has had its ups and downs, and some industries have grown much faster than others. Nevertheless, the total output is impressive. Industrial production, according to the Reserve Board Index, by 1974 was double its 1957 average. And the 1957-1959 level was two and a half times the production in 1929, the year of the Big Crash and the peak of prosperity up to that time. This achievement in the production of goods is more impressive when we realize that during the past twenty years most of the increases in man-hours of work have gone into services and government. In fact, at present more people work in services and government than in the production of goods (farming, manufacturing, and mining). This means that future increases in productivity will have to be found more in the office than in the plant.

Total income. The market side of the same picture is the overall capacity of people to buy the output. In 1929, the first year for which the Department of Commerce statistics are available, disposable personal income amounted to $83 billion. This looks small indeed from the lofty heights of 1974 when people had over $900 billion available to spend or to save. With all effects of price changes removed, and on a per capita basis so that population increases are washed out, the additions to income still look impressive. In 1958 dollars, per capita disposable personal income was: 1929, $1,236; 1950, $1,646; 1974, $3,094.

Income distribution. An outstanding economic fact and a major factor in keeping the economy in high gear is the redistribution of income, especially to the lower income classes. In 1929, only 8% of American families had incomes of over $5,000 per year; some 60% had incomes of less than $2,000. Today, over 75% have incomes of more than $6,000, and only 7% have less than $2,000 to spend. Now almost one family in two has an income of over $10,000. The "middle-class" has grown enormously. This is the group that now has "discretionary" spending power and that has been using its discretion to create a continuing demand for goods and services that make ordinary living easier and leisure more varied. This is the group that upgrades luxuries into necessities and buys huge quantities of consumer durables—color TV sets, automatic dishwashers, air-conditioners, and second family cars.

Income distribution still provides its problems. The average for nonwhite families is only three fifths of that for white families. Nevertheless, as the accompanying table shows, some progress is being made; over the 25-year period, nonwhite family income increased at a faster rate than that of white families.

Median Family Income
(Current dollars)

	Total	*White*	*Index*	*Nonwhite*	*Index*
1947	$ 3,031	$ 3,157	(100)	$1,614	(100)
1972	11,116	11,149	(366)	7,106	(440)

Stress and strain

Change, the theme of this chapter so far, produces stress in any individual or organization that goes through it. Pouring new wine into old bottles builds pressure that must be planned for beforehand or mopped up after the explosion.

The turret lathe operator who must develop new skills when electronic controls are added to his machine, the company that must change its organization structure when new products are added or when sales growth makes the old relationship among executives inefficient, the woolen-worsted company that finds its existence threatened by synthetic fabrics, and the stock-brokerage firm that loses clients to the mutual funds—all must plan for some adaptation in their way of operating or find it more and more difficult to continue.

These stresses come not only from changes initiated within the company itself. The uncertainties from the international political scene and from changes in government policy often bring a feeling of uneasy tension combined with one of frustration—a feeling that unmanageable forces might be taking one toward some impending disaster and that there is nothing one can do about it. Psychiatrists occasionally call this an Age of Anxiety.

Management has the never-ending task of providing enough stability and continuity of action to permit efficient performance, and at the same time, of adjusting company operations to the array of changes suggested in the preceding pages. The socially responsible response to a dynamic, imperfect world is to identify tasks that need doing and then to do them well.

SCANNING AND FORECASTING COMPANY ENVIRONMENT

The following chart depicts the dynamic environment in which a company operates and the changes—technological, social, political, and economic—that have an impact on it.

COMPANY ENVIRONMENT

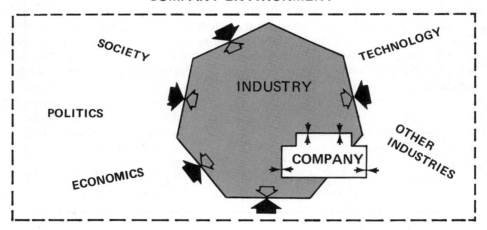

If management can forecast important changes in company environment, it clearly is in a better position to deal with the opportunities and the problems that these changes will create. But, three practical hurdles have to be crossed to capture such benefits:

1. The critical aspects of the environment must be identified.
2. Techniques for forecasting each of these factors must be selected and predictions must be made.
3. The forecast must be incorporated into the decision-making process.

Selecting critical features of the environment

The task of predicting even a dozen major variables is substantial. Consequently, central management must be selective in what it pays attention to. Boeing will obviously be more concerned with aerospace exploration than will the Coca Cola Company.

A first set of variables to be forecast can be derived from the industry in which a company is currently operating. Industry analysis, explored in the next chapter, helps spot those environmental factors most likely to change in a way that can greatly expand or seriously curtail industry growth. For the furniture industry, new home construction is significant; whereas for computers, new technology is crucial. *Each industry* must be analyzed to ascertain where to center forecasting effort that will be most relevant to it.

These easily recognized variables are not enough. Some *general* scanning of the future environment is also desirable (a) to identify possible changes that previously had been considered so unlikely or so minor in impact that they were omitted from regular examination, and (b) to pick up ideas for new directions the company might take outside its industry as currently conceived. The rise in importance of air pollution to the automobile industry illustrated (a), and new opportunities in the publishing field created by remote electronic typesetting are an example of (b). Although a company (and certainly a person) can undertake systematic forecasting of only a very select part of its total environment, the list of factors watched should be open-ended.

Forecasting techniques

Probably each of the key environmental items will require its own forecasting method. Interest rates, price movements, oil discoveries, tax exemptions, lower tariffs, cost-cutting inventions, social mobility rates, substitute products, use of leisure time, political stability in Africa, reduction of the sonic boom, low-cost water desalination, labor union power—these merely illustrate the kinds of factors that may be crucial to one industry or another. Unfortunately, no universal forecasting model exists. Two common techniques—economic forecasting and technical forecasting—will be discussed to indicate what is involved.

Economic forecasting

Gross national product (GNP). A widely used technique to predict economic conditions is in terms of the gross national product, which systematically summarizes many diverse influences in the national economy. In the words of the Department of Commerce, "The gross national product measures the nation's output of goods and services in terms of its market value." The gross national product is the sum of the market prices times quantities sold of all the goods and services produced in the country in one year.

Two views: total costs and total sales. There are two different ways of measuring total output. Since they are essentially two aspects of the same thing, they will have to add up to the same amount. First, gross national product is the sum of costs incurred in producing all the goods and services made during the year. Let's look at the table at the top of the following page.

National Income and Product Accounts
1st Quarter, 1975
(Annual rate, in billions of current dollars)

Costs of Output		Sales (or Uses) of Output	
Compensation of employees......	876	Personal consumption expen-	
Rentals paid to persons..........	27	ditures	913
Net interest	69	Government purchases of goods	
Business taxes and depreciation ..	267	and services	332
Corporate profits	93	Private investment in U.S........	163
Income of unincorporated firms ..	85	Net exports	9
Gross national product	1,417	Gross national product	1,417

On the left-hand side we find amounts paid to those who contributed toward making the gross national product. These are the costs of output. Included here are the wages of workers, net rents and royalties, net interest on capital loans and securities, business taxes and depreciation, corporate profits, and income of unincorporated enterprises and farms.

In the example given in the table, the total costs incurred in producing final goods in the economy was measured at an annual rate of $1,417 billion. In passing we may note that all these costs, except business taxes and depreciation charges, reflect a flow of earned income. This income was available for personal expenditures, income tax, or investment.

Second, the right-hand side of the table shows the uses made of the total output of goods and services. For direct and immediate consumption, people were buying at the rate of $913 billion, or almost two thirds of the total. Government bodies—federal, state, and local—used 23% of the total. Investment in private houses, plant and equipment, inventories, and the like used 12%.

One important thing to note about the gross national product is that it is a *measure* expressed in dollars. Having such a measure, subject to statistical manipulations, is a great advantage in trying to estimate the significance of changes in economic, political, and social affairs, since it enables us to avoid the confusion of merely saying "more" or "less." With gross national product statistics, we can answer the question, "How much?" We can also chart the movements of a country from depression to prosperity or its steady long-term rate of economic development.

Use of GNP in long-run forecasting. Often business strategy must be established on the basis of forecasted conditions five, ten, or twenty years hence. The impact, for instance, of adding a new product line or leasing branch plants is likely to be greatest at least ten years after the original decision is made. Clearly, many of the dynamic factors discussed in the first part of this chapter will have a bearing on that future business environment. Can the gross national product concept be helpful in forming a sharper picture of the future and thereby aid in the design of strategy?

A few examples from a forecast of 1990 will show how the gross national product idea may be used for this purpose. Among the changes discussed earlier in this chapter were rising population, shorter hours of work, and increasing output per man-hour. These facts can be used to estimate GNP for 1990:

> Since the people who will be in the 1990 workforce are already living, we can come pretty close in estimating the number of workers at that time. Assuming that the increase in the proportion of housewives and older people working will offset an increase in the number of adults in school, we can be reasonably sure that the work force in 1990 will be about 110 million.
>
> The output per man-hour has shown an annual increase during the past half-century of 2.5%. However, the rate of increase has been slowing down in the last few years, so that a projected increase of 2% per annum is more conservative.
>
> Applying the 2% annual increase to the gross national product per worker in 1973 ($14,180), we arrive at a 1990 output per worker of $19,800.
>
> Now, the forecast of gross national product in 1990 is easy. Multiplying the output per worker by the number in the labor force, the impressive result is $2,178 billion. And, this estimate makes no allowance for an increase in the general price level.

The important point in this example is not the specific figures but the way knowledge about several diverse factors can be combined to give us a prediction of the total volume of business that is likely to be done several years hence. Of course, as new facts become available, they must be weighed, and revisions of the forecast must be made if necessary. Yet the gross national product framework can serve as a summation device, much as a profit and loss statement summarizes the results of a wide variety of activities within a company.

Technological forecasting

Hazardous though economic forecasting may be, it is well understood compared with predicting changes in technology. A cure for cancer, an economic way of desalinating water (which would open up vast areas of the world to agriculture), and a practical electric motor for automobiles are just three of myriads of discoveries that might alter the lives of millions of people—and companies. We know that massive research effort is devoted to such challenges, yet our ability to forecast them is limited. Even when the underlying technology is known, our ability to say *when* and *at what cost* a process or product will hit the market is unimpressive. Witness the use of atomic energy to generate electricity; in the mid-1960's utility companies bet on nuclear plants to meet rising demands, but by 1975 nuclear plants provided only 5% of our electrical energy. Environmental issues slowed construction, and costs were far above expectations. Brownouts, higher prices, and profit declines resulted. Clearly, the forecasts had been wrong.

One method of predicting technological achievement is by analogy: "Salk discovered polio vaccine, therefore someone will discover a way to prevent cancer.'' Or, ''Costs of generating electricity have been falling by X percent a year, therefore they will continue to drop at X percent.'' As with any analogous reasoning, the reliability is greatly improved by checking the similarity of the situations. Also, if we can develop some theory of how the discovery-development process works, then we can select our analogies with even better precision. With these refinements, forecasting by analogy gives results that are somewhat better than flipping a coin!

The ''Delphi'' technique—named for the ancient oracle—uses the combined judgment of a group of experts. Various procedures for consulting the experts may be followed, such as independent conclusions, comparison of reasons supporting the conclusions, statistical analysis and feedback to the experts, unstructured discussion among the experts, and revised conclusions. This technique does result in a highly informed guess, and as a by-product it gives a list of conditioning events that can be monitored to update the forecast. The chief drawback of the Delphi technique is the expense of identifying and securing the cooperation of a panel of experts qualified to deal with the change being forecast.

Note that the Delphi technique not only merges the judgment of the panel; it also permits each expert to use theory, analogy, trends, intuition, or whatever forecasting method he prefers. Incidentally, the method may be adapted to forecasting political and social changes.

Making use of forecasts

Forecasts have no value to a company until they enter into its decision-making process. Basically, this practical use occurs when the prediction is accepted as a *planning premise,* that is, when the prediction becomes a part of the assumed environment used in formulating strategy and other future plans. The concept of a planning premise does not require a single, unalterable assumption. The premise may be stated as a range (for example, copper prices up 25% to 40%) or as a probability (20% chance of a strike at the Baltimore plant); and explicit provision may be made for revising the premise as new information is obtained.

Many of the environmental forecasts first become premises for industry analysis, to be discussed in the next chapter. For example, the 1990 forecast of gross national product quoted previously can be related to the total U.S. demand for new plant and equipment by estimating how much of the increase will be goods (rather than services) and then projecting the new plant that will be needed to produce this additional output. Allowance must also be made for replacing and modernizing existing capacity. One prediction based on this approach is that business expenditures for plant and equipment in 1990 will be running around $185 billion (1975 prices).

Some forecasts may be tied directly to company strategy, bypassing the industry analysis stage. A chemical company, for instance, predicted that social and governmental restraints on the use of insecticides would become increasingly severe during the 1980's, with biological insect control taking their place. This forecast led to a shift in research effort and also to abandoning the construction of a California plant.

Forecasting requires hard work, and operating executives often lack the patience and the objectivity needed for good long-range predictions. Consequently, a recurring problem, which we will explore in Part 3, is how to use experts for reliable forecasts and then get operating executives to accept these projections. Formal approval by central management of particular planning premises helps; but unless executives have personal confidence in these premises, the executives are likely to introduce hidden safety factors into their plans. So, when forecasting is assigned to individuals, the forecasters not only have to be right most of the time, they also have to convince a lot of executives that they are right.

SUMMARY

An essential part of company strategy is a plan for adapting company action to its environment. This is no simple matter because the environment is continously changing. New technology, social shifts, political realignments and pressures, as well as the more commonly recognized economic changes, all create problems and opportunities. The many examples of exciting new developments noted in this chapter indicate how dynamic the setting of business is. To adjust most effectively, central management should try to predict important changes before they occur. And these predictions should not only identify the new factors, they also should anticipate how such shifts in the dynamic environment will affect the company.

In practice, no company can systematically monitor every part of its environment that might change. The task is too great. So the process involves (a) identifying crucial aspects of the dynamic environment, (b) selecting a forecasting method and making frequent forecasts for each of these aspects, and (c) taking steps to insure that the forecasts are actually used by company executives in formulating plans. Since the ability to make good long-range forecasts is limited, especially in the technical-social-political areas, management needs arrangements for frequent measurement. Built-in flexibility in the planning mechanisms is also needed. In other words, the total managing process that this book examines is no one-time affair; it is a recycling, never-ending—and challenging—undertaking.

A very helpful way to relate shifts in the dynamic environment to current operations of a company is to move first from the general environment to an industry analysis, and then to assess how the particular company stands in that industry. This narrowing-down process is described in the next chapter.

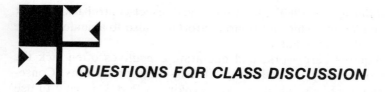

QUESTIONS FOR CLASS DISCUSSION

1. (a) Is there any reason, except tradition, why a woman should not fill *any* position in your local commercial bank? (b) What will be the effect, if any, on commercial banking of moving women into key posts?
2. (a) Assume that the president of a mobile home manufacturing company asks you, "What are the half dozen key factors in the environment that I should watch in order to anticipate the growth or decline in our industry?" Give your answer. (b) Do the same for eggs.
3. U.S. consumers spend about $5 billion annually in beauty salons and barber shops. This total has been increasing somewhat faster than the gross national product, and the trend is expected to continue. (a) Does this information have significance for your campus barber shop? (b) What other trends should the manager of that shop predict, if any? Why?
4. Some companies believe that their business would be affected by substantial growth in "black business," that is, companies owned by, staffed by, and catering to blacks. (a) Explain the method you would follow to make a 3-5 year forecast of this development. (b) Make such a forecast for a city or a state that you know.
5. The chairman of Consolidated Foods reports: "Back in colonial times 85% of our population was required to produce the nation's food supply; now the task is accomplished by less than 15% . . . Thirty years ago a grocery store handled less than 1,000 different food items; today's supermarkets carry from 4,500 to 6,000 . . . Today processed or semiprocessed foods are 80% of all groceries." (a) Do you believe these trends will continue? Why? (b) What significance do these trends have for grocery stores, vegetable canneries, mail-order houses, and kitchen equipment manufacturers?
6. In the medical field, benefits financed by the federal government and others are expanding faster than the capacity of the industry. Also, the labor supply of "dedicated" workers has been exhausted and unions are now demanding wages comparable to other industries. (a) Do you predict that these trends will continue? (b) If so, what will happen to prices? availability of services? government intervention? pressure on pharmaceutical and hospital supply firms? (c) Is a major technological change (such as occurred in food distribution) likely?
7. One of the most pervasive changes confronting a central manager is inflation. Should the manager of a small enterprise, say a dry-cleaning firm with six retail outlets, try to forecast the amount of future inflation? If so, for how long a period? How would such forecasts help him run his business?
8. Each year new forecasts of the gross national product and its components are made by professional forecasters. Explain how a company in each of the following industries could use such forecasts to its advantage: (a) air-conditioner manufacturing, (b) real estate development, (c) ski resort. In each situation, do you recommend that the forecasts be given to operating executives in their original

form, or should the basic forecasts be translated into some "intervening" variables? In the latter case, what variables?

9. In the past, international agreements to restrict the world supply of a basic product such as rubber, coffee, or copper have fallen apart within a few years. Either discord among the supplying countries and/or new sources of supply have led to renewed competition. (a) Do you think such agreement will be more stable in the future? Use crude oil as an example—or bauxite (aluminum ore). (b) After answering (a), appraise the method you used to make your forecast. What are the strengths and the weaknesses of that forecasting method?

10. The treatment of management as a *profession* is becoming more widespread. How have the major changes discussed in this chapter—such as income distribution, education, complex technology, and big government—contributed to this view of management?

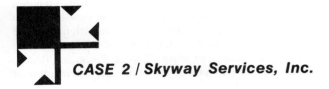

CASE 2 / *Skyway Services, Inc.*

Skyway Services faces a decision on a major expansion. The company is one of several successful "fixed base operators" that provide service to aircraft coming into Teterboro Airport. In New Jersey, 6 miles west of New York City, Teterboro Airport is used exclusively for "general aviation," that is, private planes owned by individuals and corporations. While welcoming any business, Skyway caters especially to corporate or executive planes. It has hangar space for 8 planes where it does a full range of maintenance work on radio and electrical systems, airframes, and engines; operates a profitable fuel business; and also is sales representative for one of the leading private plane manufacturers.

Five years ago Skyway established a very small branch at Stewart Airport when the former Stewart Air Force Base, 60 miles north of New York City, was converted to general aviation use. The question now is whether to expand or close the branch. Ross Webber, president of Skyway Services, has assembled the following information to help him decide his strategy.

Growth of general aviation. Shipments of new business/private aircraft doubled during the 1960's, dipped sharply in the early 1970's, and then recovered almost to their former peak—as the table on page 34 shows. Since shipments far exceeded retirements from service, the total fleet is growing; the present general aviation fleet in the U.S.A. of about 170,000 active, registered planes is expected to rise to 260,000 by 1980.

Although additions to the general aviation fleet dropped off during the recession of the early 1970's, the number of new private jets and other well-equipped planes continued to rise. Reports of general aviation movements in and out of airports, especially in California and Florida, confirm this upward trend. Travel flexibility of a private plane, highway congestion, deterioration in railroad service, and improvements in small plane performance all contributed to the attractiveness of "having your own plane."

Shipments of New
Business/Private Aircraft

Year	Units	Year	Units
1960	7,600	1968	14,200
1961	6,800	1969	12,600
1962	6,800	1970	7,400
1963	7,700	1971	7,200
1964	9,600	1972	9,400
1965	12,400	1973	13,500
1966	15,900	1974	14,000*
1967	13,800		

* Preliminary.

Nevertheless, operating a private plane with licensed pilots and careful maintenance is expensive. This makes private flying sensitive to general business conditions. So many influences are at work that it is difficult to tell how much private flying will be regarded as a luxury in the future. The economic downturn in early 1970 did put a crimp in sales of new planes by all the leading producers, including Cessna, Piper, and Beech. Industry sentiment, however, regarded this dip as a tough but temporary interruption of the basic trend.

An estimate by the Federal Aviation Administration forecast that, while the number of *commercial* aircraft handled at U.S. airports would remain stable for several years and then rise only 25% by 1982, *general aviation* aircraft handled would rise steadily and almost quadruple between 1972 and 1982 (from 4.8 million aircraft handled in 1972 to 18.3 million in 1982). These estimates, which were part of a recommendation for 1,000 new airports, were made prior to the Middle East oil compact.

Activity at Teterboro. The growth of general aviation in the New York City area, including the Teterboro Airport, has not kept up with the trend. In fact, total plane movements in and out of the New York City area have been declining since 1968—due to air congestion, larger planes, the sharp rise in fuel costs, and in 1974 a drop in passenger traffic. "In New York we are still bearing the brunt of all the industry's growing pains," explained Mr. Webber. "Actually the picture is not quite as dark as the totals suggest, especially in our particular part of the game. You can see in the table that our local business-and-private activity is up. The only big drop at Teterboro has been in student flights and that doesn't hurt us much. To understand what is going on, you have to recognize that we have a tremendous potential demand but governmental regulations are severely restricting our growth.

"During the ten years preceding the 1973-1974 oil crisis," Mr. Webber continued, "air passenger miles trebled and tons of air freight increased fivefold. New York, however, became so congested it could not grow with the total industry. Then the oil crisis hit and total flights into the area dropped 12% and passengers 3%. At the same time regulations on air pollution, noise pollution, and air safety burdened the industry. Now there is some doubt about how fast overall growth will occur. If commercial flying resumes its previous trend, two things that affect Skyway will happen. First, private/business flights into the major airports will be cut back even more, and Teterboro will be used to its capacity. Second, with all the restrictions and air congestion close to the city, a fourth major airport will become a necessity—and

Plane Movements in New York Area
(in thousands)

Year	Total Plane Movements 4 Airports *	Business/Private Plane Movements		
		4 Airports *	Teterboro	Teterboro % of 4 Airports
1965	1,029	268	143	53%
1966	1,127	290	145	50
1967	1,219	286	151	53
1968	1,235	274	151	55
1969	1,185	260	170	65
1970	1,109	263	183	70
1971	1,116	273	190	70
1972	1,126	273	186	68
1973	1,102	268	180	67
1974**	970	275	184	67

* J.F. Kennedy, LaGuardia, Newark, and Teterboro.
** Partly estimated.

Stewart, in spite of its commuting handicap, looks like the most likely location. My problem is to figure out the net effect of all these forces.''

Noise and air pollution. The substantial and politically explosive efforts to control noise and air pollution are primarily concerned with large commercial aircraft. Small planes can be aggravating to residents close to an airport, but this annoyance is so overshadowed by problems with large jets that general aviation is rarely a target.

Indirectly, however, general aviation and companies like Skyway Services are affected. First, regulations on noise and air pollution are likely to include all aircraft, and small planes may have to install equipment. This increases the cost of flying—a consideration more serious for private planes than business planes. Second, noise associated with a commercial airport is so objectionable that a location for a fourth major airport within the New York City area has been unattainable. And with limited facilities, the higher priority commercial planes tend to squeeze out general aviation. In fact, until the 1974 dip, existing facilities were so crowded that foreign and domestic airlines were ''encouraged'' to schedule new flights to cities other than New York. If the noise problem could be overcome and one or two large new airports established, the squeeze on general aviation in the New York area would be reduced.

Noise reduction is both a technical and an economic problem. New aircraft—to be delivered in the future—can (and must) be designed to make half the noticeable noise of present jets. Engineers are also working on ways to quiet down the existing fleet; some improvement is possible for an expense of $500,000 to $1,000,000 per plane. The airlines are already deep in debt, and there is great controversy over who should foot the bill.

Traffic congestion and safety. General aviation is directly involved in traffic congestion. Major accidents have been caused by collision in the air of small planes and airliners. On the runway a plane is a plane no matter its size, and serious delays in landing and takeoff do arise when the total traffic exceeds the capacity of an airport. In bad weather both the accident and the delay hazards increase. Over forty million passengers per year in the New York area alone are personally concerned that these problems be relieved.

To relieve the especially acute pressure in the New York area, the Port Authority has expanded the runways and terminals at all of its airports. General aviation use of the J.F. Kennedy, LaGuardia, and Newark airports was curtailed and shunted to Teterboro where $4,000,000 has been spent extending runways and adding taxiways. With these improvements the bottleneck, for a year or two at least, will be in the air.

The present system for regulating air traffic relies primarily on personal and radar communications between each aircraft and a ground control. Numerous suggestions are being studied for speeding up this system and/or supplementing it with instruments carried on every plane that enable each plane to keep track of other nearby planes. Also changes in the equipment, on the ground and in the planes, for landing in bad weather hopefully can alleviate delays. Such new equipment can provide the desired safety only if all planes in the air are properly equipped, *including* the business and private planes.

When agreement is reached on improved air traffic control systems, the operators of small planes will be required to install the new equipment if they wish to fly in a congested area such as New York. Operators of business planes, which already often cost between $750,000 and $2,500,000, will probably welcome the added safety and landing flexibility; but owners of small private planes, which can be purchased for as little as $5,000, may find the cost prohibitive. Such a new system probably would increase the number of plane movements Teterboro Airport could handle but nowhere near as much as the projected potential growth.

Another possible technical development is the perfection of V/STOL (vertical or short takeoff and landing) planes that could be used as air shuttles between major airports and downtown locations. If this development occurred, additional major fields could be located farther from New York City, thereby relieving the present and potential congestion in a relatively small area. (The idea of a floating airport anchored ten miles out in the ocean has received little support.)

Incidentally, the principle of satellite airports has been adapted to general aviation by Indianapolis. To take pressure off its main airport, the Indianapolis Airport Authority has several "reliever" airports around the city that handle most of the general aviation flights.

The new Stewart Airport. In 1970 the Stewart Air Force Base was converted from military to civilian operation and the fully-equipped airfield was turned over for general aviation use. Located just west of Newburgh, New York, at the junction of the New York Thruway and the east-west Interstate Highway 84, this airfield is in a good spot for motor traffic that wishes to circumvent New York City congestion. The drawback is its two-hour motor distance from downtown Manhattan. With half a dozen other general aviation airports within closer range of Manhattan, not many people flying to the city elect to stop at Stewart in spite of its superior landing facilities, and the surrounding population is not large enough to support a large private plane activity. Nevertheless, Stewart enjoyed a steady growth in traffic until the energy crisis of 1974. The proportion of business jets in the total traffic at Stewart is substantially lower than at Teterboro.

Stewart Airport has exciting possibilities. It is very well located for a satellite operation using V/STOL to Manhattan and other airports. New York State is acquiring surrounding land and planning for a major airport when demand exceeds the capacity of present Port Authority facilities. Also, William Zeckendorf is promoting a plan for high-speed urban transportation into Manhattan that would cut travel time to an hour. (This plan also embraces a new deep-sea port for containerized shipments—unhampered by New York City labor inefficiencies.) However, these plans call for public investment

**Private/Business Plane Movements
in Stewart Airport**

Year	Plane Movements (in thousands)
1970 (10 months)*	61
1971	91
1972	116
1973	136
1974	139**

* Stewart Airport opened for nonmilitary business on March 1, 1970
** Partly estimated.

of hundreds of millions of dollars and are subject to all the foibles of intrastate and interstate politics. From Skyway Services' viewpoint, perhaps the most attractive possibility is the establishment of Stewart Airport as a Customs Inspection Station. Then almost all general aviation flights from Canada and some from Europe would stop there, creating a significant need for refueling and maintenance.

Skyway Services' current dilemma. When Stewart became a civilian airport, the airplane manufacturer that Skyway Services represents at Teterboro wanted to establish a foothold at the new Stewart Airport. The manufacturer urged Mr. Webber to set up service there and become its sales representative. The implication was that some other sales representative would be found if Webber declined; and if this occurred, Skyway Services would have difficulty later in moving into the Stewart Airport because a sales affiliation with one of the leading plane producers is widely recognized as an essential ingredient for a "fixed base operator" such as Skyway.

Ross Webber was reluctant to make the $2,000,000 investment necessary to start a full-fledged service operation at Stewart Airport because the future of the airport was surrounded by so many uncertainties. So he worked out an interim plan for operating only a fueling service coupled with shuttle repair service from Teterboro. This was recognized as an inefficient arrangement, but the plane manufacturer did give Skyway a five-year option "during the transition period."

The present setup is unsatisfactory to Webber because he is losing $3,000 to $5,000 annually and because his personnel do not like the uncertainty about the future. And the plane manufacturer feels it is getting only nominal representation at Stewart Airport. The one fully-equipped fixed base operator now at Stewart represents a competing manufacturer. Both Webber and the company he represents agree that the time has come for either expansion or withdrawal, and both agree that the decision depends primarily on how much growth can be anticipated in plane movements at Stewart in the next five to ten years.

Required: Do you recommend that Skyway Services expand its activities at Stewart Airport to capitalize on the investment it has already made there?

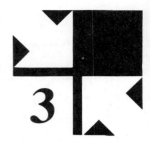

ASSESSING COMPANY'S FUTURE STRENGTHS

Analysis of industry and company

The dynamic environment, discussed in Chapter 2, does create opportunities and problems. For a specific company to respond constructively to this setting, however, it must sharpen its focus. It must (a) analyze prospects and requirements for success in specific industries, and then (b) carefully assess its strengths and weaknesses relative to competitors in those industries.

For example, the manager of Aluminum Fabricators, Inc. may foresee rapid growth in the use of aluminum wire for extra-high-voltage lines that will tie all parts of the United States into a vast power grid. But industry analysis indicates that such wire will be supplied on a tonnage basis by primary producers; and the relative strength of Aluminum Fabricators lies in the design of precise castings with unique specifications suited to each end use. Clearly, this particular company is not well suited to tackle competitors who will grasp the opportunity created by this technological development.

Such analyses of particular industries and companies provide the essential basis for wise strategy formulation, considered in Chapter 4; it also contributes important background for policy designed to execute the strategy. (Policy issues are explored in Part 2.)

Framework for analysis

This chapter explains an outline that will help to analyze industries and to position a company in each industry; it gives a way to sift and classify ideas, determine their relationships, and weigh their importance. The key topics are given in the outline on the following page.

The nature and the importance of each of these topics will be examined in the following pages. All subheadings may not be significant for a particular company, but the list as a whole suggests a range of factors that should be considered.

Of course, a company may be involved in two or more industries and may be considering many others; if so, separate analyses should be made for each

I. **Outlook for the Industry**
   A. Demand for Products or Services of the Industry
      1. Usefulness and desire for products
      2. Stability of desire for products
      3. Stage in product life-cycle
   B. Supply of Products or Services
      1. Capacity of the industry
      2. Labor costs
      3. Material costs
      4. Taxes and other costs
   C. Competitive Conditions in the Industry
      1. Nature of companies
      2. Organization of the industry
      3. Government regulation
   D. Conclusions
      1. Prospects for volume and profits
      2. Key factors for success in industry

II. **Position of the Company in the Industry**
   A. Market Position of the Company
      1. Relation of company sales to those of the industry and leading competitors
      2. Standing of company products
      3. Strength of company in major markets
   B. Cost Position of the Company
      1. Comparative location
      2. Relative efficiency of equipment
      3. Unique cost advantages
   C. Special Competitive Considerations
      1. Relative financial strength
      2. Ability of company management
   D. Conclusions
      Strengths and weaknesses of company in terms of key success factors identified in I

industry. Moreover, since the environment, industry, and company all change over time, the thinking must be updated. Having a framework of analysis makes such extensions and revisions easier to do.

DEMAND FOR PRODUCTS OR SERVICES OF THE INDUSTRY

Usefulness and desire for products

The end uses of an industry's products provide a key to future demand. For instance, if the familiar flashlight battery were used only for flashlights, the demand would be stable and mature. Actually, small dry cells are used in portable radios, cassettes, action toys, emergency lights, and a variety of gadgets. The popularity of the portable entertainment devices, especially, has contributed to a high growth rate.

Dry cells illustrate two other aspects of demand that may be significant. First, dry batteries have a *derived demand*. They are used only in association with some other product, and it is the popularity of these other products that leads to the demand for dry batteries. Many other items have a similar dependency on a different product for their sale. Manufacturers can do little to influence total industry sales; instead, their sales efforts focus on increasing their share of the market.

Second, the *focus of research and development effort* is not on new devices that will increase the demand for batteries. Of course, the manufacturers are glad to provide data to the designers of toys and radios, but these end products involve such different considerations that the battery manufacturers feel they have little to contribute. Instead, research by battery manufacturers is directed toward reduction of cost and improvement of quality.

Occasionally the possible uses for a product are not fully known. This is illustrated by vermiculite, a mineral that expands greatly upon being heated and that has unusual insulation properties. Possible uses for vermiculite are as a wall-fill insulation, a plaster base, a filter material, and also as the basic material for a light fireproof tile. In determining the demand for such a product, its probable effectiveness for these and other uses should be explored thoroughly.

After the possible uses of a product or a service of an industry have been explored, it is often desirable to classify potential customers by type and area. Thus the customers for automobile insurance may be grouped as private and commercial, and they may be further divided between states and regions. This information will be useful in determining the probable demand in the future; it will also provide a basis for sound sales policy.

Stability of demand for products

Demand for a product or a service may be steady and predictable or it may be volatile and uncertain. The following factors give insight regarding stability.

Substitutes. The desire for the utility or satisfaction rendered by a product may be reasonably stable, yet the demand for the product itself may be quite unstable because of increased or decreased use of substitutes that render this same satisfaction. Fresh oranges, a leading item in most grocery stores not so long ago, are becoming a novelty because frozen juice is an effective substitute.

**Fluctuations in Demand for Different
Kinds of Products
(Index numbers of physical volume, 1948 = 100)**

	Shoes	Automatic Dishwasher	Railroad Freight Cars	Electricity (kilowatt hours)
1948 (postwar recovery)	100	100	100	100
1954 (recession)	109	96	32	162
1965 (prosperity)	124	573	69	344
1969 (recession	109	941	61	461
1972 (prosperity)	98	1422	42	550

Chain stores have tended to replace independent stores in many lines. Television has reduced the demand for radios. In each case the problem has been not so much a decline in the demand for the service as the substitution of one product for another.

Durability of products. Durable products have wide fluctuations in demand. Houses, airports, and washing machines once constructed render services over a period of time, and consequently the demand for such products is more active during *periods of original construction* than during periods when existing facilities are merely being replaced. Also, the replacement of durable goods can often be postponed for a substantial period of time. For these reasons the demand for durable products tends to fluctuate over wider ranges than does the demand for such things as food, clothing, travel, and entertainment, which must be replenished to render additional services. Speculation may play a part in fluctuations of demand for almost any product; however, the more durable the product, the more lasting the maladjustment that may result from the unwarranted speculation.

Necessity versus luxury. Necessities, such as food and medical care and other products that people have come to regard as essential to their well being, will enjoy a more stable demand than products such as swimming pools and foreign travel that are purchased only at times when people have funds over and above what is necessary for the first class of goods. Sometimes a product or a service—for example, air-conditioning or long-distance telephoning—is a necessity in one of its uses or for one group of customers, whereas it is regarded as a luxury by another group of customers.

The federal government is a large buyer of some products. These purchases go primarily to the armed services; but from time to time, purchases for space exploration, stockpiling, atomic research, and the like assume large proportions. Here again the demand is likely to change sharply, and it is difficult to predict because it depends on national and international politics fully as much as on economic factors.

Stage in product life cycle

Many products pass through a life cycle, as shown in the chart on page 42. Although the phases vary widely in length, experience with an array of products—from ballpoint pens to automatic pinsetters in bowling alleys—does show that the concept is a useful analytical tool. Clearly, when electric refrigerators are already in 90% of the homes, growth prospects are much lower than for microwave ovens, which are in less than 1% of the homes; refrigerators have reached the maturity phase. A shift from maturity to decline typically occurs when a substitute product or service appears on the scene—witness what happened to the small-town newspaper.

In addition to a way of analyzing demand, the life-cycle concept bears directly on key factors for success. In the growth phase a company can take

CLASSICAL PRODUCT LIFE CYCLE

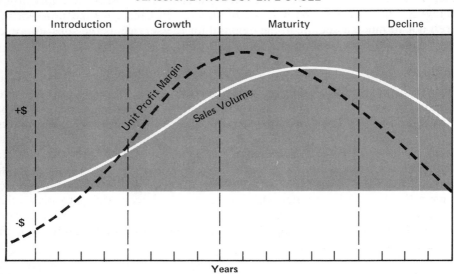

risks with overcapacity and even with quality in an effort to establish a market position; profit margins will permit production inefficiencies. By contrast, in the maturity phase efficient use of plant and close attention to production costs become much more important.

As already noted, separate demand analysis is necessary for industries with multiproducts or those serving several distinct markets. The several product-markets may be in different phases of the life cycles; one may be a necessity whereas another is a semiluxury; and each will have its own vulnerability to substitution.

SUPPLY OF PRODUCTS OR SERVICES

The outlook for profitable operations in an industry depends not only on the demand for the commodities and the services that the industry produces, but also on the available supply and cost of bringing such products to the market. This leads to questions of capacity and behavior of costs.

Capacity of the industry

In a dynamic business system, some industries are likely to have excess capacity while others have inadequate capacity. At one stage, sulfa was the wonder antibiotic drug and pharmaceutical producers expanded greatly to meet the urgent demand. Then penicillin and aureomycin came along, and the sulfa producers found themselves with large capacity that could not be utilized. In the finance field, stockbrokers have been plagued with excess capacity when interest in stock speculation declines. In addition to such drops in demand, excess capacity may result from overexpansion. Sometimes a field of business looks so attractive that too many firms enter it. Thus there may be an excess of resort hotels or office buildings in a given locality because promoters expanded their facilities too fast.

Undercapacity is common in any expanding industry. If a new service like retirement villages meets with wide public acceptance, the original facilities will probably not be able to fill the demand. Or a rapid increase in demand for, say, the Chinese language may make the number of qualified teachers quite inadequate.

Significance of undercapacity. When capacity of an industry is scarcely adequate to meet demand, most companies will enjoy profitable operations. Products will find a ready market, prices will be firm, and a high level of operation will permit spreading overhead costs over many units.

The significance of undercapacity also depends on the *ease of entering* the industry. If a new concern can be established with comparatively small capital and within a reasonably short period of time, undercapacity will probably be a temporary matter. The production of plastic toys, for example, requires little more than a few molding machines and assembly space; consequently, the capacity of a plant making this type of product can be easily expanded to meet demand. Similarly, the advertising agency industry is characterized by ease of entry. In contrast, virgin copper production requires an expensive plant and access to satisfactory ore deposits, with the result that few firms enter the business.

The possibility of expansion or contraction of *imports* from foreign countries must be taken into account for some commodities. The importation of sugar from the Philippines has long been a crucial factor in the outlook for the domestic sugar industry. Similarly, domestic paper producers must consider imports from Canada and Scandinavian countries. The extent of imports is, of course, strongly influenced by tariffs and foreign exchange, which may entirely prevent foreign goods from entering local markets or allow only certain types of goods to enter at competitive prices.

Effect of excess capacity. Excess capacity will have a depressing influence on the outlook for an industry, for it may lead to low prices, low rates of operation, and a high proportion of sales expense.

The seriousness of excess capacity depends, in part, upon how large depreciation, interest, and other expenses connected with the facilities are in relation to total costs. If, as in the chemical fertilizer industry, these overhead charges are a high percent of total expenses, the individual companies may cut prices to low levels in an attempt to secure volume and at least some contribution above out-of-pocket expenses toward the fixed burden. On the other hand, if the bulk of expense goes for materials and labor, the excess capacity will have much less effect on supply and price because the relation between out-of-pocket costs and prices will be the controlling influence—whether the plant is busy or not.

Durability of the excess capacity is also important. In the textile business, for instance, excess looms and other equipment were available for many years. The failure of a particular company did not *remove* this *capacity*, for the equipment was merely sold—usually at a low price—to another firm and again placed in operation. As a result, profitable operations were very difficult. Scrapping of existing facilities must sometimes be considered when overcapacity exists, although the usual pattern is the development of more efficient methods and machinery that make operation of the old facilities impossible at competing prices.

Labor costs

The significance of labor cost to an industry depends on whether it is *labor intensive* or *capital intensive*. If value is added primarily through the use of manpower rather than machines, then labor supply, wage rates, and labor efficiency become critical factors. The small-scale dairy farm, for instance, is rapidly disappearing because of its low return for a relatively high labor input. High-grade furniture is suffering from a similar difficulty.

In many industries the additional labor cost has been passed on to the consumer, and in some instances the contention that the additional labor cost can be offset by technological improvements is justified. On the other hand, a particular industry that is facing competitive substitution of other products or that produces an article for which the demand is comparatively elastic may not be able to increase its selling prices enough to offset the higher labor costs. In such instances the prediction regarding labor costs may be vital to a conclusion regarding general profitability of the industry. Clearly, high labor productivity will be a key to success of individual firms.

Material costs

The sheer existence of an adequate supply of raw materials may be a factor in the outlook of a few industries, notably those depending upon a natural resource such as timber, crude oil, iron ore, or other minerals. In most cases, however, the problem is the price at which the materials can be obtained.

Changes in raw material prices have varying effects on different industries. For example, public utilities have relatively stable rates, and firms selling through catalogs have fixed prices for at least a season. For such companies, a fall in raw material prices increases the gross margin, and rising prices decrease the profit margin. In other industries, such as textiles or containers, the selling price is comparatively flexible and may be adjusted as material prices go up or down.

A forecast of prices of the major raw materials of an industry requires at least a brief study of the history and present conditions in the raw material producing industry. Past prices should be reviewed for the purpose of determining any general trend or the typical behavior of the commodity price. Some raw materials show sharp seasonal fluctuations, others are characterized by very wide and rapid changes in price, while still others are typically stable or sluggish in their movements. Prices of finished steel products, for example, reveal considerable rigidity; on the other hand, a product such as raw cotton or leather fluctuates over a wide range. Generally speaking, the problem with respect to material costs is to predict the way fluctuations in both raw material prices and finished goods prices will affect the *margin* between the two.

Occasionally changes or raw material prices are less important because of the possibility of using substitutes. In the production of some steel products, for example, the proportion of scrap iron to pig iron can be varied in accordance with relative prices and availability of supply. Within limits, natural gas can be substituted for feedstock from oil refineries in the production of chemical-fertilizer. Insofar as such substitution is practical, the availability of either raw material at low prices will be a favorable factor in the outlook of the consuming industry.

Taxes and other costs

Taxes make a heavy drain on all profitable industries, but of particular concern here are special levies such as the excise tax on alcoholic beverages or a processing tax on agricultural commodities. When such special taxes are found, it is then necessary to explore (a) whether the amount of the tax can be added to selling prices and thereby passed on to the consumer, and (b) if it is passed on, whether the increase in price will be large enough to cut sales volume.

A few industries, notably oil and mining, have enjoyed tax cuts in the form of *depletion allowances* (the purpose is to stimulate search for scarce material resources). Political pressure is building up against all preferential tax treatment—tax loopholes—and the profit prospects of an industry can be seriously jeopardized by a likely reform in the tax laws.

Other costs such as rent or interest may influence the prospects for an industry. The heavy interest and retirement charges incurred by the airlines in their rush to fly superjet planes, for instance, casts a pall on the entire industry. Usually it is a specific company that is in a particularly favorable or unfavorable position because of "other costs" rather than an industry as a whole, and consequently these other costs will generally have only a monor bearing on the outlook for the industry.

COMPETITIVE CONDITIONS IN THE INDUSTRY

The outline thus far has suggested that the outlook for an industry will be determined by the balance of the various forces affecting demand and supply of the products of the industry. Competitive conditions within the industry will often affect the manner and the rapidity with which these forces work themselves out.

Nature of companies in the industry

Some industries are dominated by a few *large companies,* the actions of which are of major importance to the future profitability of the entire industry. For example, the Federal Trade Commission has alleged that profits in the farm machinery industry have been abnormally high due, in part, to the fact that this industry was dominated by two or three large companies. Likewise, the United States Steel Corporation is reputed to have "held the umbrella" over the price structure of the steel industry for a long period of years. In contrast, other industries are characterized by *atomistic competition,* in which each small firm seeks to adjust the current condition as rapidly as possible. The weaving of dress goods and numerous other branches of the textile industry typify this type of competition.

Companies in an industry also vary as to *stability* and *financial strength.* An industry characterized by firms of great instability and comparative financial weakness is illustrated by the women's ready-to-wear industry. Here firms are organized, operate for a limited period of time, and then pass out of the picture so rapidly that widespread goodwill among customers or reputation for dependability is rarely established. In other branches of the clothing industry, such as the men's shoe industry, several of the leading firms have been in operation for two or more generations and have a stability and financial backing that tend to make competitive conditions less chaotic and unpredictable.

The *attitude* of the management of companies in an industry may also affect the outlook. The typical managements in some industries are sharp and irresponsible and take only a short-run point of view. They are likely to engage in activities that may give them an immediate benefit irrespective of the future repercussions of their actions. In contrast, the typical managements in other industries tend to adhere strictly to an accepted code of business ethics and are inclined to take a long-run industry viewpoint in their actions. *Leadership* in an industry may also be characterized as aggressive and alert, as in the packaging industry. This is in contrast to unimaginative leadership, which with some qualifications was said to characterize the railroad industry during the period when trucks were taking away much of its profitable freight business.

Beware of the industry where size, strength, and leadership of companies is so weak that competition is chaotic. At the other extreme, be cautious about tackling large, financially strong, well-managed, aggressive companies—unless prospects for rapid industry growth are high.

Organization of the industry

Organized cooperative effort has a significant effect upon the outlook for some industries. There are literally hundreds of trade associations, which are the central agencies for such voluntary action. Many of these associations do little more than sponsor an annual convention and perhaps a trade paper. Others, like insurance associations, engage in research and compilation of information of interest to its members, lobby in national or state legislatures, conduct a public relations campaign, and promote fair trade practices. Some of the trade associations play an active role in government price and production controls. While the scope of such government-industry cooperation is in a state of flux, it is likely that the trade association will assume increasing importance in this regard. In any event, it is already clear that an intelligently run trade association can contribute significantly to the stability, public relations, and government relations of an industry.

Government regulation of industry

Even the most ardent advocates of "American individualism" will admit that the forces of supply and demand should not be given free sway in the contemporary business world. There are, however, wide differences of opinion regarding the extent to which government should seek to restrict and regulate these forces. During recent years government regulation has been extended on many fronts, and it appears likely that this tendency will continue.

Federal and state governments have for some time regulated in considerable detail the activities of utilities and life insurance companies. There is much discussion as to the desirability of extending this concept to other industries such as aerospace or even to all industries vital to public welfare. If for a given industry any action in this direction seems likely, it is highly important to study the nature and the effects of the regulations that might be imposed.

The government often provides *special advantages* to particular industries. Our merchant marine is heavily subsidized; many other industries are protected from foreign competition by tariffs; agricultural products have been granted large subsidies. In order to qualify for such special advantages, it is often necessary for the industry to conform to stipulations and regulations of the government. This is particularly true in the agricultural industries where the whole program of subsidies is associated with a plan for controlled production and marketing.

Government bodies exercise influence over general *trade practices*. The Federal Trade Commission Act has been strengthened so that the commission may more effectively regulate what it considers unfair methods of competition; at the same time special powers were granted over advertising of foods, drugs, health devices, and cosmetics. It is quite probable that additional statutes regulating trade practices will be enacted from time to time.

Such government action is frankly and deliberately designed to modify the underlying forces of demand and supply. It is part of the composite picture of the outlook for any industry.

Emerging synthesis

Industry analysis along the lines outlined should lead to two vital conclusions:

1. Outlook for volume and profits in the industry.
2. Key factors necessary for company success in the industry.

These conclusions will be essential inputs in the designing of an effective company strategy.

Perhaps the total picture will have to be broken down into several different industries or subindustries to highlight the opportunities and to identify what is required to achieve them. On the other hand, the conclusions need not be burdened with all the detail checked during the analysis; it is the dominant emerging factors that should be sifted out.

MARKET POSITION OF THE COMPANY

Success comes from matching opportunity with capability. The industry analyses, just discussed, should flag an array of opportunities, so we next examine the particular strengths and weaknesses of a company to grasp these opportunities.

Can the company get its share of new markets? Is it fortified against impending hazards? Does it enjoy a favorable or unfavorable cost position as compared with its competitors? Will its management make it a leader in the industry? Such factors as these will determine whether a specific enterprise will get along better or worse than the industry as a whole. Answers to these questions will also point to the particular problems that become the core of company strategy.

Relation of company sales to those of the industry and leading competitors

The ups and downs of a total industry often obscure how well a specific company is being managed. A revealing way to screen out such external influences is to watch company sales as a percentage of its total industry and its major competitors. A dramatic example of loss of industry position is Univac—the computer subsidiary of Sperry Rand Corporation. Univac's forebearer was the leading pioneer in digital computers and in the 1950's was expected to maintain its strong position. Its sales grew, but it failed to capture the lion's share of the market. Again in the 1960's Univac had an upsurge, only to lose position again to its competitors—as the following table shows.

Computer Installations
Net Additions

	Total Industry	Univac	Univac % of Industry
1962	3,280	79	2.4%
1963	5,017	365	7.3
1964	7,278	1,682	23.1
1965	7,842	1,300	16.6
1966	8,379	496	5.9
1967	12,036	375	3.1
1968	16,056	662	4.1

Here was a company very technically oriented. It was good at pioneering, and it achieved initial success with its new designs. But Univac was slow in exploiting commercially sound products. Its competitors, notably IBM, were more sensitive to customer needs and had stronger marketing organizations. As soon as the key to success embraced the market as well as the laboratory, Univac slipped.

Comparisons of a company's sales with those of its industry are usually possible in one form or another. The United States Department of Commerce and other government agencies publish vast quantities of valuable statistics; trade associations often compile figures on volume of activity; sometimes trade papers assemble data and publish indexes of activity; or occasionally a special source, such as F. W. Dodge Corporation (construction industry) or the A. C. Nielsen Company (retail grocery and drug sales), is available to subscribers. In spite of statistical weaknesses that often exist in such comparisons, some measure of the trend in a company's position is highly valuable.

Standing of company products

The market position of a company is strongly influenced by the quality and the distinctiveness of its products. The automobile that has distinctive engineering features, the motel that serves good food, the hospital equipment that has dependability and durability, or the airline with a good on-time record is the product that will improve its position on the market. In the case of each type of product, the important characteristics from the *user's point of view* should be determined and a company's products should be appraised in terms of these characteristics. In this process it is necessary to distinguish between various price ranges, because the controlling characteristics may not be the same for, say, low-priced shoes and high-priced shoes.

A classic case of a company failing to keep its product attuned to customer requirements was Baldwin Locomotive Company. For many years a leader in American industry, Baldwin insisted on making only steam engines. Even when diesel-electric engines had taken three fourths of the new orders, Baldwin executives argued that steam power would continue to be used for heavy freight runs. In fact, Baldwin's sales did increase from depression lows, but its share of the industry total dropped steadily. In contrast, Electro-Motive division of General Motors Corporation pioneered in diesel development; and because its product required less servicing, had lower maintenance costs, needed a shorter time "getting up steam," and enjoyed other operating economies, Electro-Motive's position in the industry moved from 14% to 76% in a 20-year span.

Sometimes the past success of a company is attributable to a single product, whereas future success in the industry must be built upon an *ability to develop new products*. For example, the Mead Johnson Company has enjoyed very large sales of its prepared baby cereal "Pablum," but possible substitutes or changes in ideas regarding child feeding made this single product an inadequate base for maintenance of a leading position in the industry. This company, fully recognizing the danger, developed a wide line of baby foods and then hit upon another winner—Metrecal.

Strength of company in major markets

A company's position in its industry is also affected by its reputation in major markets. For instance, some motels cater to commercial travelers and business conferences, while competitors carefully nurture the tourist trade. Supplementary services and sales promotion help, then, to focus on their target market.

Often the reputation of a firm varies by area as well as by type of customer. This is illustrated by different brands of coffee. Many local brands exist that are known in only one metropolitan area or perhaps one region; even the nationally advertised brands experience substantial differences in consumer acceptance in different sections of the country. In the same way, a particular manufacturer of farm machinery may have a strong *dealer organization* in the corn-belt states but have weak dealers and acceptance in the cotton states.

Reputation is an intangible thing including, in addition to being known, a prominence for giving service, for offering a good buy in terms of product and price, and for fair dealings. Many companies, as already indicated, have a niche in the industry where they are outstanding. For purposes of forecasting, the problem is to identify those areas or types of trade from which a company will obtain its business and then consider the prospects for such groups on the basis of the outlook for the general industry.

Note also that a relatively small firm may deliberately cater to a particular segment of the market or concentrate on a narrower line of products than do the large firms, which are obligated to offer a complete line. Crown Cork & Seal Company, for instance, has been highly successful in focusing on aerosol and beer cans; for these products its engineering and delivery service is outstanding. But it does not try to compete with the big American Can and Continental Can companies for the large-volume food business.

COST POSITION OF THE COMPANY

The position of a firm in its industry depends upon its ability to deal with supply factors as well as with demand or market factors. Its relative cost position influences the extent and the direction of company expansion and may be the key to survival itself.

Comparative location

Ready and inexpensive access to raw materials is a major asset for companies using bulky products. The newsprint mills of Canada, for instance, now have a controlling advantage over their former competitors in Wisconsin, Michigan, or the New England states because the virgin timber in the latter areas has been cut off and logs—or pulp—must be transported long distances to the mills. In fact, most of the remaining mills in these areas have turned to specialty paper products to counteract the disadvantage of their location. Ready access to crude oil is vital for an integrated petroleum concern.

Location with respect to labor is sometimes a definite advantage or disadvantage to a company. Minimum-wage legislation and union activity have greatly reduced geographic differentials in wage rates within the United States, so "cheap labor" is now obtainable only in foreign countries. Occasionally a company located in a rural area is at a disadvantage if expansion requires that skilled workers must be induced to move from the cities.

In some industries, location close to markets is crucial. This is obvious for retail stores for which buyer traffic may mean the difference between success or failure. Printing firms that wish to serve advertising agencies must locate nearby so as to provide the necessary speed in service. For heavy products like cement, shipping expense becomes a significant factor.

Industry analysis, already discussed, should have indicated the significance—or the insignificance—of a favorable location with respect to raw materials, labor, or markets.

Relative efficiency of equipment

The production facilities of a company may have an important bearing on its future success. A prime consideration is whether the plant can make products suited to the trends in demand. To take an example from a service industry, high-ceiling hotel rooms without air conditioning no longer serve the lodging market satisfactorily. Bowling alleys as a form of entertainment are in a similar fix.

Often such outmoded facilities are doubly disadvantageous because other companies are also likely to have excess equipment for the declining products; therefore, profit margins tend to be narrow, especially in contrast to margins on the expanding products that may be in short supply.

A second consideration is the operating costs of the equipment. This is illustrated in the printing industry where one-color, hand-fed presses can be used for three- or four-color work by running the paper through the presses a separate time for each color. However, an automatic, multicolor press can do the entire printing job in one operation with a single pressman. Except for special jobs, a firm with only one-color, hand-fed presses cannot compete for multicolor work because its costs are too high.

Flexibility of equipment is often a factor in operating costs. For example, large jet planes such as the Boeing 747 are efficient for transatlantic and cross-continental flights, but they are expensive and hard to handle on short runs where traffic is lighter. Smaller, flexible planes cost more to operate per passenger mile than a 747 when the latter is fully loaded on a long flight, but they have decided advantages in filling varying needs. Again, the crucial point is having equipment suited to the market the company wants to serve.

Unique cost advantages

In practice, firms often achieve cost advantages in a variety of other ways that may not be available to their competitors. The following examples merely suggest these possibilities. A patented or secret process may give a firm unusually low operating costs. In other cases a long-term contract or lease may be particularly beneficial. Some companies, through affiliations with other operating units or by virtue of their own size, are able to buy materials at lower prices because of the large quantities taken.

A concern may enjoy for a time low depreciation expense because its facilities are carried on the books at substantially less than replacement costs. This usually occurs when equipment or even an entire plant is bought secondhand at a distress sale, or the assets may have been written down in connection with a financial reorganization. On the other hand, the assets may be overvalued in terms of present replacement costs and the firm may be trying to cover depreciation charges that are substantially higher than those of its competitors.

Whatever the reason, the basic problem is to attempt to discover any significant reasons why the company in question is in a better, or worse, position than its competitors in supplying goods that are in demand.

SPECIAL COMPETITIVE CONSIDERATIONS

Two further considerations, in addition to market and supply factors, influence the ability of an enterprise to grasp new opportunities; namely, financial strength and competence of the company executives.

Relative financial strength

Adequate capital provides one of the necessary means to put plans of the business administrator into action. A company may enjoy a distinctive product, an unusually low cost, or some other advantage over its competitors; but virtually every type of expansion requires additional capital for inventory and accounts receivable if not also for fixed assets. Moreover, if a firm is to maintain its position, it must have sufficient financial strength to withstand depressions and aggressive drives by competitors for choice markets. Competition may force a company to expand the variety of products offered for sale, to establish district warehouses and local sales organizations, or to buy new equipment, and this requires capital.

The simplest way for a company to meet these capital requirements is from its own cash balances, which may be larger than necessary for day-to-day operations. Most concerns, however, do not carry large amounts of idle cash (or nonoperating assets readily convertible into cash such as government securities), in which case financial strength is primarily a question of ability to borrow net capital or to secure it from stockholders. Ability to raise new capital will reflect not only past and probable future earnings, but also the existing debt structure and fixed charges of the company. So, the entire financial structure of the company should be examined, particularly if there are likely to be major readjustments in industry operations.

Ability of company management

The most important single factor influencing the position of a company in its industry is the ability of its executives. The executives of a business turn potential sales into actual sales, keep costs in line, and face the endless stream of new and unanticipated problems.

The qualities desired for executives are numerous and vary to some extent for different types of companies; for example, the manager of a specialty shop needs a style sense, whereas the head of a hospital must have ability to supervise a diverse collection of professional employees. Industry analysis may have identified outstanding research capability as a key to success, or it may be a willingness to take risks.

No single executive should be expected to have all the talents required, but within the management group there should be vision, creativeness, supervisory ability, human understanding, diligence, and other qualities essential to the planning, direction, and control of the enterprise. In fact, partly due to age and to the personal motivations of people in central management posts, the capacity of company managements differs sharply.

In predicting the future of a business, it is also necessary to consider the extent to which success is dependent on a few individuals and the provision that has been made for a succession of capable leadership. This is a crucial factor in the outlook for a small "one-man company."

Comparison of strengths and needs

Each company has its particular strengths—and weaknesses. These can be assessed in terms of successful firms in the company's present industry (or industries). Much more significant for strategic planning, however, is to think in terms of *future* requirements in growth areas. As already noted, a vital conclusion from industry analyses is the identification of key factors for future success. Now, the revealing question is how does the company match up to these *key success factors?* If several industries or subindustries have been studied, in which do the company strengths offer the greatest advantage and in which are the company weaknesses least critical?

Rarely will the match between company strengths and key success factors be perfect. Where a mismatch appears and where weaknesses might bar success, attention can then be directed to the feasibility and the cost of overcoming the handicap. Expanded product research, stronger dealer organization, or even new central management may be required. The point here is that a comparison of company strengths and weaknesses with previously established criteria for success identifies where profitable growth is most likely and where corrective action is needed.

SUMMARY

The base from which a company strategy is developed is an insightful recognition of (a) dynamic conditions in the environment where the company operates, (b) the prospects for its industry generally, and (c) its position in that industry. A systematic analysis of each of these aspects should be made frequently by the top executives of the company. In studying the industry outlook, a continuing review is desirable of the demand for the products of the industry, the factors affecting supply, and the competitive conditions. Similarly, analysis of company position calls for appraisal of the relative standing of the company in markets and in costs, and also review of its competitive strength.

Clearly a great many facts and forecasts bear on a company outlook. Some device is needed to put these data into systematic relationship. The outlines in Chapters 2 and 3 provide a method of putting the array of data into meaningful order.

Such an analysis is far from a mechanical or routine matter, however. Keen judgment is especially vital in attaching *relative importance* to the numerous factors that have some influence on the outlook. A general outline, such as the one discussed in the last two chapters, suggests possibilities but cannot decide which are the key considerations for a specific company. To identify the key factors, ask: (1) What influences or elements are probably going to determine which companies in the industry will enjoy outstanding success and which will decline? (2) How do the strengths and the weaknesses of Company X match against the crucial factors identified in the answer to question (1)?

When a company considers shifting or expanding into a new industry, central managers should make the same kind of analysis just suggested for the company's present industry.

QUESTIONS FOR CLASS DISCUSSION

1. Using the framework for industry analysis suggested in this chapter, what do you conclude are (a) the industry outlook and (b) the key factors for success in the nursing home industry?
2. Several years ago bowling became a very popular pastime. New large bowling alleys were constructed in all parts of the country, and companies making bowling alley equipment prospered. Many people still bowl, but the rapid growth has stopped; both equipment manufacturers and alleys are in financial difficulties. (a) What characteristics of demand are illustrated in the experience of the bowling industry? (b) To what extent do you think skiing will have a similar experience? Explain the similarities and the dissimilarities present.
3. Companies often operate in more than one industry; for example, from its early beginnings Procter & Gamble has been in both the soap and the food shortening

(Crisco) industries. Consequently, when studying a company we often face a practical question of how to define an "industry." For instance, we can consider the energy business, or the petroleum business, or the fuel oil business. What are the advantages of using a broad scope? a narrow scope? Illustrate your answer in terms of the communications vs. telephone vs. long-distance conversation "industry," or some other industry with which you are familiar.

4. How does the "ease of entry" of new firms into the restaurant industry as compared to the difficulty of entry into the basic aluminum industry affect (a) the nature of competition in each industry and (b) the crucial factors for success in each industry?

5. How does the concept of social responsibility presented in Chapter 1 relate to the assessment of a company's strength? (a) Give specific points from the analytical outline on page 39 that will be affected by a strong sense of social responsibility. (b) Will the outlook for a company be improved if its central managers take social responsibility seriously?

6. Company analysis outlined in this chapter focused on profit enterprises. To test the applicability of the same approach to nonprofit enterprises, use the outline to analyze the outlook for your university or college. Use both the industry section and the company position section.

7. Lowering of tariff barriers, improvements in transportation, and greater similarities in consumer tastes due to more travel and better communications —all tend to increase international trade. How does this trend affect the outlook of an English manufacturer of men's suits? a U.S. manufacturer of children's dresses?

8. Assume that you have decided to open a new carwash establishment in the city in which you now live. Your alternatives on production methods range from a hand operation with only hoses, brushes, and rags as equipment to a fully automatic tunnel that can be run by a single individual who collects money as the cars enter. (a) Would you invest in the capital intensive process or the labor intensive process? (b) Does your answer to (a) imply a general view that new operations in your city in any line of business should be as capital intensive (or labor intensive) as technology will permit? (c) What other competitive strengths do you believe will be crucial to your success in your new venture?

CASE 3 / FACT Oil Company

The board of directors of the FACT Oil Company has before it a recommendation from the firm's executive group for the expenditure of about $2,300,000,000 on new capital investment over the next eleven years. Approval will mean a marked departure from previous company strategy and a chance to be an early entrant in a new and developing source of energy.

The company's situation. FACT Oil, unlike the integrated major oil companies such as Texaco, Gulf, Shell, and EXXON, has been primarily a transportation, refining, and wholesale distributing company. It purchases crude oil in Venezuela and from producers in the United States, refines the oil in the U.S., and sells refinery products through its own distribution network to independent retailers east of the Rocky Mountains. This way of operating has been reasonably successful in the past, but company executives, looking forward to 1990, do not believe that it will be as successful in the future.

Since they see no way to follow the strategy of the integrated majors (worldwide exploration and production, refining outside the United States, and worldwide marketing), they propose something else—becoming a raw material supplier to energy consumers in the United States as well as continuing current operations on the same physical scale. "We believe energy requirements will increase by a factor of 2 by 1995 and we want to increase our share of that growing market. Since U.S. demand is above the indigenous supply capability and while the majors in the industry plan to meet the deficiency by oil and gas imports, we have an alternate strategy—to develop 'frontier' indigenous sources and search for attractive niches on this 'frontier.'"

Table 1 and Chart 1 represent the proposal.

Table 1, Summary

	1975	*1986*	
		Stand Pat	*Proposed*
Sales (millions)	$1,700	$3,100	$4,600
Net Income (millions)	140	210	510
% on Sales	8.2	6.8	11.1
Assets (millions)	2,700	2,500-3,000	5,000

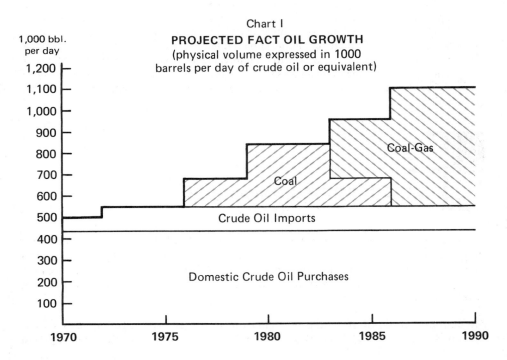

Chart I
PROJECTED FACT OIL GROWTH
(physical volume expressed in 1000 barrels per day of crude oil or equivalent)

Approval is requested for (a) the proposed coal-based concept and (b) expenditures of $200 million this year to begin mine development.

An array of facts and predictions bears on the wisdom of the proposed shift in strategy. The primary data that company management has available are summarized below.

Energy demand and supply. The United States is the world's largest user of energy. Its consumption in 1975 was 50% more than all of Western Europe, whose combined population was much larger (75%) than the U.S. total. This demand for energy comes from many sources: generation of electricity, 27%; transportation, 25%; industry (excluding electricity), 24%; residential and commercial (excluding electricity), 18%; and other, 6%. Despite many uncertainties, America's appetite for energy may almost triple by the year 2000.

Chart 2 reflects a projected annual growth rate in U.S. use of energy of 3.5%—slightly above the 1900-1975 average but well below the 1960-1975 average of 4.3%. The projections assume that prices for imported oil will drop from 1975 levels of $11 to $12 per barrel to between $7 and $9 (in 1975 dollars).

Another demand projection assuming maximum efforts in conservation in the United States has been developed by the Office of Emergency Preparedness:

Demand Projection Based on Maximum Conservation in U.S.

Year	Current Demand Projected				Demand with Conservation			
	All Energy		Oil Consumed		All Energy		Oil Consumed	
1980	96 quadrillion Btu's[1]		21 million bbls daily		82 quadrillion Btu's		16 million bbls daily	
1985	117	"	24	"	92	"	17.5	"
1990	140	"	27.5	"	106	"	19.5	"

[1] One quadrillion British Thermal Units (Btu's) equals the amount of energy produced by 172 million barrels of oil, 1 trillion cubic feet of natural gas, or 41.6 million tons of coal.

Conservation efforts required would be to: improve home insulation; upgrade commercial construction standards; shift 10% of freight from trucks to rail; set up freight consolidation centers; provide more mass transit; produce smaller, more efficient autos; design more efficient air conditioners; recycle waste heat and scrap metal; and replace inefficient industrial processes.

The Committee for Economic Development worked out the supply pattern that would be needed in 1985 to provide energy with a projected growth in demand of 2.9% per year and with strong conservation measures in effect:

Possible Pattern of U.S. Energy Supply in 1985
with Imports Held to 10% of Total Use
(quadrillion Btu's)

Domestic Production		Imports	
Oil —Conventional.................	28.5	Oil........................	8.5
—Synthetic	2.0	Gas	1.5
Gas—Conventional.................	26.5	Total.....................	10.0
—Synthetic	1.5		
Coal	21.5		
Nuclear	10.0	Total Supply, Domestic	
Hydroelectric, Solar, Geothermal	5.0	and Imports	105.0

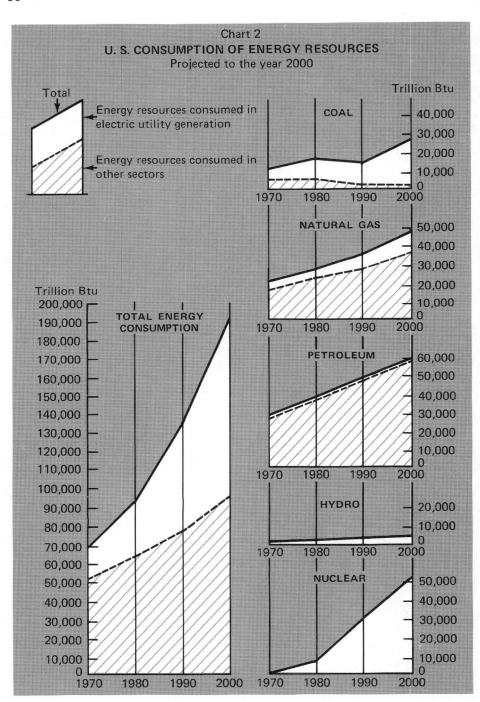

Chart 2
U. S. CONSUMPTION OF ENERGY RESOURCES
Projected to the year 2000

SOURCE: U.S. Bureau of Mines, Federal Power Commission, Resources for the Future, Inc.

Coal. In all of the energy projections given on the preceding pages, coal plays an important role.

How much coal does the United States have? There is no single answer, and expert estimates differ. The U.S. Geological Survey has identified 1.5 trillion tons—theoretically enough to last for 2,500 years at a mining rate of 600 million tons a year. But most of this cannot be recovered with existing technology at the prices current in the mid-1970's. The best estimate of readily recoverable reserves is 450 billion tons, enough to last the U.S. for 200 years beyond 1995 at a then-projected mining rate of 2 billion tons per year. And this assumes no advances in technology or in real prices from 1975 to 1995. One hundred and twenty-five million tons are low sulfur (1% S or less), and 75% of this is in the Western area that runs south from Montana and North Dakota through Wyoming, Utah, and Colorado to the Four Corners area of northern Arizona and New Mexico. Most of the western coal can be strip-mined at a cost (in 1975) of $4 to $6 per ton, compared to deep-mining costs of $10 to $15. These are costs at the minemouth, and they pertain to utility-grade coal—not the low-sulfur, low-ash, high Btu content, strong coal sold for metallurgical purposes.

U.S. Production of Bituminous Coal
(millions of net tons)

Year	Amount	Year	Amount
1920	569	1970	603
1930	467	1971	552
1940	461	1972	586
1950	516	1973	591
1960	416	1974	604
1965	512	1975	650

Predictions made in the early 1970's of greatly expanded demand for coal have been borne out by rapidly rising prices rather than increases in output. Restrictions on output have not been arbitrary but have been the natural consequence of: the time required to develop and open a new mine (2 to 5 years); delayed investment in new mines while company managements waited for clarification of federal legislation on strip mining (land restoration adds $1 to $3 a ton to costs and is impossible where rainfall is less than 10 inches per year); a 28% decline in productivity as mine-safety legislation began to be obeyed by the coal owners and enforced somewhat by the Interior Department; and shortages of skilled miners.

Despite their long experience, the managements of existing coal companies were not able to increase output substantially in an environment with new constraints to which they had to adjust.

Coal prices paid by utility companies increased, on the average, from $8 per ton in 1973 to $18.30 in 1975.

Coal gasification and liquefaction. The technology to convert bituminous coal or lignite into a gas with 900 to 1,000 Btu's per cubic foot (natural gas averages 1,032 Btu's) is a combination of the Lurgi technology developed in Germany during the 1930's to turn coal into a medium-Btu gas and a newer "methanation" process to bring the heating value up to 950 Btu's per cubic foot. Two pilot plants have been in operation since 1974.

On a commercial scale, El Paso Natural Gas and Western Gasification Company broke ground in 1975 for coal mines and gasification plants that they plan to have in operation in northwestern New Mexico in 1978. El Paso's project was announced in 1971. Four years later it had received approvals from the state and federal governments and the Navajo tribe to invest $180 million in a coal mine and about $700 million in the total project (the original estimate of the investment cost was 40% less). The crucial variable for the two projects was water, not coal. Extensive negotiations resulted in the two companies' securing rights to all the surplus water in the area (it is piped in from the San Juan river, a tributary of the Colorado).

El Paso expects its costs to be $1.60 to $1.70 per thousand cubic feet of gas in 1978. This should be compared to the $0.64 per 1,000 cubic feet for natural gas established by the Federal Power Commission as the well-head price for "new" gas in 1978 and the landed cost in California of liquefied natural gas from overseas of more than $2 per 1,000 cubic feet.

El Paso and Westco had no alternatives to trying coal gasification. They were not able to buy any more natural gas in the Permian Basin of West Texas and the Andarko Basin of western Oklahoma and Kansas.

Four processes for producing liquid fuel from coal are under study in various places around the world. All of them are expected to still be in the laboratory stage beyond 1976. One pilot plant processing 20 tons per day was opened in 1969 and abandoned five years later. Hydrogenation, the process with the most promise, was predicted in 1974 to require 10 to 20 years for development at a "prudent rate." The National Petroleum Council estimated the cost of synthetic crude from coal to be $6.80 to $7.30 per barrel (in 1972 dollars) in 1985 if a large-scale (100,000 barrels per day) plant were built by then.

The preceding technical evaluation should be judged in the context of a statement made by Dr. Robert C. Seamans, Jr. when he was appointed as head of the Energy Research and Development Administration: "Nuclear power development is still a prime research goal, but the top priority now is developing a synthetic-fuels industry that could make a petroleum-like liquid and a synthetic form of natural gas from coal. The 1985 goal is one million barrels per day (crude oil equivalent) of synthetic fuels derived from coal."

In late 1974 the Interior Department received "only three" industry proposals to participate with the federal government in building a coal-to-oil demonstration plant—far fewer than were expected. The demonstration plant was estimated to cost from $100 million to $400 million and would produce a coal liquid suitable for use as boiler fuel. An executive of one nonbidding company said that his firm decided to refrain from bidding "because of tight money and because Washington is still weighing what steps, if any, it will take to assure the ability of synthetic fuels to compete with crude oil."

Management's proposal. The presentation by the executive group to a special meeting of the board of directors of FACT Oil Company opened with a review of alternate possibilities that had been considered as a means for the company to maintain its share of the energy market.

(1) Enter into a large program of crude oil exploration and production. The risks are large (1 successful exploratory well in 10 drilled) and new operations of drilling on the continental shelf of the United States require an advanced technology that FACT Oil Company does not have, since to date it has primarily purchased crude oil. Exploring

abroad means high political risks, with ownership of any oil pools found remaining with the host government. Expansion based on foreign crude oil also contributes to the U.S. balance of payments problems and would require the company to double or treble the size of its transportation system.

(2) Expand the company's refineries in the United States and increase marketing efforts with a company brand and company-leased retail stations. Refining capacity in the U.S. is low and products are imported from abroad because refineries have had low profit margins for the past decade (a return on investment of two percentage points below that of all U.S. manufacturing). Prospects depend on competition from foreign refineries and on the stringency of environmental regulations such as those of the state of Delaware. Other oil companies are not attempting to increase market share in the U.S. by adding retail stations but are pushing marketing elsewhere in the world. There are more than sufficient retail outlets in existence to meet U.S. demand.

(3) Produce synthetic crude from either oil shale in Colorado or the Athabaskan tar sands. The technology of getting oil from shale has been stuck at the pilot plant stage since 1958 when Union Oil finally abandoned the first major attempt. Three consortiums are still working in the Piceance Basin with little chance for success until at least 1990. Use of Athabaskan tar sands, in northern Canada, has encountered much higher investment and operating costs than anticipated. One 50,000 barrel-per-day refinery has had a loss for eight years. Closing down a much larger project during construction was forestalled only by a capital injection of a billion dollars by the Canadian government.

(4) Coal gasification and liquefaction. Executives of the firm believe this path holds the best promise. Political risks of expropriation are nil. Natural gas has been in short supply in the United States for over two years and all reliable forecasts expect a continued shortage for the next 10 years. New gas wells are being drilled only in unusual circumstances when the probability of finding gas is above 0.6.

While two natural gas transmission line companies have already begun projects to turn coal into pipeline quality gas, FACT executives see this as an opportunity not really explored by the major oil and gas producers. They believe it to be a niche into which they can move and establish a solid position. Until the gasification plants are ready, coal can be mined and sold on the market—especially low-sulfur coal, for which demand appears to be increasing rapidly. The company has obtained options on low-sulfur coal leases in Montana, near the Yellowstone River, and in West Virginia. The Montana coal could be strip-mined; the Eastern coal would be mined underground.

(5) Recommendation. "That the directors approve our plan to purchase, develop, and implement the coal-based program. The project economics are illustrated in Chart 3. The predicted return on coal mining of 10% on the investment has minimal risk. Coal is a proven commodity with an assured market. The 15% predicted return on the gasification plant has some risk, but we can hold off entering the market until the price is right (about $1.50 per 10^6 Btu or per 1,000 cubic feet). We can sell the gas to utilities. Will they buy? Yes, they have contracted for liquefied natural gas from Algeria in 1972 at $1.02 per 1,000 cubic feet. Alternatively we can sell the gas to industrial users such as steel companies for furnace gas or to electric utilities if the nuclear-power programs continue to be delayed for cost and safety reasons and if the first experimental U.S. fast-breeder reactor does not come on-stream in 1985.

Chart 3
PROJECT ECONOMICS
(M = millions)

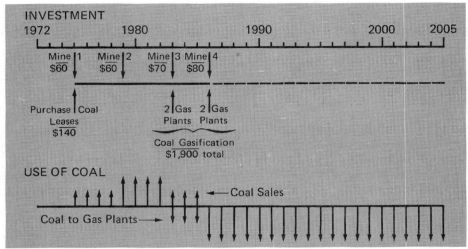

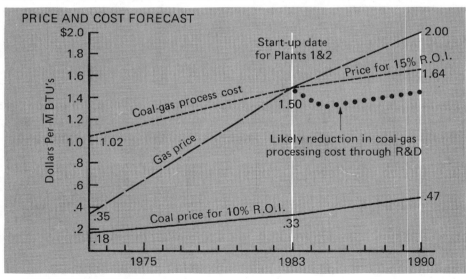

ESTIMATED RETURN

	Coal Mining	Gas
Investment	$410 M	$1,900 M̄
Production capacity	120,000 tons per day	2×10^{12} BTU per day
Product price used in estimating return	$5.60 per ton	$1.50 per 10^6 BTU
Return on investment (discounted cash flow)	10%	15%

"Therefore, we request approval of: (1) the coal-based concept so that intensive and specific planning can be undertaken, and (2) immediate approval to exercise our options to buy coal leases and purchase one existing mine at a cost of $200 million."

Required: (a) What outlook do you see for coal gasification as a source of energy in the United States? For coal?

(b) What is your appraisal of the strategy of the integrated major energy companies?

(c) As a director, how would you vote on the recommendations by the FACT Oil Company executives?

SELECTING COMPANY STRATEGY

Analysis of opportunities by itself is futile. Left alone, it serves mankind even less than making such decisions only after crises arise. Instead, we must use the analysis in selecting actual plans of action. For a company-as-a-whole, this commitment to action logically starts with designing a *master strategy* for the firm.

The two preceding chapters on dynamic environment and company strengths outline the array of forces that should be considered in designing master strategy. They set the stage. The next step is for the principal actors—central managers—to decide how the firm can best adapt to the anticipated opportunities and threats. A company strategy normally should indicate:

1. *Services* to be provided. What products or intangible services will the company sell to what group of customers?
2. *Resource conversion technology* to produce these services. What will the company make and by what processes, and what will it buy from what sources— so as to obtain a relative advantage in supply?
3. Kinds of *synergy* to be exploited. Will the combination of selected thrusts provide extra, mutually reinforcing benefits?
4. *Timing and sequence* of major steps. What moves will be made early, and what can be deferred?
5. *Targets* to be met. What are the criteria for success, and what levels of achievement are expected?

Too often statements of strategy deal with only a single dimension. A new market or a desired financial return on investment, for instance, may be labeled as "our company strategy." Such a goal may indeed be part of the strategy, but its narrowness robs strategy of a needed balanced operational quality. A company strategy should be a well-conceived, practical commitment. To achieve this realistic quality, all five of the elements just listed should be carefully considered. The resulting strategy will then be an *integrated*, forward-looking plan.

The multidimensions of strategy—product/market scope, supply technology, synergy, major moves, and target results—do not require that a strategy be detailed and comprehensive. Rather, strategy should concentrate on *key* factors necessary for success and on *major* moves to be taken by the particular company at the current stage in its development. The selectivity of key points, and by implication its designation of others as supportive, gives strategy much of its value as a planning device.

Full elaboration of plans is a necessary sequel to selecting company strategy—as we shall see in Parts 2 and 3. The role of strategy, however, is to identify primary missions and to set forth major ways of achieving distinctiveness; this is the focus of the present chapter.

SERVICES TO BE PROVIDED

Product/market scope

The starting point in clarifying the mission of almost any enterprise is to define the services it will provide. It may design and manufacture a broad range of physical products or it may merely sell advice. But to continue to exist, it must provide some package of services for which some segment in society is prepared to pay. For example, after carefully examining the anticipated growth in the use of computers for billing retail customers, two enterprising IBM salesmen set up their own firm that (1) leases time on a central computer and (2) assists medium-sized stores in adapting their records and procedures to make use of this service. Note that this young firm has a sharp definition of the kind of computer work it will undertake and the kind of customers it seeks. This definition is a key element in its strategy.

Future orientation

Strategy is concerned with where a company should be headed in the future. Possibly the existing product/market scope is so attractive that the best future course is continued exploitation of a successful strategy. Often growing competition, new demands, market saturation, and similar factors will suggest some shift in the services provided.

Commercial banks, for instance, are in a period of transition. For years banks dealt predominantly with large enterprises and wealthy persons. At most, the common man had a savings account. Then the situation changed. A large portion of the population acquired enough cash to open checking accounts; the banks needed these accounts to swell their deposits; and small fees were introduced to cover the cost of clearing checks, handling monthly payments on auto loans, and similar services. Now your friendly banker is very interested in doing business with blue-collar workers. Some banks changed their customer strategy early; others were too conservative and missed out on much of this new business. And the end of the shift is not yet in sight. Having expanded its types of customers, should a bank provide a complete line of financial services—including investment counseling, insurance sales, income tax advice, and the payment of bills?

Shifts in customer needs occur also in basic products. Even coal raises strategy questions. The Island Creek Coal Company, to cite a specific case, has large deposits of coal especially suited for the production of steel. Clearly the company should serve these metallurgical customers. But the recent growth in coal demand is to generate electricity. Island Creek is handicapped in serving this large market because its coal must be dug in high-cost underground mines and because electric utilities are unwilling to pay a premium for several of the qualities of Island Creek coal. So Island Creek must decide whether to (a) concentrate only on metallurgical customers who will pay a premium, (b) sell its high quality coal to utilities at low prices, (c) try to capture some of the utility business by buying strip mines and learning a new technology, or (d) hold onto its reserves until techniques for converting coal into gas and gasoline become practical.

Opportunities for many companies are created by external changes, as in the two examples just noted. But the future is always uncertain. Strategic choices about product/market scopes usually must be made long before the wise path is evident.

Matching company strengths and market needs

Identification of growth areas is not enough. Each company must also predict the probable competition and its own strengths and limitations in meeting that competition, as suggested in Chapter 3. The book publishing industry provides a good example. The high birth rates of the 1950's made an increase in college enrollment eighteen to twenty years later easy to predict. So a lot of publishers entered the college textbook field. Only a few of these new entrants succeeded, while most firms lost money until they returned to the markets they knew well. The difficulty arose with the publishers' evaluation of their own strengths. They were well qualified in editing and printing, but they were weak in the crucial areas of knowing good authors, evaluating manuscripts, and having a distribution system that reached professors and college bookstores.

Just as assessment of market opportunities often relies on predictions, company strengths can also include expected changes. Thus, if a company does not already possess the strengths needed to grasp an opportunity, it can start filling the gaps so that the strengths will be built by the time they are needed. Several years ago, for instance, a small nonscheduled airfreight company decided that the competition in domestic nonscheduled freight business would be so keen that profits would be marginal at best. On the other hand, there appeared to be an opportunity for an airline carrying only freight in the transatlantic business. The forecast was that the larger airlines whose primary business is passenger traffic would not give the specialized attention that manufacturers moving goods across the ocean desire. The small company had technical skill in freight handling, but it lacked large planes for transatlantic flights and approval to make scheduled flights. It risked its entire assets and its reputation to build these strengths (nearly failing in the process), but finally did muster the resources required for the transition. At the start of this risky strategy both the market and the company strengths were predictions. Fortunately for the company, both predictions came true and the business is prospering.

The aim of such an imaginative analysis of future industry environment and of company strengths is to find a service opportunity that is distinctive—to find a "propitious niche." This idea of a propitious niche is applicable to all sorts of industries. Among magazines, for instance, special-interest journals are the most successful. Volkswagen obviously exploited a particular niche in the automobile industry.

Separate definition of multiple niches

The strategic advantage of picking a niche very carefully does not mean that a company should confine its activities to a single niche. As an enterprise expands, it frequently spots an additional service it can provide effectively. Thus, IBM's strong position in computers was no bar to its entering the electric typewriter field when it developed a product superior to any on the market at that time. In our later discussion of synergy we shall note several other examples of multiple niches. The point being stressed in this section is the selection of any niche—the original one or additional ones—with an eye on the strategic advantage of providing that particular service. Each niche should be appraised in terms of future growth and profitability of the proposed product-market scope and in terms of the company's ability to provide the service with distinction relative to competitors.

RESOURCE CONVERSION TECHNOLOGY

Deciding on services to be provided is only part of a strategic plan. It is the direction, but it does not tell you how to get there. Often the choices made about the way services will be produced spell success or failure. And in making these choices, as in picking propitious niches, the manager may be dealing with a high degree of future uncertainty and with a need to secure a differential advantage over competitors.

Production of own materials

A recurring strategic issue is control of materials needed to create the service(s) that a company expects to sell. How much backward integration is desirable? If materials will be plentiful in the future, they can simply be purchased as needed. Sometimes, however, the company that has ready access to scarce materials is the only one that can grow.

A critical question for integrated petroleum companies for years has been how much crude oil to own relative to refinery requirements. In this industry an open market exists for both crude oil and refined products, so it is possible for a company to have a much larger marketing operation than its own refining or crude oil production. The strategic problem is to predict for the industry as a whole which stage in the total cycle will be relatively short of capacity. If crude is in short supply, that segment of the industry will be most profitable; whereas if total supplies exceed consumer demand, the companies with strong market positions will reap the profits. To cite a recent case, for several years British Petroleum has wanted to obtain a share of the U.S. market for gasoline and fuel oil. Its forecasts indicated, however, that being in the marketing segment alone would be extremely hazardous. Consequently, British Petroleum deferred entry into the U.S. market until its Alaskan explorations provided a promising source of U.S. crude oil. Now, with protection against a profit squeeze on either the crude oil or the marketing end of the business, the company is investing heavily in U.S. expansion.

The basic issue of vertical integration applies to parts and subassemblies as well as to raw materials. Thus, for many years automobile manufacturing involved primarily design, assembly, and marketing. Many of the parts, such as carburetors, speedometers, wheels, and even engines and bodies, were purchased from independent parts manufacturers. For years, the Chrysler Corporation followed a strategy of buying virtually all of the specialized parts. This had several advantages: capital investment was low, flexibility in the changing of parts was achieved, the company organization structure was simplified, and cost control was sharp. The company was slow, however, in noting that shifts in the industry called for a modification of a previously successful strategy. With the decline in the number of automobile manufacturers, and the two largest firms—General Motors and Ford—producing most of their own parts, many independent parts manufacturers went out of business. Chrysler could no longer depend upon several suppliers to compete for its business, nor could it rely upon them to provide technological leadership. This shift in industry structure made the former strategy a weakness rather than a strength.

Even retailers face a major make-or-buy decision. Normally, a retailer expects to buy, directly or indirectly, from a large number of manufacturers. He can select just the assortment of merchandise he believes his customers desire. However, several large retailing organizations, such as Macy's or A & P stores, are experimenting with the strategy of making several of the lines they sell. A & P's total volume of, say, bread can support an economical-sized bakery. Such a bakery has low selling costs and can easily coordinate its product specification and production scheduling with its captive customers.

In practice, the entry of retailers into manufacturing has not been outstandingly successful. Frequently the manufacturing unit becomes complacent and fails to make product and cost innovations as rapidly as aggressive competitors. Often the managements of the retail firms do not fully appreciate the problems of manufacturing, and the investment in fixed plant and equipment restrains a shift to more popular end products. These considerations lead most organizations to limit themselves to "private labeling"; merchandise is sold under the retailer's brand name but is actually produced by an independent supplier who is an expert in the production process. The rapid changes occurring in consumer buying patterns will continue to provide large retailers with opportunities to develop strategic combinations of their own manufacturing, private labeling, and use of nationally advertised brands.

The preceding examples of production of own materials—raw materials, parts, and finished goods—have focused on either owning or not owning the source of supply. A variety of other opinions exists. Many of these are more practical for small companies. Joint ventures, for example in the exploration of oil, reduce the investment required. Long-term contracts or exchange agreements may secure the protection desired without sapping the vigor of the supplying unit. These and comparable arrangements provide room for considerable ingenuity in designing a strategy for a specific situation.

Extent of own research and development

In some industries, such as pharmaceuticals or electronics, strong company research and development is regarded as the touchstone for success. Especially for firms that hope to serve new technical markets, an imaginative engineering department is vital. Two college professors, who set up a firm to design and install equipment to control air pollution of chemical processing plants, considered their research program as a key element in the firm's basic strategy.

But what is good for one firm is not necessarily wise for another. For instance, a leading British cement company relies on very good customer service, not on distinctive products, to win business from competitors. Hence it spends no money on product research; its engineering is focused on reducing operating costs. At the same time, the company does support product research by the industry trade association as a means of meeting competition by other building materials. The president of this company believes that he is receiving adequate research results at a modest cost.

A small computer firm in the United States does even less research. Its niche is in designing and programming applications of computers in wholesaling and other physical distribution centers; it also trains client personnel to use the equipment and new program. The managers of this firm admit that continued improvements in computer equipment are vital for sustained interest in their services. But they predict that the large computer manufacturers will do equipment research far beyond anything their small firm might undertake. So they deliberately follow a strategy of "intellectual hitchhiking."

Production technology

We have already noted in our earlier discussion how technological changes expand or contract particular markets. Changing technology also affects the creation of services. In fact, the amount of capital a firm risks in its decisions to adopt a new technology may far exceed the risks incurred in entering a new market.

One of the most conspicuous examples is an airline's choice of equipment. The introduction of a new type of plane, such as the Boeing 747 jumbo-jets or the supersonic Concorde, can have a dramatic effect on the airlines' competitive position. If the plane provides faster, more comfortable, or just a more dramatic ride, the airline that first puts such equipment into service will woo many passengers from competitors. On the other hand, if the plane proves to be slower or less comfortable, a continuing handicap is faced; and should one or two early accidents mar the plane's safety record, the airline's market position will be damaged for years. Orders for new planes have to be placed several years in advance, at a time when the plane's performance and the public's reaction to the new service are only estimates.

In many industries, the customer is not aware of the production technology, as he is on an airplane, yet a new production process may be critical to the success of a selected strategy. A budding financial news service, for instance, relied on the workability of a new electronic typesetting device to get its report out promptly—and promptness was an essential feature of the proposed service. To cite another example, medical diagnosis may be revolutionized by the central processing of symptoms observed by the local physician, and this will make possible new ways of running clinics. Similarly, the agricultural strategy of an entire nation such as Peru or Chile may be changed when desalinization of water, perhaps with the use of nuclear power, is feasible.

Technology relates to more than physical processes. We also have social technologies. A familiar example is retail selling. For years a customer expected to be waited on by a salesclerk who took merchandise from closed counters or shelves. Then a new type of selling based on open displays and customer self-selection was developed. Companies that foresaw the advantages and the limitations of this new technology—notably supermarkets and discount houses—were able to design a strategy that has appealed to millions of customers.

Single versus multiple locations

Still another consideration in the production of services is the number and the location of producing units. Here, we continue to use "production" in the broad sense of creating whatever services the company sells. Thus, traditionally stockbrokerage firms have confined their offices to financial districts of large cities. However, those firms that foresee widespread public ownership of corporate securities need to match their production facilities to this new market. That means opening many more offices in diverse business centers. Unless the firms adopt this strategy, they cannot cater to the growing general-public market.

Bakeries and dry-cleaning firms face a similar issue of being close to their customers while also having economical processing units.

In manufacturing, the use of multiple locations runs into a limitation of optimum size units. When heavy, specialized machinery is required, the economies of scale dictate large plants. On the other hand, customer service and transportation costs are aided by locations close to markets. Automobile companies attempt to "have their cake and eat it too" by making parts and subassemblies in single plants and then assembling these parts in different locations throughout the country.

The location issue becomes more critical as companies move into foreign markets. In addition to optimum size of plant, tariffs, currency controls, and a host of other problems arise. Despite these difficulties, Caterpillar Tractor Company adopted a strategy several years ago of opening plants in foreign locations, and it has built a strong position in world markets. Other companies, less ready to make a major foreign commitment, have found foreign plants expensive and troublesome. Clearly, the plant location strategy should be a pivotal response to careful weighing of industry prospects and competition in international markets.

Summarizing, the preceding examples of strategic issues related to the "production" of services demonstrates that the strategy involves more than selecting an attractive market. Vertical integration, research and development, technology, or location may be a key to profitable growth for a particular company. In all such situations, we are seeking a specific course of action that takes full advantage of the anticipated environment and of the unique strengths of the particular company.

KINDS OF SYNERGY TO BE EXPLOITED

The emphasis in the preceding discussion has been on identifying just a few vital elements that capitalize on the predicted environment and the relative strengths of the specific company.

We now turn to a different dimension of strategy—the way selected elements fit together. Especially as a company grows, it may seek two or more niches. Success in one market or with one production process generates a desire to conquer new territory. Or, possibly difficulty with one area leads to a search for an additional mission that will buttress current efforts. A key aspect of strategy is that any such expansion provides synergistic opportunities. *Synergy* arises when two actions performed jointly produce a greater result than they would if performed independently. A simple example is building a restaurant with a motel; the restaurant makes the motel a more convenient place to stop, and the motel contributes business to the restaurant; the total business is larger than it would be if the two units were located 5 miles apart. Often this is called the "*2 + 2 = 5*" effect. Possible opportunities for synergy are discussed below.

Optimum scale of operations

Often some asset or strength of a company is not fully utilized. If an attractive additional niche can be found that needs this unused capacity, then synergy should arise. Here are a few examples.

If the customer buys only a small quantity of any one product at a time, it may be necessary to offer him several products so that a salesperson may secure sufficient sales on each to justify the expense of making a stop. For example, for years Fuller Brush salespeople sold only brushes in their door-to-door calls on housewives. Recently, a combination of price competition on brushes plus an increase in basic wage scales has made the housecall to sell brushes alone uneconomical. So, to more fully utilize each call, the product line has been expanded to other household supplies.

A textile printing and finishing firm had expensive equipment and trained operators to produce unusual effects on woven fabrics. Profit margins were good when the equipment was operating, but the specialty nature of the service resulted in substantial idle time. To fill the gap, the firm added a line of plastic shower curtains, simulated leather, and similar products to which the specialized machinery could be adapted. The raw material was new and the customers completely different, but the firm had marked synergistic advantage in its low incremental cost of production.

Seasonal or cyclical stabilization

Synergy occurs when a company that faces large seasonal or cyclical fluctuations succeeds in finding a use for its resources that otherwise would be idle during the slack period. Until recently, for instance, electric utility companies expected peak demand during the winter months when lighting and industrial demand is higher than in the summer. Then came air conditioning, which not only absorbed previous idle capacity but has grown to the point that most utility companies now face peak demands in the summer. Since electricity cannot be stored, seasonally complementary business is particularly attractive.

The growing resort industry also faces sharp seasonal peaks. One strategy used by resort hotels is to cater to training conferences that are held in their off-peak periods. A few New England hotels have established ski runs to attract winter guests. Other companies operate in New England during the summer and in Florida during the winter; this does not relieve idle facilities but does permit companies to offer steady employment to key personnel such as chefs.

In each of the above examples, the combination of two different services provides advantages that would not occur if the activities were separated.

Cyclical stabilization is much more difficult to achieve, especially since the fluctuations are much more irregular and difficult to predict than seasonal fluctuations. One strategy used by industrial firms is to seek both military and civilian business. Military orders are quite volatile and subject to cancellation on short notice. Consequently, firms doing this kind of work prefer to also have a significant volume of civilian business that will permit them to keep their basic organization intact when military demand drops off. A second kind of synergy sought is the transfer of technical know-how; skills and knowledge acquired on a government contract hopefully will be applicable to civilian business with a much shorter learning period.

Expansion matrix

Since many of the opportunities for synergy occur when a company is expanding, a framework for thinking about expansion is desirable. The following diagram suggests that expansion arising from fuller use of productive capability would lead in quite different directions than providing the same services to a wider range of customers. With respect to synergy, as a firm moves farther away from its present customers and/or its present productive capability, the prospects for synergistic benefits diminish. At the extreme (lower right corner), if new customers are to be served with a completely different knowledge and facilities, synergy tends to disappear; the firm is then involved in "conglomerate" expansion.

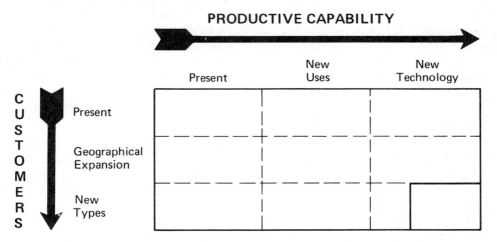

Of course, not all opportunities for synergy are suggested by the diagram. For instance, vertical integration may provide economies in marketing, purchasing, and production scheduling.

Negative synergy

Naturally a manager will seek combinations of activities that supplement or reinforce each other in a synergistic way. He should also be aware that negative synergy can occur, possibly "2 + 2 = 3." For example, a large store in an eastern city achieved prominence by selling high-quality, distinctive women's apparel. When a new management attempted to capitalize on the firm's reputation by adding a line of medium-priced clothing, the store's prestige fell rapidly and the reduction in profits on the higher margin line more than offset the gain in medium-priced goods. The shift in strategy was also complicated by a break in morale of the long-service employees who had taken great pride in the distinctiveness of the store's products and customers.

A similar issue has been bitterly argued in the life insurance industry. Several aggressive firms have added variable annuities and mutual funds to the "products" their salesmen offer to policyholders. The contention is that the policyholder will be glad to deal with a man who can offer him a full range of protection against future financial need; synergy will be at work. The other side, with equally strong convictions, has argued that a half century has been devoted to building up the image of life insurance as stable and sure, not a gamble and not associated with speculative ventures. The supporters of this view believe that the association of variable annuities with the established types of life insurance will lead to a substantial reduction in life insurance sales. Experience to date is too limited to indicate whether synergy in this instance will be positive or negative.

A shoe manufacturing firm ran into negative synergy when it added sport shoes to its more conventional line. The salesmen welcomed the change, but production scheduling and quality control rapidly deteriorated in the plant. The new line so interfered with the established flow of production that work-in-process began to pile up, shipments to customers were late and often incomplete, and the workers complained that they were not earning their production bonuses. After one season the sports shoe line was dropped, but it took several years to overcome the damage done to the production system and customer relations.

TIMING AND SEQUENCE

Strategy starts with picking an economic mission—more specifically, identifying a distinctive service, seeking a particularly advantageous way of producing this service, and combining activities to capture the benefits of synergy. These aspects of strategy, which have already been discussed, set the desired direction and scope of the enterprise. Master strategy has two additional dimensions: timing and targets.

The timing of an action is critical to its success. Since master strategy is especially concerned with a firm's adjustment to its dynamic environment and particularly to competitors' actions, the question of when and how fast to move requires close attention. Moreover, all firms have some limitation on resources, so often a manager must decide what to do first and what to defer.

What to do first

Typically, a whole set of activities must be undertaken to move toward a newly defined mission. Some actions obviously must precede others, for example, land acquisition before plant construction. But often a strategic choice can be made. In the British Petroleum move into the U.S. market, mentioned previously, the company deferred heavy commitment in marketing until a source of U.S. crude was in sight. To have started marketing alone and relied completely on local purchases of finished products would have exposed the company to very high risks. In this situation, we can also note that building or acquiring refining capacity came even later; clearly, refining capacity was not regarded as a critical factor—it could be manipulated later without paying high penalties.

A different sequence is being followed by a manufacturer of fiber glass boats. A low selling price is a key feature of the marketing strategy, and in order to achieve costs permitting this low price, a large modern plant is necessary. The company's current sales are not large enough to keep such a plant busy. Nevertheless, the management decided to build the plant and to be in a strong competitive position. While market demand is being built up, the company has taken on several subcontracts at break-even prices and is even selling some boat hulls to another boat builder to help cover overhead costs of the plant. Here is an instance of moving first into large-scale production facilities, hoping that demand will catch up.

When to act

Even after a sequence has been selected, the manager has to decide how fast to move. It is quite possible to be too early. A leading East Coast department store, for example, correctly predicted a major shift of population to the suburbs and it became a leader in establishing suburban branches. However, at the time it selected branch locations, few of the large modern shopping centers with their vast parking spaces were in existence. Consequently, the store established branches in locations that are now being passed by. Traffic congestion is not uncommon on the routes to its stores, and the desirable buyer traffic from adjacent stores is diminishing. The irony of the situation is that the management of this store was more farsighted than several of its competitors, yet because it moved too soon it is now at a relative disadvantage in suburban operations.

A serious question of timing confronts the sponsors of a major urban renewal project. This project has been initiated by an urban university that finds its campus surrounded by a black community. The plans contemplate converting a rundown area into (a) a large industrial complex at the base, (b) a series of high-rise apartment houses located on the completely covered-over industrial space, and (c) a substantial recreation area both around the apartment houses and in an adjacent location. The scheme would provide new job opportunities, significantly more and better housing than now exists, improved recreation facilities, and a financial prospect more attractive than most slum-clearance proposals. The snag at the moment is that the project requires substantial black-white cooperation. The black community is suspicious of the university, so the university cannot aggressively push the idea. Any black group that takes the leadership will be accused by other members of the community of too-close collaboration with the whites. In other words, in terms of the environment, the timing is wrong. Until confidence improves or strong leadership develops, positive action on anybody's part will probably do more harm than good.

Occasionally the timing aspect of strategy can be turned to an advantage. Mr. Nash, the president of a paper converting company (printing, cutting, folding, gluing) became convinced that vertical integration of paper manufacturers into finished products will in the future make profitable operations of firms like his increasingly difficult. After considering all sorts of alternatives, Mr. Nash concluded that eventually he would either have to liquidate or sell out to a paper manufacturer. He also knew that typically the paper industry goes through periods of under- and overcapacity: when there is undercapacity, paper is scarce and the converter is often squeezed; but when overcapacity exists, paper manufacturers are anxious to work closely with any customers to develop volume.

At the time Mr. Nash was formulating his strategy, paper mills were expanding and he predicted that within three years overcapacity would exist. So, on the basis of these conclusions about his industry, Mr. Nash decided to concentrate in the next couple of years on building volume even where profit margins were very narrow. Working closely with several of his large customers on their particular needs, he developed a new "tonnage" plant, which is not much better than a break-even operation after interest payments. Now he is waiting for a paper manufacturer to offer to purchase his entire business in order to control the volume of paper that flows through his plant. In other words, Mr. Nash has used time to make his firm more attractive. Of course, he must sell when the paper manufacturers are eager for volume; otherwise he is likely to find himself with a large, unprofitable business on his hands.

TARGETS TO BE MET

A final feature of a clear strategy is its expression in terms of targets. Here, translating and testing are involved more than new plans of action. Services a company plans to provide, the way these services will be produced, and the timing and sequence are all designed to create a set of desired results—the *targets*.

A small manufacturer of testing instruments for metallurgical industries, for instance, adopted a strategy of major commitment to research in the use of lasers. Translated into targets or anticipated results, this research commitment meant aiming for (1) a breakthrough on testing equipment in two to five years, (2) a reputation as a technical leader in this field within three years, and (3) a break-even on company profit and loss during the next three to five years. Note how much clearer the strategy is when we state *both* the means (laser research) and the ends (the three targets).

Translating a strategy into targets serves two highly important purposes: (1) the targets can be evaluated in terms of more general objectives (aspirations) of the central managers and other interest groups, and (2) the targets serve as goals in the more detailed planning of the company.

Matching strategy and aspirations

How does a manager decide that a particular strategy is a good one? On what basis does the manager decide "O.K., that's it"? Fundamentally, the process involves: (1) selecting the criteria for judging the strategy,

(2) translating and stating the expected results of the strategy in terms of these criteria, and (3) deciding whether the expected results (the targets) meet acceptable minimum levels of achievement and are better than expected results of alternative strategies.

Criteria to be considered. Several criteria are often used to evaluate a strategy, such as:

1. Return on investment (usually this is profit related to financial investment, but it might be the return on any critically scarce resources).
2. Risk of losing investment of scarce resources.
3. Company growth (in absolute terms or as a percentage of the market).
4. Contribution to social welfare (in one or more dimensions).
5. Stability and security of employment (of all employees and/or of executives).
6. Prestige of the company and of company representatives.
7. Future control (or influence) over company decisions.

Different individuals naturally stress one or two of the above criteria—finance people the return on investment, research people the company prestige, marketing people the company growth, and so forth—and occasionally they may wish to add other criteria such as cash flow or international balance of payments. Fortunately, doing well on one criterion does not necessarily detract from all of the others, so a specific strategy may be attractive from several viewpoints. In fact, every strategy has not one but a whole set of results, and the only practical way to judge a strategy is to consider several criteria simultaneously. To expedite the evaluation process, three or four of these various criteria should be singled out as dominant in the specific situation.

Expressing strategy in terms of criteria. Meaningful strategies must be conceived in *operational* terms—products to sell, markets to reach, materials to acquire, research to perform, and the like. These are the kinds of issues we have explored throughout most of the chapter. However, such actions take on value only as they contribute to desired results. And the pertinent results are defined by the criteria just discussed.

So to relate a strategy to the selected criteria, a conversion or translation is needed. For instance, the actions contemplated in a strategy have to be expressed in anticipated costs and revenues, which give us an estimated profit. Similarly, the proposed actions have to be restated in manpower terms to estimate their effect on stability of employment (if that is one of the key criteria). And likewise for other criteria.

These restatements of anticipated results become the targets at which the strategy is aimed. But since the success of any strategy is never certain, these targets will be surrounded by many ''if's'' and ''maybe's.'' Often they should be expressed as a range, not a single point, with subjective probabilities attached. Nevertheless, tentative though the estimates may be, this is the currency in which a strategy will be evaluated.

Are targets acceptable? Now, with criteria selected and the anticipated results of strategy expressed in terms of these criteria, the manager is in a position to say "Let's go" or "That's not good enough." Rarely is there a choice among several strategies, each of which is quite attractive. Instead, the pressing question is whether any proposed plan is acceptable at all. The reason for this scarcity of attractive choices is that all of us have *high aspirations,* at least for one or two criteria. Thirty percent profits, no real risk, worldwide prestige, half of industry sales—any and all of these may be part of one's dreams. The blunt facts are that few of these dreams will be realized by any strategy we can conceive. So we have to decide what *level of achievement* will be acceptable for each of our criteria.

This picking of acceptable levels is complicated by differences in values held by key executives. For instance, Strategy A may promise a 30% return on capital but with a 15% chance of complete loss and a sure transfer of ownership, whereas Strategy B promises only a 15% return on capital but with small risk of total loss and little danger of change in control of the company. The chairman of the board—say, a wealthy man and a large stockholder—may prefer Strategy A; while the president, who came up from the ranks, is age 52, and owns little stock, may prefer Strategy B. Or, if the chairman likes the prestige of his position and the president thinks the chairman is too conservative, the preferences may be reversed.

It is difficult to generalize about whose values will predominate. Generally, the most active and aggressive senior executives will establish the pattern, *provided* their objectives meet at least the minimum acceptable requirement of each interest group whose withdrawal of support could paralyze the company. In the language of Chapter 1, the "output" of the strategy must enable the company to fulfill at least minimum needs of resource contributors.

Thus, while there is no simple resolution of how high targets should be, we obviously should not evade the translation of operational plans into key targets (or vice versa). A strategy expressed in terms of targets alone is little more than wishful thinking. On the other hand, an operational strategy that is not translated into targets is primarily an article of faith. A well-developed strategy has *both* an operational plan and targets.

Targets and expansion of plans

A second strong reason for including targets in a statement of strategy is the planning and the control necessary to carry out a strategy. For this purpose, we are concerned not so much with overall probable results as with more specific and immediate results anticipated from the early moves in strategic plan. Effective company planning involves a whole hierarchy of goals, subgoals, and sub-subgoals. Thus, if the strategy requires, say, 20% of the southern market for Product X, a whole series of moves—more sales representatives, new warehouse, and the like—may be mapped out to reach the goal. Then the building of the new warehouse by September 1 of next year becomes a subgoal, and a more detailed series of steps—acquiring land, design of the building, mortgage financing, etc.—are laid out. Each of these steps, in turn, becomes a sub-subgoal, and even more specific plans are laid out to achieve each of them.

Such elaboration can be done much more easily if, at each stage, the various steps can be translated into targets. The more specific these targets are, the easier the next phase of elaboration will be. For instance, "Move aggressively into the southern market" is only general guidance and leaves vague the need for a new warehouse. In contrast, translating this general guide into a target of "Twenty percent of the southern market by 1980" provides a much sharper focus for the detailed planning that will expedite the entire strategy. Moreover, the target is a much clearer control standard and is more useful in assuring that progress is being made.

In practice managers may wisely defer precise commitments. They may wish to keep their strategy "flexible" and hence be reluctant to state targets in exact terms. Such vagueness is no serious handicap *provided* that it relates to moves which do not call for action now. However, as soon as action has to be initiated, for the strategy to be carried out, then specific targets are needed. For instance, if the "move into the southern market" mentioned above is not to occur until a new product has proven successful in the midwest, then a definite target for southern expansion may well be held in abeyance.

In conclusion, the active aspects of strategy deal with a series of moves—a course of action based on industry outlook and company strengths. These moves, however, should be translated into anticipated results or targets. The overall probable results are needed to decide on the adequacy of a proposed strategy; and the specific shorter range targets are a necessary base for elaboration of operating plans.

SUMMARY

Company strategy deals with the basic ways a firm seeks to take optimum advantage of its environment. As we saw in Chapter 2, changes in technology, politics, social structure, and economics create opportunities and problems. To bring these environmental factors into sharper focus, we urged in Chapter 3 that they be woven into industry analyses. Such industry studies identify growth and profit prospects, and also the key factors necessary for future participation in the growth. Still more pointed is an analysis of company strengths and weaknesses, and a matching of these against the key success factors for each industry.

Armed with this background, central management selects its strategy. The strategy indicates (1) *services* to be provided, (2) *resource conversion technology* to be used, (3) kinds of synergy to be *exploited,* (4) *timing and sequence* of major steps, and (5) *targets* to be met. These elements interact and they should reinforce each other.

This master plan evolves, of course. As the environment changes, some uncertainties become realities and new uncertainties arise. And the company strategy may be shifted to take advantage of the new situation. Competitors are also responding to the same environment, and their actions may open up—or require—adjusted action. Meanwhile the company itself moves forward and/or runs into snags, so it has new internal information and modified strengths and weaknesses. Inevitably the strategy needs reassessment.

Nevertheless, at any point in time, and hopefully for a long-enough span to translate plans into action, the main elements of strategy remain stable. With this overriding guidance, central management moves to elaboration and implementation of the scheme (as we do in the next parts of the book).

Small companies benefit from well-conceived strategies fully as much as large ones. Their strengths and options differ, but their flexibility and growth rate can be greater.

QUESTIONS FOR CLASS DISCUSSION

1. Several airlines have purchased resort hotels at locations they serve. For instance, Eastern Airlines bought hotels in Puerto Rico. (a) Use this development to *illustrate* each of the five elements in company strategy discussed in this chapter. (The aim of the question is to show the meaning of strategy, so make assumptions about the local situation if you need to.) (b) Now assume the airline decided to go out of the hotel business (its hotels were losing money) and sold one of them to you. How would this change in ownership affect the strategy you would recommend for the hotel?

2. Must a successful strategy have profit as its dominant target, or can we have a viable, vigorous enterprise with social welfare (or any other of the criteria listed on page 77) as the end to be maximized, with profit as a target to be satisfied but not maximized?

3. Use each of the boxes in the chart on page 73 to identify possible alternative ways of expanding for (a) a company in the office furniture manufacturing business or (b) a medical "clinic" consisting of five doctors concentrating on pediatrics (care of children).

4. Soon after the first major oil discovery on the northern slope of Alaska, the State of Alaska offered drilling leases on adjacent tracts of land. These leases were auctioned off, and almost all the larger U.S. oil companies bid millions of dollars just for the opportunity to search for oil in this remote location. What strategic considerations, in your opinion, lead companies to such an investment?

5. The speed at which tough, antipollution emission controls should be required for all autos has been intensely debated. (a) List the major arguments for quick and for slow national requirements. (b) Do the pros and cons in your answer to (a) suggest similar arguments for the speed at which: (1) a successful "fried chicken" fast-food chain should grant additional franchises; (2) an undergraduate college should establish a master's degree program; (3) a Hawaiian pineapple

canning company should develop more economical Philippine and other foreign source? In (1), (2), and (3) assume that central management has decided to make the change at some time.

6. Sears Roebuck & Company enjoys an established position in mail-order (plus telephone) and retail-store selling of clothing, hardware, and other consumer goods. Sears also successfully sells automobile insurance, mostly by mail. Recently the company entered the life insurance field. Do you think Sears will become a prominent competitor in the life insurance industry, especially in view of the practice of all leading companies to use agents to explain the product to customers? Use the strategy approach outline in answering this question.

7. One company's statement of objectives calls for "a decent return to stockholders, an example to the community of corporate citizenship, payment of better than a living wage and stability of employment for all employees, honorable treatment of suppliers, and the willingness to undertake business risks to provide an example of dynamic management." How can the concept of a "strategy" as outlined in this chapter help sharpen the meaning and the focus of such a statement?

8. Assume that you have just been appointed manager of the leading bookstore on your campus, with a free hand to make any changes you believe desirable. Outline the strategy you intend to follow.

CASE 4 / Electron Amplifiers, Inc.

Floyd Orlan, president and part-owner of Electron Amplifiers, Inc., gazed reflectively across the open court lying between the office and factory wings of his firm's leased building. As he half-saw the contrasts of palm tree shade and grass bright in the winter sun, he wondered just how to state to the directors his report due next week and covering last year's operations. "The news is good. Sales are rising, profits are high, and the future is promising. We have grown into using all the space available in this plant. How can I keep from appearing excessively optimistic to my fellow investors—directors all?"

Electron Amplifiers manufactures devices that pick up a weak electric signal from a sensor such as a thermostat or an air-pressure or liquid-flow gauge and then amplify—or increase the strength of—the signal so that it can trigger off control and operating devices such as electric switches or motors. At present its amplifiers are widely used in testing and measuring instruments and in missiles built for the Air Force. Electron buys components, assembles them according to circuits of its own design, and resells the amplifiers as subassemblies to other manufacturers.

The electronics industry is large, competitive (there are over 5,000 firms and the number continues to grow), and easy to enter, especially in the components, subassembly, and nonconsumer market segments. The relationship of various types of businesses in the electronics industry is shown in Exhibit 1 at the top of page 83. Overall growth in the past ten years has varied from 8%-10% a year, but some products grow less rapidly than others. Integrated circuits and subassembly devices based on microelectronics are predicted to grow at 10%-12% for several years to come.

Mr. Orlan and a partner who is now dead founded the company over a decade ago. Mr. Orlan supplied some of the original capital, knowledge about manufacturing, and a few sales contracts, while his partner, an electrical engineer, supplied the original circuit designs and the idea of making miniaturized amplifiers utilizing transistors. Sales and net profits for the ten-year period are shown in Exibit 2 at the bottom of page 83, and the current financial condition is shown in the current balance sheet in Exibit 3 at the top of page 84.

Early in its history Electron Amplifiers sold a limited range of amplifiers with only a few circuit designs to large producers of consumer goods and computers, including Motorola and General Electric. As a pioneer it has a large share (about 35%) of the miniaturized amplifier market. When the costs of transistors, other semiconductor devices, and printed circuit boards dropped substantially, the large producers turned to making their own amplifiers. Electron then began to specialize in the high-priced, special-adaptation market. It now makes many thousands of different amplifiers tailored to individual customers' control circuit needs and sold in relatively limited quantities. Electron has captured a position in this market by skillful sales engineering work and by careful assembly and testing operations so that the products it ships are highly reliable. Customers seldom order more than 10,000 units at one time. Orders frequently are in the low hundreds.

Electron builds its amplifiers by assembling both passive components (resistors, capacitors, and inductors) and active components (semiconductors) on a printed circuit board. Women who do the assembly work are trained on the job. The production executives have little formal training in electrical engineering but they have a great deal of experience in electronics assembly work. All parts are purchased. The smallest product is encased in a cube of black epoxy about one and one-half inches along each dimension.

Manufacturers' agents do all the selling work except in the home city, Phoenix, Arizona. Foreign agents represent the company in forty countries, and their sales now comprise more than half the total. Sales abroad have risen especially rapidly—twice the domestic rate—since the present sales manager left his post as export manager for a large, integrated electronics company a few years ago to become sales manager for Electron Amplifiers, Inc. Present plans are to continue increasing the number of foreign representatives. Domestic representatives blanket all the major electronics-producing areas in the United States, but company sales are concentrated in Southern and Central California, Eastern Massachusetts, and near Denver, Colorado. The number of customers is growing slightly more rapidly than sales volume.

One reason for the relative lag in domestic sales is increasing competition from components manufacturers who are moving into the subassembly segment of the industry through the use of integrated circuits or thin-film and thick-film hybrid technologies for building circuits. Electron Amplifiers, Inc. might, of course, meet the competition head-on by utilizing the same technologies.

Thick-film hybrid technology requires three major steps to produce a circuit that can perform an amplifying function. First a base, or substrata, is made of a ceramic material to have particular thermal, electrical, and mechanical properties. To this base are added several layers laid up as films by squeezing, one at a time, glass, ceramic, and metal pastes through silk screens that have been photographically developed. These films, when laid down, act as resistors, capacitors, and conductors. Then, in the hybridization

Exhibit 1

Electronics Industry

```
                          ┌─────────────────┐
                          │ Raw Materials   │
                          │  — Wire         │
                          │  — Silicon      │
                          │  — Germanium    │
                          │      Etc.       │
                          └─────────────────┘
                                   │
                                   ▼
                          ┌─────────────────┐      ┌──────────────────┐
                          │ Components      │      │ Non-Electronic   │
                          │  — Resistors    │      │ Components       │
                          │  — Capacitors   │      │  — Cabinets      │
                          │  — Transistors  │      │  — Knobs         │
                          │  — Vacuum Tubes │      │  — Chassis       │
                          │      Etc.       │      │      Etc.        │
                          └─────────────────┘      └──────────────────┘
                                   │                        │
                          ┌────────┴──────┐                 ▼
                          │               │      ┌──────────────────┐
                          │               └─────►│ Subassemblies    │
                          │                      │  — TV Picture    │
                          │                      │     tubes        │
                          │                      │  — Filters       │
                          │                      │  — Amplifiers    │
                          │                      │      Etc.        │
                          │                      └──────────────────┘
                          │        ┌─────────────────┐
                          ▼        ▼                 │
               ┌─────────────────────────┐           │
               │ Complete Assemblies     │◄──────────┘
               │  — TV Sets              │
               │  — Computers            │
               │  — Missiles, Radar      │
               │  — Instruments          │
               └─────────────────────────┘
    ┌──────────────┐            │
    │ Component    │            ▼
    │ Replacement  │   ┌─────────────────────────┐
    │ Market       │   │ Customer Markets        │
    └──────────────┘   │  — Consumer             │
                       │  — Industry             │
                       │  — Government           │
                       └─────────────────────────┘
```

Exhibit 2

Year	Sales	Net Profits After Taxes
Current	$10,000,000	$500,000
Previous	8,800,000	400,000
Previous	7,800,000	335,000
Previous	6,900,000	345,000
Previous	5,500,000	165,000
Five Years Ago	4,300,000	120,000
Ten Years Ago	800,000	16,000

Exhibit 3

Current Balance Sheet

Assets		Liabilities	
Cash	$ 250,000	Current	$3,900,000
Accounts Receivable	2,400,000		
Inventories	2,800,000	**Stockholders' Equity**	
Leasehold Improvements	350,000	Common Stock and Re-	
Other	200,000	tained Earnings	2,100,000
Total	$6,000,000	Total	$6,000,000

step, active devices (semiconductors) are added as individual units. They are soldered or laser-welded in place.

The major advantages of a thick-film hybrid circuit as compared to one built from micro-miniaturized components are size and low cost with volume production. The cubic space occupied by a thick-film circuit may readily be one ninth that of a circuit built of discrete elements. The cost per circuit is one quarter to one half, provided a high volume of output is attained for each circuit. A small order might be for 200,000 units at $0.26 each. Manufacturing thick-films requires skill in ceramic engineering and materials, photographic processes, and process engineering. The work does not call for separate assembly operations and requires that engineering and manufacturing departments be closely related. A minimum investment in equipment is about $135,000.

Thin-film technology utilizes the same steps as thick-film. The major difference is that metals and ceramic materials are sputtered (deposited) on the base in layers four millionths of an inch thick by stripping off one atom at a time of the layering material and depositing it on the base ceramic in an argon-atmosphere oven. Sputtering is slow but results in circuits with close tolerances, accurate performance, and high stability. Investment in a sputtering line can run $500,000 and the cost of a clean room in which to add the active transistors or diodes must be added.

Monolithic integrated circuits are built up on a tiny clip of silicon by adding precise amounts of impurities, such as boron or phosphorus, to the originally pure silicon. The end result includes active elements as well as passive elements right in and on the silicon chip. The manufacturing process is highly complex and requires special skills to grow and handle ultra-pure materials. Monolithic integrated circuits are a direct outgrowth of the work on transistors and diodes and have wide application through the entire field of electronics. When first introduced, their price dropped about 30% per year, and the down-trend still continues. Although the end-product is a low-cost device, the original cost for developing any one circuit is high and can run to $50,000 per circuit. Minimum equipment investment is about $400,000 and operation would be about $50,000 per month.

Required: (a) How do you appraise the company's situation? Do you agree with Mr. Orlan?

(b) What strategy do you recommend for the firm for the foreseeable future?

Part 2
DEFINING MAJOR POLICY

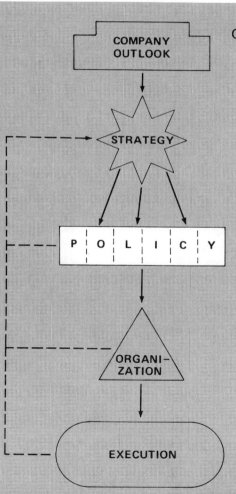

MARKETING POLICY–
PRODUCT LINE AND CUSTOMERS

Relation of policy to strategy

Strategy, as defined in Chapter 4, takes a broad, total company view and singles out major targets for company action. Its strength arises from highly selective concentration on a few critical issues. To achieve this necessary perspective and emphasis, strategy sets aside a whole array of issues "to be considered later." Policy deals with an important group—though not all—of these issues that were temporarily set aside.

A policy is a standing plan; it is used over and over to guide specific actions. For example, if a company adopts a policy to sell only for cash, all employees give a consistent answer to any customer asking for credit. Every company needs policy covering many aspects of its operations in order to simplify decision-making and to give predictability and consistency to actions taken at different times by different people.

In addition, policy serves a key role in spelling out, clarifying, and testing strategy. Frequently strategy is stated in such general terms that its interpretation can be varied. A carefully selected policy sharpens the meaning of the strategy and guides specific decisions in a direction that supports the strategy. In a sense, no strategy has really been thought through until its implications for policy (and programs) have been explored. Sometimes as our planning follows through from a tentative strategy to more specific policy we encounter a stumbling block that causes us to go back and revise the strategy. In the end, each should support the other. To be sure, some policy is adopted for administrative convenience and is not affected one way or the other by a change in strategy; our focus here, however, is on policy that does directly help implement strategy.

Basic policy issues

Since each company has its own unique strategy, its policy will also be individually tailored. However, virtually every firm faces a similar set of issues, and an analysis of policy can be expedited and improved by a systematic exploration of these basic issues. A convenient sequence for analysis is:

1. Marketing policy.
2. Production and purchasing policy.
3. Personnel policy.
4. Financial policy.

These groups overlap to some degree, and it is impossible to make final decisions with reference to one group without considering other groups. Some companies may have still another policy for specialized activities. Nevertheless, the sequence does provide a logical approach to overall company activities, so in this part two or three chapters will be devoted to each of the four policy categories.

Within the marketing policy sphere, every enterprise needs general guidelines with respect to (1) product line, (2) customers, (3) pricing, and (4) marketing mix.

PRODUCT LINE

Although company strategy defines the type of product or service to be sold—such as mobile home sites, textbooks, or sneakers—rarely does it provide answers to the following questions: How many *different* sizes, grades, and shapes of the product will be carried in the line? Just how can our products be made *distinctive* from those of competitors? Should we *change* product design frequently, say every spring, or stick with a tested model? We need standard answers—policy—on such issues for two reasons: first, to build a desired and consistent interpretation of strategy, and second because many marketing, production, and financial activities will be affected by the simplicity or the elaborateness of our product line.

Variety of products

For each strategic niche, a company must decide on the variety of products to be offered to its customers. This is a recurring problem as markets change, competition grows, and new technology becomes available.

Cost of diversity. Customers are continually asking for products that are smaller, stronger, another voltage, or otherwise different from what is offered, and salesmen will contend that the sales volume could be increased materially if they had a larger variety of products to sell.

One manufacturer of soaps yielded to this pressure. Whenever the sales manager became convinced that competitors were offering a new soap or that a number of customers had requested a new soap that differed in color, shape, fragrance, or composition, a new product meeting these specifications would be introduced. Examination of sales records showed that sales of most of these new products were satisfactory for several months but would gradually dwindle.

Apparently the initial sales were due to the enthusiasm of the salesmen for a new product and a willingness on the part of the retailers to try an original stock to see how the product would sell. After this original distribution, however, most new products were discovered to have no unique appeal. This particular company, therefore, had a large number of products for which the sales volume was inadequate to justify the cost of manufacturing, warehousing, and selling. By careful study the company was able to reduce the number of items carried to comparatively few products that really had significant differences. It then concentrated its attention on selling these products rather than dissipating its efforts on new and unnecessary additions to its line.

A common policy is to fix a limit on the number of items. Then any proposal for a new item must be accompanied by a recommendation for dropping an existing one. While exceptions may be necessary, this plan has the advantage of forcing attention to pruning along with justifying the new item.

Need for complete line. In some situations the customer desires to buy a variety of products from the same source. For example, each of us expects the local druggist to be able to fill within a few hours any prescription our doctor may write. The druggist, in turn, expects the same kind of complete line service from drug wholesalers. Since a single slow delivery is likely to result in a long-time loss in patronage, a complete line is very important.

In contrast, a policy to concentrate on only a few items may be wise for a firm seeking distinction as a specialist. A paper company may sell only newsprint, for example, or a firm may specialize in putting out fires at oil and gas wells. By focusing on a narrow line, costs can be reduced; and if the product is sold in *large enough units* to warrant separate action by customers, the lack of a complete line may be no serious handicap. A narrow line policy relies on specialization to achieve a competitive advantage in pricing, unique service, or concentrated attention.

Ways of customizing products. A middle position may be feasible. Perhaps some variety can be offered without too much added expense. Common practice with automobiles or refrigerators, for instance, is to have basically a standard product but with two or three sizes and other options as to color and accessories. The number of variations is strictly limited, and the optional items are available only by paying a premium. While inventory and production scheduling are complicated by this practice, it does give the customer some choice.

A variation of this customizing policy is to permit the customer to set the specifications on one or two characteristics instead of stipulating his options. Thus the outside frame of a machine may be made to each customer's order. Or group insurance and pension contracts can be written with special clauses modifying the standard contract to fit a unique need of a large buyer. To prevent such adjustments from leading to costly processing costs, a company policy is needed indicating what features of the product can be modified and the conditions justifying the modification.

Product differentiation

In a competitive economy every company must develop some reasons for customers to prefer its products over those of its competitors. This raises a question—in what respects will a company try to make its products distinctive? Usually the company will have a standing answer, because it wants a continuing and consistent reputation in the market and because its engineers and production people need guidance on what to emphasize.

What is quality? Quality is not capable of an exact definition. It depends on the type of customers to whom a product is sold and the nature of the appeal used in its sale. The customer of a discount store may define quality in terms of *durability,* while a purchaser of a high-priced hat who expects to use it only one season may define quality in terms of richness in *appearance.* For medical products, quality usually refers to *purity*; customers will pay a high premium for a product they feel confident is pure. *Dependability* is crucial in the space industry, and so forth.

So, if a company seeks distinctiveness on the basis of product quality, it must decide the particular characteristics it will stress. Here, desired market segmentation is the key in setting policy.

Similarly, the policy of a company in regard to style must conform to the desires of the group of consumers to whom it seeks to sell its products. A furniture producer, for example, must decide whether it will concentrate on modern furniture of the extreme type or follow more conservative lines. Firms manufacturing "period" furniture must decide whether they will copy original pieces in minute detail as an appeal to potential customers who are fastidious about interior decoration or merely use some of the characteristic features of the period. Within the furniture industry there is a well-recognized demand for what is known as "borax furniture" that tends to be gaudy, ornate, and cheap in construction.

Consumer recognition of product differences. In deciding on the kind of distinctiveness to emphasize, the company must consider not only the desires of its customers but also their ability to appreciate variations in quality. Even purchasers of hi-fi sets have limits in ability to detect differences in tone quality. The company must therefore determine (a) what characteristics of its product its customers feel are important; (b) the extent to which its customers can appreciate the differences in such features and how much they are willing to pay for this extra quality; and (c) whether the cost of producing extra features is more or less than customers are willing to pay for them.

Frequency of design change

Related to the question of how product distinction is to be achieved is the troublesome issue of how frequently changes in design should be made.

Costs of change. Design changes are costly. First comes the technical and marketing research, engineering, testing, and tooling-up for the redesigned product. For simple products, such preparation expenses often amount to thousands of dollars; for complex products, like automobiles or airplanes, to millions of dollars. Then, manufacturing costs tend to increase if frequent changes are made. New skills have to be learned, production runs are shorter, and overhead builds up.

Next, inventory problems are complicated. Enough but not too much of the old product is needed as it is being phased out, and stocks of the new product must be built for an uncertain demand. The same problem arises at each stage in distribution—wholesaler, retailer, and perhaps consumer. In fact, anticipation of new models often leads to wide fluctuations in distributors' inventory and irregular orders for the manufacturer. If the manufacturer wants to keep distributive channels well stocked, it may have to accept return of old merchandise or make price concessions.

Finally, service problems are complicated by frequent design changes. The user of the product will expect repair parts to be readily available and servicemen to understand the idiosyncrasies of each model. As users of foreign products know from bitter experience, adequate service on a product has a significant effect on its usefulness and its resale value.

But these costs—development, manufacture, distribution, and service—are only one side of the picture. In setting a policy for frequency of design changes, the manager must also consider the benefits of changing.

Pressures to change. The most recent style, as already noted, may be so important to consumers that frequent design changes are inevitable. Today even staple products are styled according to the current mode. Kitchenware and bathtubs, which still render the same service they did thirty years ago, are streamlined and styled to the modern taste. Bath towels and sheets have blossomed out in all colors of the rainbow; even steam hammers are now streamlined.

Change may be necessary for more technical reasons. Technology is advancing in many fields—in the home and in the office, as well as in the plant. New developments are occurring every year in color television, microfilming, and solid-state controls of machines, to mention only a sample. If customers are to be well served, a company must from time to time adapt its products to such technological developments.

The pressures of style or technology are strong by themselves. Competitors' actions, however, may make the need to change irresistible. When a clearly preferred product is offered by a competitor, a company must respond in some manner, usually by redesigning its own products.

Frequency of change. Several alternative ways of reconciling the pressures and the costs of redesign of products are available to managers. Annual models are often used for consumer goods. This practice tends to accentuate the changes, because strong promotional stress is laid on "new" features—whether they are significant advances or not. And the annual model may hasten obsolescence, thereby raising replacement demand. The annual change does consolidate revisions into a single package that is retained for at least a year, so the timing of production adjustments is predictable. The best known example of annual models is in the automobile industry. In recent years only some European cars have had significant success with "continuous improvements" instead of annual models.

Another tack, more common in industrial goods, is a policy of "product leadership." Here the firm wants to be first on the market with improvements, and new designs are introduced as rapidly as new technology is developed. An illustration of this practice was IBM's switch to unitized computers, even though at the time the new design was presented the company enjoyed a dominant position in the electronic computer field.

A few firms try the leapfrog approach. Once they have a good design, they stick with it, letting competitors try various modifications. Then when significant improvements are evident, they make a major adjustment— incorporating not only competitors' advances but hopefully many more. The presumption here is that production and marketing economies of few changes will more than offset a temporary lag in improvements. In those fields where technological change has been slow, this policy works well.

A straddle is to use standard parts year after year, but to combine them in different ways or to change the outside shell to give an up-to-date appearance. The Swiss and Japanese watch industries, for example, substantially follow this practice with excellent results. The standardized parts simplify manufacturing and service problems, while the watchcases can be adapted to the latest styles.

Revisions of product line policy

The question of frequency of product redesign suggests the dynamic nature of all product line policy. The success of one kind of policy may create the need for its revision. A small firm, for instance, may succeed so well with a distinctive narrow line of products that it attains the capability of becoming a leader in the field. But this implies an expansion of the line. And the tapping of new segments of the market probably calls for different ways of seeking distinctiveness in each segment. Also, action of competitors and technological development often alter the soundness of previously desirable policy. So, while the product line policy is necessary to provide a stable base for day-to-day decisions, the policy should be reexamined whenever the business setting changes.

Services and a product line policy

The issues regarding product line are easier to grasp when we use physical products as examples. However, most service enterprises face comparable problems. Consider a university. What variety of courses should it offer—in urban planning, black studies, and Sanskrit? How should it differentiate its services from other universities—what characteristics of quality are significant, and can the consumer recognize the differences? How frequently should programs change? A similar set of questions confront advertising agencies, hospitals, and management consultants. Clearly, these issues are fundamental in developing a viable, continuing relationship between a firm and the people who use its product/service output.

CUSTOMER POLICY

Customer policy, like product policy, is broadly determined by company strategy, but it needs elaboration and refinement before it gives adequate guidance to day-to-day decisions. Three kinds of issues arise again and again: What body of ultimate consumers does the company wish to serve? What channel of distribution will be most effective in reaching these consumers? And, what limits on size or other characteristics should be placed on customers with whom the company deals directly?

Consumers sought

Distinction between customers and consumers. Confusion sometime arises because of failure to distinguish between "customers" and "consumers." The term *consumer* means the one who *uses* a product (or service) for his personal satisfaction or benefit; or in the case of industrial materials, the one who so *changes* the form of the product as to alter its identity. A *customer*, on the other hand, is anyone who *buys* goods. A customer may be a consumer, or it may be a dealer who will resell the product to someone else.

The habits and the wishes of the ultimate consumer of a product (or service) are of vital interest to all businesses having anything to do with the product, for a major purpose of economic activity is to create consumer satisfaction. In the original design of a product, during its production, and throughout its distribution, consumer satisfaction is ever a controlling consideration. Consequently, a policy clearly defining the "segments" of consumers sought should be an early decision for every company—even though the company may use middlemen (for example, retailers) to actually sell to those consumers.

Types of consumers. Various kinds of consumers want services of widely different nature. Thus, the restaurant catering to business executives offers a different service from the campus kitchen seeking the trade of students. A hotel primarily serving commercial travelers must maintain a different atmosphere and render a different type of service than a motel seeking resident guests. A patent medicine company found as a result of studying its market that a major group of its consumers were people who spoke only foreign languages. These groups were located primarily in large industrial centers and could be reached by foreign language newspapers and circulars printed in foreign languages.

Even the clients of management consulting firms may be grouped into major types in much the same way as the customers of an industrial firm. Bankers sometimes desire a general survey of a business as a means of appraising its management and determining its financial possibilities. If it is the board of directors or the general manager who calls in the consultant, the problems are likely to deal with policies or organization. Department managers often call in consultants to help them with more detailed problems, such as linear programming, sales incentives, management information systems, or systems of expense control. Each type of client requires studies made from its particular point of view. Some consulting firms seek to adapt their activities to satisfy any of these consumer groups, whereas other firms follow a policy of serving only one type of client.

When a manufacturer of electric-powered hand tools decided to tap the do-it-yourself market in addition to its established market with the professional building trades, it failed to recognize the difference in needs of the two types of customers. The amateurs required more foolproof machines and elementary instruction sheets. After two years of losses, the manufacturer returned to its policy of focusing only on the professional market.

The relation of a company to consumers of its products is normally continuous over a period of years. Reputations are established, and expectations—so vital to careful planning—are built up. Consequently, a company cannot move in and out of a market from week to week. Instead, well-established and relatively stable policies regarding consumers to be served are very useful.

Location of consumers. The large mail-order houses such as Sears, Roebuck and Montgomery Ward built their business with rural consumers—people who had difficulty getting to cities to shop. But conditions have changed. Now there are fewer farmers, and they drive automobiles. One adjustment to this shift has been an impressive expansion of retail stores operated by these companies.

Nevertheless, the mail-order business also continues to prosper. How? Through a shift in definition of potential consumers. The largest mail-order market now is the suburban homemaker, whose children and other duties make shopping a chore, and her do-it-yourself husband. They find the semiannual catalogs a storehouse of merchandise information and a convenient way to select many items. To be sure, the merchandise offered has been adapted to appeal to the nonfarm consumer, and telephone ordering is replacing the mailed order. But, vital to the planning of what will be offered is a clear concept of where the potential buyers live.

Export business often is attractive. In analyzing foreign markets, as any other new markets, the added or *incremental* costs should be balanced against the added income. Once a company has completed its product engineering and is "tooled-up" for production, the cost per unit of turning out an added 5% or 10% is less than the total average cost of the basic output. If the company has idle capacity in its plant, this incremental cost may be very much lower. So, even though there are difficulties in selling abroad, the net revenue received may still be above the incremental cost.

Full utilization of an existing strength may be a factor. Most common is adoption of *national distribution* because national advertising of the company—already necessary for part of the market—is reaching consumers in all areas. In these cases, sales promotion considered to be desirable dictates the market scope, rather than consumer policy determining what promotion is feasible. A somewhat similar situation arises when a company invests heavily to acquire technical know-how for a specific problem and then feels impelled to serve all people with this problem regardless of where they are located.

Competitive tactics may also influence policy regarding location of desired consumers. For instance, Company A may immediately follow Company B into a new area—say the West Coast—because A does not want B to acquire a possible source of strength that might be extended to other markets. On the other hand, if a pattern of normal territories has evolved, Company X may not move into Company Y's home market for fear that Y will reciprocate. Such intangible considerations may result in a firm not pushing its territorial limits just to the point where incremental selling and delivery costs match incremental revenue.

Channels of distribution

By *channel of distribution* is meant the *steps* by which products are *distributed* from the one who first converts them into usable form to the consumer. Many enterprises, of course, render services rather than manufacture products—for example, airlines, banks, public accountants, and all sorts of retail stores. Because of their nature, such services are almost always sold directly to consumers. But for manufacturers the selection of the proper channels of distribution is a very real problem.

Changes in buying habits, transportation, communications, and market locations have modified methods of distribution greatly during recent years. This whole field is in a state of flux, and few companies are justified in assuming that their traditional channels are necessarily the most effective ways of reaching the consumer they prefer.

Through jobbers. For many years the jobber (or wholesaler) was regarded as the orthodox method of distribution. The jobber assembles products from many manufacturers, stores them, and sells them to retailers. In so doing, it also assumes risks of price change, damage, or obsolescence; it extends credit to retailers; and it sorts and ships products according to retailer needs.

All of these functions are essential in the distribution of merchandise; regardless of the channel of distribution used, someone must perform them. When a large part of consumer purchases was secured through small retailers scattered over a wide territory, it was more economical for the manufacturer to have the wholesaler perform these services than to undertake them itself.

During the past half century, an increased interest in style and price coupled with improved transportation have resulted in a decline in the importance of the small retail store and a growth in the discount store and the chain store. The latter types of retail outlets buy sufficient quantities of merchandise to make it economical for the manufacturer to sell directly to them. Nevertheless, a *local jobber* is still needed to serve small retailers located both in small towns and in trading centers. Also, there are auto supply jobbers who serve repair shops, plumbing supply houses that serve plumbers, and similar specialty jobbers that assemble a wide variety of supplies needed by some particular trade or industry. Thus, while the trend may be away from the use of jobbers, there are situations in which the local jobber or the specialty jobber performs a very useful service.

Direct to retailers. Distribution by the manufacturer direct to retailers has some distinct advantages. By using specialty sales representatives to concentrate on the sale of its products, the manufacturer may secure more aggressive selling efforts, for a jobber's general-line salespeople sell a wide variety of products and cannot concentrate their efforts upon the sale of one particular product. This plan may also enable a manufacturer to ascertain better the consumers' desires, since it has firsthand contact with the final "point-of-sale," namely the retailer.

The manufacturer exercises more control over the final sale of its goods if it has direct contact with the retailer. Personal relationships and goodwill are tied to the manufacturer, and consequently it is not so dependent on the jobber for sales volume. Also, the manufacturer has a better opportunity to influence retail prices, display, and other factors that affect the popularity of its product with the consumer.

The plan of selling direct to retailers, however, may lead to excessive costs if it is used unwisely. If the manufacturer eliminates the jobber entirely, it may incur unbearable costs because many retailers buy in such small quantities that the expense of selling and servicing them may exceed the gross profits on the goods they purchase.

Some companies that manufacture a variety of products set up their own *sales branches*. These branches perform in many respects like a jobber, except that they sell only products of the parent company. One firm, for example, has eleven separate manufacturing divisions—each operated like an independent company. The sales division is another fairly independent unit with several branches that perform the functions of a jobber. A sales branch with its own sales staff enables a company to secure improved selling effort and at the same time have a local distributing point. Coordination of sales and production is easier with a branch, and the branch is more willing to make market surveys.

Direct to consumers. This plan is usually employed when the product is of such a nature that the salesperson needs a high degree of technical training to sell it and when technical services must be rendered in connection with the product after it is sold. For example, this plan is used by manufacturers of office equipment such as duplicating machines, postage meters, and computers. Salespeople must be able to operate such equipment to sell it, and the manufacturer must assure itself that the equipment is kept in proper repair or the customer may become dissatisfied with it. For similar reasons most industrial equipment is sold directly to users.

Use of *exclusive dealers,* as is done by automobile manufacturers and many oil companies, combines many advantages of direct sales to consumers while retaining the initiative of local businesspeople. The dealer "runs its own business," but to retain its franchise it must join in company sales programs and conform to service standards set by the company. Obviously, the producing company must have a good enough line of products for the typical dealer to make a profit or competent people will not apply for dealerships and the whole system will collapse.

Through brokers or agents. The broker usually performs only one major function of distribution—selling. As contrasted with the jobber, it usually sells only one type of product, or at most only a few closely related products. Although the broker is employed most frequently in the distribution of producer goods, it may also be used in the distribution of consumer goods. For example, brokers are often used in the same way by small canneries that do not have sufficient output to justify a full-time sales force and therefore need the services of someone who is familiar with the potential market for their product. Anyone who has publicly announced an intention to buy a house or a suburban lot knows that brokers are also used in the real-estate field. Here, again, it is difficult for buyers and sellers to get together without the aid of someone who is in close contact with the market.

Selecting a channel of distribution. Dr. Thomas L. Berg[1] suggests that selecting a channel of distribution be viewed as an organization problem and that the activities analyzed include the total distribution system. More specifically, his approach involves:

1. Listing all actions necessary between producer and consumer—promotion, actual selling, transportation, financing, warehousing, repackaging, risk-taking, installation and repair service, and the like.
2. Grouping these activities into jobs that can be effectively and efficiently performed by separate firms. These firms may be banks or warehousemen who also do other things, or they may be firms exclusively involved in this particular channel. The crucial matter here is to conceive of jobs (packages of activities) that are the most effective combinations.
3. Defining relationships between the jobs that will assure cooperation and necessary flow of information. Also define how each firm involved is to be compensated for its efforts. And work out necessary, minimum controls to be exercised by various members over other members.

---

[1] See T. L. Berg, "Designing the Distribution System," in W. D. Stevens (ed.), *The Social Responsibilities of Marketing,* American Marketing Association, 1962.

4. On the basis of the organization design (the *policy* adopted by the designer), developing specifications for the firms that are to fill each job.
5. Then moving on to execution of the plan by recruiting people to take the specified jobs (some negotiation may arise here since independent firms will be participants), educating people on how the plan is to work, supervising the day-to-day operations, and exercising necessary controls.

One of the significant aspects of this approach is that the channel of distribution problem is not viewed as a choice between a few predetermined alternatives. Instead, each company should work out a design that is the best way to get its products to the consumers it has selected. Also implied is the idea that tasks assigned to participants are apt to need modification as economic and competitive conditions change.

Since a channel of distribution typically creates a complex set of relationships, a policy is needed to provide consistency and stability of action. And top management is vitally concerned because—as experience in the automobile, watch, liquor, and many other industries testifies—a strong, well-designed distribution system may spell the difference between success and failure of the entire enterprise.

Size of customers

Customers that a company deals with directly may be either too small or too large. The company should know how much it costs to serve each type of customer and the amount the customer must buy if its business is to yield a profit to the company. One manufacturing concern, for example, was selling to 8,000 retail accounts. An analysis of these accounts revealed that 55% of the total number purchased only 5% of its entire sales volume and that none of these 55% purchased more than $200 worth of merchandise a year. The company decided to eliminate all such accounts, which, it was thought, would not develop into better accounts, and as a consequence the number of customers was reduced to 4,000. This enabled the company to reduce its sales staff from 82 to 43 and to make a number of other substantial reductions in selling costs.

In deciding whether to eliminate customers who purchase in small quantities, consideration should be given to the potential purchases of these customers as well as to the actual purchases now made from the company. If small customers have the capacity to increase their purchases substantially, it may be desirable not to eliminate them but to concentrate on securing a larger percentage of their trade.

On the other hand, a customer may purchase too much merchandise! If a concern is dependent on one or two customers for most of its business, its position is vulnerable because loss of patronage of such an important buyer will disrupt the entire organization.

Companies in the aerospace industry often depend upon one or two large government contracts for the bulk of their business. Cancellation of or failure to win a renewal of such a contract can spell disaster for the firm. Advertising agencies may develop a similar overdependency on one or two large accounts; when the account is "dropped," the agency has to lay off most of its talented employees and may close entirely. Consequently, companies may have a policy that says no more than 20% of their business will be done with one customer.

SUMMARY

Company strategy requires elaboration to give it specificity and to put it in more operational terms. Policy is a major instrument for thinking through and sharpening such elaboration. And in this chapter we start a systematic review of key policy that almost always is involved in this "filling in of the broad picture."

Two dimensions that help shape every master strategy are the products (or services) to be sold and the customers who will buy them. So the discussion in this chapter of policy covering product line and customers is a logical starting point for this phase of company planning.

Sharpening of each product area singled out in a company strategy involves policy regarding the variety of products, product differentiation, and frequency of design changes.

Central management should also set up policy regarding the types and the location of final consumers the company hopes to reach, the distribution system to be used in getting products to such consumers, and the upper and lower limits on the size of direct customers. These adjustments to the market are vital to success; they have to be nurtured over time; and they need wise policy guidance for consistency and dependability.

There has been frequent occasion in this chapter to note how customer policy is closely related to many other aspects of a company's activities. For example, the customers sought will affect the kind of a sales promotion needed, the size of plant, the type of sales and perhaps production personnel, the need for large accounts receivable, and other phases of operations. These interrelations will become more apparent in subsequent discussion of the other aspects of management and in the analysis of the cases found throughout the book.

QUESTIONS FOR CLASS DISCUSSION

1. Does a secretarial school need product and customer policies? In your answer consider variety and quality of products, need for product differentiation, and type and location of customers.
2. Possibilities for the product line of a filling station include, in addition to gasoline and oil, the following: batteries, tires, antifreeze, oil filters, fan belts, windshield

wipers, mufflers, brake linings, tire chains, soft drinks, cigarettes, souvenirs, candy, and an array of repair services ranging from motor tune-ups, front-end repairs, body work, and transmission replacement to greasing and car washing. (a) If you owned and operated a filling station, how would you decide on your product line? (b) If you were the manager of a major oil company's nationwide chain of filling stations, what policy would you establish regarding filling station product lines? What would you insist on? forbid? leave up to the local operator?

3. Pepperidge Farm bread grew from personal sales of a housewife to regional sales in the Northeast because of its distinctive quality. Its high quality led to rapidly growing sales at a substantially higher price than most bread, with very little advertising. Then Campbell Soup Company bought Pepperidge Farm. To capitalize on the remarkable reputation, Campbell considered (1) expanding the territory in which Pepperidge Farm bread was sold and/or (2) applying the name to a wider variety of products. A related issue was the possibility of fuller utilization of the trucks that delivered the bread daily to retail stores. What would you have advised Campbell Soup Company to do at that time?

4. Most people find it difficult to distinguish between the services of real estate brokers. How might a progressive broker apply to its business the concepts of market segmentation and of product differentiation related to each segment? Under what conditions should a broker utilize the segmentation and differentiation you have developed?

5. The S and K Corporation, manufacturer of plumbing supplies, has for years sold its products through plumbing wholesalers to plumbers. It is well known in the trade but has never advertised to consumers. One of its best lines is high-quality, well-styled towel racks, soap dishes, and similar fixtures. To share in the growing "do-it-yourself" market, S and K now wants also to sell this fixture line to homeowners who install the fixtures themselves without the help of a plumber. What channel of distribution should S and K use to reach this new market? What major hurdles will have to be overcome in marketing the fixtures to these new consumers?

6. A producer of room air-conditioners for use in homes is having difficulty obtaining adequate distribution. Use the Berg approach outlined on pages 97 and 98 to build a model of the total distribution system of the industry. Then select places in that system where you believe a company with only 12% of the total market could develop some comparative advantage. Assume that the products of all competitors have about the same characteristics and quality.

7. The Lincoln Box Corporation, a producer of set-up paper boxes, sells about 60% of its output to one large candy manufacturer. There has been a close relation between the two firms for over 15 years and the two presidents are good friends. What steps, if any, might the Lincoln executives take to protect their company against the possible loss of this one customer?

8. A highly successful U.S. motorboat manufacturer is considering international expansion. Two markets being considered are (1) England and (2) Mexico. To what extent will the company's product line and customer policies need to be modified in each country?

9. The converter-resource model used in Chapter 1 to discuss social responsibility implied that relationships with each resource group are somewhat similar. Test this notion by applying the product and customer policy issues raised in this chapter to (a) labor and (b) raw material suppliers.

CASE 5 / *American Non-Woven Fabrics, Inc.*

American Non-Woven Fabrics, Inc. is in a growing segment of the U.S. textile industry. It manufactures non-woven fabrics used for filters, as backing for carpets, and as lining for the trunks of automobiles. Executives of the company have been considering a proposal made by a European firm that would take the company into a new market—for synthetic leather. Now they are deciding whether or not to recommend to the board of directors that the company agree to manufacture and sell, under license, a synthetic leather in the United States.

The industry. Non-woven products make up about 3½ to 4% of total textile products currently manufactured in the U.S. and are widely predicted to be 6% of total textile production within the next ten years.

Table 1
U.S. Output of Non-Woven Textiles
(millions of pounds)

	Quantity		*Quantity*
5 years ago	352	5 years ahead	1,430 (est.)
2 years ago	602	10 years ahead	1,816 (est.)
Current year	1,090		

Source: Company data.

Continuous, though relatively minor, technological changes are improving the performance of non-woven textile fabrics as to their mechanical strength and their absorption characteristics; improvements have also been made in the "hand" (feel) of the non-woven fabrics used in clothing. Early entry is important in this growing field. The need for continual development efforts and the opportunity for the first producer of one product type to gain and hold a substantial market share for that product type have resulted in the non-woven fabrics industry being dominated by relatively large producers.

Table 2
Non-Woven Textile Products

Item No.	Disposable	Item No.	Nondisposable
1	Sheets and pillow cases	21	Backing for carpets
2	Surgical supplies		and cushions
3	Towels	22	Carpets
4	Head-rests for seats	23	Garment padding and lining
5	Filters	24	Clothing
6	Diapers	25	Trunk-liners (automotive)
		26	Coated fabric substrates
		27	Filters

Table 3
Non-Woven Textile Producers

Producer (Item No.)	Producer (Item No.)
Pellon, Inc. (5, 23, 24, 27)	American Non-Woven (5, 21, 25)
Kimberly-Clark, Inc. (1, 3, 4)	E. I. du Pont (21)
Armstrong Corp. (22)	Monsanto Chemical Co. (27)
Kendall Corp. (2, 3, 4, 5, 27)	Ozite Corp. (22)
Ludlow Corp. (21, 25, 26)	Procter and Gamble, Inc. (3, 6)
Deering-Milliken Corp. (23)	International Paper Co. (1, 3, 5)

From the production standpoint, entry to the industry is easy since capital costs are ordinarily small and particular technologies can be secured by licensing. Fibers used in non-woven products are joined by heat-bonding, by chemical binders, and by stitch-binding, or they are needle-punched to entangle the fibers. Average manufacturing costs for the industry are: raw materials, 75%; direct labor, 10%; variable burden, 5%; fixed burden, 10%.

The company. American Non-Woven Fabrics, Inc. is the dominant producer of fabrics that are ultimately used to line the trunks of automobiles. It sells these fabrics to convertors and finishers who coat the fabric with resins or a rubberlike substance and then sell the coated fabric to automobile manufacturers or to distributors in the automotive parts supply business. American Non-Woven also has a substantial, although not the major, share of the carpet and cushion backing market. Its share of the disposable filter market is small.

In all cases, American sells to other manufacturers (predominantly [90%] convertors and finishers) using its own salesforce, which is organized geographically into sales territories.

Carpet backing and filters are made in one plant in Athens, Georgia, while the trunk-lining fabric is manufactured in the company's second plant in its headquarters city, Macon, Georgia. Each plant is currently running at about 80% of its maximum capacity. There is adequate land available for plant expansion in Athens, but none on the site at Macon. Because of expected future sales growth of its present products, production executives are now planning for additional facilities in Athens, with groundbreaking to take place one year from now.

American Non-Woven was originally financed by the sale of common stock. Its steady upward trend in total sales has been financed entirely by retained earnings with

Table 4
American Non-Woven Fabrics, Inc.
Sales and Return on Investment

	Sales Revenue (from present product line)	Post-Tax Return on Investment
5 years ago	$12,000,000	18%
Current year.........................	30,000,000	15%
5 years ahead	42,000,000 (est.)	13% (est.)

Source: Company data.

the exception of the funding for the building in Athens. This was erected by the city and is leased to the company under a long-term lease.

The opportunity. American Non-Woven has been approached by a European manufacturer with the proposal that American Non-Woven should become one of two U.S. licensees to manufacture and sell a poromeric leather that the European firm has developed and introduced successfully in some regions of the European Common Market. To date, this artificial leather has been used primarily for shoe uppers and to a lesser extent for lightweight shoe innersoles. It can be given the appearance of any kind of leather; it is more durable, and it has some of the same "breathing" characteristics as leather.

Poromeric leather (of which du Pont's Corfam was the first sold on any scale in the U.S.) is not an animal product but a synthetic leather made by coating a non-woven substrate with either a polyurethane or vinyl finish. In the case of Corfam, the substrate had three layers, including one of a woven polyester. When sales did not reach the expected volume, du Pont sold its process and remaining inventory to a Polish company.

The proposal by the Common Market firm is that America Non-Woven should manufacture the substrate (one layer of non-woven material) and coat it with polyurethane in its own plants and then sell the product primarily to shoe manufacturers, using a specialized salesforce. The European company wants American Non-Woven to carry out the entire process for both quality control and process security reasons.

The European developer seeks two U.S. licensees because a tariff of $.12 per pound plus 15% ad valorem effectively rules out at present exports to the U.S. from Western European and Eastern European manufacturers. European technology is widely thought to be 2 to 3 years ahead of U.S. technology in its development stage. The European firm expects to continue its development work and would keep American Non-Woven fully advised of any process and product advances as a part of the licensing agreement. The license fee would average about 1% of net sales.

Current U.S. efforts to manufacture an acceptable leather substitute have failed on the three desirable properties of the substrate (strength, absorbability, breathability). The European firm claims that it has exported one million square yards of its substrate to U.S. coating firms and has had good acceptance from them. Preliminary checks by American Non-Woven with three of its present customers (the coating firms) have substantiated this claim.

Market studies by the European manufacturer indicate:

Table 5
U.S. Sales and Potential Sales of Leather and Leather
Substitutes for Shoe Uppers and Innersoles
(millions of square yards)

Product	Current year	5 years hence	10 years hence
Leather shoe uppers.....................	75	n.a.	n.a.
Non-leather shoe uppers	5	37.5	46
Leather shoe innersoles...................	75	n.a.	n.a.
Non-leather shoe innersoles	1	15	20

The market study was carried out using an assumed U.S. price of $6.50 per square yard as contrasted with shoe upper leather prices of $12.50 per square yard.

The decision. Sales executives of American Non-Woven universally support the idea of accepting the licensing agreement. Their arguments are: (a) the firm would have an early entry into a rapidly expanding market and thus could capture a major market share; (b) the proposed selling price makes the synthetic leather highly competitive; (c) neither E. I. du Pont nor Monsanto Chemical is now interested in the product (du Pont's plant for making Corfam had been built to produce 100 million square yards annually, but its total sales in two years were only 35 million square yards); and (d) the American Non-Woven product would have only two layers and thus would tend to stretch and adapt itself to the wearer's foot—whereas Corfam did not.

Production executives generally oppose the licensing idea for several reasons: (a) they are busy with other plans; (b) it will take 12 months to procure the machinery to make the non-woven substrate and another six months to get production underway, and this time span might allow other U.S. manufacturers to catch up with the European technology; and (c) the coating process would be a new venture for American Non-Woven and would require a substantial investment in fixed assets and working capital equal to one half the firm's present capitalization.

The financial vice-president said: "Well, we can probably finance the investment by borrowing since, based on preliminary figures, it promises a rate of return well above the present return on our net worth. But what is the risk? What will the competition be? Will sales of our present products be affected? If sales turn out to be half the amount predicted, will the fixed overhead bankrupt the rest of the company, since the pattern of costs of this venture will be about average for the industry?"

Required: (a) Do you agree with the conclusions of the sales executives? With those of the production executives?

(b) What would you, as an executive of the firm, vote to do about the licensing proposal?

6

MARKETING POLICY–
PRICING

The particular price at which a product is sold reflects numerous influences on its production and distribution (or service) and on the desires of consumers for such a product. Moreover, legal restrictions may affect pricing policy. The final market price is the net result of these different forces.

This complexity of the pricing problem has led many managers to regard pricing as a subject that can be properly handled only on the basis of experience, and in some firms it is surrounded by an air of mystery not to be penetrated by analytical thinking. Actually, the very complexity of the problem makes necessary some general policy to guide executives in their daily actions.

The pricing policy of a company should be coordinated with its competitive strategy and its policy regarding products, customers, and sales promotion. If a company has decided to sell a product of high quality to a selective group of customers, obviously its pricing policy will differ from that of a company that plans to sell lower quality products to a wide range of customers. Thus, the pricing policy followed by the publisher of a distinctive magazine like *Fortune* must differ considerably from that of the publisher of a "western thriller."

But even after the desired strategic role of a product in a market has been selected, a set of questions regarding prices still call for answers. Most important are:

1. What will be the general relationship to *prices of competing products*?
2. What will be the relation to *costs* of production and distribution?
3. How will *prices of specific items* in the company's line compare?
4. Will all customers be charged the same price; if not, on what basis will *differences* be established?
5. How often and under what conditions will prices be *changed*?

RELATION TO PRICES OF COMPETING PRODUCTS

Prices at which competitors offer similar goods or services always have a bearing on pricing policy. They may signal a price war, precipitate extra services in "nonprice" competition, or open the way for unilateral price increases.

Even in periods of rapid price increases, customers will make comparisons with competitors' prices. In fact, the shock of high quotations may lead customers to examine alternative prices more closely than they would when prices are stable.

Comparative quality and price

Pricing of highly standardized products. The quality of some products can be accurately and readily measured, and in such instances recognized grades may be established. For example, cotton, wheat, coffee, and certain minerals and chemicals are described with such accuracy that permanent variations from going prices in a market are impossible. Insofar as the quality varies, there is a standard differential in price.

Thus pig iron is quoted at so much a ton; then, as the sulphur content increases, there is a corresponding reduction in price because this is considered an undesirable quality. If the content of manganese or other desired elements increases, the price is raised accordingly.

Companies dealing in such products must anticipate prompt reaction of competitors if they deviate for long from the established price. So, setting basic prices at the "market" is the only practical option.

Differences in quality and services. For the vast majority of products, however, there are no commonly accepted standards of quality. The quality of men's suits may vary because of differences in materials used and in workmanship, but consumers have no accurate measurement of the difference. Management, then, has some options in pricing, although customers will frequently make comparisons of products that they considered to be in the same general quality range.

Differences in services rendered also affect pricing policy. A few independent grocers still exist who deliver orders free of charge and permit customers to run charge accounts until the end of the month. This service differs sharply from that of a supermarket where the transaction is completed at the counter when the clerk exchanges a paper bag filled with groceries for a full cash payment. The service that a manufacturing concern renders its customers in such things as credit, deliveries, sales aids, and returned goods often varies more than the service provided by retail stores to ultimate consumers.

When significant product or service differentiation is achieved, the company must decide whether (a) a higher price than that of competitive products will be charged, or (b) a comparable price will be set and the superior quality or service will be used as a means of building sales volume, or (c) a high price will be used initially to "skim the cream off the market" and then the price will be cut to competitive levels. The choice of one of these alternative policies depends, in part, upon how long the product or service distinctiveness can be maintained and how much premium consumers are willing to pay for the superior quality.

In establishing a pricing policy, a company must take into consideration not only the immediate effect of a price above or below the prevailing market, but also the reaction of competitors to such a price.

Sensitivity of markets. At the peak of a recent business cycle, for example, a number of textile companies had excessive inventories of sheets that they were having difficulty in selling because their retailers were facing a declining consumer demand and wished to reduce inventories already on their shelves. There was not an immediate and drastic reduction in price because each manufacturer recognized that its competitors would probably match any reduction it might make and thereby eliminate its competitive advantage.

However, if the quality of the goods is quite indeterminate and customers cannot easily compare price schedules, the reaction of competitors may be much slower. They may decide to permit a differential in prices to exist on the assumption that the demand for their products will not be immediately affected. The prices of all sorts of intangible services fall into this category.

Influence of size of company quoting low prices. The effect of a price change on competitors will depend significantly on the size of the company. Price changes by a large and dominant firm in an industry are very likely to affect the prices of the entire industry. Thus, in the farm machinery industry a recognized *price leader* must anticipate that its price changes will be copied by most, though not all, of its competitors. On the other hand, a small company may be able to quote prices lower than those of the large competitors because its total sales volume is not important enough to the large company to warrant an adjustment of its entire price schedule. In the steel industry, for example, several small concerns have been able to increase their business by shading the prices quoted by the leading companies.

If there are two or three price leaders (ologopolistic competition), any one of them typically will raise its price only when it predicts that major competitors will follow. Such predictions are based on rising labor and material costs throughout the industry and on guesses about the competitors' desire to increase their volume—to fill up plant capacity and/or to gain market position—even at the sacrifice of profit.

Since the reaction of competitors to price changes does not always follow a fixed pattern, internal policy guidance for dealing with market response typically takes the form of "factors to consider" or "steps in assembling the best estimates available."

RELATION TO COSTS

Companies that have some discretion in pricing their product above or below the market frequently establish a general policy regarding the relation of price to cost. In fact, the pricing of personal services and of unique, special-order products almost always starts with an estimate of the necessary inputs of time and material. Pricing policy then centers on selling products at a price that permits a normal profit above cost, selling below cost, or varying the price in an attempt to maximize short-run net revenue.

Selling at a normal profit above cost

A policy to set prices at cost plus a normal profit is much more common than economic textbooks imply. It suits three kinds of situations especially well. (1) For unique services—a consultation with a doctor or the repair of furniture, for instance—there can be no market price, and the benefit received by the customer is hard to measure. So a "professional" relationship is established in which the fee is based on time spent. (2) Public utilities, other monopolies, and diverse nonprofit enterprises basically aim to set prices that cover costs and enough margin to attract capital needed. (3) Other firms may choose to subordinate price as a sales appeal and, if competition will permit, simply charge what both buyer and seller feel is a "fair" price—which typically is cost plus a normal profit.

In all such situations mutual confidence and normal expectations are essential. Consequently, policy that introduces consistency and predictability into the pricing serves an important role. Of course, from time to time the policy may be changed—in which case a new mutual understanding must be established. And there will be occasional questions about the applications of the policy to unusual transactions. But clearly the aim is to remove price as an issue for negotiation, while retaining flexibility in the actual charges.

In practice, measuring cost and profit may be complex. (The federal government has a library of manuals and thousands of accountants devoted to measuring costs on its "cost plus fixed fee" purchases.) Standard guides are needed for (a) the per diem rates to be charged for labor, (b) the way prices for materials will be determined, (c) the allocation of overhead, (d) the treatment of idle capacity, and (e) the level and base for computing normal profit.

Setting prices at cost plus a normal profit is a comfortable way to deal with a troublesome problem. But it may be too comfortable. Opportunities for more effective use of resources may be overlooked, and new competition may be invited. Moreover, a cost plus normal profit policy does not resolve issues of price lining, protection, and frequency of change—and it is hard to apply to market segmentation.

Selling below cost

Pricing on the basis of out-of-pocket expenses. A number of conditions may lead a company to establish prices below the total cost of a product. Every firm has certain expenses such as interest, rent, and executive salaries that must be paid regardless of the volume of sales. Other costs, such as materials and direct labor, vary with the volume of activity. These latter costs are *out-of-pocket expenses*, and theoretically any sale above such incremental costs will make some contribution to overhead and profit. Especially when a company is trying to gain market position, selling at incremental costs is appealing.

Strong feeling exists in many industries against selling goods at a price below the total cost. The manager of a printing establishment, for instance, recognized that he might secure additional business if he reduced his price to slightly more than his out-of-pocket expenses, but he refused to do so because he did not want to "spoil the market." He pointed out that if he reduced his price, competitors might follow suit and soon all business would have to be taken at the low price. Moreover, after the price had once been generally used throughout the market, it would be difficult to return it to the present level. In other words, pricing followed at one time may materially affect the price structure for subsequent sales.

Liquidation of inventory. When goods are already produced and on hand in the form of finished inventory, it is occasionally desirable to sell them below cost. In fact, it may be desirable in special circumstances to sell such merchandise at a substantial sacrifice. A lamp manufacturer, for example, had exhausted its cash resources and needed funds for taxes and notes at the bank. Unless it secured capital from some source, bankruptcy appeared inevitable. Under these circumstances the inventory was sold at a very low price in order to raise cash.

Even firms in a strong financial condition sometimes follow a policy of selling inventory for any price it will bring. Thus, if a general decline in prices is anticipated, a firm may be better off to dispose of its stock immediately rather than to carry it over a period when prices are dropping. A similar situation arises for firms handling perishable merchandise or goods that will soon pass out of style or become obsolete.

Some firms have a policy that their first-quality, branded goods will be sold only at a fixed price. Hence, when they want to liquidate inventory, they have to remove all brand identification and often they use entirely different outlets. Second-quality merchandise, soiled goods, and odd lots may also be sold at below-average unit costs; here again some unknown brand label is often used to avoid "spoiling the market" for the regular line.

Loss leaders. Still another reason why retail stores occasionally sell below cost is to attract customers to the store. In such cases one or more standard products are sold at a loss, which loss it is hoped will be more than offset by the profit on the sale of other merchandise to the customer while in the store or on subsequent visits resulting from the contact established by the special sale. In many states there is agitation to prohibit the use of loss leaders, but from a strictly business point of view it is difficult to see any valid distinction between incurring a loss on certain types of merchandise and spending money for other forms of advertising. (Misrepresenting the reasons for selling below cost or selling below cost for the purpose of eliminating competition are already contrary to federal law.)

A company may sell some minor item at a price below the total cost just to render a service to its regular customers. This may be done on a certain part of the product, or it may be done on a particular item necessary to complete the line. Such a practice is distinct from loss leaders in that it is done as an accommodation and is not featured.

Effect of volume on costs and profits

Variations in average unit costs. Thus far we have assumed that costs per unit were fixed and could be easily measured. In many companies, however, the total cost of products varies with the volume sold. A partially filled airliner (or classroom), for example, may handle a substantial increase in passengers (or students) with little change in total operating cost. In the production of many metal products, the cost of making dies and setting up machinery for production is often half of the total expense of producing a normal volume. This fixed expense will remain the same whether the volume is cut in half or doubled. Thus, there will be a substantial variation in the *average cost per unit*.

Note that the foregoing tendency holds true only when the production capacity of facilities is not fully used. If a motel, for instance, had to build an addition and increase its staff in order to handle additional customers, its profit on each customer might not increase at all.

There are, of course, many companies in which the fixed expenses are comparatively small and consequently the unit costs do not change greatly with the changes in volume. For example, the expenses of a commission merchant dealing in fruits and vegetables consist largely of material costs. Similarly, contractors building homes have low fixed expense.

Costs will also vary because of many other factors, such as changes in prices paid for raw materials, variations in the efficiency of the employees, and increased or decreased selling and promotion expense. All of these factors should be considered by an executive in estimating the cost for various volumes of business.

Estimating profits for different price levels. When per unit cost varies with volume, the manager should estimate the quantity of output that can be sold at different prices; the effect of change in volume on the cost of goods produced as well as on the cost of selling; and the combined effect of changes in the price, the volume, and the cost on total net profits.

A hypothetical illustration will indicate the possible variations resulting from changes in price. A company may be able to sell 800 dresses at $20 a dress. By reducing the price to $18, 1,200 dresses may be sold; and at a price of $16, 2,000 dresses may be sold. Additional reductions in price may increase the demand for the product further. The possible effects of variations in price on the sales volume, the cost, and the net results are shown at the top of the following page.

In the example the cost per unit decreases as the volume increases—a typical experience for many companies. In most instances, however, unit costs do not decline as rapidly as the prices must be reduced in order to secure the

The Effect of Price on Volume, Cost, and Profit

(1) Price	*(2)* Number of Units Sold	*(3)* Cost per Unit	*(4)* Profit per Unit	*(5)* Total Profit (2) × (4)
$20	800	$14.00	$6.00	$ 4,800
18	1,200	11.50	6.50	7,800
16	2,000	11.00	5.00	10,000
14	2,500	10.80	3.20	8,000
12	3,000	10.60	1.40	4,200

additional volume. Consequently, the *profit per unit* diminishes as is indicated in Column 4.

Profit per unit, however, is not the final answer regarding the desirability of a particular price because recognition must be given to the number of units on which this profit is earned. Thus, if an increase in price results in a significantly higher profit per unit and a comparatively small reduction in volume (from $14 to $16 in the illustration), the total profit will be increased. But if the drop in volume is sharp, it may more than offset the higher profit per unit (from $16 to $18 in the illustration).

Factors affecting response of volume to changes in price. The total profit secured at each price, as can be seen by the preceding table, depends upon the volume of sales as well as the average cost per unit. Clearly, management must estimate as best it can not only the effect of volume on the total cost but also the volume of sales that will be secured at different prices. In practice the response of volume to price changes depends upon many factors, such as the following.

The *reaction of competitors to price changes* by one company is an important factor to be considered. If an entire industry acts almost simultaneously in the adjustment of any price, then there is little reason to assume that one company will gain volume at the expense of its competitors because of the price change. Only if the entire volume of the industry expands or contracts because of the price change is it reasonable to assume that there will be a significant change in the volume of a specific company. If, on the other hand, price advances or reductions are not copied by competitors, then a company can consider the demand for its own products.

Another factor in the response of volume to price changes is the *elasticity of the demand*. We have observed that if a retail store has a big sale with prices on standard articles significantly reduced, the volume of sales will be greatly expanded. In fact, the sale of certain articles will be doubled and trebled. The use of synthetic fibers has expanded greatly as its real price has declined. On the other hand, a doctor would not greatly increase the volume of his business if he were to make a 25% reduction in his charges, nor would an electric power company sell much more current for household use if it were to make a similar reduction in its rates.

The behavior of the price of one product may affect the response of volume to price changes in another product. Packing companies have observed that if the price of pork rises while the price of beef remains constant, there will be a significant decrease in the consumption of pork. Should beef prices rise at the same time pork prices are increased, there will be a much smaller drop in the volume of pork consumed.

Professional buyers for industrial concerns, as well as retail stores, *adjust the volume of their purchases to anticipated prices* as well as to changes that have actually occurred. Thus, if a company reduces its price and the buyer anticipates that this is just the beginning of a series of price reductions, he may actually diminish his volume rather than increase it. Contrariwise, if an increase in price is interpreted as a sign of future scarcity of goods, the buyer may place large orders so as to be assured of an adequate supply at the current market price. This is one of the reasons for temporary spurts in business activities during periods of business prosperity and a sharp contraction in activity when a decline in prices is anticipated.

Other influences may affect the response of volume to price changes in a particular industry. The complexity of the problem is due not only to the numerous influences that may affect the response of volume to price, but also to the fact that it is difficult to obtain adequate information. Often the short-run adjustments to a price change are quite different from those that will occur in the long run after costs and volumes are well known.

Composite policies

Often companies use both competitors' prices and their own costs in formulating their general pricing policy. A local manufacturerer of electrical fixtures who uses price as a sales appeal, for example, follows a policy of (a) 10% below prices of a well-known competitor, except (b) this differential is narrowed to avoid selling below "cost" (total manufacturing costs at estimated sales volume), and (c) sales below "cost" are made only temporarily to close out an item or to combat a "price leader" of a competitor. In contrast, a company producing high-quality, shortwave intercommunication systems relies on technical service and quality to attract customers. This firm normally quotes prices on the basis of total engineering, manufacturing, and selling costs (with a liberal allowance for overhead) plus 15%. However, downward adjustments are made when it is known that the normal price is more than 20% above either of two reputable competitors.

POLICY REGULATING PRICES OF INDIVIDUAL ITEMS

Price lining

If a company sells several different grades of the same product, the price of one grade must be established in relation to the prices of the other grades. This problem often becomes important in department stores where a rather wide selection of each type of merchandise is handled. Some stores have established a definite policy of carrying only one or two styles of a certain product at each price level. Furthermore, they attempt to have prices spread throughout the range from the highest to the lowest rather than concentrated at some points and having wide gaps at others.

Manufacturers that sell their products under several brand names, only one of which is advertised, must decide on the differential between the advertised brand and the unadvertised brands. If a significant difference between the products exists, then each may be priced on the basis of its particular market and its costs. When the products are similar and are available to the same customers, the problem becomes more delicate. Some obvious characteristic of the product must be different if the higher-priced line is to continue to sell. Surprisingly enough, this variation may consist of a relatively unimportant change such as the kind of finish or the addition of a special gadget—for example, more chrome trim on an automobile.

Several manufacturers have a regular line of products and a deluxe line; and if price competition is keen they may add a "fighting brand," which is the basic product stripped of almost all the surface features that give extra convenience or attractiveness to the regular line. Thus, product design and pricing policy are coordinated so that the company can tap several different segments of the total market.

Using accepted market prices

For some products or services there are well-established prices in the market. Inflation long ago turned the 5-cent candy bar and the 10-cent bus fare into history. Nevertheless, even under unstable price conditions, convenient or psychologically attractive prices do gain widespread acceptance. Breaking out of these bounds causes at least temporary resentment by customers, and demand is likely to drop. Consequently, no single company (nor politician if bus fares are at issue) wants the onus of initiating such an increase. Small companies, in particular, usually secure better results if they can adjust their products and services so that the final price will conform to such accepted market prices.

DIFFERENT PRICES FOR DIFFERENT CUSTOMERS

One-price policy

Every enterprise must decide whether its products will be sold at the same price to all customers. In the United States the so-called one-price policy has wide acceptance, particularly in retail transactions. Retail stores typically have a set price marked on the merchandise, and every customer coming into the store must pay this set price. In fact, an American is frequently at a loss when buying goods in foreign countries where dealers name a high price and expect to haggle before the sale is finally made.

The horse-trading days in the United States, however, are by no means over. New automobile prices are not rigidly fixed, and the secondhand market and trade-in values retain many opportunities for deception and bargaining. A wholesale fruit company considered a one-price policy but rejected the plan because the prices in the market changed so frequently and the products were so perishable that standardization of prices would have prevented the flexibility for success in this type of business.

Discounts from established prices

Many manufacturers and other concerns wish to have the benefits of a one-price policy, but they find it desirable to have different prices for different types of customers. This is often accomplished by maintaining a list price and then granting discounts to certain classes of customers.

Discounts are necessary when a company wishes to sell to wholesalers as well as to retailers. The wholesaler performs services for which it must be paid, and unless it can buy products for a lower price than the retailer, its resale price will be so high it cannot get business. This need for *trade discounts* is generally recognized, but there is much debate as to how large such discounts should be and who are entitled to them. For example, one firm with three retail stores set up a "wholesale department" in an attempt to get an extra 20% discount. Most manufacturers would refuse to grant a wholesaler's discount to such a firm because it is not really performing wholesaling functions. In some industries, such as tires, it is a common policy to have a whole series of discounts that presumably reflect the differences in actual services performed by the various distributors. Clearly, a company's discount policy will have a marked effect on its success in winning patronage from different types of customers and hence should be coordinated with customer policies.

Quantity discounts are commonly offered to anyone who purchases in large volume. Here, again, the difficult questions are under what conditions the discounts will be granted and how large they should be. Large customers may be so important to a company that there is a temptation to give them very high discounts. Under the Robinson-Patman Act and related legislation, however, quantity discounts are limited to actual savings in producing and selling the larger orders.

There are, of course, other forms of discounts, such as cash discounts and advertising allowances, that are not intended to be price reductions. In actual practice, however, they are sometimes so large and are granted in such a way that their effect is a price reduction in a somewhat disguised form.

In addition, a company may offer price concessions in an effort to build up volume in slack periods. A 10% discount for early orders of Christmas cards is not uncommon; airlines have lower fares in slack seasons; electric utility companies offer special "off-peak" rates. When a well-recognized policy has been set up, such discounts can be granted without upsetting the basic price structure.

Regional differences in prices

Still another pricing problem deals with regional differences in prices. If the cost of shipping the finished goods from the plant to the customer is a significant part of the cost, as is true for most heavy or bulky articles, this problem can hardly be avoided. If the manufacturer pays the freight, it will receive a lower *net price* from the most distant customer.

The policy of many companies is to absorb most or all of the shipping costs to distant customers whenever a competitor is located in that territory. In some cases the courts have ruled, however, that this is an unfair price discrimination, and there are legal questions as to how far a company may go in regional pricing. Clearly, if a producer with excess capacity wants to sell products in a highly competitive, distant market at a *lower* price than it charges in its local area, it will be on sounder ground if it differentiates the products sold in the two areas.

PRICE CHANGES

Difficulty of changing widely announced prices

Not all companies are in a position to make frequent adjustments in their prices. Many companies selling industrial goods distribute a printed price list to potential customers, and it is not expedient to change such prices frequently. An increase in price is likely to cause dissatisfaction on the part of customers who have been relying upon the printed list, and even a decrease may cause some confusion in ordering and billing. Similarly, the mail-order houses cannot readily adjust prices for at least a season once their catalogs are distributed.

Several means are available to limit the adverse effect of such inflexibility. Fixed price contracts can be made with suppliers so that part of the risk of rising costs is shifted to the supplier. Of course, such contracts are a double-edged sword since they involve risk that supply prices may drop or that the quantity of goods will not be needed. Another approach is to include a modest buffer for cost increases in the announced price, and if this turns out to be unwarranted, then to cut back. The presumption here is that cuts are easier to make than increases and that volume will not suffer too much before such action is taken. A third precaution is to sharply limit the period for which the announced prices apply.

Price protection

Changes in prices on industrial raw materials create a special problem because these products are often an important item of cost to the customers. To get orders on the books and thus facilitate production planning and also to assure the customer of a supply of material at a known price, it is customary to plan orders for such material a long period in advance. The order specifies the price and protects the customer against an increase in the price of its raw materials. In practice, the customer is often permitted to defer its contract if the price falls. Thus, the customer is in a position to take advantage of a falling price or to protect itself against an increase in price as circumstances may warrant. The raw material producer follows such a pricing policy because it is the only way it can secure advance orders that greatly assist its production scheduling, and also because it is necessary if the goodwill of the customer is to be maintained.

Sometimes price increases are announced several weeks before they become effective and customers are encouraged to place firm orders at the old price. This builds volume temporarily and gives customers an opportunity to protect themselves against the rising costs.

Protection against price cuts is also granted by some manufacturers to wholesalers and retail dealers. In such instances, if prices are reduced, the manufacturer agrees to reimburse the dealer for the nominal loss in inventory value it suffers as a result of the price reduction. Tire companies, for example, have found it necessary to protect their dealers against price reductions in order to encourage the dealers to carry a complete stock. Such a practice obviously is important in maintaining a dealer's goodwill, for otherwise it might feel that the manufacturer had loaded it up with stock and then caused it to take a loss in order to compete with dealers who held off buying until the new prices were in effect.

In almost every instance the handling of a price change may create complications, and recognized policies are often essential if the transition to the new price level is to be accomplished smoothly.

SUMMARY

Every company needs policy covering the prices to be charged for its products and services. Often the setting of this price policy is one of the most complex problems central management faces.

An orderly approach to pricing has been suggested in this chapter. First, policy regarding the basic level of company prices should be considered. The policy is usually expressed in terms of relationships with prices of competing products and relationships with company costs. Then policy dealing with pricing of specific items and with price lining should be set. Closely related is policy regarding price differentials for various types of customers; there will be need for standing answers to questions regarding trade discounts, quantity discounts, freight and advertising allowances, and similar adjustments to list prices.

Once a price structure is established, there is the further issue of how often and under what conditions prices will be changed. Warning of price increases and protection from price cuts are often important in relations with customers.

Throughout this discussion of pricing policy, frequent reference has been made to the quality and the variety of all products in the company lines, the types and the sizes of customers sought, and the nature of company services and other sales appeals, as well as to many factors affecting company costs. Company strategy regarding improvement in market position versus short-run profits is also involved.

Clearly, pricing policy is intimately connected with strategy and with other policy; final pricing decisions should not be made until their repercussions on all company operations have been considered.

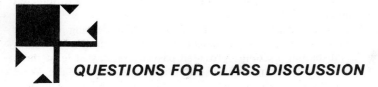

QUESTIONS FOR CLASS DISCUSSION

1. As part of its program to control inflation in expansion periods, the federal government often urges business firms to refrain from raising their prices. (For some key products such as steel, government pressure is intense.) How much weight do you recommend that a company give to such governmental requests when setting the prices of its services or products?

2. (a) In a period of general inflation many companies will own buildings and equipment that cost a lot less than their current replacement costs. Also, inventories will often have been purchased at less than replacement costs. In pricing its products, should such a company use actual costs or replacement costs when thinking about its cost/price ratio? (b) How would you answer the question if replacement costs of equipment and of inventory were below actual costs?

3. Ivar Berg personally owns a ski run located two hours' drive north of Philadelphia. It has two chair lifts, exciting slopes, and a heavy mortgage. Nearby lodges are owned and operated by other people. Berg gets virtually all his income from fees for riding the chair lifts. (His share of profits from the Ski Shop is small.) The costs for running the lifts and maintaining the slopes (with artificial snow when necessary) are affected very little by the number of people on the slopes. What fees do you recommend Berg charge for use of the chair lifts? There are no limits on the variations and the discounts you may propose.

4. What connection may there be between a company's policy to sell above, at, or below the market and its policy regarding national advertising?

5. Book publishers often sell the same book in hardcover editions and in paperback editions. Novels are usually sold only in hard covers during the first year, and a paperback edition is added if the book is well received and after much of the initial fixed cost of editing, typesetting, and makeup has been recouped. At that time the cost of putting the book in a hard cover is about 50¢ more than putting it in a paper cover. If you were the publisher, how would you determine the price differential between hardcover and paperback books?

6. In the automobile tire business, wages constitute approximately 15%, materials 43%, and overhead 42% of the total costs. The typical costs of sugar refining are labor 4%, materials 85%, and overhead 11% of the total costs. Suppose that the X Tire Company and the Y Sugar Company each suffered a 33 ⅓% decline in

volume of business. (a) Which company would have the largest increase in average total unit costs? (b) Should each company raise its price to cover the increased costs? Why?

7. Five medical doctors with diverse specialties have established in Cheyenne a private clinic for their joint practice. From society's viewpoint, how should they price their services: (a) On the basis of time devoted to a patient? (b) On the value of the services to the patient? (c) On ability of patients to pay for services? (d) On an annual service charge for all care needed? (e) On an annual service charge, with quantity discounts for families? (f) On fixed charges for each specific kind of service—tonsillectomy, broken arm, obstetrical care, infected toe, case of pneumonia, etc.?

8. The overseas airlines have used price as a major means of increasing passenger traffic. To build off-season business, the lines flying between the United States and Europe give substantial discounts provided passengers stay at least three weeks and do not travel during the busy summer months. On the West Coast-Hawaii run, fares are cut for economy class (no meals and a minimum of other services). Do you recommend that sharp cuts in certain classes of fares be introduced on domestic (48 states) flights? If so, how would you differentiate the passengers entitled to the low fares?

9. The Amsterdam Petroleum Transport Company owned and operated eight T-2 tankers. By today's standards these tankers were small and slow, and they had been operating at a substantial loss (except for brief periods of acute tanker shortage). Estimates showed that a cut in freight rates might increase the volume of business but that, even with the increased volume, depreciation and interest on the capital investment would not be earned; consequently, the vessels were sold at substantially below their book value to an Algerian concern.

The Algerian concern proceeded to cut the freight rates to a point where the tankers were kept reasonably busy. Amsterdam Petroleum Transport protested strongly against the low rates. The Algerian concern replied that, because of the low purchase price and the resulting low depreciation and interest, it was able to operate at these low rates and show a profit.

Assuming equal efficiency of operation, should Amsterdam Petroleum Transport have sold the vessels or should it have cut rates to the same level as the Algerian concern?

CASE 6 / North-Central Standard Oil Company, Inc.

North-Central Standard, a major domestic oil refining and marketing company, sells gasoline and other oil products throughout the United States west of the Appalachian Mountains. The company has had several different pricing policies during the past sixty years. Now the Vice-President for Finance is concerned about company earnings and is making a statement to the Committee for Pricing Policy. Two other executives are also appearing before the committee.

Company policy during the firm's early history was to base its wholesale (tank wagon) prices on costs plus a desired profit margin. After some years, when marketing executives gained greater influence in the company, policy shifted to meeting the prices of the largest competitor in each city or district. More recently, pricing policy has been modified to be based upon the entire competitive situation in any one locality, which includes considering the costs of various products and the types of marketing that characterize the individual local markets. (Some cities have had price competition from local refiners plus rebates, premiums, trading stamps, sales contests, and giveaways—others have not.) Pricing policy is now stated as meeting competitive conditions on both a broad industry basis and on a local market basis. If necessary to meet local competition, prices in a local market may be unrelated to company costs and primarily influenced by the local wholesale market price.

By analyzing market prices at different stages of production (crude oil, refinery door, major shipping point), the company attempts to determine what it will cost a competitor to serve a given market. Shifts in costs do not automatically affect prices but are weighed along with market trends in determining whether changes are warranted in the company's overall price structure.

The Vice-President for Finance's statement is:

"Company profits have been hurt by legislative action that changed the depletion allowance and that relaxed import restrictions on foreign crude oil. Profits may even be damaged further by changes in excise taxes or tariffs. My studies indicate that changes in the depletion allowance have cut our post-tax cash flow by $21 million. Importing foreign crude oil benefits our competitors much more than it does us, so any cut in the tariff will reduce their costs relatively. We depend on higher-cost domestic crude for most of our supply so that our material costs are, in general, higher than those of our competitors. Increases in material costs due to these factors are not under our control.

"However, we have done our best to reduce controllable costs. Our refineries have increased output over the past ten years from 300,000 barrels per day to 450,000 barrels per day. We have reduced the number of employees from 22,000 to 15,000. We have recently negotiated a three-year labor contract that will keep us free from strikes and allow us to stabilize wage costs as a percent of prices.

"The big question that remains is whether demand is increasing and will increase. If so, a price increase is warranted. The accompanying tables and financial statements explain the demand situation and fully warrant, I believe, the kind of price increase I have in mind to restore our return on assets and return on equity to acceptable levels.

"We all know that government policy and action is uncertain and will change with regard to tariffs, excise taxes, import quotas and/or license fees for imports; but some forecast has to be made, so I have used the conservative forecast of the Federal Energy Administration and modified it slightly based on our own analysis.

"Gasoline prices have stabilized and even declined slightly in some markets over the past six months. And, over the past decade, gasoline prices have still risen less than the total consumer price index. So, despite the increases of not too long ago, we still have not caught up and are justified in raising our prices further.

"It is necessary for us to maintain our oil exploration program to survive as a company. We can't cut that expense. We need to explore in northern Canada to supplement our Alaskan North Slope discoveries.

"Our goal is to realize an 8% to 10% growth in earnings per year and to increase our shareholders' return to above industry average. To do this we must continue exploration to lessen our cost of crude, and we must look forward to later acquisitions.

Table 1

U.S. Liquid Petroleum Supply and Demand
(Millions of barrels per day)

Year	Domestic Production	Imports	Total U.S. Demand
Current	10.0	6.3	16.3
Next	10.2	6.6	16.8
Five Years Hence	11.0	9.5	20.5
Ten Years Hence	12.0	12.0	24.0

Source: Federal Energy Administration, Company Data.

<table>
<tr><td colspan="3">

Table 2
Rate of Return on Equity

</td><td colspan="2">

Table 3
The Domestic Tax Burden

</td></tr>
<tr>
<td></td>
<td>All
Industrial
Concerns</td>
<td>Oil
Industry</td>
<td></td>
<td>Percent of
Gross Revenue</td>
</tr>
<tr>
<td></td><td></td><td></td>
<td>Petroleum</td><td>5.43</td>
</tr>
<tr>
<td>Current Year</td><td>13.5%</td><td>12.0%</td>
<td>Mining and Manufacturing</td><td>5.50</td>
</tr>
<tr>
<td>Last Year</td><td>12.2%</td><td>12.2%</td>
<td>All Business Corporations</td><td>4.62</td>
</tr>
</table>

"The following income statements and balance sheets show our current position and a five-year *pro forma* position assuming that productivity increases offset one half of materials and labor price increases so that we have a 3% per year rise in cost per barrel of production and refining while running at the same throughput. The statements also predict a 9% price increase the first year and price increases of 6% per year thereafter to keep up with inflation.

Income Statements
(In millions)

	Current	Pro Forma (Five Years Hence)
Sales	$1,750	$2,410
Costs:		
Production, Purchases of Crude		
Oil, Refining	$950	$1,095
Exploration	80	240
Selling and Administrative	277	412
Taxes	115	240
Depletion	145	70
Interest	24	53
Total Costs	1,591	2,110
Net Earnings	$ 159	$ 300

Balance Sheet
(In Millions)

Current Assets	$ 650	$ 900
Net Property	1,625	2,250
Total	$2,275	$3,150
Current Liabilities	$ 318	$ 440
Long-Term Debt........................	420	590
Deferred Taxes	90	120
Equity	1,447	2,000
Total	$2,275	$3,150

"For expansion we shall have to raise substantial sums of capital, and for this we need at least a return on investment equal to all industry. The solution to our problems of return on investment, financing exploration, and finding more capital is to raise prices. We should increase our prices 9% as rapidly as possible.

"As to reactions of our competitors, the changes in depletion allowances and import quotas and other legislative action will affect us all about equally. Demand studies measure national price elasticity as −0.52. As the price goes up, revenues will rise since the quantity taken falls off less rapidly than the price rises. Once again, I recommend an immediate price increase and the policy shown in the *pro forma* statements."

The Marketing Vice-President's statement is:

"In my opinion, the rest of the industry is not in the same position we are. Look at the facts. We have much less foreign oil than the other majors. Thus we cannot drop our crude costs as they can by bringing in lower-cost foreign crude from sources not in the OPEC agreement or by taking advantage of price differences among the OPEC countries. Since we buy a lot of crude oil, we will have to pay higher prices to independents who are undertaking the very high costs of domestic exploration. They will raise their prices—our costs—to maintain their earnings. Thus our competitors' costs will not rise as will ours and they will not have a need for comparable price increases—now or later.

"We should price to hold market share and regain markets. Pricing to attain a fixed target return on assets or on investment is wrong. The price we can charge depends entirely on competition. Profitability should be determined by the way we manage the company—by continuing efforts to improve efficiency and to lower our costs so that the market price will yield a satisfactory return. If we maintain the current price and do not raise future prices more than 6% per year to offset inflation, we will be close enough to the lowest seller and yet not highest in our markets so that we will hold our proper market position. I have prepared projections to show this—a 16% increase in physical volume over the five-year period and a predicted 6% per year price increase. (See the statements on page 122.) The production, purchase, and refining costs shown include a 3% per year inflation increase as well as the 16% gain in volume."

The Vice-President for Finance responds:

"I disagree. It seems to me perfectly satisfactory and the wise course to follow to have a higher price and higher margins with a lower volume and even a declining market share if this means that we can have the highest return on investment. Let those who want to run a profitless treadmill do so. We were the price leader in the past. Let's return to that policy now."

The National Sales Manager responds:

"Think back on our history. For years we lost market share and then went below 10% in our three big markets. We have won back some of our position and are now up to 13% and 14% in the Twin Cities and southern Wisconsin. Currently our prices everywhere are 4 to 5 cents a gallon above the lowest seller in the market. To move toward regaining our historically justified market position of about a 20% share, we need to lower prices 2 cents, not raise them. This increase in market share plus the usually expected 6% per year sales growth in the market, which includes an inflation factor of 3% per year on the average, should bring sales up to $2.9 billion in five years (a 32% increase in physical volume). I don't believe that general inflation is going to hit us anywhere near as hard as the rest of you assume. Even if our cost of purchases and refining to sales ratio goes up to 57.5% we will do as well as indicated in the *pro forma* statements. The better thing to do is to price this way to achieve the strongest possible consumer franchise and thus protect the company in the market."

Pro Forma Statements (5 Years Hence)

	Presented by *Marketing Vice-President*	*Presented by* *National Sales Manager*
Income Statement (In millions)		
Sales	$2,620	$2,900
Costs:		
Production, Purchases of Crude Oil, Refining	$1,245	$1,665
Exploration	220	200
Selling and Administrative	540	459
Taxes	218	180
Depletion	90	100
Interest	92	136
Total Costs	2,405	2,740
Net Earnings	$ 215	$ 160
Balance Sheet (In millions)		
Current Assets	$ 975	$1,080
Net Property	2,450	2,700
Total	$3,425	$3,780
Current Liabilities	$ 480	$ 530
Long-Term Debt................	1,015	1,505
Deferred Taxes	130	145
Equity........................	1,800	1,600
Total	$3,425	$3,780

Required: (a) Explain the effects of the three pricing policy proposals.

(b) What economic reasoning underlies the statement of the Financial Vice-President?

(c) What is your decision as to wise company policy? Explain.

MARKETING MIX POLICY

Strategy and the consumer

Many engineers and theoretical economists have contended that once policy has been set defining products to be sold, customers to be reached, and prices to be charged—issues we have examined in the preceding chapters—all significant marketing decisions have been settled. Such thinking is an oversimplification. The process of matching the creation of goods and services with customer needs is finished only when goods have been purchased and put to use.

Consequently, central management should envisage the actions necessary to complete the full transformation into consumer satisfactions. For this purpose, it is helpful for a manager to assume the viewpoint of the consumer and to think through what the company should do to encourage repeated purchases.

Rarely does a consumer merely buy a physical product. Instead, the consumer purchases a *package* that fulfills some "need," that provides a psychological pride of ownership and/or consumption, that involves a minimum of anxiety about breakdown or damage, that is considered a "good buy," that can be acquired without great financial upset, that will be delivered when wanted, and so forth. An essential part of a marketing plan, then, is to conceive of a practical package of satisfactions that will appeal to a significant number of consumers.

Normally, providing each of these consumer satisfactions involves a cost. The cost may be a direct expense incurred by the producing company, or it may be a fee or margin charged by a distributor. Keeping these costs within acceptable bounds is, of course, an inherent aspect of designing a viable package of satisfactions.

Marketing mix

In addition to seeking a winning combination of consumer satisfactions, the central manager must consider how to communicate with the consumer to present an offer. A whole array of alternative forms of advertising are available for this purpose. And the role of sales representatives and agents in this total distribution process has to be defined.

But, advertising and sales staffs involve costs, just as do the satisfactions discussed in the previous section. Inevitably, a choice must be made. How much of each—consumer services, higher quality, convenient packages, lower price, advertising, or personal solicitation? This allocation among such competing uses for the distribution dollar is called the *marketing mix*. Of course, the particular marketing mix that fits one product in one market will differ from the combination suited to other product-markets. Selling life insurance differs from selling automobile insurance; a marketing mix suited to electric typewriters differs from one for computers. Key decisions are needed with respect to:

1. Selecting *sales appeals* that are important to the customer.
2. Determining the use that will be made of *advertising*.
3. Deciding the role of *personal solicitation*.
4. Combining all marketing plans into a practical *marketing mix*.

SALES APPEALS

A variety of dimensions are available for the total service a company provides its customers. The role of policy on sales appeals is to clarify the emphasis that management believes will be most effective. Among the possible appeals often featured are:

1. Customer services.
2. Quality.
3. Style and packaging.
4. Price.
5. Reputation of company.

Customer services

Personal assistance. A recurring question is how much personal assistance to the customer should be a part of the total sales package. For example, in Honolulu a car driver who pulls up to a gas pump finds someone washing all the car windows, checking tire pressure, filling the radiator, and inspecting the battery while the gasoline is being pumped; this requires two or three attendants working simultaneously. In contrast, in a New York City service station the driver has to ask to have the windshield washed, and checking tire pressure is clearly a do-it-yourself operation. Many filling stations in London are on a complete self-service basis—except for paying the bill (and even that function may be taken over by an automatic credit card device). Maps, touring advice, washrooms, and soft-drink dispensers provide still other variations. Clearly, filling station operators must estimate which services their customers really want and whether they are prepared to pay a differential to get them.

Similarly in industrial products, some companies give their customers a great deal of free advice. Some salesmen of dairy equipment, for instance, advise a milk plant operator on his total production activities. The commercial banker, to pick another example, frequently counsels with important customers about all sorts of financial matters that may not directly relate to the bank. In contrast, the homemaker does not expect to get cooking advice from the clerk in the supermarket.

A shift is occurring in personal service in the hotel field. Motels grew up with a minimum of personal service, in contrast to the traditional hotels with doormen, bellhops, and room maids. But as motels are becoming more luxurious, they are adding more personal assistance; meanwhile, the large downtown hotels will permit guests to carry their own bags and to find their own rooms. With changing attitudes about personal assistance, matching services to a particular desired clientele calls for sharp perception.

Buying convenience. How far should a company go in making it easy for a customer to buy? A wide range of answers are found in the retail field. Department stores, for instance, provide attractive displays, wide selection, sales help, gift wrapping, home delivery, charge accounts, and return privileges. In contrast, discount houses provide few or perhaps none of these services. When discount houses were first started, the differences in their prices compared with those of the department stores were almost as great as the differences in buying convenience. More recently, the spread between prices and between services has tended to narrow. Department stores have trimmed their services somewhat and have reduced their margins, whereas the larger discount houses have done just the opposite. Obviously, retail managers believe that the differences in convenience desired by various groups of customers is becoming less sharp.

In industrial fields, buying convenience takes the form of descriptive catalogs, telephone ordering, stock held for future delivery, and acceptance of rush orders. Companies differ greatly in their policy on the extent to which they provide such services.

Maintenance and repair. One of the central pillars of IBM's marketing success is its maintenance service policy. Most of its machines are covered by a contract under which IBM provides regular maintenance service and is available for prompt repair work in the event of breakdown. Other manufacturers have a less elaborate service organization but do maintain a stock of repair parts for all equipment sold during, say, the past twenty years. The importance of repair service for durable equipment is illustrated by foreign automobiles. Neither a low price nor the latest sportscar model is an adequate substitute for keeping the car running. Consequently, foreign car sales are closely correlated with the availability of good repair service.

Policy on customer service and policy on channels of distribution are closely related. The further removed a manufacturer is from the final consumers of its product, the more difficult is control of customer service. Companies that stress service often find it necessary to maintain their own branches; some television and hi-fi manufacturers establish exclusive distributorships in order to improve the quality of repair service available to ultimate customers.

Installment credit. The day is gone when installment credit is available only on durable goods in an amount less than the resale value. Now financing may be arranged on almost any large purchase, and mail-order houses—among others—extend installment credit on an accumulation of small purchases. However, the ease of obtaining credit and the terms on which it is granted do vary. Also, manufacturers give more or less help to their distributors. Part of the marketing mix, then, is the extent to which a company gets into the financing business. Recently, companies have been turning over more and more of this function to banks, finance companies, and credit card companies; this tends to remove installment credit as a competitive factor.

Leasing equipment instead of selling it is a service provided by some manufacturers. Computers, postal meters, shoe machinery, and automatic bowling-pin setters are all available under lease. Many of these lease arrangements are similar to installment credit, calling for periodic payments during the period when the product is being used and giving the customer an option to buy the equipment at the end of the lease. The major difference is that the customer may return the equipment to the manufacturer when it is only partially used. For customers with limited financial resources or fluctuating needs, such leases can be quite attractive.

Often leasing and maintenance service are combined. This has an added attraction to the manufacturer because it then knows that the equipment which may be returned to it is being kept in good repair.

Prompt availability. This is a valuable dimension for both products and services. An employer with a potential strike, or a mother about to give birth to an offspring, wants consulting advice promptly—not next week. Similarly, a loan from the bank or a delivery of fuel oil have much greater sales value if customers know they can depend on the services being available when needed. Advance planning helps, of course; but rarely can requirements be precisely predicted, so prompt availability becomes an added aspect of service.

Small local companies can often gain significant advantage by providing this prompt delivery. They can reach the scene of action quickly, they are already familiar with local conditions, and their small size permits considerable flexibility. If larger firms choose to stress availability, they have to set up local representatives or branches and then give the local units both the incentive and the authority to meet unusual customer requirements.

Considerable choice and opportunity for creative variation is available in customer services that a company provides—as the preceding examples show. Some of these services may be so important to customers that they are regarded as part of the product itself. Since they are intimately tied up with the product in the mind of the customer, it is important that policies regarding their use be integrated with product, customer, and other marketing policies.

Quality as a sales appeal

The importance of quality in certain types of services has already been indicated in the discussion of product policies. Minimum quality standards are essential for many products, and here we are assuming that such minimums are being met. The issue in terms of sales appeal is whether quality higher than the prevailing level will be used to attract customers.

Extra quality involves extra effort and cost. Strawberry jam made with only pure sugar and no corn syrup has added raw material cost; handrubbed furniture has extra labor cost. A policy to build extra quality into our products, therefore, has to be matched up against other ways to differentiate our total marketing mix. The question is, Does distinctive quality hold strong appeal to the particular customers we are trying to reach?

One limitation to using quality as a sales appeal is that consumers may be unable to detect the difference and may be skeptical about the claims made. So, to clinch the appeal, some companies *guarantee* their products. For instance, an automobile manufacturer recently extended its guarantee from one year to three years (and on some parts to five years). The move attracted so much attention that competitors were forced to follow. In the meantime, the first company added to its reputation for producing dependable products.

Guarantees must be carefully worded to keep liability within reasonable bounds. One arrangement, common for automobile batteries, is to adjust the allowance made on a replacement downward as the normal life expires. Actually, most customers never expect to make claims under a guarantee. The fact that a company is willing to make it is the significant appeal.

Professional ethics prevent doctors or lawyers from guaranteeing the results of their services. Nevertheless, quality is especially significant in intangible services, so a professional person's reputation for quality work becomes very important.

Emphasis on style and packaging

"Pick the right style" is merely a pious wish, not a policy. However, the degree of emphasis on style in the total selling effort may be a significant policy. A French restaurant, for instance, may go to great lengths to create a Louis XIV decor and atmosphere. A few men's shoe manufacturers stress the latest style, at the sacrifice of durability. Producers of household items—from hand tools to garbage cans—need some guidance on how much to add to design and production expense to have currently popular styles and colors.

Packaging is one means of giving a product stylish appearance, but it may play a more important role in the marketing mix. Packaging can affect the product-service itself, as in the use of aerosol cans for paint. If a product is to be sold through self-service stores, the size, sturdiness, and shelf appeal of the package are critical to success. Continued usage of a returnable glass milk bottle is primarily dependent on the use of home versus store delivery. So, while a package may add significantly to the unit cost, the right kind of package can be an integral part of providing distinctive service for a group of consumers.

Typical use of price appeal

Price has some influence on the sale of all products. However, the emphasis placed on price varies widely. Large mail-order houses stress the price appeal throughout their catalogs. For some products, such as pianos, where quality rather than price is the normal emphasis, one or two manufacturers will try to tap a segment of the market by stressing their low prices.

Of course, when a standard market price exists, as with fuel oil, price will rarely be used as a sales appeal.

Effect of a company's reputation on sales

Banks, insurance companies, and other financial institutions must guard their reputations jealously because this is a major factor in the business they secure. Some manufacturers have developed a reputation for well-designed and reliable products, and they use this reputation as one of their important sales appeals. For instance, a well-regarded brand name is so important in the sale of large kitchen appliances that an unknown company has a hard time breaking into the market. The Whirlpool Corporation, to cite a specific case, for years made appliances for Sears, Roebuck & Company but was unknown to the general public; lacking a reputation with consumers and dealers, it entered into a long-term agreement to use the highly regarded RCA label. Several years later, after the Whirlpool reputation had become established, the association with RCA was dropped.

Even the highly competitive bidding process of the federal government makes allowance for company reputation. A low bid may be rejected if the bidder lacks a demonstrated ability to perform. And for high technology contracts, as in aerospace, reputation is often the deciding factor.

Good reputations are not bought on Madison Avenue. They arise primarily from a sustained willingness to devote extra effort to assure dependability and use of the latest state of the art, to avoid exaggerated claims, and to adjust such errors as do occur in a prompt and liberal fashion. Since conducting activities in this manner is sometimes inconvenient and costly, a policy on the kind of reputation the company desires is necessary. (We might note in passing that a policy on company reputation is very difficult to state in writing; here especially the policy takes on operational meaning through a succession of specific decisions that become a traditional way of operating.) If a company has earned a distinctive reputation, then it is appropriate to publicly reinforce this posture and to incorporate it in the total marketing effort.

Concluding briefly, no company can stress all the sales appeals we have discussed. Some are incompatible (for example, low price versus high quality and service); others are inappropriate; all involve some expense. In thinking through what combination of appeals makes sense for a particular company, central management should recognize (1) the differences in attractiveness of various appeals to the groups it seeks as customers, and (2) the compatibility and perhaps synergistic effect of a particular appeal policy with the product-market emphasis selected by the company and other aspects of its master strategy.

ADVERTISING

Today we are bombarded on all sides by many types of advertising. No matter whether we walk on the streets, drive an automobile on the highways, ride a bus, watch television, read a newspaper or magazine, or open our mail, we are brought face to face with advertising. This creates a difficult situation for management, for it must determine what advertising on its part will justify its cost amid the bewildering array of advertisements by other companies. Major questions of policy with reference to advertising are (1) the purposes for which it is to be used and (2) the media employed to accomplish these purposes.

Analysis shows that advertising is employed for numerous purposes. It also shows that many companies have not given adequate thought to the question of exactly what they are trying to accomplish with their advertising. Let us, then, take a closer look at the major options.

Bringing customers to the place where goods are sold

Retail stores frequently use advertising for this purpose. In such cases the display of merchandise and the efforts of salespeople are depended upon to close the transaction. We are all familiar with advertisements of special drugstore sales that feature twenty-five or fifty different items. The store usually hopes to sell substantial quantities of the merchandise advertised; but more important, it hopes to get customers into the store so that they will buy other types of merchandise and will develop a habit of coming to that establishment for their subsequent requirements.

Stores desiring to use a prestige appeal may have the author of a popular book give a lecture or may secure designers of furniture, dinnerware, or clothing to talk about these particular products. A number of stores provide space for local art exhibits or a showing of crown jewels; a pair of unusual and very expensive fur pelts or the elaborate doll houses of a well-known TV actress may be featured for the purpose of attracting customers to the store.

The point is well illustrated by a story told of two keen partners operating a store located in a very low-income neighborhood. Upon observing that a large number of customers were patronizing their nearby competitors, they set up a table filled with small articles, such as pickle forks, salt shakers, and cigarette holders. This table was placed near the front door where it would be passed by everyone entering or going out of the store. The sales of the articles proved to be very unprofitable, however, since they could easily be slipped into a pocket and the nearby door allowed easy escape for would-be purchasers. According to the story, however, there was a substantial increase in customer traffic. When asked to explain the situation, one of the partners said, "We call that our steal table. We place $10 worth of merchandise on the table each morning and know that most of it will have disappeared by evening. But when people come in to steal from this table, they have to act like customers and look at other merchandise, and sometimes they buy. They like to come to the store because they can go home with an extra 10-cent article that probably cost us 3 cents. All for $10 a day—it's cheap advertising."

Persuading the customer to ask for a specific product

This function of advertising is the likely aim of a manufacturer who wishes to create consumer demand, or at least consumer acceptance, for its brand of products. For example, a number of children's television programs are sponsored by manufacturers of food products. The program may consist of adventures in space, a detective serial, or anything that arouses the intense interest of a child. Somewhere in the program the youngsters are instructed to insist that their mothers buy the product of the sponsoring manufacturer.

This kind of advertising has proved very effective under certain conditions. In fact, almost the entire advertising programs of the large cereal companies are directed towards ultimate consumers for the purpose of getting them to ask for that specific product. Although the goods are usually sold through a jobber, who in turn sells them to a retailer and thence to the consumer, it is the policy of these companies to advertise only to the consumer and thereby to create such an active consumer demand that the retailer and the jobber will be glad to carry the products and benefit from the quick turnover resulting from the strong demand.

Any of a number of advertising techniques are used to induce the customer to purchase specific products. Some have a rational basis while others are largely psychological or emotional. Thus, when you buy aspirin, you are to insist on a given brand because it is pure, it dissolves, and it acts more quickly. At other times reliance is placed primarily upon repetition of the brand name so that the consumer will automatically select that particular product. The Coca Cola Company follows this technique extensively. Whatever the technique, the purpose is to get the consumer to ask for, or at least willingly accept, a particular brand of product.

Assisting the sales representative in making sales when calling on customers

Manufacturers use advertising extensively for this purpose. The objective is to familiarize the customer with the products and to create a favorable attitude toward the company before the sales representative approaches the customer. For example, concerns producing basic metals frequently advertise in trade papers that are read by their customers. The advertisement itself will not induce the potential customer to take any action, but it is hoped that the sales representative will receive a more cordial welcome as a result.

A firm manufacturing a line of luggage had for several years advertised extensively in national magazines. This advertising was discontinued when a special study convinced the management that style, design, quality, and price were so much more important to the ultimate consumer than a particular brand name that directing its advertising toward the ultimate consumer was not economical. Nevertheless this company does a limited amount of national advertising because retailers are more inclined to stock a product that is nationally advertised. Thus the primary purpose of the national advertising campaign of this company is to assist sales representatives in their negotiations with retailers.

Other companies provide the retailer with attractive window displays and store decorations that serve the dual purpose of creating consumer interest and providing the sales representative with a favorable reception by the retailer.

Producing direct sales

In some circumstances advertising is used for the purpose of persuading the customer to submit an order as a direct result. The catalogs of mail-order houses, for instance, present merchandise in such a way that the consumer can write out or telephone an order without going to a shopping center and without further promotional effort on the part of the vendor. Similarly, motels expect their outdoor advertising along highways leading toward a specific building to attract guests.

One company has been successful in selling men's shirts as a result of direct-mail advertising to the consumer. This company stresses a price appeal that, it claims, is justified by its distribution "direct from the factory to you." How-to-do-it and reference books that appeal to a particular type of reader are often sold by direct mail or magazine advertising.

Building institutional goodwill

Practically all advertising is expected to build institutional goodwill to some degree, but in some cases this is the primary objective. The advertising by telephone companies is largely for this purpose.

One of the leading personal finance companies has made extensive research on the problems of consumer buying and distributes a large number of pamphlets guiding housewives in the selection of merchandise. Intelligent expenditure of a limited income is, of course, related to the collection of small loans made to individuals for personal use. Nevertheless, the primary purpose of the distribution of these pamphlets is the development of goodwill toward the company.

Enough illustrations have been given to indicate that advertising may be undertaken for widely different purposes. Central management normally does not become involved in detailed aspects of advertising, but it can and should exercise a significant influence by setting policy regarding the purposes of the expenditure.

Choice of advertising media

After a company has decided on the purposes of its advertising, the media must be determined. The principal media include:

1. Magazines.
2. Newspapers.
3. Trade papers.

4. Television and radio.
5. Billboards.
6. Direct mail.

This list is not intended to be complete. Other types of sales promotion that might be included under the general heading of advertising are displays, dealer helps, and sampling.

Rarely does a single company use all of these media. It must select those that will accomplish its objectives most economically. For example, one large hosiery company that used advertising primarily to influence retailers formerly spent approximately $800,000 annually advertising in magazines having a national circulation. A survey among retailers showed that, while dealers liked nationally advertised products, they were influenced to a greater degree by dealer helps, such as counter displays and leaflets, and by cooperative advertising in local newspapers in which the name of the local dealer was mentioned along with the company's products. The expenditure of the company on magazine advertising is now less than $50,000 a year.

An airline company faced a serious problem in the selection of media to build familiarity and goodwill among a large number of people. Advertising that would produce traffic on its planes immediately was also wanted. For this latter purpose expenditures are confined primarily to direct-mail letters, TV commercials, and announcements to business executives and other people believed to be potential passengers in the near future. Considerable effort is directed toward passengers on its planes because these passengers as a general rule do not travel by air as much as they might, and the fact that they do use planes occasionally indicates they are interested in this method of transportation. The institutional program consists largely of magazine advertisements and general newspaper publicity.

We see in both of these cases the need to match media and purpose carefully. Too often the virtues of a particular medium are advanced without reference to the mission of the advertising.

The chart at the right shows the relative importance of the major types of media for all U.S. advertising. Total annual expenditures for advertising recently passed $25 billion.

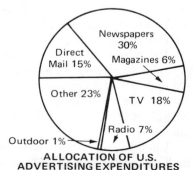

**ALLOCATION OF U.S.
ADVERTISING EXPENDITURES
AMONG TYPES OF MEDIA**

Other advertising problems

Problems of advertising are by no means limited to a determination of the major purposes and selection of media. In addition, decisions must be made as to the general type of advertising to be used. Some companies feature testimonials; others employ cartoons to a large extent. Some use flashy advertisements and large print; others make their advertising more dignified. The use of premiums and of contests can open up many additional possibilities for the imaginative copywriter. Then there are numerous questions regarding such things as layouts. Primarily these are questions of advertising techniques rather than general sales promotion policy.

PERSONAL SOLICITATION

Although sales representatives must be used to some degree in nearly all types of selling, the extent and the purpose of personal solicitation vary greatly.

Differences in the use of sales representatives

The nature of the product to be sold, the type of customer to be solicited, the channels of distribution to be used, and the types of sales appeals to be employed all affect a company's policy regarding personal solicitation. An accounting firm, for example, operates on a professional basis and consequently is prevented from using advertising beyond a few dignified announcements. Such a firm secures its business primarily through personal solicitation. As a general rule, specialized representatives are not employed. The partners and the supervisors are expected to seek new business among their acquaintances, but in so doing they must maintain the professional dignity of the firm.

The selling activities of a clerk in a variety store consist of little more than making change and wrapping packages; therefore, the amount of constructive selling such a clerk can perform is very limited. In contrast, good insurance salespeople are usually well-versed in problems of personal finance in addition to knowing facts regarding insurance premiums, cash reserves, cash surrender values, mortality rates, and contingent beneficiaries. They must also have considerable skill in approaching people and developing their interest in insurance to a point where a policy is purchased.

Some companies use what are known as missionary sales representatives. Most of the leading cracker manufacturers, for instance, distribute their products through grocery wholesalers. Experience has shown that the sales staff of these jobbers handle such a wide variety of products that they do not effectively promote the sales of a particular brand of cracker. As a result, cracker manufacturers employ sales representatives to travel among retailers, sometimes with the jobber sales representatives, to advise the retailer regarding its problems connected with selling crackers and to secure its cooperation in promoting the company's products to the retail consumers. The jobber fills orders, keeps the accounts with the retailer, and makes collections; it also contacts the retailer at more frequent intervals than is possible for the specialty sales representative. The missionary sales representative, however, is an essential part of the sales promotion program of the manufacturer.

Sales personnel, organization, and techniques

From these examples it is evident that every company should adopt definite and clear-cut policy regarding its use of sales personnel. It is essential that the company not only must decide the extent to which sales representatives are to be used but also must clearly define the purpose of their activity. Unless such a program is adopted, a considerable amount of misdirected sales effort and expense will result. The administration of a sales force involves, of course, many problems in addition to the establishment of general policy. There will be personnel policy relating to selection, training, and compensation of these salespeople. A sales organization must be provided, and detailed techniques must be worked out for specific activities to be performed. These problems are discussed in later chapters of this book.

MARKETING MIX

Finding an effective balance among the alternative measures a company can take to build sales volume involves analysis, imagination, and judgment. Too often the task is done a piece at a time without relating the pieces to a grand design.

An approach to sales promotion

At a minimum, the various facets of sales promotion should be tied to a common purpose. One analytical method that helps put various promotional devices in perspective is to answer these four questions:

1. *Who consumes the product to be sold or alters it so that its identity is lost?* The answers to this question should be found by a study of the customer policies of a company.
2. *Who makes the final decision as to the products that the ultimate consumer buys?* A study of this question will often lead to interesting results; for some products it is the housewife; for other products it is the breadwinner or the head of the family; and for still other products the ultimate consumer actually has little influence in the choice of the product. For instance, in purchasing fresh meats, the housewife usually is not interested in the packing company from which the retailer secures the products. It is the meat purchasing agent of the retailer who determines whether the beef comes from Packing Company A or from Packing Company B. In the same way the student buys the textbook specified by the instructor, and consequently sales promotion efforts of a textbook publishing company are directed toward the teacher rather than the student.

   On the other hand, the ultimate consumer usually makes the decision in the selection of the brand of cosmetics bought. The purchaser of producer goods is often influenced by several individuals. For example, the engineering department, the production department, and the purchasing department may all exercise an influence in selecting the company from which steel or coal is bought.

The answer to this question is often the key to a proper sales promotion policy. It certainly was for a company manufacturing piston rings for automobiles, since the entire advertising program depended upon whether the car owner or the garage manager actually selected the brand of piston rings that was to be used in the repair job.

3. *What factors influence those who make final decisions?* Note that this question focuses attention upon the factors that influence the person making the decision. The more common factors have been discussed in detail under sales appeals, and added illustrations are not necessary at this point. For example, a small difference in the price of piston rings is of little importance to the ultimate consumer, nor is he concerned with the delivery service of the manufacturer since he depends upon the local garage owner to carry a supply of such parts. If, however, the garage owner makes the decision regarding the rings to be used, then some of these things become of vital importance.

4. *How is it possible to influence these factors by means of sales promotion?* To what extent is it possible by national advertising, by sampling, or by personal solicitation to influence the thinking of those who make the final decision regarding the purchase of the product? There are some factors, such as the price or delivery service, that no form of sales promotion can change. On the other hand, an explanation by a salesperson may be effective in pointing out the distinctiveness of quality and design of a particular product, and an advertising program may greatly affect the reputation of the company.

The approach to sales promotion problems indicated by a discussion of the foregoing questions does not provide a ready answer, but it will often lead to very significant conclusions. As the advertising manager of a company securing annual sales of approximately $100 million said, "I have asked a large number of advertising people those four simple little questions and frequently found a lack of adequate understanding of the problems they were pretending to solve. The questions are keen because they go right to the heart of the problem."

Relating marketing to other policy and strategy

The effectiveness of sales promotion is improved by synergy. We have already noted how, say, technical bulletins and engineer-trained salespeople or well-styled products and magazine advertising can reinforce each other. Likewise, sales promotion and other policy should be synergistic. IBM's repair service, leasing machines, capital financing, and high wage policy, for instance, each gives added impact to the other.

The final marketing mix selected need not be complicated if a relatively simple combination fits the basic mission of the company. Here are three examples:

1. Handy & Harman, a leading processor of silver, makes bimetals, brazing compounds, and a variety of other fabricated silver products for industrial uses. To reach the industrial users, stress is laid on (a) closely controlled quality, (b) engineering advice to customers by sales representatives backed up by technical bulletins, (c) sales representatives who understand the problems of their respective industries, and (d) company reputation built up over a hundred years. A relatively high amount of money is spent on the first two appeals. In contrast, advertising is very low (occasional ads in trade journals and Christmas

greetings), price is simply kept "in line" with competition, and no thought is given to style.

2. A prominent correspondence school offers courses in computers, programming, mathematics, and a wide variety of semitechnical subjects. It concentrates heavily on advertising in trade and do-it-yourself magazines and by direct mail. A low price is featured, that is, low in relation to potential earnings resulting from a course. Also, considerable effort goes into "product design" so that courses are up-to-date and easily grasped by the students. The school has no sales representatives, quality of performance is not stressed, and reputation of the institution is not a major appeal.

3. The Paper Wrapper Company prints and finishes wrappers for bread, candy, and other food products. It obtains business primarily on the basis of low price, willingness to accept short runs, and personal friendships of sales representatives. It does no advertising, provides no technical advice, and gives no special emphasis to style, reputation, or quality.

Each of these companies has a marketing mix carefully designed to fit its master strategy. They differ sharply, but this is a reflection of very different jobs to be done. In each example the marketing approach builds on company strengths and avoids efforts that would create internal strain with other activities of the company.

SUMMARY

In moving a product from the plant to consumers, a variety of activities are undertaken—and each of these involves an expense. The marketing mix policy of a company guides the selection of these activities and the allocation of marketing funds. The aim, of course, is to create a final package of satisfactions that are attractive to the specific groups of customers identified by customer policy.

Services cannot be stored, and so they move directly from their creator to the user. Nevertheless, an array of attributes also surrounds each service. Here, too, there is a marketing mix, and the customer is attracted by the total package of attributes provided.

Components of a marketing mix policy include: (1) the sales appeals that the company will stress, such as customer service, unusual quality, style and packaging, low price, and company reputation; (2) the nature and the use of advertising; and (3) the functions to be performed by sales representatives. Selection of an optimum combination is crucial. It calls for empathy with various target customer groups balanced against realistic understanding of incremental expense.

Policy regarding marketing mix should be compatible—hopefully also synergistic—with production, purchasing, personnel, and financial policies. For instance, stress on quality affects production, delivery service is related to purchasing, leasing increases capital requirements, and so forth. So, as we examine these other types of policy in the following chapters, we will often need to think back to the package of consumer satisfactions that has been adopted for our marketing mix.

QUESTIONS FOR CLASS DISCUSSION

1. Two of your friends like outdoor work and have decided to set up a landscape gardening business. In the beginning they hope to get regular customers for whom they will mow the lawn weekly, trim shrubbery, fertilize, etc. Their location will be in an upper-middle class suburban area north of Cincinnati, hopefully focused in a five-mile radius to reduce travel time. Once established, they expect to add contract planting and estate work. They have enough capital for necessary equipment. "You've studied business," they say. "How should we market our services? Will advertising pay?" What marketing mix do you recommend?

2. Explain how a change in strategy of a company making automobile air conditioners from (a) sales only to automobile manufacturers to (b) sales also to car owners for installation after the automobile has been driven affects the market mix that is appropriate.

3. (a) If each package of cigarettes had to contain a list of the amount of nicotine, tar, and other potentially harmful ingredients in the contents—based on government tests—do you think the sales volume of cigarettes would drop? (b) Should all claims made in TV advertising be considered "guarantees" with the sponsor being liable if the product failed to live up to the guarantee? What effect would such a law have on sales volume and on advertising? (c) Should adoption of the metric system of weights and measures be opposed because consumers might be misled by it? (d) What other new laws should be passed to protect the consumer?

4. (a) What justification can you see for the business ethics of the legal and medical professions forbidding advertising and personal solicitation as practiced by a commercial enterprise such as a washing machine company? (b) How can doctors or lawyers promote their businesses? (c) Do you think it might be desirable to require all businesses to restrict their sales promotion to such means?

5. A method of approach to sales promotion problems has been outlined on pages 134 and 135. Apply this outline to the development of a sales promotion program for (a) a breakfast cereal, (b) tents for camping, (c) sightseeing tours in San Francisco, and (d) a World Trade Center (office building) in New York City.

6. "In the typical product life cycle (see page 42) a manufacturer should stress market position during the growth phase and then stress total profits—volume X margin—during the maturity phase." Assuming that a producer of electronic pocket calculators accepts this advice, what changes—if any—should it make in its marketing mix when it decides that its product has moved from growth to maturity?

7. Compare the marketing mix of the correspondence school described briefly on page 136 with the marketing mix of (a) a summer camp for boys aged 12 to 15 years and (b) the college you are attending.

8. In the pharmaceutical industry products are divided into proprietary drugs (products with brand names often widely advertised to consumers who buy from

the drugstore the items that they think will help them) and "ethical" drugs (products sold by drugstores only on prescription from a doctor). Since the purchaser of ethical drugs does not decide which product to buy, special problems of marketing mix arise. Pharmaceutical manufacturers spend large sums sending representatives, called detail persons, to doctors to explain the merits of their products and to encourage the doctors to prescribe such products by the company trade name. (It is strictly unethical for a doctor to accept any financial inducement from a manufacturer or a drugstore.) The cost of detail persons is subject to much debate. Manufacturers of ethical drugs contend that such persons perform a vital educational function; critics recommend use of generic (not company) names and reliance on professional journals to keep doctors abreast of new discoveries. In addition to detail persons, ethical drug producers can promote their products by publishing research reports and by direct-mail advertising to doctors with stress on quality, pricing, service to drug wholesalers and retailers, etc. (a) Which sales appeals and forms of sales promotion do you believe will be most effective and profitable for a manufacturer? (b) Is the marketing mix you recommend in answer to (a) in the best interest of the consumer? If not, what can be done about it?

CASE 7 / *Early Learning Associates*

Early Learning Associates is a relatively large supplier of equipment and materials to kindergartens, nursery schools, day-care centers, and other preschool educational programs. Its product line embraces most of the things used within the classroom, including: (a) environment for learning—tables, chairs, mats, lockers, storage units, etc.; (b) active play—vehicles, sand and water, woodworking, slides, etc.; (c) dramatic play—dolls, utensils, hand puppets, etc.; (d) block-building—large, small, etc.; (e) creative art—easels, paint, scissors, paste, etc.; (f) sound and rhythm; (g) puzzles and games; (h) perception-measurement, eye-hand coordination, etc.; (i) sciences—biology, chemistry, math, etc.; and (j) reading readiness.

"Our emphasis is on education, not merely entertainment," says Ms. Mary Gleason, the president. "The founder of Early Learning had the vision of being more than a toy supplier, and in twenty-five years he built up a million dollar business. Unfortunately, he ran a one-man show, and when I came over from juvenile book publishing there was no other professional backup here. Catalogs were mailed at irregular intervals to 12,000 institutions, and that was about it.

"Three years ago the company was acquired by a large conglomerate that believes education is a growth area. Mr. Early retired, and we were given the encouragement and the capital to expand. I'm a strong advocate of preprimary school child development, and I am convinced that we can be of real service to thousands of teachers who feel the same way.

"We now have a strong team. Dr. Ann Brewington is a full-time educational consultant; she helps with product selection, counsels with our school representatives, and represents the company at all sorts of meetings. Then we convinced Hilda Hirsh that she could do more good with us than in a school system; her enthusiasm and drive helps her supervise our growing field force. Michael Sherman gives our catalogs a real professional tone; he knows how the products can be used and has a gift for selecting pictures that communicate to teachers. The work of these people and their associates shows up in results. Our sales last year were over four million. As volume grew, we soon discovered that our warehouse and shipping procedures were antiquated, so we brought in a new warehouse coordinator. Also we added a supply coordinator to pick up part of the buying responsibility.

"Of course, we're not alone," Ms. Gleason continued. "Childcraft and Novo on the East Coast, for example, also push education. But our location in Ann Arbor, Michigan, gives us better contact with the Midwest. The local jobbers—and there must be several hundred of them—pick up the routine supply business. Someone estimated that they sell 10,000 different items, seven times what we carry, though they don't actually stock anywhere near that number. As a matter of fact, jobbers don't attempt to give professional service. They are just order-fillers; many are small family firms, and they may do office supply as well as school supply. A few manufacturers sell their products directly to schools—Creative Playthings, for instance, and there is even a harp maker going direct—but most manufacturers rely on firms like ours and on jobbers. Outdoor equipment is different; we're not in that business.

"We work closely with our major suppliers and check their quality very carefully. We may suggest changes to fit school needs better. Then we work out annual supply arrangements. Of course, we try to get exclusive designs, but products are quickly copied so we don't insist on it. Our products are distinctive because they are carefully selected by people who understand education and because we are very particular about quality—durability, good colors, safety, designed for school use, and the like. By dealing with Early Learning, the teacher gets sophisticated professional help in creating an attractive learning situation."

Dr. Ann Brewington, the educational consultant of Early Learning Associates, in a speech to the Illinois State Conference of Social Workers predicts continuing growth in the company's market:

"Several social factors bear on the future of preschool education:

1. Kindergarten attendance will remain stable. Although the drop in national birthrates will lead to a continuing decline in the number of children of kindergarten age, urbanization and other social forces point toward an increase in the percentage (now about 75%) of such children who will attend preschool.
2. The percentage of 3- and 4-year olds in nursery schools and other programs is still small—less than 15% for the 3-year olds and below 35% for the 4-year olds.
3. The Head Start program established a precedent for federal support of preschool education for the underprivileged. Our nation is committed to external supplements to inadequate home training.
4. Mothers of children under 6 are entering the work force in increasing numbers. Children of such mothers are expected to increase from 4.2 million in 1970 to 6.6 million by 1985.
5. Educators are stressing early learning as never before.

"For these and related reasons, we expect that the proportion of 3-to-5-year olds participating in some formal preprimary educational program will increase from two fifths to one half over the next 10 years."

In an estimate for Early Learning, Dr. Brewington states: "Examination of kindergarten and nursery school budgets indicates that expenditures for the kinds of products we sell range between $12 and $15 per pupil per year. Over the next 10 years the total population of 3-to-5-year olds probably will drop from about 10,500,000 to 10,000,000, and program participation probably will rise from two fifths to one half. These estimates indicate an increase in market potential from $50,000,000-$63,000,000 to $60,000,000-$75,000,000, with no allowance for inflation. If we assume inflation at 5% per year, the 10-year projection becomes approximately $100,000,000-$125,000,000.''

Ms. Hilda Hirsh, the school service director, explains: "Most school suppliers rely solely on their catalog to explain what they have to offer. Early Learning is one of the few companies that sends people into the field to counsel teachers and supervisors. We now have 15 representatives, all experienced educators. Their service to teachers is helping to build a distinctive reputation for Early Learning.

"Each representative has a territory with about 200 key schools—schools with at least 150 pupils. The representative is expected to know personally the main people in each school and to help them in any way she can. In addition, if we receive a request for help from smaller schools in a territory, the representative follows up with a visit or at least a phone call. You'd be surprised how this sort of personal attention helps. Naturally the representatives are present at conferences and meetings attended by teachers from their territory, especially if we have an exhibit there.

"Of course, this kind of service costs money. We are now paying a base salary of $16,000—somewhat more than most representatives earned at their previous school job. And then they receive 6% on all Early Learning sales to their key schools, plus 6% on sales to schools requesting help during the 6 months after the request was serviced. We expect these commissions to build up as a representative becomes better known; even now commissions already average $4,000. We pay all travel expenses from the representative's home to her territory—about $6,000 per year. So we provide a stimulating and rewarding job to an energetic person.

"I believe we should keep on expanding this kind of service as fast as we can find and train good people—say, 5 to 10 per year as we have done. It clearly pays off. Even at the present level the typical representative earns commissions on $67,000 sales. The gross profit on that alone is $31,500 compared with total cost of a person in the field of $26,000. That's right now, in the short run. But those representatives are building goodwill for Early Learning that will last for years to come.

"We're still learning ourselves. Maybe after a territory is well established a representative can cover more than 200 key schools—but when you consider the number of school days in a year and the need to see teachers when they are not busy in the classroom, I have my doubts. One point is clear—we must have inventory to ship when an order is received. It's terrible when a representative has generated enthusiasm for a type of program and then has to return an order with, 'Sorry, out of stock. Will ship in two months.' The next time our representative shows up, she gets a chilly reception."

Viewing the national market, Michael Sherman, the communications director, says: "There are about 200,000 teachers working with the kindergarten and nursery school group. Some teachers in nursery schools are only baby-sitters, but most recognize that the 3-to-5-year old is learning fast and developing lifelong attitudes and skills.

"Communicating with those teachers is a challenge. Nursery schools are held in churches, homes, community buildings, and empty storefronts. They come and go much more than kindergartens, which typically are attached to a public school system. Nursery school programs also vary more than kindergarten programs. Some stress social development, others ooze child psychology and psychiatric adjustment, while many try to speed up first-grade reading and arithmetic—just like the fourth grade now teaches calculus. Usually a teacher has no more than 15 to 20 children, and she either determines or strongly influences what happens in her classes—and what supplies she uses. There may be a director if the school has two or three classes, and the director sets the tone, largely by selecting teachers who are sympathetic with her views on education. Often the parents get into the act.

"Now, to reach that highly dispersed market we use catalogs. Over half the products are pictured, preferably in use by a happy child. The teacher should grasp quickly how the product would be helpful to her. Our catalog has over 500 such messages to get across. (Different sizes or colors add up to 1,400 items sold.)

"Each year we have sent out more catalogs to teachers, with a 120,000 nationwide mailing last year. Also last year we experimented with a smaller catalog mailed to 10,000 consumers. Our sales results show that the catalog to teachers pays off. The current costs of preparing and mailing a catalog break down like this:

Catalog Costs

	To Teachers	To Consumers	
	Large catalog* (148 black-white pages, 4-color cover, 4 photos per page)	Large catalog* (148 black-white pages, 4-color cover, 4 photos per page)	Small catalog (48 black-white pages, 4-color cover, 3 photos per page)
	120,000 copies	10,000 copies	10,000 copies
Preparatory costs (copy, photography, layout, typography, mechanical preparation)	$ 46,000	$46,000	$16,000
Reproduction costs (plates, makeready, printing, binding)	110,000	23,000	8,000
Mailing costs (envelopes, addressing, stuffing, postage)	47,000	4,000	3,000
TOTAL	$203,000	$73,000	$27,000

* Preparatory and reproduction costs could be reduced $20,000 and $5,000, respectively, if the company chooses to put out an ordinary catalog. A large catalog for consumers was never prepared; the estimated cost figures given above are shown for comparative purposes only.

"Since the marginal cost of an additional catalog is low, we might as well send to all the good addressees we can get. Of course, we do pay something for use of mailing lists.

"We went west of the Rockies for the first time last year, and returns were low. But that was the first those people ever heard of Early Learning. Also, we have a lot of competition in New England and the Atlantic States, and the f.o.b. warehouse pricing puts us at a disadvantage there.[1] Nevertheless, the gross margin on shipments to the East is double the related catalog costs.

---

[1] Early Learning's selling terms are like those of its competitors: no discounts to anyone; customer pays shipping charges; 30 days credit to established customers; $15 minimum order.

"Inflation creates pricing problems. An annual catalog commits us to fixed prices for a year. Since we don't want our prices to be clearly out of line with competitors, we hesitate to anticipate future increases in costs to us. So we have been absorbing suppliers' price hikes made during the year. We tried sending out price change notices, but nobody paid any attention to them and we just had a lot of confusing correspondence. One very real possibility is to issue semiannual catalogs.

"Actually, small differences in price are not critical to making a sale. The typical teacher has an annual budget of, say, $300 for everything, and she can't save enough by shopping around to enable her to vary her program. As I see it, so long as she has confidence in the supplier and feels that its prices are fair, other selection factors predominate—the appeal of the product, the way it is presented, confidence in durability and quality, good experience with delivery, and the like. But if we increase prices after a catalog is issued, and then either hold up shipment while corresponding about the higher price—or ship goods that create budget problems for the customer—we're in trouble. From the teacher's viewpoint, we have failed to give good service."

Comparative balance sheets and income statements for the last year under the former management, the transition year, and the two years under present management are on the following page. In commenting on these, David Rubin, the chief accountant, says: "Customers in this industry are inherently slow pay. Our accounts receivable ratio to sales is in line with those of our competitors. But the inventory is running wild. In the name of 'service' our stock turnover has fallen below 3. As a consequence, Early Learning is just soaking up capital. The treasurer at the holding company—really my boss—is about to blow the whistle, and some heads will roll. Here's a rough breakdown I prepared for him on increase in expenses during the last 3 years."

3-Year Increase in Expenses Under New Management

Sales representatives	$ 390,000
More catalogs	250,000
Order handling (10% on increased volume)	290,000
Salaries and related office expenses of 5 new executives	200,000
Increased promotion at conventions and meetings	100,000
Other	85,000
Total increase under new management	$1,315,000

Required: What should Early Learning Associates do to improve sales and profits?

Balance Sheets
as of December 31st
(in 1,000's)

	Last Year	Preceding Year	2nd Preceding Year	3rd Preceding Year
Current Assets:				
Cash	$ 147	$ 49	$ 48	$ 17
Accounts receivable (net) .	892	711	326	254
Inventories	981	557	217	148
Prepaid expenses	85	119	23	—
Total current assets	2,105	1,436	614	419
Fixed Assets:				
Office and warehouse				
equipment (net)	273	287	141	16
Other	64	41	19	19
Total assets	$2,442	$1,764	$ 774	$454
Liabilities:				
Accounts payable	$ 223	$ 146	$ 91	$ 73
Bank loans	500	500	—	100
Accrued items	106	72	43	114
Total current liabilities ...	829	718	134	287
Term loan from affiliate	600	100	250	—
Total liabilities	1,429	818	384	287
Equity:				
Common stock	200	200	100	20
Capital surplus	800	800	400	—
Retained earnings or (loss) .	13	(54)	(110)	147
Total equity	1,013	946	390	167
Total liabilities				
and equity	$2,442	$1,764	$ 774	$454

Income Statement
(dollar figures in 1,000's)

	Last Year Amount	%	Preceding Year Amount	%	2nd Preceding Year Amount	%	3rd Preceding Year Amount	%
Net sales	$4,112	100	$2,871	100	$1,423	100	$1,260	100
Cost of goods sold .	2,181	53	1,548	54	867	61	741	59
Gross profit	1,931	47	1,323	46	556	39	519	41
Selling and admin-								
istrative expenses	1,765	43	1,213	42	651	46	450	36
Interest charges	99	2	54	2	15	1	6	—*
Profit or (loss)								
before income tax	67	2	56	2	(110)	8	63	5

* Less than 0.5%.

INTEGRATING CASES / Strategy and Marketing

THE ARCHITECTURAL GROUP, INC.[1]

Four years of nearly steady growth in its number of projects has brought enough financial success so that the two founders of The Architectural Group, Inc. believe that their original investments are now safe. Their earnings are also high enough so that their standard of living equals that which they would have enjoyed had they remained as employees of other firms.

The Architectural Group has succeeded mainly in marketing its services for the design and building of churches, small office buildings, retail stores, apartments, and expensive, individually-designed houses. It now does work in towns up to 100 miles distant from its home city (Albuquerque). The Group participates in about 25% of the available construction projects in this particular part of the architectural market. The owners find it difficult to envision capturing a larger share of these kinds of jobs since they compete with seventy other architects or architectural firms in the city.

During the past three years, three more architects have invested in the company and become active principals.

Along with the growth have come questions about what directions to follow in the future and, indeed, whether to attempt to expand at all.

The beginnings

Rather than starting small in a backroom or a basement (the usual practice), John Givens and William Walton, the founders, rented substantial office space in one of the city's secondary office centers that had a large volume of traffic pass its doors.

Their original idea—the basic service offered—was, as they called it, "the team concept." Externally, their efforts would closely involve the client and the contractor in design and construction decisions. Internally, they would support one another.

They tried to time their entry into the market to catch the beginning of a recovery by business in general from a recession and to be on the upswing of a construction cycle. This meant a year's wait after their decision to found the firm.

Two of the rules-of-thumb for new architectural firms are: (1) bring some clients with you when you begin; (2) work weekends and evenings at the new business—keep your old job as long as you can. The Architectural Group broke both of these rules. Givens and Walton believed it morally wrong to attempt to bring old clients with them. They assumed zero revenues for their new firm for six months. Each provided his own funds for living and provided the firm's working capital in exchange for common stock.

---

[1] See the Appendix to this case for information about the work of architects, pricing of their services, and professional certification.

Early on, potential clients came in with 1, 2, or 3% commission jobs. It was hard to turn these jobs down when the firm had no revenue. But an early decision had been to turn down jobs at below standard rates. Eventually one client walked in off the street with a house he wanted designed—at the full rate. A few others followed.

Little revenue and a relatively large organization expense forced the founders to search for work. Fortunately, in a way, an urban development project was partly—but incompletely—planned. Decisions already made by city planners and elected officials had frightened off established firms. Concepts firmly fixed included adaptation to territorial and mission styles and a made-from-adobe look for the finished buildings. Plazas, shops, and individualized offices were to be on a small and intimate scale analogous to those of the Chocolate Factory in San Francisco or the shopping terraces and courts of Sydney, Australia, and Singapore.

When the Group became interested in the project and began to sell their efforts, they found that, although they were technically well prepared for designing and producing buildings, they were not well prepared for managing an architectural firm in the sense of making client contacts and actually carrying out effective relationships with the client and the contractors.

The Architectural Group's idea for Urban Center (as the project was called) was finally sold basically on its character as a solution to the three design criteria mentioned above and as an attractive way to refocus the interest of the city's people on the Urban Center area. No overriding systems approach could be used because decisions already made had led to the need for a complex set of services. But there was a great deal of architectural design work needed to carry out the character sketches for the 335,000 square feet of the Center.

The product

John Givens said: "Communication with the client is a major part of our concept of the provision of architectural service. A frequent problem is keeping clients in a position so that they know what is occurring. We build models to do this and provide blueprints and perspective drawings. With each client it is a continuous educational process. A second problem is to bring clients into the decision-making for the development stage.

"We work hard to educate owners to the fact that they must tell the architect—rather than the contractor—about changes. On small jobs this is a major difficulty.

"The architect's true role when construction begins is to represent both the contractor *and* the client. Clients do not understand this even though it is spelled out in the contract.

"Every client turns out to be different. Our standard approach works, but we might do more if we could develop a way to understand how to handle the differences and then carry out the understanding.

"Everyone in the firm is attempting to reach one goal—'trying to do better architecture.' On one level this means winding up with a happy client. If we have not done this, then we have done no good. But a client may want to use a bad color. This leads to the second level, which is to satisfy our own ideas about what is good."

Organization

Mr. Givens and Mr. Walton found almost immediately that they could not do the necessary promotional work or even send out letters without a secretary. One was hired and the staff grew as the workload increased. The principle was to keep a stable staff and to feed it with work. A second principle was to select people to fill voids in the services and do the selection so that those hired would work together. An interiors group (not just one specialist) was opened within the firm—as was a planning and scheduling group.

For work not related to architectural skills, the firm used consultants. In establishing the firm, the partners attempted to find the best legal organization in the city. The benefits from using high-priced talent were expected to outweigh the costs. Then the founders met with the lawyers at least once per week so that they could understand just what the legal firm was doing or attempting to do for them.

The founders and the principals in the firm each take a direct part in the work of the firm. For example, Mr. Armando is responsible for all promotional activities, but he also spends half of his time working as an architect on specific projects. As new projects come in, they are assigned to be the responsibility of one officer or another. A fixed principle of the practice of architecture appears to be that ''clients want to talk to principals.''

The five officers all like to think that they will always be doing professional work as architects and project managers as well as having their functional responsibilities for promotion, production, design, accounting, and office management. But, if growth continues, how will additional officers and owners fit into this idea of executive tasks?

General policy decisions are now made in round-table discussions. Since the five officers were trained the same way and have the same goals and ideas, there are few matters on which they disagree. Often matters need not come to a vote but are settled by consensus or by relying on the particular expertise of one officer. Mr. Wilks commented: ''I take the attitude that I am responsible to my partners for the work I do for the firm.''

Promotion

Mr. Drollinger said: ''When we first started the firm, we were continually being asked what experience we had. This still continues in some markets such as schools. Our experience with schools has been zero to this day.''

Developing contacts with clients was, naturally, a major early concern. The plan was for everyone to devote a major share of his attention to promotion through these activities: (a) legwork—visiting every contractor and mortgage banker within the city; (b) ears open—using all social occasions to briefly chat about their new group and to listen for any response; (c) media—press releases, visits with broadcasters of local news and with feature writers; (d) public agencies—contact with all city, county, state, and federal agencies that had anything to do with housing in the city; and (e) hope—that a client would walk into the office on his own.

The point of most of the contacts was to find out who was the decision-maker or the decision-making committee in an organization with whom they might potentially work, to submit the Group's name or sketches and models, and to maintain an up-to-date list of the decision-makers and the status of any projects with which the potential client organizations might be concerned.

At one point, the Group made a special study of libraries since none of them had had experience in designing and building a library. They learned how to handle the problem of getting ready to construct a library. To date, no library job has been obtained. One principal said, ''We must have a constant attitude of promoting ourselves. This is uncomfortable at first, but we have to get accustomed to it.''

Presentations to potential clients include not only sketches, drawings, and models, but also specific attempts to explain how the architects hope to work with the client and what architectural, space design, and space-use goals they have with and for the client. They attempt to sell the idea that the job is going to be interesting to the client and that the client has information that will be needed regularly during the project but mainly as input at the design and scheduling phases.

The team concept is used on all jobs. Some clients are surprised to be called upon continuously. A significant minority of clients object to more than a few meetings with the architect at the onset of a project.

Issues to be faced

What roles, as architects, can the members of the firm play in society today? They have consistently attempted to be public relations men for an idea—to convince people that they can function better in a good space. Thus they have been promoting architecture that is promoting an ideal. Is this useful socially?

Projected growth, if it continues, will mean adding three more principals within the next two years. Then not all will be able to work in two roles. "We now have considerable momentum," John Givens observes, "and are regarded by people who know us as a progressive, growing firm. Naturally we would like to take advantage of this image. Adding principals and staff to support them will increase our fixed costs substantially, which could be serious to all of us if construction hits a tailspin. On the other hand, with a larger volume of work we should be able to utilize our existing staff support more effectively." The five officers can, of course, agree not to attempt further expansion of projects and activities. This will leave them in comfortable positions. And they will be able to be selective to some extent about their future work.

If new officers or principals are added to the firm, they will have to make a financial investment by buying a share of the common stock. Each man thus sees his work as, in part, a contribution to the firm's return on the financial investment. But, as one of the original architects said, "Not one of us would stay if we did not like to work together."

The Architectural Group has decided, for individual homes, to change its pricing system from the customary practice of charging a percentage of the total construction costs—a higher rate for smaller projects—to a fee system. Present practice includes making presentations on speculation at the expense of the firm. The fee system for individual homes is now 2.75 times the direct hourly payroll of those who work on the project with a maximum of 10% of total costs. This maximum is 2 percentage points less than the recommendation of the American Institute of Architects, but The Architectural Group believes it to be more just.

Should the Group change to a system with fees specified for all tasks undertaken—including an hourly charge for developing presentations or space concepts? The historical method is understood and generally acceptable to clients. The fee system is not widely known but is much more flexible for the architects and is thought to be more suitable for the presentation of a wider range of ideas and architectural choices to existing and potential clients.

The present physical space is just adequate for the number of architects, draftsmen, technicians, and office workers now in the firm. Finding more space will not be difficult nor will it impose any financial strain. But a lease commitment would mean a choice for continued growth.

Since architecture, tied as it is with construction, is cyclical, the five have considered other kinds of ventures. "When you work on your own, you begin to think of all sorts of things you never thought of before. We have wondered whether it would be wise to try other cities, repeating the kind of work done here. Or should we attempt land development—which requires a considerable financial commitment, much negotiating, a long-term plan, and close supervision of contractors as well as costs?"

QUESTIONS

1. What promotional, pricing, product, and customer policies might The Architectural Group follow to be consistent with continued growth?
2. Do you see an advantage for the firm in remaining at its present size? Explain. What policies will then be useful?

Appendix

Nature of Architectural Work

An architect plans buildings (houses, apartments, schools, factories, office buildings, churches, synagogues) to serve the many purposes of the owners and the inhabitants. An architect may, on a large scale, design useful and beautiful neighborhoods, cities, and metropolitan areas. An architect is, first of all, an artist who tries to provide beauty in the shapes, forms, and spaces of the buildings as well as usefulness to those who live and work within them. But an architect also needs the skills of a businessman and an engineer to keep the costs of the buildings reasonable, to meet project deadlines, to use materials effectively, and to work within building codes.

To provide usefulness for clients (who may be private individuals, governmental officials, contractors, or business executives) the architect works with them to learn their goals—expressed and unexpressed. The architect helps in the acquisition of a site or studies one chosen by the client so that the plans may be related by comparison or contrast to the form of the land and to nearby structures. With the client, the architect prepares a detailed program that outlines the requirements to be met as to a building's size, location, and general appearance as well as the proposed budget. Following a sequence of decisions made by the architect and the client on the basis of rough sketches, room plans, section drawings, and elevation and perspective drawings, the architect prepares a basic design for the client's approval. The presentation may also indicate why and how the design meets the standards of good architecture.

The basic design is reviewed again for costs, alternative methods of construction, building code standards, and acquisition of a building permit. On large jobs the architect may call in specialists in interior design, heating and air conditioning, foundations, or landscape design at this stage of the project. Once the design is accepted by the client, the architect prepares working drawings, specifications for materials, and the document of general conditions that describes the rights and duties of the client, the architect, and the contractor in working together. During construction, the architect evaluates progress against the plans, checks on materials and equipment used, approves subcontractors, and makes large-scale drawings of decorative details to guide the workers. After a final review, the architect's responsibility to the client for administration of the contract ends. The architect then, hopefully, receives the fee.

Fees, customarily, are negotiated as a percentage of the construction cost. Typical fees are 12% for an individual, custom-designed home; 8% for a church built for $100,000; 6% for a privately-owned building costing $1,000,000; 6% maximum for any state-owned building; a negotiated percentage for buildings of the federal government with a 6% maximum for small projects; 1% for a tract development of 40 to 50 houses selling for $25,000 to $35,000 each.

Those architects who have changed their pricing to either the cost-plus or the fixed-fee basis submit bills to the clients at various stages of the project. Ordinarily the amounts billed under a fixed-fee contract are: schematic phase, 15%; development phase, 20%; construction contracts document phase, 40%; the bid-negotiating phase, 5%; contract administration, 20%.

Since new buildings are, ordinarily, rare events for the owners, architects seldom work with a particular client more than once. Even if they do so, the relationship is not continuous but sporadic, with jobs for the architects occuring at varying intervals of several years. Construction cycles add another dimension of complexity to the flow of work available for architectural firms.

In most states, architects must pass a licensing examination to open an office. Qualifications to take the examination ordinarily include five or six years of professional training beyond high school to earn a degree in an accredited architectural school and three years of practical experience in an architect's office.

ROYAL HAMBURGERS, INC.

The widow, weeping in her weeds, and the executor of the estate of the owner of Franchise Systems Company, have approached Royal Hamburgers, Inc. in an attempt to persuade the firm to repurchase the franchise license originally bought from Royal Hamburgers as well as the equipment and the leases of Franchise Systems' 8 fast-food restaurants. Royal Hamburgers, Inc., a nationwide chain of fast-food drive-in restaurants, has at present no fixed policy on the reacquisition of licenses but has dealt with such requests on an *ad hoc* basis. It has purchased some licenses and taken over the associated leases, referred other requests to applicants on a waiting list, offered managerial assistance in other cases, and done nothing in a few instances. Executives of the company believe that now is a propitious time to consider a policy and that this should be done in light of the long-run future for fast-food enterprises, the current situation, and company plans for expansion.

Fast-food restaurants are classified as a part of the "away-from-home" food and beverage industry, which last year had sales of about $27 billion, distributed as follows:

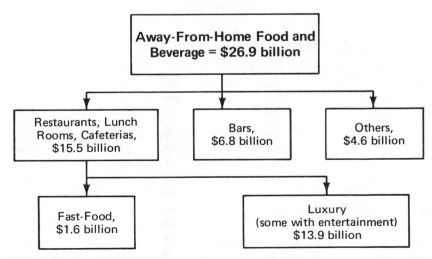

Source: U.S. Bureau of the Census.

A bright future for the industry is generally foreseen, as indicated by the following table:

Sales Results and Predictions

	Percentage Increase		*Fast-Food Dollar Volume in Constant (last years) Dollars*
	All Restaurants	*Fast-Food*	
5 Years Ago	7%	15%	—
4 Years Ago	8	15	—
3 Years Ago	8	28	—
2 Years Ago	9	30	—
Last Year	9	25	$1.6 billion
Current Year	10	25	2.0 "
Next Year	10	25	2.5 "
Succeeding Year	10	20	3.0 "
" Year	10	15	3.6 "
Five Years Hence	10	15	4.5 "
Ten Years Hence	11	9	6.5 "
Fifteen Years Hence	11	8	8.1 "

Source: Marketing research consultants to the company.

The 5-to-14 age group in the United States is predicted to increase from 39 million to 45 million in the next fifteen years, and the young adult group should grow from 58 million to 80 million over the same time span. The potential effect of these population changes is indicated in the following figures:

Population Changes

Age of Head of Household	*Average Annual Expenditure per Family on Away-From-Home Food*	*Family Income*	*Average Annual Expenditure per Family on Away-From-Home Food*
Under 25	$243	Under $ 3,000	$ 89
25–30	269	$ 3,000– 5,000	180
35–44	319	5,000– 7,500	230
45–54	301	7,500– 10,000	330
55–64	248	10,000– 15,000	486
65+	118	Over 15,000	788
Average	$253	Average	$253

Source: U.S. Bureau of the Census.

With the growth in the age groups that tend to eat out, in people's mobility, and in industry sales, the number of organizations in the field has increased rapidly. About 300 franchising organizations sell fried chicken, hamburgers, roast beef sandwiches, pizza, egg rolls, and tacos through more than 30,000 franchise units.

In many communities "franchise rows" have sprung up and more units compete for space along the same strips. The prospect of a shake-out from increased competition leads not to backing out by fast-food companies, but to scrambling to snap up the remaining good locations and thus to gain a foothold in the local market.

The explosion in fast-food companies (up 44% in two years) brings talk among industry analysts of impending market saturation. In the past year the big portion of the sales gain went to 6 companies. Many smaller operators began to lose volume. Near Cleveland, 14 franchise restaurants line a 2-mile roadstretch near a large shopping center. Profits of 8 are sharply down. Two of these say they are near bankruptcy. But McDonald's Corporation increased the number of units by 17% and Jerry's jumped its outlets 72% in just one year. Behind the scrambling is the belief that independents and weak franchise companies will be driven out of business by those with national marketing power, leaving the survivors with a market that is just beginning to be penetrated. "These young people have been trained to eat in fast-food places and they won't change when they get older," says one executive.

The readiness of large food corporations to enter the field shows the attractiveness of the fast-food industry. Companies that have acquired fast-food subsidiaries recently include Pillsbury Co. (Burger King), General Foods Corporation (Burger Chef), Ralston Purina Co. (Jack-in-the-Box), Pet Milk Co. (Stuckey's), United Fruit Co. (A & W Root Beer), and Consolidated Foods Corporation (Chicken Delight, Big Boy restaurants). Pillsbury budgets about $7 million on advertising and expects to triple this amount in five years.

Fast-food franchising expanded rapidly in the 1960's, cashing in on general prosperity, the opportunity for a franchisee to own his own business, and decreased labor costs because of automation. Tight credit limits expansion, as does the dwindling number of good locations. Labor is a constant problem since the great majority of employees are part-time high school and college students.

Difficult times for franchisers also arise from government hearings into various business practices—including the notorious accounting technique of including in earnings the full amount of an initial franchise fee even though the entire payment may not be made for many years, if at all. Court challenges have arisen to contracts that require the franchisee to buy supplies through the parent company at prices in excess of those offered by competitive suppliers.

Top Wall Street analysts generally agree, however, that some companies can achieve annual earnings growth of at least 20% to 25% over the long term. One says: "We'll have a saturation point eventually. I don't know when. But the demand will continue to grow as long as many mothers work, as long as adolescents continue to have more money to spend, and as long as we continue to have a mobile society. This will be as long as competition continues to keep prices in line and quality high."

In the restaurant end of the away-from-home eating industry, the chef is vanishing—to be replaced by frozen dishes. Precooked and frozen main dishes widen the variety on the menu, cut waste enormously, and save space and labor. With kitchen help fast disappearing and 250,000 unfilled jobs in the restaurant industry, frozen entrees are seen as an important way to ease the strain of that shortage. They work, if reheating directions are followed exactly and if the processors avoid some sauces that curdle, some spices that strengthen when frozen, and some ground meat products (such as hamburgers and some kinds of sausage) that do not freeze well.

Royal Hamburgers, Inc. has sold hamburgers, cheeseburgers, french-fried potatoes, soft drinks, milk drinks, and cherry pie through both franchised and company-owned drive-in restaurants and hamburger stands for over a decade. The president, Mr. Roy A. Royal, pioneered in developing automatic equipment, a kitchen layout, and a limited menu that proved successful in his first drive-in restaurant in Dallas, Texas. Success led to success, and now the company logo and trade mark (a hamburger with a crown) is seen on installations in 40 of the 50 states. Mr. Royal attributes this success to low prices, excellent quality for the price, and efficient, courteous, and rapid service (see Exhibit A). Selected financial information over a period of years and the current balance sheet for the company are presented in Exhibits B and C.

Exhibit A

Outline of Mr. Royal's Recent Speech
Keys to Success in the Fast-Food Industry

I. Profit formula
   (High volume × Low margin) − Low expense = High profits

II. Low labor cost in relation to sales
   (a) Degree of self-service
   (b) Nonprofessional labor

III. High productivity per employee
   (a) Equipment
   (b) Plant design

IV. Standardized menu
   (a) Limited number of items
   (b) Close portion control over size and weight of portions
   (c) Convenience foods

V. High traffic density location

VI. Establish an identity
   (a) Trade mark
   (b) Advertising

VII. All of these to keep at bay our competition from:
   (a) The home   (d) Vending machines
   (b) Motels and hotels   (e) Other fast-food
   (c) Luxury restaurants   —Chains
                                —Independents

VIII. What is going to happen?
   (a) To population, discretionary spending, where people live
   (b) The effect of this on away-from-home eating
   (c) Luxury restaurants have problems—availability and price of labor
   (d) Through the growth of chains, fast-food will grow more rapidly for five years. Then will vending machines and luxury restaurants cause a slackening in fast-food growth?

Exhibit B

Royal Hamburgers, Inc.

Selected Financial Information

(All dollar figures in 1,000's)

	Five Years Ago	Four Years Ago	Three Years Ago	Two Years Ago	Last Year	Current Year	Next Year	Succeeding Year	Five Years Hence
Total Number of Units	322	364	426	472	501	640	750	875	1,250
Company-owned Units	64	65	64	63	85	104	160	235	535
Revenue from Company-owned Units	—	—	—	$19,600	$35,300	$46,140			
Revenue from Licenses and Rents	—	—	—	$15,000	$13,000	$18,000			
Direct Cost of Company-owned Units	—	—	—	$ 3,200	$28,700	$37,000			
Direct Cost of Licensing Income	—	—	—		$ 3,830	$ 6,000			
General & Administrative Expenses and Financial Overhead Expenses	$2,447	$3,110	$4,030	$ 4,826	$ 7,300	$10,700			
Net Profit	$1,070	$1,819	$2,346	$ 3,175	$ 4,420	$ 5,300			
Direct Costs as Percent of Revenue	68%	67%	67%	61%	65%	67%			
Average Sales per Unit	$ 225	$ 248	$ 278	$ 297	$ 333	$ 391	$405	$430	$490
Average Sales per Company-owned Unit	$ 150	$ 202	$ 236	$ 312	$ 415	$ 450			
Average Direct Costs per Company-owned Unit	$ 129	$ 174	$ 203	$ 258	$ 337	$ 356			

Exhibit C

Royal Hamburgers, Inc.
Current Balance Sheet
(000's omitted)

Assets

Current Assets:

Cash and Certificates of Deposit.........................	$ 6,000	
Short-Term Investments...................................	2,000	
Notes Receivable..	800	
Accounts Receivable.....................................	1,500	
Inventories (at cost)....................................	600	
Prepaid Expenses..	500	
Construction Costs Advanced Prior to Sale.................	6,000	
Total Current Assets....................................		$17,400
Other Assets and Deferred Charges...........................		3,000
Net Property, Plant, and Equipment..........................		47,000
Intangible Assets Including Acquired Franchise Rights...........		4,900
Total Assets...		$72,300

Liabilities and Stockholders' Equity

Current Liabilities:

Accounts Payable.......................................	$ 4,000	
Accrued Liabilities.....................................	1,000	
Federal Income Taxes...................................	3,500	
Long-Term Debt Due Within One Year....................	4,500	
Total Current Liabilities................................		$13,000

Long-Term Debt:

Mortgage Notes..	$13,000	
Notes Payable to Insurance Companies.....................	16,000	
Total Long-Term Debt.................................		29,000
Security Deposits by Lessees...............................		5,000
Total Liabilities...		$47,000

Stockholders' Equity:

Common Stock (no-par value, 25 million shares authorized, 8.3 million shares issued and outstanding)..................	$ 7,000	
Retained Earnings.......................................	18,300	
Total Stockholders' Equity..............................		25,300
Total Liabilities and Stockholders' Equity....................		$72,300

Company-owned units are concentrated geographically around Dallas, Houston, San Diego, Los Angeles, San Francisco, Phoenix, and Austin, Texas, because of economies and administrative efficiencies associated with proximity (see Exhibit D). Units repurchased from licensees have often been resold since, under independent ownership and lower overhead costs, they produce a profit satisfactory to the owner.

Exhibit D
Regional Strength of Royal Hamburgers, Inc.

Region	Percent of Total Away-from-Home Meals	Percent of Royal Meals
Pacific	16%	31%
Mountain	4	8
West South Central	8	13
West North Central	7	12
East North Central	20	17
East South Central	4	4
South Atlantic	13	7
Middle Atlantic	22	5
New England	6	3
	100%	100%

All Royal units are built according to company specifications. Older units have a building of about 800 square feet with paved parking space for 20 to 30 cars. Units built within the last three years have a 1,200 to 1,500 square foot building with indoor seating for 50 persons and parking space for 50 cars on a minimum land area of ½ acre. The latest design calls for a building area of 1,800 to 2,200 square feet, seating for 55 to 100 persons, and space for 75 cars on a minimum land area of 35,000 square feet. All buildings are built and owned either by the company or by the owner of the land and are leased or subleased to the operator by the company. Equipment and fixtures are specified by the company but purchased and owned by the unit operators.

Methods of food preparation and serving are prescribed in detail and are inspected by the company. Specifications for menu items, such as meat, potatoes, buns, condiments, and beverages, as well as paper and equipment are provided to the unit operator. Fresh food and some condiments are bought from local purveyors who meet and maintain the company's quality standards and specifications.

The company inspects units to ensure that standards are closely followed by the operator and that product quality, customer service, and cleanliness of units are maintained at prescribed levels. The company continually advises and consults with unit operators, develops equipment and techniques, and formulates national, regional, and local advertising and promotional campaigns in which the unit operators are required to participate.

Each unit operator invests $100,000 to $150,000 (depending upon the size of the unit) for initial license and location fees, lease security deposit (refundable later), signs, equipment, inventory, and working capital. He is required to select, train, and employ the personnel for his own unit. Employees per unit range from 15 to 50, with an average of 33. Wages paid are at the low end of the spectrum of all wages but tend to grow at 4%

to 6% per year. Payroll and employee benefits average 21% of sales as compared to 24% for all classes of restaurants in the United States.

The offer from Franchise Systems Company covers 5 units in Rome, Utica, Syracruse, Rochester, and Albany, New York, and 3 units in the Springfield-Mt. Holyoke-Amherst region in western Massachusetts. (There are no other Royal franchised or company-owned units in these cities.) Sales and operating profits of each unit last year were as follows:

Franchise Systems Company

Location	Last Year's Sales	Last Year's Operating Profit
Rome	$ 210,000	$ 20,000
Utica	180,000	3,000
Syracuse	560,000	120,000
Rochester	280,000	25,000
Albany	250,000	5,000
Springfield #1	390,000	40,000
Springfield #2	480,000	70,000
Springfield #3	520,000	100,000
Total	$2,870,000	$383,000

Franchise Systems Company's total general, administrative, and financial costs were $203,000 and income taxes amounted to $90,000 in total.

The former owner, who died recently of a heart attack, is survived by a widow and nine children. He, together with an accountant, a food buyer, two secretaries, and four clerks, had directed the firm and administered all its affairs except for the details of operations of the individual restaurants. These were handled by the eight unit managers.

His executor and his widow have asked for either $1,800,000 for the capital stock of Franchise Systems Company or $3,800,000 (the book value) in payment for the total assets (including land and buildings) without the liabilities. (All the family funds, including insurance proceeds, are tied up in the affairs of the company.) They will take either cash (preferably) or sufficient common shares of Royal Hamburgers, Inc. to equal these amounts at a price of $15.50 per share (50 cents below the current price on the American Stock Exchange).

QUESTIONS

1. Should Royal Hamburgers, Inc. continue to stress expansion, using its present marketing policy?
2. Should Royal Hamburgers, Inc. buy out Franchise Systems Company, and if so on what terms? Should this action be regarded as setting a policy on reacquisitions?

8

RESEARCH AND DEVELOPMENT POLICY

The creation of services is just as indispensable as their distribution, which we have been examining in preceding chapters. Company strategy embraces both. In fact, it is often the ingenious marriage of producing and marketing that gives a company unique strength. And as with marketing, policy is needed to elaborate and sharpen the broad strategic choices that have been made for the production of services that are to be sold. This amplification of directions for creating services will be discussed in this chapter on research and development policy, and in the following two chapters on production policy and procurement policy.

ROLE OF RESEARCH AND DEVELOPMENT

Some firms quite wisely do virtually no research and development. Others rely on their "R&D" for continuing survival. Between these two extremes there are many variations in purposes and emphasis. Because of this array of options, policy guidance on the role of research and development is sorely needed.

Scope

This chapter deals with activities from basic research to placing a product on the market or utilizing a new process. We are primarily concerned with *innovation*—the effective application of a new idea. Innovations occur in all kinds of human activity, but here we are focusing on technological changes in products and processes.

Clearly, the business manager is concerned with more than *invention*—the conceiving of a new and useful idea. Invention is an essential part of the total process, but it is only a part. Companies may engage in activities that lead to inventions; but if they do, they must also devote a great deal of effort to converting the invention into a practical application.

Stages

When planning for R&D, a recognition of the stages involved in innovation is helpful. The normal stages of technological innovation are:

1. Basic research—the scientific investigation of a physical phenomenon without any defined use that might be made of the resulting knowledge.
2. Applied research—studies designed to identify specific potential applications of general knowledge.
3. Development—testing and elaborating a potential application into a model or a set of specifications that demonstrates the physical "doability" of a new process or product.
4. Pilot plant testing—testing the economic as well as the physical feasibility of actually using a model or specifications emerging from the development stage.
5. Manufacturing, tooling, and debugging—designing and assembling new manufacturing equipment, then testing and modifying it until full-scale operations at acceptable efficiencies are possible.
6. Marketing startup—overcoming any new technical problems of physical distribution and customer use.

The following table presents an outline of the six stages of technological innovation with respect to output, predictability of results, and types of personnel involved:

Normal Stages of Technological Innovation

Stages	*Output*	*Ability to Predict Results*	*Kinds of People Involved*
1. Basic research	Knowledge	None	Madmen and dreamers—young, professionally oriented
2. Applied research	Directed knowledge, leading to identified applications *	Little	May be prickly personalities
3. Development	Product or process model—operational feasibility		
4. Pilot plant	Cost knowledge—economic feasibility	Some	Engineers—organization oriented
5. Manufacturing, tooling, and debugging	Total operating system, specifications, and process costs	High probability	Persons with efficiency and effectiveness as values
6. Marketing startup	Product acceptance		

* Many inventions by individual tinkerers arise without knowledge from basic research; all major inventions sparking the Industrial Revolution were of this sort.

In practice, the separation of these six stages of technological innovation is fuzzy. Problems encountered at any one stage may require backtracking to a previous stage. For instance, a difficulty uncovered in a pilot plant may signal the need for further development or even applied research effort. Similarly, good management practice requires forward bridging. Thus, basic research shades into applied research, and applied research shades into development. Especially important in private R&D work is a frequent checking of market potentials and market requirements during all of the stages except basic research.

In setting policies for R&D work, it is important to recognize that research expenses are normally very much smaller than development expenses for a successful project. Statistics on this point are far from precise, but the following chart does indicate a "rule-of-thumb" distribution.

TYPICAL DISTRIBUTION OF COSTS IN SUCCESSFUL PRODUCT INNOVATIONS

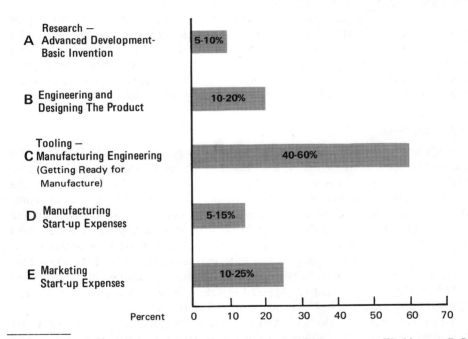

Source: *Technological Innovation: Its Environment and Management,* Washington, D.C., Department of Commerce, 1967, page 9. In terms of stages listed in first part of chapter: A covers approximately Stages 1 and 2, B covers Stage 3, C and D together cover Stages 4 and 5, and E matches Stage 6.

The reasons for high expense in later stages are not hard to find. Many manhours are required to design and test each of the subparts of a new product or process. Moreover, as the work progresses it must be done on a larger and larger scale, requiring greater inputs of materials and machinery. In some instances, such as the development of penicillin, entirely new processes for acquiring raw material in the quantity and the quality desired have to be invented. The identification and the recording of all the specifications in an experimental model is time-consuming. Clearly, any company that engages in applied research must be prepared to invest substantially larger additional amounts if it is to reap full benefit from its research efforts.

Progress by increments

A single dramatic invention such as Carlson's Xerography or Land's Polaroid camera catches our attention when we think about innovation. However, it is a mistake to assume that the success of all R&D work depends upon major discoveries. Much more common is a succession of small improvements, one built upon another, that in total add up to a major change. The development of mobile homes and self-service stores are examples of innovations that occurred in this incremental fashion.

This incremental process permits several different companies to participate in an innovation. Frequently one firm builds on the advances of another, and it is possible to enter the game late and still be successful. Of course, a basic invention protected by a patent is of great competitive value, but a great majority of R&D work is not of this character. Most firms advance a step at a time, and R&D success is measured by who is stepping fastest.

Risk entailed

Both uncertainty and expense permeate the design of all R&D policy. Of course, the total U.S. investment in R&D of about $25 billion per year (two thirds of this in government money) produces a stream of new products and processes, but the output of a single company laboratory is by no means sure. For example, laser theory was discovered and published by Charles Towne early in the 1950's. Many different laboratories started applied research with this new concept, but fifteen years later a significant industrial application had not yet appeared. R&D managers estimate that less than 20% of the ideas that look good enough to move from applied research to development actually end up in a marketable product (or applied process), and only a part of these are commercially successful. Uncertainty in R&D is real.

Moreover, R&D work is expensive. When technical assistants and other laboratory expenses are added to salary, a scientist or a senior engineer may cost a company from $60,000 to $100,000 a year. Of course the cost of routine engineering is lower, but so is the useful output. Projects that call for a team approach quickly entail a significant investment. Such cost, coupled with uncertainty of outcome, put pressure on central management to think through carefully how R&D should be used.

Among the key issues for which policy guidance is needed are the following:

1. Targets for improvement.
2. Depth of research effort.
3. Offensive versus defensive R&D.
4. Getting R&D done by outsiders.
5. Limits on total commitment.

TARGETS FOR IMPROVEMENT

R&D activities tend to wander. Researchers and engineers must be given considerable freedom to organize their own work, and each person prefers to move in directions that are intellectually exciting to that individual. No company can afford such a diffused effort on a large scale, although occasionally a company does permit its researchers to devote, say, 20% of their time to anything that intrigues them. Instead, guideposts—policy—are established to focus the effort. The guides should be directly derived from company strategy.

Product versus process focus

A recurring question is how R&D effort will be divided between developing new and improved products or seeking improvements in production processes. The key to a policy on this matter lies in the *industry analysis,* which we have urged as a prerequisite for drawing up company strategy. In a mature industry where low cost is necessary to meet price competition, for instance, R&D effort on processes may be crucial. On the other hand, newly designed products may be the primary success factor in another industry, so here R&D should focus on products.

A large chemical company used this simple but fundamental approach to sharply alter its R&D targets. For years this company had focused on tonnage production of carbon compounds. It was an efficient producer and maintained a steady position in its segment of a growing industry. Good process R&D was an important contributor to this achievement. Then the oil companies entered the chemical industry on a large scale. In terms of tonnage and low cost, the oil companies had some relative advantages: ready access to low-cost carbon inputs in the form of oil and gas, and a large cash flow available for the huge investments needed for new plants. Analysis of these developments led the independent chemical company to conclude that maintaining its position in the tonnage business would probably yield a declining return on its invested capital. Prospects were brighter for complex products that produced special effects and carried greater added value. Consequently, a new strategy was adopted of gradually phasing out the heavy petrol chemicals and replacing this business with newer complex products. To implement this strategy the R&D policy was sharply altered. New products became the dominant theme, whereas process research was confined to modifications of existing plants.

Adoption of the policy change just cited was no easy matter. For years the company had prided itself on being an aggressive, successful competitor. The personal careers of several of the key executives were based on this success. To them the policy change was like forfeiting a football game in midseason. Of course, the firm would continue to be a major factor in the segment of the industry these individuals knew so well, probably beyond the date of their retirement, but they were well aware that the change in the R&D policy would probably shape the character of the company in the future.

Existing lines versus new lines

A decision to support product research still leaves open the question of what type of product to concentrate on. For example, a jet engine manufacturer sticks to its existing products. It believes that the future market in this line alone is very large and that technological improvements from company R&D will be the key determinant of who gets the lion's share.

In contrast, Minnesota Mining and Manufacturing Company, makers of Scotch tape, photographic material, and a variety of other products, has achieved considerable success with R&D focused on new lines. The company does have a clear policy about the kinds of products on which money is to be spent. The emphasis is to be on products that are (a) new, (b) patentable, and (c) consumable (heavy repeat business). Here again, the R&D policy is a direct extension of the expansion strategy that this particular company has selected.

One dimension of a product line sometimes covered by R&D policy is the amount of forward integration. For instance, should a transistor manufacturer do research on products using transistors? In its fiber division, the Du Pont company has stayed away from end-products such as hosiery, shirts, rugs, and the like. The R&D people must know enough about the subsequent processing and final consumption of its fibers to build desirable characteristics into its products, but that is as far as its R&D people are expected to go. Incidentally, when there is no clear breaking point, Du Pont does carry its research clear to the consumer level, as in paints. Nevertheless, for years the company's basic policy was to stick to chemical manufacturing. This forward limit has had a significant effect upon the character of Du Pont research and the innovations it has produced.

Process improvements that count

In process R&D, as with product R&D, policy guidance is needed on where to focus attention. One approach is to deal only with those aspects of production where significant savings are possible. Thus a farm equipment manufacturer turned down a proposal from its engineering department to develop a new way of heat-treating a special type of steel. Even if the project had been as successful as hoped, it would have cut total manufacturing costs only by a fraction of one percent. The company preferred to concentrate its limited resources where the potential payout was greater.

The number of units affected by a process change is also critical. A large copper company, for instance, devoted substantial effort to finding ways to improve the recovery of copper from its ore crushing process by just a small percentage. Since literally millions of tons went through this process, even a small improvement in recovery could be significant. Unfortunately, a special study showed that the R&D department of this company was proceeding with equal zeal on the recovery of other metals that were produced in minor amounts as by-products of the copper operation. The study resulted in a sharper definition of what kind of process improvements to seek.

Policy defining the direction of R&D effort should provide for some degree of freedom, especially in the research stages. Many new discoveries have come through serendipity—finding one thing when looking for another. Penicillin and X-ray are examples. However, an interest in bright ideas that may be unrelated to the purposes of the project at hand does not diminish the value of policy about where to put the major effort. With such policy, most of the output will be directly usable by the company. Additional insights are welcome by-products, but they should be treated as by-products.

DEPTH OF RESEARCH EFFORT

Identification of a promising research area still leaves management with a question of depth or effort. For example, does a research interest in vertical takeoff planes mean that the company will undertake theoretical research in aerial dynamics or structural properties of lightweight metal? Where in the continuum from a search for new knowledge to practical specifications for a marketable product should the XYZ Company focus its efforts?

Basic research versus applied research

No company authorizes its research department to study anything that intrigues its scientists. Even basic research will be in areas related to the company's strategic mission—biochemistry for pharmaceutical companies, geology for oil companies, and the like. The issue is whether (a) simply to investigate a phenomenon without any specific idea of how the new knowledge acquired will be used (basic research), or (b) to pick a potential application of knowledge—human need—and try to devise ways of meeting this need (applied research). The distinction is like studying the geography of Central Africa just to learn more about it versus identifying attractive sites for hydroelectric power plants in Central Africa.

Exceptional companies in basic research. A few companies have had outstanding success with their policy of doing basic research. A notable example is the work at Bell Telephone Laboratories on semiconductors. Because of a possible connection with solid-state amplifiers, Bell Labs set up a semiconductor basic research group of physicists, chemists, and metallurgists in 1946. In the process of their investigation they discovered the transistor in 1948, and by 1951 they had developed the theoretical knowledge on which transistors with all their manifold applications are based. In passing, note that the initial effort took over five years of basic research by a whole group of scientists and that ten to fifteen years elapsed before the transistor was in widespread commercial application.

The Du Pont discovery of nylon is another classic example of where basic research paid off. Here, the research was on polymerization and by accident one of the researchers discovered that the fiber formed by pulling a stirring rod out of an experimental batch had unusual flexibility and strength. This led to a change in the direction of the research; but after two years of intensive work, the results were so discouraging that the entire project was almost abandoned. It took seven years after the initial discovery before nylon could be produced on a commercial basis. Just when this undertaking moved from "basic research" to "applied research" is hard to define. But it is clear that the basic research provided the situation in which the initial discovery was possible.

Occasional commercial success growing out of basic research, however, does not mean that all companies interested in new products and processes should embark on basic research. In fact, most companies have concluded that the costs and the hazards of basic research make it an unwise investment of company funds. Even large research-minded companies like Union Carbide Corporation and Monsanto Company have recently redirected their R&D effort to applied market-oriented projects.

Policy criteria for basic research. If a company is going to undertake basic research, it should meet the following criteria: (1) be prepared to take the risk of long periods of research without discovering ideas that have commercial value; (2) have a "payout" period threshold that permits a long time between investment and return (over twenty-five years elapsed between Fleming's discovery of penicillin and its large-scale production); and (3) possess enough capital to exploit discoveries when and if they are made—often millions of dollars are needed after the discovery to bring it into commercial use.

In addition to the three preceding criteria, which are essentially financial, a fourth operating consideration is usually necessary to justify basic research: (4) be sufficiently large in the industry where the discovery is applied to take full advantage of the new concept. This means that the company should have an existing position that will permit it to obtain synergistic benefits when the new product or process is introduced. Of course, a company can license or sell its patents to other companies, or it might enter a new industry in an effort to exploit a discovery it had made; but the return from such use of a new idea is much smaller than enhancing an existing market position or production capability.

Government financing of research can mitigate these rather severe criteria. In the aerospace industry and some other industries, government financing does permit a lot of *applied* research and development. To a much smaller extent, this same approach can be utilized for basic research (typically, however, government funds for this purpose go to universities or other nonprofit research institutes). Of course, government financing means that the company will not have exclusive use of the knowledge obtained, but direct access to scientists familiar with the latest developments might be advantageous for the company.

Applied research versus development

If basic research looks nebulous for a company, maybe it should also back away from applied research. Instead of spending time and money in finding how to accomplish a desired end, perhaps effort could better be concentrated on developing economical methods of utilizing ideas that are already known to work.

The considerations in making this choice are similar to those just listed for basic research, but here the risks are less and the payout periods somewhat shorter. The main advantage of sticking to "development" is assurance that results will reinforce existing activity. Thus the outcome can be directed toward strategic objectives (new products or production economy) rather than toward less predictable outcomes of applied research, which at least occasionally go off on tangents.

One category of applied research has a different twist. A company may develop a store of background knowledge about a phenomenon it often confronts. Then, as specific problems are faced, the research findings expedite solutions. For instance, a relatively small company making automatic materials-handling systems frequently needed to know how different materials (flour, paint, pigment, fertilizer, and cement) flowed; any tendency to lump, dust, or bridge required special design modifications. A research project on all factors affecting the way materials in general flow created a bank of information that enabled the company to give its customers distinctive advice on materials handling. The desirability of such applied research depends, of course, on the kind of service a company seeks to provide. One oil company may study the behavior of lubricants in Arctic temperatures, whereas an oil company selling only to Midwest customers would not bother. Policy guidance, geared into strategy, on how far to push such research is needed.

OFFENSIVE VERSUS DEFENSIVE R&D

Company strategy strongly influences R&D policy in terms of its emphasis on being a leader or a follower.

First with the best

If company strategy endorses a strong leadership position in any industry where technological change is a significant factor, an aggressive R&D program is essential. Money, time, and executive effort must be devoted toward this end.

Maxwell House Coffee, the largest division of General Foods Corporation, illustrates the price of such leadership. Having won a preeminent position in the U.S. coffee market by pioneering instant coffee, the division might have concentrated on maximizing short-run profits. Instead, the basic strategy was to retain this strong position over the long run, and this required product leadership. Consequently, Maxwell House retained a large research effort on ways to improve its product—notably to capture the aroma of freshly ground coffee. The freeze-dry method of making instant coffee was finally perfected in the laboratory and, despite the company's existing market leadership, additional millions of dollars were spent on tooling-up and introducing this new type of coffee to the consumer. Incidentally, Nestle's developed a freeze-dried coffee about the same time, and if Maxwell had not engaged in "offensive R&D" during the preceding ten years Nestle's probably would have captured a large piece of the Maxwell House business.

The fact that a company adopts an offensive R&D policy does not, of course, guarantee a dominant position such as Maxwell House gained. RCA, for instance, spent millions of dollars pioneering in color television. It was successful in being an early entry into this vast market but other companies quickly followed, each with its own modifications, so the market has always been shared with half a dozen other leading manufacturers. Also, even a successful R&D effort, to be effective, must be combined with good production and marketing for the investment to pay off. We noted in Chapter 3 that Univac did very well with its offensive program in computer research but then failed to capitalize on its initial technological advantage.

Running a close second

The price of being first is high. Many firms, especially those not giants in their industries, adopt an R&D policy that they hope will enable them to defend themselves against advances made by competitors. The policy has two phases. First, a systematic scanning—including planned intelligence—of research effort and results by others is maintained in all fields that could seriously upset present competitive strengths. Such surveillance requires a few men of high technical perception but does not require large outlays of money for laboratory and staff. Second, the company needs unusual competence to perform development work; its engineers must be able to move rapidly and be ingenious in devising methods of accomplishing results someone else has demonstrated as possible. The aim is to match competitors' offerings before the delay seriously upsets market positions.

Such a defensive policy has advantages. The most obvious is avoiding long, unproductive expenses for applied research and perhaps basic research. In addition, typically a new product does not work well in all its early applications; these initial problems create customer dissatisfaction, delays, and perhaps makeshift remedies. For instance, despite all the testing, a really new model of an automobile usually develops a series of weak points that require tedious trips back to the shop. If a second-runner can avoid these difficulties, it may rightfully claim it has the more dependable product. So, for that very large part of innovation that is developed by a series of modifications rather than a dramatic "breakthrough," a defensive R&D policy may not be a serious handicap.

Patents do create difficulties for the company using a defensive R&D policy. Basic patents are the serious ones because they may cut off an entire new area; for example, Hall's patent on electrolytic reduction of aluminum prevented new entry into the basic aluminum business until the patent expired. Patents for modifications or refinements are less troublesome because often the same effect can be achieved in a slightly different way. In some industries, such as pharmaceuticals and automobiles, cross-licensing of the use of patents is fairly common. Nevertheless, the possibility of a patent block is one of the hazards that must be weighed in considering the defensive policy approach.

A varied attack

The R&D policy does not have to be the same for all product lines. A medium-sized pharmaceutical company, for example, concluded that it could afford applied research only in two fields—tranquilizers and anesthetics. In seven other areas it adopted a defensive policy of follow-the-leader, and for two older product lines it simply continued production of established items with existing facilities—doing no R&D.

In practice, this mixture of defensive and offensive R&D created some internal misunderstandings. The need to select a limited area for concentrated research was understood, although not everyone agreed on the selections made. Confusion sometimes did arise when high priority was given to intensive development effort on one side of the other lines—to catch up with competition. "Why don't they make up their minds whether to stay in that business or not? For six months, all hell breaks loose and then we lapse back into our 'do-nothing' policy." The idea that the company was playing *both* a offensive and a defensive game was hard to accept by people who found themselves shifted suddenly from one project to another. But, to the executives who wanted to get maximum return from a limited R&D budget, the mixed policy made sense.

GETTING R&D DONE BY OUTSIDERS

R&D does not have to be done "in house." As with other inputs desired by a company, the R&D results may be acquired from outsiders. This is the familiar "make-or-buy" issue.

A firm may consider the use of outsiders for several reasons. Much R&D work requires a minimum-sized effort to be effective; the minimum "critical mass" usually consists of at least two or three scientists, some laboratory technicians, physical facilities, a flow of information and raw materials, travel money, and overhead services. Also, while an improvement in a product or process may be desired by an industry, the potential use by a single company may be too small to justify the cost of the necessary R&D. Or, a company may have more attractive use of its funds; a quicker cash flow return will be preferred, particularly by a company in a tight capital position. For any of these reasons, a company may hesitate to back a proposal with its own R&D effort, yet strongly desire the result.

Buying R&D effort

Like preparing advertising copy, making a computer analysis, or running a training course, R&D effort can be purchased outside the company.

Tapping expertise of others. In many fields, good independent research laboratories have been established to do special research for people who lack their own facilities. The Battelle Institute, for instance, did development work on Carlson's Xerox invention (the patent was subsequently sold to what is now the Xerox Corporation). The staffs of these institutes often include a wider array of specialists than many companies can retain on their permanent staff. Especially when a company only occasionally needs a particular type of R&D work, temporary access to such experts may be of great help.

Universities are a second major place to buy research effort. Occasionally a contract is made with the university itself, but more often individual faculty members are employed to work on projects in their special field of expertise. Pharmaceutical companies, for instance, frequently support the private research work of professors in the biochemistry field. The development of one of the oral contraceptives, to cite a specific instance, was done by university professors on sponsored research projects. Normally when university facilities are used, the results of the research must be made public; the sponsor gains by having the task done and being among the first to know about the results.

Joint ventures in R&D. If a project will be of value to several companies or perhaps an entire industry, several companies may join in financing the study. Currently, several studies on the control of pollution are being handled in this fashion. In some industries, such as coal and cement, a trade association conducts research for the entire industry. Incidentally, the common practice in the oil industry of several companies sharing the cost of an exploratory well is a variation of this general policy of joint ventures in research. In all these instances, the research cost to a single company is lowered and frequently the quality of research is improved; the disadvantage—which may not be serious—is that the results of the research must be shared.

Relying on others to do desired R&D

A firm's outlay for R&D can be even further reduced without sacrificing all of the benefits from such effort. This policy need not be passive; a company can actively encourage and assist work in particular directions.

Pay license or royalty fee. In industries where cross-licensing is an established practice, a company can make known in advance its willingness to enter into such agreements. This knowledge, combined with similar assurances from other firms, may encourage a member of the industry or an outsider to conduct research in desired areas. A medium-sized oil company, for instance, concluded that the research it could afford in refining technology was too small to keep it abreast of its competitors. Instead, it publicly announced its willingness to pay substantial royalties for improved technology developed by others. After two decades of experience, the management feels that it has been at no serious technical disadvantage to competitors and that royalty payments, while high, total considerably less than would have R&D effort to achieve similar results. Obviously the feasibility of this policy rests upon a prediction that licenses will be available.

Seek foreign licenses or patents. Technical know-how is a significant item in international trade. U.S. companies receive approximately $800 million annually in payment for their technical know-how, patent royalties, and the like. The flow into the United States is only about a fifth of this size, but it does reflect a potential source of technical ideas.

Often a foreign company lacks the desire or the capital to enter the U.S. market, and it may welcome an opportunity to get some additional return on its technical knowledge and designs. The U.S. company will probably have to take some initiative in working out the agreement, and it must be prepared to do considerable engineering work to adapt the foreign concepts to local conditions (just as is necessary in the reverse flow). Nevertheless, our debt to foreigners for important contributions to products ranging from helicopters to ballpoint pens indicates the potentiality of this approach.

Encourage equipment or materials suppliers. In a number of industries, the suppliers rather than the fabricators themselves provide most of the innovation. This is clearly true of the textile industry where most R&D activity has been carried on by producers of man-made fibers and by equipment manufacturers.

A company can encourage such external developments. For equipment, the most common practice is to place an order for an experimental model or to agree to pay a rather high price for the first two or three units of a product that meet certain performance specifications. Vast sums are spent by the U.S. government in this fashion, and most of the high-speed railroad equipment has been developed on this basis. The amount of premium a company must pay for newly designed equipment naturally depends upon the size of the market the manufacturer anticipates if the equipment works well. Incidentally, from the equipment manufacturer's viewpoint, it is getting a customer to help underwrite its R&D expense.

Similar cooperation between customer and supplier can relate to raw materials. If the materials supplier sees a large and continuing market, it will foot most of the development expense. Even in such instances the supplier often wants trial runs in actual production conditions. The user contributes its plant for such testing. In return it hopes to have an edge in the early use of the new material.

Promote government research. The federal government spends between $10 and $15 billion a year to finance R&D work. Most of this goes to defense and space projects, but the remaining amount is still very large. The pressure for use of these funds is tremendous and the allocation is based primarily on potential contribution to public welfare. However, since many companies wish to pioneer in the same directions that the government is promoting, the possibility of having government finance expensive research exists. The production of gasoline from oil shale, improved means to control injurious insects, better urban transportation, use of plankton from the ocean, and less expensive hospital services are merely illustrations of the diversity of government interest in R&D work. A company can actively encourage the government to sponsor research that may make technical contributions of interest to the company.

Of course, if a company's strategy includes seeking the government as a customer, possibly the government will also underwrite company R&D effort. Usually this possibility is open only to companies with strong R&D departments. In this section, however, we have been exploring ways a company could obtain R&D results without having a large research operation of its own.

In conclusion, enough alternatives to in-house research have been mentioned to indicate that a company need not abandon all interest in R&D if it cannot do the work itself. Most of the possibilities for getting others to do desired research involve sharing the results. Nevertheless, when the magnitude or the duration of the necessary effort is beyond the resources of a single company, initiative in getting others to help share the load may bear fruit. Finally, a mixed policy is again possible: a company can do its own R&D in some fields and work with outsiders in others.

LIMITS ON TOTAL COMMITMENT

The wide range of possible R&D effort, which we have already indicated, adds up to a substantial undertaking for most companies. Like most budgets, when one totals all the things it would be desirable to do, the sum can be staggering. Central management has the task of setting some kind of a limit that maintains a desired balance of R&D work with other activities of the company. This decision as to "how much" probably involves as much subjective judgment as any faced by central management. The uncertainty of results, what competitors will do, and the contribution of technology to long-range strategy—all are based on intuitive judgment more than on objective facts. Nevertheless, if R&D is to proceed with vigor and on an even keel, guidelines for the magnitude of the effort are needed.

Policy regarding the size of R&D commitment is usually stated in terms of the key considerations that will be used in setting annual appropriations. A useful approach is the following.

Use percent of sales or gross profit for maximum range

To get some kind of a handle on R&D expenditures, central managements often use "percent of sales." Sales volume does indicate the principal cash inflow of the company and thus provides a gross measure of the total annual resources from which outlays for R&D will be drawn. For example, a company with $100 million in sales can undertake more R&D than a company with $10 million in sales.

At best, this is a crude guide. The gross profit on a dollar of sales may be only 15% in a distribution firm compared with more than 60% in a pharmaceutical firm. Indirect expenses like R&D obviously must come out of the margin remaining after the costs of materials, labor, and other direct expenses are met. Consequently, it makes more sense to relate R&D outlays to gross profit rather than ·to sales.

Clearly, there is a limit to what proportion of this gross profit a management can allocate to R&D without eroding current profits so much that the company's financial strength is in danger. The permissible maximum depends upon the urgency of other claims upon the company's "discretionary income." Somewhere in the range of 5% to 20% of gross profit—depending upon the industry—is a limit beyond which a company cannot prudently go. While imprecise, this consideration does establish the order of magnitude for the maximum R&D expenditure in a normal year.[1]

Use competitors' actions for minimum range

In technologically based industries, any company that wishes to maintain (or achieve) a particular position in the market must do enough R&D to keep up with the parade. In other words, the magnitude of the research effort by competitors sets a minimum floor below which it is hazardous to go. Such a minimum is an approximate figure. No two companies have exactly the same product line. Based on its technological forecasts, a company may decide to pursue an offensive policy with respect to some products, a defensive policy with respect to others, and the phasing out of its remaining products. Allowances must be made for differences in this mix when comparing research efforts of competitors. However, after making such adjustments, a study of competitors' actions does provide some guidance as to the minimum level of R&D that a company with given market targets can safely undertake.

Use "expected" profit between minimum and maximum

A third way to set limits on R&D is in terms of "expected" profit. If no uncertainty were present, this would simply involve estimating the total outlays and the total incomes for each project and then, using discounted cash flow or some other appropriate procedure, computing the rate of profit. Unfortunately, both future outlays and incomes are highly uncertain. Theoretically, the decision-maker should think in terms of a frequency distribution for each of these figures, compute "expected" value, adjust for differences in time, and compute the "expected" profit. Rarely does the accuracy of the estimates justify this refined estimating procedure, but the underlying concepts can be used to size up the attractiveness of a series of proposed R&D projects.

---

[1] For an exceptional project, *new capital* may be brought into the company just to finance the necessary R&D. This is an unusual situation and goes beyond a policy for internal growth.

Then, if the major R&D projects a company contemplates are ranked according to their attractiveness in terms of expected profits, a cumulative total may be computed running from highly desirable to least desirable proposals. The final step is to see where the cumulative annual expense for these projects falls within the previously established maximum and minimum. If the analysis shows that the company has an ample supply of very attractive projects to utilize the maximum that can be allocated for R&D, a strong case can be made for a policy of spending this maximum amount. On the other hand, if the company would be undertaking projects of marginal attractiveness with an outlay, say, halfway between the maximum and the minimum, then the policy should set an overall limit close to the minimum outlay. The reason for setting the combined total somewhat lower than the expected profit analysis of individual projects suggests is the optimistic bias that almost always exists in such estimates. Experience indicates that the ceiling should be low enough to encourage frequent review of projects in process so that the ones turning out badly can be dropped promptly to make room for exciting proposals that had to be temporarily deferred.

Adjust for stability and capacity to absorb

Two further considerations are important in setting a limit on the total R&D effort. Some stability in the level of activity is highly desired. Effective R&D cannot be expanded and contracted on short notice. Time is required to hire good scientists and engineers, to build facilities, to establish working relationships, and to get a program underway. Consequently, central management should establish a policy that it expects to continue for several years, and the value of momentum should be recognized when changes in policy are considered.

A final factor in setting a limit is the capacity of the company to absorb the output of its R&D department. If the company lacks the capital, the managerial talent, or other resources necessary to exploit, say, two new products a year, then an R&D department that is likely to produce five such ideas is out of balance.

Subjective judgments and imprecision permeate the approach we have just outlined for establishing policy limits on total R&D commitment. Unfortunately, this is inherent in the nature of the problem. Our contention is only that the proposed approach is far better than dealing with this important subject on purely an intuitive basis.

SUMMARY

R&D very much needs policy direction in terms of (a) targets for new products and/or processes that are important to company success, (b) the areas in which the company wishes to push back from development work into applied research and possibly basic research, and (c) the areas where an offensive effort is called for and the areas where a defensive posture makes more sense. These guidelines define the mission of R&D activities.

Part or possibly all of this R&D mission can be met through the use of outsiders. So, policy is needed on subcontracting, joint ventures, licensing, and encouraging suppliers or governmental research. Here, as in each facet of the mission, a mixed response may be dictated by policy—the approach to be taken depending upon the kind of R&D being considered.

With the scope of R&D effort thus defined, limits on total resource commitments provide a third dimension. Financially, a policy maximum often is a percent of gross profit, the minimum is a sum necessary to keep up with competitors, and within this range "expected" profit of projects sets the level. The capacity of management and other aspects of organization may also set limits.

We have stressed repeatedly the need to relate R&D policy to master strategy. The R&D mission finds its *raison d'etre* in company strategy; the use of outsiders is a special aspect of the fundamental make-or-buy issue; and overall limits on R&D take their cue from strategy for the inevitable rationing of scarce resources. By interlacing strategy and R&D policy, we harness the potentialities of modern science to the management of an enterprise.

QUESTIONS FOR CLASS DISCUSSION

1. Additional sources of energy and improved output of present sources are desired to increase the total energy available and to reduce dependence on crude oil imports. This will require massive R&D effort. What role should private industry play in this total effort? What kinds of companies not now in the energy business should try to take advantage of this opportunity for growth?

2. More people in the United States are engaged in service industries than in "production" industries (manufacturing, mining, and agriculture). (a) Do you believe as many opportunities exist for innovation in services as in "production"? Give illustrations. (b) What does your answer imply regarding the nature and the directions of R&D work in service industries?

3. Although it sells to a variety of customers, Island Creek Coal Company is known as a producer of coking coal used by the steel industry and for other metallurgical purposes. Its mines and its coal reserves are predominantly "underground" (i.e., not strip or surface), and consequently its production costs are comparatively high. The quality of its coal is good. Almost all of Island Creek's R&D effort is devoted to improving mining efficiency and to sorting the coal into different grades. "We concentrate on producing a quality product at a reasonable cost.

That's a major task. We let our customers do the research on how to use the product; that is not our game. Most of our competitors do less R&D than we do.'' Do you think Island Creek's R&D policy is wise?

4. Urban housing and urban transportation are two areas of recognized need for substantial improvement. (a) For what kinds of companies do these needs provide attractive R&D opportunities? (b) Can these problems be solved largely by innovations introduced by private enterprise?

5. A leading publisher of high school mathematics textbooks wants to add a "teaching machine" to its product line. The machine will be used by individual students with an instruction booklet, and it will give the student immediate feedback on the correctness of his answers to a series of questions. Various programs can be placed in the machine, and each student can progress at his own speed. The question now facing the publisher is how to get a good machine designed. For textbooks the publisher relies on teachers to write and test the basic text; the publisher advises, edits the text, arranges for printing and binding, sells the book, warehouses and ships, extends credit, etc. Printing and binding is done by an outside firm. For the new machine, teaching methods and instruction programs have to be developed as well as the machine itself. What parts—if any—of this R&D work do you recommend be done by outsiders? Give your reasons.

6. A small group of scientists and engineers have formed a company to design, manufacture, and sell an atomic-powered heart pacer. Thousands of people already have battery-powered heart pacers in their chests; use of atomic energy will reduce the size of the pacer and avoid biannual operations to replace the batteries. To date the company has focused entirely on the very exacting design problems and on obtaining FDA (government) approval of the device. (a) Assuming this effort is successful, what major problems will the company face? (b) What are the pros and cons of continuing into manufacture and sale of the device as an independent company versus selling or licensing the device to a large established firm already serving the medical profession? (c) If the company decides to undertake the manufacture and sale of the heart pacer, should it also continue R&D effort on other complex health devices?

7. One offshoot of work with cable TV is the idea of eliminating the need for meter readers. Electric, gas, and water companies face high expense getting their people into homes to read meters as a basis for charging customers; with more women away at work, finding someone at home is increasingly difficult. Several technically possible ways are known that would automatically "observe" a meter in a home and transmit the information via telephone lines to a central recording station. However, much development work remains to make such a system economically feasible. Assume that you had to decide for your company whether to invest in such development work, and that your president wanted to know the *expected value* of an investment on this R&D project. Explain (a) what factors you would consider and (b) how you would combine estimates regarding each of these factors into an "expected value."

8. Several of the more innovative companies in the mobile homes industry are subsidiaries of lumber concerns or metal producers. Assume that you are president of one of these subsidiaries and have been given a free hand to develop your company as you think best. In what ways, if any, would you want your affiliation with a materials supplier to influence your R&D effort?

CASE 8 / Grayson Pharmaceutical Company

Company background. The Grayson Pharmaceutical Company is an ethical pharmaceutical firm with sales in excess of $200 million. The company held substantial market positions in the tranquilizer, anti-obesity, gastrointestinal, respiratory, and diuretic markets. Grayson Pharmaceutical was deeply committed to growth through new product development, as evidenced by a research and development budget of $20 million. This R&D budget placed it among the five largest research performers in the industry. R&D expenditures at Grayson had increased at an average annual rate of 10% during the previous decade.

Research and development at Grayson. The search for new products within Grayson's R&D Division is performed in two distinct stages: (1) research programs and (2) development projects. Basically, research programs are designed to discover new drugs. Grayson, as do most firms in the industry, focuses its research programs around sets of animal tests designed to uncover desired types of biological activity.

The first checkpoint in the development of a new drug occurs when a research program yields a chemical structure with desired biological activity. At this point, a preliminary estimate of the chemical structure's medical utility is made to determine whether the compound should proceed to development or be rejected. The animal pharmacology and toxicity data compiled during the research program are used to predict the potential efficacy and safety of the compound in man. The areas of probable effectiveness for the compound and its chances of superiority or distinctiveness in these fields are the major criteria used to make this judgment.

Development at Grayson also proceeds in two stages: (1) pilot development and (2) full development. During pilot development, animal testing is expanded to obtain a complete laboratory profile of the compound. Human pharmacological studies and limited chemical testing are initiated under the direction of three to six expert chemical researchers. If pilot development indicates that the compound is sufficiently promising to warrant full-scale clinical development and premarket testing, a full development project will be established. The three major steps in a full development project within Grayson Pharmaceutical are: (1) large-scale clinical testing, (2) final product formulation, and (3) surveys of market potential.

During the past ten years the proportion of the Grayson R&D budget allocated to development averaged 55%. Research programs received 35% of the funds, with the remaining 10% devoted to other R&D activities such as post-marketing product support. Of the 134 full development projects conducted by the firm in the last seventeen years, 75 had resulted in a marketed new product.

Meeting of Grayson's Executive Committee. In mid-September the Executive Committee of the Grayson Pharmaceutical Company convened to review the research plan proposed by the R&D Division for the following year. The Executive Committee was comprised of the president, the executive vice-president, and the vice-presidents of Grayson's six functional divisions.

Reade Exton, president of Grayson Pharmaceutical, opened the Executive Committee meeting:

"It has now been six months since Glenn Overton assumed the leadership of our Research and Development Division. Since you are well aware of the events that led to Glenn's appointment, I will not dwell on past history. Suffice it to say that our profitability and market position in the various ethical pharmaceutical submarkets have been declining in each of the last five years. R&D had contributed only one significant new drug during this time period, and there were no promising new drugs on the horizon. In short, Glenn's mission was to get R&D moving again.

"Today, Glenn will have an opportunity to discuss the research section of his proposed operating plan. We have all had an opportunity to review a copy of the plan during the past few weeks. I, for one, believe that this proposal is notable for the definitiveness of its objectives and for the clarity and enthusiasm with which they have been described. I'll now turn the meeting over to Glenn."

Glenn Overton rose to speak:

"Thank you for that glowing introduction, Reade. Since you've all received copies of the operating plan, I prefer not to dwell on the specifics of the plan. Instead, I'd like to provide you with some insight into the thinking that underlies the research section by making some general comments. I'll then invite you to raise questions.

"During the past six months my staff and I have identified a new set of research goals for our division. We have selected five research areas for their pharmacologic and medical importance [see Exhibit 1], for the extent and strength of our resources to explore them, and for the potential of discovery in them of agents both valuable to therapy and profitable for the corporation. These five areas are: mental and emotional disease, cardiovascular disease, arthritis-rheumatism, respiratory disesase, and gastrointestinal disease.

"The selection of these five major areas has required of us decisions that were frequently difficult: to leave an area of research in which an initial success might have tempted us to seek others; in some areas, though staying in them, to turn away from a basically defensive program of product improvement and replacement toward an offensive program of therapeutic innovation; and elsewhere, to select or design for our laboratories new methodologies for research into the underlying causes of a disease process rather than that of mere symptomatic control.

"In reviewing our selection of research areas, I think it important to recognize that this selection must be made with some sensible relation to research as a whole—to research throughout this country and the world. Though we, as a corporation, spend a healthy percentage of our sales dollars on research, we must recognize that the percentage of total research we can perform is small.

"We are all aware of the size of the federal research budget, but we must appreciate its significance for our research planning. The National Institutes of Health will next year spend in one week more than our R&D division will spend all year, and that huge program is still less than half of the research that will be publicly and privately supported in the government, in the universities, and in industry. This overpowering aggregate of research programs puts two somewhat paradoxical questions to the management of small, private R&D organizations such as ours. First, can we sensibly attempt any of the truly basic research from which will come the breakthroughs that Grayson's growth

Exhibit 1

National Annual Economic Costs of Major Diseases

	Direct Cost[1]		Indirect Cost[2]		Estimated Pharmaceutical Sales[3]	
	$ Millions	%	$ Millions	%	$ Millions	%
Infective & Parasitic Diseases	502	2	890	4	45	2
Neoplasms	1,279	6	1,335	6	60	2
Allergic, Endocrine, Metabolic, etc.	903	4	607	3	130	5
Diseases of Blood, etc.	166	1	48	neg.	120	5
Mental Disorders	2,402	11	4,634	19	180	7
Diseases of Nervous System Sense Organs	1,415	6	1,825	8	165	7
Diseases of Circulatory System	2,268	10	4,146	17	325	13
Diseases of Respiratory System	1,581	7	3,306	14	400	17
Diseases of Digestive System	4,159	19	1,344	6	175	7
Diseases of Genito-Urinary	1,210	5	546	2	160	7
Maternity	1,391	6	34	neg.	40	2
Diseases of Skin & Cellular Tissue	248	1	132	1	85	4
Diseases of Bones & Organs of Movement	1,430	6	1,231	5	100	4
Symptoms, Senility, & Ill-Defined Conditions	624	3	322	1	65	3
Accidents, Poisonings, & Violence	1,703	8	2,052	9	90	4
Special Conditions Without Sickness	966	4	12	neg.	285	12
Miscellaneous	293	2	1,309	5	2	neg.
Totals	$22,540	100%	$23,773	100%	$2,427	100%

[1] Includes expenditures for hospital and nursing care, physicians' and dentists' services, and other professional services.

[2] Productivity losses due to illness, disability, and premature death.

[3] Retail and nonfederal hospital sales of ethical pharmaceuticals reclassified by major disease areas.

demands? Second, should we not instead ready ourselves to recognize and exploit incipient breakthroughs anywhere along the broad front of research as a whole?

"Our answers to these two questions, which have determined the profile of the research program outlined in our annual plan, interlock. We believe we must depend largely on research as a whole, profiting from it where we have the talent to exploit its advance. It is unrealistic to believe that we can deploy men along any sizeable sector of the research front in any effective depth. We must look to research as a whole. On the other hand, we cannot develop or maintain the talent to profit from advancement anywhere along the front unless we involve ourselves in carefully selected basic research.

"I think it would be appropriate for me to terminate my formal remarks and give you an opportunity to raise questions."

Ted Byron, vice-president of marketing, was the first to speak:

"Glenn, let me first second Reade's earlier remarks regarding the comprehensiveness and clarity of your operating plan. My questions deal with some of the research areas that you and your people have decided to drop. Some of these areas are programs that Grayson has pursued over a number of years. We in marketing, for example, are stunned that you've decided to terminate our diuretic [kidney and related ailments] research program. Our two most recent new products have been diuretics, and the market has been rapidly growing. We've developed considerable selling experience in this market and had assumed that we'd continue to capitalize on our experience and investment as future diuretic products were forthcoming."

Overton replied: "Frankly, Ted, we can find little to recommend in the diuretic area in the short run. With the introduction of furosemide and ethacrynic acid, good treatment is available for all patients and there is little chance of finding an agent in the next few years that shows improvement over available drugs."

Byron countered: "Although you may estimate that the probability of technical success is quite small, we think that the substantial payoff for that superior product offsets this low probability. Suppose, however, that we grant you your assumptions concerning diuretics, how can you explain the decision to terminate the analgesic [pain-killer] research program? Here's a $90 million retail market showing good growth. There's an established need for a potent nonaddicting analgesic. Moreover, we know that the leading product in this market is not considered as good a drug as its sales might lead one to think."

"Ted, let me try to explain our reasoning," answered Overton. "There are a number of disadvantages to pursuing research in this area. At the present time, clinic evaluation is particularly difficult in mild to moderate pain. Since we have limited facilities for demonstrating the lack of an addiction liability, it would take three to four years to demonstrate this effect. Perhaps the most telling argument against continuing analgesic research is that the wide acceptance of aspirin as an analgesic agent makes it difficult to penetrate this market."

Olive Whittier, vice-president of administration, was next to speak:

"My reservations are not along the same lines as those of Ted. Whereas he's upset at our leaving certain areas of research, I'm concerned that the five research areas selected do not represent a significant enough departure from past policies. Why don't we move into some new research areas for us, such as cancer drugs or oral contraceptives?"

"Let's take those one at a time, Olive. Sure, oral contraceptives sold nearly $70 million in this country last year. Five to six million women are using oral contraceptives, and this figure is expected to double or triple in the next decade. Our problem is that we missed the boat ten years ago. We simply do not have enough scientific resources in the area of reproduction physiology to mount the kind of effort needed here. The cost would be staggering."

Overton continued, "Now let's consider the possibilities in cancer research. Cancer is one of the leading causes of death in this country. It is an area to which the government is heavily committed both in terms of research for drug therapy and in support of fundamental and basic research. At the moment, we do not think of this as a promising area for us because of the large amount of government resources being expended in the area and the relatively heavy and long-term efforts of other firms in the industry. In addition, the profit margin on a product with a broad spectrum of application could be restricted by government involvement."

Carter Johnston, executive vice-president, was next to join in the discussion:

"As I listen to this discussion, it becomes clear that we have to be explicit about the criteria we are using to select research areas. So far we've mentioned such criteria as size of market, cost of research, technical capability, probability of technical success, quality of existing products in a market, Grayson's current sales in a market, and the degree of government involvement. The list seems endless. We certainly aren't agreed on what our criteria should be. Isn't it necessary for us to agree on the criteria for selection and the relative importance of these criteria before selecting research areas?"

"Isn't there the equally important issue of *whose* criteria we use?" asked Mort Jensen, vice-president of finance. "One of our past problems was the isolation of the R&D division from the rest of the company. My impression was that we were seeking to achieve more interdivisional cooperation and involvement through reorganizing and changing personnel. Shouldn't the establishment of criteria and the selection of research areas be an Executive Committee responsibility rather than a unilateral R&D function?"

At this point, Reade Exton noted: "I have been carefully following the various issues raised here today. Glenn, with due apologies to you, perhaps we've put the cart before the horse. Before you begin to defend the particular research areas selected, I think it best to discuss the issue of what criteria we used to select research areas and the role of the Executive Committee in relation to the R&D division in the selection process."

Required: (a) How valid are the objections raised by Grayson executives to the R&D operating plan?

(b) How should Grayson select research areas? What criteria should be utilized in the selection process? Which of these criteria should receive priority?

(c) What role should the Executive Committee play in the selection process? What should be the role of R&D?

PRODUCTION POLICY

Company strategy, as we saw in Chapter 4, involves effective integration of the supply of goods (or services) with their marketing. Somehow, someplace, the goods must be procured. In the preceding chapter we discussed the creation of *new* products and processes. Now we turn to key issues in buying and/or making all the products that a company sells.

Many firms have separate departments for purchasing and production, but the basic problems that demand attention of central management are so entwined that it is simpler to consider production policy and purchasing policy together. This chapter and the next chapter should be considered as a unit.

Although our discussion of production will deal primarily with manufacturing—the physical fabrication of products—a comparable set of problems arise in the creation of intangible services. Banks, brokerage houses, consulting firms, and retail stores, for instance, face issues of capacity, technology, make-or-buy, and purchasing that are just as vital as production problems in a factory. With relatively minor adjustments, the points raised can be applied to intangible as well as tangible "production."

Historical changes in procurement problems

For many years procurement of merchandise was the primary problem of business people. The rounding of the Cape of Good Hope and the discovery of America were actually attempts to find new trade routes. The enterprising merchants of those days were seeking products of the Far East because these products had a ready market in European nations. For centuries thereafter merchants searched the four corners of the earth for goods that they might bring back to sell in their home markets. These early merchants had some sales problems, but their major task was that of finding goods to bring to the markets.

Following the Industrial Revolution in the latter half of the Eighteenth Century, with its application of power and large-scale production methods to the processing of goods, more attention was given to the production than to the buying of goods. In the United States particularly, businesses gave their energy to exploiting natural resources, developing more efficient methods of production, and harnessing steam and electric power. Nevertheless, the problem still remained one of securing goods that could be offered for sale.

During the last fifty years problems confronting central management have shown a still further change in emphasis. The great increase in variety of goods produced and the improvements in transportation have compelled businesses to give added attention to marketing their wares. This increasing attention required by the marketing end of business has changed procurement problems in some respects but cannot be said to have diminished them. Because of the increased competition for markets, more attention must be given to timely production, keeping costs low, and maintaining quality standards.

In the future, world shortages of basic resources will raise the strategic importance of production. The supply of energy, mineral deposits, fresh water, even fresh air cannot expand at the fast-accelerating rates of use. And these restraints will create other shortages. Moreover, environmental protection will slow up readjustments. In our opinion the industrial system will not collapse, but resource availability and efficient use will certainly command closer attention.

Issues requiring central management attention

Production and purchasing, like other phases of a business enterprise, involve a myriad of detailed problems. At this point, however, we will focus on broad policy issues that need the attention of central management. Many, if not all, of these issues have a profound effect on the destiny of virtually every firm.

These major production and purchasing policy issues will be discussed under the following headings:

1. Deciding the extent to which vertical integration is strategic.
2. Selecting the general processes to be used in production.
3. Setting total capacity and facility balance.
4. Providing basic guides for maintenance and replacement.
5. Resolving make-or-buy questions regarding services and supplies.
6. Selecting vendors from whom purchases should be made.
7. Correlating purchasing, production, and sales.

The first four sets of problems will be considered in this chapter; the last three in the next chapter.

EXTENT OF VERTICAL INTEGRATION

"Should we manufacture what we sell or should we buy it? If we manufacture, should we just assemble purchased parts or should we make the parts? Should we make or buy raw materials for the parts? Should we produce the supplies needed to make the raw materials?" These are questions of vertical integration. Every firm faces them, and for many firms a sound answer is the key to long-run success.

Vertical integration in the automobile industry

The problem of deciding whether to make or buy products is well illustrated in the automobile industry. Forty years ago the typical automobile manufacturer bought most of his parts from other manufacturers. The entire body of the car might be purchased from one manufacturer, the motor from another, and the differential from a third manufacturer. In fact, a substantial number of the so-called automobile manufacturers did little more than assemble these various parts into a complete automobile. They frequently exercised considerable influence over the design of parts, but the actual production operations within their own plant were quite limited.

Since that time large automobile manufacturers have decided to manufacture many of the 15,000 parts that go into a typical car. They may stamp and weld the metal that goes into the automobile body, and they often cast the original parts that go into making the engine. It is interesting to note, however, that even the large manufacturers do not make certain automobile parts. The production of a speedometer is a specialized operation, and most automobile manufacturers have considered it more economical to purchase their supply from a company that specializes in the production of speedometers for several different makes of automobiles. This specialized company can make speedometers more economically for several manufacturers than one automobile company can make a limited number for its own automobiles.

Piston rings and tires are other examples of purchased parts. Expertise is the main reason piston ring manufacturers have withstood the swing to vertical integration. For tires, an added factor is that most successful tire companies make a wide array of other rubber products and the automobile firms do not want to become involved in activities so far removed from their main business.

Combining publishing, printing, and paper making

The sharp differences in integration in the publishing field throw more light on the nature of the problem. Most book publishers do not print or bind their products. Their printing needs fluctuate in volume; one week they may have six typesetters and printers working for them and the next week none at all. Also, being free to get printing done anywhere gives them greater flexibility in the design of their books. On the other hand, contract printing is expensive. The former president of the company publishing this book, for example, often said as he passed the plant that did most of his printing, "My business made the owner of that company wealthy. But, I have enough worries already."

In contrast to book publishing, larger newspapers always do their own typesetting and printing. Probably this saves them money. The dominant consideration, however, is the need for very close coordination—literally down to a few minutes—between writing copy, setting it in type, proofreading, headlining, layout, and printing. And when a hot story breaks, much of the work may be redone in an hour or two. Such fast coordination can be best supervised by a single management.

Fewer newspapers have their own paper mills and timberlands. The big papers and the chains have a large, fairly steady need of a single product. Production economies are a natural result. To be sure, these same economies might be obtained by an independent supplier under a long-term contract, but some risk would remain for both newsprint producer and newspaper. So, at least those papers that predict a long-term rise in newsprint prices and that have capital for investment try to reduce supply risks by integrating clear back to the forest. Even so, newsprint shortages curtail output from time to time.

To farm or not to farm

Still unsettled is the extent to which frozen food companies should raise their own vegetables and fruits. Seabrook Farms, to cite one case, is heavily engaged in farming. Most firms, however, rely on local independent farmers. Farmers tilling their own land conform to the centuries-old cultural pattern; and reliance on independent growers presumes that the resourceful, close supervision of farmers over their crops will be more effective than hired management. But the frozen food packer must be assured of a supply of quality produce suitable for freezing. So it signs annual contracts with farmers well in advance of planting, provides selected seed, and offers advice. We see here, not vertical integration in the usual sense, but an arrangement with supply sources that accomplishes several of its benefits.

Key factors in vertical integration

The examples just discussed show that a variety of factors may influence a decision on when to integrate. Among the many possible considerations, the following are likely to be key ones.

Possible savings resulting from coordination. If a company manufactures the products or the materials it needs, the promptness of delivery and adjustment to emergencies may be easier. When the parts have to fit together into a complex balance, the engineering may be more easily coordinated. Unusual quality requirements may be easier to meet. A firm knowing its own needs and being assured of continued use of equipment may develop more specialized machinery than is feasible for an outside supplier.

Elimination of marketing expenses. If a firm produces its own materials, the selling expenses incurred by the outside vendor are automatically avoided.

Lower supply risks. If there is reason to doubt that raw materials will be readily available, then a company may acquire its own sources as a means of protection. For example, virtually all the basic metal processors mine their own ore, and the leading oil companies want a controlled supply of at least part of their crude oil requirements.

Effect of patents. The control of patents by other companies may make economical manufacture impossible; but if the company itself should obtain control of patents, then a policy of manufacturing may be particularly desirable.

Flexibility. Vertical integration tends to limit flexibility in product design. Heavy investment in plant or raw material sources hampers the shift to completely new designs or materials, whereas the firm that buys its requirements is not concerned with making a large investment obsolete.

In the short run, too, the nonintegrated firm may cut down its purchases or shift to another supplier, whereas the integrated firm must recognize the effect of such action on unabsorbed overhead. To guard against such a stultifying effect, General Motors has a longstanding policy that none of its divisions is required to buy from another division if the profit or the long-run development of the first division would suffer from doing so.

Volume required for economic production. Many small companies simply cannot consider backward integration because the volume of their requirements for any one part or material is too small to keep an efficient plant busy. Also, the requirements may be so irregular that a plant would be kept busy only part of a year (like a college football stadium). Occasionally a company builds a plant larger than needed for its own use and then sells the balance of the output to other users. Such an arrangement, however, does divert both financial resources and managerial attention from the major activity of the firm.

Financial status of the company. Many firms have only enough capital to operate their principal line of business and may not be in a position to acquire new capital under favorable conditions. This precludes substantial investments in manufacturing facilities for the production of parts or raw materials. On the other hand, financially strong companies may undertake vertical expansion because their suppliers are financially weak. In such circumstances, the added financial strength may permit substantial improvements in the manufacturing operation.

Capacity of management to supervise additional activities. In a great many instances, a decision to produce products that formerly were purchased means that the executives of the company are undertaking activities of a distinctly different nature from those with which they are familiar. While they can employ an executive from that industry, central management cannot escape giving some attention to the new undertaking and bearing responsibility for making final decisions regarding it. Sometimes central management becomes so absorbed in directing the new activity that it fails to give adequate guidance to the older part of the business where it has demonstrated competence.

On the other hand, if inadequate managerial attention is given to the new venture, expected savings may not be realized. Perhaps low cost will exist when production is first started because the new plant will have new equipment and the latest methods; but with only secondary attention by central management and the opiate of an assured market, there is real danger that the plant will fail to keep up with other concerns.

General conclusion. Vertical integration decisions of the type that we have been considering in this section are of substantial magnitude. Each proposal should, therefore, be thoroughly examined in terms of the key factors listed, estimated ratio of savings to investment, and unique considerations such as idle plant or lack of technical knowledge. But underlying such a detailed analysis—and guiding a decision to devote time and energy to the study in the first place—should be a consciously determined disposition (policy) to move toward vertical integration or to stay away from it. Such a general policy should be based on an appraisal of what is required for success in the industry, the distinctive competence and resources of the company, desire for diversifying economic risks, and similar factors reviewed in Part I. Few policies are more crucial to the long-run development of a company.

PRODUCTION PROCESSES

Closely related to decisions on what production activities the company itself will perform are choices of pressures to be used. Broad issues in this area are:

1. Choice of technology.
2. Extent of division of labor.
3. Extent of mechanization and automation.
4. Size and decentralization of plants.

Choice of technology

In the production of many products the manager has no choice regarding the process to be used. Thus, a manufacturer of wallboard, using fiber of sugar cane as its primary raw material, need be in no quandary about the process to be employed in removing the small quantity of sugar remaining in the cane after it passes through a sugar mill. The only commercially practical method is fermentation. By allowing the sugar to ferment, it can be almost completely removed and the remaining fibers are then in a light and workable state. Since this is the only feasible process, the manufacturer really faces no problems in this regard and turns its attention to the detailed methods and facilities for carrying out the process.

Not all manufacturers can solve their production process problems as readily as the wallboard company. Small airlines, for instance, that provide local feeder service to major cities must decide whether to use jet or prop planes. In the same way a company manufacturing steel must decide upon the extent to which it will use electric furnaces, open-hearth furnaces, or oxygen inverters. Stemming from such basic decisions will come a whole array of plans for equipment, personnel, methods, and organization.

Technology is not confined to physical processes. Universities, engineering firms, and mental hospitals—to mention only a sample—face similar choices. A management consulting firm, for instance, can either design standard solutions (statistical quality control, sales compensation plans, budget procedures, and the like) and adapt them to each client, or it can make a fresh analysis of each situation with no preconceived ideas about the solution. The choice here does not involve large investment in facilities, but it does affect personnel, organization, sales appeals, and other facets of the business.

A recurring issue of "production technology" in a business school revolves around the use of cases versus lecture-discussion. And in elementary education the busing of white children to black neighborhoods and vice versa is even more controversial. These examples suggest that when output and processes become more human and less physical, choice of technology has a lot of subjective value overtones.

Extent of division-of-labor

Practice differs among manufacturers of inexpensive dresses as to the use of the "section system." Sewing constitutes a major part of production activity, and under the older system each sewing machine operator did a whole series of operations on either the blouse, the skirt, or the other parts of the dress. The newer system has each operator do a much smaller piece of the work and then pass the garment to the next operator for another small seam. Thus, when work can be standardized and secured in sufficient volume, the idea of line production is applied. While not so called by people in industry, students of economics will recognize this as an example of the *extent of division-of-labor*.

Fine division-of-labor has been a common, and usually productive, policy in business operations since the establishment of pin factories in the early days of the Industrial Revolution. Recently it has faced two challenges—mechanization and automation of routine work, and "job enlargement" in which the duties of workers are deliberately diversified to give them more nearly a "whole" operation. In deciding how much emphasis to give division-of-labor, then, managers should weigh their policies regarding standardization of products, mechanization, type of labor to be employed, and style of motivation.

Extent of mechanization and automation

Some companies adopt definitive policies regarding the extent to which they will automate their operations. One manufacturer of automobile frames, for example, established a policy that operations would be mechanized from start to finish. As a result, the final product might carry the same label as appears on some food products, "Not touched by human hands." Many banks use computers to clear checks and to post to checking accounts; but the extension of such mechanization to trust accounts and noncash items is a debatable economy.

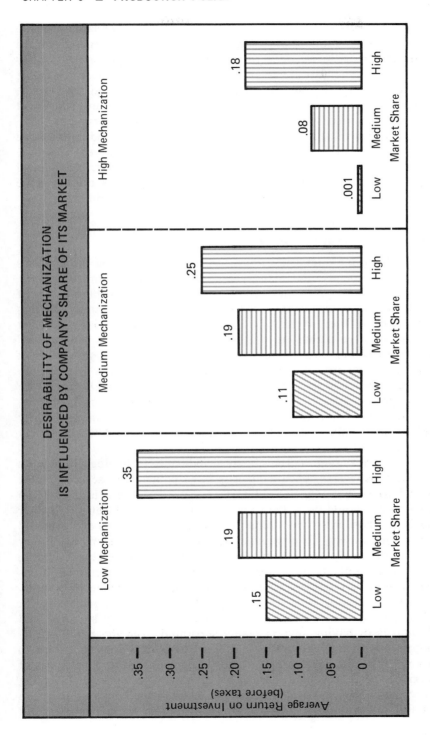

DESIRABILITY OF MECHANIZATION
IS INFLUENCED BY COMPANY'S SHARE OF ITS MARKET

High Mechanization

Medium Mechanization

Low Mechanization

Average Return on Investment
(before taxes)

This chart is based on the analysis of the experience of several hundred self-contained businesses, or "companies," conducted by PIMS (Profit Impact of Marketing Strategy) sponsored by the Marketing Science Institute. Mechanization is measured by company's ratio of fixed capital investment to sales. A company's return on investment is, of course, affected by other factors in addition to market share and capital intensity.

The rising cost of labor and the inflexibilities in the use of labor that are being introduced as a result of unionization and government regulations are leading more and more companies to mechanize wherever practical. They recognize that machines also are often inflexible, but machines are tractable and their costs do not rise after they are placed in operation. Moreover, ingenious electronic controls now can instruct some machines to make short runs of various dimensions, thereby overcoming the inflexibility.

A similar decision regarding mechanization has been followed on the large collective farms in Russia and the large farms in the United States. In the South, crop dusting from the air, flame throwers for killing weeds, mechanical harvesting equipment, and other power driven machines are creating a change that alters the plantation more than did the Thirteenth Amendment.

Size and decentralization of operating units

Large manufacturing companies have considerable choice in the size and the location of their plants. For many years, most of them assumed that the larger the plant, the more economies would be possible; transportation costs of raw materials or finished products were usually considered the limiting factors on the size of a plant. Present thinking challenges these assumptions. At least the advantages of large plants are not taken for granted.

A firm in the clothing industry has a clear-cut policy toward separation of production into several operating units. Production technology does not require large-scale operations, and the company believes the optimum size plant is one just large enough to support specialized service divisions such as accounting, personnel, and maintenance. In this case, plant location is determined primarily by nearness of consuming markets and availability of women workers—but again, not in a big city.

In some industries, such as the chemical industry, technology requires a large-scale plant. However, once a plant is large enough to use economical processes and to support specialized service divisions, there is a question whether expansion should be at the same plant or at a new location. Smaller plants, especially those in smaller communities, have advantages of closer and friendlier relations among all employees (operators and executives), easier identification of the worker with the product being produced, less bureaucracy, more face-to-face contacts in place of expensive and impersonal communication systems, executives who have first-hand knowledge of what is going on, less commuting time and expense for employees, and so forth. Moreover, modern means of communication and transportation have reduced the disadvantages of having several plants separated from the home office.

The dispersion of plants and offices out of urban centers does contribute to unemployment difficulties in depressed areas. Recognizing the seriousness of the urban crisis, several companies are experimenting with a policy of locating some production operations in city slum areas. Initially such plants usually are high-cost units, but the hope is the new ways of training and supervision will turn the plants into economically sound ventures. Again, small-sized plants are better suited to this policy.

A similar challenge to size of operating unit is occurring in the retail field. Here, traffic and transportation congestion in large cities has led department stores to open branches in suburban locations. These branches cannot, of course, offer customers the same selection of merchandise as the larger downtown stores. Several different policies are used to overcome this limitation. Some firms have their branches carry only certain lines, such as women's ready-to-wear and domestics, and do not attempt to stock all kinds of merchandise. Other companies place at least samples of a wide variety of goods at their branches and rely upon the main store to supply a full range of sizes and colors. Still other firms have only large branches and stock each with almost as wide a selection as the main store. The decision as to which of these policies to follow makes a fundamental difference in the branch operation.

The smaller company with a single place of business does not face this issue, but for larger companies a wise policy regarding the optimum size and location of operating units is of crucial importance.

HOW MUCH CAPACITY

Data from a variety of sources must be brought together to estimate the productive capacity a company needs. Sales forecasts of physical volume, policy decisions on what will be purchased instead of made, engineering estimates of machine productivity, and production plans on how equipment will be used all contribute to projections on size of plant needed. In addition and overriding such data are several central management policies regarding capacity desired. These policies deal with provisions for peak versus normal requirements, backward taper of capacity, allowance for growth, and balance of facilities.

Peak versus normal load

A completely stable level of operations is virtually impossible. All types of business activity are affected by cyclical fluctuations, and most industries experience seasonal, daily, or even hourly variations in volume of business. In addition, the demand for a company's product may increase or decrease because of wars, government regulations, inventions, floods, changing fancies of the consumer, and many other influences. Moreover, mere random distribution will lead to peaks and valleys. Management must decide whether it will provide capacity large enough to satisfy all demands during peak periods, knowing that some of this capacity must remain idle during slack periods, or whether it will maintain a smaller capacity and hope that failure to render service during peak requirements will not have unbearable consequences.

A leading example of companies that try to meet peak requirements is found in the electric utility industry. On dark winter evenings or hot summer days, we hope to have current available on the flip of a switch. Utilities have a policy of building capacity to meet such peak demands (occasionally there are some restrictions on industrial customers). Fortunately, the demand is predictable; nevertheless, the investment made for peak needs is tremendous.

Most companies follow a policy of letting the customer bear part of the peak load burden. This is obvious to the subway or bus commuter during rush hours and to the Christmas shopper on December 24. Neither the bus company nor the retail store is indifferent to crowds of customers. They provide capacity several times their volume during slack periods. The problem is one of balancing the amount of delay and inconvenience of X% of the customers versus the cost of providing the increment of capacity to meet the peak. Perhaps the policy will be to meet 90% of the requirements without delay. (When peaks occur in random fashion, queuing up theory is useful to estimate customer inconvenience.)

Other means of meeting peak capacity will, of course, be incorporated in the policy regarding maximum capacity. (a) Manufacturers of standard, durable products may manufacture stock during slack periods. This arrangement is explored in the next chapter. (b) Overtime work may be feasible for operations not already run twenty-four hours a day. (c) Obsolete or high-cost equipment may be maintained on a standby basis and placed in service just during the peak. (d) Some of the work may be subcontracted, although this is often difficult because potential subcontractors are likely to be busy during the same peak period. (e) Off-peak discounts, "mail early" campaigns, and other measures may be used to induce customers to avoid peak periods. These devices also involve extra expense and may be more or less satisfactory to customers. Clearly, policy guidance is needed to indicate the reliance on these various ways of responding to peak needs.

Backward taper of capacity

Vertically integrated companies may deliberately follow a policy of backward taper of capacity. Such firms normally perform final operations on all their finished products, but they manufacture only parts of their material requirements. A tire manufacturer may have its own textile mill in the south to weave tire fabric. This mill will probably have the capacity to supply only the minimum needs of the tire manufacturer. Additional fabric for peak requirements will be purchased from outside concerns. Such an arrangement has the obvious advantage of keeping the units in the earlier stages of production operating near their productive capacity. The feasibility of this policy depends on the presence of potential suppliers who are willing to supply fluctuating amounts of material.

Provision for growth

Experience indicates that a business enterprise does not stand still. During the last century, many executives were warranted in anticipating an increase in the volume of their business. Whether the executive who built facilities 50%

larger than needed for current operations had a clear vision into the future or was simply lucky, the decision was justified in a great many instances.

It is both expensive and inconvenient to customers and employees to have additions to facilities made at frequent intervals in piecemeal fashion. On the other hand, the financial downfall of many firms can be traced to the construction of excessive facilities, which construction absorbed a large part of the company's liquid capital and entailed annual charges that further depleted the company's resources.

Again, some middle ground is desirable if it can be arranged. Often provision for expansion may be included in the amount of land purchased and the shell of the building, while only part of the equipment is purchased initially and a work force is hired as needed. Perhaps the original plant can be used for both manufacturing and warehousing, and then a warehouse may be added later. Offices may be treated in a similar fashion. Whatever the specific scheme, the basic decision to be made by central management is how much growth to anticipate and the extent to which investment will be made now in anticipation of that growth.

Balancing capacity

Each phase of an operation—materials handling, office processing, warehousing, selling, and the like, along with their subdivisions—has its own capacity. A recurring task is trying to keep the volume of business that each subdivision can perform about equal.

Lack of balance shows up quickly in a cafeteria line when customers stack up at perhaps the sandwich counter or the cash register. The difficulty here—and on a larger scale in hospitals, plants, and offices—is that the optimum size unit for various activities differs. Several stock brokerage firms, for instance, got into serious trouble because their optimum size selling activity was larger than the conventional "back office" (paper processing) could match. Deliveries were slow, accounts were not posted daily, and errors could not be located. To avoid catastrophe, sales had to be restricted until a new system permitted enlarged capacity of the back office.

Even if balance is achieved through careful planning, it is hard to maintain. Over time, the character of work may change, small modifications will be made in the techniques employed, and people will move about. With such shifts, some one operation becomes the bottleneck. Consequently, there seems to be a neverending task of overcoming one bottleneck after another. On the other hand, there is the task of trying to reduce the expenses in those phases of operations where the workload has dropped off.

Most of the examples of problems with capacity have been in terms of physical facilities. Nevertheless, similar issues arise in stores, offices, and firms dealing with intangibles. How to deal with peak requirements, what provision to make for growth, and how to balance capacity are questions likely to arise in any kind of enterprise.

Integrated systems

Often process, capacity, and make-or-buy choices are interrelated. We must look at the total system. At MacDonald's and most other fast-food restaurants, for instance, the amount of work done on the premises, the way food is prepared, and the size and location of each outlet all fit into a whole system. Similarly, in branch banking the optimum size of a branch depends partly on the technology used, and the best technology depends on how self-sufficient the branch is to be.

A specific production system is good only when it supports company strategy. MacDonald's system would be a disaster in Maxime's in New Orleans.

New systems can be devised by combining the elements in fresh patterns, of course, but time is required to discover and learn the new harmony. For example, one-room schools, regional graded schools, and open-classroom schools each fit particular needs. However, if we decide to switch from one to another, pupils, teachers, and facilities all have to be adjusted. So in each situation we need a well-conceived policy for general guidance and consistency of action.

MAINTENANCE AND REPLACEMENT

Closely associated with issues of how much capacity should be provided and the design of an integrated system are questions of maintaining and replacing existing capacity.

Levels of maintenance

The statement ''Captain Svenson runs a tight ship'' conveys meaning to any sailor. It refers to much more than caulking the hull; everything throughout the vessel—engines, galleys, winches, and whistle—are kept in excellent running condition. Sloppiness and procrastination are not tolerated.

Similarly, a tourist driving through Kansas can easily tell when he is in a Mennonite section. The fences are mended, the barns are painted, the fence rows are weeded, and the crops look good.

Plants and offices, likewise, may be run like a ''tight ship'' or in a more casual and relaxed fashion. The level of maintenance results partly from the personal preferences of key executives, perhaps a cultural value inherited from their forebears. It may also reflect a calculated decision on the kind of maintenance that will most effectively support the other objectives and policies of the particular company. Maintenance involves expense (the Mennonite farmer in Kansas works hard and long). And the ''tight ship'' approach may be unwarranted in, say, a sawmill located on a tract that has just been cut over. Railroads appropriately vary the level of track and right-of-way maintenance on their main lines compared with a branch line soon to be abandoned. Incidentally, railroads also accelerate or hold back on deferrable maintenance depending upon their financial condition from year to year.

Preventive maintenance

Prevention of breakdowns, rather than repair after a stoppage has occurred, is now widespread practice. This is achieved by proper use and care of production facilities, coupled with regular inspections to identify potential trouble. Repair of worn or defective parts is then scheduled when it will cause the least disruption to regular operations. We are all familiar with this approach in the care of an automobile—regular greasing and oil changes, driving within prescribed limits, 5,000-mile checkups, prompt inspection of unusual noises or performance, and replacing tires when they are worn. Observing such practices enables us to depend on the automobile instead of wondering when we will have a flat tire or whether the motor will start. The same general concept can be applied to a sales organization or an accounting office, except that here we deal with people, social relationships, paper forms, and procedures.

Again, there are questions of degree. The attention given a fire engine should differ from that given a wheelbarrow; an integrated chemical plant, from that given a roller rink. If a breakdown can be repaired quickly without serious interruption, the intensity of preventive maintenance can be relaxed.

Scheduled replacement

In this day of mass production, regular replacement may be simpler than careful maintenance. The typical trouble-free life of electric bulbs, autos, water meters, and airplane engines can be measured and replacements made regardless of the apparent condition of a specific piece of equipment. Compulsory retirement of air pilots at age 60—or professors at age 70—is based on the same logic. The replaced item may be salvaged for use, or it may be rebuilt, but the aim is to make the change before performance falters.

Central management rarely becomes involved with maintenance or replacement of specific units. To maintain effectiveness and efficiency, however, senior executives need to provide guidance on how tight to run the ship, when and where to slow down or push ahead maintenance, the level of preventive maintenance desired, and the extent of scheduled replacements.

Purchasing policy, also intimately related to productive capability, is examined in the next chapter.

QUESTIONS FOR CLASS DISCUSSION

1. Legislation requiring tighter control on air, water, and other forms of pollution has limited processing options and added over 40% to the investment and operating costs of numerous manufacturing processes. New safety laws have the same effect. (a) Do you think this kind of regulation will be a more serious

obstacle to large or small businesses? (b) Who will ultimately bear the added cost? (c) Under what conditions is such regulation likely to lead to significant modification in a company's strategy?

2. (a) Which of the potential advantages and disadvantages of vertical integration discussed on pages 182-185 apply to a chain of food stores? (b) Why are most of the items carrying the private label of a retail food chain purchased instead of produced by the chain?

3. Does a trend toward increasing freedom of trade among nations add to or detract from the attractiveness of vertical integration? Illustrate in terms of a company dealing (a) in watches, (b) in paper, and (c) in men's and women's clothing.

4. The principle of "modular production"—the combination of standardized parts or modules in various ways to create varied end products—has been applied to automobile production. Explain how the same principle can be used in producing prefabricated homes. What happens to production costs under such a system?

5. (a) Mechanization in agriculture is leading to larger units of operation, just as mechanization of the textile industry did two hundred years ago. Do you foresee farming being organized and managed by large companies? (b) What are the implications of your answer to (a) for the strategy and production policy (1) of a dairy company and (2) of a meat packing company?

6. (a) What effect, if any, do you think the policy of some companies to set up smaller decentralized operating units will have on opportunities for "small business" in those industries? (b) Do you believe operating units will become larger or smaller in the following fields: (1) hospitals, (2) dry cleaning, (3) the leading industry of your own state, and (4) universities?

7. In home construction the use of specialized subcontractors and of prefabricated materials is increasing. Separate contractors are often used for excavation, masonry, plastering, roofing, painting, plumbing, tile laying, flooring, and electric wiring. Prehung doors, glazed windows, finished cabinets, finished stairs, and installed garage doors illustrate prefabrication. (a) How do you explain this trend toward buying rather than making by the general contractor? (b) How does the trend affect the contractors' cash flow, capital requirements, and potential sources of capital? (c) What are the principal services now rendered by a general contractor; that is, what has happened to his economic mission?

8. Among the possible ways of improving the ratio of actual operation to theoretical maximum capacity are: (1) not accepting peak business, (2) manufacturing to stock, and (3) buying goods or otherwise using idle capacity of another company in the same industry. To what extent can these three ways of reducing necessary capacity be used by (a) a typical electric utility plant, (b) a dress factory, (c) a restaurant, and (d) a brick factory?

9. (a) What do you think is the optimum size for an undergraduate school of business? For a university? (b) What assumptions about educational processes did you use in arriving at your answer to (a)? (c) Do assumptions regarding vertical integration affect your answer?

10. An Eastern railroad, in financial trouble, had postponed and slowed down expenditures on maintenance-of-way until it was now necessary to reduce freight train top speeds from 60 to 50 mph over the system if a sustained maintenance improvement program was not introduced immediately. Train schedules and interchanges with other roads would be considerably affected by the reduced

speed. How much could not be completely determined. A maintenance program could be carried out (1) by the old system of section gangs using temporarily hired labor or callbacks from the layoff board, or (2) in half the time by investing heavily in mechanized equipment that would have to be financed by borrowing at high interest rates. Detailed quantitative studies had led to the qualitative conclusions just stated. What would you recommend?

CASE 9 / Fayette Grain & Produce Co.

Chicken production is big business. Small barnyard flocks are as obsolete as the horse and buggy. Companies such as the Fayette Grain & Produce Co. each raise 50 to 100 million birds every year. These chickens have genetically controlled ancestors, eat a menu calculated by an electronic computer, grow under the close surveillance of veterinarians, and reach the market in refrigerated trailer trucks ready to put in the oven. The U.S. annual volume is 3 billion birds.

Improvements in production efficiency far exceed those in most industries. Over the past thirty years the average size of a broiler bird (the primary type of bird sold as meat) has increased from 2.8 pounds to 3.8 pounds, while production time has dropped from 12-14 weeks to 8-10 weeks. Meanwhile, the pounds of feed needed to create a pound of chicken declined from 4 to 2.2. Mortality rates have dropped from 10-20% to less than 6%. And, manhours required for 1,000 broilers decreased from 250 to 15!

These production improvements have contributed substantially to the increase in per capita U.S. broiler consumption from 0.5 pounds in 1934 to 43 pounds in 1974 and a projected consumption of 60 pounds in 2000.

Fayette Grain & Produce Co. made its start in the grain and feed business in northern Alabama and then moved into chicken production as a way of increasing its profit margin on feed. Now Fayette has breeder flocks that lay the eggs, hatcheries, contracts with 700 farmers who raise the chickens, and processing plants. Of course, Fayette's feed mills supply the feed for both breeder flocks and the farmers who raise the broilers.

Competition in the poultry industry is extremely keen. New technology and new strains of birds are rapidly adopted by alert competitors, with the result that profit margins are narrow. But an overriding problem is the sharp fluctuations in cost of feed and in selling prices of dressed birds. Although costs and selling prices tend to move up or down together, the movements are by no means synchronized nor of the same amplitude, and profit margins may be squeezed. For example, during the acute grain shortage of 1974, feed prices rose so much that variable costs of broilers exceeded the selling price. The situation as of July was as shown at the top of the following page.

Fayette's costs are slightly better than the industry figures just cited. And, there will be short periods when prices are high relative to costs. Nevertheless, Fayette must find ways to improve and stabilize its profit margin. The following possibilities in the production area have been suggested.

Improved technology. Fayette already has moved aggressively into automation. It has large automated hatcheries, one of which can hatch over 500,000 chicks weekly. Its four

Estimate of industry averages by *Cargill Market Letter*

	Per pound of chicken
Feed costs:	
1.43 pounds of corn	8.51¢
.77 pounds of coybean meal	6.44
Supplemental nutrients	2.00
Total feed costs	16.95¢
Chick cost	4.50
Out-of-pocket overhead: fuel, medication, grower payment, hauling, administration	5.00
Cost per pound gross weight	26.45¢
Adjustment for yield of finished product from gross weight: 73%	36.23
Processing cost	8.50
Freight to Chicago	1.25
Variable cost delivered in Chicago	45.98¢
Broiler selling price (futures)	40.95
Gross margin	−5.03¢

processing plants each have a capacity of over 7,000 birds per hour. The feed mills are tied into a computer that calculates the optimum proportion of ingredients based on nutritional needs and current prices. Raising of chicks is done by farmers who provide the houses, equipment, and labor—while Fayette provides chicks, feed, veterinary service, and other advice.

In each of these operations the plants appear to be at optimum size and utilizing the latest techological developments. Fayette might raise its own birds instead of using the present "grow out" system with farmers; however, the farmers handle the chickens on a marginal labor basis, and the advantage of Fayette having its own employees do this is not clear. Equipment manufacturers are working on further automation of processing equipment, which Fayette can buy when and if it is perfected.

Unique breeder stock. Fayette could extend its activities farther back in the chicken-egg-chicken sequence. At present, additions to its breeder flocks (which each year lay the 75,000,000 eggs that become broiler chickens) are purchased either as chicks or as eggs. It is the suppliers of these chicks and eggs who do the genetic work of developing strains that grow rapidly, have a high proportion of meat, are disease-resistant, and consume a small amount of feed per pound of growth.

Companies engaged in this early stage of chicken production work closely with the government-supported research organizations—usually at state universities—and make their results available to everyone in the industry. Fayette might do its own R&D genetic work with the hope of developing its own superior strain, which would give it at least a temporary production cost advantage.

Computer forecasts of prices. Ernest Doan, head of Fayette's computer unit, suggests that a forecasting model be designed which would predict feed prices, broiler prices, and profit margins. Then Fayette could expand or shut down its output depending upon the profit outlook.

Many studies have been made of factors affecting prices of agricultural products. For example, the aggregate demand for meat of all kinds is known to fluctuate with consumers' real income, though with some "stickiness" as eating habits become traditional. Also, something is known about consumer switches between kinds of meat. The demand for and the price of chicken, for instance, depend to some extent upon the price of beef and pork. Factors affecting the price of feed are more numerous because the world supply and demand for grain are involved.[1]

The lags in adjustment to changed conditions are significant. Calves born today will not reach the market for about two years. Although grain and chicken production cycles are shorter, the human and physical resources committed to the production of a particular product can be transferred to another product only after a lapse of time. Such inertia affects short-run profit margins. And for Fayette's purposes, these short-run highs and lows in margin are very important.

Hedging in futures markets. Futures contracts for various grains have been bought and sold for many years. More recently, a futures market for broilers has been established. Emil Hampel, treasurer of Fayette, proposes that the company hedge on both markets, as necessary, to avoid unexpected squeezes in its profit margin. The idea is that whenever the spread between feed prices and broiler prices is attractive, Fayette would buy grain futures and sell broiler futures. Then it could convert each contract into physical deliveries in its normal operations without being concerned about the spot prices on the particular dates when the physical transactions occurred.

Andrew Crawford, president, is not enthusiastic about this approach. "There is no way futures can make our business profitable when broiler prices are low relative to feed costs. And when the margin is right, any efficient producer should make a profit. Sure, we occasionally get hurt when prices drop while we have an inventory of chickens eating high-cost feed—as happened in 1974—but we are in close touch with the markets and have a pretty good sense of which way prices will go. Besides, we can't shut down plants and give grow-out contractors no business for a year, and then have an effective organization ready to produce 80 million broilers the next year."

Transfer of know-how to catfish. Catfish are now being raised in freshwater ponds, and during any overall food scarcity a good demand for fillets and other end-products exists. The structure of this new industry is similar to the broiler industry. A central operator provides baby fish, feed, and advice to farmers who create the ponds and raise the fish; then the central operator takes the adult fish to its processing plants for cleaning, etc., and final sale. Raising catfish has two advantages over raising broilers: (1) Less feed (mostly grains) is needed per pound of finished product. (2) Once grown, catfish can be kept in the ponds with very little additional feed, whereas adult chickens eat a lot; this gives more flexibility in the timing of harvesting.

Although the catfish is a more efficient converter of grain than the chicken, the human inputs to catfish-raising are still on a relatively small scale and consequently less efficient. Fayette clearly understands the elements of chicken production, and the suggestion has been made that this know-how might be profitably applied to the raising of catfish.

Required: What do you recommend Fayette Grain & Produce Co. do to lower its production costs and improve its profit margins?

---

[1] The outline for industry analysis presented in Chapter 3 suggests additional factors that should be included in a forecasting model.

PROCUREMENT POLICY

MAKE-OR-BUY SUPPLIES AND SERVICES

Every company uses a variety of supplies and services—paper, soap, transportation in and out, telephone, electronic computing, packaging, heat, power, and many other items. Time and again the question arises of whether to make or buy these supplies and services. The following examples suggest the nature of the problem.

Production of containers and printed forms

All firms must decide whether to purchase or manufacture printing and packing supplies such as cans, cartons, and seals. Some companies have a small printing shop in which they print their own forms, circulars, and notices, and do other job printing. While this practice is convenient, a single firm rarely has enough printing of a similar type to justify the most economical machine methods. Consequently, the wiser policy usually is to have such printing done by an outside firm that has a large number of customers.

A similar situation exists in connection with packing boxes. For example, the Taft Pharmaceutical Company, which had its own box shop, needed boxes in a considerable range of shapes and sizes for the packing of its various products. Because of the variety, several different machines were needed; however, most of these machines were used only part of the time. While the boxes made in the local shop were satisfactory, an independent check showed that it would be less expensive for the company to purchase boxes from a manufacturer specializing in this type of work. This also gave the company more flexibility to shift to plastic containers.

On the other hand, a leading manufacturer of prepared breakfast foods concluded, after an exhaustive study of the relative costs of manufacturing and of buying packages and cartons, that a considerable saving would result from its own manufacture of these products. In this instance large quantities of identical boxes and cartons were required, and the cereal company was able to install as efficient machinery as the independent box companies. Furthermore, under this arrangement the company was able to exercise direct control over all phases of production and to coordinate under the same roof the manufacture of the packing boxes with the packing of the final product. This same company, however, decided that its job printing could be done more economically by an outside concern.

Company power plants

Larger companies must decide whether they will produce their own power and light or buy all their electric current from a public utility. The policy sometimes followed in this case is to manufacture the minimum load and to purchase from the public utility only for the purpose of meeting peak requirements. Thus, the company plant can be operated continuously and the burden of fluctuating demand can be shifted to the public utility. The feasibility of such a plan depends, of course, upon the rates charged by the public utility. If the peak demand for a particular company occurs at the same time that other utility customers have peak demands, the rates charged are likely to be high.

Emergency power supply for hospitals, alarm systems, dairy farms, and the like is quite a different issue. For safety, in-house generators or batteries are needed.

Guides to make-or-buy policy

The following line of analysis provides an answer to most make-or-buy questions relating to supplies and services.

1. Does a dependable outside source exist? If the answer is "no," then we presume that our own production is best unless unforeseen obstacles arise. For instance, a cement plant in Chile has its own foundry and machine shop because no reliable source of repair parts is within reach. Similarly, most large industrial plants in Argentina have their own power plants because public power is unreliable.

2. When a dependable outside source does exist, we will use it unless a strong case can be made for not doing so. The reasons for this preference include simplifying the total managerial burden, focusing executive attention where major opportunities lie, reducing capital investment, retaining flexibility regarding sources, and—in competitive markets—gaining some of the economies that suppliers serving several customers will obtain.

3. Possible reasons for making exceptions to the preference for buying, just stated in (2), are: (a) Coordination with outside sources would be very cumbersome; for example, although office buildings frequently contract for janitor service and window washing, industrial plants rarely do so because cleaning up is intimately related to plant operations. (b) A large volume of a uniform item would result in unusually low costs. (c) The supply source is unwilling to provide special services (for example, speedy delivery or unusual sizes) we desire.

This approach at least puts the burden of proof on the executive who suggests deviating from the main activities on which the firm is staking its success.

SELECTION OF VENDORS

Regardless of how a company resolves its problems of vertical integration and of make-or-buy supplies, some sorts of goods must be purchased. The manufacturer must buy raw materials and factory supplies, the retailer must buy finished goods, even the professional firm must buy office supplies. In most businesses it is possible to purchase satisfactory products from several vendors; these may be local or foreign. This raises the question of whether purchasing from several vendors is wiser than concentrating the business on only one or two. Even after this policy is settled, the type of vendor that will be the most satisfactory source for materials has to be settled.

Number of vendors

The number of suppliers of at least the essential products purchased by a firm should receive careful attention. Entire operations of the firm can be jeopardized if this issue is not wisely handled.

Allocating buying to secure vendor's services. A school supply jobber, for instance, followed the practice for a number of years of buying from as many different manufacturers as possible so that the firm name might be widely known. The company later became involved in financial difficulties and regretted its policy of using a large number of vendors. The purchases it made from any one manufacturer were not important enough to that manufacturer to justify granting special credit terms, and each vendor sought to collect bills promptly. Had this firm concentrated its purchases to a greater extent, it might have induced its vendors to be more lenient in making collections during the period of financial stress.

Advantages and dangers of concentration. A few companies that buy large quantities of merchandise concentrate their purchases to such an extent that they buy the entire output of the supplier. By doing so, they are able to secure favorable prices because the manufacturer is relieved of all selling cost and is able to concentrate its production operations on just those commodities desired by its one customer. The danger in this practice is that the manufacturer may fail to make delivery because of labor troubles, lack of capital, fire, or some other catastrophe, thus leaving the company deprived of its supply of products at a time when they are sorely needed.

A large mail-order house that was buying the entire output of a refrigerator plant guarded against this danger to some degree by having at the plant its own representative who watched accounting records and was familiar with plant operations. Such a representative could warn the mail-order house of any impending difficulties. Another large firm followed the policy of buying no more than 25% of its requirements of any one product from the same manufacturer. If for any reason something happened to one of these sources of supply, the company would be able to continue to get at least 75% of its requirements from its other vendors. When buying abroad, use of several alternative sources gives protection against political interruptions—as petroleum companies using Middle East crude oil well know.

Many firms follow a policy that seeks to gain the advantages of both concentration of purchases and multiple vendors. They find that buying most of their needs of a particular material from one source is desirable; the quality, price, delivery service, or some other factor makes concentration clearly the best arrangement. So, they give 70% to 80% of their business to this one vendor. The remaining part of the business is divided among several other suppliers. In this manner, business relations are established, specification problems are met and resolved, and the way is prepared for much larger purchases at a later date. Placing these small orders with several vendors is probably more expensive than buying all requirements from the chief source, but it serves two important purposes: (1) if a strike, fire, or other catastrophe hits the main supplier, the firm can shift to other suppliers much more quickly than it could if no relationship had been established; and (2) the main supplier is "kept on its toes" because the buyer is in close touch with the market and in a position to shift to other suppliers if the price, quality, or service from the main source does not continue to be the best.

Buying distress merchandise. Some retail stores appeal to their customers primarily on the basis of price, and in order to make a profit they continually seek to buy merchandise at "distress" prices. These stores usually offer to pay cash for merchandise, and they are not particularly concerned about being able to secure additional products from the same company. Such stores will deal with any vendor who has merchandise to offer for sale at a reasonable price, and they are continually "shopping around" for more favorable terms. Although such a policy appears to be good for companies operating on a purely price or cut-rate basis, most concerns have learned by experience that it is preferable to cooperate with vendors. A cooperative relationship will not be disrupted by either party because of apparent temporary advantages that may be obtained from time to time under special conditions.

Factors determining number of vendors. These illustrations show that there are both advantages and disadvantages to limiting the number of vendors from whom purchases are made. It is often necessary to balance the advantages of better service and quantity discounts that can be secured by concentrating business with a few vendors against the disadvantages of possible failure of supply and the passing up of occasional bargain merchandise. The problem often resoves itself into the following questions:

1. Can a limited number of vendors supply the variety of products required?
2. How much special service and price concession will result from concentration?
3. How important is such service to the purchaser?
4. Is the company too dependent upon any one company for materials?

Type of vendors

The type of vendors selected by a company will depend on the company's requirements in regard to quality, service, reciprocity, and price.

Importance attached to quality. Selection of vendors by a company will be influenced, in part, by the quality of the products that it wishes. Thus a publishing house, desiring all its books to be made of a high-quality material, buys only from mills that make paper of dependable quality. Although the paper is purchased according to detailed specifications, the company is aware of the difficulty every paper mill has in controlling the quality of its product. The publishing house therefore prefers to pay somewhat higher prices to those mills that have a reputation for exercising care in maintaining the quality of their product.

Even a product that is highly standardized and that has a recognized market price may be purchased from one vendor rather than another in order to secure certain intangible qualities. Operators of textile mills, for instance, point out that there is considerable variation in the way raw cotton of identical staple and grade will work up in cloth. Consequently, when a textile mill discovers that cotton coming from one region through a given broker is more easily handled on their equipment than cotton from any other region, that mill will try to concentrate its future purchases on cotton coming from that particular section.

Service of vendors. Vendors may be selected because of the service they render their customers. For example, companies manufacturing computers, duplicators, and other types of office equipment often give their customers a great deal of aid in designing office forms and in establishing new systems. Most of these companies also maintain an extensive repair service. If a machine should break down, it may be quickly repaired without serious interruption in the work of the office using the equipment.

The importance of such service became striking in Brazil when that market was flooded with relatively inexpensive office equipment of German manufacture. The machines had entered Brazil under a barter agreement in which Brazil exchanged coffee and other raw materials for a specified quantity of machinery from Germany. Inadequate provision had been made for servicing the German machines, however. Consequently, when one of these machines broke down, it was both expensive and time-consuming to get it back into working order. As a result, many of the office managers were turning to more expensive American machines because of the repair service maintained by the American manufacturers.

Under some conditions promptness of delivery is a controlling factor in the selection of vendors. This has been one of the primary reasons why small steel companies have been able to secure in their local territories business that otherwise might have gone to the big steel companies. With standardized products and uniform prices prevailing in the industry, such special services as delivery often become controlling influences. The large companies have recently given more recognition to this factor and have spent substantial funds in an effort to expedite the handling of customers' orders.

Reciprocity. Under special circumstances vendors are selected on the basis of reciprocity. Thus, railroads are careful to place orders with concerns that are in a position to route a large quantity of freight over their lines. Sometimes the reciprocity may be a three-cornered deal. For instance, a Great Lakes steamship company decided to place a large order for motors with a particular manufacturer as a favor to a pig-iron producer. The pig-iron producer shipped large quantities of ore and could therefore demand favors from the steamship company in exchange for a contract to transport ore. To complete the circle, the pig-iron producer used its controls over the order for motors in selling pig-iron to the motor manufacturer. Hence, each of the three concerns selected vendors with an eye to the indirect effect such election would have on sales.

Formal reciprocity agreements have been challenged legally as a restraint of trade, but this aspect is very cloudy. Much more common is the objection of "professional" purchasing agents. In fact, a policy on reciprocity is often necessary to keep peace between the purchasing department and the sales department.

Role of price. Thus far, no mention has been made of price in connection with the type of vendors. Prices for many products are uniform, and for other products the differences are not of sufficient importance to offset such factors as quality and special service. It should be clear, however, that price is an ever-present consideration, and if for some reason one vendor charges higher prices than another, the former is automatically eliminated unless there is some special reason for dealing with him. As already noted, the significance of differences in prices depends partly upon the emphasis that the company buying the material gives to price in reselling the material, and also upon the importance of that particular product to the total cost of the company.

Gifts and friendship. Especially when large purchases are to be made, gifts and lavish entertainment may be offered to the person who selects the vendor. In its gross form this is clearly bribery. But the line is hard to draw; for instance, is a free lunch unacceptable? While not so strict as government on rules regarding favors, most companies do have a clear-cut policy forbidding the acceptance of any significant gifts from vendors.

More subtle is the question of friendship. Business relationships naturally lead to numerous contacts and mutual dependence—as we noted in Chapter 1. Friendship often grows out of such contacts. And cooperation between friends typically flows in both directions. In the United States the principle that we assume should guide business relations between friends is clear enough: cooperate to the hilt as long as the interests of the two companies are compatible (and such action is legal), but when interests conflict always give one's own company uncompromising priority. This norm is so widely understood it is rarely stated as a policy.

Summary regarding selection of vendors

In selecting vendors a company is responding to the *sales appeal* of the numerous companies desiring to sell merchandise of the type used by the company. The point of view, however, is essentially different because the purchasing company is concerned only with its own specific problems and has no interest in the sales activities of the vendor unless these activities are of some value to it. There are also a number of questions, such as the number of vendors, that do not have an exact counterpart for the seller. The more important factors that should be considered in making vendor selections are indicated in the following table:

Factors Influencing Vendor Selection

Capacity and Willingness of Vendor to Meet Company Needs	General Characteristics of Desirable Vendors	Factors Limiting the Choice
Quality of product: Specifications Dependability Services offered: Delivery Technical aid Repair Credit terms Guarantees Adjustments Price: Competitive level Inclination to squeeze Protection on changes	Size of vendor: Interest in our business Financial stability Geographic location: Support of "local" industry Dispersion of risks Manufacturer *vs.* jobber Maintenance of alternative sources: Divide equally One main source, others minor	Reciprocity Time and expense of locating and dealing with new vendors Habit and conservatism: potential "headaches" in new relationship Friendship and loyalty Willingness of using departments to try new vendors

Company policy is needed to show which of these factors should be given primary consideration and which should be disregarded.

COORDINATION OF PRODUCTION, PURCHASING, AND SALES

Even after policies regarding integration, capacity, processes, procurement of supplies, and selection of vendors are clear, a cluster of problems on *timing* of purchasing and production remain. We are concerned here not with specific programs—a topic explored in Chapter 21—but with several underlying guides that must be established before programs can be built. As a basis for coordination of purchasing and production with sales, central management should set policies regarding:

1. Procurement "to order" or for stock.
2. Minimum inventories.
3. Size of production run or purchase order.
4. Stabilization of production operations.
5. Adjustments in inflationary periods.

Procurement "to order" or for stock

The made-to-order policy. Coordination of procurement with sales is accomplished in some industries by buying or making goods only if the customer's order is already received. The purchase of raw materials and supplies is not undertaken and production is not started until the order is actually in hand. Manufacturers of heavy machinery—or space ships—almost always follow such a make-to-order policy.

Other companies, such as producers of radio and television broadcasting equipment, make finished products only "on order"; but, in fact, they produce many parts and even subassemblies for stock. Then when an order is received, only the final assembly operation has to be done according to customer specification.

Concerns manufacturing high-class upholstered furniture may follow the same policy to even a lesser extent. In this industry, it is customary to manufacture the furniture up to the point where the upholstery is to be put on. This final covering is not applied until a specific order is received from a customer designating the kind of cover desired.

While a policy of making-to-order does reduce inventory risks and gives the customer just what he wants, it also has serious drawbacks. Delivery is inevitably slow and costs tend to be high because mass production techniques cannot be fully utilized.

Carrying stock. The majority of products are purchased or produced long before the customer's order is received. Orders are filled from inventory already on hand. This is true of most of the products that we, as ultimate customers, purchase, and it is also true of a great many products purchased by industrial concerns.

A compromise policy is followed by some firms that carry only standard products in stock. If their customers want an article that is not standard, the merchandise will be purchased or produced according to the customer's choice. For example, a shop dealing in dinnerware and glassware may carry an open stock of certain popular patterns. Should a customer wish other patterns, the manager of the shop will be glad to order them from the factory.

Since there are various degrees of making-to-order and of carrying stock—as the preceding examples show—and the degree affects purchasing, production, and selling activities, management should provide policy guidance. This is not a decision to be made from the viewpoint of any one department alone.

Minimum inventory

If stock is to be carried, a company must establish some general guide to assist the purchasing and production departments in determining how much inventory to have on hand at any one time. Let us look first at the more mechanistic aspects of the problem—ordering points, size of production runs, and purchase quantities—and then note two main reasons for further adjustments, namely, stabilization and speculation on price changes.

How low should inventories be permitted to go before they are reordered? Each retail store in a modern grocery chain, for instance, is expected to maintain a minimum of all items regularly sold. Since the store gets frequent deliveries of additional merchandise, the minimum may be only a week's supply. In contrast, because of slow turnover the minimum inventory carried by many independent furniture stores is equal to a full year's sales.

Manufacturing firms must establish some general policy for minimum inventory for both finished goods and raw materials. Thus, a manufacturer of rugs had a policy of carrying finished merchandise only at the beginning of each selling season and gave no assurance to its customers that it would carry an inventory throughout the year. On the other hand, it did wish to carry a minimum stock of raw materials so as to avoid possible delay in production operations. Here the policy was to carry approximately three months' supply of yarn and other raw materials.

A general rule for finished merchandise is that the stock level at which replacements will be ordered should approximately equal the sales of that merchandise during the period required for replenishment. Thus, for stock that can be replenished within two weeks, the reordering point would be approximately two weeks' sales. If it takes three months to procure new inventory, then the minimum at which orders should be placed would be correspondingly higher. The same general idea can be carried back into the inventory of raw materials. Of course the rule does require estimates of future sales and of the speed of procurement, and these may be quite unstable.

Since the sale or the use of stock on hand will continue during the period of replenishment, it is customary to add a reasonable margin of safety to any such reordering point as a protection against possible contingencies. The size of the safety margin will depend upon the likelihood of delays in getting replacements and the seriousness of the delay to production operations or customer service. These considerations lead many firms to follow a policy of carrying a minimum inventory much higher than strict interpretation of the replenishment rule requires.

Size of production run or purchase order

When reordering is necessary, how much should be ordered? Primary considerations are economical production runs in a company's own plant or quantity discounts offered by vendors due to economic production runs in the vendor's plant or warehouse.

A company producing printed plastic bags for bakeries and candy companies, for example, found that the cost of preparing plates, setting up plates in the printing presses, threading the proper weight of plastic film through the presses, and making other preparations necessary for actual printing was often a substantial part of the total expense incurred on small orders. It was found that labor and idle machine charges were often $150 per order, and when this cost had to be charged to a few hundred bags, the cost per unit was quite high. If the order was for several thousand, the expense could be spread over the entire order and thus the cost per unit could be lowered.

To meet this situation, the company often printed more bags than were actually on order by the customer, thereby securing a low production cost per unit. The extra stock was then held until the customer placed a reorder. This policy substantially increased the company's inventory but was the only way that the company could secure satisfactory production costs.

Policy regarding size of purchase orders, like policy regarding size of production runs, may be stated in total quantities or in so many weeks' or months' supply. Then order standards for specific items may be computed, giving effect to economy of large lots, cost of storage, perishability and obsolescence, and related factors.

If the time at which sales orders will be received (or supplies needed) can be predicted with reliability, at least for a frequency distribution, and dollar values can be attached to carrying inventories, to savings on large quantities, and to loss resulting from failure to accept or deliver a sales order—then minimum inventories, ordering points, and size of production runs or purchase orders can be calculated statistically. Even then, however, the judgment of central management is needed to establish safety margins on receipt of goods and to evaluate the seriousness of disappointing a customer. These judgments are often stated as policies. Moreover, management may choose to modify statistically optimum schedules (a) to stabilize production or (b) to adjust to price changes.

Stabilization of production

The business of every company fluctuates by seasons and by cycles. For example, a manufacturer of electric blankets may find that it sells two thirds of its products in the last half of each calendar year, and a manufacturer of gloves may find that it sells 45% of its products in the last three months of the year. Even articles in daily use, such as cosmetics, have a seasonal fluctuation.

Production for stock. Faced with such a seasonal fluctuation, a company may decide to synchronize procurement with its sales volume so that it will not carry inventory in excess of its sales needs at any time. Most women's glove manufacturers, for instance, do not attempt to produce very far ahead of the season in which they will sell their gloves. Frequent style changes may make gloves produced in advance of the season unsalable, or salable only at a reduced price. But, unfortunately, seasonal production means unstable employment.

Other firms produce at approximately a level rate throughout the year. This means that they accumulate during the seasons of slack sales an inventory to satisfy demand during the peak periods. One of the leading manufacturers of skis follows this policy to avoid having an idle plant during part of the year and to keep a group of efficient workmen employed the entire year.

Theoretically, a similar policy of production stabilization could be applied to cyclical fluctuations. But few companies have financial strength to do more than stretch out a product for a few months while looking for a prompt recovery in sales. (The massive stabilization programs undertaken by the federal government for agricultural products involve resources far greater than any company possesses.)

Any company that considers producing during slack periods for sales in later boom times must reckon with obsolescence, deterioration, storage costs, and financing. Fully as important is the ability to forecast the duration and the amplitudes of downswings and upswings. Even seasonal drops are difficult to interpret during the downswing because a manager usually cannot tell *at the time* how much of the change is random, trend, or seasonal. So, an important aspect of a policy to stabilize production is how long production will be maintained above sales—or how large an inventory will be built up—in the face of below-normal sales.

Other ways of dealing with fluctuations. Production in excess of demand during slack seasons is not the only way companies have sought to adjust to fluctuations in sales volume. We have already seen that some companies have been successful in adding to their line products that have complementary seasonal fluctuations. The combination of the TV and electric refrigerator business was among the illustrations cited.

Subcontracting at times of peak demand has been used by some companies in place of a temporary expansion in their own work force. This is not always practical, however, since subcontractors are likely to be busy just at the times when the prime contractor has his peak load.

The automobile industry changed the date for bringing out new annual models from the spring to the fall in an effort to level out seasonal fluctuations. A large number of people prefer to buy new cars in the spring of the year. When the new models were brought out at this time, there was a double incentive to buy during the months of March through June. By changing the time of introducing the new models to the fall, the companies were able to attract customers in the fall of the year who otherwise might have purchased in the spring.

These methods, like almost all stabilization devices available to private enterprise, apply best to seasonal fluctuations and have only limited application to cyclical changes.

Adjustment in inflationary periods

Many companies adjust their purchasing and production schedules in anticipation of changes in prices of raw materials and finished products. When price increases are anticipated, goods will be procured in excess of immediate requirements; and when declines are forecast, inventories will be reduced. In this way the companies hope to secure additional profits. This practice is so hazardous—and yet in inflationary periods so necessary—that the elements involved should be separately evaluated.

Total inventory position. Exposure to inventory price risks involves commitments as well as physical goods in the warehouse. Firm orders to purchase entail just as much price risk as goods in-house. On the other hand, firm orders from customers with fixed prices are an offset against goods on hand. The amount of exposure is the net total of these commitments and goods on hand. In fact, a company making products such as aircraft, which are ordered several years in advance, may have a negative inventory exposure. When we establish policy regarding inventory price risk, the focus should be on net exposure.

Case against speculation. There are three main reasons why merchandising, manufacturing, and nonprofit enterprises should not attempt to make an extra profit from varying the size of their inventory in an attempt to buy-low-and-sell-high. First, it detracts from the primary function of the enterprise, and most managements have all they can do to accomplish their primary mission. Second, every enterprise is exposed to a wide variety of risks that cannot be avoided; it is desirable to try to minimize these risks rather than add others. Third, if someone within the company has exceptional price forecasting ability, he should resign and concentrate all his talent on speculation. Perhaps he can join a trading firm where speculation is part of the mission.

This injunction against speculation is generally accepted. But it applies to the more extreme situations, and it leaves unresolved a lot of inventory variation that most managers insist is not "speculation." These remaining price risks arise directly from performing the regular business. The question is how to deal with them prudently.

Assuring uninterrupted operations. Availability of goods often fluctuates with price. At times of rising prices, demand is brisk and it may take twice as long to get delivery as is necessary when business is dull. Consequently, purchasing agents who are responsible for having an adequate supply of inventory on hand may buy ahead in boom times just to make sure that they get goods on time. On the downswing, prompt deliveries are easier to get and the purchasing agents may safely cut back their inventory.

Thus, in times of material shortages—and these are likely to occur during a period of general inflation—a company quite properly protects itself by building inventory. However, practical limits arise because some inventory may become obsolete—due to changes in style or engineering specifications—or may deteriorate as do many food products and sensitive chemicals. Also storage and other carrying costs may be quite high. These factors place an outer limit on the physical supply it is practical to hold. But within these limits, inventory accumulation is desirable if it is needed to assure uninterrupted operation.

This kind of inventory buildup is not really an anticipation of price changes. The underlying reasons for expansion and contraction are so entwined with price fluctuations, however, that they are difficult to separate. The motive is availability of supply, but an accompanying side effect is exposure to inventory price fluctuation.

Known risks of not buying. Interwoven with problems of having inventory when needed are adjustments to "known" price changes. Sometimes suppliers announce price increases in advance of an effective date. Clearly, when this occurs, a company should buy its future requirements as far ahead as it is practical to store goods.

More common are situations where the odds are, say, 80% that prices will rise in the near future. For instance, the supply may be known to be tight, a labor contract providing higher wages has just been signed, prices of competing products have already gone up, or the world price may have firmed. And there is certainty the price will not fall in the near future. Under these conditions a firm is assuming greater inventory price risks from not buying than from buying.

Limits on exposure. Inventory buildup for the two reasons just discussed—assurance of uninterrupted operations and reduction of "known" risks—should be subjected to one other influence. A company's total risk posture may place constraints on the amount of inventory risk assumed. Overall business uncertainties usually set a time span beyond which it is dangerous for a company to cover its specific needs. Just as we consumers don't buy an oil filter replacement that our car is likely to need two years hence, there are limits on how far ahead a company has full confidence in its detailed projections. In turbulent periods the possibilities of an international monetary crisis, war, overthrow of the government, drastic government intervention, or comparable events may make firm commitments beyond six months unwise. Under more favorable conditions management may feel reasonably confident about the shape of events for a year or more ahead. Regardless, then, of specific expectations about a particular material or part, management often sets a general horizon beyond which commitments should not go.

Likewise, as we shall see in Chapter 13, the scarcity of capital may require a company to set some limits on the total sums tied up in inventory.

Summarization. A strong case can be made against out-and-out speculation on inventories—except for a trading company organized for such a purpose. Nevertheless, especially in periods of inflation, adjustment of inventories in anticipation of external shortages and price shifts may be prudent. An approach to this troublesome issue is (a) to focus on inventory necessary to assure uninterrupted operations—within the practical limits of holding such inventory. In addition, (b) inventory may be built up when the price outlook makes the risk of not doing so quite high. Here, again, the inventory is confined to future operating needs. Finally, (c) the accumulations for either (a) and/or (b) should be restricted to a general commitment horizon and financial allocation set by central management.

Conclusion regarding timing of procurement

In producing and in buying, wide differences exist in anticipating consumers' actions or waiting until orders are in hand. Many companies carry larger stocks than are required for customer service to secure economic production runs or to obtain discounts from vendors. Sometimes the procurement of merchandise is adjusted in an effort to stabilize production operations, but more frequently it is adjusted in anticipation of price changes or to assure adequate supply.

The more important factors that an executive should consider in dealing with such timing issues include:

1. Customer requirements for specially designed merchandise or for prompt deliveries of standard merchandise.
2. Economies possible from larger production runs.
3. Economies that may be secured from level production, including maintenance of a well-trained labor force, more complete utilization of facilities, and possible reductions in tax burdens.
4. Expenses of carrying goods in inventory, including the storage charges, the financial cost, the insurance expense, and the deterioration or obsolescence of merchandise.
5. Accuracy with which price changes may be predicted.
6. Accuracy of prediction of the volume and nature of products demanded at a subsequent period of time.

This list, though incomplete, does indicate that the timing of procurement is a complex problem. Central management should provide policy guidance in this area because actions will affect the company's ability to render good customer service, influence its operating costs, change its circulating capital requirements, and bring about special losses due to adjustment in inventory valuation.

SUMMARY

Every business enterprise will face many of the production and procurement issues discussed in the last two chapters. There is the inevitable question of "make-or-buy," and this applies to the whole range of finished products, parts, supplies, and raw materials used.

Production processes must be selected, and here policy regarding division of labor, automation, size of plant, and process research is needed.

Then comes the issue of how much capacity. Plans for meeting peak loads should be set up. Provision for growth, balance between departments, and backward taper of capacity also have to be fitted into the general scheme. Guidance on the level of maintenance and on replacement should be correlated with product line, customer service, and financial policy.

For goods to be purchased, policy dealing with the number and the types of vendors is necessary. And there are basic issues of when and how much to buy and to produce.

In this array of issues we are concerned with the company's basic strategy for generating the goods and the services that its marketing strategy requires. Each part of the total production plan should support the other and also should be consistent with personnel and financial policy—to which we now turn our attention.

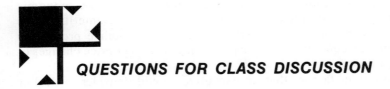

QUESTIONS FOR CLASS DISCUSSION

1. In all large cities, firms selling computer time have sprung up. The services of most kinds of computers are available; consequently, a company need not buy or rent its own computer in order to be able to use one. If you were advising the president of a company regarding the advisability of having its own computer(s), what factors would you consider?

2. The manager of a local lumber and building supply firm explains: "We concentrate our purchases for each type of product that we buy with a single supplier. And we let the supplier know that we are relying on him and giving him all the local representation we can. In return we hope to get more extended credit terms and to receive our proportionate allocation of products that are in short supply. Of course, we really are small stuff to most vendors. Our total sales are only about $1,000,000 annually. We buy from over one hundred companies, but only from about a dozen of those in fairly significant amounts. Nobody would pay any attention to us if we spread our purchases around." (a) Do you think this policy is wise for most small companies? (b) At what stage in growth or under what conditions should a company shift to multiple sources?

3. Which of the factors listed in the table on page 204 do you think should carry the most weight in selecting vendors by (a) an electric public utility? (b) a hospital?

(c) the operator of a group of 20 overnight cabins—now called a "motel"? (d) a city such as Denver, Colorado?

4. Several laws have been proposed that would make reciprocity in buying illegal. This would be a facet of antitrust legislation designed to maintain free and open competition. Opponents of such proposals contend that a business firm should be permitted to favor its friends if it so desires. Do you believe such legislation is desirable? Give reasons supporting your position.

5. Many of us regularly buy most of our gasoline from one service station; it is easier and more convenient to do so. (a) At times of gasoline shortage do you think the service station should give preferred treatment to its regular customers? (b) Should all government-sponsored rationing plans prohibit preferred treatment of regular customers because such practice results in inequitable distribution? (c) Even in normal times, doesn't preferred treatment to regular (and large) customers result in social injustice?

6. Vertically integrated firms can achieve substantial stabilization in earlier stages of production if they "taper" capacity—that is, have capacity in an early stage or in a service only up to minimum needs and then buy their remaining needs, which fluctuate, from outside sources. What are the implications of this method of achieving stabilization for the basic strategy of a company?

7. Most discussions of stabilization of production, including that in this chapter, accept fluctuations in sales and consider ways of adjusting production to those sales. An alternative approach would be to set the production volume—at a stabilized level—and consider ways of adjusting sales to production. The second approach (widely used in Japan) enables companies to provide stable employment and helps maintain the Gross National Product. Would such a practice be socially desirable in the United States? What would companies have to do to operate in this manner?

8. (a) At what point should company policy bar the acceptance of gifts and entertainment from vendors: lunch at a local restaurant, golf game at an exclusive club, three-day technical seminar at a comfortable inn, Christmas calendar, bottle of Scotch, electronic watch, theater tickets, mink coat, opportunity to invest in Florida real estate, assistance in getting son a seat on a booked-up plane flight, employment for Uncle Ben, $10,000 to a pet charity, $50 bet at favorable odds, you name it? (b) Should the company policy be the same with respect to company bankers? union leaders? advertising agents? customers?

9. "When selecting vendors, we carefully consider service, price, and other factors affecting our operations. However, we do not feel that we should interfere with the way the vendor runs its business. Specifically, its decisions on equal employment opportunity, pollution, foreign military contracts, and such matters are not our responsibility. We run our company as we believe is right, and the other company is entitled to the same respect." Do you agree? Does a bank have any more obligation to "interfere" with the way its customers operate than a steel company does its customers?

10. (a) A Wall Street analyst says: "During a period of inflation the smart person owns things, even if he has to go into debt to do so. A company has an even better built-in opportunity to own things and should buy inventory to the extent of its financial capacity." Do you agree? Why? (b) How should a company take advantage of inflation?

CASE 10 / Hammond Engineering Products Corporation

Hammond Engineering Products Corporation makes a variety of metal products—boilers, valves, fin pipe, cooling units, radiators, heat exchangers, and copper tubing—for the air-conditioning and chemical industries. In manufacturing these products it uses copper in large quantities. And there is the rub. For the president spends 30% to 40% of his time on the single task of buying copper on the London Metal Exchange and the New York Commodity Exchange—an arrangement necessary under current conditions, which outrages the directors and which has sent the vice-chairman of the board and the chairman of the finance committee on a journey to find copper.

Why do they want their own source of assured supply and why do they travel away from Baltimore by airplane, taxi, automobile, truck, horse, burro, and shanks' mare in an attempt to find it? Because they think they can cut costs, reduce the risk of inventory losses, and get the president off the telephone and out of the wire room onto more far-seeing tasks.

Engineers of the firm, an ingenious crew, recently designed and built a continuous casting machine, a piercing mill, and a copper tube extruding mill to supply company needs. With an assured source of supply and operation at 80% of capacity, the mills will produce tube at $.15 per pound below the price paid a supplier for volume purchases and at $.35 per pound below the off-the-shelf warehouse price. There is an investment of $7 million in these mills and associated equipment. If all goes well, they will run efficiently for 10 to 12 years.

To equal competitors' costs of finished tubing, radiators, etc., the president calculates that he must bring refined (99.9% pure) copper into the plant at $.08 a pound above the current U.S. producer price. This allows for shipping costs plus the cost of a small percent of foreign copper added to obtain the necessary total pounds.

Copper is sold to buyers in the United States at two current prices. One, called the U.S. producer price, is the price charged by the largest domestic producers (Anaconda, Phelps Dodge, Kennecott, and American Smelting & Refining) to their old and established customers. The second, the world price, is set daily on the London Metal Exchange in a free market. Prices on the New York Commodity Exchange closely match the LME prices. The LME current prices fluctuate widely. The price difference above the U.S. producer price has ranged from $.15 to $.76 in the past six months. Five years ago the variation during the year was from equaling the U.S. producer price to $.55 per pound above. Two years ago the LME price was $.10 to $.20 below the U.S. producer price.

Futures prices make up a third price that can be paid for copper. Futures are quoted both in London and in New York.

Price differences among the various copper prices are shown in the table on page 215.

For the past six months Mr. Sorenson, the president, has bought heavily in the futures market. The company is now taking delivery on copper it contracted for at a price that nets out at the factory door to be $.05 a pound below the domestic producer

Price Differences

	London Metal Exchange Current Price (per pound)	New York Commodity Exchange Futures Prices	
		6 months delivery¹	12 months delivery¹
Today	$.05 above U.S. producer price	$.15 below U.S. producer price	$.10 below U.S. producer price
Last Month	.22 " " " " "	.05 " " " " "	.01 " " "
Last Year	.77 " " " " "	.30 above " "	.68 above " "
Two Years Ago	.13 " " " " "	n.a.	n.a.
Five Years Ago	.05 below " " "		
Ten Years Ago	.04 " " "		
Fifteen Years Ago	.03 " " "		

¹ If Hammond buys copper today at the future prices for twelve months delivery, it then actually receives the copper at its plant twelve months from today and pays for it at the future prices quoted today. For example, last month Hammond could have bought at a futures price for six months delivery at $.05 below the then-existing U.S. producer price. Then, six months later (five months from now), the company would have the copper delivered at its plant and pay the price it earlier contracted for—$.05 below the producer price of last month.

price. At present Mr. Sorenson is attempting to decide whether or not to commit the firm for another year's needs (7,000 short tons) at the twelve months futures price. His decision has to be made in light of unfavorable news, which includes U.S. government investigations of copper pricing, foreign government intervention to stabilize copper prices, and releases of copper from various stockpiles. Typical of the forecasts available is the following one covering the near term: "The price in London is 'unsustainably high.' It will weaken over the next few months. Factors are a normal summer slowdown by fabricators, a lag in U.S. business, and the Japanese release of 18,000 tons for export." A typical forecast covering the longer term is: "The president of Kennecott Copper said that there should be some easing of the tight supply situation over the next two years with the addition each year of about 400,000 tons of new annual Free World capacity—a 6% rate of increase. Demand grows about 4½% per year."

Will there be a one-world price for copper? "It would have happened before now if it had been easy to do," said the chairman and chief executive officer of American Metal Climax Company. Big suppliers and customers appear to have mutual desires to stick with each other during surpluses and shortages alike. The large suppliers are concerned that higher prices would bring large-scale substitution of aluminum and plastic for copper. There is an industry rule of thumb that aluminum begins to replace copper in electrical uses when the price of copper climbs to more than double the price of aluminum.

Mr. Schlesinger, the chairman of the Finance Committee, and Mr. Califano, the vice-chairman, had a mixed reception on their calls on U.S. producers. At the headquarters of various firms they were received with great respect, listened to carefully, and treated to statements of considerable sympathy and clear understanding. It is, nevertheless, the firm policy of the producers to take care of the needs of their old customers first. Despite the obviously unfortunate position of Hammond Engineering, the producers are obliged to respect the obligations of established trade relations. Some sales executives entertained Mr. Schlesinger and Mr. Califano lavishly, others were barely civil. "We allocate the copper here—not those fellows downtown you talked to."

In addition to seeing some spectacular scenery, the two gentlemen learned a bit about mining economies on their visits to Arizona, Montana, and New Mexico. Following the required course of exploration, development, and stripping the overburden to bring a new open-pit mine into production would require 6 to 7 years and an investment of $300 to $350 million. The mine would then produce copper at an average total manufacturing cost of about $.50 per pound for the refined copper. Such a mine would include the digging, crushing, and concentrating stages. Its output would then go to a smelter and refinery for production of copper electrodes that were 99.9% pure. Mine production would be 55,000 tons of copper annually for about 20 years with present-day technology. With normal luck and good management, the return on investment for such a mine would be 20% after all taxes—assuming that the U.S. producer price would match changes in operating costs.

Negotiations with the developers of a mine now being opened are stalled at the latest offer from the mine owners. They want a 5-year guarantee from Hammond Engineering for the purchase of 5,000 tons per year at the U.S. producer price plus a premium. This arrangement would bring the copper to Hammond's door at a fluctuating price $.10 per pound above the current producer price, which is $.70 per pound. The owners await Hammond's acceptance—but not very eagerly, they say. This mine's smelted concentrates would be shipped to a Baltimore refinery that has occasional excess capacity for refining outside ores.

Refinery time is not entirely impossible to obtain provided Hammond can offer the necessary semiprocessed copper to the refiner. Mr. Schlesinger and Mr. Califano have found a Belgian refinery that will take any smelted ore concentrates they may have in substantial quantity and trade refined copper for it at the relevant free-world prices. Transportation costs overseas are about $.03 per pound one-way.

To supply semiprocessed copper to an independent refinery, Mr. Schlesinger and Mr. Califano have located an old mine with an exhausted ore body but with substantial tailing dumps from which copper can be leached by trickling sulfuric acid down through the dump. The resulting solution can be treated to remove the copper for later stages of refining. The quality of the copper is not as good as that obtained from virgin ore bodies, but it is satisfactory for making tubing. The copper would ultimately cost about $.66 per pound after refining and before any shipping costs. Required initial investment in the land and the associated chemical plant will be $8,000,000 to $10,500,000 depending on the desired output, which could range from 5 to 10 tons of copper per day. Development time is 1 year and useful life would be 10 years.

During the executives' search, Hammond engineers have been busy designing and building a pilot plant for a new method—called "electrowinning"—of extracting copper from ore bodies that can be leached. They believe that the equipment design has overcome the problems of corrosion that have been a stumbling block to other developers attempting to do the same thing. A pilot plant—which can be moved on a railroad flat car—is under construction at the factory. The engineers' cost estimates indicate that 99.9% pure copper can be produced at a total manufacturing cost of about $.45 per pound by this process of leaching, concentrating the solution, and then precipitating the copper electrically. This process avoids all pollution problems usually associated with smelting and refining. The necessary investment for full-scale operations will be about $10,000,000 to $11,000,000. Finding a surface ore body that could produce 3,000 short tons of copper per year for 10 years in total from ore containing 0.6% to 0.75% copper in acid soluble form, delineating the ore body, developing the mine, and building the plant will take 3 to 4 years—provided the process proves out.

Not all companies are happy about the problems of being in the copper tubing business. One of the larger metal-working and electrical goods companies (last year's sales $280,000,000) recently announced: "We have decided to sell our two-year old Virginia tube mill and cease operations in the tubing business. The decision is dictated by the current high prices and by our inability to obtain prime copper at reasonable prices . . . Although our plant is a modern, integrated facility with the lowest possible operating costs, we have been unable to obtain copper at a price that will allow us to compete profitably in the highly competitive community tube market."

Executives of Hammond Engineering Products Corporation welcome any decline in competition but believe that the firm should continue with its historical product line.

Mr. Califano explained the board's view of company strategy: "We have to put ourselves in sound financial shape so that a public offering of our stock will be a success or so that we can attract a favorable offer of merger with a publicly owned corporation. This means a 4-to-5-year record of sustained growth in both sales and pre-tax profits. A 15% annual growth rate would certainly do it, and it is possible that a 10% rate might be enough."

Company financial data for Hammond Engineering Products Corporation for the past 5 years is given in the following table:

Financial Information

Year	Sales	Net Profit	Total Assets	Long-Term Debt	Total Equity
Current	$74,000,000	$5,300,000	$82,000,000	$32,000,000	$41,000,000
Last Year	76,000,000	6,000,000	77,000,000	25,000,000	39,000,000
Previous Year	71,000,000	5,600,000	75,000,000	24,000,000	36,500,000
Previous Year	69,000,000	5,900,000	74,000,000	22,000,000	34,500,000
Previous Year	64,000,000	4,900,000	72,000,000	21,000,000	32,000,000

Required: (a) Outline the alternatives available to the company.

(b) What decision would you make about copper supply?

(c) Explain how your decision would be useful in meeting company objectives.

PERSONNEL AND INDUSTRIAL RELATIONS POLICY

Every enterprise requires labor inputs. Survival depends upon continuing cooperation of the men and women who convert inert resources into services. Moreover, any strategic redirection of a company's mission is possible only if human resources can be focused on the new tasks.

Distinctive personnel challenges

Human resources differ from machines, materials, and capital in two major respects. (1) People care deeply about the way they are used. The amount of effort and initiative people contribute reflect not only off-the-job rewards; the work assigned, relations with co-workers, and the manner of supervision also are part of the bargain. So, when we assess the workability of a particular strategy, we must consider both the availability of kinds of skills required *and* the attitudes of the people we will employ toward the work itself. (2) Society, too, cares about the way manpower is used. In terms of social responsibility, as defined in Chapter 1, managements must keep abreast of dynamic changes in the work force. A continuing exchange of labor inputs for satisfaction outputs is possible only when the terms of exchange are updated to fit new facts of life. And society keeps on changing the rules. Managers have the difficult task of adjusting personnel policy so as to support revisions in company strategy and at the same time to meet requirements arising from points (1) and (2) above.

Important changes affecting labor supply include the following:

1. Pressure is high to increase the proportion of black and other minority employees and of women employees in skilled and managerial positions and to provide "equal opportunity" in all respects.
2. Attitudes toward work are making motivation increasingly complex. Workers are shifting their ideas of success; fewer accept the Protestant work ethic; and alienation from traditional social values regarding marriage, children, and behavioral freedom carry over to roles in organized effort.
3. The work force includes an increasing proportion of people who prefer part-time work and short-term jobs. Also, the supply of migrant labor willing to do physical labor is dropping.

4. The education level of the total work force is rising rapidly. This changes not only the ability but also the expectations and the attitudes of young workers.
5. Labor unions are becoming more skilled and less hampered in the exercise of monopoly power, especially in the public and service sectors.
6. Business is expected to participate actively in rehabilitation of hard-core unemployed and, more generally, to assist in overcoming urban blight.
7. Meanwhile, accelerating social and technological changes increase the value of an adaptable and responsive work force.

Each company must work out its own adjustment to these pressures. The approaches tried should be at least compatible with the overall strategy, and, as we have repeatedly stressed, the preferable policy is one that has a synergistic effect—that is, it provides extra strength to the company while meeting the social situation in a constructive way.

Personnel decisions

As with marketing and production, a wide array of detailed personnel decisions must be made. To explore these fully is far beyond the scope of this book. However, the intimate, essential, and inevitable relation of personnel to successful execution of a strategy does deserve emphasis. Again, our focus here is on policy issues that are likely to demand central management action. We will illustrate possibilities of this kind in the following basic areas:

1. Selection.
2. Development.
3. Compensation.
4. Supplemental benefits.
5. Industrial relations.

Because of its importance, executive personnel is discussed in a separate chapter (Chapter 19). Here we will deal with policy guides covering manpower as a total resource.

SELECTION

"Selection" is used here to embrace all policies a company may have regulating the choice of employees. In this broad sense, it includes not only the *hiring* of new employees but also the selection of employees to be *promoted* and the further problem of *discharging* employees. The process of selection goes on almost continuously.

Hiring new employees

An ideal employee for all companies does not exist. Just as the raw materials a company needs depend upon what it makes, so do the kinds of employees needed depend upon both strategy and technology. This fitting of company recruiting practice to requirements for future operations is not simple; during the same period when shifts in company operations call for a change in personnel policy, the external labor supply is also changing. Here are a few examples.

Matching growth strategy. Communications Systems, Inc. is a growth company centered around some patented devices that transmit and receive multiple electronic messages. These devices are particularly well suited to handle communications between branch offices and a centralized computer. The company founder and president, however, regards the equipment merely as the base from which all communications systems can grow. Among the possibilities already worked on are central inventory control of multiple warehouses, central payroll records for all branches of a state government, logistic systems for the Air Force, a nationwide bidding system for commodity exchanges, and complete integrated data processing systems for business firms.

With these possibilities in mind, the firm expanded rapidly. Its stated personnel policy was "to attract the best brains in the country." The glamor of the company objectives enabled it to hire both theoretical and applied experts in systems design, communications equipment, computer technology, and the activities to which the systems might be applied.

The match between the mission conceived for the company and the kinds of people employed was excellent. But serious difficulty developed in terms of the rate of growth. Communications Systems was employed to make a variety of pilot studies, but full-scale applications proved to be complex and costly. Concepts such as national bidding on commodities require legal and institutional changes that probably are several decades away. The result was that many members of the high-powered staff that was employed became frustrated. The high morale in the early stages turned to internal criticism and disappointment with lack of personal advancement. Since many of the people employed were indeed very capable, they began taking other jobs. Turnover accelerated. Hiring mistakes during the initial expansion became conspicuous because these individuals tended to stay with Communications Systems. The company is still in business, but it now has a poor name rather than a good name in its particular labor market.

Hiring policy has a quantitative as well as a qualitative aspect, as we clearly see in the preceding example. While this was an extreme case, other companies have discovered they moved too fast in the right direction. (It *is* possible to have too many bright young MBA's.) Excess inventory of talented manpower is both hard and expensive to keep in storage.

Adjusting to new labor market. For years a drug wholesale company followed a policy of hiring high-school graduates to staff its large warehousing operations. These people stacked, marked, and kept track of the thousands of different items involved; assembled orders for prompt delivery to retail druggists, priced the order, and computed the bill; kept track of back orders; and helped maintain records needed for buying new stocks. High-school graduates were found to have the accuracy and the dependability required, and at the same time they did not find the highly standardized operations offensive. The more energetic employees became supervisors, sales representatives, buyers, and perhaps branch managers.

The company now finds that the supply and the quality of high-school graduates is changing. Most of the more able and energetic high-school graduates now go to college. Efforts to use men and women who want a full-time job while working their way through school, or those who have temporarily dropped out, have shown unsatisfactory results because many of these people become bored with their routine work. Attempts at further mechanization has somewhat reduced the human effort per unit of output, but the basic skill requirements remain much the same. So, some modification in hiring policy clearly was called for.

A modification in the *structure of jobs* was the first move. Instead of assuming that everyone would have a basic competence to perform a variety of tasks, the work has been more sharply graded in terms of reading, writing, and arithmetic skills. This permits relaxation of the high-school graduation requirement. Also, more black and Puerto Rican people have been hired even though some are weak in desired basic skills at the time of employment. This new type of employee is given intensive training on limited tasks. Turnover is high during the early months of employment, but out of the group come a significant number who can do the simpler tasks well and quite a few who quickly move on to the more skilled jobs.

In addition, provision has been made for hiring a few college graduates and moving them rather quickly through various operations with the expectation that they will qualify for buying, selling, or supervisory jobs. This *career path* is considered necessary because the bright energetic youngster who previously might have sought employment on graduation from high school is now likely to go on to college—and the company needs its share of this kind of talent.

The revised policy has some disadvantages. The work force is less flexible; it is more difficult to move people from task to task to meet peak requirements. More significant, lost is the feeling that everyone starts out on an equal basis and progresses to more difficult positions on the basis of demonstrated merit. Even though it is now possible to move up through the hierarchy, and some people do, new employees enter the company at different levels. This generates an undercurrent that some people—because they are lucky enough to get more education—continue to receive favored treatment.

Racial discrimination. No institution such as business can stand aloof from major social issues. In the case of racial discrimination, business firms cannot rely on legal requirements to define the action they will take on this important matter. Each company must decide how its personnel policy will reflect the pressure for equal employment opportunity.

The table at the top of page 223 shows a breakdown of occupational distribution of white and nonwhite employed persons in the United States.

OCCUPATIONAL DISTRIBUTION OF EMPLOYED PERSONS IN THE U. S., 1972
(in percent of total employed)

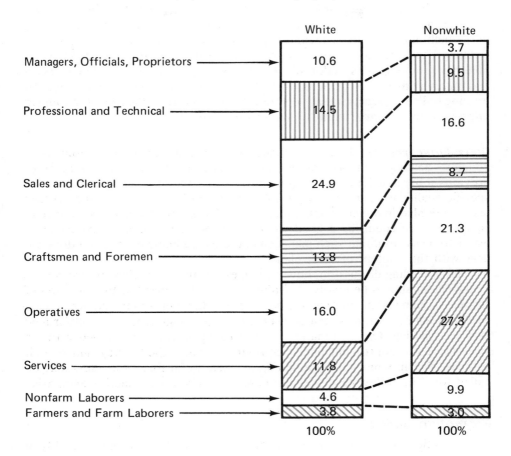

One response to racial discrimination is to increase the proportion of blacks in the total work force. For instance, a consumer credit company has a policy of employing 32% blacks—the same percentage that blacks are of the total population in the area. At present, over 80% of the employees are white. Consequently, white applicants must have most unusual qualifications to get a job—because they are white. Although the policy is probably a technical violation of the law against racial discrimination, the management feels that it must quickly redress past injustices if its objective to provide credit service to all segments of the population is to be realized.

In contrast, a major airline takes the position that color will play no part in the selection of flight crews. The management of this company feels that safety is such a crucial aspect of its strategy that there should be no tampering with the top priority given technical qualification. The president says, "We employ a lot of blacks, but not on a quota basis. In our business, technical excellence comes first.''

A leading advertising agency gives still a different emphasis in its policy. The president sees the task as one of modifying social mores so that classes of jobs—including managers, technical people, and account executives—do not ''belong'' to a racial or religious group. He is pushing to have members of minority groups in all sorts of jobs but not on a quota basis. Primary stress is laid on breaking down social barriers. The policy, then, affects counseling and training fully as much as initial selection. We will return to the role of training in improving racial opportunities later in this chapter.

Other hiring policies. Every company will have a variety of employment policies—dealing with promotion from within, health, age, sex, number of previous jobs, association with competitors, and the like—as well as a set of specific qualifications for particular jobs. Recruiting, interviewing, and perhaps testing are also involved. Such policies, standards, and procedures contribute significantly to acquiring a good work force. Normally, central management wants to be assured that such management tools are being used, but it does not deal with the content of such plans.[1]

The preceding discussion, however, does illustrate situations where central management should be involved. Adjustments in the speed or the direction of strategy, changes in company environment that permit or require a new company adaptation, or social pressures of major magnitude may call for new personnel policy. On such matters central management is concerned with the wisdom of the adjustment and a consistency with other policy and overall strategy. Possibly more subcontracting or a search for foreign markets may be called for. The following discussion continues this same selective emphasis.

Promotion policy

Promotion policy has a significant effect on the ability and the versatility of employees within a company. And, in turn, such characteristics of key employees should be closely correlated to company strategy.

Promotion of women. Due to traditional attitudes about men's jobs and women's jobs, some discrimination against women occurs in initial hiring. More significant is the reluctance to promote women into managerial posts. In many firms custom dictates that women will not be considered for key posts. And because such positions have never been open to them, the number of

---

[1] Central management also wants assurance that personnel practices meet our increasing complex legal requirements. For example, the Supreme Court in its Griggs vs. Duke Power Company decision ruled out many previous selection tests. Now each test must measure a person for a specific job; unless a test is validated it may be considered a discriminatory device. Discriminatory pay rates, good faith in collective bargaining, and many other personnel actions now have legal definitions. So legality as well as effectiveness must be watched.

women who aspire to such jobs and have prepared themeselves—technically and psychologically—is small. However, a fundamental change in attitudes is occurring. Prodded by legal pressures, companies now face the necessity and the opportunity to tap a new source of technical and managerial talent.

A generation ago, bank tellers were men. Now almost all tellers are women. Aware of such shifts, a grocery chain is experimenting with women as store managers—traditionally a man's job. The personnel vice-president says: "Women run clothing shops, so why not grocery stores? Both jobs involve dealing with the public, supervising personnel, and inventory control. We hope to gain real competitive advantage by quickly moving women into these jobs."

As with hiring and promotion of blacks and other minorities, each company must decide whether to adopt a policy of "reverse discrimination." Breaking tradition may require giving women preferential treatment. The risk in doing so, of course, is that unprepared women will be thrust into conspicuous posts; their failure in such posts could set back the entire movement. Consequently, most companies are sticking to a promotion-on-merit policy, but they do devote more effort looking for qualified women and more quickly restructure jobs to fit the abilities that available women possess.

Horizontal versus vertical promotion. A strategy that stresses frequency of change and adaptability can be executed best by employees who themselves are able to shift quickly from one operating pattern to another. Employees differ in their response to change. Some are very effective only as long as they work with a familiar technology in a known social setting. Other people find new situations challenging and are stimulated by a change in pace. These attitudes toward change can be modified to some degree by a company's promotion policy.

Horizontal promotion encourages versatility. By horizontal promotion we mean transferring employees to a different kind of work rather than promoting them vertically into the positions of their bosses or to more sophisticated jobs in the same department. The horizontal transfer may be to a job of the same level of difficulty, but it is regarded as a promotion because it is part of the normal path of advancement in that company. IBM has used horizontal promotion extensively for many years (executives insist that the company's initials stand for "I've Been Moved"). A large portion of its production and finance executives, for instance, have had sales experience sometime during their career—and this contributes to a customer orientation of many IBM decisions. Individuals may eventually land in their bosses' positions, but they know that they typically will hold one or two positions outside of the department before being moved back at the higher level.

Such a promotion policy accustoms people to change. Because of the varied experience, the people bring a somewhat broader perspective to each of their assignments. From the employees' point of view, a horizontal promotion policy increases the number of potential openings; they do not have to wait for their bosses to retire to get a promotion. Among the disadvantages are a significantly higher training cost—each individual has more to learn on the new job—and a greater risk that decisions will be made on an incomplete understanding of the total situation.

Career paths for individual contributors. Business needs experts as well as generalists. The knowledge explosion in virtually all fields creates a need for specialists. In particular, companies that stress leadership in scientific development as part of their strategy must have people thoroughly informed on all relevant research. In addition, experts may be needed in such fields as patent law, foreign exchange regulations, and even the personal likes and dislikes of indispensable customers.

Horizontal promotion certainly does not develop this kind of expertise. Moreover, in most companies the high-status and high-paying jobs are managerial. So, often outstanding individuals—researchers, sales representatives, or engineers—must be promoted vertically to a manager's job to keep them within the company. The experts may be poorly suited to managerial tasks, and their new assignments may seriously interfere with their doing the kind of work that they enjoy and in which they can make the greatest contribution to the company.

A career ladder for the "individual contributor" provides a way around these difficulties. Exceptional performers are promoted and at the same time their unique capabilities are enhanced. General Electric Company pioneered this approach, and now several other firms follow a similar policy. The idea is simple. A few prestige jobs with high status and high salary are created. Individuals in these positions outrank their supervisors (just as TV stars outrank their managers), although the need for managerial direction must be respected. Thus the possibility of promotion is held open to the really outstanding people who prefer to remain specialists.

This policy does require a sophisticated understanding and acceptance of the roles of both unusual specialists and managers; a delicate balancing of ego-satisfactions is required. Nevertheless, the policy is particularly well suited to those companies, or departments, where the harnessing of unusual human talent is a part of the strategy.

Discharge policy

Turning now to a less pleasant aspect of selection, circumstances do arise when employees must be chosen for discharge. The way this issue is handled can have a profound long-run effect on a company's strength. With a weak discharge policy, a firm may find itself saddled with a large number of ineffective employees. A leading manufacturer of farming equipment, for example, went bankrupt partly because management had failed for a period of years to cleanse itself of inferior workers. Moreover, the cost of dismissing a long-service employee is increasing rapidly. So, any firm whose strategy calls for competition on a cost basis must be particularly careful about its discharge policy.

Transfer or dismissal. One set of issues involves the transfer of employees who simply do not perform their assigned tasks satisfactorily. For a new recruit a trial period is customary; presumably if he is incapable he will be discharged immediately. The catch is that a person's ability *and* willingness to do an assigned task may be difficult to judge within the trial period. And, in times of labor shortage, a supervisor is tempted to hang on to anybody he can get.

Once a person has been employed for at least a year, many companies have a policy of transfer prior to dismissal. The assumption is that the person may have been assigned to the wrong kind of work or that the trouble may be due to a personality clash with his particular supervisor. Both in fairness to the person and to save the company recruiting expense, the employee is given "another chance." Vigilance is necessary to avoid abuse of this policy. It is easier and more pleasant to keep on transferring marginal employees than to dismiss them. Especially in large companies, negotiating a transfer of a misfit becomes almost a game. The cumulative effect of such practice, unfortunately, can be a heavy burden of unproductive workers.

Seniority and layoffs. Quite a different problem arises when a worker's performance is acceptable but the company wishes to reduce the total number employed because of a drop in the volume of work to be done. Widespread policy, reinforced by union contracts, is that regular employees be discharged (and reemployed) on the basis of seniority; that is, when operations are curtailed, the newest employee is the first one to be discharged and the employee with the longest service is the last one.

The effect of a seniority policy depends in part on whether it relates to a small section, a type of job, or an entire plant or office. If the scope is wide, the dislocations can be extremely burdensome. The people with low seniority may not be on jobs to be cut back, and consequently a whole series of transfers may be necessary each time a reduction is made. This results in many people being on new jobs with new relationships with the accompanying inefficiencies that always occur during a shakedown period.

More serious in the long run is the fact that efficiency and length of service are rarely closely correlated. Except for personnel considerations, it makes more sense to discharge the least efficient worker first and to keep the more efficient ones on the payroll. If work is machine-paced, then differences in ability may be insignificant; on the other hand, the more important the personal ability, skill, and motivation in performance—as in professional and managerial jobs—the more onerous a straight seniority policy becomes. Consequently, because people do differ in ability and because massive reassignment of work is costly, most companies try to confine their formal seniority policy to relatively small homogeneous groups of routine or semiroutine jobs.

Incidentally, the use of seniority complicates the task of increasing the proportion of black or other minority groups in a work force. Since the persons being added inevitably have low seniority, they are the first to be laid off when work slackens. Only a persistent infusion of black workers over a period of time will remove this effect.

Dismissal range. We have suggested limitations on the use of seniority and implied that ineffective employees should be weeded out of the work force at all levels. Nevertheless, most managers feel that a successful company does have some obligation to employees who have served the company to the best of their abilities for several years—the longer the service, the greater the obligation. A general policy is that (a) an ineffective person should be removed from a job, and (b) any obligation of the company to the person should then be met in ways that do not interfere with optimum execution of company strategy.

Several ways of meeting service obligations to employees are available: (1) A search may be made for a vacancy in the company that the individual can fulfill satisfactorily, and he should be given an option to take this job. (2) The company can assist the person in finding a job with another employer. Just because an individual no longer fits in one company does not mean that he may not be highly desirable to another. (3) If a person is approaching retirement age and the company has a retirement plan, early retirement may be arranged. Usually this means that the company makes a special, and often substantial, contribution to the retirement fund so that the person is able to retire without too great a reduction in the annual amount he receives. (4) A dismissal wage can be paid of perhaps two week's salary for each year of service. The aim in this case is to provide a person an income while he is establishing himself in a new job.

A number of foreign countries have laws requiring the payment of dismissal wages of one to five years' salary. In effect, wages become a fixed cost much like interest on long-term bonds. U.S. concerns much prefer a more flexible arrangement suited to the particular circumstances and the individuals involved. If our companies do not handle this problem in a manner generally regarded as equitable, some form of legislation is a real possibility.

Technological unemployment. The kind of situation where dismissal wages are most strongly advocated is technological unemployment—that is, where people lose their jobs as a direct consequence of technological improvements within their company. The feeling is that the worker should not bear the brunt of the greater mechanization.

In fact, some companies state as a general policy that "no one will lose his job as a direct consequence of technological changes made by the company." This strong position is felt to be necessary to overcome resistance to change. When a company is operating in an expanding market and the technological unemployment is small, such a policy is feasible because the displaced persons can be absorbed in new jobs elsewhere. However, when major changes are involved, as has occurred in coal mining, the "no loss of job policy" would be unworkable. A more flexible arrangement for technological unemployment is to provide either another job or a dismissal wage.

No company should undertake a strategy that includes substantial technological change without thinking through the effect of such changes on who will have to be discharged and under what conditions.

Selection: a recurring issue

Policy guidance is needed on the intake, internal movement, and discharge of people—a key resource for every company. Hiring the right number of particular kinds of people is complicated by the way central management decides to respond to past discrimination against nonwhites, other minorities, and women. Also, past hiring policy must be adjusted to changes in education and interest in full-time employment of the current labor supply.

Movement of people up, around, and out of a company is becoming more and more fenced in by external regulation. Consequently, policies covering promotion and discharge should be matched carefully with the expected frequency of technological change and with the availability of skilled workers on short notice.

DEVELOPMENT

Two underlying considerations shape a personnel development policy. First, the need for learning is pervasive and never-ending. All employees—from the president to the lowest unskilled laborer—have to learn new information and skills when they take their jobs. And, this is a continuing process because requirements of the jobs keep changing. Second, such learning occurs primarily as a result of the desire and the effort of each individual. Without the active cooperation of the learner, company efforts have only slight impact.

Nevertheless, while most development is self-development, a company can play a role in guiding, encouraging, and assisting the process. Personnel development policy defines the scope and the degree of such company involvement. As we shall see, a wide choice exists in how far a company should go in various development activities.

Learning before and after employment

The scope of a company development program depends, in part, on the training and skills an employee is expected to have prior to employment. The greater the pre-employment training, the less is the need for company concern.

Technologically advanced companies often depend upon someone else to provide training of their key employees. For example, RCA ran a half-page ad in the *New York Times* with a banner headline reading:

RCA DEFENSE ELECTRONIC PRODUCTS WINS THE NAVY'S ADVANCED MISSILE SYSTEM CONTRACT
    This contract offers engineers in a wide range of electronic and scientific disciplines one of the major challenges of the 1970's. If you are the type of individual that would like to be part of this combination of exceptional skills, facilities, and resources, and desire professional growth, we want to hear from you. You should have a minimum B.S. degree with at least five years' experience in one or more of the following areas: Systems Analysis, Missile System, Tracking Radar, Ship Integration, Interface Definition, Standardization Engineering, . . . (Sixteen different specialized areas were listed.)

In this situation, RCA policy was not to train its own engineers. Undoubtedly, the company would grant time and financial assistance for its engineers to attend conferences, and it might underwrite the cost of evening study. But, predominantly, the company expected these people to be already prepared to do the work to which they were assigned. Company training, aside from experience on the job, was to be at a minimum.

In contrast, the wholesale drug company referred to earlier in this chapter followed a policy of providing virtually all of the specialized training needed by its employees. The young recruits were first given training on the job; then, as they were promoted to jobs with greater responsibility, they studied company manuals and other instruction materials; as they moved into supervisory positions, they attended a whole series of one- or two-week courses run by the central personnel department. A major task of every supervisor was recognized as training and coaching his subordinates. The company did have a tuition refund plan for night school work, but this was regarded more as a fringe benefit than an essential part of employee development.

These two examples suggest that a policy of training is best suited to relatively simple operations. This inference is wrong. Many companies with simple operations do no systematic training.

The primary factors in choosing between "raising your own" versus "hiring seasoned workers" are, first, the probable length of employment. Industries such as construction or the theater, which work on relatively short projects, typically assemble the talent needed for immediate purposes and leave the task of training to the individual and to other institutions. Staffing of government contracts in the space and defense industries largely falls into this category. Of course, any company that undertakes to enter a different industry on a large scale lacks time to do very much training. Second, the existence of well established skills or professions affects the need for in-company training. Thus, printers, doctors, and welders are usually hired as experienced individuals. By comparison, if the work of a particular company is primarily unique, internal training is necessary to assure the skills required.

Companies that are technological leaders in their field are always faced by a problem of training people who then go to work for competitors. A substantial number of engineers and sales representatives in the computer industry, for instance, have been trained at IBM expense. If a company's strategy is to be a leader, it should anticipate not only the cost of overcoming the pitfalls of a new product or process, but also a personnel development cost. Moreover, the company will probably have to be a leader in compensation and supplemental benefits in order to keep its turnover low.

Overcoming employee obsolescence

Rapid change creates employee obsolescence. In the electronics and chemical industries, for example, a much-sought-after specialist may be obsolete in ten or fifteen years. A similar problem arises with sales representatives—and college professors. Normally, the individuals are more competent in their specialties than they were when they were originally hired. What they have to offer simply becomes less relevant to current problems.

A fairly widespread approach to this problem is to leave the burden of obsolescence to the individual. As job requirements change, if existing personnel are not qualified, new people are hired. In fact, from a short-run point of view, the company gains by keeping people on jobs they already know well. Quite aside from humanitarian considerations, such a short-run policy eventually generates the need for discharges with all the burdens of dismissal wages and related headaches discussed earlier in this chapter.

An alternative policy is to provide time, financial assistance, and perhaps company training programs to assist employees to keep current in their field. The most effective techniques for such adult education are not yet well developed. Short refresher courses are common, but sabbatical leaves—customary in the academic world—are very rare in business. Moreover, since so much development is job-related, the structuring of work to avoid obsolescence is more important than external training programs. Such restructuring of jobs is likely to be expensive because it cuts down on the efficiency of doing familiar tasks. The company that embarks on a program to avoid employee obsolescence must be prepared to spend money currently for (a) future productivity and (b) improved employee morale.

Assisting in professional growth

An increasing number of people view their work as a profession. Purchasing agents, copywriters, computer programmers, credit managers, salesmen, and training directors are only a few of the many classes of business having their own professional associations. To be sure, neither entry nor licensing is as rigid as in medicine or law, but other aspects of professionalization are being developed. Knowledge requirements for entrance, advancement of the state of the art, ethical standards of behavior, objectives of serving society, pride in doing one's job professionally—all are aspects of a professional viewpoint.

Now the question for company development policy is how much encouragement to give such professional movements. In many ways, a professionally oriented employee is a better worker. From the company standpoint, however, two drawbacks arise: (1) Professionals are more independent in their behavior; they derive some of their objectives and standards from the profession rather than the company and they have a narrower span of legitimate guidance from their supervisors. (2) Professionals are more mobile; they have recognized skills that can be used by other companies, and their professional acquaintances give them information about vacancies.

A few companies, notably in the service industries, actively *encourage* their employees to become prominent professionals. McKinsey & Company, a leading management consulting firm, urges its staff members to devote 20% of their working time to professional advancement. The Bell Telephone Laboratories give their scientific personnel similar encouragement. In each of these instances, having a strong group of professional employees is an integral part of the company strategy. The belief is that this type of personnel is most likely to enable the company to achieve its service mission.

On the other hand, many central managers believe that the employees' first loyalty in their work activities should be to their company; if people carry their professionalism to the point where they cannot enthusiastically promote company objectives, then they are in the awkward position of trying to serve two masters. Companies with this lukewarm viewpoint typically pay for memberships and attendance at one or two professional meetings a year in the belief that some professional contact will help to make the individual a better employee. Of course, the ideal solution is to have no incompatibility between company objectives and professional conduct; but with literally hundreds of professional organizations, such a beautiful synthesis is difficult to achieve.

A third policy is one of *no support* for professional growth—what employees do on such matters is their personal affair. Managers taking this view are not necessarily callous; they may ardently believe that the company has a worthwhile mission and that employees have ample opportunity for self-fulfillment in working for this cause. Incidentally, some of the sharpest conflicts between professionalism and organization goals arise in nonprofit enterprises such as family welfare agencies, avant garde schools, and the like. To managers in this last group, professionalism leads to conservatism and to a preoccupation with means rather than with ends. "The professional is a person who always plays safe." So, we see here again that the policy relative to support of professionalization is directly related to the character of the enterprise.

Special training for minority employees

Many business firms are having difficulty increasing their promotion of minority employees as rapidly as they desire because they cannot find qualified candidates. We have already discussed problems associated with preferential treatment of blacks and other minorities in hiring and promotion. To the extent that company training can help to overcome knowledge or skill deficiencies, the whole process can be expedited. Consequently, many companies follow a policy of being sure that company training resources are made available to minority employees as rapidly as they have the desire to undertake the development activity.

Unfortunately, this policy works well only to the extent that a company has exceptional minority employees who have the capacity to advance rapidly. For many employees, the difficulties go deeper. Home and school background have given inadequate preparation. Attitudes developed in a minority neighborhood do not easily fit middle-class white norms. Outside pressure against being an

"Uncle Tom" cannot be ignored. The practical questions facing a businessman are how far a business firm should go in trying to assist in the total adjustment and what it is equipped to do in a constructive fashion.

This development problem is illustrated in the extreme by the experience of a number of leading companies with special training programs for "hard-core unemployed." One company undertook to train 40 such young men to be mechanical servicemen—an important semiskilled job in this particular company. It quickly ran into difficulty with ability to read instructions and to make simple calculations; deficiencies in early schooling had to be overcome. Several of the men did not understand the process of asking for help in overcoming a difficulty, taking instructions, and practicing the new operation; their process of learning was different than the instructors knew how to teach. The self-discipline involved in daily attendance at regular hours also was a stumbling block; in this matter there was lack of reinforcement in the home situation. And, a question of financial motivation arose because the more aggressive young men could make twice as much money per week pushing dope as they would receive when they successfully completed the training program. After a great deal of effort, the company did wind up with 8 very good employees. Even when allowance is made for the fact that the company was inexperienced in this kind of training, the cost was high for the results achieved.

This company is continuing its policy of providing special training for both present and potential minority employees because it is convinced that significant increases in the proportion of minority employees cannot be achieved without special training assistance. At the same time, (a) the nature of the training activity is still very experimental, and (b) closer cooperation with other agencies in the community that are better equipped than the company to handle certain difficulties is being developed.

SUMMARY

Thinking through a strategic plan includes weighing its impact on company resources. In its role as a resource converter, the company must attract the particular kinds of resources needed to execute its selected strategy. If a workable exchange of inputs and outputs cannot be arranged, then the strategy itself must be altered. For example, relations with present and potential employees can affect the feasibility of entering a new line of business, moving from a city location to the suburbs, replacing clerical operations with a computer, or shifting the degree of vertical integration.

Building a basis for continuing cooperation with human resources is difficult because (a) the kinds of inputs needed change, (b) the available supply and personal expectations change, and (c) the contributions actually made depend significantly on the current feeling of the people toward their jobs and their company.

Selection and development of company personnel is one part of such resource mobilization. The changing composition, attitudes, and expectations of the U.S. labor force imposes a dynamic aspect on approaches that will be effective in this area.

Hiring policy should be geared to planned growth rates and to new job structures. At the same time, policy must reflect external changes such as the rapid rise in educational levels and in pressure to upgrade jobs provided to black and other minority workers.

As company strategy is adjusted to the accelerating accumulation of knowledge, the practicality of using horizontal promotion to develop a versatile work force and/or the provision of career ladders for employees who assume specialist roles should be considered.

An unwelcome consequence of changing strategy will be technological unemployment. This raises policy questions about transfers, layoffs, and dismissal wages.

The prevailing tradition of bringing people in at the bottom and promotion from within rests on a high degree of training-on-the-job and other company-encouraged development activities. Closer examination reveals that such a training policy fits only some firms. Where tenure of employment is short and external training facilities exist, in-company training can be limited. On the other hand, companies that elect to be technological pioneers may find themselves training for an entire new industry.

Employee obsolescence and professional growth are becoming more pressing issues. Companies whose strategy stresses frequent change face especially acute problems in these areas.

Superimposed on these issues is the knotty question of what and how companies can accelerate the development of minority and women employees at all levels.

Each of these issues has its own ramifications, but the primary task of central management is to assure an *integrated* adjustment to the needs generated by strategy decisions and by a dynamic environment.

QUESTIONS FOR CLASS DISCUSSION

   1. For the following positions do you recommend a hiring policy giving preference to women, giving preference to men, or based solely on objective measurements: (a) Taxicab driver? (b) Hospital dietitian? (c) Coal mine superintendent? (d) Office secretary? (e) Army officer?

   2. The president of a large Midwest commercial bank has actively supported the hiring and promotion of blacks in his community and in his own institution. Several officers and over a dozen supervisors are blacks. Although there is only

minor resentment among other employees over the rapid rise of these executives, a more serious difficulty is the feeling of the blacks themselves. One vice-president says, "I got here because I'm black. Now the question is, can I live up to the opportunity?" Self-respect and self-confidence are still needed. In a situation like this, how fast should blacks be promoted?

3. What kinds of firms, if any, should attempt in the process of hiring people to screen out those who feel alienated toward capitalistic society and who have "anti-Establishment" feelings? How should a company try to learn about a person's feelings on such matters?

4. A manufacturer of stainless steel tubing plans to open a small plant in the Piedmont region of North Carolina. The new plant will concentrate solely on automated production of quality tubing for hypodermic needles. Thus the new plant will avoid problems of frequent shifts in sizes and materials that occur in the main plant. Should the selection and training policies of the new plant differ from those of the main plant? If so, in what respects?

5. (a) What might Communications Systems, Inc., described on page 221, have done to keep its corps of competent young persons interested in working for the company? (b) Assuming that a reduction in staff was necessary, how could the company have avoided the adverse "selection" by the technical persons who resigned?

6. National Bakeries has a policy of increasing the percentage of its black employees. Roger, a black, was transferred from his first assignment at the end of three months (the "temporary worker" period at National) because of unsatisfactory work. He has been in his present job for six months and his work is still substandard. The union shop steward reminds the plant manager of previous grievances regarding management's right to dismiss "regular employees" on the basis of low productivity, and he asks the plant manager if a new precedent regarding ability is established. Roger was hired on the recommendation of a civil rights leader. What should National Bakeries do about Roger?

7. In government services of all kinds there is a strong movement toward the hiring of "professionals." (a) What consequences do you predict will arise from such professionalization? (b) Do you recommend encouraging this trend in government service? (c) Should a similar trend be encouraged in private business?

8. "A seniority policy for layoffs may be okay for routine workers, but it should not apply to key persons." Assuming that central management wished to follow such a policy, how would you define "key persons" (a) in an advertising agency, (b) in a hotel, (c) in a telephone company, and (d) in a professional baseball club?

9. Most large book publishers have moved their main offices to the suburbs. Here the primary functions are editorial, warehousing, bookkeeping, and sales promotion (typesetting, printing, and binding are almost always subcontracted). Most publishers hoped to tap a new labor supply in the suburbs—mostly women living within easy commuting distance. They now find that many potential employees are second wage earners in the household and want only part-time jobs, often with irregular hours. How do you suggest the publisher utilize this potential resource? What are the implications of using such personnel on the way the business is run?

CASE 11 / Chapparal Memorial Hospital

John Chavez, Personnel Director of Chapparal Memorial Hospital, is concerned by information he has received over the past several months. It seems to indicate that some personnel policies of the hospital might be ineffective. He personally is proud of these policies, for he has played a major role in their establishment during the past three years. He does not want to see them fail. But the situation in Foods and Nutrition Service is not what it should be.

Chapparal Memorial Hospital in Rincon, a major city in the southwestern part of the United States, is a complete general hospital with beds available in medicine, surgery, psychiatry, neurology, physical medicine, and pulmonary diseases. Specialized treatment includes a hemodialysis unit, equipment for the treatment of cancer, and a renal transplant unit. There are about seven hundred full-time employees as well as many part-time employees, volunteers, and attending physicians.

The Foods and Nutrition Service of the hospital is responsible for all aspects of planning, preparing, and serving meals and special diets for the patients, both bedridden and ambulatory, and for the staff, volunteers, and visitors who use the hospital's cafeteria. Tasks, reporting, and responsibility relationships of the Foods and Nutrition Service are shown in the diagram on the opposite page.

Mr. Chavez recalled that the medical director of the hospital has often spoken with pride about the inclusion of dietitians in the "full-service patient-care team" that is responsible for the diagnosis, treatment, and care given patients during their stay in the hospital or their attendance at the out-patient clinics. The dietitians themselves indicate that they frequently work with doctors, nurses, pharmacists, rehabilitation specialists, and social workers on various aspects of the treatment of patients. Mr. Chavez knew from his personal experience that the food served in the hospital's cafeteria, although occasionally colder than he would have liked, is tasty and varied. It was never criticized for being the same from week to week nor for "institutional blandness."

Working conditions in the kitchens are generally recognized as not ideal. One factor in the position description of a Grade 4 Food Service Worker reads:

> Working areas are often warm and noisy. Employees are exposed to minor cuts, bruises, burns, and scalds. There is danger of slipping on floors which are wet from daily mopping or spillage. Some workers are exposed to extreme temperatures of the hot kitchen and the walk-in refrigerators.

Mr. Chavez recalled being told during one of his customary walking tours of the hospital that a cook had complained to Mrs. Salgado, the Section Head for Program Management and Planning, that the air-conditioning and venting was inadequate during the summer months. She responded: "In October, nature will take care of the heat problem."

About half of the long-service (5 to 20 years) workers in the Foods and Nutrition Service are ex-military personnel who have retired after long years in the Armed Services and some duty time at a major defense installation close to the city of Rincon.

Foods and Nutrition Service
CHAPPARAL MEMORIAL HOSPITAL

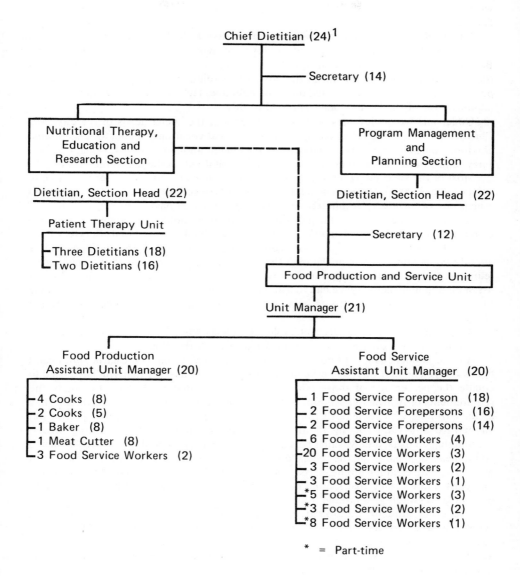

Chief Dietitian (24)[1]

Secretary (14)

Nutritional Therapy,
Education and
Research Section

Program Management
and
Planning Section

Dietitian, Section Head (22)

Dietitian, Section Head (22)

Patient Therapy Unit

Secretary (12)

- Three Dietitians (18)
- Two Dietitians (16)

Food Production and Service Unit

Unit Manager (21)

Food Production
Assistant Unit Manager (20)

Food Service
Assistant Unit Manager (20)

- 4 Cooks (8)
- 2 Cooks (5)
- 1 Baker (8)
- 1 Meat Cutter (8)
- 3 Food Service Workers (2)

- 1 Food Service Foreperson (18)
- 2 Food Service Forepersons (16)
- 2 Food Service Forepersons (14)
- 6 Food Service Workers (4)
- 20 Food Service Workers (3)
- 3 Food Service Workers (2)
- 3 Food Service Workers (1)
- *5 Food Service Workers (3)
- *3 Food Service Workers (2)
- *8 Food Service Workers (1)

* = Part-time

[1] The numbers in parentheses indicate the rating grade for the position.
Grades 9 and below are paid by the hour, grades above 9 are on a biweekly
salary, and grades above 19 are managerial.

This includes 2 of the dietitians and the 3 unit managers. Of the part-time workers, 3 are high school students employed in a federal program designed to keep them in school and the rest are students at a local university. The latter have all told Mr. Chavez that they were attracted by the hospital's policy of paying higher than the normal wages in the community.

Jobs in Rincon are not and never have been easy to find despite the city's growth rates in population, total income, and employment, which are above national averages. Based on the evidence from a University of Chicago study, Mr. Chavez had concluded that a high-wage policy minimized the costs of searching for employees and attracted persons who, on the whole, turned out to be effective. He had eventually convinced the administrator of the hospital and its board of this.

Under another policy, designed to meet some of the social needs of the city, Mr. Chavez had seen to the hiring of 4 graduates of a local vocational school for exceptional children, some of whom have handicaps of one kind or another. These 4, Delia, Charles, Jerry, and Louise, have come to work at the hospital within the last three years.

Most of the succeeding information about the Foods and Nutrition Service came to John Chavez in exit interviews he held with some of the college students. This group had a high rate of turnover, despite the attraction of the wages paid.

One student said: "I read the general indoctrination booklet everyone gets when he comes to work at Chapparal and the employees' handbook for the Foods Service. They were pretty helpful. Then, after I had worked for a month, one of the dietitians had us attend two meetings at which she read the handbook to us. She closed the meeting by telling us to be sure to change our underwear daily. I asked my foreman and also the assistant unit manager why we had to listen to her read the book to us. They just told me that everyone had to listen to its being read once a year and that the best way to get along was to take it easy.

"Abe, one of the retired sergeants, told me to relax when I was doing some cleaning. 'Don't do such a good job. They'll want it that way all the time.'"

Another student said: "I know why you hired Louise, Delia, and Charlie, but I can't figure Jerry. The first three have Spanish surnames and I assume that you have tried to equate the percentage of those who work here with that in the city to satisfy the requirements of Affirmative Action. But Jerry is less capable than the other three. They all have trouble with some of the jobs that we all have to do (pushing carts, putting out silverware and then sorting it later, cleaning, washing dishes, counting meals, maintaining utensils, and washing pots and pans). Louise gets confused when she has to count meals or separate all the special diets. Charlie can't do any heavy lifting and walks away from any cleaning job he is assigned to. Delia cries if she is assigned to scrub pots and pans. I don't think that I could have stood this place as long as I have if we hadn't been able to switch jobs around a lot."

One other student mentioned in his exit interview that, since he majored in accounting at the local university, he had once asked Mrs. Salgado whether the hospital used program budgeting for the work in Foods and Nutrition. She had told him that accounting was the responsibility of the accounting section of the business department, that the dietitians were concerned with equipment and programs to provide the best health care possible for the patients in the hospital, and that he should stop wasting his time and hers with questions that were not relevant to their jobs and get on with his work.

During his reflections about the Service, Mr. Chavez recalled what Mrs. Nunez, the Food Service Foreperson, Grade 18, and a close neighbor, had recently told him about some administrative matters. "Our special employees—Louise, Delia, Charlie, and Jerry—have difficulty with some of the tasks that all food service workers have to do, but our checking system is such that we catch most errors before they get out of the kitchens. Once in a great while a nurse or ward attendant will call down about a wrong tray, but that is rare. We certainly haven't poisoned any babies by putting salt rather than sugar in their formulas, as did that hospital in the East some years ago.

"Those college students whom you hire are a special problem. They work hard when they are here, but they certainly are sick often on Fridays or Mondays. If we did not have everyone else coming in steadily, we would often be in difficulty on those days. The college boys are also the center of a group of about nine persons in Foods and Nutrition who spend a lot of time complaining about how the system works, about how the dietitians won't listen to them, and about how the other workers are stealing food. They seem to think their ideas about how the hospital should be run should be listened to, put into practice at once, and then enforced by a group of policemen who would run around checking on the laws laid down by the students. Well, all of them aren't that bad, but I wish the university would teach them how to work with other people and keep their mouths shut some of the time. Then they might have a chance to look and see how Foods and Nutrition has to act to do an effective job in this hospital."

Mrs. Frances Ivey, the Chief Dietitian, had also spoken to Mr. Chavez. "The policy of hiring college kids may help them get through college but I sometimes think that they are more trouble than they are worth. They come in to see me every once in a while about pay problems or work problems and I always ask them if they have checked with Mrs. Nunez. Well, usually they haven't and they seem surprised when I won't talk with them about what they think is a problem but tell them to see her. She has the administrative responsibility here and handles it well. As a matter of fact, I am glad that that leaves us free to deal with all the technical questions we have in the Service and to work with the physicians on nutrition problems of the patients."

Required: (a) What personnel policies do you find in action in Chapparal Memorial Hospital?

(b) How are they working out?

(c) Does the case reveal other personnel and administrative problems in the hospital?

(d) In Mr. Chavez's position, what would you do? Be specific about what action you think is wise. What would you say to whom?

12

PERSONNEL AND INDUSTRIAL
RELATIONS POLICY (CONCLUDED)

COMPENSATION

Compensation is a sensitive area. It warrants special attention because (a) a significant part of total costs are involved and (b) the ability of the company to attract and hold desirable employees, in part, depends on its compensation policy. Especially firms whose strategy calls for distinctiveness on the basis of low cost must seek a judicious blend of economy and incentive. Key issues include:

1. The general level of pay in relation to local labor markets and to the industry.
2. An internal alignment of compensation that employees feel is equitable.
3. Recognition of differences in individual performance.
4. Use of incentive plans.

General level of pay

Most companies follow a policy of paying competitive rates, that is, salaries and wages in line with those paid by other employers in the local labor markets and in the industry.

Relation to local rates. Changes are made in starting rates and maximums in accordance with "the market." The aim of such a policy is to neutralize pay as a competitive factor. The company hopes to be regarded as being fair, but it relies on factors other than pay to attract and hold its employees.

A higher wage level than that prevailing in the community is paid by some companies in an effort to secure the "cream of the crop." For many years this was the policy of the Ford Motor Company. Workers differ substantially in their ability to do a given job. By offering to pay more than average compensation, companies hope to secure the best workers. In other instances, the higher rate must be offered to offset an unfavorable location or poorer working conditions. Low labor turnover is still another reason for paying employees above the general competitive rate; such a policy might well be followed by a company that wishes to give its customers distinctive personalized service.

If satisfactory results can be secured from mediocre employees, a firm may follow a policy of paying comparably low wages. A retail store, for example, that expects the salesclerks to do little more than make change and wrap packages may quite legitimately have a lower wage scale than a store that expects its salespeople to give intelligent counsel and advice to customers. Of course, in this illustration the two stores desire a different quality of worker, and actually each store may be paying the competitive rate for the type of employee that it is seeking.

Industry rates. In some industries, primarily as a result of union pressure, the industry-wide wage level is more important than the wage level in the local labor market. A national union, after being recognized in key plants throughout the country, may choose to negotiate wages with most or all of the employers as a group instead of dealing with each firm separately. In these circumstances, comparison with local rates is usually less significant than ability to pay, changes in cost of living, and general bargaining strength of the two parties. In fact, there is no agreement as to what should be the basis for establishing industry-wide wage levels once the union secures and operates as a national monopoly of the labor supply for that industry.

The policy questions facing a company in these circumstances are largely concerned with the extent of joint action with other managements in the industry. This subject is considered at the end of the chapter.

Internal alignment of pay

Increasing recognition is being given to the comparison of compensation paid to different employees within a company. Several psychological studies of the attitude of workers revealed that they are as interested, if not more so, in how their pay compares with that received by their fellow workers as they are in the actual amount they receive.

To meet this situation, a company may adopt a policy of using a consistent wage scale for all employees. The application of this general policy is illustrated by the compensation plan of a utility company that was formed through the consolidation of nine separate corporations operating in more than one hundred cities. As might be expected, these different companies had followed different wage policies, so that when they were consolidated, there was considerable variation in the amount that was paid to people doing identical work in different cities.

In order to develop a fair basis for wage differentials, it was necessary to evaluate each of the numerous jobs. Each job was rated in terms of the education and experience required, the degree of supervision received, the degree of supervision exercised, the nature of duties performed, and the working conditions surrounding the job. The *job evaluation* provided a basis for classifying all jobs up to the executive level into fifteen different grades. Jobs in any one grade are about equal in difficulty and importance, and hence are entitled to the same pay. In other words, the company adopted a policy in which the pay differentials between *jobs* would be based on systematic job evaluation.

This rationalization of its pay scales was important to the utility company not only in terms of employee morale. The new system also helped the company justify its costs in its rate case before the state public utility commission.

Recognition of differences in individual performance

Sound policy regarding external alignment of the wage level and internal alignment of individual jobs will go a long way toward a satisfactory wage plan for a company. A third factor should also be recognized. The quality and the quantity of work turned out by individuals on the same job are not equal. Rarely is a person recently assigned to a job as valuable to the company as a fellow worker who has been doing that kind of work for several years. Most companies believe it is desirable to adjust pay in recognition of these differences in individual performance.

If a company uses piece rates, commissions, or other forms of incentive compensation, individual differences in performance will be reflected directly in the pay envelope. For a great many jobs, however, output bonuses are not practical. Consequently, companies often have a range of pay for each job or job grade. Beginners will be paid at the minimum of the range; then, as they improve their skill and usefulness, their pay is increased up to, but not above, the maximum of the range.

The public utility already discussed decided it wanted a range of pay for each of its job grades. It made provision for five in-grade increases above the minimum, each of approximately 5%, giving an overall pay range from the minimum and the maximum of any grade of about 28%. The resulting salary schedule (including several adjustments made since the plan was first installed) is shown at the top of page 243.

A company following this plan must decide how wide its salary range is to be. If the nature of the work and the management of the company is such that employees can exercise considerable initiative, or if there are other reasons for a wide variation in individual performance, then the salary range should be wide. Most companies, if they have a salary range at all, allow for a spread of 20% to 35%.

There are several drawbacks to a wide spread, however. Control of salary costs is more difficult. People in low salary grades may be earning as much as or more than people holding considerably more difficult jobs, and this can create a bad morale. Also, for certain kinds of labor, notably in the skilled crafts, it is a tradition in some markets to have a single rate, or at most only a 5% or 10%

Salary Scale Used by Public Utility Company
(in Communities of 15,000 to 100,000 Population)

			Weekly Pay for Steps Within Each Grade			
	A	*B*	*C*	*D*	*E*	*F*
Job Grades	*Learning*	*Mastery*	*Skill*	*Versatility or Skill and Long Service*	*Exceptional or Versatility and Long Service*	*Exceptional and Long Service*
15	$467	$491	$515	$540	$567	$595
14	423	444	467	491	515	540
13	384	403	423	444	467	491
12	348	365	384	403	423	444
11	316	332	348	365	384	403
10	287	301	316	332	348	365
9	260	273	287	301	316	332
8	236	248	260	273	287	301
7	215	225	236	248	260	273
6	195	204	215	225	236	248
5	176	185	195	204	215	225
4	160	168	176	185	195	204
3	145	152	160	168	176	185
2	132	138	145	152	160	168
1	120	125	132	138	145	152

differential, for all workers in that craft. The implicit assumption here is that anyone who qualifies as a regular carpenter or plumber is as good a worker as anyone else in the same trade.

A salary range permits recognition of intangibles—and it opens the possibility of favoritism or discrimination. For instance, if black technicians (or professors) are in short supply, should they be paid more than whites? Or if an ample supply of women exists for, say, security analyst positions, should they be paid less than men doing the same work? What recognition, if any, should be given to future potential? Should cheerfulness count, or being a star on the bowling team? What about loyalty? Being intangible, such issues are hard to treat in an explicit policy. A company may simply say that it will, or will not, include intangibles in determining an individual's pay. And it may adopt a few specific negative policies such as no differentiation in pay because of one or more of the following: age, military service, family connection, education, previous earnings, number of children, health, or similar factors. (Differentiation in pay because of race, religion, and sex is illegal, so policy—if any—on these factors deals with the way the law will be interpreted and applied.)

Use of incentive plans

Individual merit increases, as just described, provide a general incentive to people in the lower part of their range, but the spur is lost after individuals reach their top. Almost never under such a plan do persons move down because their work slips. Consequently, the idea of tying people's pay more closely to their output appeals to any executive attempting to improve output and to keep costs from rising.

Virtually all financial incentive schemes have a guaranteed minimum salary in some form—a minimum regardless of output, a salary plus bonus, or some similar arrangement. Even sales representatives on commission usually have a "drawing account." Moreover, the aim is to enable people with "normal" performance to earn at least as much as they would under a fixed wage or salary. The incentive plan, then, works no hardship on an effective employee. It does bring pressure on the individual who gets lazy and it does reward the one who is extra productive.

Problem of installing incentive rates. The design of a satisfactory incentive plan is not easy. For example, a company dealing in air-conditioning equipment wished to put its sales representatives on an incentive wage, but it found this difficult because many sales were made on a contract basis for which there was no standard price. The sales representatives, in their desire to increase sales volume, were likely to offer the product at such a low price that the company could make no profit on the transaction.

As an alternative it was proposed that before a contract order was accepted, the company engineers make an estimate of the total cost of installation. Sales representatives would then be paid a percentage of the margin between the estimated installation cost and the price received from the customer. Under this arrangement sales representatives would be interested in profitable business rather than mere sales volume. The difficulty with this suggestion was that the company often wanted to accept business at a very narrow profit margin in order to keep its plant active. In such a case the sales representative would receive very little pay for selling an order. The management recognized that some form of compromise between these two bases might have been developed. The company felt, however, that such a system would be so complicated that it would be difficult to administer and that the sales representatives would not respond because they would not understand just how the system worked. Consequently, the idea of an incentive plan was at least temporarily set aside.

Plans for incentive do not always work just as anticipated. When quality work is desired, an incentive on volume of output may lead to difficulties. A company manufacturing electrical appliances experienced a sharp increase in complaints from customers shortly after its incentive plan was installed, and only after a new quality control procedure was established did the incentive plan work satisfactorily.

Conditions affecting success of incentive wage policy. Many conditions affect the success of a policy of paying incentive wages. Among the most important are:

1. The final result must truly reflect the effort of the worker. In many types of work the nature of the job, the raw materials, the conditions surrounding the work, and other factors outside the control of the worker are primarily responsible for the accomplishments achieved. If workers see that their efforts do not affect the final outcome very much, the incentive will not be effective.
2. All important elements that are subject to the control of the worker should either be included in the compensation plan or be carefully controlled by other means. Output or sales are frequently not the only factors that must be controlled. Quality of output, waste of materials, care of machines, selling expenses, prices received for products, cooperation with other employees, and service rendered to the customer are some of the details that may suffer under an incentive form of compensation. Frequently, however, such details are included in the basis on which the compensation is computed or are controlled by other means.
3. The method of computing compensation must be simple enough so that the employees can readily understand it. Unless the employees recognize the connection between their actions and their wages, the incentive form of compensation will likely be ineffective.
4. The effect of good performance on the amount of compensation received should become apparent quickly so that the worker will realize the importance of good performance. If the typical employee is not rewarded until a month or perhaps a year after exerting the extra effort, the reward will lose much of its potency.
5. The confidence and the cooperation of the employee should be secured. If workers believe incentive wages are merely a device to cut wages or to increase the amount of work without added benefit to them, the plan is likely to run into snags. On the other hand, if they believe the management is fair and is offering them an opportunity to secure extra pay by added effort, the whole system is much more likely to succeed.

Unless these conditions can be reasonably met, the better policy would probably be to pay employees on a time basis.

SUPPLEMENTAL BENEFITS

Sharp challenge has been raised to company policy that intrudes into the private lives of employees. Paternalism is frowned upon; modern attitudes require that employees be regarded as mature, self-respecting individuals. Why, then, should any company go beyond proper selection, development, and compensation?

The answer lies in the fact that each employee is a whole person. The employee's working self is the same personality who is head of a family, goes to a ball game, and argues about politics. The contention is that a person whose total life is satisfactory is more likely to be a productive employee. Even if this somewhat debatable premise is accepted, there remain serious questions about the areas and the degree to which a company should undertake to help provide a "good life" for its employees. Let us review briefly some of the supplemental benefits a company can provide and then note considerations in establishing a policy regarding such matters.

Vacations and holidays

Paid vacations ranging from 2 to 4 weeks are now customary. There is, however, considerable variation in the length of service an employee must have to qualify for the longer periods.

Opinion differs among executives regarding the purpose of granting vacations. Some executives contend that a vacation is an opportunity for employees to get a change from their regular daily routine so that they may come back to work refreshed, rested, and prepared to render more efficient service to the company during the balance of the year. According to this philosophy, a vacation is not something to which the employees are entitled. Consequently, the employees do not have a claim to vacation pay if they voluntarily leave the company, nor can vacations be carried over from one year to the next.

Other executives look upon vacations more or less as a bonus or a special compensation. One large company, in which approximately 90% of its 23,000 employees are eligible for vacations with pay, permits its employees to work during the vacation period and to take extra compensation in lieu of time off if they so desire. Incidentally, the cost to this company of granting vacations is approximately $8 million per year.

With a 2-week paid vacation, a 40-hour week, and the customary 8 paid holidays, "full-time" work accounts for less than 25% of a worker's total time. The shifting occurring in many service companies to a 35-hour week and a 4-week vacation reduces the working time to under 20%. Yet many people regard this as a tough schedule. To a considerable degree, holidays, vacations, and working hours are like a standard of living—one feels either rich or poor depending upon what one is accustomed to.

Protection against risk

At the same time that federal and state governments have undertaken vast programs of social security, unemployment insurance, and medicare, companies have also stepped up the financial protection they provide against risks that formerly were borne by children, parents, relatives, the local community, and the individual himself. Here is a list of the possible kinds of protection a company can provide.

Illness. In addition to the usual on-site medical office, a company may protect against a burden of illness through sick leaves, hospital insurance, surgical insurance, and major medical expense insurance.

Unemployment. Supplementing the state plans, the automobile companies and some others have their own unemployment insurance. Sometimes this is called a guaranteed annual wage and in other cases an annual salary plan.

Premature death. A group life insurance plan may provide protection ranging from a few thousand dollars to double an employee's annual salary.

Old age. During the past 35 years, old-age pension plans have become increasingly popular. For employees with long service, the pensions may amount to as much as 50% of annual salary.

The cost of this kind of protection is high. Pension costs alone are skyrocketing. Increasingly, pensions are being geared to the highest salary a person earns (not the average salary on which reserves were set aside), and cost-of-living supplements to offset inflation are being added after a person retires. A liberal company plan for an array of risks can easily add 30% to basic salary expense.

As with vacations, the purpose of protection plans is being debated. One view of company pensions is a quid pro quo for long, loyal service; the employee stays with one company and gets a pension in exchange. Turnover, especially of older employees, is reduced. An opposite view is that employees earn their pensions as they work and are entitled to take all accrued claims with them whenever they decide to quit—even when they go to work for a competitor.

Social and recreational activities

Companies vary a great deal in the extent to which they sponsor social and recreational activities. The basic aims are to create a friendliness among employees and to have employees remember pleasant associations when they think of the company. Athletic teams, picnics, musical organizations, company libraries, and company magazines are typical of such activities. Often these activities are run by the employees themselves, with the company providing encouragement and financial assistance.

To lead or to follow?

No company can ignore supplemental benefits. Social custom now requires a company to make some provision for vacations, employee risks, and social activities away from the job. The basic policy question is whether merely to follow general practice as it develops or to take the lead in one or more of the various areas we noted above.

Sharing the costs of pioneering. The costs of supplemental benefits are substantial, and the company that pioneers in liberal pensions, early retirement, or guaranteed annual wage may find itself at a competitive disadvantage because of high costs.

One policy is to have the employee share the cost of a new benefit. This has been done for medical insurance, pensions, and even recreational activities. In addition to cutting cost, a benefit of this arrangement is that most of us prize those things for which we have made some sacrifice. Thus, an employee may appreciate major medical insurance more if he contributes to its cost.

Usually, if employees contribute to the cost of a benefit, their participation should be voluntary. Then, as time passes, if the benefit ceases to be distinctive from what is done by other companies and employees are complaining about the burden of payroll deductions, the company may take on the total expense and provide the benefit for everyone. Of course, at this point the benefit becomes just another part of the total work package and drops out of the pioneering category.

Employee expectations. Not so long ago all regular employees expected to work at least half a day on Saturday. Now, an employee who doesn't get a 2-day weekend feels abused. The attitudes toward other supplemental benefits follow this same pattern. Consequently, if a company expects to generate strong employee enthusiasm because of its supplemental benefits, it must be prepared to keep adding new ones.

   Also, what interests an employee shifts over time. The automobile and the television set have radically changed the social structure and the recreational patterns at the place of employment. Suburban living segments a person's life. Added purchasing power permits diversified and dispersed recreation. Living patterns diminish the feasibility of mutual family assistance. Government aid reduces the tradition of self-dependence. Because of such changes as these, a supplemental benefit that was heralded a generation ago may generate little excitement today. Consequently, the firm that seeks leadership in this area must be both sensitive and imaginative.

Showing genuine concern. Mayo found in his famous Hawthorne studies that the employee's belief that the company was concerned about him as an individual and was interested in his work and welfare was more important than the particular actions the company took. This insight suggests that supplemental benefits cannot be passed out with the assumption that the employees will be grateful. A policy of pioneering in this area must be accompanied by other demonstrations of genuine concern about the employee as an individual. Organization, personnel development, and supervision—discussed elsewhere in this book—are all part of the picture. In the proper combination they give synergistic effects.

Operations responsive to supplemental benefits. For reasons just outlined, central management must carefully analyze the particular operations of its company when deciding what supplemental benefits to stress. Generally speaking, companies that want to hold their employees over long periods and have low turnover will probably find their employees more responsive to supplemental benefits. In contrast, companies that use many part-time employees or have wide fluctuations in employment, as in the space industry, are more likely to find their employees saying, "Put it in the pay envelope." Location in or outside a big city will also affect the social and recreational activities that are attractive to employees. The general age of employees is still another factor. In personnel, as in marketing or research, being a successful pioneer requires keen discernment.

INDUSTRIAL RELATIONS

For managers and employees to work together to accomplish the objectives of an enterprise, they must agree on wages, hours, and other conditions of employment. For many years these agreements were made primarily between managers and individual employees. Even today, over two thirds of the employees in the United States bargain individually with their employers. However, there has been a dramatic rise in the power of labor unions, and the agreements reached with the unions set the pattern for many of the individual agreements.

Some people contend that the existence of a union makes the objective consideration of personnel policies futile. The assumption is that if management is not entirely free to make final decisions on such matters, the alternative is an irrational patchwork of agreements based on the bargaining surrounding each issue. Such a view is both unrealistic and unproductive. The manager designs products in terms of what customers will buy, sets prices on the basis of competition and within the limits permitted by law, and buys materials and borrows money under terms he can negotiate with the supplier. The views and the strength of the union will, of course, influence the personnel policy finally established, just as the operating situations influence other policies. But the fact that the decisions are not made by the manager alone does not remove the desirability of a workable, integrated plan of action. The need for unemotional, careful analysis remains unchanged.

Policies regarding the selection and the development of a work force, compensation, and supplemental benefits have already been discussed; consequently, attention here will concentrate on the way relations with unions are conducted. In this connection, a company should establish its policy regarding:

1. Character of union relations.
2. Scope of bargaining.
3. Recourse to outside agencies.

Character of union relations

A key aspect of all union relations is the underlying approach of a company to its relations with the union. The following examples illustrate the wide choice and the importance of this policy.

Belligerent policy towards unions. Companies engaged in interstate commerce are required by federal law to bargain with unions that represent a majority of their employees. Similar state laws require collective bargaining by most local businesses. Nevertheless, some employers balk at union activities whenever possible and do anything in their power to weaken the union.

Such a policy usually stems from a conviction that unions are antisocial. It may be supported by experiences with corrupt union officials, or communist-led unions, or unions that fail to live up to their contracts. Whatever the causes, there is strong dislike and mistrust of the union by the company executives. They try to conduct themselves so as to discredit the union in the eyes of the employees. They hope that sooner or later the employees will repudiate the union and it will no longer have to be recognized as the bargaining agent.

Obviously such a militant policy keeps the union stirred up; it will probably continue to use scurrilous tactics in its organization efforts. At best there will be only an armed truce between the two factions.

The horse-trading approach. Another view accepts the union as being inevitable but conducts relations along horse-trading lines. The union is assumed to be unreliable and conniving; consequently, negotiations are conducted in an air of suspicion and sharp bargains are quite in order. In keeping with this approach are deals that resolve immediate difficulties but that violate sound principles of human relations. As one advocate of this policy said, "It is just a question if you can outsmart the other guy."

Follow the leader. Often smaller companies try to establish an understanding with the union that the company will grant any wage increase or fringe benefits that have been agreed to by the leading companies of the industry, or sometimes in the local labor market. These firms feel that they are too small and weak to stand out against the union. The most they hope for is to be no worse off than their large competitors.

This is undoubtedly a practical policy in some circumstances. It does, of course, have the weaknesses of any policy of appeasement. Naturally, the union is going to ask for, and probably get, the most favorable clauses that are granted by any of the leading companies. Having won these points, the union leaders may ask for even more, particularly if they face political problems within the union and feel they must win further concessions to strengthen their own position. Moreover, one important way a small company competes with a large one is by making special adaptations to the local situation. The follow-the-leader policy sacrifices this potential strength insofar as industrial relations are concerned.

Straight business relationship. When both company executives and union leaders take a mature view of their relations, a company may approach union negotiations as a straight business proposition. This can occur only after union recognition has been accepted and the bitterness so often associated with such activities has passed into the background. There is mutual confidence, respect, and trust, just as there should be between the company and its major suppliers of raw materials.

This sort of business relationship does not mean that there will be no disagreements. The company may take a firm, even tough, position on certain matters; but the positions it takes are based on long-run business considerations, and there is a strong undercurrent of sound personnel relations.

Company executives must recognize that union leaders hold elected offices and that at times they must press grievances simply in response to pressure from some of their constituents. Under the straight business policy, this does not create a strong emotional reaction but is regarded simply as a normal part of the relationship. This type of relationship is often found in industries that have been organized for several years by a union which itself is stable and follows a bread-and-butter philosophy.

Union-management cooperation. Still another policy is to regard the union as an ally in improving the efficiency of the business. One of the best examples of union-management cooperation is the agreement developed over a generation ago between Hart, Schaffner & Marx and the union representing its factory employees. The union recognized that the company was in a highly competitive industry; consequently, it helped make improvements in labor productivity. On the other hand, the company acceded to demands for higher wages and better hours.

From the start there was emphasis on settling disputes by arbitration. The arbitrators have been highly respected individuals and always insist that questions regarding interpretation of an agreement be examined objectively. Even more important than wise administration of fixed agreements, however, are the methods developed to deal with technological and economic changes in new agreements. The actual operation of the plan has required a great deal of patience. Nevertheless, there is substantial evidence that employer and employees alike have benefited by the spirit of cooperation and tolerance created by working together under such circumstances.

Union-management cooperation has taken different forms in the steel industry and in other places where it has been tried. In some cases a sharp distinction has been made between cooperative activities at the plant and bargaining over a new contract. In other instances, as in some agreements in the hosiery and ladies' garment industries, plans for improving productivity have become part and parcel of the basic contracts. Whatever the form, the important point here is that the company followed a basic policy of union-management cooperation.

The foregoing illustrations, ranging from a belligerent policy to union-management cooperation, are among the more common policies followed in union relations. Of course, many other variations are possible. Until a company formulates some kind of policy on the character of its union relations and gets this policy thoroughly accepted through its executive ranks, there is little hope for consistent and really effective industrial relations.

Scope of bargaining

Recognition of a union does not, of course, indicate what activities are to be covered in the union-management relationship. By tradition and law, questions of wages, hours, and physical working conditions are normal subjects of collective bargaining. More recently, employee pensions and similar benefits have been added to this standard list. Most companies would also agree that job assignments, the use of seniority or other factors in selecting employees for layoffs or promotions, and other supervisory activities were legitimate subjects for discussion, although they might firmly oppose any written agreement as to how these matters were to be handled. As soon as discussions extend beyond these traditional subjects, questions arise as to whether the union is interfering with ''management prerogatives.''

Employees clearly have a real stake in the stability of their company. Their income and their economic future are strongly influenced by the prosperity of the firm for which they work. If the union function is to protect the worker's interests, is it not reasonable then that the union should participate in decisions regarding pricing, new customers, product line, and similar matters?

This line of reasoning led unions in postwar Germany to insist on membership on boards of directors and other means of co-determination. With a few exceptions, American unions have shied away from such arrangements. Union leaders have recognized that if they participated in such decisions, they would share responsibility for them. By staying away from such matters, they avoid managerial responsibility and continue to be in a position to criticize (a significant weapon in union politics).

While neither union nor management leaders want unions to become involved in the entire managerial process, it is likely that an increasing number of topics will fall within the orbit of union-management relations. Unions can be helpful on such matters as absenteeism, productivity, and installation of new processes. They are concerned about changes in plant locations and mechanization.

Some firms follow a policy of keeping unions as far away from such matters as possible. In other cases, such as the union-management agreements on mechanization of hosiery mills and contracting in the garment industry, union contracts deal with what typically are regarded as management matters. A more common and more flexible policy is to restrict the formal collective bargaining process to conditions of employment and to work out other matters of mutual interest in a much more informal manner.

Recourse to outside agencies

Union-management relations are not confined to an individual company and the unions representing its employees. Other parties may enter the picture, and a company will do well to clarify its policy on recourse to outside agencies.

Impartial arbitration. Most union contracts provide for arbitration of disputes over the interpretation and the application of the contract. Typically, a dispute follows a grievance procedure moving up from the worker and his first-line supervisor through several administrative levels. If the matter cannot be settled by management and union representatives, an impartial arbitrator is called in to make a decision that becomes binding on all parties concerned.

Some such provision is necessary if strikes are to be avoided during the period of the contract. Where a single impartial arbitrator has been used over a period of years, a sort of "common law" develops. Once this common law becomes accepted, many potential disputes are settled without ever reaching the arbitrator. Many companies take the position that minor disagreements can be worked out best by the parties directly concerned and follow a policy of minimum use of outside arbitrators.

Group bargaining. The negotiation of a new labor contract is quite a different matter than its interpretation, which has just been discussed. The distinction is like that between the legislative and the judicial branches of the government. Usually the company itself works out the new agreement with its employees. To an increasing extent, however, employers are joining together in groups to negotiate new contracts with labor unions. Roughly a tenth of all contracts in effect are negotiated through employer groups, and these cover approximately a fourth of all workers under union agreements.

Industry-wide bargaining is used in a few industries, such as coal mining and glass. More often, group bargaining covers employers in a city or a region. A company might want to join such a group for several reasons. The executives in small firms lack the time typically consumed in negotiations. In many instances they are not as skilled in the process as the professional union representatives with whom they must deal. Even the larger companies that have full-time industrial relations men may join an employer group in an effort to increase their bargaining strength. Moreover, the union has less opportunity to play one company against the other, pushing for different concessions with the several companies and then requesting everyone to agree to the most favorable concessions any competitor made.

On the other hand, such group bargaining makes it much more difficult to adapt the agreements to the particular situation of a given company. Also, at times the company may find itself being pushed into agreements that it would not make had it bargained alone. Consequently, companies whose industrial relations policy differs significantly from others in the industry, or whose economic position is distinctive, are often reluctant to participate in group bargaining.

Government mediation and arbitration. When a company and a union cannot agree upon a new contract and a strike threatens or actually begins, it is possible to call for assistance of a government *mediator*. This person explores the dispute and tries to find some basis on which the two sides may agree. The company will determine in part when a mediator should be called in and how effective he is likely to be. Some companies believe that this type of mediation is very helpful, while others resent the intrusion of an outsider.

If the impending strike is of sufficient importance to the public interest, the company may face other forms of outside assistance. Public utilities and basic industries are subject to fact-finding boards and impartial commissions of various kinds, depending upon the state or federal laws under which they fall. In this country we have not yet adopted *compulsory arbitration* in which parties to such a disagreement have to submit the dispute to an arbitrator whose decision is binding. But government seizure and other forms of pressure bring us pretty close to that point.

Each dispute has its own unique problems, and a general policy governing the way a company will conduct itself in this type of negotiation is difficult to establish. Nevertheless, some companies very carefully steer away from government intervention, whereas other firms either are willing to submit to government decision or they permit themselves to be jockeyed into that kind of position. The reason why the general policy of resorting to government intervention has detrimental value is that the whole preliminary bargaining process tends to break down if it is assumed that the dispute will be carried to mediators, political bodies, and public opinion. Strong pressure for the negotiators to arrive at agreement is lacking if they feel that a final settlement will not be reached at their level. On the other hand, if the feeling is that some type of an agreement must be hammered out without recourse to outsiders, then local negotiations can be carried on in an atmosphere where results are likely to be achieved.

SUMMARY

Selecting and developing a work force suitable to company needs was the focus of the preceding chapter. In this chapter we considered several key problems of making the company attractive to the desired employees. Fair compensation is crucial. Here, policy is needed on (a) a reasonable alignment with what other companies are paying, (b) differentials between jobs within the company based on differences in job difficulty and importance, and (c) recognition of variations in individual performance.

In the right situations, this compensation may be paid in the form of a financial incentive. Such incentives stimulate effort and provide an automatic reward for superior results. They are likely to be successful, however, only if results and efforts are closely related, noncompensated factors are controlled, the plan is simple and prompt, and mutual confidence prevails.

In addition to financial remuneration, every company must decide how far it wishes to go with supplemental benefits. Vacations, holidays, recreational activities, and a whole array of protections against economic risks such as sickness, old age, and unemployment should be appraised. Few companies dare lag behind general practice in such matters, so the major issue is in what ways a company wishes to be a leader in granting special benefits.

Finally, relations with unions must be considered. The underlying approach of a company, which may be anywhere from a militant policy to union-management cooperation, will permeate all union contracts. Within this general policy, more specific guidelines regarding support to existing union organizations, the scope of topics that will be discussed with the union, and the extent to which the company will join in group bargaining and use outside arbitrators need to be clarified.

Just as viable, continuing relationships with customers and suppliers are essential to a firm's existence, so, too, are its relations with its employees. The ritual of collective bargaining in no way diminishes the value of objective analysis in formulating a pattern of relationships with employees that are suited to the mission and the technology selected by central management.

Having discussed policy issues in three areas vital to every business enterprise—marketing, production, and personnel—we turn in the next chapters to a fourth inherent dimension—finance.

QUESTIONS FOR CLASS DISCUSSION

1. The regional manager of a franchised chain of Pancake Shops (fast-food restaurants) says her only personnel problem is finding good owner-managers and training them to train their workers. "Each shop is an independent enterprise. It has its own employees (15 to 30 people, since we are open 24 hours a day, 7 days a week, and use some part-time help), and sets its own pay. The turnover is fairly high, and we have no unions. It would be a mistake for us to try to develop personnel policies, because one of the advantages of a franchise system is to let local managers run their business in a personal way like all the early business enterprises in this country did." (a) Do you agree with this viewpoint? (b) Is this a good example of the advantages of a small business with respect to personnel and industrial relations?

2. Several studies show that when men and women hold the same kinds of jobs, the average pay for women is less than the average pay for men in comparable jobs. Sometimes the jobs of men doing about the same work as women are in higher classifications than the jobs of women. (a) What factors do you think may account for this difference? (b) If you were president of a company in which such a situation was brought to your attention, what would you do about it?

3. Several large companies recruit business school graduates (both four-year graduates and MBA's) as potential candidates for key jobs. Starting salaries are high, often equal to those of good employees with ten years of experience occupying second-level supervisory positions. (a) What problems will such salaries create for the company? (b) What problems will such salaries create for the newly hired business graduate? (c) What should companies do to utilize these young people most effectively?

4. An automobile company executive said privately: "Our wage rates should continue to be among the highest in the country. Our competitors will have to match any increases we give, and the higher wage cost can be passed on to the consumer." The treasurer of a competing company believes: "We have a social

responsibility to check this wage-price spiral. Our people are already well paid, and further increases only add fuel to inflation.'' (a) Under what conditions can a company ''pass on a wage increase to the consumer'' through a rise in prices? (b) How much attention should a company give to inflationary effects of wage increases—the second point quoted above?

5. For years hospital employees were paid relatively low wages. This was possible partly because many employees felt that they were helping their fellowmen and consequently did not press for maximum financial rewards. With the more recent rapid expansion in medical services, hospitals find that they cannot attract enough workers without paying close to prevailing market rates. Also, unions have called strikes in order to press for higher pay and shorter hours. Assuming that you were administrator of a large hospital, what wage level would you try to maintain?

6. ''Business firms and other employers should get out of the welfare game. Let the U.S. government follow the lead of other Western nations and finance more and more of health care, old-age benefits, and the like. Business can't compete in playing Santa Claus. Instead, it should put all it can in the pay envelope. And inflation will provide an opportunity to withdraw gracefully. By freezing existing dollar commitments, the percentage cost will drop as prices and wage levels rise. Any increase in compensation can then go into immediate pay—which employees will need very much to cover rising living costs.'' (a) Do you think this proposal is wise policy for a company to follow? (b) Does the proposal make more sense for some types of companies than others? Explain.

7. The aluminum industry has an agreement with the United Steelworkers of America regarding pensions which includes provisions (1) that the pension will be based on the highest job grade an employee reaches during his career and on his length of service, and (2) that cost-of-living additions will be made to persons already on pension if prices rise. These provisions contrast sharply with typical pension plans for university employees in which the amount of a person's pension is based on the contributions made to a pension fund, by the university and the individual, which are typically a percentage of each year's pay. (a) What benefits do you think aluminum companies will get from their more liberal plan? (b) Should aluminum companies be required to ''fund'' their anticipated pension payments, that is, make annual contributions to a fund that will make the fund large enough to finance anticipated future payments? (c) What effect, if any, does the character of business—aluminum vs. university—have on these pension arrangements?

8. Should unions as representatives of employees have more—or less—participation in company discussions regarding expansion, product lines, mechanization, location, and vertical integration than representatives of (a) customers, (b) major suppliers of materials, (c) government, (d) bondholders, and (e) stockholders?

9. The union business agent representing the workers of the Superior Hosiery Company has objected to the company's subcontracting some of its knitting and has asked that the company come to an understanding with the union on this issue. Do you think the company should bargain with the union on this issue? Do the reasons for the subcontracting have any bearing on whether the union should have some say in the matter? Would your answer change if the subcontracting is to be done in a foreign country?

CASE 12 / Western Steel Bar Company

Western Steel Bar Company, of Dallas, Texas, bought a marginally profitable manufacturing firm in Houston, Texas, to extend its marketing area. Both plants make steel rods and bars used to reinforce concrete for buildings and highways. In addition, the parent company melts steel and casts it into rod form in the Dallas plant. Two years after the purchase, certain output, delivery, and safety problems of the Houston plant have been brought under reasonable control, but the new management is having considerable difficulty with product quality. Ronald Bert, manager of the Houston Division, attributes the quality problems to the failure of employees to respond properly to changes in the compensation system and in job methods.

Steel rods, ¼ inch to 2 inches in diameter and up to 80 feet long, are shipped by rail from Dallas to the Houston plant. Rods for cutting and bending or for shearing only enter one end of the plant, which measures 160 feet wide and 200 long. Overhead cranes lift bundles of bars from the railroad cars, move them to cutoff tables next to the shears, and carry the finished items to loading docks at each end for shipment by truck to various construction sites. Scrap accumulates in the middle of the plant until it is moved for shipping to Dallas. The Houston Division's function is to get and fill orders for bars of a specified grade, quantity, length, diameter, and shape.

The Houston shop employs 40 to 60 men on two shifts, depending on the season and the construction cycle. All nonsupervisory employees belong to a local of the United Steel Workers of America. Nationwide bargaining by the international union determines the wage rates that apply to various skill levels in the shop as well as the fringe benefits. Two foremen supervise the day shift where the high-seniority employees work. One foreman handles the night shift. Exhibit 1 presents the organization chart for the Houston shop.

Stockmen are responsible for unloading railroad cars and for supplying the shears with bars of the proper grade and diameter.

Shearmen work in pairs—an operator and a helper on each of four shearing tables. They cut the 60- to 80-foot bars to lengths specified by production control cards and are responsible for length and quantity on each order. Cut bars are sent either to the benders for further processing or to a loading dock for shipping.

Benders receive some of the cut bars and shape them as specified by the job order card. (Common shapes are U, L, and J.) Large-diameter rod is bent on the four heavy benders operated by two men each. Smaller rod is processed on three light benders operated by one man each. Benders vary by the kinds of kinks they can curl into the steel.

The floorman handles scrap and occasionally assists with other jobs assigned by the foremen.

New employees learn all aspects of each helper's job (bending, shearing, or shipping) and move freely from one task to another. All training is on the job. Seniority and a foreman's request are the two determinants for training for a higher-rated job.

Job classifications, skill indices, and pay differentials in accordance with the collective bargaining agreement are given in Exhibit 2.

Exhibit 1

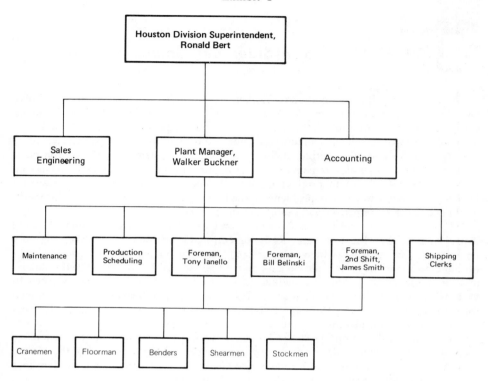

Under the previous management, work conditions that had evolved over time prevailed. The plant manager spent no time on the floor. The production scheduler and the foreman worked together to move the orders through the shop. The men freely rotated assignments. Coffee breaks and card games often ran for half an hour, but the men always met the daily output requested by the foremen. Once the quota was reached, the workers freely left their jobs—occasionally one or two hours before the end of a shift. Drinking on the job was common and was done openly. All men in the plant lived in the same neighborhood, and many were related by blood. Men with serious personal problems got substantial help from the plant manager.

During this regime, absenteeism was low, employee turnover was minimal and limited to seasonal or cyclical needs, there was always a waiting list of job applicants, and there were never any strikes of any kind (a competitive advantage for Western in an industry in which strikes over contract negotiations are common). However, the plant had the worst accident record of any reinforcing-bar shop in the Western District as well as the lowest output-per-man-hour record. Although daily delivery promises were always kept, the firm was profitable only part of the time. Its return on investment was less than half that of the industry average.

Immediately upon their arrival in Houston, Mr. Bert and Mr. Buckner set to work to improve the shop's safety record. Their purpose, as often stated to the men, was to

Exhibit 2

Skill Indices and Pay Rates by Job

Title	Job Class per the Collective Bargaining Agreement	Degree of Training Required [2]	Physical Effort Required [2]	Pay Differential Above Guaranteed Hourly Rate
Bender's Helper	3	3	8	Base Rate
Shearman's Helper	3	2	8	Base Rate
Shipper's Helper	3	1	8	Base Rate
Floorman	5	1	4	+ 6 percent
Shipper	7	8	1	+12 percent
Craneman	8	4	1	+15 percent
Shearman	8	4	5	+15 percent
Stocker	8	2	2	+15 percent
Light Bender	7 while training, then 9 [1]	5	8	+12 percent +18 percent
Heavy Bender	9 while training, then 9	8	7	+18 percent
Maintenance Man	10	9	4–7	+21 percent

[1] Training period is 520 hours on the machine.
[2] As rated by Ronald Bert on a scale from 1 (lowest) to 10 (highest).

make the shop a better place to work and to improve the men's lot by reducing the number of missing fingers, broken toes, wrenched backs, and injured or blinded eyes.

Mr. Buckner rigidly enforced regulations requiring the men to wear safety shoes, helmets, safety glasses, and leather arm sheaths. All items were provided by the company except shoes. One offense meant a written warning. Two warnings meant three days' suspension without pay. The men enthusiastically adopted the bright yellow helmets and the arm sheaths, but they complained bitterly about the safety glasses. They gave headaches, slipped off, got in the way, became clouded with sweat and dust, etc. Within a year the only noticeable improvement in the safety record was a marked decrease in the incidence of eye injury.

Additional rules and regulations were introduced and enforced. The first blast of a new siren announced the beginning of a ten-minute coffee break. Mr. Buckner patrolled the shop to cut down horseplay and early leaving. The siren signaled starting and quitting time.

To ease the physical effort required of men on the shear line, Mr. Buckner ordered and had installed electric rollers that did away with the need to manually push steel bars into the cutting heads. The number of helpers on each shear was reduced from two to one. Two automatic (and faster) benders replaced old models of the heavy benders.

With these changes, men were reassigned, old work groups were broken up, and mobility among jobs was considerably reduced. Foreman Ianello was assigned responsibility for the stockmen, floormen, shearmen, and the crane operator. Foreman

Belinski was responsible for bending operations and for one craneman. The foremen then controlled hiring, the assignment of helpers, and training for higher job classifications; however, they had to secure Mr. Buckner's concurrence for each decision. For the first year Mr. Buckner made all the choices as to who would be hired. This resulted in fewer relatives on the job.

After the new equipment was installed and the job reassignments made, two industrial engineers came in from Dallas to time-study all the jobs in the shop. Eventually they introduced an incentive system. Shearing and bending teams now get an incentive above the guaranteed rate based directly on daily output. All other plant personnel, including the foremen, are paid an incentive bonus on the basis of the entire plant's daily output. The output index is calculated from a complex formula that has, as independent variables, the metallurgical grade, diameter, quantity, length, and weight of the bars; and, for the benders, the number of bends per bar. Neither the union committeemen nor the foremen can explain the formula. Daily results are printed out on a computer terminal in the accounting office on the day after the accounting department sends data to the computer department in Dallas.

It did not take long for the operators to learn that small bars offer the best chance to make money. They then put out a major effort on those sizes of bars that they believe offer a chance to exceed 100% of standard by a large margin. The incentive pay system operates only when output exceeds standard. Below that output rate, employees are paid the guaranteed hourly rate.

Shift foremen now distribute job assignments and decide who processes what orders. Tony Ianello, recently promoted, is noted for favoring those operators who show the highest percentage performance. Workers make this judgment on the basis of the daily list that Mr. Buckner posts. It carries the names of the men whose output is below standard and by what percent.

Union committeemen now spend a fair proportion of their time bringing grievances to Mr. Buckner and appealing them to Mr. Bert. The complaints are mainly about equipment and working conditions. Both men have adopted a hard line toward the grievances and ordinarily respond that the equipment is the best available in the industry—and it is.

Demand is now at an all-time high and the United States Steel Corporation has seized this opportunity to gain a share of the market by doubling the size of its reinforcing-rod plant in Houston. Its plant is now slightly larger than the Houston Division of Western Steel Bar Company.

In the past three months, during vacation time, several job openings for heavy benders became available. No regular employees bid for these jobs. Bill Belinski put no pressure on his men to do so and claimed that his section could still do its job. However, output was below that desired by Mr. Bert.

Other incidents have disturbed the tranquility of the shop. Mr. Buckner's automobile was vandalized while parked during the day next to the building. On two occasions, bars of steel have come hurtling through Tony Ianello's office door. Loud disagreements and threats are common among the shearmen. Three employees are now under suspension for "horseplay."

With heavy pressure from customers and the sales department, the plant now works overtime. The day shift is scheduled for 10 hours except for Saturdays when it works 5 to 8 hours. The night shift regularly works 10 hours and frequently is scheduled for a week of five 12-hour days. The men complain about being tired, and the union has asked that more men be hired. Since all machines except the new benders are staffed and running, Mr. Buckner has refused to hire any men. He has pushed the foremen to look for men from outside the old neighborhood, and Tony Ianello believes that he can persuade two friends to come in from Galveston. Mr. Buckner has also authorized a modification of one of the heavy benders to allow greater operator control over the machine.

With the long hours and incentive pay, machine operators' take-home pay is often $350 to $400 per week. Total output is high and satisfactory to Mr. Bert. The plant is turning away orders for larger sizes of rod, and has subcontracted for replacement orders of 1,200 tons of steel returned by customers as not meeting grade and length specifications. Although Western was low bidder, it lost three orders totaling 500 tons (at $200 per ton) to U.S. Steel last month. Mr. Bert is not unhappy since he thinks this will give the plant a breathing space to work on the quality problem. Poor quality and late delivery by Western led to U.S. Steel's getting the orders.

Mr. Buckner posted a memorandum stating the facts about the lost orders and said that he would change the jobs of workers whose output percentage was below 90 or whose quality was below specifications.

During the week before last Labor Day, the men worked extra overtime in an attempt to bring the production schedule up to date. Although output was unusually high during the week, work was still scheduled on Saturday via a notice posted Friday morning. The men protested to Mr. Buckner, but to no avail. Most of them came in on Saturday (those who did not were suspended without pay for 5 days), but there was an unusual crop of accidents on that day. One shearman dropped a wrench into the shears of the highest producing team and damaged a blade. This accident shut down the shears until Tuesday. The crane operators and the stockmen spent most of their time in the locker room and toilets claiming that something they ate at a party the night before made them ill. One light bending machine operator shut down his machine claiming that it was out of alignment. All other benders supported him, and the maintenance man was unable to make the proper adjustments.

Mr. Buckner now seeks out individual employees whom he thinks might be having some difficulties with which he could help or who might want a temporary change in shifts. He takes care of any problems directly. From one man whom he has helped he learned that the men are looking forward to going on strike during the wage negotiations that come up in another four months and that they are seeking disaffiliation from the present local. Mr. Bert has opposed making any concessions to the union and has insisted that every grievance brought to him be submitted to arbitration. This policy has been financially burdensome for the local union and has led to extra assessments.

Turnover is still low. Only one man quit last year. A hard core of high-seniority employees works year-round. Under the existing union contract, they cannot be fired unless their infractions of work rules exceed a certain number within a given year. Mr. Buckner has observed that almost all the men come close to that number of infractions and are suspended for a predetermined number of days at particular intervals, such as deer-hunting season, fishing season, major holidays, etc. The last man who accidentally damaged a shear (the benders very rarely seem to break down) was cheered as he left the plant two hours prior to the end of his shift. Appeals by Mr. Buckner to the union committeemen for some help in getting the operators to live up to their responsibility under the contract to do a fair day's work and to use reasonable care toward the equipment meet with no response.

Mr. Bert believes that, under existing conditions, he is getting maximum output from the plant, that as many orders as can be taken are being processed, and that the safety problem is now less than before. Sales are well above two years ago and profits are proportionately much higher. Mr. Bert is concerned about the question of product quality and believes that something will have to be done soon to preserve Western's market share. In the long run a cyclical downturn could possibly trigger a heavy erosion of the firm's market position.

Required: (a) Describe current company policy on compensation, arrangements for work, employee services, union relations, support of unions, and recourse to outside agencies. What are they?

(b) Explain changes in compensation methods, union relations, informal social organization, and foremen's behavior during the past two years. What effect have these changes had on the workers' behavior and attitudes and on productivity?

(c) Explain changes in managerial action during the past two years. What effect have these had on output and productivity of the plant?

(d) What problems do you see for the Houston Division and what can usefully be done about them?

INTEGRATING / Strategy and the Creating
CASES / of Goods and Services

ESSEX CREEK DISPOSAL CO.

Essex Creek Disposal Co. faces difficult questions about who should take the initiative and who should bear the cost of "environmental protection." Company officers are subject to several conflicting pressures.

The company itself was born an unwanted child of an outlying housing development. The builders of Essex Manor, a 300-unit garden apartment and home development, had to include sewage disposal in their plans for converting a large farm into a modern housing complex. Lewis Township[1] has no general sewage system—other than septic tanks for individual homes—but insisted on a biochemical plant for a population concentration like Essex Manor. To meet this need, Essex Creek Disposal Co. was formed.

Essex Creek Disposal Co. is a small, privately owned public utility, chartered to serve Essex Manor. It owns collecting lines, pumping equipment, and a treatment plant 2 miles from Essex Manor. Its effluent (which is potable) is discharged into Essex Creek. Initially the company was owned and operated by the promoter of Essex Manor. The promotor donated to the company about two thirds of the original investment and also set service charges low enough—$20 per quarter—to appear minor to prospective buyers of houses and apartments.

After the Essex Manor development was completed, the promoter wanted to move on to new ventures, so it sold all the common stock of Essex Creek Disposal Co. to a group of investors for a nominal amount. These present stockholders have diverse experience with local public utilities, and they bought the company with the belief that the state Public Utility Commission (which must approve changes in utility rates) would agree that the heavy investment justifies some increase in service charges. Mr. Boynton Boyd, Jr., president of Essex Creek Disposal Co., says, "The $600,000 invested in this company entitles the owners to roughly $36,000 income per year, even under the very limited profits allowed public utilities."

During its six years of operation the company has never made a profit. Costs of chemicals, power, and labor have risen while service charges remained constant—with a resulting increase in annual deficits. (The condensed balance sheet and income statement for the past year are shown on the following page.)

Obtaining approval to increase the service charges has proved to be more difficult than the present owners anticipated. Two current complications are new antipollution equipment and possible plant expansion to serve a new high school.

---

[1] Lewis Township is a subdivision of Clark County. The government provides all the local governmental services (education, police, etc.) for a 35 square mile area—except for two incorporated villages.

Condensed Balance Sheet

Assets		Liabilities and Equity	
Cash	$ 540	Accounts payable	$ 34,170*
Accounts receivable	2,268	Accrued items	9,606
Total current assets ...	$ 2,808	Total current liabilities .	$ 43,776
Utility plant & equipment:		Long-term debt	75,000
Cost $596,777		Contribution to aid	
Depr. 71,613	525,164	construction...........	379,752
		Common stock	100,000
		Retained earnings	(70,556)
		Total liabilities and	
Total assets	$527,972	equity	$527,972

* $30,000 of notes due to company officers are subordinated to other claims.

Condensed Income Statement

Total revenue	$ 25,920
Operating deductions from revenue:	
Operating expense	$ 22,495
Maintenance expense	4,382
Depreciation expense	11,377
Taxes other than income taxes	3,855
Total operating deductions	$ 42,109
Interest expense..	$ 4,930
Total deductions	$ 47,039
Net (loss)...	$(21,119)

Who pays what for cleanliness?

Detergents used in homes for washing clothes and dishes have sullied our natural environment. First, in the 1960's high-foaming detergents that do not break down in the earth through biological action began accumulating at alarming rates; surface wells in some areas produced sudsy water! To correct this problem, detergent manufacturers substituted phosphates. Phosphates do a good job of cleaning and they foam only a little. But they do remain in disposed wash water, and this creates a different kind of pollution. Phosphates are excellent plant food—as their use in fertilizer attests. In water, phosphates stimulate the growth of algae and other plants, especially in warm shallow ponds and lakes. The algae die, rot, and use up the oxygen in the water, the fish die, and the whole body of water becomes a stinking mess. The more phosphates in the water, the greater the mess.

Phosphates in our lakes and streams were identified as a villain just as public concern with ecology accelerated. Since then, state health boards and others have demanded a reduction in the inflow of phosphates. One route is to ban the use of phosphates in detergents, but there is no convenient substitute that does not have its own polluting effects. (Besides, public authorities are embarrassed to ask detergent manufacturers to stop using an ingredient they were forced to adopt a few years earlier.) Another route is to remove the phosphate from the waste water before it is released back into the environment. It is this latter approach that complicates life for Essex Creek Disposal Co.

In response to the public outcry about polluted waters, the state Department of Health is urgently seeking ways to reduce the discharge of phosphates. And, the effluent from the Essex Creek Disposal plant is clearly high in phosphates (as are discharges from most other sewage treatment plants). An engineering firm, the Chemical Equipment Company, has invented a chemical process for removing phosphates from sewage, and the Department of Health is pressing Essex Creek Disposal Co. to install the process even though it is still in the development stage. Company executives feel that they are being used as an experimental guinea pig, perhaps because the company is small, but state officials deny this.

Following negotiations with Chemical Equipment Company, Essex Creek Disposal Co. decided to pursue the plan urged by the Department of Health—provided the cost of doing so could be recovered in service charges to its customers. Toward this end the company petitioned the Public Utility Commission for permission to increase its basic rate for each living unit, or equivalent, from $20 to $75 per quarter. The requested increase explicitly included both an adjustment to overcome past deficits and projected costs of the new phosphate removal process. The key table supporting the request is summarized in the following pro forma statement:

Pro Forma Annual Income Statement
Showing Effect of Proposed Rates and Phosphate Removal

	Present	*Projected*
Total revenue		
(324 residential units, at $80 and $300)	$ 25,920	$97,200
Operating expenses:		
Operating labor	$ 3,052	$15,600[a]
Power and fuel	3,633	5,433
Chemical expense..................................	1,754	7,154
Miscellaneous supplies and expense	438	3,138
Administrative expense.............................	8,458	8,458[b]
Office supplies and expense	2,385	2,385
Professional services	2,275	588
Property insurance	500	945
Maintenance of plant and equipment	4,382	4,382
Transportation	——	750[c]
Depreciation......................................	11,377	14,892[d]
Taxes—payroll, gross receipts, franchise, excise	3,855	15,242
Income taxes @ 22%	——	2,927
Total operating expenses	$ 42,109	$81,894
Operating income or (loss)	$(16,189)	$15,306
Interest charges:		
Interest on long-term debt	4,500	4,500
Other interest	430	430
Total income deductions	$ 4,930	$ 4,930
Net income or (loss)	$(21,119)	$10,376

[a] Addition of full-time operator stipulated by Department of Health.
[b] Administrative expense includes part-time salaries of all officers.
[c] Station wagon for operating personnel.
[d] All depreciation charged at 2% per year, except 33% on station wagon and 20% on new laboratory equipment.

Pro Forma Estimate of Return on Investment

Rate base:

Present plant and equipment, depreciated		$525,164
Add: New investment in phosphate removal		
Plant and equipment	$70,745	
Transportation equipment	4,500	
Laboratory equipment	3,000	78,245
		$603,409
Less: Contribution to aid construction		379,752
New rate base		$233,657

Return on investment at proposed rates:

Projected operating income	$ 15,306
Divided by new rate base	$223,657
Equals rate of return on investment	6.84%

This proposed rate increase of 275% was greeted by howls of protest from residents of Essex Manor, many of whom had already strained their financial resources when moving into the new development. The Public Utility Commission's hearing on the proposal was a stormy session. Shortly thereafter the Commission ruled the company was not entitled to relief for phosphate removal since the equipment was not installed and working properly. However, the Commission did authorize an interim rate increase from $20 to $31.25 per quarter to overcome current cash deficits. The ruling also indicated that if and when the company had a phosphate removal system installed and operating properly,[2] and had experience with additional costs, a request for further increase would be appropriate. Of course, no commitment was made as to the amount that might be allowed under such conditions.

Now, the company must decide what to do about phosphate removal. (1) It can proceed as the Department of Health is urging—i.e., invest $78,000 in new equipment, hoping that the system will be effective, and then go back to the Public Utility Commission for a further rate increase. *Or* (2) it can stall. Under this second alternative the Department of Health will probably obtain a court order compelling the company to remove the phosphates. (The company could argue that a state or country prohibition of the sale of detergents containing phosphates would be more effective, but such action is unlikely because it would be unpopular with detergent users and opposed by manufacturers.)

The second alternative differs from the first primarily in four respects. Essex Creek Disposal Co. will be regarded as uncooperative by the Department of Health, Lewis Township officials, and ecology buffs. There is a possibility, though very small, that the order compelling Essex Creek Disposal Co. to install the new equipment will not be issued. The need for action will be postponed for about six months. The company's posture in appealing for a rate increase will differ, but whether the Public Utility Commission will be more—or less—considerate of the company if it is acting under court order rather than its own initiative is unknown.[3]

---

[2] Proper functioning is defined by the Department of Health as removal of at least 95% of the phospate coming into the treating plant, and less than one part per million in its discharge.

[3] The Public Utility Commission is an independent body with its own due process procedures. There is no possibility of a working agreement between the Commission and the Department of Health, especially on a very small case such as this.

Either alternative is risky for the company. The process may not work satisfactorily; the company would then be stuck with ineffective equipment with no one to pay the bill. The Department of Health has much enthusiasm but no money to underwrite experiments. Even if the equipment works properly, there is no assurance that the Public Utility Commission will permit the company to pass off the entire operating and capital cost to users of its services. Yet everyone agrees that phosphate pollution of waters should be reduced.

New customer on the horizon

Essex Creek Disposal Co. has another opportunity that is related to its action on phosphate removal. Lewis Township is building a new high school close to the company's sewer line and clearly will need arrangements for disposal of sanitary sewage.

When plans to build the school—to provide for a growing population—were first announced, Mr. Boyd recognized that a large potential customer would be created. However, he decided not to seek a tie-in of the school with company facilities for the following reasons: (1) The treatment plant would have to be expanded. Although some excess capacity exists, the addition of the high school would create a risk that the existing processing tanks might overflow into Essex Creek before treatment was completed. To maintain a comfortable safety margin, a 25% increase in capacity would be necessary. (2) The service charge to support this additional plant would look high to school and township officials. More than half of the construction cost of present facilities was donated by the developer of Essex Manor, and prevailing residential rates do not provide reasonable earnings even on the residual investment. So, charges that would provide a reasonable return on the added investment needed to serve the new school would appear high in comparison to residential rates.

The company charter does not require the company to serve new customers such as a high school. Since the company was created explicitly to solve a problem related to the Essex Manor development, it is not part of a scheme to serve the total township or county. In fact, the company has accepted about 30 residential customers located outside Essex Manor, but these could be easily handled with existing capacity.

Recently Mr. Boyd discovered that the school architect assumed that sanitary sewage would flow into Essex Creek Disposal Co.'s line. Contracts have been let and construction is under way based on this assumption.

Thus, the company is in an unusually favorable bargaining position. For the school to build its own treating plant would cost more than the addition to the Essex Creek Disposal Co. plant. Moreover, planning and construction of a separate plant would delay opening the school for perhaps a year, whereas no delay (though perhaps a short-run pollution risk) will be involved in a tie to company facilities.

The relation of the new school to phosphate removal is explained by Mr. Boyd as follows: "If Essex Creek Disposal Co. has already embarked on a phosphate removal program when school officials approach us—as they undoubtedly will—the school can be expected to bear a reasonable share of that expense. On the other hand, if we are still arguing with the Department of Health, then the school people will focus on our present costs and rates, and phosphate removal will come as a separate issue on top of that.

"As you know," Mr. Boyd continued, "I wish the high school problem had not come up, because I doubt that we can make a decent return on the necessary investment. It complicates our picture, and we'll end up having another group—the Board of Education—trying to tell us how to run our business."

QUESTIONS

1. What action do you recommend Mr. Boyd should take with respect to removal of phosphates?
2. What should he do about the new school building?
3. Do you think that pollution issues reported in this case were properly handled? If not, who should have done what?

WARDWELL VINYL COATINGS, INC.

Wardwell Vinyl Coatings, Inc., of Charleston, West Virginia, designs and produces vinyl-coated fabrics for the automobile, luggage, shoe, and furniture industries. Wardwell's fabrics cover interior panels of the Ford Thunderbird and the Cadillac El Dorado, and they grace Knoll Associates' line of Saarinen-designed chairs.

Since sales have grown and profits are at an all-time high, Beckley Wardwell, the president, has begun to think about his political career. He contemplates with some satisfaction reducing his operating responsibilities, changing his position to chairman of the board of directors, and beginning an effort toward a higher post in the state legislature. Occasionally, in an off moment, Mr. Wardwell muses: "If a Rockefeller can do it, why not a Wardwell?"

The family-owned firm has competed successfully for years in the fabric coating industry with subsidiaries of B. F. Goodrich and the other major rubber companies, with divisions of General Motors and Ford Motor Company, with departments of E. I. du Pont de Nemours, Monsanto, Eastman Kodak, and Dow Chemical Company, and with a host of smaller competitors.

George Wardwell, grandfather of the current president, built his first factory fifty years ago to produce chemically treated canvas. After being shut out of the large chemical plants in Charleston because of alleged assaults on several plant managers, George opened his own shop.

Some ten years later, during a depression and shortly after the Wardwell firm had begun to make artificial leather by coating cloth with pyroxylin, the original plant burned down. The company then moved to an abandoned steel warehouse on the Kanawha River. This structure, slightly modified, is still the site of operations.

Marketing

Harleton Rowe, the sales manager, came to Charleston three years ago after a fifteen-year career as salesman and product manager with eight garment manufacturers and textile producers. His first move was to add a man who specialized in sales to the furniture industry. Before, Wardwell Vinyl Coatings, Inc. had sold only through manufacturer's representatives whose total compensation was an 8% commission.

Half of the manufacturer's representatives have now been replaced by six company salesmen who specialize by industry. They are guaranteed an annual salary of $20,000 and are then paid by commission at an increasing rate when their sales exceed $500,000 annually up to a maximum rate of 8%.

Beckley Wardwell approved the changes in salesmen and their compensation as being consonant with his belief in putting great trust in his senior managers and in allowing them all the responsibility they were willing to take. Harleton Rowe had come highly recommended by some old family friends of the Wardwells who were associated with the J. P. Stevens Company.

Beckley Wardwell started in the firm as a salesman on house accounts and has continued to sell to some customers as his duties in the organization changed. At present, he still does all the sales work with the two largest customers, whose purchases are now $1,950,000 annually.

Responsibilities of other executives are indicated in Exhibit 1. This diagram is not circulated in the company since Beckley Wardwell does not believe in formal charts. He is convinced that their development tends to make the organization too rigid and that their publication leads to status jealousies and bureaucratic infighting.

Exhibit 1

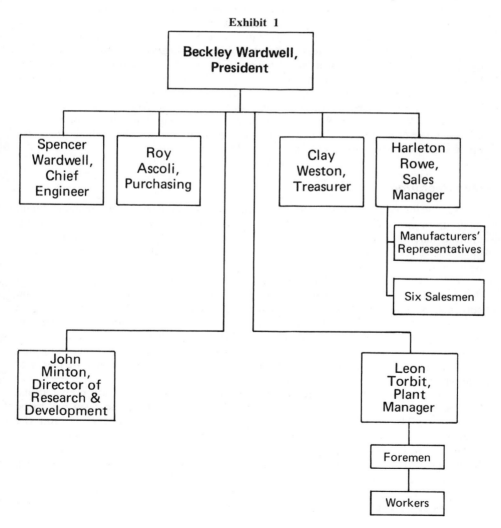

Products of the vinyl resin coated fabric industry are upholstery for vehicles, coverings for luggage, engine, and equipment covers, baby carriages, casings for typewriters, yard goods sold by mail-order houses and department stores, shoe materials, furniture upholstery materials, shower curtains, wall coverings, surgical tape, ribbons, and other applications. Major producers in the industry include rubber and chemical companies that specialize in organic and polymer chemistry and a large number of smaller producers who purchase their resin in bulk from a major supplier and concentrate their efforts on the production process of coating fabrics at the lowest possible cost.

Buyers want their color, finish, and durability needs met carefully. Successful selling depends also on preconsultation with designers about the various fabrics needed in the customer's line. Frequently a salesman works for several days, at various intervals, with a customer's designer. A supplier is also expected to furnish samples—even of new materials—rapidly when new items are being considered for a customer's line.

Automobile manufacturers and the consumer divisions of the rubber companies—which do not necessarily buy from producing divisions of the same firm—generally place large orders. Furniture, shoe, and luggage manufacturers tend to place small orders and to repeat them frequently if sales of the item for which the coated fabric is used catch on. A customer's pressure for a low price is related to the number of yards of coated fabric bought and to the ultimate price line at which its product—be it baby carriages or washable wall covering—is offered to the great consuming public.

Harleton Rowe said that Wardwell succeeds by marketing a high-quality product to a large number of customers who desire fast and accurate service. Individual orders are often small, but they are repeated eight to ten times a year.

Manufacturing

Wardwell coats the cloth it purchases from textile producers with a resinous liquid made up of either chloride or acetate compounds. The mixture can be sprayed on by coating machines—as is common practice in the industry—but Wardwell uses a calendering process to control the amount of liquid applied, its spread-rate, and its penetration.

Fabric is bleached, stretched, and then run between calenders (large steel rollers) to dry it and smooth it before coating. Vinyl resin, in combination with color pigments and solvents, is applied on the coating machine as the cloth is pulled through to a drying oven at the end of the coater. Coated cloth is later finished by stamping or by rolling it on embossing machines to impart a grain, a raised surface (such as pigskin texture), or any other finish desired. Until recently, each of these three processes—bleaching and smoothing, coating, and then finishing—has been done in batches on separate pieces of equipment.

Coating is the crucial production department. Resin ingredients are prepared and applied under closely controlled conditions. Tensile strength of the resin has to be related closely to the speed of coating machines. Both temperature and the concentration of chemicals have to be held within exact tolerances. Stains left by the rollers or rips in the fabric cause spoilage losses or reduce fabric quality. Close attention by the plant workers to the fabric belt as it is calendered and rolled is required for a satisfactory product.

The process is dangerous to unskilled or careless employees. Machinery is heavy and runs at high speeds. Chemical odors are stong and cannot all be removed in the present building even by the best of ventilating and solvent extraction processes. While the equipment is kept in the best of repair, the rest of the plant is old and facilities are rundown.

Worker turnover is high. Experienced men can be hired from the glass factories or the chemical plants near the city. When absolutely necessary, new men are taken on from the large pool of migrants from the hill country and are trained at some cost in lost productivity or rapid turnover.

Last year a Teamster's Union local was voted in to replace an AFL craft union. After one month, the company settled a strike for higher wages for 85% of the union's demand. The plant manager, Leon Torbit, told Beckley Wardwell that he was satisfied with the settlement since he believed that the men would now work harder than they had before and that the company would be in a better bargaining position when the new two-year contract ran out.

Leon Torbit rose through the ranks. He knows the process and the equipment and he demands careful attention to plant activities by his foremen. The foremen spend most of their time supervising production runs closely to minimize spoilage and waste. Leon Torbit also spends at least half of his time touring the plant, checking on the status of individual orders and questioning various machine operators. He knows most of the hundred plant employees by sight, but few by name. Hiring, firing, and discipline are entirely the responsibility of the various foremen—subject to negotiation on some disciplinary matters with union stewards.

Chemical research and development

Chemical research and development is done in John Minton's workshop. His six assistants have had university training in chemistry, but they basically "engineer" his suggestions. John Minton earned an advanced degree in organic chemistry years ago and has since followed the old tradition of experimentation. Chemical research at Wardwell is really "mixing and brewing" and relies but little on modern quantitative polymer theory. John Minton firmly believes in using "art" and experience in his formulations.

Each year cooperative students from the University of Cincinnati work a semester at Wardwell, and the personal relations between these undergraduates and John Minton have been very warm. Professional conflicts arise occasionally because John diverges in some instances from currently accepted laboratory and analysis techniques. The students have learned that his methods are often quite ingenious.

The present vinyl resin resulted from "rational" trial and error that converged on the successful mixture. Knowing the desired properties of the finished compound and the characteristics of the component chemicals, John Minton exhausted many combinations of reactors, allowing for fine differences among different brands of the same product.

John Minton also adapted other processes to vinyl manufacturing. For example, the dyeing process used at Wardwell came from an industrial magazine article about coloring fabrics in the garment industry.

Wardwell's vinyl resin has advantages over its competitors' products. The coating is less likely to crack, has better tensile strength, absorbs dye more easily, and can be applied at lower temperatures. It is a quality product demanded for more expensive applications, yet its production cost is not much higher than common vinyls.

Working at first with little money, John Minton discovered some very simple procedures for improvements. He modifies his processes if manufacturing difficulties arise, and he constantly checks the application of his new product ideas to make sure they work out in the plant.

John Minton plans to retire within the next three years. "I'll be seventy years old then, and threescore and ten is enough for anyone," he said. Transferring his experience gained over thirty years of work with vinyl will be difficult. Any new man will probably be accustomed to using more sophisticated equipment. New methods might be incompatible with the existing staff of technical people, who must then be retrained. The greatest incompatibility to a modern researcher will be the responsibility for watching after the production process. Any new man will also probably be surprised with the autonomy given him to perform his development activities.

Engineering

Process development, that is, the improvement of equipment used in manufacturing, is carried on by Spencer Wardwell, the president's cousin and a mechanical engineer trained at California Institute of Technology. He devotes his time to machine design, to some outside consulting work, and to a complete factory redesign now in process. The goal of this change is a factory that will produce fewer defects while utilizing much less labor.

In the present plant, new drying ovens contrast sharply with some "Pittsburgh 1895" equipment surrounding them. Two years ago a wall was knocked out and the factory floor space was extended by about a third. The result was a longer, more efficient linear series of rollers that made each run easier to mount, process, and finish.

Wardwell depends on a manufacturing process that has little down-time and that can handle orders in a very short time.

Increases in roller speed have reduced the crucial turnaround time, but on the very oldest equipment they have also led to increased defects as tension overcame the fabric's tensile strength. Workers cannot follow the process at very high speeds. Even at lower rates a marred roller—which leaves a mark with each revolution—is difficult to detect.

A pilot model of a new coating machine is under test to prove out its design characteristics of a 50% reduction in labor hours and a 10% increase in fabric output. Discretionary settings have been reduced substantially, mechanical handling has been substituted for manual, and tension controlling devices have been added to reduce tearing.

Spencer Wardwell once said, "Every company needs a dreamer, and I'm the one here." Of the six assistants, who work on outside consulting engagements as well as Wardwell projects, three are skilled machinists and technicians. The others are graduate mechanical engineers.

Engineers seldom stay with the company more than three years. As one said, "I learned a great deal from Spencer about both mechanical engineering and consulting and put up with him to get this knowledge. In a weak moment he once told me that company policy was to kick the worker when he didn't produce and to reward him as little as possible when he did. Of course, that was only Spencer's idea of it. I never did get to see how Torbit carried out any policy."

Spencer Wardwell believes that his cousin and Clay Weston, the treasurer, try to hold him down too much. "Those two haven't yet got it through their thick heads that the future for this outfit is in cutting its labor costs and that I am going to do it. We need longer runs. Over four years our yardage output has gone up 40% and we only need 100 plant workers now—not 120. The two of them almost stopped me from building that pilot model because, they said, sales to the automobile companies were off and we had to conserve cash. Baloney.

"That model is a necessary step toward the automated plant we are going to have here in a few years. When I get it, we'll need only 10 workers. Then we won't have any union troubles, we won't have any training or turnover problems, and we can pay these ever-loving workers enough so they will think six times before they quit us to go to work across the river at Union Carbide. Well, maybe we'll need 20 men, because I am going to build enough machinery to double the number of yards we are turning out. Then we can cut down on the number of orders, triple the length of each run, and do away with half of this silly setup and changeover time that keeps us from really being efficient. Our manufacturing cost should now be 15% less than it is. Just give me five years and ten million dollars."

General management

Beckley Wardwell believes in getting outside expert advice. One consulting firm recommended the recent plant expansion.

Another firm recommended increased coordination among the managerial group and attempts at cooperation through dinner meetings and general discussion. Dinners were held for awhile and then discontinued when Spencer Wardwell had to be out of town.

Meetings led by Leon Torbit for the plant foremen were discontinued when the bleaching, coating, and finishing foremen argued at length over technical matters.

Beckley Wardwell spends 20% of his time with two customers and, at times, assists individual salesmen with difficult relationships with other customers or accompanies them on visits to celebrate unusually large orders.

The balance of his work is mainly on financial matters. He analyzes cash balances and cash flows each day with the treasurer. He looks at actual and predicted budget comparisons for previous and succeeding months. He, the treasurer, and the purchasing agent check the investment in inventory each month—both in total dollars and by reviewing summary tally sheets prepared from the detailed records.

With the purchasing agent, Beckley Wardwell reviews individual purchase orders amounting to more than $2,000 and analyzes alternative sources of supply for new items.

Beckley Wardwell says: "Weston and Ascoli are perfectly competent executives, can perform all the duties asked of them, and do careful work. I spend time with them to keep myself informed. I need the data to press for increased revenues and decreased costs. In my view, a chief executive's major role is to establish the rate of return on investment and the rate of sales growth that he wants and then to push continuously for these. Secondly, I need it to keep the family happy.

"Spencer Wardwell is the only family member in the firm. I was lucky to attract him away from his full-time consulting business with the help of a special stock option arrangement. No one member or one branch of the family has a controlling stock interest, but they all have a personal interest. One or two of them are in the investment business and are convinced they know as much about coated fabrics as anyone else. A few of the others I would call professional Monday morning quarterbacks; this is not something I have not told them directly.

"While a few nephews, cousins, uncles, and aunts have asked for jobs here, I have refused to hire them—except for Spencer. I can't see that they would be any more competent than the people we already have, and none of them seems to want to start in the coating room.

"Judge our managerial methods by our results. Sales are now $15,000,000 a year, whereas they were $9,000,000 five years ago. Our manufacturing cost is 65% of sales—4 percentage points lower over the same period. We now spend 7% rather than 9% of sales on our total marketing effort. Research and engineering cost us 9% of sales. That compares well with any of the big chemical companies. After taxes, we net out 9% of sales, which is even better than General Motors. A dividend payout ratio of 60% takes better than adequate care of the three branches of the family.

"Look at our balance sheet (Exhibit 2) and I think you will have to agree that I can begin to satisfy all those impulses I have had toward politics in recent years. I'll give up my sales work and that will free up a lot of time. Harleton Rowe can handle all our marketing effort. School board membership, chairman of local welfare organizations, and one term in the state legislature has not been enough. I've traveled this state—and the country—widely over the past eighteen years and have gotten to know a fair number of people. I think I can contribute politically."

Exhibit 2

Wardwell Vinyl Coatings, Inc.

Current Balance Sheet
(In Thousands of Dollars)

Cash..........................	$ 2,400	Accounts Payable..............	$ 480
Receivables, Net..............	1,275	Accruals......................	1,950
Inventory....................	2,400	Long-Term Debt *.............	2,000
Marketable Securities.........	2,000	Common Stock and Retained	
		Earnings...................	6,845
Plant and Equipment, Net......	3,200		
Total Assets.................	$11,275	Total Liabilities and Equity.....	$11,275

* Debt due in equal amounts over a ten-year period. Current amount carried as an accrued item.

QUESTIONS

1. Assume that Mr. Beckley Wardwell has asked you what steps should be taken so that he can become chairman of the board and less active in the company. What is your answer?
2. What personnel problems, if any, do you foresee for Wardwell Vinyl Coatings, Inc.? What should be done now to mitigate them?
3. Do you agree with Spencer Wardwell's plans for production? Explain.

FINANCIAL POLICY–ALLOCATING CAPITAL

13

Need for capital

Capital, like personnel, is an essential resource for every enterprise. Equipment must be obtained, materials purchased, employees paid, sales and administrative expenses met—all before goods are available for sale. Then a month or more may elapse before customers pay for purchases. Even a law firm selling only services will incur payroll expenses and have accounts receivable. Capital fills the gap between the time outlays are made and revenues flow back in.

In formulating policy regarding uses and sources of capital, *cash flows* require primary attention. Capital already invested in fixed assets or debts already incurred become active when they affect the inflow or the outflow of cash. Occasionally direct exchanges are made of, say, company stock for land, but these are exceptional shortcuts. Most pressing problems relate to (a) getting capital in the form of cash and (b) allocating cash (liquid capital) to the most propitious uses.[1]

In this chapter we discuss central management's guidance of capital allocation for fixed assets and current assets, the use of cash for dividends, and the related issue of calculation of profits. Then the obtaining of new capital is examined in the following chapter.

Relation of strategy to capital allocation

In a sense, financial policy concerning the use of capital does not stipulate the *specific* uses of capital; these are determined by other management decisions. Plans for sales—such as products to be sold, sales appeals to be stressed, plans for production and purchasing, decisions to "make" rather than

---

[1] Remember that accounting profit or loss does not refer to cash. A profitable company may be short of cash when expanding sales call for additional inventory and accounts receivable; likewise it is quite possible for a losing company to liquidate assets (turn them into cash) at a faster rate than losses occur and thereby increase its cash position. Of course, profits do sooner or later generate cash; the question for financial management is when this cash will be available and whether the flow is large enough to meet cash requirements.

"buy," heavy use of automation, and other comparable plans—dictate the uses of capital. Nevertheless, capital plays an essential supporting, facilitating role.

Strategy lays out the positive direction a company will take. Executives throughout the company then create plans for carrying out their respective parts of strategy. And from these plans come specific requests for capital and other resources. Specific allocations of capital can be made only after the creative planning process has generated alternative proposals.

In a well-managed company, however, planning is not done in isolated bits. Instead, tentative ideas are passed back and forth among departments, alternatives are suggested, rough estimates are provided, and objections are raised while plans are still being formed. A vital part of this give-and-take process is checking on the availability of capital and other resources that each alternative would need. And as we have already seen, often a resource—people, plant capacity, vendors' cooperation, capital—can be provided only if certain conditions are met. Bargaining and trade-offs occur. Eventually out of this discussion specific requests for capital emerge.

Financial considerations enter into this planning process in two highly important ways: (1) Financial policies are set that provide guidelines in advance on how capital may or may not be used and how recurring needs will typically be met. The availability of such guidelines expedites the planning process described in the previous paragraph. (2) Targets for financial results are one dimension of company strategy (see pages 76-79). These targets and subgoals derived from them serve as standards to evaluate various proposals.

REGULATING INVESTMENT IN FIXED ASSETS

General restrictions

In every active enterprise, from landscape gardening to generating electricity, all sorts of proposals are made for additions to facilities. Executives concerned with a particular operation naturally think of new equipment that would enable them to do their job better or at lower operating expense. One way to regulate such proposals is to set forth general areas where investment will or will not be made, or criteria that must be met.

Consistency with long-range plans. Company strategy often stipulates the markets to be sought or the production technology to be used. Such aspects of strategy can be translated into more specific policy guides.

A paper company with a mill in northern United States, for example, became concerned about the increasing costs of its pulpwood. Careful study showed that on many of the types of paper it was making, southern mills using southern pine enjoyed a cost advantage. While shifting to specialty papers was a possibility, the company concluded that the best strategy was to move closer to large raw material sources.

Consequently, a policy of making no major investment in fixed assets in its northern mill was adopted. Only the purchase of miscellaneous equipment necessary to operate existing machines would be permitted, and installation of new machines or substantial expenditures on the existing building would be postponed at least until the outlook for a northern mill improved.

Another firm adopted a similar policy because the probable shift in demand for its product would make its present plant somewhat obsolete. If new processes had to be adopted, then the firm wanted to move into a new building in a suburban location. In the meantime it chose to keep itself in a flexible position and made only essential investments in fixed assets.

A policy that places definite limits on the use of capital for fixed assets must be administered with discretion. A change in technology may necessitate installing new equipment if a company is to continue to compete in a particular industry. If the concern wishes to render distinctive service to its customers, investments in fixed assets may be essential. Nevertheless, investment policies should be disregarded only in unusual circumstances.

"Hurdle" rate of return. The policy just illustrated stipulates a type of fixed asset to be avoided or encouraged. A different kind of investment guide is a minimum rate of return that must be anticipated if capital is to be assigned to a proposal. For example, the policy might be that any new investment in fixed assets must earn at least 15% annually on the initial investment after provision for depreciation and taxes. Then, a proposal to buy an accounting machine costing $10,000 that was expected to result in an average net saving of $1,200 per year during its life would be rejected because the 12% return falls below the acceptable minimum.

For such a policy to be useful, the method of calculating the rate of return should be defined. Depreciation, taxes, interest, net investment, and several other items can be treated in different ways. So, to avoid ambiguity, the policy should indicate the formula that was assumed when the minimum was set.[2]

Theoretically, the minimum permissible rate of return should be the average cost of capital to the company (a weighted average of the company's long-term borrowing rate and the earnings/price ratio of the company's common stock). In practice, desire for expansion, willingness to sell more stock, funds already available, judgment about future risks, and similar considerations affect management's choice of the minimum rate. Since most executives who propose new investment in fixed assets tend to be optimistic in predicting the benefit of the action, central management of many companies counter by setting the "hurdle" rate higher than the theoretical minimum.

Risk classifications. Many investments are so risky that they should have an expected return higher than the basic hurdle rate. Uncertainty surrounds every investment. The activity made possible by the investment may not work as

---

[2] For most situations the estimated rate of return in a typical year or average year is as precise as the underlying data warrant. However, for proposals involving long time periods in which the cash outflows and cash inflows will occur at sharply different and irregular dates, the estimated rate of return should be made by the discounted cash flow method.

predicted; workers may like the change or they may sabotage it; materials and energy inputs may cost more than expected or be unavailable; customers' tastes may shift; competitors may react vigorously; pollution controls may be more severe than predicted. Since one investment often is subject to many more such uncertainties than another investment, we cannot compare them without making an adjustment for differences in risk.

One way to deal with differences in risk is to place proposals into classifications reflecting the odds for success. The following table is a simple example:

Risk class	Extra discount factor for risk	Representative investment
High risk	0.2 or more	Exploratory oil well
Medium risk	0.5	R&D development of disposable oil can
Low risk	0.8	Expansion of frozen food display cases
Minimum risk	1.0	Replacement of 40-year old elevators

A company can either set a minimum acceptable return for each risk class, or the predicted result of an investment can be multiplied by the appropriate discount factor to obtain an "expected return." If the classification and the discount factor are accurate, the "expected returns" for all investments have been adjusted for risk and can be compared with one another.

In theory, discounting for risk can be greatly elaborated. A whole array of possible outcomes with probabilities for each can be projected. Successive contingencies can be recognized in a "decision-tree" computation. Risk discounts can be combined with time (interest) discounts. Rarely in practice do the underlying data warrant actual computations of this sort, but the concepts may help clarify the degree of risk involved. More significant and subtle is the absorption of risk by people making various estimates. Central managers should know how much allowance for risk their subordinates have already made in the figures submitted before they do their own classifying or discounting.

The simplest way to use risk classifications is to establish a hurdle rate for investments in each class—say, 15% for minimum risk investments and 30% for medium risk investments. The "expected return" computations give synthetic figures which are best suited to capital budgeting.

Capital budgeting

Frequently, a company has many more possible investments in fixed assets than it can prudently finance. The issue then becomes which projects to endorse and which to reject. *Capital budgeting* is a method for making this selection.

First, all major proposals for additions to fixed assets are described and analyzed and predictions are made of the amount of the investment and the resulting benefits of each proposal. Obviously, this analysis and prediction must be carefully done because the soundness of all subsequent steps can be no better than the data fed into the process. The whole task will be simplified by promptly screening out all proposals not consistent with marketing, production, purchasing, and personnel policies and with the general investment policy just discussed.

Next, the predicted investment and results should be expressed in dollars insofar as possible. The figures that are pertinent are *additional outlays* the company will make if the project is undertaken and *additional receipts* (or reduced expenditures) that will result from the project. Intangibles should also be recognized, both intangible costs and intangible benefits—for example, flexibility or strategic advantage of entering a new market. These intangibles must be listed because the budgeting process deals only with dollar figures and time; it tends to de-emphasize intangibles and strategic considerations.[3]

Then, proposals should be ranked, with those showing the highest rate of return to outlay at the top and those with the lowest return at the bottom.

Finally, management can proceed down the ranked projects until (a) the capital available is exhausted, assuming overriding reasons exist for keeping the total within a fixed amount, or (b) the rate of return falls below the minimum acceptable rate. Before projects below the cutoff point are completely rejected, intangible benefits should be appraised to decide whether the added advantages are important enough to move a project up into the acceptable list. Similarly, intangible cost of projects above the cutoff point should be assessed with an eye for projects that might be dropped.

Investment mix

Every firm makes some high-risk investments and some low-risk investments. The proportions, however, among high-, medium-, and low-risk commitments can vary a lot. Just as the "marketing mix" (see Chapter 7) used by a company should be adapted to its strategy, so also should the "investment mix." All high-risk investments make a company too unstable; all minimum

---

[3] Theoretically the dollar estimates can include contributions to strategic moves or detractions from them. In practice, these broader effects are difficult to estimate (and may not be fully understood by people making the specific proposal), so they are normally treated as "intangibles."

The scope of each proposal determines which intangible factors should be weighed. If the proposal deals only with, say, replacing autos used by sales representatives, we disregard many intangibles because all alternatives assume the same people doing the same work. However, if closing a branch or dropping a product line is at issue then many questions about employee morale, competitors' reaction, and the like must be included.

Note that the rate of return based on incremental results and incremental investment differs from the overall average. For instance, assuming we stay in business, the incremental value of a telephone vs. no telephone will be very high. One of the major reasons for prior screening of capital proposals against strategy criteria, suggested above, is to clarify the assumptions and to narrow down the factors to be weighed for a particular proposal.

risk forces liquidation. A healthy arrangement is some mixture—like a healthy human diet provides a mixture of nutrients and energy.

Risk profile of a small firm. Alain Ribout, the owner-manager of a successful motel in the Laurentian mountain region of Canada, faces several attractive propositions: enlarge and improve his present kitchen and parking facilities, add a large wing to his present building, build a new motel 30 miles away at the site of a proposed new ski lift, and invest in the new ski lift. Both the uncertainty and the potential rate of return rise in the order in which the four alternatives are listed.

Selection of any one investment will affect Ribout's interest in making the other investments. For instance, commitments to both the new motel and the ski lift, Ribout feels, would be risking too much on the success of one development. Likewise, if he embarks on a new wing expansion, he hesitates to also be starting a second motel. But he does want to share in the growth of the area. So to keep his overall risk exposure in balance, Ribout is now inclined to make two moves: (1) ensure continuation of his present success by improving the kitchen and parking, and (2) take a high risk by investing in the ski lift.

A Missouri farmer, to cite another case, is being encouraged by a poultry processor to double his capacity to raise broilers from chicks. This would involve a $100,000 investment in highly mechanized facilities, which could be recovered in four to five years *if* the demand for broilers continues to grow. The farmer actually spends most of his time raising corn, but with present equipment this is not profitable. A shift to large-scale mechanized methods for raising corn would require changing fences and fields and buying at least $85,000 of new equipment. An alternative is to use the fields for grazing beef cattle and to take a job that will provide cash income for current expenses. Since the family can easily muster the small additional labor to care for the expanded broiler activity, the farmer could handle both the broiler and the new corn venture. But he hesitates to take both risks at once. He prefers a choice between (1) the new corn operation plus present broiler activity or (2) expanded broiler activity plus cattle grazing and cash income from an outside job.

A mixture of high-risk and low-risk investments with an eye on dependable cash flow is needed in both of these examples. Since a choice of any one alternative modifies the attractiveness of the others, a policy dealing with the total mix is desirable.

Diversification in multiproduct company. A policy regarding investment mix is also useful in large companies. Here the focus is often on product line diversification. The aim is to develop or acquire a portfolio of products—like a portfolio of securities—that balances the overall risks and the cash flow for the company. For instance, the Boston Consulting Group has developed a theory calling for a combination of products in different stages of their life cycle. Since products in the development and expansion phases require net cash investments, they should be combined with mature products that generate net cash outflows. Ideally, at least some of the developing products move into maturity as still older products are liquidated, thereby providing a continuing flow of cash needed to nourish another generation of new products.

For this type of analysis, products are classified into four categories—stars, cash cows, problem children, and dogs—as shown in the following matrix:

MATRIX SUGGESTING FINANCIAL CHARACTER OF PRODUCT LINES

Company share of the market

		High	Low
Product growth rate	High	Stars 1	Problem children 3
	Low	Cash cows 2	Dogs 4

1. *Stars* are products in the introduction and growth stages of their life cycle in which the company has a high market share. Future prospects are bright, but it is important to focus on building market share during the growth stages. This requires investment in marketing effort, inventories, accounts receivable, R&D, and production facilities. As volume rises, the costs per unit should drop; so after the introduction stage some profit will be earned. However, the growth needs will call for much more cash than is generated by profits.
2. *Cash cows* are mature products. The company has a high market share and a high volume that gives it relatively low production costs per unit. Now effort shifts from building market share to profits and cash flow. Production capacity should be used to the maximum, inventories and receivables should be carefully controlled, and R&D should be focused more on product differentiation that will enable the company to get the higher quality-wider gross margin business in what may become a very competitive market. Cash flow is high. When the product moves from maturity to decline, investment is even more restricted, losing segments of the business are quickly dropped, and the ratio of cash flow to sales can be even higher.
3. *Problem children* are products doing only moderately well in a favorable, growing market. Unless remedial action is taken while past growth makes improved market share easier to obtain, the product will become a "dog." This means that substantial cash investment in marketing, R&D, technological changes, and perhaps vertical integration must be made to move ahead rapidly. Such effort clearly involves higher risk than promoting growth of stars. Consequently, the company should persist with only a limited number of

problem children, and these should be carefully selected. Other problem children should be promptly discontinued.

4. *Dogs* are products that should be disposed of as expeditiously as possible. Since the company's volume is low relative to that of competitors, the costs are probably higher and the profit margins unattractive. And the growth prospects do not warrant investment for future returns. If the product line and related facilities cannot be sold, the line should be placed in a liquidating status and investment of cash (and management time) should be stopped.

Classification of products into these categories contributes to financial policy in two ways: (1) A guide for investment or disinvestment in each product line is provided. (2) The company can deliberately move toward a selected combination or portfolio of several lines that gives the balance of risk and of cash flow contemplated in its strategy.

The concept of investment mix has application beyond the particular examples for small and large firms just cited. Single-product firms face questions of acquiring raw material sources or mechanization, an art museum must select the kinds of art and the kinds of services it will provide, and even universities venture forth in some directions and hold back in others. The investment policy on such matters is midway between broad strategy directions and specific projects. It identifies, for all persons involved, areas where investments will be encouraged and other areas where investments will rarely be made. Clearly, the investment mix approach is less mechanistic and more sophisticated than capital budgeting.

Summarizing. Policy guiding the use of capital in fixed assets takes several forms. First, we set up general restrictions that screen out many proposals. These restrictions often state the kind of activity that will, or will not, be supported—based on company strategy. Also, hurdle rates-of-return, perhaps refined for different risk classifications, narrow the projects that receive serious consideration. Then, to select among remaining proposals we can either employ capital budgeting or seek a balanced mixture of high- and low-risk ventures.

Leasing versus purchase of fixed assets

Analysis of investment proposals may reveal more attractive opportunities than can be absorbed by a company's normal financial structure. When this occurs, long-term leasing instead of buying the fixed assets should be considered.

Of course, reasons other than financing may make leasing attractive. The outlook may be so uncertain that owning your own building is imprudent, or prospects of rapid expansion and relocation may suggest flexibility in asset commitments. However, in the present discussion we are concerned with leasing as a way of reducing the need for tying up capital in fixed assets. Here is the way it works. An investor, perhaps an estate or an insurance company, with funds for long-term investment buys a building we want to use and at the same time leases it to us for a long period. The rental payments are high enough to cover real estate taxes, depreciation, and repairs, as well as interest on the capital tied up. Note that these are all expenses we would have to pay if we owned the building. The main difference between owning and leasing is that with a lease we show neither the building as an asset nor the source of funds as a liability on our balance sheet.

If the asset to be leased has to be constructed for our own peculiar requirements, we may actually build and equip the structure and then *sell and lease back*. Also, we may have an option to buy the asset when the lease expires, 10 or 20 years hence, at a depreciated value. Both these provisions make leasing even more like owning. The investor, in turn, is in much the same position as a mortgage holder; it relies on our contract for its interest and the return of its investment.

A few companies have a *policy* to lease rather than to buy certain types of assets. For example, oil companies and retail chain stores may regularly use such an arrangement for their many retail outlets. Most firms resort to leasing only occasionally for some large asset. Whatever the frequency, the operating cost and the tax implication should be carefully studied because a long-term lease obligation is just as binding as mortgage or debenture bond obligations even though it does not so appear on typical financial statements.

Since a long-term lease creates a continuing financial burden in many respects comparable to owning fixed assets, it must not be used promiscuously. The general policy of a company regarding its investment in fixed assets and capital budgeting comparisons of alternative uses of company resources should normally apply to property leased for a long term as well as property that is purchased.

POLICY RESTRAINTS ON CURRENT ASSETS

Operating needs for inventory

The size and the composition of inventory should be determined primarily by operating needs. As explained in Chapter 10, the following factors should be considered—minimum inventory necessary for uninterrupted operations, economical size of purchase orders and of production runs, production for inventory to stabilize employment, advance purchases to get seasonal discounts, and anticipation of price changes and shortages of supply. Inventory policy blending all these considerations is one of the main issues in wise procurement. Financial limitations are a different and additional constraint.

Budgetary limits on inventory

Inventory absorbs capital. The cash spent for finished goods, work in process, and raw materials is not available for other uses as long as these stocks remain on hand. Consequently, financial policy dealing with the allocation of capital to competing uses frequently places an overall limit on the size of inventories.

A common way to limit inventory is to budget the total size month by month. Each time the budget is revised, the use of capital for inventory is weighed against other needs. This establishes a mechanism for seeking the optimum use of capital throughout the company. Of course, since inventory serves as a buffer between purchasing, production, and sales, the actual inventory may deviate from the budgeted amount, but the guide to desired inventory levels is clear.

Budgetary control of inventories is particularly well suited to companies that have wide seasonal fluctuations. In the automobile industry, for example, cutting-back of production and disposing of inventory of one model while scheduling startup on production of next year's model is a tactical problem of considerable significance. Similarly, the buildup and disposition of Christmas merchandise and agricultural supplies calls for short-run adjustments.

Policy on inventory turnover

A second way to limit inventory is in terms of turnover ratios. Thus, a retail shop may aim for an inventory in relation to sales of 25%, or 4 turns per year. The turnover standard creates pressure to dispose of slow-moving, obsolete stock; accumulation of such stock is likely to lead to future losses. Moreover, high inventory relative to sales increases the company's exposure to price fluctuations. And, since inventory turnover is frequently used by outside credit analysts, a company's credit standing can be improved by fast inventory turnover in relation to industry averages.

For internal administration, separate turnover ratios for raw materials and for finished goods, perhaps broken down by type of product, are more useful than a total composite figure. Often the turnover will be stated in terms of months of supply to avoid arguments about values to be used. A primary purpose of this kind of policy is to induce inventory managers to decide what kind of stock is worth holding and to clean out past mistakes.

Note that as inventory policy becomes more specific, it shifts from a general financial guide to an operating control. This fuzzy dividing line between finance and operations is characteristic of many financial issues and unless adroitly handled becomes a source of jurisdictional dispute.

Investment in accounts receivable

Central management's concern with accounts receivable is similar to inventory. First, the company credit policy should aid the execution of strategy. This means that liberalness in granting credit to customers and in making collections should be consistent with stress placed on credit as a sales appeal. Defining the function (service) that it is to perform is primary. Second, budgetary limits may then be set for the total capital allocated to accounts receivable. These limits will arise from the capital-allocating process and will reflect a balancing of alternative uses of capital. And third, turnover ratios can be set to check the soundness of accounts and to avoid future losses from an accumulation of uncollectible accounts. As with inventory, even more detailed constraints—such as "aging" the accounts receivable, that is, listing those 30 days overdue, 60 days overdue, etc.—move from general financial limitations into operations. The basic task of central management in the area of accounts receivable, then, is to set policy regarding (1) purpose, (2) allocation of capital among competing uses, and (3) maintenance of the quality of the asset.

A special issue is the *use of outside financial institutions*—banks, credit companies, and factors—to provide customer credit. Outside firms will be glad to extend installment credit because this is profitable business by itself. For help in carrying regular commercial accounts receivable, the company must pay a fee, the size of the fee depending on who makes the credit investigation, who collects the accounts when due, and who bears the risk of bad accounts. The basic question that central management must resolve is whether to reduce capital needs for accounts receivable by turning to outside firms. The answer hinges on two factors: (1) How important to the company is close customer contact and integration of credit with other services provided to the customer? (2) How does the cost of outside service (the fee paid or the installment profit foregone) compare with income that can be earned by using the capital saved for other purposes?

CALCULATION OF PROFITS

Allocating capital among fixed and current assets, the problem we have just been discussing, is part of a broader task of guiding the flow of capital in, around, and out of the company. Clearly the allocation of cash for dividends is another part, and we explore that question at the end of this chapter. Before doing so, we need to look at a subtle issue that bears on dividends and a whole array of financial matters—policy affecting the calculation of profit.

Management has significant discretion in how profit is calculated. And, more than protection against unwarranted dividends is at stake. Income taxes, reputation in the financial community and hence ability to raise new capital, perhaps executive bonuses—all are affected by this calculation. The three main areas where policy guidance is needed on this matter in a going concern are:

1. Accounting reserves.
2. Capitalization of disbursements.
3. Inventory valuation.

Accounting reserves

The extent to which accounting reserves are set up may affect company profits significantly. The issue is what expenses to anticipate in accounting reserves and what decline in asset value to show in such reserves.

Expenses that involve an immediate outlay of cash or those for which there is written evidence, such as a bill from a vendor of raw materials, are easily recognized. On the other hand, expenses that require no immediate outlay of cash but that must be met eventually are subject to greater error or manipulation. Depreciation of equipment and buildings, provision for uncollectible accounts, and anticipated expenses such as unassessed taxes or contingent losses are examples of this latter type. Often the amount of the expense is not known accurately, and opinion as to how much should be charged against the operations of a particular year may differ.

The customary way of handling such items is to make a reasonable estimate of the amount to be charged against operations each year, and then to include this figure along with other expenses as a deduction from gross income in the calculation of net profit. At the same time a so-called "reserve" is set up on the accounting books in anticipation of the time when the cash payment or the discarding of assets will take place. It should be remembered that this reserve is not a special cash fund put aside to meet an anticipated cash payment. Such an account does, however, perform an important function in preventing the overstatement of profits.

A conservative policy is to create large reserves even though this cuts stated earnings. Conversely, a company wanting to show immediate profits may build accounting reserves slowly. For example, a steel company may depreciate equipment that will not wear out with 20 years of continuous use at the rate of 10% a year because improved methods of operation will probably make this equipment obsolete in 10 years' time. In contrast, a large resort hotel depreciated its equipment at an average rate that would have taken 50 years to cover the original cost, even though this hotel catered to high-class customers who expected up-to-date service and modern equipment.

Capitalization of disbursements

A similar issue arises in the treatment of product development expenses and improvements of fixed assets. Here the cash has been paid out, but the question is whether to treat the disbursement as an expense in the current year, and thereby reduce profits, or to *capitalize* it.

The treatment of patents illustrates the problem. If a company buys a patent, it clearly has an asset the cost of which should be charged as an expense, not all at once, but year-by-year during the life of the patent. But when a patent comes out of the company's research laboratory, the situation is not so clear. How much research cost should be attached to that patent, treated as an asset, and written off year-by-year? The more cost that is capitalized as an asset, the higher the profits in the current year.

Likewise, when a wooden floor in the plant is replaced with a concrete one, should the cost be treated as a repair expense or should at least part of the outlay be shown as an asset? Disbursements for intangibles like training or advertising a new product are regularly treated as expenses, but what of the cost of an elaborate demonstration motel built for a World's Fair though to be used for several additional years?

Inventory valuation

Still another fuzzy area in the computation of profits is valuing inventory. Judgment has to be exercised in deciding what is obsolete, damaged beyond its point of usefulness, or missing an essential bearing. Value depends on future demand as well as on physical condition of the inventory; but future need in the company for repair parts, or demand by customers, often is uncertain. Someone has to say that a specific item is still a good asset or that it should be written off (or down). Here, again, the higher the value attached to inventory carried as an asset, the higher the current profit.

Policy issues in profit determination

Limitations surround the size of reserves, the capitalization of costs, and the valuation of inventories. The public accounting profession has devoted much effort to establishing "acceptable practice" in these and related areas. Federal tax regulations of what may be treated as an expense on income tax returns (and hence not taxed) are comprehensive and complex. Securities and Exchange Commission stipulations stress full disclosure in annual financial reports. Nevertheless, a substantial latitude for management action in these areas remains.

Central management does not, of course, deal with the numerous specific entries involved in profit computation. Instead, it should set general policy indicating the degree of conservatism to be followed throughout the company. When room for judgment is present, should it be resolved in favor of low value of assets, large reserves, and, to the extent that these entries are acceptable to the Internal Revenue Service, low taxes? Or will the policy be to show as high a profit as is legitimate within the area of judgment?

A related policy issue is *when* guides for profit computation should be changed. If a given method for computing profits is followed consistently year after year, the effect of the method chosen tends to balance out—profits postponed from last year show up this year and largely offset this year's potential profits that have been deferred until next year. However, if a conservative policy is followed one year and then a liberal policy the next, the effect on results reported for any one year can be much greater. Consequently, many prudently run companies stress *consistency* fully as much as the particular valuation methods employed. Other companies have a policy to postpone and *minimize income taxes* in any legitimate way, including a shift in treatment of matters of judgment if such should be propitious.

Like so many other policy problems we have examined, calculation of profits is interrelated with several aspects of central management. Protection of capital calls for conservative estimation of profits; but income taxes, executive incentives, and ease in raising new capital also should be considered. In addition to these explicit factors, the policy should reflect the kind of company envisaged in its strategy. A risk-taking, fast-growth, volatile firm needs a public image quite different from a dependable, steady-growth, stable enterprise.

DISTRIBUTION OF EARNINGS

Net profits of a company after income taxes belong to the stockholders. This does not mean that stockholders will receive a cash dividend equal to their share of the profits, because the board of directors may decide that part or all of the profits should be kept in the company. Policy regarding the disposition of profits varies widely.

Plowing back profits

A very common practice in American business is to use profits as a source of additional capital. Profitable enterprises typically are growing concerns, and additional capital is required to finance this expansion. Rather than distribute profits in the form of dividends and then seek new capital from other sources, many managements believe that it is wiser to use their earnings to meet this need.

One prominent company manufacturing office equipment has relied exclusively on profits to finance its expansion. The founder of this company had an idea but no capital. A loan from a bank was therefore sought to launch this enterprise. The unsympathetic treatment that the founder received at the hands of the bankers made him resolve never to seek their aid again. Finally a partnership was formed with a man who had some capital. The partnership soon became successful enough to finance further expansion from its earnings. This meant, however, that the original partners could not withdraw any profits from the business and that the use of this single source for additional capital would not permit a rapid expansion or exploitation of the market. On the other hand, it did permit a healthy growth of the company, which now enjoys freedom from any long-term financial obligations.

The process of plowing earnings back into the business rather than distributing them in the form of dividends has proved to be such a desirable practice in the past that some authorities advocate a standard policy of distributing no more than half of the profits to the owners in the form of dividends. Such a policy certainly contributes to the financial strength of a company, but it may lead to the accumulation of unnecessary capital if the company is not expanding the scope of its operations. One small company, for example, kept about 20% more capital than it needed for over 10 years simply because the board of directors thought it was "sound" to plow back half of the earnings.

Except in special circumstances, traditional attitude frowns upon the payment of dividends in excess of earnings. For instance, one company seeking the aid of investment bankers in the public sale of a large block of its stock was required to make a detailed explanation of its dividend policy because it had paid out more money in dividends during the preceding year than it had earned. Without a good explanation, this was regarded as a blot on the record of the company and a handicap to the sale of its securities.

Stable dividends

Another dividend policy, and one that is sometimes contradictory to the idea of plowing back at least part of the profits, is the payment to stockholders of a regular amount of dividends each year. Of course, the payment of regular dividends on cumulative preferred stock is not uncommon, because companies wish to avoid large accumulations of back dividends that must be paid before any dividends can be paid to common stockholders. Common stock and preferred stock on which dividends are paid regularly tend to have a better market and are more likely to be regarded by purchasers as an investment rather than a speculation.

To maintain a stable dividend rate, it is often necessary to retain part of the profits earned in prosperous years, irrespective of the present need of the company for additional capital, so that dividends in less prosperous years can be assured. Thus, a company might pay dividends of $2 a year over a 10-year period rather than pay dividends of $4 a year for the first 5 years and no dividends for the next 5 years. This policy, however, is likely to lead to the payment of dividends in excess of earnings during depression years. If it is clear that a company has refrained from paying large dividends in prosperous years in order to be in a position to continue the stable dividend rate in lean years, then payment of dividends in excess of earnings need not be condemned. On the other hand, if profits are retained in order to provide needed capital, then the payment of dividends in excess of earnings may lead to an inadequacy of circulating capital.

The dividend record of the Todd Shipyards, shown in the accompanying table, clearly reveals more attention to a stable rate per share of common stock than a tie to earnings. The company paid dividends even in years when a loss was incurred, but note also that it was slow to increase the rate when profits returned. Recent policy of the company is to set a rate that can be maintained over a period of years and to raise this rate only when management believes the higher figure can be continued on an uninterrupted basis.

Need for adequate retained earnings

Net profits left within a company are generally shown in a surplus account, which is more aptly called "earnings retained in the business."[4] It is illegal to pay dividends that wipe out the retained earnings account and create a capital deficit; in fact, most companies prefer to show a surplus that is much larger than current dividend payments. A relatively large retained earnings account is desired because any operating losses or dividends in excess of profits may be charged against this account without impairing the original capital invested.

Before leaving this topic, one distinction should be made clear. The condition of the retained earnings account may be a restraining factor on the

---

[4] Surplus may, of course, be created in other ways, such as by purchasing bonds at less than par value and retiring them or by reducing the par or stated value of stock.

Net Profits and Dividends
TODD SHIPYARDS
1948–1973

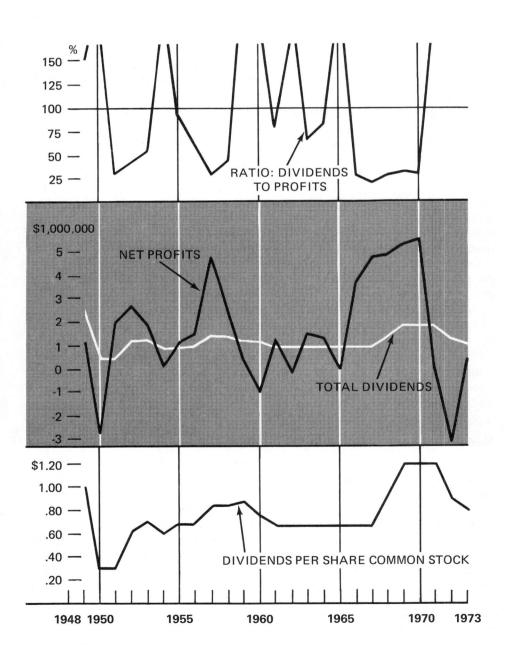

payment of dividends if the account is not as large as the management believes it should be. On the other hand, a large retained earnings account does not mean that the company is in a position to pay dividends. The capital represented by this account may be tied up in buildings or inventories, and dividends are paid in cash—not bricks or commodities. In addition to adequate retained earnings, there must be adequate cash in order to pay dividends. This goes back to the need for additional capital that has already been discussed in connection with plowing back earnings.

Conclusion regarding dividend policy

Major factors to be considered in the distribution of profits are:

1. Present cash position and need for additional capital.
2. Desire to maintain a stable rate of return to stockholders.
3. Adequacy of the retained earnings account to meet present and future reductions due to dividends and losses.

In establishing a dividend policy, the attitudes of people outside the company should be considered as well as those inside. A stable dividend payment, for instance, will affect not only the income of present stockholders but also the marketability of stock to new holders. Likewise, care to maintain a strong cash and retained earnings position will influence the credit rating of a company and its ability to borrow long-term capital. In addition, the effect of high income taxes on large individual stockholders should be kept in mind when the dividend policy is set.

SUMMARY

Policy guiding allocation of capital cuts across and intertwines with almost all other policy of the enterprise. (a) Restrictions on inventory are directly involved in the coordination of procurement and sales. (b) Credit limitations tie in with customer service policy. (c) Fixed asset controls will affect, to some extent, almost all divisions of the business.

Financial policy should not attempt to stipulate the *specific* uses of capital, as this would extend the financial arm too far into the responsibilities of other departments. Instead, policy on use of capital is primarily concerned with general soundness, total size, and balance between various types of assets.

Capital allocation is not a mechanistic activity based on numerical estimates alone. Instead, allocations are made within the boundaries of service aims specified in company strategy. Judgment about acceptable degrees of risk are introduced either by varying the hurdle rate-of-return or by reducing estimated income to an "expedited value." Moreover, the total risk exposure—and the prospective drain on cash—is brought into balance through policy on the investment mix.

The use of cash for dividends should be done on a policy basis because stockholders and creditors develop expectations as to a high but fluctuating payout, a stable rate, or a 100% plowback for future growth. The dividend policy combined with announced strategy enables investors to characterize the company in terms of growth rate, capital gains, current income, and so forth.

Related to this whole cash flow picture is the calculation of profits. Management can emphasize current earnings versus future earnings by the policy it follows on accounting reserves, capitalization of disbursements, and inventory valuation. The result has bearing on earnings available for dividends and also on the company's ability to attract new capital—a major consideration that is discussed in the next chapter.

QUESTIONS FOR CLASS DISCUSSION

1. Apply the portfolio matrix concept presented on pages 281-282 to investment policy for: (a) a coal mining company, (b) a chain of fast-food restaurants, (c) a privately supported university, and (d) an IBM computer business.

2. Assume that the economist for your company forecasts an average rate of inflation of 8% a year for the next 10 years. How would this premise affect the financial policy you recommend for inventories, accounts receivable, and fixed assets?

3. Assume that Alain Ribout sold his motel to an aggressive, financially strong motel chain and that he is now a district manager for that company. (a) How should he decide which of the investment alternatives listed on page 280 to recommend to his new employer? (b) If you think he should recommend more investment than he would have made as owner, do you conclude that big firms do and should take more risks than small firms?

4. The Nelson Construction Company, which specializes in building highways, has a clear policy of selling its bulldozers, cranes, heavy trucks, cement mixers, and other equipment as soon as a major job is completed. What reasons do you think account for this policy regarding fixed assets? What effect does it have on capital requirements and on operating costs?

5. A professional football team, the Black Knights, finished last season in the middle of its league. Most of its players will be available to play again next season if you want them. Assume you are asked to prepare an "investment policy" for the payment of bonuses to college stars for contracting to play with the Black Knights. Bonuses annually range from $5,000 to $100,000, depending on a player's demonstrated ability and his position. The total you have to invest in new talent is $300,000. On the average, fewer than a third of college stars who try professional football become regular players, and the odds for becoming a professional star are lower. How do you recommend the $300,000 investment be allocated (number of new players, size of bonuses, and positions)? (To simplify matters, assume trading of players between teams is not permitted.)

6. A successful fertilizer manufacturer says: "We are definitely pushing foreign production and sales because our industry can serve a great need in many areas

of the world. At the same time, our policy is to invest no more dollars abroad than we have to." (a) What reasons do you think lie behind the policy to keep foreign investment low? (b) How can a company such as this avoid tying up U.S. dollars? (c) Should the amount of hunger in different countries be a factor in selecting countries in which to invest? (d) Should the same hurdle rate-of-return be used for each country?

7. Saturn, Inc. has ten years of successful experience with service and repair work on astronomical and highly technical optical equipment. Two years ago the central management decided, on the basis of its knowledge of what was needed in this field, to develop some equipment of its own design for sale to its present customers. As anticipated, the outlays for this new venture have absorbed all the company's available cash and the new products are not yet ready for the market. In the past Saturn had no difficulty getting short-term bank loans because of its profitable operations. The president contends that operations are still profitable, but to show this on his accounting reports he must capitalize the development costs of the new products. (a) What factors should be considered in deciding whether to capitalize these outlays? (b) What do you recommend be done?

8. (a) Would you, as a stockholder, prefer the distribution of a large or a small percentage of net profits in the form of dividends? (b) If you were a member of the board of directors and had shared responsibility for deciding what dividends to pay, would your answer be the same? (c) Finally, if you were an executive of the company, interested in building up the financial strength of the company so as to ensure continuation of your job, would your answer still be the same?

9. (a) Make an outline of the marketing, procurement, and personnel policies discussed in Chapters 5 through 12. Indicate how, if at all, choice of policies in each of these areas will affect the need for capital. (b) How can policies covering the use of capital be set so that they will not usurp the significance of these other policies?

CASE 13 / Delta Engineering, Inc.

Delta Engineering, Inc. is one of the thousands of firms in the so-called "military-industrial complex." Founded eleven years ago by three electronic engineers, the firm continues to work on the frontier of rapidly changing technology. However, being a very small part of the vast defense hardware industry is both risky and strenuous, and the three owners of Delta Engineering are wondering how to utilize their currently strong financial position to aid future stability and growth.

Delta Engineering got its start in military electronic-countermeasure-systems (ECM's). ECM's are used to defend against electronic systems of the enemy. For example, if an enemy radar "locks-on" to an aircraft, the aircraft's ECM devices will cause false indicators of its range and azimuth (i.e., distance and direction) for the purpose of confusing and deceiving the enemy radar operators. Of course, other designers will work to incorporate counter-countermeasures into their radars which will reject the false indications. This, in turn, triggers a second round where the ECM schemers must now overcome the improved radar, and so on. The equipment incorporated into ECM's is complex and on the outer fringe of the scientific state-of-the-art.

Broadly, three types of companies are engaged in the technical defense business: (1) Large prime contractors who supply the military services with total systems. (2) Numerous and often small equipment manufacturers who make components for the prime contractors (just as separate manufacturers make antenna, speakers, turntables, record-changers, and the like for hi-fi systems used in homes). (3) Materials and parts producers who make wire, transistors, metal boxes, insulation, circuit boards, etc., for the component manufacturers. Delta Engineering has always been in the second category—a manufacturer of specialized components.

The particular niche of Delta Engineering is amplifiers, mixers, microwave relay links, and closely related equipment. These devices must be very precise and must withstand wide temperature ranges, shocks, salt air, and other adverse operating conditions. Improvements in design are frequent. For instance, over a ten-year period successive steps have resulted in the following improvements in the logarithmic, intermediate-frequency amplifiers:

	Early Units	*Current Units*
Models Available	2	40
Center Frequencies	to 60 MHz	to 200 MHz
Bandwidths	to 10 MHz	to 100 MHz
Risetime	200 nanosec.	10 nanosec.
Dynamic Range	50-70 db	80-90 db
Accuracy	± 2.0 dd	± 0.25 db
DC Response	No	Yes
Temperature Stabilized	No	Yes
DC Input Power	25 watts	1.5 watts

Products originally developed for military use are also sold to universities and industrial laboratories engaged in advanced electronic design. Sixty-five percent of Delta Engineering sales are to 250 customers, including many of the largest and most discriminating users in the world. Customer engineers are very sophisticated, so selling is done on exact specifications. Technical catalogs are widely distributed, and manufacturers' agents "bird-dog" new prospects.

Actually only a third of Delta Engineering sales are previously designed catalog items. Two thirds of the dollar sales are special orders ranging from minor variations on catalog items to original engineered subsystems. Delta Engineering's competitive strength lies in its ability to couple advanced engineering with quality production and to make deliveries when promised. Its 50 employees are accustomed to this highly technical, special-order business, and all senior people are skilled engineers. Last year the company processed about 700 orders ranging in value from $300 to $100,000.

The company has grown in volume and profits, as indicated in the table showing operating results. Variations in recent years reflect primarily fluctuations in military purchases of specialized equipment (Delta Engineering is not prepared to make large runs of standardized items). All growth has been financed through retained earnings. No dividends have been paid on common stock. Internal growth also applies to personnel; relationships are informal, and everyone from president to secretaries may join in a special effort to complete a rush order. The profit-sharing plan applies to all employees (32) with more than 2 years of service.

Operating Results
(dollar figures in thousands)

	Sales (Shipments)	Net Profits Amount	Net Profits % of Sales
Last year	$2,286	$141	6.2
Previous year	1,863	49	2.6
" "	2,041	87	4.3
" "	1,979	110	5.6
" "	1,864	107	5.7
" "	1,713	95	5.5
" "	1,116	45	4.0
" "	897	39	4.3
" "	522	24	4.6
" "	288	8	2.8
First Year	36	− 3	−8.3

Earnings Statement
(Last Year)

Sales		$2,286,000
Cost of sales:		
Opening inventory	$ 120,000	
Materials purchased	735,000	
Direct labor	319,000	
Factory overhead	497,000	
Total	$1,671,000	
Closing inventory	156,000	
Cost of goods sold		1,515,000
Gross profit on sales		$ 771,000
General & administrative expenses (net)		487,000
Operating profit		$ 284,000
Provision for federal & state income taxes		143,000
Net profit		$ 141,000

The balance sheet shows a very liquid position, with cash in excess of all liabilities. However, possible uses of available capital being considered by executives far exceed what is currently available. The various alternatives are briefly as follows.

(1) New product development. To date, Delta Engineering has combined product development with engineering design of special orders. When a growing need—within company competence—is identified, the marketing people seek out and aggressively bid on jobs that include the new product. Although the price may be low and the specifications tight, the hope is that experience with the order will provide the knowledge necessary to quickly design a new product that can be added to the catalog.

The above practice works well for extensions of the existing line. Attempts to get really new lines by this route, however, have been unrewarding. Often a great deal of engineering effort goes into a difficult order that proves to be unique.

An alternative is to assign one or more creative engineers, with technical assistants, exclusively to R&D work. They would seek new catalog products to sell to existing

Balance Sheets—as of December 31
(000 omitted)

Assets	Last year	Previous year
Current assets:		
Cash or equivalent	$ 322	$188
Accounts receivable	362	267
Inventory	156	120
Total current assets	$ 840	$575
Fixed and other assets:		
Machinery and equipment	$ 247	$230
Furniture and fixtures	26	26
Autos	24	21
	$ 297	$277
Less Depreciation	128	107
	$ 169	$170
Prepaid expenses	12	11
Cash surrender value-		
officers' life insurance	46	35
Total fixed and other assets	$ 227	216
Total assets	$1,067	$791
Liabilities and equity		
Current liabilities:		
Accounts payable	$ 81	$ 56
Accrued items	68	45
Due to profit sharing	76	59
Income taxes payable	80	10
Total current liabilities	$ 305	$170
Equity:		
Common stock	$ 60	$ 60
Undistributed earnings	702	561
Total equity	$ 762	$621
Total liabilities and equity	$1,067	$791

customers. This would require hiring more engineers—either to relieve persons already in the company or to do the work themselves. To achieve momentum and a "critical mass," at least $100,000 per year should be budgeted, not counting the time of marketing and production people who would be frequently consulted. The outcome of such work is uncertain, of course, but the present executives and staff are so busy on existing business that moves into really new lines are unlikely to occur without the concentrated attention that typified the early history of the company.

(2) Promote microwave relay links to TV broadcasters. Two years ago Delta Engineering launched an effort to reduce its dependence on military purchasing. The company bid successfully on a solid-state microwave relay to transmit television signals from a downtown studio to the broadcast tower. Recent developments in microwave equipment make it more dependable than telephone lines for such purposes, and Delta's customer is highly satisfied with the performance of the new installation.

Selling the relay link to other TV stations has proved to be difficult. Station engineers don't buy on technical specifications but on demonstrated performance, and they are rightly concerned about very prompt repair service. Consequently, if Delta Engineering is to sell its relay link to any significant portion of 800 potential TV customers, it must (a) acquire agents who are familiar with this industry, (b) stock demonstrator units that can be temporarily installed in TV stations and towers,[1] and (c) establish (or tie in with) a reliable service organization.

Private microwave systems are also being installed for data transmission, for example by Western Union, and by railroads and pipeline companies. Competition from large manufacturers of electronic equipment is keen.

(3) Manufacture circuit boards. Producers of small lots or individual units of electronic equipment, such as Delta Engineering, now buy transistor chips and affix them to ceramic circuit boards. (Assemblers who put the parts together use high-powered binocular microscopes and vacuum tweezers to handle the parts, which are extremely small.) Large-scale electronic production, in contrast, can utilize a more integrated process.

Because the demand for ceramic boards from large manufacturers has dropped off, almost all independent suppliers of this material have discontinued its production. This leaves companies such as Delta Engineering with a difficult supply problem. One solution is for Delta Engineering to integrate backward and make its own ceramic boards.

These ceramic boards are coated with layers of chromium, nickel, and gold and must be carefully made. If Delta Engineering establishes a plant, it will sell boards to other firms like itself. Possibly a joint venture and/or an acquisition of existing facilities can be arranged. Between $250,000 to $500,000 minimum capital will be required.

(4) Buy its own building. Delta Engineering has always occupied rented space. Presently it has a 10-year lease on a newly constructed building in a good location in Southern California where all its activities are carried on. Space is ample, and about a quarter of the building is sublet to another concern for a branch office and warehouse.

The lease has 4 years to run. However, Delta Engineering has an option to buy the land and the building for $400,000, which—because of inflation—is about 40% below current replacement costs. The building could easily be mortgaged for $300,000. If the building is purchased, the carrying charges (including interest on the mortgage) will almost equal rental charges; current net earnings would be increased by only $6,000 per year. Nevertheless, the company would immediately have a potential capital gain, and it would gain from further appreciation of these fixed assets.

(5) Dividends. Mr. Arnold Beame, Delta Engineering's president, says: "Of course we should also consider substantial dividends to the stockholders. Bob Morganthau, Ron Javitz, and I are so deeply involved in making the company go we rarely take an objective look. Defense expenditures have stabilized and may go down. The big companies are likely to do more of their own subsystem work 'in-house' to keep their own people busy. So if further investments involve the kind of chances we took when we founded the company, maybe we should start drawing out capital. There is no precise way to measure which direction to go. We try to forecast where there is an opportunity for us and then assume we are smart enough to make money doing it. The record is not bad."

Required: What uses of capital do you recommend for Delta Engineering, Inc.?

---

[1] Each set of broadcast and receiving units costs between $10,000 and $15,000.

FINANCIAL POLICY—
SOURCES OF CAPITAL

The cultivation of adequate sources of capital is of prime concern to central management. Other aspects of company operations may be just as crucial to success, but none is more relentless in insisting on proper attention. For small and medium-sized firms especially, the supply of capital is frequently a restraint on the successful execution of their preferred strategy.

The principal sources of capital available to most companies are:

1. Owners.
2. Long-term creditors.
3. Short-term creditors.

We shall first review the typical ways capital is obtained from each of these sources and shall then consider how a management can combine the use of various sources to form a financial structure suited to the strengths and the needs of its specific enterprise.

INSTRUMENTS USED TO OBTAIN CAPITAL

Owners

Some cash for investment is generated within a company—if it is at least breaking even financially. Much of this results from a bookkeeping reduction in the value of assets, called depreciation, which is an "expense" but involves no disbursement of cash. Sooner or later, however, cash from such depreciation charges will be needed just to maintain existing capacity.

The second internal source of cash is *retained earnings*. As noted in our discussion of dividend policy, owners normally leave a large portion of the company profits in the enterprise to finance expansion. This flow of funds has become increasingly inadequate—as the table on the following page clearly shows. Retained earnings financed almost one quarter of the new investments during the expansion in the latter 1950s but less than one tenth of the expansion in the early 1970s. So, for major growth in most firms, either present owners or additional owners must contribute more capital.

**Relative Importance of Various Sources of Fund
in Three Periods of Expansion
(Estimates for all U.S. nonfinancial corporations)**

	Depreciation & Depletion Allowances	Retained Earnings	Stocks, Bonds, Mortgages	Short-Term Loans	Other
1954-57	38.8%	23.9%	16.3%	8.3%	12.7%
1961-64	47.7	20.9	15.6	4.6	11.2
1971-73	42.3	9.4	25.8	12.3	10.2

Source: *Survey of Current Business*, April, 1974.

The amount of additional direct contributions from owners will depend upon the legal form of organization and the particular rights granted to each class of owner. In a sole proprietorship the amount of capital is limited by the personal resources of the individual who has complete control of the business. Partnerships expand the potential resources, but the lack of stability of partnerships limits their usefulness. So, as soon as capital needs of an enterprise exceed the wealth of one or two persons, a corporation usually is created. Then, raising ownership capital becomes a matter of selling stock.

Common stock. A share of common stock is simply a small percentage of the residual ownership of a company. If 100,000 shares are outstanding, each share represents 1/100,000 of the owner's claim on profits—and on assets if the corporation is liquidated. When additional shares are sold, profits have to be divided into more pieces—which the original shareholders will not like unless the total earnings increase faster than the number of shares; they get a smaller portion of what they hope will be a bigger pie. The new stockholders pay in capital primarily for the right to a piece of this bigger pie—usually expressed as "earnings per share."

If the common stock is *split* (several new shares issued to holders of each old share), of course the earnings per share go down. The individual shareholders retain their percentage claim on the total, however, since they now own more shares.

Preferred stock. Some investors are willing to buy stock having a limit on the dividend they will receive if they also get assurance that special effort will be made to pay such dividends. More specifically, if a company issues $7 preferred stock, a $7 dividend must be paid on each share before any dividend can be paid on common stock. In addition, preferred stock dividends are usually cumulative. Thus, if no dividends were paid on the preferred stock just mentioned for two years, $14 for back dividends and $7 for current dividends would have to be paid on each share of preferred stock in the third year before any dividend could be declared on common stock. Less significant, a preferred stock typically also has prior claim on, say, $100 of assets if liquidation should occur.

Normally, after the preferred dividend has been paid on preferred stock, all remaining dividends are divided among common stockholders. In exceptional situations the preferred stock *can* be made "participating," which means that both the preferred stock and the common stock will share in dividends after a stipulated amount has been paid on each type of security. Participating preferred stock may be issued, for example, to some stockholders who are reluctant to approve an expansion program; they get preferred treatment if any dividends are paid at all, and if the expansion proves successful they also share in the profits from growth.

Frequent use of stock to raise capital. The sale of additional stock is often used to raise money for expansion. To attract particular types of investors, the rights of an issue may be specially tailored. Different issues of preferred stock will have priority in rank and often will vary in the amount of the preferred dividend; voting rights will vary; occasionally preferred stock will be convertible into common stock; and so forth. A package of preferred and common may be sold as a unit. Sometimes *warrants* entitling the bearer to purchase common stock at a stated price are included with a share of preferred stock or common stock, thus giving the holder of the warrant an opportunity to benefit from a price rise. Or, to assure that a new issue of common stock will be sold, existing stockholders may be given *rights* to buy stock at slightly less than the prevailing market price. These special provisions, however, do not modify the basic transaction of securing additional capital through the sale of additional shares of ownership.

Long-term creditors

In addition to investments by owners, capital may also be secured by borrowing it from long-term or short-term creditors. Long-term borrowing as a source of capital is discussed in the following paragraphs.

Trading on the equity. The advantages and the disadvantages of obtaining capital from long-term creditors are illustrated in the situation facing the Red River Power Company. This local electric company, with assets of about $40 million, wished to finance an expansion program that would cost $9 million. The new expansion might have been financed by the sale of additional stock. The present common stockholders, however, did not wish to use this source of capital because (a) high income taxes make earning of net profits more difficult than earning bond interest, and (b) all profits would have to be shared with the new stockholders.

Interest on borrowed capital is an expense deducted from income *before* income tax is computed. Profits available for stockholders are net income *after* income tax has been paid. Consequently, a corporation in the 50% income tax bracket has to earn $2 for each dollar available to stockholders. If capital is borrowed, less earnings are needed to pay for the use of the capital because the tax collector has not yet taken his toll.

The effect of these factors on the Red River Power Company can be seen by comparing the disposition of operating profits (before paying bond interest) under bond and stock financing. The Red River Company already had outstanding $14,000,000 of 8¾% bonds, $9,000,000 of 9% preferred stock, and $9,000,000 of common stock. It was estimated that an average annual operating profit of $5,000,000 would be earned when the expansion was completed. The effect of borrowing the necessary $9,000,000 at 8¾% or selling common stock at par would have been:

	Borrowing $9,000.000 at 8¾%	Selling $9,000,000 of Common Stock
Estimated annual operating profit	$5,000,000	$5,000,000
Less bond interest	2,012,500	1,225,000
Net profit before income tax	$2,987,500	$3,775,000
Income tax @ 50%	1,493,750	1,887,500
Net profit	$1,493,750	$1,887,500
Less preferred stock dividends	810,000	810,000
Available for common stockholders	$ 683,750	$1,077,500
Rate of return on par value of common stock outstanding	7.6%	6.0%

The present stockholders would profit by borrowing because a larger rate of return would be earned on capital than would be required for interest. If for some unforeseen reason, however, the operating profit of the company should fall to $4,400,000 or $3,600,00, the earnings on common stock would have been:

	Rate of Return on Common Stock Outstanding	
Annual Operating Profit	Borrowing $9,000,000 at 8¾%	Selling $9,000,000 of Common Stock
$5,000,000	7.6%	6.0%
4,400,000	4.3	4.3
3,600,000	−.2	2.1

Thus, by borrowing, the common stockholders increase their possibilities for profits but also incur a greater risk of loss. Such use of bonds for raising capital is referred to as *trading on the equity.*

Instruments for long-term borrowing. Trading on the equity may be accomplished through the use of any of the following instruments:

Mortgages. To attract long-term capital, a mortgage on real estate or other assets may be given as security. If the interest and the principal of the loan are not paid on schedule, the lender may force the sale of the mortgaged property and use the proceeds to repay the debt. If the proceeds do not cover the entire debt, the borrower is still liable for the remaining balance.

Bonds. To borrow large amounts, the total can be divided into a series of identical bonds that can be sold to as many leaders as necessary to secure the sum desired. The bonds may be *secured* by a mortgage or other pledged asset, or they may be *debentures* that rely only on the financial strength of the borrower. Typically, the borrower must continue to meet stipulated requirements such as minimum working capital, no senior debt, conservative dividends, and the like. Also, most bonds either call for *serial* repayment year by year or have a *sinking fund* in which money to repay the debt is accumulated. Bonds usually are *callable* by the borrower if it is willing to pay a premium. These provisions are stated in the *bond indenture* and are administered by a trustee.

Long-term notes. Increasingly, large sums can be borrowed from a single financial institution like a life insurance company or a trust company. Here, dividing the loan into bonds is unnecessary. Instead, 10-, 15-, or 20-year promissory notes are used. There is, however, an agreement similar to a bond indenture stipulating various protective measures and the repayment schedule. Such *private placements* avoid underwriting costs. Their use depends largely on the total to be borrowed and the comparative interest expense.

Variations. As with preferred stock, numerous variations are used to tailor long-term securities to attract particular groups of lenders. In addition to the interest rate, maturity dates, and protective features mentioned above, some loans are *convertible* into common stock. If the stock price rises above the specified conversion rate, the lender has the option to switch to an equity security at a low cost. Thus, convertible bonds give the investor the security of fixed debt plus the possibility of benefiting from a rise in stock prices. Another variation is to issue warrants along with bonds. In tight money markets, offering a security that appeals to special classes of lenders can reduce interest expense significantly.

Anyone who lends money for a long term is concerned about the continuing ability of the borrower to meet its obligations. Hence, new companies lacking a record of demonstrated ability and companies in risky industries may be unable to borrow for long terms. In contrast, loans will be easier to obtain by an established firm that over the previous ten years has earned at least twice the interest on proposed new debt and in no year has failed to at least equal the fixed payments. Although future earnings are what really matter, past earnings are often used to decide a company's credit worthiness.

Short-term creditors

The sources of capital discussed thus far provide capital for a long period. Short-term creditors, however, are better adapted to supply funds for seasonal requirements or other temporary needs. The most common short-term creditors are (1) commercial banks and (2) merchandise vendors.

Commercial banks. The most desirable way to borrow from a commercial bank is to establish a *credit line.* Under this arrangement, the company anticipates its needs for temporary cash and works out an understanding with the bank, prior to the time the cash is required, that credit up to a certain maximum will be available. This gives the bank ample time to make its customary credit investigation, and it also enables the company to plan on the bank as a temporary source of capital. The bank wants to feel confident that the company will pay off the loan within a year; consequently, it checks the character of the people running the company, the nature of its existing assets, use to be made of the money borrowed, obligations already incurred, and the earning record of the company. The bank is also interested in the company's budget of monthly cash receipts and disbursements during the coming year. The aim of the bank is to avoid embarrassing bad debt problems by not making dubious loans in the first place.

For some types of business a commercial bank makes loans that are secured by collateral. For example, an investment house pledges stocks and bonds as security for its bank loans, and a dealer in commodities backs up its loans by means of warehouse receipts or bills of lading. When such security is provided, the preliminary investigation by the bank is less rigorous.

Commercial banks do also make some mortgage loans and buy marketable bonds, but this is not a primary service they render to business firms.

Merchandise creditors. Companies normally purchase products and services ''on account''; that is, they make payment thirty to sixty days after products are shipped. With a continuing flow of purchases, some bills will always be unpaid. In effect, the vendors are supplying part of the capital needed to carry on operations. If a company is slow in paying its bills, it may have accounts payable equal to two months of its purchases.

Extensive use of such trade credit is usually unwise. Vendors often offer substantial discounts for prompt payment of bills, which means that this is an expensive source of capital. Furthermore, a company with a reputation for slow payment will not receive favorable treatment from vendors when there is a shortage of merchandise or when closeouts are being offered at low prices.

It will be recognized, of course, that buying on trade credit is but a counterpart of the use of capital to finance accounts receivable from customers.

Other short-term credit. Selling on the installment plan clearly increases a company's need for working capital. As we noted in the preceding chapter, special arrangements can be made with finance companies either to take over or to lend money on such accounts receivable.

Postponing payment of taxes, installment payments on machinery, loans against inventory placed in a bonded warehouse, and even advance payments by customers can be resorted to in periods of stringency. Few companies care to have a continuing policy of obtaining short-term capital from such sources.

With this summary view of possible sources of capital in mind, we can now turn to this issue of how to combine their use in a sound financial structure.

FINANCIAL STRUCTURE

Meaning of financial structure

The various sources of capital used by a company make up its financial structure. In establishing policy for obtaining capital, the overall general structure must be considered because the relative importance of one source will affect the desirability of others.

The size of the company, the nature of its assets, the amount and the stability of its earnings, and the condition existing in the financial market at the time the capital is raised, all have an influence on the sources of capital used by the company. From time to time changes will be made, either because capital can be secured more advantageously from another source or because some lender decides to withdraw its capital. Expansion or contraction of the total amount of capital used also will affect the relative importance of the various sources.

At any given time the right-hand side of the balance sheet of a company will reflect its financial structure. So, to review the policy followed by three different companies, we will examine briefly their condensed balance sheets.

Financial structure of Schultz Electronic Controls, Inc.

The balance sheet of Schultz Electronic Controls, Inc. shown below is typical of many comparatively small manufacturing companies.

Almost three fourths of the total capital of $2,685,000 was supplied by owners of this company. Par value of preferred and common stock is $1,600,000, and earnings retained in the business have increased the

Schultz Electronic Controls, Inc.
Balance Sheet
December 31, 19—

Assets		Liabilities and Stockholders' Equity	
Cash	$ 140,000	Accounts payable	$ 117,000
Accounts receivable (net)	410,000	Accrued liabilities	84,000
Finished inventory	196,000	Long-term serial notes	550,000
Materials and in-process		Preferred stock, 5½%	600,000
inventory	439,000	Common stock	1,000,000
Fixed assets (net)	1,500,000	Earnings retained in	
		business	334,000
		Total liabilities and	
Total assets	$2,685,000	stockholders' equity	$2,685,000

stockholders' investment by another third of a million dollars. Limited use of long-term notes is shown. These notes are only about one third of the depreciated value of fixed assets and thus appear to be protected by an ample margin of assets. The serial feature provides for a regular reduction in the amount of the long-term debt.

The short-term debt of the company at the time of this balance sheet was comparatively small, the accounts payable to trade creditors being only a fraction of the total assets and actually less than the cash on hand. The company did, however, have a bank line and normally used bank credit to finance a seasonal peak in inventories and receivables from March through August.

Financial structure of the Red River Power Company

The sources of capital used by the Red River Power Company reflect the difference in the nature of operations of an electric utility company compared with a manufacturing company such as Schultz Electronic Controls, Inc. The balance sheet below shows the financial condition of Red River Power Company after its expansion program was completed.

Red River Power Company
Balance Sheet
December 31, 19—

Assets			Liabilities and Stockholders' Equity	
Cash		$ 600,000	Accounts payable	$ 600,000
Other current assets		400,000	Accrued taxes, etc.	200,000
Fixed assets ... $55,100,000			Mortgage bonds, 8¾%	23,000,000
Less allow-			Preferred stock, 9%	9,000,000
ance for de-			Common stock	9,000,000
preciation ...	7,600,000	47,500,000	Retained earnings	6,700,000
			Total liabilities and stock-	
Total assets		$48,500,000	holders' equity	$48,500,000

Perhaps the most striking feature of the financial structure of this company is the large bond issue that represents almost 50% of the total assets. This company could obtain such a large bond issue at favorable rates because of the stable earning records of operating utility companies and also because of the large amount of fixed assets that the company could pledge under a mortgage issue. This company has also issued both common and preferred stock. Earnings retained in the business instead of being paid out as dividends amount to about 27% of its total proprietorship.

Inasmuch as there is no such thing as inventories of finished goods in a utility company and accounts receivable can be collected from customers promptly, the assets of this company are virtually all in the form of fixed assets. The company has used bank loans to finance temporarily the expansion of its facilities.

Financial structure of The Long-Shot Printing Company

The balance sheet of a company financed on the proverbial shoestring offers an interesting contrast to those already considered. At the end of its first year of operation, the financial condition of The Long-Shot Printing Company was as follows:

The Long-Shot Printing Company
Balance Sheet
December 31, 19—

Assets		Liabilities and Stockholders' Equity	
Cash..........................	$ 5,200	Trade accounts payable........	$ 61,600
Accounts receivable—net.......	28,400	Notes payable...............	18,000
Inventories...................	52,500	Accrued liabilities............	7,600
Total current assets............	$ 86,100	Total current liabilities.........	$ 87,200
Deferred charges.............	3,000	Mortgage on equipment.......	72,500
Machinery and other fixed		Common stock..............	40,000
assets—net................	115,300	Retained earnings............	4,700
		Total liabilities and stock-	
Total assets.................	$204,400	holders' equity..............	$204,400

The owners of this company have actually contributed less than 22% of the total capital and are relying heavily on both long-term and short-term creditors. Machinery, which is the principal fixed asset of the company, was purchased on time payments; and the vendor, in order to protect its claim, still holds a first mortgage on the machinery amounting to almost two thirds of its book value. It is doubtful, however, whether even the book value could be realized if it became necessary to sell the machinery at a forced sale. Credit from material suppliers has been used to a point where it exceeds the value of the inventory actually on hand. This means that the vendors are not only financing the entire inventory of the company but other assets as well.

Fortunately, the notes payable are due to an affiliate company that will probably not force their collection at maturity but will accept new short-term promissory notes in exchange for the old ones. Nevertheless, the current ratio is approximately 1 to 1, and any shrinkage in the value of current assets would probably cause immediate financial complications. The company has no bank loan and has been unsuccessful in securing a line of bank credit that it may use in an emergency. It is doubtful if new capital can be attracted to correct the existing weak cash position, with the possible exception that the company might offer a new investor the speculative possibility of sharing in future profits if they are earned. Under such a plan, however, the present management would probably be required to give up part of its control over affairs of the company.

In this situation the company must adopt a strategy of improving short-term earnings with existing assets—a very different strategy from that of Red River Power Company where physical expansion financed by debt with a fixed interest cost was the strategic direction to higher earnings per share. In fact,

The Long-Shot Printing Company decided to operate on a three-shift basis, cutting its prices close to incremental cost if necessary to keep the plant busy.

The close interrelation between overall strategy and financial structure is evident in all three of these examples.

SELECTING CAPITAL SOURCES

Industry patterns

Typical financial structures of companies in its industry will give management a lead on what the financial community will accept as satisfactory. Oftener than not, however, wide variations in assets, in earnings, and in existing capital structures, in addition to the differences in management, make reliance upon typical industry patterns both unsatisfactory and even dangerous. The policy adopted should suit a particular company and the conditions existing at the time plans for the financial structure are made. Important factors to consider are:

1. Use to be made of the capital.
2. Cost of this capital.
3. Rights granted to persons or concerns from whom capital is secured.

Use of capital

Funds to finance seasonal peaks or other temporary needs can probably best be obtained from short-term creditors, such as commercial banks. This is a comparatively inexpensive way of raising capital and permits an immediate reduction in the total amount owed after the peak requirements are over. On the other hand, capital for fixed assets or for circulating capital that will be permanently retained in the business calls for a different solution. Because the company cannot expect to have cash to return to the lender for several years, owners or long-term creditors present a more logical source for such funds.

The use of capital will also affect the ability of the company to offer the lender some special security for its loan. As an effective guarantee that a loan will be repaid, a company may pledge as security one or more of the following assets: inventories that can be readily sold on the market, machinery that is standard in design and that can be easily moved from one plant to another, buildings located and designed so that they are suitable for use by other companies, or marketable securities. If valuable collateral can be given to the lender, borrowing will be much easier. If the funds are to be used for purposes that cannot be made to yield cash readily, the raising of capital from owners is indicated.

Cost of capital

To ascertain the cost of capital, consideration should be given to the original cost of obtaining it and also to the compensation to be paid for its use. In sole proprietorships and partnerships, capital is usually secured by negotiations between the owners and those with whom they are intimately acquainted. Other persons or concerns not personally acquainted with the owners are unlikely to provide capital to such organizations. The cost of procuring such capital, if it can be obtained at all, will therefore usually be nominal.

Underwriting and registration. In the case of a corporation, securing capital by issuing bonds or selling stock to the public often involves a considerable expenditure. Frequently these securities are sold through an investment banker who is equipped to reach prospective purchasers of securities, and in most instances substantial commissions must be paid to the investment bankers for these services. Also, complicated legal requirements must be complied with before such securities can be sold. Federal legislation requires the registration of all widely distributed securities with the Securities and Exchange Commission, and the expense involved in preparing the detailed statements required for registration is quite large. In fact, the minimum cost of registration is so large that it makes the public offering of less than $1,000,000 of securities uneconomical.

Private placement of bonds and long-term notes also entails legal and accounting fees and perhaps a fee to a consultant who helps arrange the loan, but the total expense of procuring capital in this manner is normally less than half the expense of a public sale.

Use of rights. Some companies are able to sell securities directly to present stockholders. This applies particularly to the sale of additional stock similar to that already outstanding. The charters of many corporations require that when additional stock is to be sold, it must first be offered to the present stockholders; and if the new stock is offered for sale at a price somewhat lower than the current market price, the present stockholders will probably exercise their right to buy the new issue. When this procedure is possible, the cost of securing additional capital may be reduced substantially. If, however, there is any doubt about stockholders exercising all of their rights, it may be necessary to employ an investment banker to underwrite the issue, in which case many of the expenses incident to an initial public sale of securities must be incurred.

Adjusting sources to prevailing interest rates. The compensation, or interest, that must be paid for the use of capital not only varies according to the use to be made of the capital, but also is often affected materially by the state of the financial market. To note an extreme case, during the 1940's the rate of return on call loans fell as low as a fraction of 1%; by 1975 it had risen to 12¼%. Although the interest rate on other types of loans will not fluctuate over such a wide range, it does vary; and if a long-term loan is being negotiated, the fluctuation in the interest rate will affect the cost of capital for a period of many years. Changes in corporate financing costs in recent years are shown in the following chart:

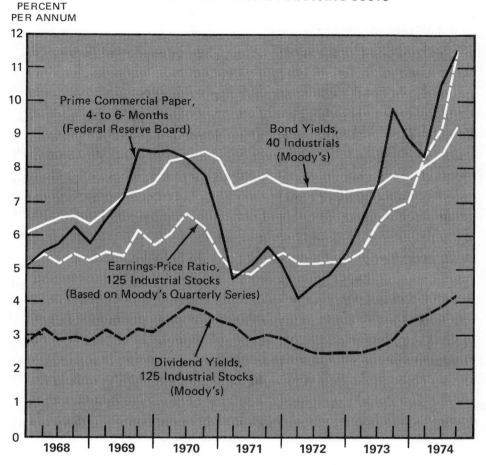

CHANGES IN CORPORATE FINANCING COSTS

When interest rates are high, a company may choose short-term obligations, with the expectation that these can be paid off from the proceeds of long-term bonds that will be sold at a later date when interest rates are lower. The success of such a plan depends, of course, upon the accuracy with which movement in interest rates is forecast. There is always the danger that the interest rate on the long-term obligation will be even higher when the short-term notes mature, or other changes may occur that will make it difficult for the company to sell its long-term obligations as planned. Income taxes play such an important part in corporate profits that the timing of changes in capital structure may be based on an attempt to get the most favorable tax status.

Return paid on new stock. When common stock is sold to obtain additional capital, the company does not agree to pay a specific amount of interest for the use of the new capital. Nevertheless, the new stockholders will share in any dividends paid, which will reduce the amount of dividends available to the former stockholders. This sharing of dividends is a cost of capital so far as the former stockholders are concerned.

Many companies prefer to secure capital from the sale of stock, even though it is anticipated that earnings necessary to support this stock will exceed the interest that would have to be paid on bonds. Their willingness to pay this larger cost lies in the fact that dividends do not have to be paid when there is not a sufficient amount of earnings or cash to justify their declaration. Conversely, interest on bonds must be paid regardless of the amount of earnings and the cash on hand. If this interest is not paid on time, the stockholders run the risk of losing control of their company and perhaps their investment in it.

We have assumed that capital can be secured from any source at any time provided the compensation offered for its use is high enough. As a practical matter, the sale of bonds or stock becomes so difficult in some phases of the business cycle that new capital is virtually unobtainable from these sources.

Rights granted with new securities

A final factor to be considered in selecting the source from which capital should be secured is the authority exercised by the different contributors of capital.

Rights granted to creditors. If capital is obtained from short-term creditors, they usually have no control over the affairs of the company. Of course, if the obligations of these creditors are not paid at maturity, they have the right to bring legal action against the company to enforce their claims.

Likewise, long-term creditors ordinarily have no voice in the current operations of the company, although a bond indenture may impose certain restrictions on the management. For example, the indenture may restrict the amount that the company can invest in fixed assets, it may restrict the future debts that the company can incur, or it may require that the ratio of current assets to current liabilities be not less than 2 to 1.

The loan agreement may also restrict the freedom of the company to pay dividends. Some agreements provide that dividends cannot be paid if the ratio between various types of assets is below the standards established or if there is any default in the payment of interest or principal on the long-term obligations. If any of these requirements are not met or if any interest or principal payments on the bonds are not made, the company may be declared in default. In case of default, the bond trustee has the right to take legal action against the company in order to enforce the payment of the *total* amount of the bonds. These restrictions may become so burdensome that the management prefers to seek capital from other sources.

Rights granted to stockholders. If capital is secured by the sale of stock, the new stockholders have certain rights with reference to the company. The new stockholders frequently have full voting rights, and they thus become participants in the future management and control of the corporation. Sometimes present stockholders wish to retain a balance of control of the company and do not care to grant participation to others outside their group. The possibility that the sale of stock will change the balance of power in the board of directors depends, of course, on the relative size of the new issue as compared with the stock already outstanding, the amount of stock held by those already in power, and the extent to which the present stockholders exercise their right to purchase the new issue.

Preferred stockholders normally do not exercise control over company operations. They usually, though not always, have the right to vote for directors just as do the common stockholders. The par value of a share of preferred stock, however, is typically higher than that of common stock (often $100 and $10 respectively), so a given investment in preferred stock gives considerably fewer votes than an equal investment in common stock. The common stockholder usually runs a risk of losing control to preferred stockholders only if preferred dividends are unpaid for several years and if the charter provides that voting powers of the preferred stockholders are increased under such circumstances.

SUMMARY

An important task of central management is to see that capital necessary to execute the company strategy is provided at a reasonable cost and with a minimum of risk. Short-term creditors, such as commercial banks and suppliers of materials, can be used to cover seasonal needs or other temporary requirements. It is risky, however, to place too much reliance on short-term loans because the capital might be withdrawn when business conditions become unsettled. If used to the maximum for continuing needs, short-term credit will be unavailable for temporary rises in capital requirements.

Long-term loans in the form of bonds or long-term notes are a natural source of capital for companies with relatively stable income. Since the credit is extended for a period of years, various types of protection may have to be granted to the lender, such as mortgage liens, regular reduction of the debt, and limits on additional debts. The greater the stability of a company's earnings and the greater the protections offered, the easier long-term loans will be to obtain and the lower the interest rate. Conversely, unless a company can meet these conditions, few, if any, lenders will extend long-term credit. And, from the viewpoint of the company, heavy fixed interest and debt retirement charges may cause financial disaster for concerns with volatile earnings.

Owners' contributions of capital may take the form of either preferred or common stock. The special provisions of preferred stock, like those of bonds, should be tailored in terms of conditions prevailing at the time of issue. Moreover, the total owners' contribution should be a large enough part of the whole financial structure to be able to absorb shocks and losses of bad times.

Typically, the owners' capital is increased by retention of earnings as a company grows, as discussed in the last chapter.

Company strategy influences many of the factors that shape financial policy—for example, movement into risky ventures, building new plants to cut production costs, emphasis on keeping a steady flow of standard business, or limiting research and development expense to enhance current earnings. These kinds of decisions affect the earning base, the kind of assets available for security, and the degree of uncertainty around which a financial structure must be designed. And because of this interdependence of strategy and financial policy, a major change in strategy usually necessitates an adjustment in company financing.

QUESTIONS FOR CLASS DISCUSSION

1. You are one of five officer-owners of a company pioneering in the design and manufacture of atomic-powered heart pacers. The company has recently received final approval from government authorities to sell its compact, long-lasting pacer for use by humans. Because of the product's superiority over battery pacers, a rapid increase in sales is anticipated. Financing such an increase in operations will require an estimated $5,000,000. The present owners have already paid in $500,000 for common stock; this is all the capital they have, so outside financing must be obtained. A very wealthy Saudi Arabian is seeking equity investments in the United States and has offered to invest $5,000,000 for two thirds of the common stock of your company. A New York investment banker explains that venture capital is very scarce, but it thinks it could sell $5,000,000 of common stock to about 100 investors. The banker would expect a 10% commission. Also the banker suggests that the existing equity be treated as worth $2,000,000. What action do you recommend the company take?

2. Nelson Nursing Home wants to finance a large expansion. About a million dollars will be needed—a third of the present equity. Mortgage money is scarce even though the Home expects to earn twice the 12% projected interest cost. One investment banker suggests that convertible bonds would attract investor attention and cut the interest rate a full percent; each $1,000 bond would be convertible into 10 shares of stock that currently have a book value of $80 per share and a market value of $90 per share. Current earnings per share are $11, but the Home's management expects this to increase to $13 within the next few years. Do you recommend that the Home finance its expansion by selling convertible bonds?

3. Bob Palmer and Arnold Jones have developed a profitable landscaping business in the seven years since they got out of the Navy and took over the business from Bob's father. Primarily they have secured contracts to take care of lawns in several prosperous suburbs. By hard work, use of labor-saving equipment, and

employment of high school dropouts whom they carefully train and supervise, their gross income is approaching $100,000 annually. To cut labor costs they have a wide variety of power-driven equipment, four trucks, and a trailer. All this equipment is either bought on installments with the maximum time period or financed with a term bank loan. Bob and Arnold have growing families, need cash, and say they believe in trading on the equity. (a) Do you think they are wise to go into debt in this way? (b) What will happen to the landscaping business if Arnold accepts his father-in-law's invitation to join him in the contracting business?

4. A paper company is seeking to sell 11% mortgage bonds to finance a major expansion. The company has been earning a small return on invested capital, and the president hopes the new mill will increase profits substantially. The earnings record of the company leaves some doubt whether interest will be earned in slack years. Compare the likely attitudes toward this proposed issue of (a) an investment banker asked to sell the bonds, (b) a preferred stockholder, and (c) a common stockholder.

5. Look up the current interest rates on bank loans and on high-grade bonds and the dividend yields on utility company stocks. On the basis of this information and your forecast for the future, how do you recommend that Red River Power Company raise $4,000,000 which it needs for transmission lines to tie into a multistate power grid? Assume the existing financial structure of Red River Power Company is as shown on page 305, that it can obtain funds at generally prevailing rates, and that the transmission line must be built to maintain service (estimates show a 12% return on the investment after income taxes).

6. (a) What effect does an inflation rate of, say, 5% to 8% per year have on the availability and the cost of capital obtained from (1) stockholders, (2) short-term creditors, and (3) long-term creditors? (b) If your company is expanding and in need of additional capital, how will a forecast of 8% inflation vs. no inflation affect the sources of capital you would choose?

7. The balance sheet of a strong regional trucking company, whose ton-miles of freight carried had grown more rapidly than the national average but that had still seen some cyclical variations, showed long-term debt amounting to 40% of total liabilities and stockholders' equity. Since this was well above the industry average of about 20%, it had been suggested to the treasurer that he "clean up" the balance sheet by a sale and leaseback of company-owned terminals to reduce the debt ratio to 25%. He, too, was worried since current liabilities amounted to 38% of total liabilities and the equity base thus seemed very thin. Should he pursue the suggestion?

8. "Pollution controls are killing us," says Gerald Cox, the owner of a small iron foundry. Sales have been dropping and a new government requirement for a $40,000 exhaust control would add only expense and no income. Joe and Dawn Sandusky, a husband-wife team, have a growing precision alloy casting business and need a larger building. Cox's building is very well suited to their requirements, so Cox proposes to sell out to the Sanduskys. Cox wants $120,000 for his total business—plant, equipment, accounts receivable, inventory. The Sanduskys can scrape up only $20,000 cash; they already have $30,000 in their business. An insurance company is willing to buy the plant for $85,000 and lease it to the Sanduskys. If the Sanduskys liquidate the iron casting inventory and receivables gradually, they might realize $65,000; a quick sales of these assets

would yield only $15,000. But they would have to install the exhaust control if they continue to run the iron foundry. Cox recommends that the Sanduskys continue both businesses and indicates that he will accept one fifth of the stock in such a venture in place of $35,000 of his sales price. The supplier of the exhaust control equipment will take 25% down and a 5-year installment mortgage note for the balance. What do you recommend the Sanduskys do?

CASE 14 / Longhorn Refining Co.

"The energy crisis has forced us to recast our strategy for survival," says Mr. Myrdal, president of Longhorn Refining Co. Longhorn Refining is a successful maverick in the petroleum industry. It neither produces its own crude oil nor sells to final consumers. Instead, it concentrates only on refining. Its efficient 50,000-barrel per day refinery, well located near Houston, has good pipeline connections with Texas crude oil sources and it also has a deepwater terminal. Domestic crude oil is purchased, typically on annual contracts; and refined products are sold wholesale to "independent" distributors of gasoline, fuel oil, etc. Since it spends nothing on R&D and little on marketing, Longhorn Refining is a low-cost operator.

The financial results, shown on the next page, while not outstanding, have enabled Longhorn Refining to maintain its independence in competition with the very much larger "major" oil companies.

"We now foresee great difficulty in obtaining a steady supply of crude oil when our present contracts expire," explains Mr. Myrdal. "Restrictions and price of foreign crude, a widening gap between domestic crude supply and domestic requirements, and the national policy of greater self-sufficiency in energy, all will make Texas crude very hard to acquire in the future. And without a dependable flow of raw material to keep our refinery running near capacity, our type of operation is doomed. This year we will make a good profit, maybe next year. But soon we will be entirely dependent upon government allocations to take care of the little guy.

"The best way we know to survive in the future is to become a contract refiner for the major oil companies which will control their own supplies of crude. Under this strategy we will seek long-term processing agreements with two or three of the majors.[1] Here's our rationale: (1) There will be a nationwide shortage of refining capacity, as well as crude supply—about 5,000,000 barrels per day within the next ten years. Meanwhile, environmental regulations will force a shift to no-lead gasoline and to low sulfur in all products. That calls for an industry investment of well above $10 billion—on top of the billions needed to find and produce additional crude oil. (2) To meet this need the majors will build very large refineries to process foreign, high-sulfur crude. But these refineries will not be used efficiently if they run small batches of domestic, low-sulfur crude, nor with blends of foreign and domestic crude. (3) We can modify our refinery to be

---

[1] Longhorn Refining does occasional contract refining now. Under such processing agreements Longhorn refines the other company's crude oil for a fee. Refined products are made to specification and sold by the major company.

Annual Income Statement
(in millions)

	5 Years Ago	4 Years Ago	3 Years Ago	2 Years Ago	Last Year
Sales	$84	$85	$98	$101	$111
Manufacturing costs	$67	$69	$82	$ 80	$ 90
Selling and administrative expenses	8	9	9	10	11
Interest and other expenses..............	1	1	1	1	2
Total	$76	$79	$92	$ 91	$103
Income before income taxes...........	$ 8	$ 6	$ 6	$ 10	$ 8
Income taxes	4	3	3	5	4
Net income	$ 4	$ 3	$ 3	$ 5	$ 4

Balance Sheet as of December 31st
(in millions)

	5 Years Ago	4 Years Ago	3 Years Ago	2 Years Ago	Last Year
Assets					
Current assets:					
Cash	$ 5	$ 6	$ 9	$ 7	$ 8
Accounts Receivable ...	8	8	8	9	10
Inventories...........	12	12	11	12	14
Total	$25	$26	$28	$ 28	$ 32
Fixed Assets:					
Land	$ 6	$ 6	$ 7	$ 7	$ 7
Refinery (net)	17	16	16	18	19
Other.................	8	8	7	9	9
Total	$31	$30	$30	$ 34	$ 35
Total assets	$56	$56	$58	$ 62	$ 67
Liabilities and Equity					
Current liabilities:					
Accounts payable	$11	$ 9	$10	$ 11	$ 9
Long-term debt due within one year	1	1	1	1	2
Accrued items	2	3	3	3	3
Total	$14	$13	$14	$ 15	$ 14
Long-term liabilities:					
Bonds-20 yr. serial 6% .	$13	$12	$11	$ 10	$ 9
Notes-5 yr. serial 8%...					4
Total	$13	$12	$11	$ 10	$ 13
Equity:					
Common stock (2 million shares outstanding) ..	$20	$20	$20	$ 20	$ 20
Retained earnings	9	11	13	17	20
Total	$29	$31	$33	$ 37	$ 40
Total liabilities and equity	$56	$56	$58	$ 62	$ 67

especially suited for producing nonleaded gasoline (and related heavier products) from low-sulfur domestic crude. Our processing costs, with our low overhead, will be as good as or better than the majors can do for this refining task. (4) By entering into processing agreements with us, the majors can avoid the dilemma of either processing domestic crude in refineries not designed for this purpose or adding a specialized refinery to their already staggering capital budgets.

"To play this game, we must modify and expand our refinery. We have had engineering studies made, and to have a fully modernized plant that fits into the proposed strategy we must invest $20 million. Mr. Samuelson, our treasurer, has been exploring ways of raising that capital."

Mr. Samuelson reports: "The proposed refinery addition is an attractive investment. It will enable us to produce nonleaded gasoline with satisfactory octane rating, and it will expand overall capacity 30%. To have included in the new addition disulfurization of foreign crude would have put the costs clear out of sight.

"To compute a return on investment, the engineers estimated what last year's results would have been if the addition had been in place and had operated 320 days, as the present plant did. Earnings before interest and income taxes would have been $4 million higher. That's a 20% return on the investment. Actually, the importance to Longhorn Refining is even greater because if we don't have nonleaded gasoline in the future our earnings will disappear.

"But finding the necessary $20 million is tough. We have been reinvesting our annual depreciation (about $2 million per year on the present plant, which cost around $30 million) mostly on air and water antipollution improvements, so we don't have a cash backlog. Selling more common stock in today's depressed stock market is out of the question. Our stock is currently traded on the Exchange at around $10 per share, and we'd have difficulty floating a big issue at that price. That means we'd have to give new owners more than half the total equity in exchange for an addition to the plant.

"We did talk to underwriters about a preferred stock issue. Tentatively they suggested 200,000 shares of $100 par, 10%, convertible preferred. Dividends would be cumulative if unpaid, and the preferred stock would participate share for share in any dividends on common stock in addition to the $10 preferred dividend. Preferred stockholders would have an option to convert each preferred share into 7 common shares. Here's the way such an issue works out using last year for a base as the engineers did.

Pro Forma Results of
Proposed Convertible Stock Issue
(in millions)

	Present Plant	Plant with Addition
Earnings before interest and income taxes	$ 9	$ 13
Interest (6% of $10,000,000 + 8% of $5,000,000)	1	1
Earnings before income tax	$ 8	$ 12
Income tax	4	6
Net earnings	$ 4	$ 6
Preferred stock dividend		2
Available for common stock and preferred stock participation	$ 4	$ 4
Net earnings per share	$2.00	$1.82

"If we borrow the $20 million, debenture bonds are the best form. Our term loan would have to be paid off, so the total issue would be $24 million. In today's money market we would have to pay 12% interest and make the bonds convertible to stock. The underwriters suggest 15-year serial bonds ($1,600,000 maturing each year) convertible at the owner's option into common stock at $15 per share. Of course, the bond indenture would provide various protective clauses, including a prohibition on dividend payments unless at the date of declaration and of payment (a) the ratio of current assets to current liabilities exceeds 2, (b) the ratio of equity to total assets exceeds ½, and (c) earnings before interest and income taxes during the preceding year are at least 1½ times total interest and debt retirement during that year.[2] The pro forma results of this way of financing the expansion would be:

**Pro Forma Results of
Proposed Debenture Bond Issue
(in millions)**

	Present Plant	Plant with Addition
Earnings before interest and income taxes	$ 9	$13.00
Interest	1	3.50
Earnings before income tax.......................	$ 8	$ 9.50
Income tax	4	4.75
Net earnings	$ 4	$ 4.75
Net earnings per share	$2.00	$ 2.37

"The bonds are more attractive if all goes well," observes Mr. Samuelson, "but we could get into serious trouble if we had a couple of bad years. It will take two years to build the plant—and to negotiate processing agreements—and a lot can happen to the oil industry during that time. However, we do not dare sign contracts for the plant unless we know where the capital is coming from."

"Fundamentally," Mr. Myrdal says, "we are thinking of three alternatives: (1) continuing as is, (2) building the addition and becoming a contract refiner, or (3) finding a large oil company to acquire us. We did have a feeler about a takeover from one company, with the suggestion that our stockholders take Company X stock on a ratio based on earnings per share. They are earning $6.50 per share compared with our $2 per share, so the ratio would be 3.25 Longhorn shares for one of theirs. In the current market, where all oil company stocks are depressed, their stock is selling for $29 per share. I personally don't like the idea of selling out because I'd probably lose my job!"

Required: (a) Assuming the plant addition is to be built, how do you recommend it be financed?

(b) Do you believe the company should build the plant financed in the manner you recommended in (a)?

---

[2] Annual dividends on common stock have been 50 cents per share for the past 8 years.

MERGERS AND ACQUISITIONS

Mergers are exciting. They make headlines; new thrusts into growth areas are foreshadowed; realignments of supply are imminent; the status, security, and social relationships of many people are affected; large blocks of capital are involved; government agencies gird for action.

For managers of a specific enterprise, however, the excitement of a merger is incidental. A merger with another company is a major event in the life of an enterprise; it may be the key to success or failure. And like the marriage of a man and a woman, it has deep emotional as well as economic effects. Mergers are an integral part of strategy, but we have deferred discussing them until key policy issues have been examined. Policy implications of a master strategy need to be thought through first so as to grasp the full-blown concept of the enterprise. In practice, this policy is refined through experience; we have a going concern with organization and people as well as plans. Talk of mergers makes sense only after we know the strengths and the limitations of this business entity that will be our part of the transaction.

We approach mergers, then, from the viewpoint of a manager of a going concern, who faces three basic questions:

1. What benefit can my company gain from combining operations with another company?
2. How can such a merger be financed?
3. What steps need to be taken to assure that the anticipated benefits will be realized after the merger takes place?

These questions apply to both mergers and acquisitions. Formerly, the term "merger" applied to the consolidation of two companies about equal in size, whereas "acquisition" involved a larger firm taking over a smaller one. Since this distinction is no longer consistently observed and is not significant to our analysis here, we use the words interchangeably. The focus is on the mergers of related businesses, because such combinations offer higher potential benefits than a conglomerate of unrelated businesses.

BENEFITS SOUGHT BY MERGING WITH ANOTHER COMPANY

The major benefits sought in combining operations with another company are financial gain and improved productivity.

Predominantly financial gains

An increasing proportion of mergers are made for narrow financial reasons; the operational, productive activities of the business are not directly affected. Very briefly, here are some of the possibilities.

Use excess cash and/or borrowing capacity. A company may find itself with more actual or potential cash than it can use profitably in its regular line of business. So it looks for other companies that it can buy. Unless attractive uses of these funds are found, stockholders will expect liquidating dividends—or the company will become a prime target for a "takeover" by someone else.

Take advantage of high price-earnings ratio. Suppose the stock of the Apple Company is selling at 20 times its earnings per share and the stock of the less glamorous Orange Company at 10 times its earnings. Then if Apple acquires Orange and its price-earnings ratio stays at 20, the capitalized (market) value of Orange's earnings has doubled. Under such circumstances, which do occur, the management of Apple Company is under strong pressure to acquire all the Oranges it can find so long as they do not undermine the high price-earnings ratio.

Diversify risks. A highly successful aerospace firm found its future entirely dependent on large government contracts. To spread the risks of sudden reduction in business, the firm merged with a company making industrial testing and control equipment. In this instance, the plants were located in different parts of the country and there was no intention of transferring personnel; so the stability sought was only financial.

Use tax loss carryover. Income tax regulations permit large losses in one year to be used to offset profits earned during the next five years.[1] Thus a company with a large tax loss carryover may retain all its earned profits instead of paying approximately half of them as taxes to the government. So if a profitable firm is merged into one with a tax loss carryover, the taxes that the profitable unit would otherwise have to pay can be avoided.

Get into a more profitable industry. A company in a declining industry may acquire a firm in a growing industry simply to place its resources where profit prospects are brighter. When the resources transferred are only capital (that is,

---

[1] More specifically, the loss is first used to offset any profits earned during the three preceding years before it can be carried forward. To aid a merger, only a carry-forward is attractive because it can be applied against the profits of a second corporation only after the merger is completed.

no use of know-how), a "conglomerate" is created; each division of the merger continues to deal with its separate operating problems.

When a merger creates *only* financial gains such as those just listed, we often find ourselves with some weird combinations. The task of central management is complicated and the opportunity for synergistic gains is small. Often short-run benefits lead to long-run difficulties. However, if one or more of these financial gains can be *combined* with productivity improvements—discussed on the next pages—then a merger becomes especially attractive.

Improved productivity

Sometimes a merger improves operating effectiveness. The synergistic effect of combining the two companies may lead to more and better services and/or to lower costs. Thus the new combined structure is a more economic social enterprise. Here are several possibilities of the way such improved productivity may be achieved.

Broader use of company strengths. The Campbell Soup Company provides a well-known example. Over the years this company has built up a strong national selling organization for its soups. When it acquired Pepperidge Farm, an East Coast producer of specialty breads, cookies, etc., it used its marketing strength to give the Pepperidge Farm products national distribution.

The company strengths as applied to the newly acquired company may be in any function. An office equipment manufacturer, for example, developed substantial research and development strengths related to small computers. Then, when it acquired a company that distributed a wide variety of printed office forms, it had the technical background to quickly adapt many of these forms for use in an integrated information system that took advantage of computers where appropriate. Incidentally, the office form company had entree into many companies that were potential users of the company's small computer. The basic source of benefit from this type of merger is the more extensive use of an outstanding capability that one of the companies possesses.

Acquire needed resource. A merger may be the most expeditious way to obtain a much-needed resource. A diversified company, for instance, wanted to employ an outstanding young entrepreneur to head one of its ailing divisions. The man recognized the challenge but was reluctant to give up the small business he had carefully nourished. So the larger company bought the entire business as a necessary step to get the man as one of its key executives.

Several years ago, Crown Cork & Seal Company acquired the Mundet Corporation primarily for its plant, which is ideally located to serve the New York metropolitan area. Mundet's insulation and plastics business was sold off and can-making equipment was installed in its place. The acquisition was an important part of a plan to improve Crown's service in the large New York market.

Perhaps the resource needed is established access to markets. This certainly was the prime consideration when a leading U.S. encyclopedia company acquired W. M. Jackson, Inc., publishers of reference works and encyclopedias sold in Latin America and Spain. To have entered these markets fresh would have been slow and costly.

Raw materials may be the objective of a merger. Lumber and plywood companies often engage in a series of mergers with companies that hold timberlands in areas convenient to a new plant site. An assured source of raw materials is a prerequisite to a large investment in new facilities. Here, as in the previous examples, mergers provide the most expeditious way of acquiring a specific resource.

Correct stodgy performance. Occasionally a company sees a unique opportunity to correct management weaknesses in another firm. McGraw-Hill's acquisition of the Gregg Publishing Company is a good illustration. Mr. Gregg had built a dominant position in the shorthand market throughout the country and had tied in with this other secretarial training aids and supplies. In the latter years of his life, however, Mr. Gregg ceased to pioneer, and following his death the company lacked strong leadership. This made the company an attractive acquisition to McGraw-Hill because, with the injection of good management, the unique prestige of the company in its field could serve as the basis for renewed expansion.

By no means rare are companies with managements that dislike decisive action. The president of a medical supply company had placed close friends in charge of branch operations and was unwilling to replace these executives in spite of submarginal performance. Nevertheless, this company was attractive for merger because the elimination of two losing units and the change of one additional executive made the remaining activities a successful venture. Quite clearly, managers with an objective viewpoint, introduced following the merger, were all that was needed.

Vertical economies. Mergers can be used to build vertical integration—either forward to the company's customers or backward to its raw materials and supplies. The pros and cons of backward integration have already been indicated in our make-or-buy discussion in Chapter 10. Under some circumstances, but by no means always, economies can be obtained from central management of several stages of production. Forward integration offers similar potential benefits—simpler coordination, priority of supply, reduction in selling cost, and similar economies.

Mergers simply provide one way to bring two or more stages of production and distribution under common management. Vertical integration can arise from "internal" growth. However, when very dissimilar activities are involved, the combination of two or more existing enterprises may be more expeditious. A relatively small company making metal powders, for instance, requires an unusual grade of iron. Relative to other uses of iron, its demands are tiny and it had difficulty getting deliveries of the particular specifications it needed. Consequently, it acquired a small iron mine, and the two units of the merged company now work closely on meeting the unusual quality specifications for this special product. The powder manufacturer had no competence whatever in mining, and a merger provided the quickest way to bring skill within the family.

Economies of scale. Mere size—up to a point—may lead to economies. Mergers of companies in similar lines of business may produce a combined volume that makes these economies possible.

Hospitals are sometimes merged together to achieve an optimum size that can support modern laboratories and highly specialized equipment. Similarly, in recent years small local banks have often merged to reach a size where modern bookkeeping and check-clearing technology can be effectively used. (The enlarged resources also permit the bank to safely extend a larger line of credit to a single customer).

Size is also a factor in effective marketing. We have noted elsewhere that oil companies now feel that there is significant advantage in selling a single brand nationwide. This has led to acquisitions of regional chains of filling stations so that a company will be represented in all parts of the country. The companies that are moving from local distribution to national distribution, perhaps because they have decided to use national advertising media, are most interested in mergers that will give them broader coverage.

Quantity discounts rarely are important enough to be the primary motive for a merger. However, if size can be combined with substantial increases in standardization, as is beginning to occur in some types of housing construction, purchasing economies may give a real push to consolidated action.

All these examples of possibilities for improving productivity—broader use of company strengths, obtaining a key resource, providing managerial drive, economies from vertical integration, economies of scale—presume that a merger will result in significant changes in the way the combined companies operate. The common reassurance, glibly stated with the announcement of most mergers, that "No changes are contemplated in the management" must be taken with a grain of salt. Instead, if a merger for the reasons just reviewed is successful, change must occur. In strictly financial and conglomerate mergers, this presumption of change is not present.

Antitrust restrictions

Many potential mergers that would improve productivity are illegal! So before management spends much time exploring a possible acquisition, it should "see its lawyer."

To protect the free enterprise system, the United States government has a battery of antitrust laws and regulations. Unfortunately, much uncertainty and disagreement exists regarding the application of these laws; each new U.S. Attorney General brings a different viewpoint, and court decisions provide no clear-cut guidelines.

It is helpful to recognize the basic premise of antitrust effort—broadly, that competition is best protected by having many small, viable, locally owned competitors in each industry. Of course, competitors cannot be created by the passage of a law; instead, the antitrust laws try to prevent actions that reduce the number of effective competitors.

More specifically, the Antitrust Division is likely to challenge the acquisition of a competitor (a horizontal merger) if (1) only a few companies already dominate the relevant market, (2) either of the merging companies already serves over 20% of the market, (3) the merger decreases the number of companies in an expanding market, or (4) the merger makes entry of other companies quite difficult. So, except for very small firms, horizontal mergers are forbidden. The chief ambiguity arises in defining "industry" and "market." For instance, are skis just a small part of the sporting goods industry or an industry of their own? Is a major milk distributor in Los Angeles within or outside its market if it acquires a milk distributor in San Francisco? On such questions as these, see your lawyer.

A vertical merger (acquisition of a supplier or a customer) gets into trouble when a new supplier would have difficulty entering the market or a new customer would have difficulty obtaining supplies—because the merger forecloses part of the market. Here again, the bigger the company, the more likely the objection. Recently, further uncertainty was added when the wording of the Clayton Act was amended to cover mergers that *may* substantially lessen competition or *tend* to create monopoly. Under this revision, the effects of a merger on potential, as well as on existing, competition must be considered.

These expanding legal constraints, which are vigorously enforced, have forced many companies to sharply alter their merger policy. Especially the larger companies are placing increasing reliance for growth on their own research and development because antitrust considerations virtually preclude expansion within their existing industries via mergers. The recent rise in mergers is predominantly in the conglomerate area. Except for conglomerates, mergers must be a highly selective aspect of company strategy.

Why seek benefits via mergers?

In addition to antitrust hurdles, every merger directed toward productivity gains involves financial negotiations, revamping organizations, career readjustments, perhaps physical moves, and other changes. A manager could avoid these burdens by expanding from within instead of merging with a stranger. Clearly, then, a merger must offer strong advantages over internal expansion. Typically, a sound merger must provide major benefits in terms of (1) time, (2) expense, or (3) physical possibility.

The mergers of local banks to take advantage of new technology, mentioned previously, provide the needed volume of activity quickly; slower internal growth would postpone the use of new methods for years. Similarly, when Du Pont Laboratories was successful in discovering several new drugs, a marketing organization capable of contacting doctors throughout the country was needed immediately. Building such an organization from scratch would have taken a long time, so Du Pont acquired Endo Laboratories with its established marketing know-how and contacts in the ethical pharmaceutical field. Incidentally, this was the first exception in twenty-four years to Du Pont's general policy of expansion from within rather than via mergers.

Expense as well as time is often critical. Creating a new "going concern," especially in a field already keenly competitive, can be costly in terms of initial investment and losses during the buildup period. And if rare assets are needed—Crown Cork's can plant within the New York metropolitan areas, or the talent of an outstanding entrepreneur—a merger may be the only feasible way to obtain the resource.

FINANCING THE MERGER

Once a potential merger is identified that offers some combination of the benefits just described, the second major question is, "What financial arrangements will be attractive to both companies?"

Every merger has its unique features, and the financial arrangements must reflect these. Nevertheless, we can suggest an approach to the main issues that arise in most mergers. Think of a merger as a swap. The company being acquired is trading a business for cash or securities of the surviving company. Involved in this trade are two packages of assets and two sets of owners; *each* owner attaches its own value to the assets it is giving up and to the assets it receives. The crux of negotiating the swap is to devise an arrangement that leaves each owner with a new package of assets that it prefers over the assets it has parted with.

To apply this approach, we must understand (1) the value both parties attach to the business being traded and (2) the value to both parties of the payments to be made. The illustration at the top of the following page indicates the main elements involved in a merger and the value assigned to these elements by each party.

Value of business traded

In valuing the business being traded, agreement must be reached on what is to be traded and the value to be attached to it.

What is included. A company may be acquired either by taking over ownership of the corporation stock or by purchasing the assets. When stock ownership is the mechanism, the entire legal entity with its intangible assets and liabilities is acquired. Later the corporation may be dissolved and a complete melding occur, but at the time of the merger we think in terms of the complete enterprise. (If minority blocks of stock remain outstanding, clearly only a percentage of the ownership is traded, but it is still a percentage of the total concern.)

Main Elements in Negotiating a Merger

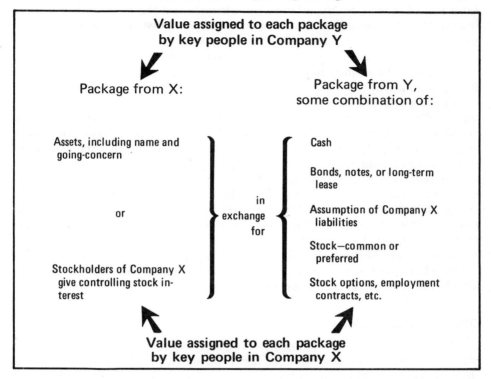

Sometimes a corporation owns assets that the acquiring firm does not want, for example, a large tract of land or a company store. Or there may be serious disagreement over the values attached to a separable asset or liability. In such cases, the tangible and intangible assets along with current liabilities and mortgages are transferred. This leaves the old corporation still with the same set of stockholders, but the corporation now holds the cash or the securities received in the trade instead of its former operating business, plus assets excluded from the trade.

Basis of evaluation. With agreement on what is to be traded, attention shifts to the subjective values each party attaches to its business. Obviously, subjective values differ. People and companies vary in their needs, opportunities, and resources. So, no bookkeeping figures or a simple formula can produce a value acceptable to everyone. Historical costs, book value, and market price (if the stock does have a market price) may influence the evaluation, but usually each individual feels that a particular package of assets is worth more, or less, than these conventional measures show.

A rational basis for setting a value is to estimate the incomes that the company (or its assets) will provide over a period of years, including the disposition of the assets at the end of the period; to adjust these annual estimates of income for uncertainty (for example, cut the figure in half if there is only a 50-50 chance that the estimated net income will arise in the specified year); and finally to reduce each of the adjusted or "expected" incomes to present values by allowing for alternative uses of the resources that are being committed to the venture in question. This gives a discounted present value of future incomes.[2]

But note that present owners and the acquiring company will come out with quite different answers even if they use the same "rational" approach. The acquiring company will manage the assets differently and it expects to obtain synergistic benefits from the consolidation; consequently, its estimated incomes, uncertainties, and alternatives are unlike those of present owners if the merger is not consummated. In any economically sound merger the minimum the owners will accept (their value of the property if the merger is not completed) should be well below the maximum the acquiring company might pay (the present value of all incomes including the expected benefits arising from the merger). The spread between these two figures leaves a wide margin for bargaining. These outer limits are rarely revealed in the negotiations because both parties seek a substantial part of the margin and because they also attach different values to the payment package.

Other considerations

Present value of future company income, just discussed, is not a complete picture—especially to the owner of a family business. People who have devoted their lives to building an enterprise normally have deep concern about perpetuating the company name and reputation; their interest is in the future welfare of their employees; they want the company to continue to give support to the community in which they live. Also, in selling the company, these individuals may be sacrificing an attractive salary and a prestigious position.

The acquiring company has no such emotional attachments to the firm being absorbed, but it does know that such considerations cannot be ignored. To a large extent, the combined company can meet the social obligations to the community; in fact, it may make substantially larger community contributions than would be made if the companies continued separate existence. Brand names and perhaps company names are often continued because of the goodwill attached to them. Employment may actually increase, although some individuals will suffer. The acquiring company may have a more liberal pension plan (and if past-service credits are large, the final merger arrangement may be adjusted to cover them). Often key executives are given an employment contract for three to five years, and the senior executive may be elected to the board of directors of the combined company.

---

[2] We have deliberately used more general wording here than is found in the typical "discounted cash flow" procedure because company owners usually have personal values that are broader than the strictly financial figures commonly used in cash flow analysis.

Unless the executives of the company to be absorbed feel that these "other considerations" will be reasonably met, serious negotiations may never start.

Value of payment to be made

The second half of a merger trade is a package of cash or securities exchanged for the acquired business. This *quid pro quo* must be attractive to the buyer and at the same time must not involve too high a sacrifice for the seller. Here, again, we must consider what is being traded and the value each party attaches to that package.

Form of payment. The most common type of payment in mergers is stock of the surviving corporation. For instance, Radio Corporation of America gave 3,450,000 shares of its common stock for the F. M. Stamper Company, a privately held frozen food concern. RCA stock with a quoted market value was attractive to Stamper stockholders; on the other hand, it was newly issued stock, so existing RCA operations were not hampered by the acquisition.

Payment in the form of common stock is especially likely when that stock has a high price-earnings ratio. Thus, electronics Company A with a price-earnings ratio of 20 would find it advantageous to use its stock to acquire Company B having a price-earnings ratio of only 8. In the simplified illustration below, the market value of the shares of the combined company has increased $6 million as a result of using Company A's price-earnings ratio on Company B's earnings. In the example, two thirds of this increase goes to Company A stockholders and one third to Company B stockholders.

**Illustration of
Effect of Price-Earnings Ratios
(Assume one share of A is exchanged for two shares of B, and
A's price-earnings ratio remains constant)**

	Shares Outstanding	Total Earnings	Earnings per Share	Market Price per Share	Imputed Total Market Value
Before Merger					
Company A	1,000,000	$1,000,000	$1	$20	$20,000,000
Company B	500,000	500,000	$1	$ 8	4,000,000
					$24,000,000
After Merger					
Company A	1,250,000	$1,500,000	$1.20	$24	$30,000,000
Former owners of Company B	—	—	—	($24 $\div$ 2 = $12)	($ 6,000,000)

Cash is, of course, the simplest form of payment. It is used when the acquiring company is highly liquid and sellers are not confronted with high capital gains taxes.

Many other forms of payment are used to meet particular circumstances. Preferred stock gives the sellers greater assurance of dividends. Debenture bonds or notes provide even greater security but are less favorable from a tax standpoint. Bonds or preferred stock may be made more attractive by having them convertible into common stock. Or stock options (rights to purchase common stock at a fixed price) may be used to give the seller an opportunity to benefit from company growth.

Frequently, a combination of several forms of payment is used. The Ingram Company, for example, received cash for its net current assets, 20-year mortgage bonds for its fixed assets, and a large block of stock options that gave it an opportunity to share in any synergistic gains that might grow out of merged operations.

Tax on payment. Sellers are concerned about the income tax they will have to pay on the package of cash and/or securities they receive. If they get only voting stock in the surviving company, as in the RCA example on page 327, the transaction is tax-free. The stockholders are merely exchanging one form of equity for another; no capital gains have been realized, and hence there is no basis for levying an income tax. (Of course, if stockholders subsequently sell their stock, any appreciation over their original cost is taxable.)

In contrast, payment in the form of cash or bonds that have a fixed value does establish a capital gain that is taxable. And some stockholders may find such a tax quite onerous. One way to avoid the tax pressure on stockholders is the sale of assets by the corporation. If a corporation exchanges its assets for cash and/or bonds, *it* will be subject to capital gains tax on any appreciation over its "cost," but the stockholders incur no tax obligation since they simply continue to hold the same stock in the same corporation.

Market liquidity. In addition to tax implications, the response of a seller will be influenced by liquidity. Stockholders of corporations whose stock is closely held often have difficulty selling their stock quickly. Family-held companies are the prime example, especially when cash is needed to pay inheritance tax. So, in appraising any merger proposal, the stockholders will be concerned about the salability of the securities they receive. Stock in a large corporation that is actively traded on a major stock exchange is attractive because it is liquid. Of course, the significance attached to liquidity, or to a tax-free exchange, depends upon the specific financial position of each stockholder.

Financial structure of acquiring company. The acquiring company, likewise, evaluates the alternative forms of payment in terms of its particular situation. Cash may be readily available or extremely scarce. Long-term debt of the company may already be so high that the issuance of additional bonds would be imprudent. Of course, if the assets acquired can support more debt, than a loan from a third party may supply cash to use in partial payment to the seller. (A sale-and-leaseback of the fixed assets can be used in the same way.) But normally the acquiring company must guarantee repayment of the loan, and this becomes a contingent liability even though it does not show on the balance sheet.

Perhaps convertible preferred stock will appeal to the owners of the prospective acquisition, but a relatively small issue of an additional form of stock would interfere with larger financing by the surviving company in the future. In other words, both debt and equity payments should be appraised in terms of their effect on the total financial structure of the acquiring company.

Loss of control. When common stock is used for a large acquisition, one or two of the new stockholders may become the largest owners of stock in the surviving corporation. They are then in a strategic position to gain control. Perhaps this prospect will be unattractive to the executives currently in charge of the acquiring corporation.

Dilution. Stockholders of an acquiring company will also be concerned about "dilution." Usually dilution refers to a reduction in earnings per share. For example, assume that Company A with 100,000 shares of stock outstanding gives an additional 10,000 shares to acquire Company B. If Company A's previous earnings of $500,000 are increased to only $535,000 when A and B are combined, then Company A's stockholders will see their earnings per share drop from $5.00 to $4.86. Although the management of Company A can enthusiastically report increased sales and higher total profits, the picture on a per-share basis is the reverse. Presumably such dilution is only temporary; a sound merger should help increase earnings proportionately more than the increase in shares outstanding. Nevertheless, any merger proposal that shows short-run dilution will require strong justification.

Negotiating a "good" merger

Clearly, a variety of considerations enter into a good merger. We start with a potential combination of businesses that will generate productivity gains and perhaps also strictly financial benefits. Our task then turns to devising and winning acceptance of a trade that is attractive to the management and the stockholders of both the acquiring firm and the acquired firm. The following brief case illustrates the adaptation that may be necessary.

The Enid Corporation of Ohio was highly successful in manufacturing and selling indoor-outdoor acrylic carpeting in Midwest and Eastern United States. It had annual sales of over $50,000,000 and profits of around $3,500,000, or $1.75 per share of common stock. The stock was listed on the American Stock Exchange and had been selling in the $26-$35 range. West Coast sales, however, had declined for four years following the death of Enid's original representative in Los Angeles. To correct this situation, Enid wished to acquire Thomas & Son, an aggressive wholesale floorcovering distributor in San Francisco. This firm had been earning after taxes about $200,000 per year and the senior Mr. Thomas was ready to retire. Executives of both Enid and Thomas thought a merger "made good sense."

Enid first suggested a simple exchange of stock, mentioning 100,000 shares of its stock, then selling at $30 per share. This would have given Thomas a price of 15 times its earnings while avoiding a dilution of Enid's earnings. Thomas felt the price was low because its earnings did not reflect two pieces of undeveloped land that Thomas believed could be sold for as much as a million dollars. Also, the debt position of Thomas & Son was complicated by the financing of this and other real estate.

The discussion then shifted to the purchase of all assets except real estate, which would remove the threat of a capital gains tax on stockholders. Thomas then said the corporation would rather have cash than stock. Enid next proposed a package consisting of: $500,000 cash; $1,800,000 in 6% notes, maturing $100,000 per year over 18 years; a "consulting" contract with Mr. Thomas, Sr., of $35,000 per year for 10 years; and an employment contract with Mr. Thomas, Jr. for $30,000 per year (his present salary) for 10 years. Later, to recognize goodwill and growth potential, Enid added stock options giving Thomas & Son the option to buy 100,000 shares of Enid common stock at $33 per share any time during the next 5 years. And on these terms the deal was made.

Both sides were happy. Mr. Thomas, Sr., said: "We keep all our real estate, get a steady flow of cash into the corporation, I'm on a liberal pension, and Tom has a good job. All these incomes add up to $2,950,000 or about Enid's original offer. Then top it off with an option that should be worth another million in five years."

Enid's president was equally pleased. He reasoned: "Our major gain is strong distribution on the West Coast, with young Thomas committed to stay on the job. Mr. Thomas, Sr., has been drawing big bonuses, so much of his pension can come out of a reduction in executive compensation. Any way we figure it, the $400,000 pre-tax earnings will more than cover the interest, capital cost, and other charges. So we expect to get an immediate improvement in net profit. True, the book value of the assets we acquired is a bit under the $2,300,000 we paid, but within a few years our profit from West Coast operations should be at least $500,000."

Note that each man used different criteria to place a value on the business being transferred and the package of payments being received. Both packages of assets had been tailored to fit the particular situation. The swap was good. Nevertheless, the long-run soundness of the merger remains to be demonstrated in the profitable growth of Enid's West Coast business.

MAKING MERGERS SUCCESSFUL

Many mergers fail. Often the anticipated benefits do not develop, at least to the degree predicted, and unforeseen problems arise. Some of these failures are due to poorly conceived combinations—the marriages of convenience that never were thought through. Others are high-risk ventures that turn up in the losing column. Rarely can managerial skill save such ill-fated mergers.

More disturbing are the well-conceived matches that do not work out. Such results usually can be avoided by proper managerial action. Experience with successful mergers suggests a twofold approach: (1) perceptive, careful management and (2) special attention to communication and motivation.

Perceptive management

The first step in making mergers successful is a *specific program* to bring about the projected results. This requires spelling out the necessary changes and the resources—new engineering, new equipment, hiring and training people, advertising, etc.—and then setting a timetable. Probably the program will need adjustment, but this adaptation will be easier if the various moves have been delineated in advance. In addition, changes needed to reconcile the policies and the procedures of the merged companies should be identified and scheduled. Such programming demands a lot of time and thought by key people (one of the reasons it is often neglected), but it pays off because in the merger process individuals who have never worked together before are expected to do new work.

A second step is realignment of and staffing the *organization* needed to execute the program. Every merger upsets the subtle understandings of status and power in the two companies; the jockeying for new positions is inevitable. Although the situations may be too fluid to define detailed relationships, placing responsibility and providing a prompt means for resolving differences of opinion are essential for positive action. The new mixture of personalities in every merger makes this reorganizing a very delicate task.

Installing dependable *controls* is a third essential element. Cash controls and accounting reports usually are quickly adapted to a format familiar to central executives. However, meaningful cost data and information on market development, research and development effort, management development, and other intangibles are rare. Many a merger has foundered because executives lack a means of knowing what was really happening in their new operation.

Communication and motivation

Cutting across the more explicit management actions just described is a critical need for communication and motivation. A merger signals change. Just what will be changed is unknown, so anxiety builds up in many people whose jobs might be affected. Rumors substitute for facts and spread rapidly.

In such circumstances, key executives should make their plans known just as soon as possible. If some matters are unsettled, they can at least indicate how and when these will be resolved. The communication should be two-way, giving employees an opportunity to ask questions and to hear frank answers. New executives have low *credibility* in the early stages of a merger, and they need to explain what will be done and then see that it happens. Suspicion of motives is apt to flare up at any time during the first year or two, and executives need to be available to make personal explanations of actions they take.

An aspect of communication is when to discuss problems and with whom. One successful pattern is to explore what changes are necessary and how merged operations will be organized *before* the agreement is final. Usually these discussions include all key executives who will have to work together. If a marriage does take place after such a frank exchange, its chances of success are high. The chief drawback is that airing of problems may cause one party to withdraw. But if the courtship cannot survive frank recognition of what living together involves, then major personnel and morale difficulties should be anticipated.

Coupled with as full communication as possible should be positive reinforcement—tangible or intangible rewards—of desired behavior. By emphasizing the achievements of a merger and rewarding them, management builds a new morale. Employee attention shifts from concern with the past to interest in the future.

We shall examine programming, organizing, communicating, and controlling more fully in later parts of this book. As indicated, mergers generate some especially difficult tasks of execution. Unless these receive their full share of attention, the entire merger effort may be futile.

MERGER VIA TAKEOVER

The vast majority of mergers are "friendly," that is, they are recommended by the directors of both companies. But recently the business world has been dazzled by a rash of "takeovers" in which the acquiring company gains control of another concern without the cooperation of its existing management. Here the "raider" gets control of the majority of the stock, ousts the existing management, and then arranges a favorable merger.

Use of tender offers

A raider may gain control of the desired merger partner in several ways: (1) by joining forces with key stockholders not supporting the management (for example, Hilton acquired the Statler Hotel chain in this manner); (2) by acquiring stock on the open market (for example, James Hill's classic fight for the Burlington Railroad); and (3) by soliciting proxies of stockholders (Young used this route to gain control of the New York Central Railroad). Today, these methods are either unavailable or becoming very expensive.

Currently, the popular path to control is a "tender offer." Here the raider makes a public offer to buy or exchange stock. The terms may be any one of the alternatives we have already discussed under friendly mergers—cash, common stock, convertible preferred stock, and so forth. However, the offer has a value well above the prevailing price of the stock being sought—typically 25% to 30% higher than the market price under the old management. In other words, the
~ bypasses company management and appeals directly to stockholders.

~ to the passage of new laws regulating tenders, this was a
d-dagger game. Surprise offers, secret deals, extra commissions to

brokers, counterattacks, splitting stock, and legal injunctions were all employed in a manner reminiscent of the battles between the industrial barons of the 19th century. Slowly the process is becoming more open and orderly.

Who is vulnerable?

No company will attempt a takeover unless it sees an opportunity to substantially improve the return to its stockholders by better management and/or by synergistic benefits of a merger. Consequently, a firm is vulnerable to takeover: (1) when it shows poor performance relative to other firms in its industry, and especially when its dividends are declining more than those of its competitors; (2) when it has surplus liquid assets or large unused borrowing capacity; (3) when it holds assets that could be sold for more than their market value; or (4) when potential synergistic benefits are being disregarded.

The best defense against a takeover is, of course, managing the company so that its assets are wisely deployed, its earnings record creates a good price for its stock, and synergistic benefits are aggressively exploited. Under these conditions, a stockholder gains little or nothing by transferring the stock to a raider.

Such a sound defense against a takeover takes time. If a company is really vulnerable and finds itself being raided before it has time to put its house in order, the management can, and often does, seek a friendly merger with some other company on terms as attractive as those of the tender. Management casualties are usually lower in a friendly merger!

Economic effects

The immediate effects on a company of a takeover are costly. Anxiety is at a peak, personal hostilities are generated, and none of the perceptive management steps discussed in the previous section can occur in advance. Nevertheless, a takeover does serve as one way of deposing a stodgy management. More important, the possibility of a takeover lurking in the background serves as a spur to management. No longer can executives be complacent just because company stock is dispersed among so many stockholders that no one can make a significant complaint.

From the point of view of society and of a stockholder, then, the potential threat of a takeover stimulates good management. All parties—stockholders, society, *and* management—will be better off if the company is administered so that the costly process of takeover is impractical.

SUMMARY

Merging with another company can be a major step in carrying out a desired strategy. The acquired company may provide a much needed resource, give access to a new market, extend company operations back into earlier stages of production, provide a scale of operation that will support improved technology, or improve company services and productivity.

Not all mergers are so well conceived. Some are opportunistic, taking advantage of short-run financial gain. Ideal, of course, is a partner that both pushes us forward on basic strategy and is financially advantageous.

Whatever the fit, the "price" paid must also be weighed. A heavy debt burden, troublesome stock options, and exhaustion of cash reserves can result—and this unhealthy financial condition can seriously deter execution of other facets of company strategy. Or the package given to owners of the acquired company, say common stock, may create no strain. Since we know that a strong financial structure is closely related to future growth, both the *quid* and the *quo* of the merger deal require close scrutiny in terms of their impact on the master strategic plan.

Even soundly conceived mergers fail if the two institutions are not melded by good follow-up action. Numerous internal adjustments in both companies need careful planning, organizing, and controlling; new motivations and communication flows have to be established. These are problems that we examine more fully in the next two parts of this book.

CONCLUSION TO PART 2

A brief re-emphasis of the role of policy in the total management process is desirable here at the close of Part 2, "Defining Major Policy." Three basic points should be kept in mind.

A. Policy amplifies and clarifies strategy. We have seen this in our exploration of product lines, customers, pricing, and product mix in the marketing area; in research and development, production, and procurement in the service creating area; in selection, development, compensation, and industrial relations in the personnel area; and in capital allocation, capital sources, and mergers in the financial area. In these—and other areas not discussed—a variety of questions keep bobbing up that should be answered in a way that reinforces company strategy. Policy provides these needed guidelines and the bridge back to strategy.

Strategy quite appropriately stresses major directions and criteria. Its strength arises partly from its selectivity in emphasis. To specify all the ramifications would becloud the central theme. Instead, strategy leaves this amplification to policy. What is the implication here? What should be done there? How does strategy limit action in this field? What priorities are implied? These are legitimate questions that management should answer, and it does so largely through policy.

B. Establishing policy, in fact, is more complex and disorderly than we have implied. By stressing the way policy grows out of strategy, we inevitably give an impression that policy formulation is a neat, deductive process. "First pick the strategy, then figure out the necessary policy'' is the implied formula. To a substantial degree this is what should be done. But it is an oversimplification. Three important elaborations help to round out the process:

1. Not all policy is deducted from strategy. Policy may arise from at least two other sources. First, managers and the decision-makers respond directly to pressures from the environment. For instance, employing more blacks, reducing oil imports from the Middle East, posting interest charges made on installment accounts—all are probably direct reactions to external events rather than interpretations of strategy. Second, a series of similar actions in specific situations may become a custom, and then this custom becomes so established that it is treated as a policy. Overtime work or customer discounts may be guided by policy that arose in this way. Hopefully, these policies originating in the field of action are compatible with company strategy even though they were not initiated to execute strategy.

2. To some extent existing policy influences future strategy, rather than the reverse. Strategy, we have said, is designed to take advantage of company strengths and to minimize the effect of company weaknesses. In other words, when mapping out a new strategy, the company is treated as an established institution with recognized characteristics. And one of the elements that gives a company its ''strengths'' and ''weaknesses'' is its policy. The existing policy may be so ingrained that it is treated as fixed when new strategy is drawn up.

3. Most important, revisions and restructuring of policy occur frequently. Change—in the company environment, in the action of competitors, and in the company's own size and resources—requires adaptation. As time marches on, the strategy may be revised, policies may be modified, organization may be restructured, resources may be shifted, and systems of motivation and control may be revamped. If we were to take an annual picture of the total management structure, each year would differ from the preceding one. Just as an automobile company is designing a new model before this year's model reaches the market, so central management is continuously predicting and responding to change. The dynamic company, like a growing city, seems always to be under construction. So, forming policy is a never-ending process responding to influences in addition to strategy.

C. This untidiness in policy formulation increases the value of a conceptual framework. In a situation where pressures push in opposite directions and where people differ on priorities and values, a mental framework that puts facts and ideas into some kind of order is a great help. Granted that the convenient sequence of industry analysis → company strengths → strategy → policy → organization → execution does not always work in just that order. Nevertheless, the model does enable us (1) to sort out and arrange the pieces into familiar categories, and (2) to have a set of logical relationships between the categories that suggests priorities and dependencies. The power of the model is its contribution to both orderly and comprehensive thinking in bewildering, complex situations.

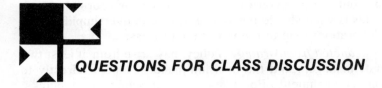

QUESTIONS FOR CLASS DISCUSSION

1. Consider the possibility of merging the college you are now attending with the nearest comparable college. Would there be significant benefits? To whom? What do you think would be the most difficult obstacles to such a merger?

2. Most U.S. railroads have experienced a sharp drop in passenger traffic and are in financial difficulty. One of the most popular suggestions for dealing with this problem is "merger." (a) What potential benefits do you see from merging railroads? What disadvantages? (b) To what extent, if any, is the discussion of financing a merger on pages 324-330 relevant to railroad mergers?

3. (a) Companies that stress long-range planning often become involved in mergers. This is especially so when the long-range planning focuses on strategy rather than on budgeting. How do you explain this tendency? (b) Review the key elements of strategy outlined in Chapter 4 and identify the areas where a merger is likely to be an attractive way to proceed.

4. In the Enid-Thomas merger described on pages 329-330, *assume* that the following difficulties arose after the merger was completed: (a) anxiety and communication difficulties during the first year reduced the effectiveness of the Thomas employees; (b) the Thomas product line needed trimming and more emphasis placed on Enid products—a switch that was not readily accepted by the Thomas group; and (c) Thomas, Jr. wanted to take independent action on a variety of matters and was "too rich to be motivated from Ohio" so he resigned after three years. What action might Enid executives have taken to minimize or forestall these difficulties?

5. "Takeovers should be encouraged because they protect stockholders against an 'in-group' of managers who may be protecting their own jobs." "The only successful takeovers are those that give the stockholders a better deal than they have had or expect to get." "The takeover is a raider's device. Usually it wants to liquidate or milk the company for immediate financial gain without regard to its social responsibilities to employees, customers, and the community. Consequently, takeover bids should have to go through the same advance warning, full-disclosure process with the SEC as a new financial offering." With which quotation do you agree? Do you have any other suggestion for regulating this kind of activity?

6. The reverse of a merger is a "spin-off"—the separation of a single company into two or more independent concerns. In practice relatively few spin-offs or divestments occur, and most of these arise from antitrust activity of the federal government. (a) How do you account for the much larger number of mergers than spin-offs? Are the economic advantages predominantly in favor of increased size? What of other social considerations? (b) Assume that you as president concluded that dividing up your company made good sense. What problems do you foresee in accomplishing the split-up? (c) Do your answers to (a) and (b) apply to profit decentralization—that is, establishing semiautonomous self-contained divisions?

7. In the medical field, both hospitals and nursing homes are trying to find the optimum scope of their services. (a) What advantages do you see in a merger of a community hospital with one or more nearby nursing homes? What disadvantages? (b) What guidelines for mergers of other kinds of enterprises does this analysis suggest?

8. "If we carefully work out our strategy and the policies to implement it, we can meet today's challenges very well. But the more committed we become to that plan, the more difficult it is to adjust to tomorrow's opportunities." (a) How can such inflexibility be avoided? Should formally stated policy be avoided in order to retain adaptability? (b) Who should be accountable for initiating changes in strategy and policy at the proper time?

9. Financial policy seeks a good adjustment of the company to suppliers of capital; personnel policy, a good adjustment to suppliers of labor; purchasing policy, a good adjustment to suppliers of things; marketing policy, a good adjustment to suppliers of outlets. And the list can be extended to other important resource groups. (a) How does social responsibility fit into this array of policy? (b) Does the answer to the previous question differ for small vs. large companies?

CASE 15 / *Brunswig Corporation*

"Well, Martin, that's the twenty-sixth offer we've had to buy us out in five years. Why do we listen to all these people? I'm not sure this one is as sound as the last one from Allied Machinery Products Corporation. What do you think?"

"I'm surprised. Schneider Transmissions, Inc. must have heard about the Allied offer and cooked this deal up in a hurry. Even though they are just across town, they have never given us a hint before that they were interested in an acquisition. Well, let's think about it. The first thing I want to do is to check with some of the boys. Those who have worked at Schneider might have a few clues."

Martin Brunswig, Chairman of the Board and President of Brunswig Corporation, and Walter Brunswig, Executive Vice-President and Chairman of the Finance Committee, left the University Club—one for the main plant and the other for a family council at the Brunswig Country Club. This new, and unexpected, merger offer promised to delay the process of persuading 92 other family members to accept the brothers' opinion—that it would be only sensible to sell out to Allied Machinery Products Corporation.

Brunswig Corporation's principal business is the manufacture and the sale of a wide range of types and sizes of gears, gear drives, and shaft couplings for transmitting power in ranges of 1 to 30,000 horsepower or more. Brunswig's gears are found on tilting drives for basic oxygen steel furnaces, kiln drives for cement processing, paper machine drives, oil refinery compressors, as reduction gears for river towboats, mixer drives for penicillin manufacturing, and as equipment for satellite tracking and radar installations.

Brunswig produces a wide line of standard gear drives and speed reducers as well as special gears and shaft couplings made to order in sizes from 1 inch to 24 feet in diameter and from 1 pound to over 40 tons in weight. It sells directly through its own salesforce working out of 39 district sales offices in the principal industrial markets of the United States as well as through more than 250 distributors. Brunswig products are basic components of industrial machinery, do not have a seasonal sales pattern, and are not dependent on any one industry or industry grouping; but sales volume is affected by the general level of industrial activity.

The company's sales and distribution organization is widely recognized as among the most effective and efficient such networks in U.S. industry.

Brunswig is a leading producer in its lines. It has substantial competition for shaft couplings and smaller gears but very limited competition in the sale of large gears and very large couplings. Market share is as high as 40% to 60% in some lines. To maintain its position, Brunswig engages in sales engineering, applied product engineering, and testing, together with some development work on methods of mechanical power transmissions. It has 100 engineers and machinery designers engaged principally in these programs on which it spent $2,500,000 last year. The firm has secured some patents, but it does not depend for its business on any one or a group of such patents.

About 2,800 employees work in three plants in the same Southern Ohio city. None are represented by unions, and there has been no strike in the hundred-year history of the company. Hourly and salaried employees share in a trusteed, noncontributory, incentive profit-sharing retirement plan to which Brunswig contributes a share of net income. Salaried employees also have a contributory pension plan.

Brunswig owns the three plants of varying ages and of cement and steel construction. Its buildings and machinery are well maintained and adequate for the presently anticipated volume of business.

Family members own a majority of Brunswig common stock and have administrative control over the corporation. Martin and Walter own 35,000 and 40,000 shares, respectively. Other directors who are family members own 50,000 shares amongst them. The over-the-counter price is currently $31 bid and $33 asked. The price range last year was $22-$30 and the year before was $26-$36. Pertinent financial data for Brunswig Corporation are given below and on page 339.

Brunswig Corporation
Statement of Income
(000's omitted)

	5 Years Ago	Preceding Year	Preceding Year	Last Year	Current Year
Net Sales..................	$48,494	$58,837	$66,753	$63,621	$58,405
Cost of Goods Sold.........	33,013	38,671	43,251	41,294	38,300
Depreciation...............	1,850	2,093	2,213	2,609	1,943
Selling & Administrative Expense..................	8,455	9,724	10,978	11,101	10,766
Interest Expense............	326	366	200	283	414
Net Income after Taxes.......	2,399	3,906	5,069	4,372	3,396
Per Share of Common Stock: Net Income.............	$2.47	$3.90	$4.88	$4.13	$3.18
Cash Dividends Paid.....	.825	1.05	1.20	1.25	1.40

Brunswig Corporation
Balance Sheets
(000's omitted)

	Last Year	Current Year
Current Assets.........................	$29,397	$29,099
Investments...........................	1,669	1,704
Net Property & Plants..................	19,380	19,946
Other Assets..........................	4,751	4,595
Total Assets...........................	$55,197	$55,344
Current Liabilities....................	$ 9,617	$ 8,683
Deferred Liabilities...................	2,509	2,644
Long-Term Debt......................	7,472	7,456
Common Stock (authorized, 2,500,000 shares; issued 1,077,000 shares)...............	2,692	2,692
Additional Contributed Capital..........	4,611	4,621
Retained Earnings.....................	28,296	29,248
Total Stockholders' Equity..........	$35,599	$36,561
Total Liabilities and Equity.............	$55,197	$55,344

Schneider Transmissions' offer, in general terms, is to merge Brunswig Corporation into Schneider Transmissions, Inc. through Schneider's purchase of up to 49% of the outstanding shares of Brunswig common stock for $60 per share in cash and the exchange of 1.54 shares of Schneider Transmissions common stock for each share of Brunswig common for the balance of the outstanding shares. The most recent closing price of Schneider common on the New York Stock Exchange was $40 per share. The stock is ranked A by Standard & Poor's.

Schneider Transmissions has three product groups:

1. Mechanical components such as chains, sprockets, flexible couplings, gears, speed reducers, clutch plates, and pumps.
2. Engineered systems, such as bulk materials handling equipment for mines, lumber and steel mills, and power plants, and equipment for the biological and mechanical treatment of sewage, refuse, and waste water.
3. Construction machinery such as concrete mixers, highway pavers, and maintenance equipment.

Schneider Transmissions sells in the United States and Canada through company offices and local distributors. It has regional distribution centers in 11 cities. Abroad, the company has 11 sales offices as well as manufacturing and warehousing operations in Argentina, Australia, Brazil, England, France, Italy, Germany, and Japan. The main manufacturing facilities are in various southern Ohio cities.

Development engineering and sales engineering are the responsibility of each product group. The company spent about $4 million last year on this work.

Acquisitions in the past three years include two major manufacturers of quick-opening fasteners, a specialized gear manufacturer, a valve manufacturer, two sewage disposal manufacturers, and, recently, a medium-sized company that makes gears, speed reducers, clutch plates, and couplings. This latest acquisition, when combined with the firm's other gear manufacturing facilities, has allowed Schneider Transmissions to become a significant—but by no means the most important—factor in gear and coupling manufacturing. As it consolidates its organization in these lines and, above all, when it combines the sales work and develops a tested marketing capability, the company will be a very strong competitor in the mechanical power transmission industry. Market share in the gear and coupling lines may well increase to 15%-18% if the marketing work is done effectively.

Selected financial data for Schneider Transmissions, Inc. are as follows:

Schneider Transmissions, Inc.
Selected Financial Data

Year	Net Sales	Net Income	Times Interest and Preferred Dividends Earned	Dividend per Share of Common Stock	Price Range of Common Stock on NYSE
	(000's omitted)				
Current	$217,000	$ 9,610	3.36 times	$1.50	$44–$40
Preceding	191,200	8,928	4.14 "	1.50	52– 34
"	185,000	8,463	n.a.	1.50	55– 30
"	165,400	10,843	n.a.	1.50	36– 25
"	159,600	8,020	n.a.	1.20	36– 24

Schneider Transmissions, Inc.
Balance Sheets
(000's omitted)

	Current Year	Last Year
Cash and Marketable Securities........	$ 5,600	$ 7,000
Accounts Receivable.................	41,100	37,000
Inventories.........................	54,300	43,700
Total Current Assets.................	$101,000	$ 87,700
Net Property........................	41,300	36,200
Other Assets........................	7,700	5,500
Total Assets........................	$150,000	$129,400
Total Current Liabilities..............	$ 35,900	$ 19,300
Long-Term Debt....................	14,800	14,500
$2.50 Cumulative Preferred Stock (570,000 shares outstanding)........	11,480	11,420
Common Stock (2,992,000 shares).......	29,992	29,453
Capital Surplus......................	11,473	12,502
Retained Earnings...................	46,355	42,225
Total Liabilities and Equity...........	$150,000	$129,400

Allied Machinery Products Corporation proposes that substantially all of the Brunswig assets and business be transferred to a wholly owned subsidiary (to be organized by Allied) in exchange for Allied preferred stock and common stock and the assumption by the subsidiary of substantially all the liabilities of Brunswig. Employees of Brunswig will become employees of the new subsidiary, which will continue to conduct Brunswig's business with Brunswig's name after the closing. The present Brunswig Corporation will be dissolved.

Allied's plan is to distribute 0.4921 of a share of Allied voting $3.50 cumulative convertible preferred stock and 0.32 of a share of Allied common for each share of Brunswig common stock.

Allied makes proprietary hydromechanical and electromechanical systems and components and proprietary machining systems. Its principal offices and plants are in a city about a hundred miles distant from the plants of Brunswig.

The proprietary systems and the components are parts sold as original equipment to the aircraft and aerospace industries, the mobile equipment industry, the oil heating industry, and the petrochemical processing industry. These components account for about 82% of sales, while the balance is made up of machine tools and total machining systems sold to the general metalworking industry. Both the machine tools and the component parts require a high degree of research, development, engineering, and manufacturing competence. For all products, Allied has patents or some special processes and trade secrets that give it special property rights.

The components sold as original equipment include hydraulic pumps and motors, pneumatic starters, underwater power plants, hydrostatic transmissions, and constant speed drives that convert variable input speed from a jet or turbine engine to constant output speed to drive alternating current electrical generators. They also include electronic controls and instruments, oil burner fuel units, lubrication pumps, condensers, and evaporators for use in air-conditioning and refrigeration systems.

The numerically-controlled or direct-computer-controlled multi-operational machining systems perform a variety of metal-cutting operations and can change from one operation to another without interrupting the manufacturing process. The machines are highly accurate and are best suited for low-volume metalworking operations such as the production of prototypes and small-lot runs.

Allied exports from its own plants and has licensed other firms in all the major industrial countries in the world to produce its components and machining systems. It has three plants abroad in Sweden, Switzerland, and France.

A technically-trained salesforce and independent distributors sell the Allied line. Field engineers provide technical services to support sales effort. Other firms compete with Allied on one or more products, but none duplicates more than a small portion of its business.

Allied owns a large number of patents that are important in the aggregate to the conduct of its business. About 700 graduate engineers and engineering employees work on a wide range of applied research and product development programs that are conducted in addition to the regular product adaptation and testing work of the sales engineering group. Company policy is to spend about 5% of net sales on research and development work.

During the past two years, Allied has acquired eight small to medium-sized manufacturing firms that produce electronic systems and special alloy castings. For these it paid, in the aggregate, $6,400,000 in cash plus 612,000 newly issued shares of common stock and 252,400 shares of $3.50 cumulative convertible preferred stock.

Allied employs about 11,000 people, of whom 6,700 are production and maintenance employees. About 2,500 of these workers closed down two plants for 40 days and 40 nights earlier in the year as part of an effort to win a new 3-year contract. They succeeded. The company has various retirement plans, including pension, profit-sharing, and money purchase plans covering most of the employees.

Selected financial data for Allied Machinery Products Corporation are as follows:

Allied Machinery Products Corporation
Selected Financial Data

Year	Net Sales Net Income (000's omitted)	Times Interest and Preferred Dividends Earned	Dividend per Share of Common Stock	Price Range of $3.50 Preferred Stock NYSE	Price Range of Common Stock [1] NYSE
Current	$242,000 $14,300	4.3 times	$.80	$95–75	$91–64
Preceding	215,000 11,246	3.6 times	.80	83–71	87–29
"	152,000 8,020	n.a.	.60		30–18
"	122,000 5,253		.50		37–20
"	109,000 4,095		.50		24–18
"	108,000 2,581		.50		28–19

[1] This stock is ranked B+ by Standard & Poor's.

Allied Machinery Products Corporation
Balance Sheets
(000's omitted)

	Current Year	Last Year
Cash and Marketable Securities	$ 4,657	$ 5,904
Accounts Receivable	45,600	41,246
Inventories	91,023	87,690
Total Current Assets	$141,280	$134,840
Net Property	80,087	74,339
Other Assets	5,007	4,702
Total Assets	$226,374	$213,881
Total Current Liabilities	$ 61,855	$ 84,270
Long-Term Debt	70,648	65,730
$3.50 Cumulative Convertible Preferred Stock (3,000,000 shares authorized)	200	197
Common Stock, par value $1, (15,000,000 shares authorized)	4,853	4,124
Additional Contributed Capital	46,139	21,492
Retained Earnings	42,679	38,068
Total Liabilities and Stockholders' Equity	$226,374	$213,881

A week after the surprise visit and presentation by Schneider Transmissions executives, the Brunswigs—Martin and Walter—sat at lunch. Martin said to his brother:

"I believe what the Allied people told us. Their goal is to increase earnings per share of stock by increasing their market share, expanding their balance sheet leverage, and developing improved products to increase profits. They are clearly organized for action on mergers and, on the other hand, they are determined to avoid a takeover of their own company by making it too expensive. Their policy is to strive for a consistent improvement in earnings and, through this, to influence a high valuation of their stock by analysts as well as the general public.

"They have also defined their basic characteristics as being a 'mechanical engineering company' with interests in special market segments that have a relatively high growth potential. Of course, we know their special skills and advanced competence in aircraft and aerospace components and machine tools.

"But, in talking with them, I am impressed as much by their knowing all the financial moves—straight-line depreciation rather than sum-of-the-digits, smoothing profits through the development cost account, having high debt-leverage so that a raider can't buy you with your own money, diversifying to give a raider potential antitrust trouble, LIFO inventory, not amortizing goodwill, etc.—as by their knowing that our gears can be coupled with their hydrostatic equipment to develop a continuous speed device using an electric motor. This will expand the range of any electric motor well beyond the limited number of r.p.m.'s that it was originally built for. You and I know that our product lines are complementary and that there are many mutual development opportunities.

"How are we going to persuade the rest of the family? The yield on Allied common stock is very small (see Exhibit A), but the use of both preferred and common stock will get dividends to them. And the preferred is not callable for the first five years. The exchange of stock with Allied is tax-free at present, and a capital gains tax would only have to be paid if the stock were sold some time in the future. But the Schneider proposal is nontaxable now only on the common stock part. Anyone who holds some of our original shares might have to pay capital gains on the cash portion. The maximum this would be per share would be \$13.17 (25% of \$60—\$7.313).

"Allied management knows how to run a diversified company. Look at their proposal for a separate subsidiary. No one will be hurt by that move.

"And there is a final reason that I may have to pass up in public discussion. It will be a real pleasure to deal with stockholders who understand technically what this company is all about and to work with a technically-oriented management in a similar line of business.

"But what are the arguments in favor of Schneider Transmissions that we may have to meet? Schneider is local. We know the people and can trust them. And those whom we can't we can keep a good eye on. Their asset size is closer to ours so we will be a more important part of the merged operation. Schneider is expanding, but not so rapidly as to destroy any sense of where we have been and where we are going. The people there are not trying to play any go-go conglomerate role. The money looks good. And certainly the products match. Schneider has no labor or union troubles. Why turn elsewhere for a partner when you've got the fellow down the street?

"Well, we'll have to persuade the others and then set up a special stockholders' meeting soon. It looks as if the Allied common stock will be close to \$65 a share for awhile and the price of the preferred will be about \$77 a share.''

Exhibit A

Comparative Per-Share Data

	Preceding Year	Last Year	Current Year	Net Book Equity
(1) To Brunswig Shareholders:				
(a) Net Earnings:				
Actual	$4.88	$4.13	$3.18	$34
Pro Forma, assuming merger with Allied Machinery:				
Common Stock	.79	.87	.90	
Preferred Stock	1.72	1.72	1.72	
Total	$2.51	$2.59	$2.62	$48
(b) Cash Dividends:				
Actual	$1.20	$1.25	$1.40	
Pro Forma, assuming merger with Allied Machinery:				
Common Stock	.19	.26	.26	
Preferred Stock	1.72	1.72	1.72	
Total	$1.91	$1.98	$1.98	
(2) To Allied Shareholders:				
(a) Earnings Applicable to Common Stock:				
Actual	$1.84	$2.38	$2.72	$16
Pro Forma, assuming merger	2.46	2.72	2.84	$12
(b) Cash Dividends:				
Common Stock	.60	.80	.80	
Preferred Stock	3.50	3.50	3.50	

Required: (a) What alternatives do you see for the Brunswig Corporation shareholders and management?

(b) As a member of the Board of Directors of Brunswig Corporation, what would be your vote on the various alternatives? Explain.

INTEGRATING CASES / Strategy and Financing

POWDERED METALS, INC.

"During our first eight years we had to take large risks," said Mr. Hubler, president of Powdered Metals, Inc. "Bankruptcy was always a threat, but we had no choice. We simply proceeded on faith that our small company would master the art of making high-precision parts out of powdered metal, and then the leading companies of the nation would be glad to do business with us. Now, we have mastered the art—at least to some extent—and we are doing business with the Xerox's and the IBM's. But the risk problem has become tougher because we now have choices. We can use our profits to pay off debts and remove the threat of bankruptcy—or we can seize the opportunity we worked so hard to create and help push powdered metal parts into every sophisticated machine that's made—or we can decide to do something in between."

Product/market target

The company makes an array of specially shaped gears, bearings, and other machine parts. Instead of starting with the usual casting or forging process, the new metallurgy injects a finely powdered form of iron, steel, or other alloy into a mold and packs the powder together under high pressure. The "raw" part is then placed in a furnace where high temperature unites the fine particles into a solid form.

It is the combination of (a) high-pressure molding in very precise molds with (b) heat treatment ("sintering") that makes the company products distinctive. The molding process enables the company to make oddly shaped parts that are difficult or impossible to produce by ordinary machining. And the sintering process imparts strength and hardness matching or exceeding conventionally formed metal parts. Moreover, the process significantly reduces unit costs, virtually eliminates waste and scrap, and can be used for rapid mass production.

Actually, the technique of producing metal parts by compacting powders has been in use for many years. Early applications were limited to small, relatively crude parts not subjected to heavy bearing or shock loads. The process gained acceptance by providing lower costs than were available through conventional machining or forging methods and by providing unique compositions not readily obtained through conventional melt-alloying methods.

As powder compacting techniques were refined and improved, the competitive advantage broadened dramatically. It is common practice today for engineers to design components specifically for production by the powdered metal process. Load-bearing characteristics, density, dimensional and shape conformity, and ease of machining can now meet a wide range of requirements once considered available only from wrought materials.

345

The powdered metal industry is generally expected to continue to expand at its current rapid rate because the competitive capability of the process is gaining wider acceptance in all sorts of uses. The largest *tonnage* consumer is and will continue to be the automotive industry: bearings, gears, oil pump vanes, etc. However, the largest *number* of parts, requiring a high degree of precision, are being consumed in home appliances, business machines, recreational products, and the electrical and electronics industries. It is to this latter segment of the market that Powdered Metals, Inc. has directed its efforts.

Some of the more intricate precision parts made by this latter segment of the industry cannot be directly compacted to exact finished dimensions and contours and thus require secondary or finishing operations, generally by machining. Powdered Metals, Inc. has a unique capability in this area, shared with only 4 or 5 other of the 90 noncaptive powdered metal parts-makers in the country. The success it has attained in becoming a primary vendor to IBM and Xerox is testimony of Powdered Metals, Inc.'s competence in the high-value-added portion of the market. The company has the "know-how" to continue to penetrate premium markets where its proven competence and highest-grade tools and equipment are demanded.

Four years ago total industry sales of powdered metal parts was $108 million. By last year the sales had risen to $217 million, more than doubling in three years' time. About $120 million of last year's total went to the automotive industry, the balance to the more specialized markets. And this second part of the industry grew somewhat faster than the total, almost 30% per year. This rate of growth may not be maintained, but industry speakers predict an average increase over the next decade of 20% to 25% per annum.

Powdered Metals, Inc. hopes to increase the number of different customers it serves; it is now somewhat vulnerable because two large firms account for over half of its business. However, because of the cost of making precision molds, reorders of specific parts are likely to be placed with the company that produces the original run. An industry rule-of-thumb is that, on the average, a machine part will continue to be used by a customer in making new machines for seven years. Powdered Metals, Inc. has not yet had much experience with such reorders.

The company is well equipped to seek orders for complex parts. It has a very good machine shop where molds are made, its compacting presses and sintering furnaces are new, and it has equipment for secondary machining if this is required. Both Mr. Hubler and Mr. Chang, the chief engineer, are recognized for their specialized knowledge, and the company has established a reputation for high-quality output.

Progress to date

Mr. A. B. Hubler dropped out of engineering school, became a machinist in the Navy, and later worked at this trade while completing his engineering training at nights. He was a partner in several small firms, and in one of these he hired a bright young engineer, J. K. Chang. These two men soon developed the idea of a new firm in the powdered metals field. Four years later Mr. Hubler had assembled the initial capital and Mr. Chang had studied the latest technological developments. The new firm was launched in a suburb of Columbus, Ohio.

The early years proved to be even more difficult than anticipated. Learning how to get dependable quality from new equipment, training personnel, obtaining test orders from customers and waiting while they evaluated the products in their own shops—all took time and money. But now, eight years later, Powdered Metals, Inc. is a profitable business.

The plant is running on a two-shift basis. The margin between prices and costs is improving, reflecting both an ability to get more attractive orders and improved efficiency in the plant. And the company has a four-month backlog of orders. Exhibit 1 shows the improvement in income over the last five years, from a staggering deficit to a 19% return on the book value of stockholders' equity.

Exhibit 1
Income Statement
(in 1,000's)

	Last year	2 years ago	3 years ago	4 years ago	5 years ago
Net sales	$3,732	$3,019	$1,778	$ 821	$ 316
Cost of sales	2,631	2,262	1,325	644	530
Gross profit	$1,101	$ 757	$ 453	$ 177	$−214
Selling, general & administrative expenses	797	484	386	294	189
Net income	$ 304*	$ 273*	$ 67	$−117	$−403

* No income tax has been paid because of loss carryovers for preceding years. At the beginning of the present year the remaining loss carryover was $370,000.

Present financing

Obtaining the capital necessary to finance Powdered Metals, Inc. has been a strain. During its early years the company relied on equity investments by Mr. Hubler and his friends. Equipment—especially compacting presses obtained from a Japanese manufacturer—was usually purchased at least in part with chattel mortgages, and other loans were secured.

About three years ago the company was successful in a significant recapitalization: (a) 50,000 shares of common stock were sold to the public at $10 per share by a local investment banker; (b) the Buckeye SBIC[1] made a $2,000,000 mortgage loan to the company; (c) debts outstanding at that time were either paid off or converted to common stock. The Buckeye SBIC loan runs for 10 years with $50,000 maturing quarterly ($200,000 per year); the interest rate is 8½% per annum. As part of the deal, Buckeye received warrants (rights to buy) for 50,000 shares at $8 per share, which can be exercised any time during the 10 years that the loan is outstanding.

This injection of capital, helpful though it was, has not been adequate to support expanding production. New equipment to expand capacity has been financed with chattel mortgages; $300,000 of such mortgages were outstanding a year ago, and an additional $600,000 were issued during the past year. These chattel mortgages mature at the rate of $100,000 per year and bear 10% interest. Incidentally, the Buckeye SBIC was willing to subordinate its claim on this new equipment because the added capacity increases the chance that its warrants will become valuable.

The present financial structure of the company, reflecting these capital inputs, is shown in Exhibit 2.

---

[1] SBIC's (Small Business Investment Corporations) are private lending organizations that are granted federal tax advantages because they concentrate on lending money to small firms that are having difficulty obtaining long-term capital.

Exhibit 2
Balance Sheet—End of Year
(in 1,000's)

	Last Year		Preceding Year	
Assets				
Current assets:				
Cash......................................	$ 199		$ 89	
Accounts receivable, net....................	650		651	
Inventories	637		308	
Prepaid and deferred items	89		61	
Total current assets		$1,575		$1,109
Plant and equipment:				
Land and buildings	$ 941		$ 909	
Machinery and equipment....................	2,853		2,244	
Furniture and fixtures	260		230	
	$4,054		$3,383	
Less depreciation reserve	−747		−531	
Net plant and equipment		3,307		2,852
Research and deferred charges		74		83
Total assets		$4,956		$4,044
Liabilities				
Current liabilities:				
Current portion of long-term debt	$ 300		$ 200	
Accounts payable	517		345	
Accrued liabilities	109		73	
Total current liabilities.....................		$ 926		$ 618
Long-term debt:				
Long-term loan	$1,600		$1,800	
Equipment mortgages	800		300	
Total debt due after 1 year		2,400		2,100
Stockholders' equity:				
200,000 shares outstanding, par value $1	$ 200		$ 200	
Capital in excess of par value	1,800		1,800	
Retained earnings (deficit)...................	(370)		(674)	
Total equity		1,630		1,326
Total liabilities and equity.................		$4,956		$4,044

Future opportunities

"At long last," Mr. Hubler observes, "we have the opportunity to have a balance sheet look the way the bankers like it. Assuming earnings just stay steady, our cash gain from operations each year will be:

Net income	$304,000
Depreciation	216,000
Available	$520,000

"With that amount of cash we can make our annual debt repayments of $300,000 and still increase current assets $220,000. In two years our current ratio would be 2:1 and our long-term debt would be only 82% of stockholders' equity. For anyone who has been squeezed for capital for eight years, that kind of a picture has much attraction. And maybe the equipment people would stop insisting on my personal guarantee of those mortgage notes.

"But we didn't enter the powdered metal business to stay even. We believe the industry will continue to grow rapidly, and naturally we'd like to benefit from that growth. The future is never certain, of course; too many competitors may enter the business or some new technique may replace powdered metals. But powdered metals have grown much faster than the industries we serve—business machines, electronics, home appliances, and the like—and Powdered Metals, Inc. has been growing faster than its competitors. So I feel that 20% increase per year for us is very conservative. We should be able to do that and at the same time be more choosy about the orders we take—which will help our profit margin. Of course, if a real recession descends on us, it's a new ball game.

"The main catch is that fast growth takes more capital—capital we do not have. With an additional $500,000 in equipment we could produce a volume of $5,000,000 in sales. The building is big enough to handle $7,000,000—with a bit of squeezing. But as we move beyond $5,000,000, all kinds of machinery will be needed, on the average of 80¢ per every additional dollar of sales or $1,600,000 of new equipment for the expansion from $5,000,000 to $7,000,000.

"In addition, more sales require more working capital. Inventory, accounts receivable, accounts payable, and accrued items all go up. My rough estimate is that the net increase in working capital would be about one sixth of the annual sales. Where is all that money coming from? Retained earnings will help, but in any one year during the growth period the profit on the added volume (say, 9%) doesn't provide necessary working capital (17%).

"I've asked our treasurer, P. L. Jablonski, to explore all the different ways we might finance the business that I'm sure we can get during the next four years. With all those alternatives before us, we can sit down and figure out whether it is wise to go plunging ahead."

Alternative sources of capital

Ms. Jablonski summarized the various potential ways Powdered Metals, Inc. might finance its growth as follows:

1. The company's commercial bank suggests no growth this year and cutting inventories $100,000. These actions would allow the company to significantly improve its working capital position. Then the bank would make a short-term loan of $500,000 (perhaps requiring the pledging of accounts receivables if the inventory reduction was not feasible). The interest cost would be prime rate plus 1½% and maintenance of a bank balance of 20% of the loan.[2]
2. The investment banker who helped sell company stock three years ago thinks that improved company performance would create an interest in an additional issue, in spite of the present depressed condition of stocks generally. However, the selling price to the public would be only $7.50 per share, and after underwriting charges and other costs the company would receive $6.70 per share. Thus an issue of

---

[2] The minimum balance requirement, a customary banking practice, means that the company would get only $400,000 for other uses. Assuming an 8% prime rate, the interest cost would be 9½% of $500,000, or $47,500 per year. On $400,000 this is equivalent to almost 12% per annum.

75,000 shares would yield $502,000. Such an issue would improve debt/equity ratios. It would be "expensive" for present stockholders—for example, after such an issue, the people who invested $500,000 three years ago when risks were greater would hold only 18% of the total equity whereas the new stockholders would have 27% of the total equity.

3. An investment broker, recommended by the commercial bank, suggests a "sale and leaseback" of the company's land and buildings (for $800,000) plus the new equipment (costing $500,000). The $800,000 would be used to pay off existing chattel mortgages on equipment. The company would pay an annual rental equivalent to 9½% on money advanced (a total initially of $1,300,000) plus 5% depreciation on the building and equipment. The lease would run for 20 years, at which time the company would have an option to repurchase the land, buildings, and equipment at 20% of the total $1,300,000 advanced.[3]

4. Mr. Bender, a Cleveland financier and president of Empire Investment Co., proposes a merger with another small firm that he controls. The firm, a profitable truck-leasing operation, would be merged into Powdered Metals, Inc. so that the profits from the trucking operation would be offset by the tax loss carryforward of Powdered Metals, Inc. Empire Investment Co. owns the trucking firm and would get 75% of the shares of the merged companies. Mr. Bender says he can always find capital for profitable investments, and he would be able to devise some scheme to provide whatever capital the powdered metal activities can use effectively.

5. Buckeye SBIC is willing to advance more capital if the total debt structure is improved. It proposes a combined package: (a) a $500,000 loan for the new equipment on the same terms as its present loan, plus (b) purchase of 80,000 shares of stock at $6 per share. The $480,000 from the stock sale, $100,000 from reduction of inventories, and current earnings are to be used to retire the equipment mortgages.

Ms. Jablonski notes, "All five of the proposals focus primarily on raising $500,000 to expand production facilities. This will enable Powdered Metals, Inc. to increase its sales to $5,000,000. At the projected rise in sales, that takes care of us for only about eighteen months. Consequently, any plan adopted must also consider the ability of the company at that time to raise further growth capital."

QUESTIONS

1. Do you recommend that Powdered Metals, Inc. buy the $500,000 worth of new equipment at this time? If so, how should the expansion be financed?
2. Assuming that your recommendation is accepted and that you have $5,000 available for investment, what price per share would you be willing to pay for Powdered Metals, Inc. common stock?

---

[3] The company would continue to pay real estate and property taxes and insurance just as though it owned the property. The interest portion of the rent would drop as the depreciation portion retired the loan. Broadly speaking, the company would be getting a 20-year loan at 9½%, except that it would have to pay 20% to retrieve its property at the end of the period. There also would be a book loss on the land and buildings at the time of the transaction ($941,000 minus $800,000), but this is not a real loss since the property could eventually be recovered on the basis of the $800,000 figure. Presently, depreciation on the buildings is about $25,000 per year. It is anticipated that Buckeye SBIC will waive its mortgage lien on the land and buildings because it will obtain a first lien on equipment when the $800,000 chattel mortgages are paid off and because its warrants become more attractive.

WESTERN PLYWOOD MILLS, INC.

Western Plywood Mills, Inc., a company engaged principally in the manufacture and sale of Douglas fir plywood, is subject to financial pressures from many sources. The proposed acquisition of new timberlands for an assured source of supply of logs, the expansion of plant to maintain its position in the industry, the addition of warehouses to meet competitors' selling methods, and pressure from stockholders for increased dividends are currently straining the company's financial resources. These pressures are likely to increase in the future, and it is necessary for the officers of the company to review thoroughly its capital structure in order to maintain a sound financial position.

This company was organized about fifteen years ago by a group of employees who saw the possibility of a major expansion of the plywood industry. This method of organization and ownership is fairly common in the industry, and currently about 15% of total production is carried on by worker-owner companies. Since its founding, the company has been successful, and its sales now amount to about 4% of the industry total. However, its portion of industry sales is not as large as before. Five years ago Western's sales were 6% of the industry total and its share has dropped steadily since then.

Plywood is made from many different kinds of softwood and hardwood. The major species used, however, is Douglas fir, which is also known as Oregon pine. Douglas fir plywood is widely used for many exterior and interior construction purposes. Fabrication begins with the debarking of choice "peeler" logs. These logs, sawed into sections, are first skinned with a debarking knife. They are then centered on a lathe that rotates the section against a long, hollow-ground blade, and a sheet of smooth veneer is cut from the entire length of the section. This wide ribbon of veneer is cut or "peeled" from the section much as a large roll of paper is unwound. The veneer is then carried on a conveyor to the clippers where it is cut to the desired width. After sorting for quality, the sheets are conveyed to an oven dryer. Following the drying, waterproof glue is applied by rollers to the surfaces of the veneer layers, and the plies are cemented together with the grain of each sheet at right angles to that of its neighbor. Heat and pressure in a hot press weld the panels together to form a permanent bond.

A tremendous expansion has taken place in the industry, which in the past thirty years has increased plywood production from about 235 million square feet to about 10 billion square feet.

In making plywood, only the bottom 55% of a Douglas fir tree can be used. The top 10% is used for making sawmill or dimension lumber and the balance for shop lumber that goes into doors, pipes, tanks, etc. To meet the growing demand for plywood, the industry has moved south from Washington through Oregon into California in its search for good supplies of top-grade peeler logs. Less than one third of all fir logs are of peeler grade, and clear-growth, virgin timber with knot-free trunks is fast disappearing.

Shortages of high-quality logs and continued expansion have forced some of the larger companies to purchase their own timberlands so as to assure themselves of logs at a constant price. On the average, the cost of logs amounts to 55% of total manufacturing costs. Once timberlands are purchased, it is necessary for a company to enter other parts of the lumber industry so as to utilize the balance of the fir tree that cannot be used for plywood. Roads and sawmills have to be built, and investment in machinery must be made in order to develop the timberlands.

A revolution in industry marketing practices has gone along with the expansion in production. At one time the plywood mills sold through agents who handled the entire distribution program. Now marketing emphasis has shifted, and a large proportion of output is sold through controlled channels. The major companies have their own warehouses and their own salesmen. Some of them engage in extensive brand promotion. For example, United States Plywood's consumer advertising program featuring its brand name "Weldwood" is very extensive. Western Plywood currently markets 13% of its ouput through its own warehouses. It would like to extend its chain of warehouses and its dealer promotion program so that 50% of its sales are made through these channels within the near future. This will give it a good start towards a strongly competitive marketing organization.

The original group of 49 worker-owners who started the company have, by now, changed their attitude toward the use of profits. From the beginning, the company has financed its expansion by plowing back profits, as is shown by the increase in earned surplus to about $5.5 million. Many of the older owners have retired or died and only half are still active in the company. More of these will retire in the near future. Their interest is now in having a higher percentage of profits paid as dividends. They also want a ready market for their stock so that it can be sold quickly, thus providing an emergency source of cash. Some of them would like to sell their stock now, so that they can diversify their investments. In the past, the company has purchased common stock from estates of deceased partners, and several retired partners are urging that the company adopt a policy of buying back any stock that former partners wish to sell. Retained earnings have provided the major source of funds in the past, as is indicated in the table below. The treasurer is, however, by no means sure that profits will be sufficient for the capital needs that he sees arising in the near future.

Sources of Funds
(000's omitted)

	Current Year	Last Year	Preceding Year
Net profits..........................	$644	$1,600	$1,390
Depreciation and depletion...........	247	121	179
Long-term bank loans................	(94) minus	(111) minus	384
Liquidation of other assets............	....	62	302
Total.........................	$797	$1,672	$2,255

Uses of Funds
(000's omitted)

	Current Year	Last Year	Preceding Year
Increases in working capital...........	$(252) minus	$ 449	$ 218
Plant and equipment additions.........	593	699	208
Timber additions :...................	162	30	1,350
Dividends..........................	258	398	398
Investments.........................	....	75	13
Deferred assets......................	36	21	68
Total.........................	$797	$1,672	$2,255

The company estimates that an expenditure of $3,600,000 during the next year will enable it to acquire timberlands that will be adequate to provide the supply of logs necessary within the foreseeable future. Executives believe these timberlands could be purchased at an average cost that would yield 7% per annum before income taxes, based on current log prices, when all the timber is cut. It might be anywhere from fifteen to thirty years before all the timber is cut, however, and the realized profit would depend upon the trend in prices during that interval. The profit earned in any one year would depend upon how many logs were cut, and the margin between the current value of the logs and depletion, property taxes, logging, and other costs.

Additions to plant and equipment, necessary to exploit this supply of logs, will call for expenditures of $1,000,000 within the next two years. Finally, an additional $1,200,000 will provide the working capital necessary for extended production operations and for expanding the company's marketing program. Executives are confident that these additional investments in production and marketing facilities will yield about the same profit as the company is earning on its present assets, assuming industry conditions continue as they have prevailed in the last few years. Detailed estimates have been postponed until the basic policy regarding expansion is settled.

The past profit history of the company has been good, as is shown by the following income data:

Selected Income Data
(000's omitted)

	Net Sales	Net Profit	Dividends
Current year	$7,475	$ 644	$258
Preceding year	8,590	1,600	398
" "	7,500	1,390	398
" "	5,450	789	89
" "	5,170	233	...
" "	5,430	304	...
" "	6,025	338	...
" "	5,650	352	42
" "	5,520	596	168
" "	3,860	339	310

Continuous future profits are not assured, however. Plywood has shown considerable price instability in the past. This affects sales and also causes inventory losses, as was true in the last year. Price drops are caused largely by the activity of small manufacturers who buy veneer and make plywood from it. These companies are typically weak financially and will often cut prices rapidly and drastically in an attempt to maintain sales volume. Although sales prices of the finished plywood may fluctuate widely, costs typically do not. Both log costs and labor costs (which together make up 85% of total costs) have risen rather steadily since the founding of Western Plywood. Log prices on the open market occasionally drop 10% from one year to the next, but more commonly increase because of the shortage of peeler logs. Labor rates have risen 110% on the average in the past ten years.

Besides the problem of how much capital the company needs and how it should be obtained, the treasurer is concerned with the allocation of any funds obtained among the various claims on capital. The officers feel that it would be highly desirable for the company to own additional timberlands and would prefer to buy them if the capital is available. Purchase of timberlands is not absolutely necessary, however. The government owns two thirds of the timber in the Northwest and each year cuts and sells at auction enough peeler logs to meet about one quarter of the industry's needs. In addition, there are private timber operators who supply logs to the open market. Thirty years ago, most plywood companies bought their logs on the open market and some of them have continued to do so since. Open market prices of logs naturally fluctuate and may rise quite steeply when the demand is high. Three years ago, for example, they increased 33% over the year before. A decision not to buy timberlands would also mean a reduction by about one half of the contemplated expenditures for additional plant and equipment.

The company sees no other way of meeting competition than to continue the planned marketing program, which calls for additional warehouses, more finished inventory, and expanded sales promotion efforts.

The desires of the stockholders pose a difficult problem. The treasurer is not sure just how far the company should go toward increasing annual dividends, nor is he certain what should be done about the stock held by retired employees.

The company's balance sheets for the current year and past year are shown below.

Balance Sheets
(000's omitted)

	Current Year	Past Year
Current Assets		
Cash...........................	$ 675	$ 569
U.S. Government Bonds..............	262	262
Accounts Receivable................	609	405
Inventories.......................	869	1,508
Total..........................	$2,415	$2,744
Investments.........................	544	544
Plant and Equipment, net...............	2,315	1,917
Timber............................	1,930	1,820
Deferred Charges.....................	266	230
Total Assets......................	$7,470	$7,255
Current Liabilities		
Loans Payable......................	$ 180	$ 94
Accounts Payable and Accruals........	837	1,000
Total..........................	$1,017	$1,094
Long-Term Loans [1]....................	179	273
Capital Stock........................	414	414
Capital Surplus......................	367	367
Retained Earnings....................	5,493	5,107
Total Liabilities and Capital..........	$7,470	$7,255

[1] Repayable at a future rate of $74,000 per year.

QUESTIONS

1. What strategy do you recommend that Western Plywood Mills, Inc. follow?
2. What financial policy with respect to uses of capital, sources of capital, and dividends do you recommend for the next few years to implement this strategy?

Part 3
ORGANIZING FOR ACTION

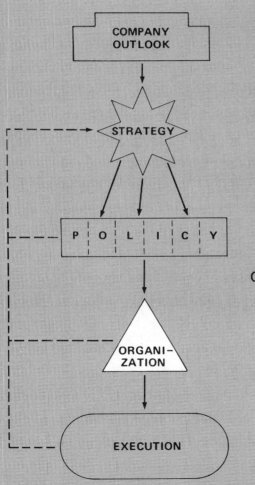

Chapter

16

MATCHING ORGANIZATION
WITH STRATEGY

Organizing for growth

A change in a company's strategy and policy usually leads to realignment of its organization. Some activities will be expanded, others curtailed; new priorities will determine which divisions report directly to senior executives. Unless these adjustments are in tune with the shift in objectives, the anticipated growth may never materialize.

In designing an organization we are concerned with the way the myriad of activities required to operate any firm are assigned to people. To be effective, each person has to focus on particular segments of the total task. At the same time, each person's work must be coordinated with the work of others. All sorts of grouping of activities and of interconnecting links are possible—just as letters of the alphabet can be combined in numerous ways—but the particular combination into subgroups and these subgroups into larger divisions has a profound impact on the successful execution of any strategy.

Central management must frequently review the interaction between strategy/policy and organization structure. This matching of strategy and structure shows up most dramatically as a firm moves through different stages of growth. So this chapter deals especially with issues arising in the shift from one stage to another. Chapter 17 then examines the way staff, services, and other divisions provide connective tissue between the basic divisions that we discuss in this chapter. Two further issues—the organization of central management itself and the staffing of positions created in the organization design—become the foci of the following chapters.

Need for activity analysis

Just as the selected strategy and its implementation policy are unique for each enterprise, so too is the organization design. Organizing calls for perception of subtle differences, imagination in devising special combinations, judgment in balancing benefits and drawbacks, and human understanding in turning an intellectual concept into a social reality. Although common patterns exist, we can't jump from a particular strategy to a predetermined form of organization.

The link between strategy and organization design is activity analysis. What work—planning, operating, controlling, and so forth—must be performed to execute a specific strategy and its associated policy? We need this transformation into work or activities because at least the formal aspects of organization deal with who does what work.

When the J. C. Penney Company, for example, gave up its long-standing "cash sales only" policy and started to grant credit, an array of new activities arose in the accounting, customer credit, and financial control sections of each store as well as in the home office. Likewise, Dole Pineapple Company's decision to make rather than buy its tin cans in Hawaii added activities ranging from purchase of tinplate to running a conveyor from the can shop to the warehouse. It is these new activities that are the grist for any organizational change that may be needed.

When thinking about organizing a large department or an entire company, as central managers must do, a comprehensive review of *all* activities necessary for successful operations is desirable. To examine only a part—the "squeaky wheel"—is likely to lead to a remedy that creates as many new problems as it removes old ones.

The degree of detail to which this analysis should be carried depends upon the scope of organization being considered. When an executive is studying broad, overall organization structure, a listing of major activities is usually adequate. However, when the organization of individual jobs is the aim, listing of minute details may be useful. In either case a lot more detail is analyzed in the design process than appears in the final conclusions because (1) the organizer must be sure to have a complete and realistic grasp of the work involved, and (2) novel and strategic combinations of duties are apt to be missed if the organizer thinks only in terms of large customary groups of work. Also, greater detail should be considered in those areas that are new, that are especially crucial to success, or that have been sources of trouble.

With the activities in mind, our next step is to decide how they can best be grouped together into manageable divisions, departments, sections, or other units. In management circles, this grouping is called *departmentation* even though the final units are not necessarily named departments.

STAGE I–ONE DOMINANT INDIVIDUAL

The simplest form of organization is one key individual with a group of helpers. The central figure is aware of the details of what is happening and personally gives instructions to the helpers as to what they should do. Of course, the helpers learn the routines of repetitive activities and can proceed with minimum guidance. And they may become specialized in their normal assignments—for example, accounting, dealing with customers, or making repairs. But changes from customary patterns and initiative in moving in new directions rest with the boss.

DISTINGUISHING CHARACTERISTICS OF STAGE I ORGANIZATION

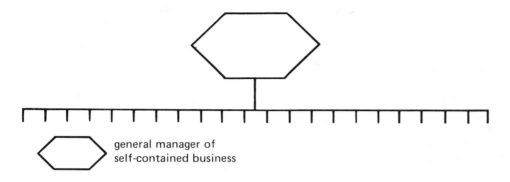

general manager of
self-contained business

Many small businesses—dress shops, drugstores, filling stations, etc.—are operated in this fashion, often with remarkable success. The key individual normally has high energy and skill, doing part of the work himself as necessary. Even though the business may be legally a corporation, action pivots around the moving spirit. One such self-made businessman, for instance, excused himself from a budget discussion at a directors' meeting to help repair a broken air-compressor that had brought the shop to a standstill.

Organizations dominated by one individual can change strategy quickly *if* the change is within the capacity and the interests of the central person. A lawyer can easily decide to enter the real estate business, or the TV repair shop can add home alarm systems to its line. A few more helpers with technical knowledge will suffice. The key uncertainty is the central person. Thus, an expansion of a Canadian motel, described briefly in Chapter 13, depended on whether Alain Ribout was prepared to supervise the building and running of a nearby unit. Too often the necessary adjustment in managerial organization is overlooked; an energetic entrepreneur pushes ahead on an attractive expansion without analyzing the nature and the volume of new activities and then discovers the difference in Stage I and Stage II organizations.

STAGE II–FUNCTIONAL DEPARTMENTS

Dividing the managerial load

Functional departments become necessary when the entrepreneur alone can no longer keep track of all of the operating activities. As the business expands, there are just too many people to be seen, quotations to check, letters to answer, inventory to watch—even for the most energetic manager. Especially when the business involves nonroutine activities and frequent emergencies, the manager must be free of normal day-to-day operations. Otherwise mistakes are made, opportunities are passed by, and the work of helpers is slowed down waiting to see the boss.

DISTINGUISHING CHARACTERISTICS OF STAGE II ORGANIZATION

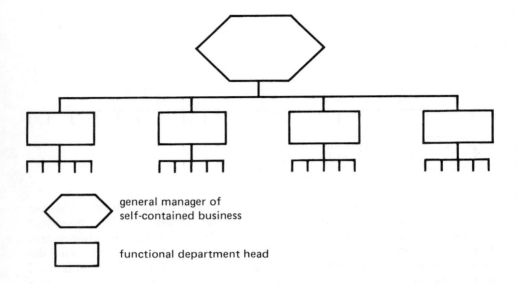

general manager of
self-contained business

functional department head

The normal remedy is to appoint functional managers—one for selling, another for accounting, a third for production, and so on. These people (or *their* helpers) answer most of the questions that bubble up from activities; they check on progress and expedite lagging action. Being specialists, they are likely to be more expert in their particular field than the general manager. And because they focus on a narrower array of work they become more sensitive to its particular needs and opportunities.

With such help, the behavior of the general manager should differ sharply from that of the dominant individual in a Stage I organization. The general manager has to be willing to delegate. This means no longer knowing just what is happening day-by-day and accepting decisions that are not quite the way the general manager would have made them. A cardinal purpose of creating functional departments is to give the general manager time to focus on interdepartmental coordination and on policy and strategy issues. Many executives whose success as Stage I managers makes possible a Stage II organization find this required change in their personal behavior very difficult and sometimes impossible.

An organization made up of functional departments is well suited for single-product line companies. For example, firms concentrating on automobile insurance typically have departments for sales-underwriting, claims, finance, investment-treasurer, and legal. Similarly, a hi-fi equipment manufacturer will probably have R&D, production, marketing, and finance as basic departments. With only a single line, coordination between departments can be handled through procedures, scheduled meetings, and mediation by the general manager. Each department continues to render the same kind of service, so neglect of parts of the business is unlikely. And a general manager concentrates on maintaining effective teamwork.

A strategy of a "full line" of services to a single set of customers also matches a functional setup reasonably well. In "one-stop banking," for instance, a customer contact (branch office) department will be aided by headquarters departments dealing with checking accounts, small loans, commercial loans, safe deposit, trust, and other services. Here the relationships overlap more and competition may arise for the concentrated attention of the customer contact personnel, but customer service provides the mediating objective.

Defining the scope of a "function"

The use of functional departments creates some problems of its own: (a) What constitutes a function—how shall the boundaries be set? (b) How should activities within a function be organized? Until we have at least a way to approach these questions, the concept of a Stage II organization is difficult to apply to enterprises ranging from aviation and banking to yacht building and zoo-keeping.

Functions singled out for separate status as a department often reflect the particular thrust of a strategy. A department store that places great reliance on advertising, for instance, treats advertising as a major function—and not as a subordinate part of marketing. Companies that rely on leadership in product design will treat R&D as a major department. Perhaps purchasing will be separated from other operations to give it strong emphasis.

In addition to such strategic functions, every firm has a variety of activities that do not neatly fit into a limited number of major departments. Two general guides are helpful in this respect:

1. Place in the same department those activities that have the same immediate objectives. For example, activities as diverse as running a cafeteria, performing medical service, and administering a pension plan may be placed in the personnel department because all of these contribute to the objective of building an efficient work force. In the same manner, the management of salespeople and of advertising may be placed under the sales manager, because the objectives of both these activities is the same—to procure sales orders.

2. Place in the same department activities that require a similar type of ability and experience for their efficient management. For example, in pharmaceutical companies quality control is often placed in the research department. Control of the quality of pharmaceuticals requires someone who is objective, analytical, and expert in laboratory techniques. These similarities with research seem to warrant combined supervision even though the mission of the two activities differs significantly. Budgeting and finance might be placed in the same department for similar reasons.

Advantages of functional departments depend partly upon the integrating theme for the particular unit. Expertness with a similar type of problem, adequate attention to an activity that otherwise might be given hurried treatment, consistent action in such matters as price concessions, and easy coordination of activities having a common purpose are among the benefits often secured.

Except in unusual circumstances, the number of major functional departments (not counting staff and services) in a Stage II organization should not exceed about six.

Organizational options within departments

Although a small functional department can be organized on the one-dominant-individual basis, its own size and the need for systematic relations with other departments soon call for orderly grouping of internal activities. One form is, of course, further assignment of work by subfunctions. There are other options. Among the common bases for further subdivision are:

Products. For many years in the typical department store the buyer was king. There would be separate buyers for hosiery, jewelry, gloves, shoes, millinery, and dozens of other products. Normally, each buyer was responsible for the purchase of the merchandise, its pricing and display, and its sale. Of course, there were storewide departments for such activities as building operations, delivery, finance, accounting, advertising, and personnel. Nevertheless, the very crucial trading function remained the domain of the respective product buyers. This provided close coordination of buying and selling each product, and it aided control by localizing responsibility.

With the recent substantial expansion of suburban branches, the role of the department store buyer has been changing. Because of the distance factor, buyers cannot directly supervise the people selling their products in the several outlets and they have difficulty maintaining their former close observation of display and proper maintenance of stocks. Buyers are becoming primarily providers of merchandise and sales promotion planners. Nevertheless, divisions by product line remain very important.

Product subunits are also often introduced in engineering and production. And as we shall see, building around products is a key feature of Stage III organizations.

Processes. Manufacturers—and government offices—often perform several distinct processes that may serve as the basis for organizational units. For example, in steel production typically we find separate shops for coke ovens, blast furnaces, open-hearth furnaces, hot-rolling mills, cold-rolling mills, and the like. Each process is performed in a separate location and involves a distinct technology.

Libraries, to cite another field, normally divide their work into units dealing with book acquisitions, cataloging, circulation, and reference. There may also be separation by type of "customer" such as children, schools, and adults.

The grouping of activities by process tends to promote efficiency through specialization. All the key people in each department become expert in dealing with their particular phase of the business. On the other hand, process classification increases problems of coordination; scheduling the movement of work from department to department on each order becomes somewhat complex. Also, since no department has full responsibility for the order, a department may not be as diligent in meeting time requirements and other specifications as a group of people who think in terms of the total finished product and their customers.

The organization issue just posed—product versus process grouping—has additional ramifications. It ties in with the desirability of subcontracting, extent of mechanization, and of course the characteristics of executives needed.

The conflict between the desire to increase skill in performance through specialization and mechanization, and the need for coordination to secure balanced efforts recurs time and again in organization studies. Insurance companies, hospitals, and even consulting firms face the same issue.

Territories. Companies with salesmen who travel over a large area almost always use territorial organization. Large companies will have several regions, each subdivided into districts, with a further breakdown of territories for individual sales representatives. Airlines, finance companies with local offices, and motel chains all by their very nature have widely dispersed activities and consequently use territorial organization to some degree.

The primary issues with territorial organization are three:

1. What related activity should be physically dispersed along with those which by their nature are local? For example, should a company with a national salesforce also have local warehousing, local assembling, local advertising, local credit and accounting, and local personnel? And how far should the dispersion occur—to the regional level or to the district level? Typically, whenever such related activities are dispersed, they are all combined into a territorial organization unit.
2. How much authority to make decisions should be decentralized to these various territorial units? In other words, how much of the planning and control work should go along with the actual performance?
3. What will be the relations between the home office service and staff units and these various territorial divisions?

We will discuss these last two issues in the next chapter, but it is important to recognize that they must be satisfactorily resolved if territorial units are established.

The major advantage of territorial organization is that it provides supervision near the point of performance. Local conditions vary and emergencies do arise. Persons located a long distance away will have difficulty grasping the true nature of the situation, and valuable time is often lost before an adjustment can be made. Consequently, when adjustment to local conditions and quick decisions are important, territorial organization is desirable. On the other hand, if a lot of local units are established, some of the benefits of large-scale operation may be lost. The local unit will probably be comparatively small, and consequently the degree of specialization and mechanization will be correspondingly limited.

Customers. A company that sells to customers of distinctly different types may establish a separate unit of organization for selling and servicing each. A manufacturer of men's shoes, for instance, sold to both independent retail stores and chain stores. The chain-store buyers are very sophisticated and may prepare their own specifications; consequently, any salespeople calling on them must have an intimate knowledge of shoe construction and of the capacity of their company's plant. In contrast, sales representatives who call on retailers must be able to think in terms of retailing problems and be able to show how their products will fit into the customer's business. Few sales representatives can work effectively with both large chain-store and independent retail customers; consequently, the shoe manufacturer has a separate division in its sales organization for each group.

Commercial banks, to cite another example, often have different vice-presidents for types of customers—railroads, manufacturing concerns, stockbrokers, consumer loans, and the like. These people recognize the needs of their particular group of customers and they also are in a good position to appraise the credit worthiness.

Ordinarily, customer groups include only selling and direct service activities. Anyone who has been shunted around to five or six offices trying to get an adjustment on a bill or a promise on a delivery will appreciate the satisfaction of dealing with a single individual who understands the problem and knows how to get action within the company. On the other hand, this form of organization may be expensive, and a customer-oriented employee may commit the company to actions that other departments find hard to carry out.

Summarization. This short review of product, process, territory, and customer departmentation indicates the many variations that are possible in organizing within a major department. A full analysis of the various options would go beyond our main focus on central management. However, even this brief discussion does indicate the necessity of clearly relating central organization to basic operations "where the real work is done." Also a by-product of this review is to mention alternatives to functional departments. In special circumstances we may decide that, say, an international department or a government contract department fits a company strategy better than a functional department.

This necessary elaboration of a Stage II organization does not change its basic features. We start with a sharply focused product/market mission, and then we establish specialized departments each of which has a different though important contribution to make to that mission. The work of these departments is interdependent, so the entire operation has to be managed as an integrated whole. The role of the general manager of such an organization is to find department managers who will be responsible for day-to-day operations while the general manager concentrates on integration and longer-run strategy and policy issues.[1]

STAGE III–SELF-CONTAINED PRODUCT OR REGIONAL DIVISIONS

Successful enterprises outgrow a Stage II organization. They become too large or too diversified. As a Stage II company grows from less than a hundred to over a thousand employees, communications become more formal, standard procedures prevent quick adjustments, the convenience of each department receives more consideration than company goals, and people feel insignificant in terms of total results. Careful management can diminish these tendencies, but sooner or later sheer size saps vigor and effectiveness.

In addition, successful companies take advantage of opportunities to diversify product lines, to develop new sources of materials, and to provide new services in response to changing social needs. This adds complexity. But large functional departments often give secondary attention to such opportunities; they are busy doing their established tasks well. So the new developments fail to receive the attention and the coordinated effort they deserve.

Unless a company makes a deliberate strategic decision to stay relatively small and clearly focused on a particular mission—a strategic option few U.S. companies elect—a shift in organization becomes necessary.

Concept of semi-independent divisions

The basic remedy for oversize is to split up into several Stage I or Stage II divisions. A series of small businesses are created within the larger company.

Establishing manageable "businesses." Ordinarily these divisions are built around product lines. That part of marketing dealing with a particular product is transferred from the marketing department to the product division. And likewise with production, engineering, and perhaps other functions. Ideally each division has within it all the key activities necessary to run independently—it is *self-sufficient.* Moreover, the management of the newly created division is given a high degree of authority, making the division *semiautonomous.* The general manager of such a division then has virtually the same resources and freedom of action as the president of an independent company and is expected to take whatever steps are necessary to make the "little business" successful.

Even when it is practical to place within a division all of its own marketing and production activities, some central services are retained. Obtaining capital,

---

[1] The department managers should participate in strategy and policy formulation, as will be pointed out in Chapter 18. Their primary duty, however, and the viewpoint they are expected to bring to central management deliberations, is that of running a specialized department very well.

DISTINGUISHING CHARACTERISTICS OF STAGE III ORGANIZATION

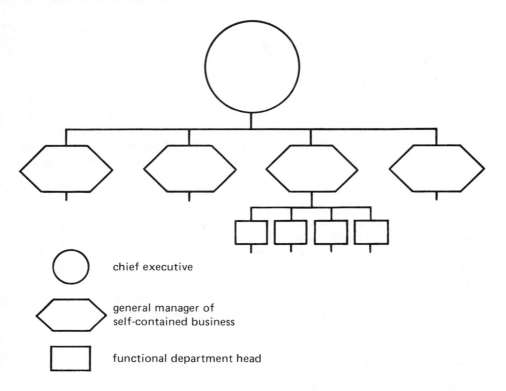

○ chief executive

⬡ general manager of
self-contained business

▭ functional department head

exploratory research, and staff assistance on labor relations, law, and market research, for example, usually can be performed more economically in one place for all divisions of the company. Such central assistance gives operating divisions an advantage over fully independent companies.

Typically, self-contained divisions are built around product lines. A company may have anywhere from two to (for General Electric Company) a hundred such product divisions. The same idea, however, has been applied by department store chains on a territorial basis. And large metal fabricators place their mining and transportation activities ("process" units) in self-contained divisions.

Advantages. Breaking a large firm into several self-sufficient, semiautonomous divisions has several managerial advantages:

1. Morale is improved because people see the results of their own efforts and feel the importance of their action.
2. Communication is faster, often face-to-face, and the significance of information is easier to recognize.
3. Adequate attention can be given to individual customers, product adjustments, and other matters that may be brushed over in a larger organization.

4. Coordination of production with sales, costs with income, personnel training with needs, and other interfunctional adjustments are improved.
5. Control can be exercised more promptly and with fuller appreciation of the total circumstances.

With more manageable and sharply focused divisions, changes in strategy can be put into effect more rapidly.

Difficulties with optimum size

In applying the concept of small, self-contained divisions we soon discover that functional departments often cannot be neatly divided. Technology and other forces dictate an *optimum size* for various activities. For instance, an oil refinery to serve Spokane, Washington, alone would be much too small to be efficient. On the other hand, the task of increasing employment of minorities can readily be handled by separate divisions.

The optimum size issue is complicated because optimum volume is not the same for each function. A men's clothing firm, for instance, found that plants with two to three hundred employees could achieve virtually all economies of scale in production and that larger plants generated more personal problems. However, the output of one such plant would be far too small for marketing purposes. National advertising and promotion were the key to the firm's marketing success, and the sales volume needed to support national distribution was six times the output of a single plant.

The optimum size of an elementary school, to cite a very different industry, would be small if we think of travel time for pupils, and quite large if we focus on the cost of heating and maintaining the buildings. Professionals in the key function—education—want classes of an optimum size, say thirty plus or minus five. Assuming the main criterion is quality of education, then the optimum size will be based on the number of pupils—thirty times the number of grades. (A change in educational "technology" to the ungraded system would probably lead to a different answer.)

These differences in optimum size affect the number of self-contained divisions we establish. In a steel company, for instance, marketing considerations call for twenty or thirty separate divisions, each focused on a product/market target. Production technology, however, dictates that almost all the end-products come out of a few large plants. These plants can't be split up by product lines. So twenty or thirty self-sufficient product divisions are impractical. The best we can do is break out a few products, such as oil-field pipe or barbed wire, that have separate plants for their final stages of manufacture. In fact, a review of self-contained divisions in a wide variety of industries indicates that most of them have a volume of work that is below the optimum size for one or two functions and above the optimum size for other functions. The aim, of course, is to build divisions that are optimum in size for critically important functions, even though this results in some diseconomies in other areas.

Compromise arrangements

Companies often try to get most of the benefits of self-contained divisions and also keep functional operations at optimum levels. For instance, one paper company leaves production in a single functional department, but it breaks product engineering and marketing down into strong product divisions. The division managers are expected to act like "independent businessmen" except that they must contract for their supply of products from the production division.

A comparable arrangement is used by a food processor, except that in this instance it is selling rather than production which is centralized in one department. Each product division does its own product design, engineering, buying, production, merchandising, and pricing, but it utilizes the sales department to contact customers. The rationale here is that a single field organization can cover the country more effectively for all divisions than they could do separately.

Whenever a product division has to rely on an outside department for a key activity, problems of adequate attention, coordination, and control become more difficult. Occasions for bickering jump dramatically. Central management has to judge whether the harm done by restricting the self-sufficiency idea is offset by the benefits of the larger-scale activities in the functional department.

All sorts of compromise arrangements are found in practice. Sometimes the product division has the option to buy services from outside companies instead of using the inside department if it can obtain better service at less cost. This clearly puts pressure on the central department to be responsive to the needs of the divisions. In other cases the centralized department merely notifies the divisions what capacity it has available, and the divisions must live within this limit. Understandings are needed on the planning horizon, transfer prices, emergency changes, quality of service, risky experiments, and the like. Basically such issues should be resolved in terms of what contributes most to company strategy, and this interpretation usually must be made by central management.

The compromises just discussed all presume self-contained product or regional divisions will be the primary organizational form of the company with an exception being made for some one functional department. Two other kinds of modifications, midway between Stage II and Stage III formats, are also used. One leaves the functional departments intact and merely establishes a so-called "product manager"—really a staff person who keeps track of his products in the various departments and attempts to negotiate adjustments that will aid his line. As with any staff (see the next chapter), the strength of a "product manager's" influence can range from merely raising questions to suggestions that carry the weight of commands. The second kind of variation, found in the space industry, construction companies, and consulting firms, is "project management" (sometimes called matrix organization). Here competent individuals are temporarily assigned by the functional departments to a project team. This team, usually with its own manager, runs the project somewhat like a product division might; but when the project is completed, members of the team return to their functional base.

Organizing for strategic benefits

The difficulties of achieving a smoothly running set of self-contained operating divisions, just discussed, naturally raise the question of when a shift from a Stage II to a Stage III organization is worth the effort.

Twenty years ago a group of progressive business executives admitted that they postponed the shift until the burdens of size forced them to take some action.[2] Today the nature and the benefits of a Stage III organization are better understood. Consequently, the pros and cons of setting up self-sufficient, semiautonomous divisions are likely to be explored as soon as a company is committed to multiple products or widely dispersed activities. Each new division should have, or should expect soon to obtain, at least enough volume to support the overhead expenses of a small business. Moreover, there should be considerable continuity in this volume—say, ten years or more—to warrant the extra effort necessary to break with tradition and build a new social structure.

Assuming these minimum conditions are met, then the key question is whether a separate division will gain strength in its *strategic thrusts.* Our discussion of industry outlook in Chapter 3 urged the identification of crucial factors for success in the industry. Then in Chapter 4 on designing strategy, we advocated picking particular moves or thrusts that would give the company distinctive strengths with respect to the crucial success factors. On the basis of this kind of analysis, central management should already know the strategic thrusts for each of its product lines or its market locations. These are the areas where excellence is highly important. If shifting to a division setup will give added impetus in such areas, the move should be made promptly. Contrariwise, if anticipated benefits lie largely in noncritical aspects, then the move can be deferred.

An aviation equipment manufacturer, for example, wanted more Air Force business and concluded that greater flexibility in meeting technical requirements would help toward this goal. Central management set up a separate ''government-business'' division, even though it entailed more overhead and some resistance in functional departments, primarily to gain the desired flexibility in meeting technical requirements. Similarly, a women's shoe company decided to integrate forward into selected retail outlets. This marketing thrust might have been assigned to the existing sales department.

---

[2] The consensus of senior executives from fifteen outstanding corporations was that ''rarely do companies foresee the need for basic organizational change in time to prepare for it.'' W. H. Newman and J. P. Logan, *Management of Expanding Enterprises,* New York: Columbia University Press, 1955, p. 90. This report examines an array of problems in moving from a Stage II to a Stage III organization.

However, management decided on a separate retail division because analysis showed that adjusting store inventory to local tastes was vital; a separate division was expected to be more objective and to act more quickly in this critical area.

A decision *not* to set up a separate carton division was reached by a paper company. Here investigation revealed that this segment of the industry was already mature and that low cost was crucial to success. So the company strategy was to operate only its most efficient plants as near capacity as possible. Although a separate carton division would have provided more intensive marketing effort, it would have contributed little toward cost reduction. Consequently, the proposal to form a self-contained carton division separated from the larger container branch was turned down.

The concept of a series of self-sufficient, semiautonomous divisions is an appealing answer to the problems of size. However, designing divisions that are optimum in size and that strengthen strategic thrusts is not a simple task.

STAGE IV–CONGLOMERATE ORGANIZATION

Conglomerate organization differs from a Stage III organization of self-contained divisions primarily in the absence at headquarters of service and staff units and the limited attempt to secure synergistic benefits among its components. Typically, conglomerates are built from previously independent companies, each with its own traditions and a full complement of central services. Moreover, these companies are not expected to contribute to each other's business. So there is little to be gained from "coordination" and from overall service units. A conglomerate truly is a collection of disassociated businesses.[3]

Primary attention to provision of capital

The main benefits of conglomerates are financial. Operating companies are brought together for one or more of the financial gains listed in our discussion of mergers on page 318 and amplified on pages 327-329. "Corporate planning" in the majority of conglomerates consists entirely of looking for attractive acquisitions and does not deal with businesses already in the fold. The presumption is that each operating unit will do its own strategic planning—except for major questions on sources and uses of capital.

Since the interactions between the central office and the operating companies in a conglomerate are largely limited to finance, the basic organization structure can be simple. The chief executive in each operating company reports to the president or a group vice-president in the central office.

---

[3] A conglomerate differs sharply from a mutual fund. The conglomerate owns all of or a controlling interest in its companies and accepts final responsibility for their overall management. A mutual fund owns only a small fraction of the stock, takes no responsibility for management, and simply sells its stock if it is dissatisfied with company results.

DISTINGUISHING CHARACTERISTICS OF STAGE IV ORGANIZATION

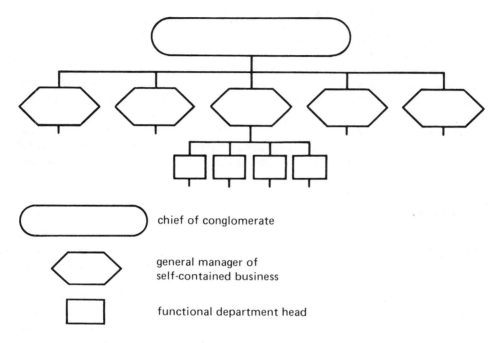

chief of conglomerate

general manager of self-contained business

functional department head

In addition, there will be the usual transfer of funds and upward flow of financial reports. That is all that's needed.

Of course, each operating company has its own organization; this may be a Stage I, II, or III organization or any variation that best suits the needs of the particular company. Incidentally, the legal status of the operating company is not significant from the viewpoint of managerial organization. Each operating unit will be treated as a separate company even though its corporate identity may be washed out for financial reasons.

Role as "outside" member of board of directors

Although the organization may be simple, the role that the supervising executive from the central office plays in the management of an operating company can be extremely valuable. This executive should be an ideal "outside director."

Every company needs objective senior counsel to its chief executives, as explained in Chapter 18. Presumably this independent counseling is the main job of an outside member of the board of directors. Unfortunately, all corporations face severe difficulties in attracting to their boards of directors individuals who are (a) wise, courageous, and well informed, and also (b) sufficiently concerned to devote energy and initiative to the affairs of that particular company. Obtaining good outside directors is a chronic and serious problem.

A conglomerate, however, can overcome this difficulty. It has sufficient stake in the success of its operating companies to locate and employ individuals who are fully qualified to be good "outside directors." Such a person should devote full time to serving as a member or head of the board of, perhaps, half a dozen operating companies. By assuring that major decisions are wisely made, insisting that unpleasant action be taken promptly, and counseling on future possibilities (as explained in Chapter 18), a strong director can stimulate operating executives.

By aiding with finance and by providing able outside directors, then, conglomerates help make their operating companies strong. Most of the central management functions, however, should be left to fully staffed operating companies.

SUMMARY

Company strategy and policy set directions, limits, and goals. But these broad plans must be matched by a corresponding managerial organization to carry out the implied array of activities. In this first chapter of Part 3 we have focused on basic structure. Two themes keep reappearing: (1) structure depends upon size and complexity, and (2) structure should reinforce vital strategic thrusts.

As a company succeeds and grows, it must change its organization. Four quite distinct stages are clear. Stage I represents the small, budding enterprise in which *one dominant individual* does both long-range planning and day-to-day managing. Sooner or later the business exceeds the capacity of even the most energetic single manager, and a shift must be made to Stage II in which day-to-day operations are delegated to *functional departments*. Then as the firm expands and diversifies, the functional departments become too large and bureaucratic, so a further shift is necessary to a Stage III organization composed of *self-contained product or regional divisions*. Finally, though not necessarily, a collection of independent companies may be combined into a Stage IV *conglomerate organization*.

Many variations and compromises are essential to fit the organization to the specific technology, optimum size, resources, and other features of a specific firm. A cardinal aim in making such variations should be to strengthen the company in those areas it has chosen to build strategic distinction. In this way the organization gives potency to the unique services the company wants to provide.

Every organization consists of more than the primary operating divisions—the topic of this chapter. Questions of decentralization, the placing of staff and services, communications systems, the organization for central management itself, and providing people to fill the proposed positions—all call for careful attention. These issues are discussed in the following three chapters.

QUESTIONS FOR CLASS DISCUSSION

1. Jean Stevens is the owner-manager of a very successful restaurant. Located on a main highway in an attractive setting about 20 miles outside of Atlanta, it is a favorite place to have "a really good dinner" for both people in the area and from the city. There are tables for 200 people in addition to the bar and a large terrace. The restaurant reflects Ms. Stevens' personality and ability, and it has grown as a Stage I organization. (a) Now Ms. Stevens wants less burden of day-to-day operations. Do you recommend a Stage II organization? If so, define the functional departments. (b) What problems would arise if Ms. Stevens, or new owners, tried to expand to several other locations? Would you recommend a Stage II or a Stage III organization for the expanded operations?

2. The Mercedes Bicycle Company is doing a flourishing business with its "Syncro-Shift" and "Mountain King" models, and it now has some international as well as national sales. Contributing to its success is the engineering design and quality control in its Indianapolis plant. Assume that your uncle is president of the company and seeks your advice, as a student of management, on organization. To date, organization has been based on expediency, but your uncle feels "the time has come to build our organization around some consistent principle." Assuming a Stage II organization, what basis would you recommend be used for organizing within the production department? Within the marketing department?

3. (a) A university could be organized so that each course ran as a separate, self-contained unit (the students would sign up, use equipment, and pay for each course just like they do for private airplane flying lessons). Or each department might be so organized; or each division. What are the key factors that determine what separations, if any, of this type should be made? (b) Should any of the following be seen as self-sufficient divisions: dormitories; bookstore; intercollegiate athletics; eating halls? Should they be expected to at least break even financially?

4. A successful TV set manufacturer with a Stage II organization has just completed arrangements to take over a small electronics plant in England as a first move in international expansion. The English plant will become a production base for the British market. A major anticipated gain will be use of U.S. engineering and production know-how in the newly acquired plant. Should the manager of the British plant report to the production vice-president in the home office? If so, what happens to marketing and finance of the British operation?

5. Expansion into the total packaging field has created organizational problems for a successful producer of tin cans. For years the company had plants located throughout the country. Strong functional departments in sales, production, and finance maintained close watch on sales to specific customers, costs, and full utilization of investment in equipment. The executives knew the can business thoroughly and "ran a tight ship." The recent expansion includes acquisitions of companies producing plastic, paper, and glass containers for food and many

other consumer products. The new strategy is to provide a complete packaging service adapted to improved technology and changing consumer requirements. Each segment of the packaging industry involves mass production, and price competition is keen. What kind of organization structure do you recommend to match the new strategy? Make clear which units are to be primary operating departments and what relationships service divisions (if any) are to have with the operating departments.

6. (a) "The conglomerate concept has a great future in its application to small businesses. These firms need the counsel that a conglomerate executive can provide as a member of the local board of directors, and they need the centralized access to capital markets." (b) "Conglomerates won't work for small businesses for two reasons. The small firm cannot support its own professional management. And, a small firm needs the strong incentive that comes with ownership." Do you support either statement? Explain how you believe the conglomerate concept can best be adapted to small business, if at all.

7. (a) Many executives regard acquisition of their company by a conglomerate with fear. The idea of being "taken over" comes as a great psychological blow. How do you account for this feeling? (b) Do executives have more, or less, opportunity if the company they work for becomes part of a conglomerate? (c) Is there any reason to presume that the conglomerate executives will push for actions contrary to healthy growth and good service of the operating unit?

8. Discuss the alleged danger that continued growth of conglomerates will result in a concentration of wealth and power that is socially undesirable. What social values are threatened? What structural designs are created? Do you agree that conglomerates should be prevented from owning companies that buy and sell to each other (the aim of such a law would be to assure that all competitors have equal opportunity to seek business with divisions of the conglomerates)?

9. (a) In analyzing the administrative problems of a business, what advantage is there in considering strategy, policy, organization, and executive personnel in that sequence? (b) Under what conditions might it be desirable to deal with these four topics in some other way?

CASE 16 / University Student Enterprises, Inc.

The most complicated and divisive problem yet to confront University Student Enterprises, Inc. (U.S.E., Inc.) was the proposed merger of ten unincorporated, student-managed agencies into the structure of U.S.E., Inc. The Assistant Vice-President for Financial Aid of the University actively supported the move and stood ready to subsidize the cost of the physical transfer of the agencies from his offices to those of U.S.E., Inc. The Chairman of the Board of University Student Enterprises, Inc.—who was also Assistant Treasurer of the University—opposed the move and, so it was rumored, would try to use his influence with the alumni and with other members of the administration of the University to work against the proposed merger.

In the midst of the argument was Al Soto, a senior at the University and the Student Treasurer responsible for the finances of all student-managed agencies. The Assistant Vice-President for Financial Aid had asked Al Soto to find a way to work out the problem.

University Student Enterprises had originally been established as an independent corporation to operate summer charter flights to Europe without any liability to the University. Its character allowed other agencies to be included in its organization. Subsequently, the Europe-by-Car Agency, the Tutoring Agency, the Typing Agency, and the Magazine Agency had been added. The corporation had then attempted to operate as a nonprofit membership corporation, but a ruling of the Internal Revenue Service prevented this. The IRS maintained that charter flights, the principal activity, offered no direct educational benefits.

The corporation was nominally controlled by an eleven-man board of directors consisting of three students (the Treasurer, the Charter Flight General Manager, and a third member-at-large) plus one faculty member, two alumni, and five University administrators. This group met twice each year. Interim decisions and control over operations were exercised by a five-man executive committee (the Chairman of the Board, the Treasurer, the General Manager, the Board Secretary [a member of the University Controller's office], and the Assistant Vice-President for Financial Aid.)

Other student-managed agencies in the University were generally supervised by a member of the Financial Aid office.

The responsibility and reporting relationships of the present arrangement can be visualized as shown in the organization chart on page 376.

Impetus for the unification of all the agencies as part of U.S.E., Inc. (which would always have to be a separate entity because of the charter flights) came first from the Financial Aid office. The Vice-President felt that the office's facilities were being strained by the excessive amount of office and secretarial work involved with the agencies and that the consequent indirect subsidy to the agencies by the Financial Aid office was getting too large. An absolute maximum of one half of Jerry Osterman's time for assistance and advice to the ten agencies had had to be imposed. The Assistant Vice-President for Financial Aid proposed a temporary subsidy of $6,000 to the agencies from his budget as an incentive toward their removal from his office.

Moving outside the University would also eliminate the indirect subsidy of financial record keeping by the Controller's office. The various student managers believed that this office was habitually slow and inaccurate in its operations.

The Charter Flight Manager, a student who was also a part-time general manager for all of U.S.E., Inc., saw some potential advantages in bringing the other agencies into U.S.E. A full-time general manager could be hired to take over the responsibilities now split with the Student Treasurer. Since the Charter Flight Agency had its peak workload in the spring, the seven students and two secretaries of that agency could devote time to other agencies that had earlier peak loads (such as the Souvenir Agency at Christmas and the Refreshment Agency at the six home football games and the twelve home basketball games). A computerized payroll system could be engaged privately to replace the University's system.

Profits from the various agencies had always been a source of conflict among the managers since the monetary reward at times had little to do with the effort expended by the manager(s) but much more to do with the type of agency. The Refreshment Agency, for example, generated large profits, but the major amount of work associated with it occurred during six weeks in the autumn. Past practice had been to recruit workers for

U. S. E., INC.

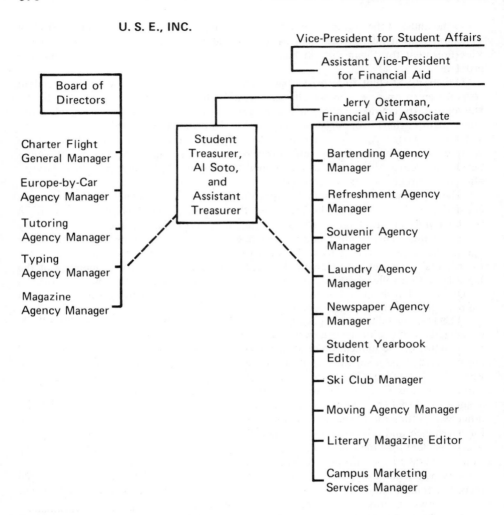

the agencies as freshmen and then promote those who gave competent service to a managerial position. Competent candidates from larger agencies that had only one or two promotional positions open might be appointed to a managerial position in a smaller agency that offered much less opportunity for a reward in the form of profits. In a typical year the range of profits was from $600 to over $12,000.

Following some long meetings and bitter discussions, the Council of Managers came to its first and only general agreement—a proposed way to reward the agency managers and to contribute to the overhead of U.S.E., Inc. The agreement essentially consisted of guidelines as to a fair wage for a manager with an ordinary year's volume of business and for a varying split of profits above the wage with decreasing returns to the manager and increasing returns to U.S.E., Inc. But first a fixed charge toward the general overhead expenses of U.S.E., Inc. (salaries of the General Manager, Treasurer, and secretarial help, the payroll system, rent, and office expenses) was to be assessed each agency before the normal period salary figure was to be paid.

Among the students, only the managers of the Refreshment Agency opposed the proposed wage and expense plan and the merger of all agencies into U.S.E., Inc. They preferred the existing arrangements, which, they said, worked well from the standpoint of providing financial aid to students.

The financial situation before the merger was as follows:

U.S.E., Inc.
Financial Data, Current

Budgeted gross margin from charter and group flights and automobile rentals	$50,000
Budgeted administrative and selling expenses including rent & payroll taxes	51,000
Budgeted net loss	$ 1,000

Cash in bank	$10,000	Retained earnings	$10,000

Note (A): Rules for chartered air flights set by the International Air Transport Association include a prohibition of the retention of any funds not used for ordinary expenses of the charter flights. Surplus funds after expenses are to be refunded to the passengers. Profits on group flights (a small part of the total) may be retained.

Under the proposed merger, the nonincorporated agencies would be assessed $7,150 for their contribution to the overhead of U.S.E., Inc. In addition they would become responsible for the employer's contribution to social security taxes. Projected budgets forecast total net profits available to managers of $35,000 (equivalent to last year's profits). The pro forma administrative budget after the merger showed a net contribution to retained earnings of $3,500. Expenses of this administrative budget included one new item—the salary of a full-time general manager. Ingeniously, so they thought, the Council of Managers had specified that his salary would not be a fixed amount but would be 50% larger than the median salary offered all the University seniors at the time of their graduation during the previous year. (The median was to be calculated by the University's Placement Office.)

Al Soto found, during his investigation, that various managers expected their businesses to expand and efficiencies to develop in the operation of the office if the merger took place. Coordination by the General Manager, leveling-out of workloads over the year, and having a staff available to take telephone messages (which the managers now refused to take for one another during various busy seasons) were cited as sources of savings.

The principal opposition to the merger came from Frank Espino, Chairman of the Board of U.S.E., Inc. He had had a principal role in establishing the student-managed businesses at the University and had been associated with them in various capacities. He said to Al Soto: "You and Jerry Osterman forget that the prime reason for the existence of these agencies is financial aid to students. They should be organized and administered for that purpose. They do in fact provide well over $200,000 in part-time earnings to the students. Since the objective of the agencies is, and should be, financial aid, they should all be consolidated and administered out of the Financial Aid office. That includes the tutoring, typing, and magazine agencies.

"Now the managers—even though they are students—are trying to turn these operations into little businesses and are trying to run them for maximum profits as part of a corporation. This is subverting their main purpose. The reorganization is moving toward the wrong ends.

"Also, the working capital base for the projected corporation after the merger is too small. Should there be serious losses by the Charter Flight Agency or other agencies, the whole corporation will be endangered. I don't think that you can find a suitable general manager. Students are not good managers. They are not supposed to be. They are supposed to be at the University to learn, with financial aid available to help them cover educational expenses. They are not supposed to be here to practice being business managers.

"Finally, the Charter Flight Agency is a business. It has to be, according to the Internal Revenue Service. Therefore, it should be separated, along with Europe-by-Car, from the other agencies and run as a business but not as a way to absorb the expenses of the Financial Aid office. With money left over after the expenses of charters, we can make refunds to the passengers rather than help subsidize ambitious little businessmen. Refunds will build goodwill and add to our sales."

Al Soto, undecided, saw the possibility of recommending to the Assistant Vice-President for Financial Aid that (1) the relationships among the various agencies, U.S.E., Inc., the Student Treasurer, and the Financial Aid office remain as they were, or (2) that all agencies be merged into U.S.E., Inc. or (3) that the Tutoring, Typing, and Magazine agencies be brought into the Financial Aid office for coordination and control along with the others.

Required: (a) What do you think the objectives of a student-managed agency should be?

(b) How might the agencies be used to further educational objectives?

(c) What should Al Soto recommend about the organizational status of the agencies and the various relationships of responsibility?

BUILDING AN INTEGRATED STRUCTURE

The grouping together of major activities discussed in the preceding chapter does not complete the organization structure. All but the smallest firms need a variety of auxiliary units. And the relationships of these units to the basic operating divisions must be clarified. To achieve a total, integrated organization design, attention must be given to:

1. Location of service units.
2. Decentralization within functional departments.
3. Roles assigned to staff.
4. Use of committees.
5. Management information systems.

These aspects of organization are important in welding the several parts into a coordinated, overall structure.

SERVICE UNITS

Most operating activities belong in the departments and divisions described in the previous chapter. Nevertheless, some auxiliary operations can be performed better in separate units.

Nature of service units

The distinction between operating departments and service units has been very helpful in one of the large rubber companies. After careful study, this company decided to establish separate organizational groups dealing with the following activities:

1. Tires
2. Footwear
3. Mechanical
4. Chemicals
5. Crude rubber
6. International
7. Advertising
8. Industrial relations
9. Public relations
10. Engineering
11. Research and development
12. Purchasing
13. Traffic
14. Legal

This is an imposing list, and if all groups were treated alike, the president would have a difficult task in securing coordination. To overcome this difficulty, the company has identified the first six units as "operating divisions." These are the units in which the basic consumer services are created. Each is large enough to have its own production and selling units, and each is responsible for showing tangible operating results. Thus, the basic structure is a Stage III organization.

All the other groups in the foregoing list are called "service units." Each of these units has relatively few employees compared with the operating divisions. There is a clear understanding throughout the company that the purpose of these auxiliary units is to help the operating divisions do their jobs better. Only in this way can the existence of the service units be justified. In this particular company, finance and accounts are treated as a third category and report directly to the board of directors; most other companies with large product divisions, however, consider these functions as services.

While this example emphasizes units serving the entire company, the same general idea is often found in the organization within a large department. Production departments, for instance, often have their own production scheduling, toolroom, stockroom, quality control, and other auxiliary units that serve the production shop. Similarly, large sales offices have units dealing with travel, customers' correspondence, display material, and the like.

Service units simply perform certain work for the benefit of the operating departments. This is usually work that the department itself would have to perform if it had not been assigned to the specialized service unit. For example, a filing section may relieve the sales department of the bother of keeping all records pertaining to each of its many customers; a computer center may do mathematical work for engineering and other departments; and a warehouse may relieve the sales supervisor of all problems connected with the physical handling of goods.

In situations such as these, the relationships between the service units and the operating departments are relatively simple. There should be a clear understanding of (1) just what services are to be performed, including questions of speed and quality of work, and (2) how the service unit is to be notified as to what is needed. Of course, supervision will be necessary to make sure the work flows as planned, but the organization is simple and clear cut.

Benefits and drawbacks of separate service units

The facilitating, supporting role of service units should never be overlooked. There is a tendency, particularly on the part of people in the service units, to recommend the transfer of more and more duties and control to the service unit. Up to a point, this may be quite desirable. Members of the service unit may have *special skills and knowledge* about such matters as traffic, real estate, or engineering. Moreover, they will not be so involved with operating details and will be able to give *adequate attention* to these functions. However, the activities are not ends in themselves. Any increase in the size of a division must continually meet the test: "Is this work adding to the overall effectiveness of the company, and can it be done better by separating it from operating activities?"

The chief reasons, then, for setting up service units are to get the benefits of specialization and adequate attention. The drawbacks of service units should not be forgotten, however. Most obvious is additional overhead expense. Salaries of specialists in the service units must be paid, and usually offices and equipment must be set aside for their use. Unless the service unit can create significant economies in operations, these overhead expenses may absorb all the benefits from a separate unit.

Less tangible but often more important is the added complexity that service units create. More units are involved in day-to-day operations, more relationships must work smoothly, and the task of coordination may be complicated. Sometimes members of a service unit become so interested in their particular activities that they lose sight of overall company goals. Consequently, we should guard against the assumption that separate service units are always desirable.

Location of service units

If agreement exists that a service activity should be separated from operation, further questions arise as to how many such units are needed and when to place them in the total structure. The chief considerations are economies of single unit versus coordination of the service with basic operations.

A single service unit is often able to secure the maximum economy, particularly in a medium-size or small firm, through concentrated attention, standardization of routine, specialized technical knowledge, and distinctive skill of the central unit. Moreover, the volume of work may warrant only the employment of a single set of experts in, say, insurance or traffic, or a single installation of expensive equipment such as a computer.

Single units, however, increase coordination difficulties. The farther removed—physically and organizationally—the service unit is from the operations it serves, the greater are the problems of coordination. Communication is more difficult and the service unit is less responsive to the needs of local people. Since the aim of the unit is to facilitate operations, ease of coordination weighs heavily.

The main alternative locations for service units are shown in the chart on the following page.

DECENTRALIZATION

Grouping activities into operating companies, divisions, departments, and service units is the most easily recognized aspect of organization. A second

ALTERNATIVE LOCATIONS OF SERVICE UNITS
(Shaded Areas Indicate Service Activity)

(A) Organization with no service unit; each operating section performs its own auxiliary activities.

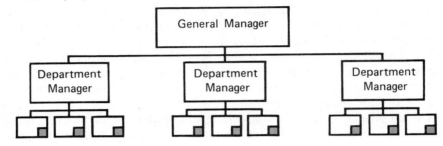

(B) Organization with service units in each operating department.

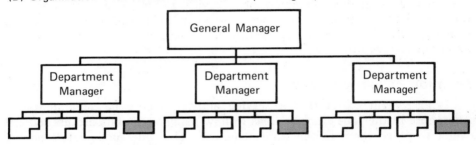

(C) Organization with separate service unit.

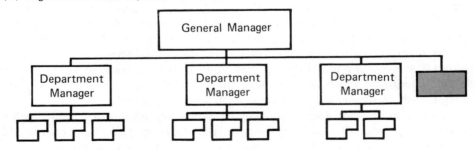

(D) Organization with multiple service units.

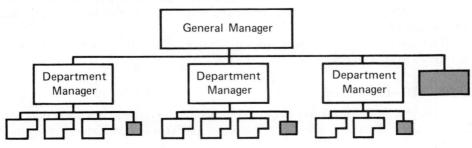

essential aspect, which does not appear on the organization chart, is deciding the level at which decisions should be made. Decentralization is concerned with who in a vertical hierarchy really "calls the shots."

Decentralizing to match stage of growth

The four stages of growth discussed in the preceding chapter clearly imply different patterns of decentralization. In Stage I, primary authority remains centralized in the one dominant individual. Of course, subordinates decide whether a particular request or condition fits the normal way work is done. They may be highly skilled people, and the boss may get their advice about plans in their field of specialty. But the dominant individual chooses new directions of effort, allocates resources, keeps track of progress in diverse areas, approves subordinates' proposals, initiates changes when necessary. Often relationships are informal, and subordinates learn from experience what is desired behavior. Significant exceptions to the normal patterns, however, are first checked with the central figure.

Growth forces decentralization, at least from the top person to the department heads. The manager of a charter airplane service in Alaska faced this change suddenly when oil was discovered on the Arctic coast. Prior to the oil boom the company had six planes; the manager, with the advice of his pilots, decided on what business to accept, which planes to use, when to do maintenance work, how to pay for planes, and the like; flying and landing the planes was left to the pilots. With the intense oil activity, business of the company mushroomed; a traffic manager, a flight supervisor, a maintenance engineer, and a treasurer were quickly added to the headquarters. And who should decide what had to be clarified. Stage II had arrived.

While in a Stage II organization authority and supervision of regular operations shifts from the general manager to the functional department heads, the degree of further decentralization within the various departments depends upon the size and the kinds of work. We will suggest guides for shaping these intradepartment relationships in the next section.

Each division in a Stage III organization has within it all of the delegation issues of the Stage II setup (or of Stage I if the division is that small). In addition, since such divisions must be semiautonomous to obtain the desired benefits of adaptability to special opportunities, substantial decentralization should prevail between the chief executive and the division general managers. Communication is a prime consideration here. This became apparent to the president of an advertising agency that expanded from its consumer product business to financial institutions. The ideas and the problems of the personnel working with the new type of client did not reach the president in their original form. After passing through a couple of layers of supervisors, an idea was likely to be modified, warped, and misinterpreted. Even if the basic idea was retained, a considerable period of time elapsed before a meeting of minds could be achieved. In this case the president finally recognized that he had to delegate a high degree of freedom to a vice-president to run the new type of business according to the latter's best judgment.

Because conglomerates, in Stage IV, typically arise from merging previously independent companies, high decentralization between the chief executive and the general managers of the operating companies is normal. In fact, the typical issue is how central management can participate in company planning more rather than less. The relationship suggested in the previous chapter is that of an active outside board member. Such an arrangement leaves operating decisions and the initiative for broad planning with the general managers, but it ensures compulsory consultation before major decisions become final.

Decentralization within functional departments

Just as the grouping of activities *within* functional departments varies widely (see pages 362-364), so does the degree of decentralization. In departments such as research, projects can proceed on their unpredictable course quite independently. By contrast, high automation of an oil refinery leaves limited degrees of freedom to local operators.

The usual situation calls for a mixture, some topics being decided by the department head and others decentralized well down the line. Consider, for example, a Midwest grocery chain. The functional departments in this case included buying, warehousing and transporting, finance, public relations, locating and constructing new stores, and "store operations." A major issue arose over discretion to be allowed each store manager compared with regional branch offices. After much study the company concluded:

1. Some of the functions obviously have to be placed under the jurisdiction of local store managers. This includes authority over the following activities:
   (a) Arranging displays and maintaining the store so that it will be attractive to customers.
   (b) Selling merchandise to customers. All stores have cashiers, stockclerks, and salesclerks, and the responsibility of selling includes selection, training, and general supervision of these employees.
   (c) Under certain conditions, buying a few products, such as butter and eggs, from their customers. Also, paying incidental expenses.
   (d) Keeping some simplified records of sales, stock, cash receipts, and cash disbursements.
2. The responsibilities of the branch office are considerably greater than those granted to the individual stores. In addition to supervising the operation of stores, the branch office has authority over:
   (a) Selecting the merchandise from that supplied by the central purchasing department that the local stores will carry in stock.
   (b) Determining the price at which each article of merchandise should be sold, and making such adjustments to the price as current competitive conditions and the size of inventory necessitate.
   (c) Directing the advertising for all stores of the branch, and working out plans of sales promotion to be followed by the store manager.
   (d) Compiling and analyzing accounting and statistical information regarding the operations in the branch area, which will aid the branch manager in appraising

the results of past activities and in making decisions regarding future activities.

Each department in a company should be given separate attention. And as external and internal conditions change, the decentralization of particular types of problems may have to be increased or decreased. The optimum setup can usually be determined by carefully weighing the following:

1. What factors must be considered in making the decisions, and at what point in the organization it is easiest to get current information about these factors.
2. The ability of the members of the organization to whom the authority is to be delegated.
3. The need for speedy "on the spot" decisions.
4. The importance of the decision to successful operations.
5. The need for consistent and coordinated action by several divisions of the company.

Delegation of authority and the task of control

The separation of planning and making of decisions on specific problems from the place where performance occurs inevitably creates control difficulties. Thus, a sales manager sitting in the home office who decides to solicit sales in a new territory also needs a control mechanism to insure proper execution of the plan. Or, if authority as well as performance is decentralized (for example, the sales representative is given authority to decide which customers to solicit), a different control mechanism is required. In the first situation, a means of making sure the sales representatives did an effective job of calling on the specified customers is needed; in the second case, a measure of how wisely the sales representative selects customers would be helpful.

ROLES ASSIGNED TO STAFF

The rounding out of an organization design should consider, in addition to service units and decentralization, possible uses of staff.

Numerous criss-crossing of influence and communication is an essential part of every organization design. Procedures establish normal, routine paths for passing information, and many other lateral contacts are incorporated into systems for planning and control. Moreover, advisory or "staff" relationships play an increasingly important role as a company grows and engages in more complex activities.

In practice, the scope of a staff assignment may vary widely—from office flunky to a key member of central management. Consequently, care is needed in figuring out just what staff relationships will aid in the execution of a new strategy in an existing organization.

General staff assistants

In its simple form, the idea of staff is used when a busy executive appoints an assistant to help do the work. At first, an assistant may be primarily a *fact*

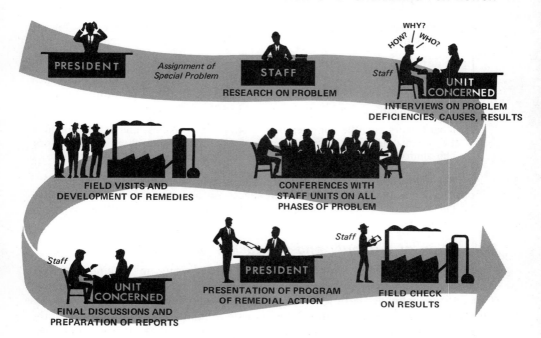

Chart used in company training manual to explain role of staff.

finder, gathering and analyzing information for use by the executive in resolving troublesome problems. As the assistant gains experience, the executive may ask for *recommendations;* in fact, the assistant may prepare written instructions so that the executive receives recommendations and papers needing only the executive's signature to put the proposal into effect. This kind of help enables an executive to deal with problems in a relatively short period of time; in fact, a more careful study of the problem may have been made than if the busy executive tried to do it alone.

Good staff assistants also work with other subordinates of the senior executive and with people outside the department and the company. They must, of course, contact such people in the process of gathering information. In addition, they normally discuss possible solutions to a problem with all people concerned. It sometimes happens that in this examination and exchange of ideas, the problem resolves itself. The staff assistant has served in the capacity of a *catalyst* or a *mediator* and therefore needs only report to the senior executive that the problem is solved.

On other problems that require centralized decision, the staff assistants may play an important role in *explaining* and *interpreting* the plan of action. Their detailed knowledge about the problem and intimate association with the senior executive put them in a good position to explain what is wanted. This interpretative function of a staff assistant again saves the time of a busy executive and improves mutual understanding throughout the enterprise.

In still other situations, the busy executive may ask the staff assistant to keep an eye on some particular aspect of operations, such as expense ratios, governmental regulations, or inventory turnover. Then, if there is need for executive action, the assistant takes the initiative in preparing a recommendation and calling the whole matter to the superior's attention. In this way the staff assistant serves as *eyes* and *ears* for the boss.

Specialized staff

The general staff assistant, such as has just been described, typically carries the title of *Assistant to* the sales manager, the president, or whoever the senior may be. These assistants may be asked to help with any or all of the activities of the executive.

The staff concept also may be applied to assistants who concentrate on some one function, or aspect, of operations. For instance, one staff specialist may concentrate on legal problems, while another works on public relations. Perhaps enough engineering problems arise so the executive needs personal help in this area. The chief executive of a large company may have a specialist on organization planning, another for expense control, and still a third working on executive personnel.

Although such people may be specialists in some one area, the nature of their relationship with the senior executive and with other employees is like that of the general staff assistant. They investigate, recommend, interpret, and follow up on problems in their particular sphere. Being specialists, it is quite likely that they possess technical knowledge that may be superior to that of anyone else in the organization. Through the staff arrangement, this technical knowledge is put at the disposal of the senior executive and all subordinates who come in contact with staff personnel.

The work assigned to a staff specialist may become so heavy that additional personnel are needed to help with the work. Consequently, there may develop a small organization unit on public relations, expense control, or other fields. This group may be called an ''office'' or a ''service division.'' Size and title, however, do not change the nature of the relationship.

Essential factors in good staff relationships

The preceding illustrations of staff have assumed that it always is a full-time job. While this is often true in larger companies, full time is not a necessary feature of the staff concept. The important thing is the relationship, and it is entirely possible for an executive to devote part time to staff work.

The staff relationship implies that the individual is working on behalf of an executive; is doing things the executive would do if time permitted; has no authority to issue orders, but may pass along instructions or interpretations in the name of the senior executive.

Staff relationships may be used in any department of a business enterprise. Most of the examples already cited have been of staff work directly under a chief executive, but the idea has many other applications. The sales promotion director in the sales department, the industrial engineer in the production department, the cost analyst in the accounting department, the economist in the purchasing department, and the safety director in the personnel department are all positions where a considerable amount of staff relationship typically is found.

Use of functional authority

Occasionally a staff person may be given functional authority with respect to certain types of problems and may work in an advisory capacity over a much wider area. Functional authority is permission to issue directions to people not under your line supervision; such directions deal only with specified activities or certain aspects of those activities. Except for their source of issuance, these directions are to be treated as though they came from the senior executive.

The use of functional authority is illustrated in a manufacturing firm that has a general office in Chicago and plants in Kansas City, St. Louis, and Cleveland. Each plant manager "runs" his plant. He has line authority over all employees at the plant, including local accountants. On the other hand, the chief accountant at the central office is responsible for maintaining accounting records for the entire company; he has functional authority over *how* the records are kept at each branch.

The reason for granting functional authority in this instance is fairly clear. The weekly sales report of the company might be misleading if one branch accountant reported orders received as sales, whereas another unit of the company did not report goods as sold until they had actually been shipped. Likewise, one branch accountant might charge depreciation on machinery at his plant at a much lower rate than was used by another branch, with the result that the combined figures for the company as a whole would lack the consistency needed for comparisons and for income tax returns.

A large part of the authority of several important departments is functional. For example, an industrial engineering unit in a factory often selects equipment and prescribes the tools and the methods to be used in production operations. The sales promotion departments of some companies stipulate the methods for presenting new products and the time the products will be introduced.

In all these examples, the executive with functional authority does part of the planning of the activity. The functional executive may prescribe policy, set up methods, or determine the time when activities are to be undertaken, thus saying how the activity is to be performed. The line executive, on the other hand, is responsible for seeing that the instructions issued by those with functional authority, as well as instructions "coming down the line," are carried out.

Functional authority is a useful concept in the proper situations; but like many good things, if used in excess or at the wrong time, it can cause trouble. Among the dangers and the disadvantages of functional authority are:

1. If several different people exercise functional authority over a given operating executive, that individual may be swamped with specialized instructions.
2. The effectiveness of line supervisors may be weakened by heavy use of functional authority. As more and more instructions come from the functional specialists, the status of the line boss may be undermined.
3. Functional authority sometimes leads to autocratic and inflexible administration. Functional specialists may become narrow in their viewpoint and insist that their plans be followed even though they are not well suited to a specific local situation.

For these reasons functional authority should be granted only when it is clearly desirable, and provision should be made to see that it is not used arbitrarily. Functional authority works best when (a) only a minor aspect of the total operating job is covered, (b) technical knowledge of a type not posssessed by the operating executives is needed, and (c) consistency of action in several departments is important.

Composite relations

A single executive often has a variety of relationships, depending upon the subject and who the other person is. A controller, for instance, normally will (a) have line authority over employees in the department who keep company books and prepare reports, (b) have functional authority throughout the company over accounting systems, and (c) act in a purely staff capacity when suggesting how expenses may be cut. Similarly, a personnel director is likely to (a) have line authority over the employment office, cafeteria, and other employee service operations; (b) exercise functional authority with respect to compensation ranges, length of vacations, dismissal procedures, and the like, and (c) provide much constructive advice regarding training, promotion, motivation, etc., in an advisory capacity.

These illustrations show that designating a person as "line" or "staff" is at best vague. For a real grasp of relationships, the authority or the influence of each executive should be defined for each subject dealt with and for various groups contacted. *Customary* roles help clarify such definitions, but we should guard against oversimplification.

USE OF COMMITTEES

Management organization is primarily concerned with the duties and the relationships of single persons. This concentration on the individual as the basic operating unit is necessary for efficiency in action and for purposes of control.

There are situations, however, when several individuals acting as a group can do a particular task better than a single individual. When a management task has been assigned to a group, rather than parceled up among several individuals, a *committee* has been formed.

When to use committees

Use of committees is a widespread practice; in fact some astute students of administration believe that committees are so widely used that they become a serious drawback to efficient operation. Executives may use committees to avoid making difficult decisions; whenever they are in a tough spot, they "appoint a committee." All too often the committee is "a group of men who keep minutes and waste hours." Consequently, we should be careful just how and where committees are fitted into the organization.

Situations in which committees have been found to be helpful include the following:

1. Management committee composed of all department heads and the general manager in a Stage II organization. Weekly meetings of such a committee provide an occasion for *exchange of information* and a clearing-house for interdepartmental troubles.
2. Salary committee composed of a personnel staff representative, department head, and immediate supervisor. To avoid charges of favoritism, such a group must approve any changes in salaries. This adds *safety and acceptability* to the decisions.
3. Community chest campaign committees composed of representatives from each section in the organization. Here the main benefit is to *secure cooperation*.

Committees may be useful in many other situations. The foregoing cases merely illustrate how committees may be helpful in promoting coordination, providing integrated group judgment, and securing cooperation in the execution of plans. Committees can also be effective training devices. Through participation on committees, executives become aware of major company objectives and of effective ways of achieving these objectives. Training, however, is a secondary benefit because rarely is it practical to set up a committee primarily for the purpose of training its junior members.

Situations where committees are ineffective

One drawback of committees is that they are often *slow* in reaching a decision. This was well illustrated by a pricing committee in a metal cabinet manufacturing company. Just after a competitor announced a price increase, one committee member—the marketing manager—left on a sales trip. Before he returned, a second member—the controller—started his vacation. Thus, the committee seriously delayed the response to the competitor's move.

Another company drastically modified its use of committees after the board of directors found it almost impossible to place responsibility for some poor investments. The decision to make these investments had been made by a committee. When the decision turned out to be unwise, each member of the committee said that he had not really been in favor of the action but had simply gone along with the others. The net effect was that *no single person could be held accountable* for the action that was taken.

When decisive action is important, committees are often of little help. The balanced, tempered decision that presumably comes from committee consideration may, in fact, be simply a *compromise* that is neither "fish nor fowl." The management committee of a medical supply company, for instance, could not agree on how much to spend for advertising. After long discussion, they decided on about half of the amount originally requested by the sales manager. Unfortunately, this drastic cut made the advertising campaign ineffective. It would have been better either to have cut the advertising expenditure to a nominal figure or to have undertaken a campaign large enough to impress hospital buyers.

Committees are a relatively *expensive* way of arriving at a decision. If half a dozen people spend from 9:00 A.M. to 10:20 A.M. in a committee meeting, a whole executive-day of time has been used up. Outside preparation time and the effect of interrupting other work add substantially to the time actually spent in meeting.

Benefits and limitations of committees

No standard answer can be given to the question of the nature and the number of committees a particular company should have. The most common advantages and disadvantages are summarized briefly in the diagram below.

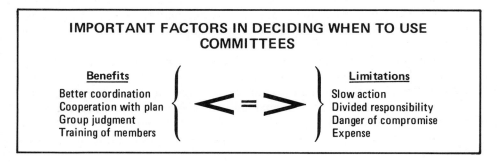

IMPORTANT FACTORS IN DECIDING WHEN TO USE COMMITTEES

Benefits
Better coordination
Cooperation with plan
Group judgment
Training of members

Limitations
Slow action
Divided responsibility
Danger of compromise
Expense

In addition, before establishing a committee, thought should be given to the social setting in which it will work. This will include such things as the availability of competent members, the prevailing attitude toward committees, and the techniques of supervision normally used. It is safe to conclude that the appointment of committees should *not* be the standard answer to difficult problems, nor a standard device to cover over weaknesses in management.

MANAGEMENT INFORMATION SYSTEM

Both staff and committees supplement the elementary structure of divisions, departments, and sections in an organization. In performing their assigned tasks they help tie together the various parts. More important, however, in assuring smooth relationships and integrating action is the management information system.

The management information system consists of designated communication channels for various kinds of information related to company activities. Formal instructions follow the chain of command, but information must flow more widely and quickly. Three essential elements of every information system are the (1) data base, (2) report flow, and (3) communication of intangibles.

Data base

Operating procedures. The most obvious part of any information system is the flow of business papers from section to section. A sales order, for instance, conveys vital information from customer to sales representatives to sales headquarters to warehouse (and if a special order, to engineering and plant) to shipping to credit control to billing. Similar procedures exist for purchasing, employment, capital expenditures, and a host of other normal transactions that are repeated time after time. These procedures are crucial for effective day-to-day operations, and they interlace all segments of the organization.

In passing, note that operating procedures spell out organizational duties. Each step in a procedure is part of a bundle of duties assigned to someone; it stipulates from whom information (usually on a piece of paper) will be received, what action that person will perform, and to whom the processed information should be sent. Thus, clarifying procedures is one way to clarify an organization. Of course not all duties are parts of procedures, but a large segment of total company activity can be viewed in this manner.

Information systems use these operating procedures in two ways: (1) The procedures themselves contain a lot of instructions on who tells whom what. (2) Summaries of work flowing through one or more steps in a procedure can be used as measures of what is happening—for instance, a monthly summary of new orders received, of export shipments, or of the number of employees added to the payroll will be significant pieces of information to several managers.

Accounting records. A second major data source is accounting records. Financial accounting's first obligation is to give outsiders—stockholders, bankers, vendors, and others—a consistent digest of the total company status. But the financial records typically are expanded to gather a wealth of data useful for internal management. In fact, a good internal accounting system classifies financial data according to organizational units.

Accounting data always constitutes a major input to the information system; in small companies it may be almost the only formal input. Because of wide use, much debate occurs about the way expenses and income are allocated and summarized. Part of the art of designing internal accounting systems is to provide information in a form that will be most useful to management.

Other sources. Many companies regularly compile data on industry prices, market position, employee absences, and a variety of other subjects, but there is no common practice on what to include. Also, the company control system—which will be discussed in Chapter 22—frequently calls for systematic observation of selected control points.[1] Here again, selective identification of data that will be truly valuable to a company decision-maker is needed.

Report flows

Fully as important as deciding what information to compile is determining to whom the data will be communicated. This question quickly gets us back to departmentation and decentralization because company design of these matters determines who can make use of particular batches of information on a recurring basis. Also, the effectiveness of staff personnel depends on their receiving current information as the basis of their advice. So we establish a standard pattern specifying what information goes to each executive.

On the other hand, sending reports to people who find the data irrelevant to their work simply clutters up and confuses their assignments.

Keeping such an information flow in tune with changes in organization and strategy is no easy task. When a company adds a product line, decides to make rather than buy materials, or otherwise modifies its strategy, shifts occur in the kinds of data needed. When the organization is reshuffled—as is often desirable to match the new strategy—executives needing particular reports change.

Communicating intangibles

The information system we have been discussing deals with recorded "facts," most of them conveniently expressed in numbers. Significant as such data are, they give only part of the picture. Missing are reasons why, feelings about the facts, guesses on how other people will respond to the same data, new ideas, and a variety of other more subjective types of data. And communication of this kind of information is as essential as communicating hard facts.

Information about intangibles is typically transferred orally. The information system should deal with these personal communications just as it does with written reports, indicating the kinds of data that are to go to designated people. Job descriptions often include paragraphs stating "Keep (service manager) advised of . . ." for this purpose.

Unfortunately, this part of the system is more difficult to operate. Face-to-face meetings with individuals are hard to arrange, especially if they are very busy, and there is no objective way to keep track of what information passed between them. Physical proximity of offices, field trips, review

---

[1] Some executives who stress control consider the information system to be a subsidiary part of the control function. We prefer separate treatment of the information system because it nourishes planning as well as control and because it has a marked effect on the interpersonal relationships within an organization.

sessions, intercom equipment, and closed circuit TV are all devices that aid desired communication flow; but chief reliance must rest upon customary behavior and expected roles. As we round out an information system, then, we move from routine, mechanistic reports to highly personalized communication of subjective impressions. And when we want to modify an information system to fit a new strategy, it is the latter behavioral features that are most difficult to readjust.

Use of computers

Computers, and even more the peripheral communicating equipment, are useful in classifying and speeding up the flow of standardized information. For example, a dress buyer for a national chain of women's ready-to-wear shops can have on her desk in the morning a complete analysis of yesterday's sales throughout the country, and for high-style merchandise such information is very valuable. The elements of the information system—identifying useful basic data, deciding how to classify and summarize them, picking people who should receive the information, and getting it to them—have not changed; but with computers, once the system is designed it can work automatically and rapidly. In fact, many executives find they are now receiving too much rather than not enough of such mechanically processed information; this criticism, however, is really a matter of refining the system.

Computers are of little help with subjective data, and they have no way of knowing what different kinds of data might be useful in dealing with unique situations. So a major task in redesigning information flows to take full advantage of computer capabilities is to preserve a balance. The intangibles have always been the more troublesome part of a total information system, and with a plethora of computer sheets waiting to be studied, the danger increases of skipping lightly over key intangibles.

SUMMARY

Organization design should begin with the major structure of operating activities—discussed in the preceding chapter. Much elaboration is necessary, however, to achieve a balanced, integrated pattern of behavior. And a good design yesterday may be outmoded today.

When a company changes its strategy and policy, then the whole fabric of relationships that ties the work of employees together may need readjustment. For instance, when a petroleum company decides to move into petro-chemicals, it faces new markets, rapidly changing technology, and large investments; decentralization of this segment of the company soon becomes a necessity. At the same time, the benefits of nationwide advertising and marketing of gasoline are creating a centralizing pull in the gasoline end of the business; here enlarging the influence of the central marketing staff, including greater use of functional authority, makes sense.

Five ways to refine an organizational design have been discussed in this chapter.

(1) Distinguishing between operating and service units helps to clarify the structure. It aids in defining relationships and also is useful in allocating manpower and in resolving jurisdictional conflicts. Fundamentally, a service unit exists only to facilitate the work of operating departments, and its performance may be judged in these terms.

(2) Decentralization of decision-making by chief executives and general managers is broadly set by the "stage" format they select. Within departments, however, wide variation in the degree of decentralization is possible. Strategy and policy indicate the relative weight to be assigned to flexibility, efficiency, etc., and these considerations determine the level at which specific types of issues can best be decided.

(3) Although adding complexity, staff assistants can provide relief to an overburdened manager. Also, staff specialists can provide technical advice that otherwise would not be available within the company. For carefully defined subjects, staff may be given functional authority that expedites the handling of matters of secondary importance.

(4) Committees can supplement and strengthen individual effort. In the right situations, they aid in securing coordination, cooperation, and group judgment on important problems. As a management tool, however, they are expensive and slow; responsibility is diffused and hence control is more difficult. For these reasons, care should be exercised in using committees to strengthen the organization structure.

(5) Finally, the management information system builds essential links between the many specialized activities. Each time a change is made in strategy or policy, or in the organization design, provision should be made for getting new kinds of information to selected people—and for weeding out information flows that no longer serve a useful purpose.

In our dynamic world every enterprise is continually adjusting to new opportunities and problems. The organization structure that is designed to help meet these challenges should also change. It can and should be a responsive tool of central management.

QUESTIONS FOR CLASS DISCUSSION

1. (a) A stockbrokerage firm with one main office is considering "contracting-out" (having an outside company do the work) all its computer work rather than enlarging its own computer service unit. Assuming the cost is the same, what difference, if any, will this choice make to the operating people using the output of the computer? (b) The firm is also considering contracting-out its janitor work.

What difference, if any, will this make to operating people? (c) How would your answers to (a) and (b) be affected by the firm's having ten offices instead of one?

2. (a) Compare the role of *purchasing* in (1) a hospital and (2) a women's ready-to-wear store. What organizational provision for purchasing do you recommend in (1) and in (2)? (b) Does your answer with respect to purchasing in hospitals have a significant bearing on the rising cost of medical care? (c) Do you have suggestions for building morale and at the same time controlling costs in hospital purchasing offices?

3. The First National Bank is permeated with dignity, tradition, and conservatism. Of its 800 employees, 20% have more than 20 years of service, and many officers entered the bank years ago as clerks. The personnel department has long confined its attention to recruitment, records and payroll, cafeteria, medical service, and employee activities. A new president has just promoted a 40-year old junior officer to a newly created post of personnel vice-president. In addition to directing the existing personnel department, the president wants the vice-president to "modernize the personnel practices of the bank" with respect to salary administration, training-on-the-job, systematic retirement, and executive development. What authority should be given to the vice-president for each of these activities?

4. (a) Assume you are a sales representative for a company that builds and equips outdoor swimming pools at private residences. How much authority to decide on the following would you want: Which potential customers to call on? What pool designs to offer? What price to quote? What payment terms to grant? What delivery date to set? What guarantees to make? (b) You have just been promoted to regional sales manager. Now, how much authority should each sales representative have? (c) If you were president, where would you locate decision-making authority for each subject?

5. Colleges and universities are under pressure to provide "black studies." Because of traditional attitudes and of continuing burdens with other areas of education, many proponents feel that black studies will receive inadequate attention in existing departments. Should a staff unit be created to aid in the introduction of black studies material into many courses? Or, should a new department of instruction—like the history or chemistry department—be established? Why?

6. (a) In the charter plane service described on page 383, what relationship do you recommend be stipulated between the pilots and the new (1) traffic manager, (2) flight supervisor, (3) maintenance engineer, and (4) treasurer? Is any staff work or functional authority involved? (b) Assume now that the entire operation was acquired by a much larger charter service—the Lucky Tigers. At the Lucky Tigers headquarters there is an executive for each of the four functions listed in (a). Explain the relationship you recommend between these Lucky Tigers executives and (1) the pilots and (2) the new local executives. (c) What added competence are you assuming the Lucky Tigers people will provide? What is the benefit of the merger to the local operation, if any?

7. Compare the need for and the possible duties of a "management committee" composed of key subordinates of the top executive in a Stage I, Stage II, Stage III, and Stage IV organization.

8. (a) Do you think every major department of a company is entitled to a representative on each standing committee? (b) Would you consider the same

factors in deciding on the size of and in selecting members for a (1) budget committee, (2) shop grievance committee, (3) salary committee, and (4) safety committee?

9. When a firm decides to expand from domestic to international operations, the difficulties of effective communication increase. (a) Illustrate this proposition in terms of expansion to any specific foreign country with which you are familiar. Consider all aspects of a management information system identified in this chapter. (b) What can central management do to minimize these difficulties?

10. (a) What contributions should an internal management information system make to the total data needed to formulate company strategy? You may wish to review Part 1 to identify data needed. If you believe the industry affects the internal data that will be relevant, select an industry or a company to make your answer more specific. (b) Where will the additional data needed come from? Who should collect it?

CASE 17 / Mercy Hospitals of Adelaide

Sister Marguerite Perry, Sister Administrator of the Mercy Hospitals complex in Adelaide, South Australia, has before her a second consultant's report on what the consulting group sees as the administrative and organizational difficulties of the hospitals and its recommendation for action. Should she accept the report and pass it on to the Board of Counsel with her recommendation for the Board's approval?

There are four Mercy Hospitals in Adelaide—Mothers' Hospital, Children's Hospital, Heart and Chest Disease Hospital, and St. Nicholas Hospital of Mercy—each in a separate building but all on the same site and connected with each other and with the central services of pathology, radiology, induction training, general administration, and staff housing. The hospitals were founded by and are, in a sense, still owned by a Catholic order, the Order of Sisters for Apostolic Service. The Order had been formed to do apostolic witness, and the hospitals are one of its activities. Others include a school, an orphanage, and several halfway houses.

Sister Perry, in her duty as administrator, is responsible to the Board of Counsel of the Mercy Hospitals and to the President of that Board, Sister Anna Reardon, who is also President of the Advisory Board of several of the other institutions. Both nuns are members of the Order of Sisters for Apostolic Service. The Mother Superior of the Order is also resident in Adelaide.

Of the four hospitals, St. Nicholas Hospital of Mercy is unique in that its capital funding comes from the federal government in Canberra and its operating funds are supplied almost entirely by the city of Adelaide through payments for hospital services supplied to those qualifying for city support under the level-of-income criterion. This means that the City Auditor is involved in the analysis of costs and services. Funds for the other hospitals come from public appeals, from payments by the national health insurance plans, and from private payments.

Exhibit A indicates the existing formal organization structure of the Mercy Hospitals.

EXHIBIT A

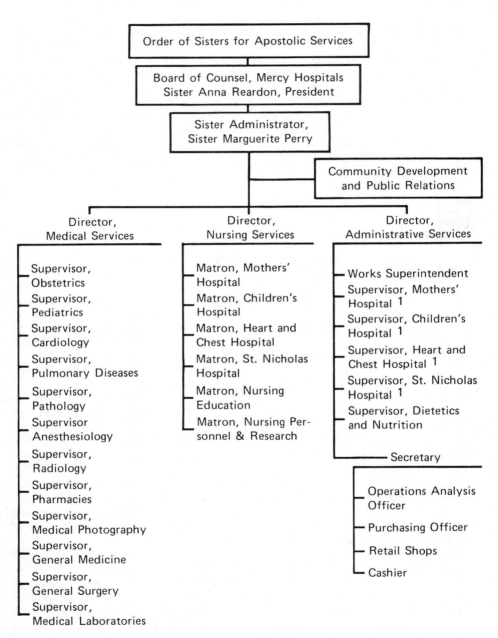

¹ Each Hospital Supervisor had reporting to him a Personnel Officer, a Medical Records Section, a Maintenance Officer, a Chief Wardsman, a Receiving and Billing Officer, and a Budget Officer.

Members of the Board of Counsel, in addition to Sister Anna Reardon, President, are the Director of Medical Services, the Matrons of Mothers', Children's, and Heart and Chest Disease Hospitals (all Sisters of the Order), the legal counsel to the Order, the Chairman of the Adelaide Ecumenical Council, and three medical consultants who are also professors at the Medical School of the University of Adelaide. The membership of the Board of Counsel had been established at the time of formation of the three older hospitals and well before Mercy Hospitals became large enough and with a sufficient medical staff to be teaching hospitals for the Medical School.

Sister Marguerite Perry, the Sister Administrator, had come to her position in Adelaide from a smaller hospital in Brisbane. Within two months after her arrival she had noted what she believed to be serious administrative problems and had persuaded the Board of Counsel to engage a well-known Australian management consulting group to survey these problems for her. The preliminary report of this group did not recognize nor analyze three of what Sister Perry regarded as major problems for Mercy Hospitals: (1) strong representations from the Medical School of the University that the education of its clinical students and of the interns was not being adequately coordinated, planned, and controlled; (2) reports from the City Auditor that Mercy Hospitals' costs for patients when expressed in dollars per bed, per patient, per patient-day, and per square foot were all higher than the same costs in Royal Brisbane, Royal Perth, and Royal Adelaide Hospitals—which had about the same number of beds and staff members as Mercy Hospitals and which were also teaching hospitals; and (3) information about patients in the wards was incomplete for other operative subunits also treating the patient, and feedback to ward records was also incomplete. Record forms varied from hospital to hospital.

Sister Perry then dismissed the group and hired another consulting organization. The main points of the analysis and recommendations of the second group are summarized in the following paragraphs.

All staff consider themselves highly trained, with a high level of education, and thus expect to be brought into the decision-making process and to have their opinions sought and considered before major decisions are made. The Residents Staff Association, the Nurses Staff Association, the Technicians Staff Association, and the Interns Staff Association[1] have all been formed to make representations on these matters to Sister Reardon, Sister Perry, the three directors, the various supervisors, and the Board of Counsel. Usually the staff associations cannot act until after various decisions have been made and the information is available to the members of the associations; then they may react forcefully.

The nuns who serve as paramedics, nurses, and matrons (about 7% of the Hospitals' personnel are Sisters of the Order) do, as a natural aspect of their community, discuss and bring common problems to the Mother Superior. If she believes that the issue is serious enough, the Mother Superior instructs the Sister Administrator in a way to alleviate the problems of the nuns. As one example, the Sisters receive special time off to attend retreats and do apostolic work in the community that is unrelated to their work as technicians or nurses. Lay personnel have, of course, standard time allowances for sickleave and holidays.

Many of the nuns, particularly the younger ones, believe that their hospital work is routine and mundane and can be better carried out by lay staff. They believe that their apostolic role is often submerged and thus feel frustrated and unfulfilled in their work.

---

[1] Analogous to local unions in U.S. terminology.

The matrons have inherited special status from the days when the patient care offered was less complex and when the hospital was nonteaching. They tend to follow an old British tradition of rigid status differentiation and of control by the matrons over the nurses, the wardsmen, and the interns. Their position on the Board of Counsel reinforces this. The Board, as a result of its composition, is primarily concerned with medical problems and its decisions are medical in nature. For example, one question before the Board is whether to spend $100,000 on some new equipment for the care of premature babies or to use the same funds for the intensive-care cardiac unit. Sister Perry had resolved this issue, she thought, after discussion with the three directors, but later she noticed it as an agenda item before the Board.

The Board of Counsel has considered for years the question of adding a geriatrics unit to St. Nicholas Hospital but has never reached a conclusion even though the Chairman of the Adelaide Ecumenical Council and the legal counsel believe that geriatric medicine is a serious issue for the state of South Australia.

There are some problems of communication among the staff members. Two prominent examples, mentioned by both parties, are communications between the Works Superintendent and the various medical and surgical supervisors. Issues of equipment, laboratory design, and operating theater design are often hard to resolve. The directors of Administrative Services and of Medical Services delegate these issues to their subordinates since the issues are highly technical. Doctors are not trained in the necessary negotiating and discussion skills; instead they are accustomed to acting as experts in a one-to-one relationship.

As their approach to dealing with these issues, the second consulting group made five major recommendations:

(1) Revision of the membership of the Board of Counsel.
(2) Establishment of an Executive Management Board.
(3) Functional Committees modeled on Likert's "linking-pin" theory of administration.
(4) A new approach to measuring the Hospitals' major objective of providing competent patient care.
(5) Committees on Medical Education.

The Board of Counsel is to remain advisory to the Order of Sisters for Apostolic Service. Its revised membership should include a President nominated by the Order, the Hospital Administrator, the three Directors, one representative of the State Health Department, and four lay members nominated and appointed from the public at large. These members should be qualified and professionally able lay people in any field of endeavor.

To implement policy and to have responsibility for the operations of the hospitals, the Executive Management Board should consist of the Hospital Administrator, the three Directors of Services, the Secretary, and one other member nominated and appointed by the Hospital Administrator.

Functional Committees (three in number), chaired by the respective Directors and including either the Director or a Supervisor from each of the other two service areas, are to discuss, review, and report to the Hospital Administrator once per month on all important matters involving each Service. It is expected that each Service will form further Functional Committees to be concerned with the major departments of each Service and to include representatives from other Services.

The consulting group was unable to determine how the comparative costs of service cited by the City Auditor were determined and the Auditor would not reveal the cost-

APPENDIX A
PATIENT CARE ASSESSMENT

WARD:			M	T	W	T	F	S	S
WEEK COMMENCING:	TIME:								
	DEPENDENCY CATEGORY:								

DIRECT CARE   POSSIBLE SCORE

A. PATIENT
1. Position — 10
2. Safety — 10
3. Hygiene — 10
4. Nutrition — 10
5. Bed Unit — 10
6. Privacy — 10

B. TECHNICAL SKILL, NURSING KNOWLEDGE AND JUDGEMENT
1. Drug Administration — 10
2. Charts and Observations — 10
3. Protective measures — 10
4. Appliances and special equipment — 10
5. Physiotherapy — 10
6. Wounds — 10
7. Pain Relief — 10

C. PRE/POST OPERATIVE OR PRE/POST INVESTIGATION (DIAGNOSTIC PROCEDURES AND TESTS)
1. Patient Knowledge — 10
2. Preparation/specific treatment — 10

D. PSYCHO-SOCIAL
1. Emotional)
2. Social   ) — 10

E. REHABILITATION
1. Involvement of outside agencies)
2. Involvement of patient & relatives) — 10

INDIRECT CARE

F. ENVIRONMENT
1. Immediate)
2. General) — 10
3. Noise   )

G. WARD ADMINISTRATION
1. Hospital Policies & Procedures)
2. Equipment and stores   ) — 10

DAILY TOTALS:

GRAND TOTAL FOR WEEK: FINAL _____

NB. MARK N/A IF ANY POINT NOT APPLICABLE.

POINT ALLOCATION — EVERYTHING SATISFACTORY   = 10
A FEW THINGS WRONG   = 5
MORE THAN A FEW THINGS WRONG = 0

determination process used, so the consultants took the problem of measuring patient care to the Nursing Personnel and Research Department. After lengthy consideration by discussion groups at all levels, the major points to be appraised in judging the quality of patient care were divided into two categories—Direct Care and Indirect Care (see Appendix A for the complete document). The proposed standard is 85%. A percentage result above that would be characterized as Very Good.

The Committees on Medical Education are to be chaired by the supervisors of the various medical services and are to include the chief resident for that service, a representative chosen by the Medical School of the University of Adelaide, two interns, a block matron or a ward charge sister, and a representative from Administrative Services chosen by the Secretary or one of the hospital supervisors.

Interestingly, the first and strongest objection to the idea in the consultant's report (which Sister Perry discussed with all the senior administrators and the presidents of the various staff associations) came from the Director of Medical Services. He stated that his work schedule was already overfull and that adding committee meetings—even meetings of the proposed Functional Committee—would completely overload his position.

Required: (a) List the problems seen by Sister Perry and the consultants. Explain, to the extent you can, how the recommendations will help to resolve the problems.

(b) Do you see any further problems or consequences that the consultants do not deal with?

(c) Would you, as Hospital Administrator, pass on the recommendations to the Board of Counsel?

BOARD OF DIRECTORS AND CENTRAL MANAGEMENT ORGANIZATION

Vital to the success of every enterprise is the organization for central management itself. We have just examined major issues that central management should consider in organizing the total enterprise, but we touched only briefly on arrangements for the small group of key people who decide on such matters as company strategy, policy, and organization structure. The need for a workable understanding of "who is to do what" is fully as important for activities of senior executives as it is for people in a laboratory or a branch office.

First, let us summarize central management tasks, noting especially the distinctive aspects of the work. Then we shall consider how the board of directors, the senior executives, and other groups can contribute to the performance of these functions.

DISTINCTIVE TASK OF CENTRAL MANAGEMENT

Members of central management—president, vice-presidents, general managers, chief financial officer, and others charged with running the company as a whole rather than one segment—have supervisory duties just like every executive. They must guide, motivate, and control their immediate subordinates; and they will have some ordinary tasks like signing papers or greeting visitors that do not differ significantly from activities of many others in the company.

These duties are not unimportant. They should be done well because they contribute to the effectiveness of the company and because they will be regarded as examples for others to emulate.

Critical issues

In addition, central management has an array of pivotal duties it cannot delegate. Subordinates or consultants may assist, but the judgments are so critical to long-run success or the impact is so pervasive that the actions must be taken by the senior executives. The following brief description gives the flavor of these distinctive tasks of central management.

Setting company strategy. When W. R. Grace & Company decided to diversify into chemicals and other activities not associated with its steamship business, the company sharply altered its course. Accompanying the expansion of product lines was a new spirit of aggressiveness and risk-taking.

Ideally, strategy is set on the basis of a long-range forecast. Thus, when a manufacturer of fishing nets foresaw a decline in its traditional market, it moved into nets for all kinds of sports where growth could be confidently predicted on the basis of population statistics. Of course, long-range forecasts may also indicate that an enterprise should stick to its present business. Such was the conclusion when a medium-sized oil company decided not to become involved in international operations; diversion of the company's limited financial and personal resources in foreign activities might well have undermined an attractive and safer development in the particular domestic market the company served.

Establishing major policy. A selection of policy also calls for broad judgment. The J. C. Penney Company, for example, built its nationwide chain of stores partly on a cash-and-carry policy. A common joke in the company was that Mr. Penney established the policy because his middle name was "Cash." Whatever its origin, the policy worked well. However, a dramatic shift occurred in the prevalence of consumer financing. The Penney company then decided that a policy which had been an asset for over half a century had now become a liability, and it reversed its position on granting credit to customers.

In other instances, central management may decide to stick with a basic policy. General Foods Corporation provides a dramatic example in its decision to maintain a policy against the union shop. The company was confronted by a very strong union on the West Coast, its position in the frozen food business was in jeopardy, and only half a dozen employees did not want to join the union. Mr. Clarence Francis, then head of General Foods, felt that the integrity of its entire personnel policy was at stake, so the company stuck with its refusal to grant a union shop. Fortunately, Mr. Francis was able to convince the union that the company's record did demonstrate fairness and liberality, and the union shop demand was dropped. In deciding to maintain its former policy, the board of directors had to match up the possible losses in an important segment of its business against the ramifications of a shift in policy on future employee relations throughout the company.

Long-range planning and timing. In addition to strategy and policy, long-range programs typically incorporate the timing and the magnitude of future actions. These are major decisions, as executives in every airline that has shifted to large jet planes can readily testify. In fact, several major lines found themselves in serious financial difficulties because their long-range planning for new equipment was faulty.

Timing often enters into long-range planning. For example—shifting the illustration from airlines to aircraft manufacturers—Boeing invested several million dollars designing a large jet cargo plane at a time when neither the Air Force nor the commercial airlines showed any interest. The company's forecast of aircraft trends proved to be correct and Boeing not only secured large military orders but won a major position in the commercial aircraft field. In contrast, Convair Division of General Dynamics Corporation overcommitted itself in an attempt to catch up in the jet race and lost $350 million (probably the largest civilian mistake up to that time).

Changing organization structure. When Mr. Ralph Cordiner became president of General Electric Company, he accepted the position only after the board of directors agreed to support a major reorganization. He recognized that the change would cause temporary disruption, risk of loss during the transition, and opposition by members of the old guard. Such a rocking-the-boat while a company is profitable takes foresight and courage. At about the same time, the president of a much smaller chemical concern chose an evolutionary approach to the organization structure he believed the company needed. Even though he moved slowly, the changes were recognized by central management as having a profound effect on the company's ability to expand in the future.

Selecting key personnel. A delicate, and in some ways the most critical, task of central management is the selection of a chief executive and the people who report to that person. These people not only dominate the success or the failure of existing policy and strategy, they also typically are key figures in formulating new plans. Often the person selected reflects a judgment of what the company most needs at that time. For instance, a large insurance company that had been highly successful in expanding its position in the industry selected a conservative financial man as its new president. This move came as a surprise because another younger, dynamic vice-president was much better qualified to continue the successful practices of the retiring president. Actually, in the expansion process expenses had gotten out of line and the older man was selected because it was anticipated he would insist on a tightening up that was needed at that time. He was due for retirement in a few years, and then the younger man was placed in the top post. If the older, conservative man had been president for ten or fifteen years, the company might have lost much valuable momentum; but a shakedown for a much shorter interval probably added long-run strength to the company.

Approving large capital expenditures and contracts. When a company commits, say, 3% or more of its total assets to an investment that will be recovered only over a period of years, central management should take a good hard look at the soundness of the venture. For example, when a department store invests in a new branch in a suburban shopping center, someone must doublecheck not only the ability of the store to manage such a branch, but also the specific location, capacity, and design of the building to be constructed. Since capital expenditures are relatively easy to identify and control, some central managements insist on reviewing small as well as large projects. The question then arises whether such a review is the most effective way to use the time and the talents of these men.

Fully as important to long-run success, though less tangible, are long-term contracts. Thus, a highly successful manufacturer of detergents quite properly gave long consideration to the granting of an exclusive franchise to sell its products in Europe. Often a purchase contract or a retirement plan may involve as much money over a period of years as a new building. We have already noted in Chapter 13 that long-term leases are an alternative way of acquiring the use of fixed assets. The length of such commitments, as well as their amount, makes their review by the same group of people who are thinking in terms of long-run objectives and policy desirable.

Negotiating mergers and major agreements. Typically, members of top management are active participants in major negotiations. The merger movement of stockbrokerage firms in the 1970's, for example, probably absorbed more time of the senior executives of the firms involved than any other problem. Such agreements are always complex, and other matters seem insignificant when a merger is in the offing.

Other major agreements may be of such significance to the company that its senior officers personally devote important blocks of their time to negotiation. The president of a company seeking to install cable television, for instance, spent more than half of his time securing the necessary approvals from federal and state regulatory commissions and companies affiliated in the venture. Similarly, the president of a nonscheduled air freight line made government approval of transatlantic flights his top priority task for over two years. Subordinates could do the spadework, but the importance of the agreement and the attitude of outside parties required that the company be represented by a senior executive.

Officially representing the company. Many people represent a company—sales personnel, purchasing agents, union negotiators, and others. On some occasions this representation must be done by a member of central management. When a congressional committee calls upon a president to testify, this senior executive rarely sends a subordinate. Likewise, security analysts much prefer to quiz the president—and to contribute to the company's financial standing, this officer usually meets with them. Charitable and civic groups also much prefer to quiz the president—and to contribute to the company's financial companies. The benefits of such activities are intangible and perhaps small, yet they are an inescapable part of business citizenship.

Approving annual budgets. Annual budgets can be a primary device for guiding and coordinating company operations. The budget presents, in condensed form, the financial aspects of an overall company program. Because of its terseness and comprehensiveness, many central managements use the annual budget—within stipulated limits—to control a whole array of more detailed plans. Review of the budget provides an opportunity to check the integration of short- and long-range plans, to iron out unresolved differences in emphasis, and to set short-range targets. Central management endorsement is necessary if the budget is to serve these purposes well.

Coordinating and controlling. Although central management is predominantly concerned with the future, it must maintain a guiding influence on current activities. Any firm with a group of vigorous executives will occasionally encounter sharp differences of opinion. Central management has the task of "umpiring" so that action may proceed.

Finally, as stewards for the entire enterprise, central management must keep a watchful eye on current results. If operations are unsatisfactory, someone must be objective enough and tough enough to insist on remedial action. The decision of RCA to admit that its enormous computer effort was a flop and should be discontinued—even though millions of dollars had been invested—was certainly difficult to make. Pride and personalities were involved. By decisive action, continuing efforts on a losing proposition were checked and resources were redirected to projects that held much greater promise.

Most of the preceding examples of critical central management problems deal with large firms. Small companies also face similar issues that to them are just as crucial. The aim of the above review has been merely to emphasize the nature of the central management task, the organization of which is the theme of this chapter. Since the entire book takes a central management viewpoint, a more systematic and complete list of problems that may land on the desk of a senior executive can be obtained from the outline of each of the chapters.

Characteristics of central management problems

Emerging from this review of critical issues faced by central management are four characteristics that appear again and again. These do not describe the total job, but they help to identify its distinctive nature. In general, central management is concerned with problems that are:

1. *Important.* Importance, here, may be tested in relation to (a) income, (b) survival, and (c) other basic objectives of the enterprise.
2. *Long-range.* In an established, ongoing, social institution, central management can influence today's actions only slightly. By contrast, it is in a unique position to shape long-range strategy, policy, and actions bearing fruit in the future.
3. *Company-wide.* Due to its position, central management can appreciate the impact of action in one department on other parts of the enterprise. It must seek strategic emphasis and balance in the total effort.
4. *Qualitative.* Many judgments of people, events, pressures, risks, and other intangibles must be made, and relative values must be attached to predicted outcomes.

On another dimension, if central management is to deal with problems having these characteristics, it needs a high degree of objectivity and wisdom, coupled with decisiveness and courage. We are not claiming that senior executives are, in fact, paragons; we are only identifying the qualities that appear to be especially important to provide in an organization for central management.

ROLE OF BOARD OF DIRECTORS

Although corporations make up only one tenth of the total business firms of the country, they contribute nearly three fourths of the income produced by business firms. Most business concerns with a hundred employees or more are incorporated, as well as a very large number of nonprofit enterprises; consequently, it is appropriate to inquire how top management functions should be organized in a corporation. (Later discussion of the use of executives and staff applies to proprietorships and partnerships as well as to corporations insofar as such enterprises organize for central management functions.)

Legal theory

Stockholders of a corporation are not expected to perform management functions, and typically they are even more passive than they need be. Except for rare insurrections, stockholders do little more than vote for directors, approve recommendations submitted by management, and hopefully collect dividends. Normally they simply sell their stock if they do not like the way the corporation is run.

Large stockholders may be active, to be sure, but this is almost always done as a director or perhaps as an officer of the corporation. Once in a while, when a corporation is badly mismanaged, a group of dissident stockholders will wrest control from the existing management. However, they too pass management responsibility to a "new" board of directors. So, the stockholders *per se* do not provide central management.

According to legal documents, the board of directors establishes objectives, sets policy, selects officers, approves major contracts, and performs many of the other functions described in the preceding section. Unquestionably the board has authority to do these things. The practical question is, Can we expect the board to perform these functions well or should most of the initiative and activity be delegated to executives of the corporation?

An inactive board

The activities performed by boards of directors vary widely. Until recently, most boards left the entire administration of the firm to executives.

The rationale for such an arrangement is that operating problems can be settled best by people who have an intimate acquaintance and long years of association with the company. These people can dispose of problems in their normal daily contacts without bothering with a meeting of the directors. The directors then confine their attention to formal action on dividends; to the election of officers; to the approval of any public reports; and to decisions on various minor matters, such as the approval of a given bank to be used as depository for company funds or the granting of a power of attorney to some trusted employee. Most of these actions are taken upon recommendation of the senior executives, and consequently the meetings of the board of directors are perfunctory affairs.

Membership of the board

Recognition that the board of directors can and should perform a more vital role has been growing. However, the nature of this role depends upon the composition of the board.

An inside board. Often a board of directors consists largely, if not entirely, of executives of the company. Such directors are well informed about internal operations, the success of the company is of great importance to them, and they are readily available for discussion when critical issues arise.

Unfortunately, operating executives have difficulty taking a long-run objective view of their company. They are inevitably immersed in day-to-day problems and they are emotionally committed to making certain programs succeed. Moreover, they cannot disassociate themselves from social pressure of their colleagues and particularly of their bosses; they are naturally concerned with maintaining the goodwill of these persons who can make life easy or hard for them. To assume that these operating executives can change their perspective and their loyalties when they walk into an occasional board meeting is unrealistic.

A board of directors composed of executives can function as a top management committee. Under favorable conditions, as we shall note later, they do contribute a valuable point of view to central management problems. Rarely can they unaided develop an objective, independent, and tough-minded view of the company as a whole.

A few conspicuous exceptions exist; Standard Oil Company of New Jersey is probably the best known. In this instance, a majority of directors are full-time employees of the company, but they are relieved of all operating responsibilities and focus their attention solely on central management problems. Very few companies can afford such a full-time board of high calibre executives (the direct expense of this board is over $2 million per year). A modified version is to have an executive committee of the board composed of persons who devote their full time to central management. This arrangement is also rare because of the expense involved.

An outside board. As the name implies, an outside board of directors is composed of men whose principal interest is in some other company or profession. A banker, a prominent attorney, and senior executives of companies in other industries are commonly used as outside directors.

The advantages and disadvantages of outside directors are just the opposite of those for inside directors. The persons coming from the outside have independence of judgment and objectivity; they can see the company from a different point of view, and they are not wrapped up in short-run problems. On the other hand, they lack an intimate knowledge of the company operations and its relations with outside groups. More serious, they lack time to become fully informed; having major commitments in their principal line of activity, they cannot be expected to devote more than a few hours a month for the nominal directors' fee that is customarily paid. All too often people accept a directorship for the prestige attached or as a friendly gesture. They are willing to give advice, but they cannot be expected to exercise initiative in seeking directions for the company to expand or in weighing the likely consequences of proposed changes in company policy.

Slow growth is occurring in the use of professional outside directors. These are usually people of broad experience, either as former executives or as consultants, who devote a significant amount of time to any directorship they accept. In return, they are paid a fee (often $5,000 to $10,000 a year) to compensate them for their services.

Since outside members and inside members each have their advantages and limitations, progressive companies now attempt to get a balance between the two groups. The aim is to get a board of directors with varied experience, talent, and viewpoints, provided each person has a dominant concern for the long-run effectiveness of the enterprise.

Social responsiveness via the board

Proponents of social reforms in which corporations play a part frequently suggest that their cause should be represented on boards of directors. Thus, we are confronted with proposals that each of the following should be represented by one or more members: women, blacks and other minorities, conservationists, unions, local government, consumer interests, youth, internationalists, and other interest groups. Add to this list representatives of narrower interests such as suppliers, dealers, bankers, bondholders, and various groups of stockholders.

From the viewpoint of an interest group, several possible benefits may result from representation on a board of directors:

1. Representation is *symbolic*. The recognition helps promote the cause generally, even when the actual influence of the representative is small.
2. *Advice* to the board from a specialist point of view is provided. This assures that, say, consumer interests are taken into account when decisions are made.
3. A *"watch-dog"* is established. The representative's constituents can be warned of pending adverse action.
4. The representative, especially in coalition with other board members, may have *power* to insist on one course of action or block another.

In terms of effective operation of an enterprise, selecting board members primarily because they represent special interest groups has serious drawbacks. The members have divided loyalties, and if they are largely watchdogs, frank and creative discussion within the board becomes difficult.[1] Also they may lack the capacity and the interest to deal with overall company problems. Such weakening of the board is a high price to pay for endorsement of a cause and/or for partisan advice that can be secured without granting membership on the board.

No single resolution of these diverse pressures exist. The resource converter model, introduced in Chapter 1, stresses the importance of continuing support of all groups whose inputs make the enterprise possible. And under some circumstances granting membership on the board of directors may be wise. When this is done, however, the contribution that we can expect from the board is reduced. Consequently, some reallocation of central management functions may become necessary. Formally or informally, the focus of influence will, and should, shift if the board is inadequate to perform the functions listed in the following section.

Feasible duties for a board

Because of the membership problems just discussed, it is unrealistic to assume that a typical board of directors will perform the functions assumed in the legal theory. The board, as such, cannot be expected to provide the initiative and the creative drive needed in central management. In fact, a company will be fortunate in attracting to its board a group of persons who can provide wise counsel. We do not mean to underrate the value of a strong board of directors; the point is that even a good board cannot be expected to do the total central management job.

What, then, should be the role of the board of directors? A practical assignment for a typical board should include these duties:

1. *Approve major changes in strategy, policy, organization structure, and large commitments.* This assumes that carefully prepared recommendations on such matters will flow up from the senior executives. Even if the board approves a large majority of the recommendations made, the necessity for developing a thoughtful justification of the proposals stimulates executives to think through such changes from all angles. This careful preparation of a recommendation by executives may be as valuable as the combined judgment of the board of directors.
2. *Select top executives, approve promotions of key men, and set salaries for this top group of executives.* This assignment is both delicate and highly important. It requires independent and yet informed judgments. The board of directors is in a better position to perform this task than anyone else.

---

[1] A line of thought diametrically opposed to interest representation is being pursued by antitrust lawyers. They contend that directors should have no conflict of interests—pushed to the extreme this would eliminate bankers, lawyers, and consultants as well as suppliers, customers, and union representatives.

3. *Share predictions of future developments, crucial factors, and responses to possible actions.* Here the board is contributing to planning in the formulative stage. The benefits of the broad experience and the diverse points of view are made available to the executive group. Outside members of the board can provide this sort of counsel without unrealistic demands on their time.

4. *Evaluate results and ask discerning questions.* The board should appraise operating results both for prudent control and to obtain background information. This evaluation process should include the asking of a variety of penetrating questions. Most of these questions will be readily answered, but a few may set off a line of thought previously overlooked. Both directors and executives should recognize that the prime purpose here is to see problems from new and useful angles.

5. *Provide personal advice informally.* Already familiar with the company, a director may be an excellent source of advice to executives. The treasurer may call a banker-director about a recent change in the money market, or the marketing vice-president may call another company executive about a new advertising agency. Or the president may want to test out an idea before a formal recommendation is presented to the board as a whole. The informality of these contacts encourages a free exchange of tentative ideas and intuitive feelings.

A board performing the functions just described is particularly valuable because such a check and independent viewpoint can rarely be developed within the executive group.

SENIOR EXECUTIVES

Although the board of directors has an essential role, the major burden of central management must be carried by full-time senior executives.

Legal titles

Officers of a corporation—president, vice-presidents, treasurer, secretary, etc.—are formally elected by the board of directors in accordance with provisions of the company's bylaws. Occasionally, the bylaws also contain a realistic job description for these officers; but typically the bylaws simply make some sweeping statements about the duties of the president and the treasurer and say little or nothing about other officers. Often a senior executive such as a general manager is not a legal officer at all, whereas an individual performing perfunctory duties in the secretary's office may be formally elected by the board. Common practice is to leave the legal authorization quite general, because this is difficult to change; instead, the actual working relationships are developed orally, by exchange of memoranda, or possibly in a company organization manual.

Legal titles, then, give us only vague clues about how a top management actually functions. Usually the role of the various executives is developed first and then any necessary legal formalities are performed later. It is entirely possible for a vice-president or even a president to have no operating duties at all. Consequently, from the viewpoint of the actual management of the business, legal titles tell us little.

Tasks to be performed

However the legal titles may be arranged, senior officers have vital duties to perform. They are the persons who must work out operational definitions of strategy and policy based on a careful appraisal of trends, company strengths, obstacles to be overcome, impact on the rest of the company, and the like. The executives, with rare exceptions, negotiate major agreements for the company. They are the ones who represent the firm to congressional committees. A review of the annual budget with an understanding of its implications is an assignment senior executives are best able to perform.

A quick review of the distinctive tasks of central management presented in the beginning of this chapter will reveal that much of the work must be performed by full-time, thoroughly informed company executives. If the company is to be strong, these senior executives must provide initiative and leadership. Others may help, but in a typical enterprise the senior executives must provide the dynamic force.

Of course, senior executives may also be owners and directors; but as we have seen, they are not in an optimum position to provide strong leadership in those capacities.

The chief executive

Normally, the chief operating executive also serves as the focal point for central management. This individual usually holds the title of "president" but for diplomatic reasons may be named chairman of the board, executive vice-president, or perhaps general manager. Ideally, this individual has vision; lays plans for 5, 10, or 20 years ahead; is a master of strategy and a negotiator; has the ability to pick able men; stimulates and leads both immediate subordinates and employees throughout the company; is a popular and effective leader in civic and industry affairs; expects high standards of achievement by subordinates; and courageously takes remedial action when all is not well.

Again, realism forces us to admit that no single person can excel in all these respects; and even if one had the ability, that individual would not have the time to do all these things personally. Consequently, wise chief executives try to see that important activities they cannot perform themselves are done by someone else in the company. This conclusion leads us to the question of how the chief executive's "office" can be organized.

Dual executive

The most common way to relieve the central management burden on the president is to share the job with another senior executive. Various combinations of titles are used: chairman of the board and president, president and executive vice-president, or president and general manager are examples. Whatever the titles, the two individuals have to develop their own unique way of splitting the total task. The division is likely to reflect the particular interests and abilities of the two individuals. One person may handle most external relations, while the other works with executives within the company. One may focus on long-range development, and the second may deal with current problems. Sometimes the division is along functional or product lines. Perhaps no continuing pattern exists; each works on whatever seems most pressing at the moment. Regardless of how the work is shared, an intimate and frequent interchange is desirable so that the two individuals function as a closely integrated partnership.

Occasionally, three people work together as peers, but the integration of their thoughts and activities into a single president's office view is difficult.

The dual executive arrangement works better in the top job than in other executive positions—probably because a higher proportion of the total work involves planning and deliberation and less time is involved in supervising daily activities. Nevertheless, it is a delicate arrangement and depends on getting the right combination of personalities.

Management committee

Another sharing device is the management committee, perhaps called policy committee or planning committee. Here all senior executives serve on a committee that deals with several central management tasks. Establishing strategy and policy, building long-range programs, appraising capital expenditures, and reviewing annual budgets are typical activities.

A top management committee has all the inherent advantages and limitations of any committee, as discussed in the preceding chapter. It clearly is a good coordinating mechanism; but if it is just an added assignment for executives who are already fully occupied with managing their respective departments, not much creative central management work will be accomplished in committee meetings. The firms with best success with a genuine central management committee have deliberately relieved its members of a significant part of their supervisory burdens, often by placing a single deputy under each member. The members are then expected to devote a quarter to half their total time to central management problems assigned to them by the president.

Central management staff

Another well-recognized way to assist the chief executive with central management tasks is the use of a staff. Several leading companies, for instance, have a staff group working on *long-range planning*. These people study future trends, explore possible additions to the product line, project requirements for buildings and for training personnel, and prepare similar data and recommendations for consideration by the president. The organization for long-range planning is a special problem in itself because central staff should tap the ideas of thinking people throughout the company. A few firms rotate young executives in and out of the long-range planning group for this purpose. Decentralized companies may select a long-range planning person in each operating division; the ideas of these persons are then funneled up to a coordinating staff, the chief executive, or to the management committee if one exists.

The use of an *organization planning* staff reporting to the president is becoming more common. Such a unit assists in adapting the company organization structure to changing needs. A related task sometimes combined with organization planning is *executive personnel development*. Executive development may simply be part of the training activity of the company; but in some cases the personnel staff advisor to the president shares in the selection, development, and compensation planning for senior executives.

The role of the *business economist* is often confined to making cyclical forecasts of volume and prices in the industry; however, in a few instances he has become an active participant in central management discussions. Similarly, *financial analysts* occasionally become advisors on central management issues.

These are merely illustrations of the kinds of problems the top staff may handle. Such people do more than assemble information specifically requested by the president, helpful though this may be. To be a really significant member of the team that assures that central management tasks are performed well, a staff member must be a respected, intimate advisor of the senior executive. Such staff members are hard to find, and not all chief executives know how to use staff effectively on difficult, intangible problems.

SUMMARY

In addition to the many—and important—problems of current daily management of an enterprise, an array of distinctive tasks must be performed by central management. Important among these tasks are formulating company strategy, establishing major policy, developing long-range planning, changing the organization structure, selecting key personnel, approving large capital expenditures, negotiating major agreements, officially representing the company, and coordinating and controlling the overall company actions.

Most companies can handle such issues best by a combined effort. The board of directors has an essential role of objective evaluation, independent approval, and injection of varied ideas and viewpoints. To perform this role well the board usually should consist of both inside and outside directors.

The major burden for central management, however, must be carried by full-time executives. The chief executive serves as the focal point but needs assistance. This may be provided by having dual top executives, a management committee, staff assistants, or a combination of all three. All such arrangements are delicate and call for individuals of outstanding ability. The particular organization adopted in a specific company will depend both on the personalities involved and the issues that are critical.

Small firms cannot support so many participants. Nevertheless, two or three outside directors can be carefully chosen, and one of the executives—the president or perhaps a vice-president—can be assigned a light enough supervisory load to permit concentrated attention on the longer-range, broader issues of central management.

An established business may coast for several years with weak central management. For long-run success, however, nothing is more crucial. Through some kind of organization, the job should be done and done well.

In the preceding chapters on organization, we discussed matching organization with strategy and building an integrated structure. We have now emphasized another vital element—the provision of some kind of organization to perform distinctive central management tasks. Of course, sound organization alone is not enough; it must be manned by good executives. The next chapter is devoted to this related topic of executive personnel.

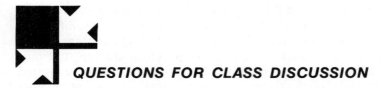

QUESTIONS FOR CLASS DISCUSSION

1. (a) Does a Stage 1 enterprise—one dominant individual—face the kinds of problems listed on pages 403-407? (b) To what extent does such an enterprise need a separate check on the chief executive to perform at least the duties listed on pages 411-412? (c) How do you recommend that a small, privately owned enterprise obtain the kind of guidance you suggested in answering (a) and (b)?

2. To avoid any possible "conflict of interest," should we have a law prohibiting a person being *both* a director of one corporation and (a) a director, (b) an officer, or (c) an employee of another company that sells goods or services to the corporation or that is a large customer of the corporation? Why?

3. Chapter 1 presented an argument that the socially responsible company should seek an exchange of inputs and outputs with each resource group that is mutually beneficial on a continuing basis. Developing such an exchange involves both cooperative effort and some bargaining. In what ways would this process be aided, and in what ways hindered, by having a member of the company's board of directors designated by the resource group?

4. (a) "Students should select at least one of their numbers, and preferably two or three, to serve on the Board of Trustees of their university." Do you agree? Why? (b) Should employees of a university have a representative on the Board of Trustees? Why? (c) Would your answer be the same for customers and employees of (1) an airline and (2) a telephone company? Why?

5. Compare the duties you would assign to the board of directors of a typical non-profit, nongovernmental hospital with the duties of a board of a typical pharmaceutical manufacturing firm. How will any difference in duties affect the types of persons you would recommend for membership on the respective boards?

6. (a) Do you recommend that corporations make special effort to find women to appoint as directors? Should they give preference to women over men in such appointments? (b) Answer the same questions with regard to blacks. (c) Answer the same question with regard to American Indians.

7. Special studies of the membership of the Young Presidents' Organization (president before age 40 of a firm with 50 or more employees and sales of $1 million, or $2 million for a nonindustrial company) have indicated that the presidents are typically "unabashed egoists" who demonstrate daring, initiative, and rugged individualism and have an urge to build rather than to manipulate. "The . . . compulsion and obsession is not to make money, but to build an empire." Do these findings have any relation to the tasks and the duties of chief executives stated in this chapter? What do they indicate about the problem of who should take responsibility for the major duties and the critical issues of central management?

8. To assure an objective check on the management of large publicly owned corporations (and also endowed, not-for-profit corporations), several astute observers recommend greater independence of the board of directors from the chief executive. To help achieve that end, the proposals include a separate staff group that reports directly to the board and serves the board by making external and internal studies. Also suggested is the nomination of replacements on the board by a committee of the board—not by full-time executives of the company. Do you endorse these proposals?

9. Wise company strategy is concerned with keeping company activities in tune with its changing environment, as discussed in Part 1. What organizational provisions can be made to assure (a) sensitivity to and preferably anticipation of significant changes in the environment, and (b) prompt adjustment to such changes? Who perceives and who initiates?

10. Several research studies have identified one of the key tasks of central management to be coordination of the functional departments or operating divisions of a company. Should this task of coordination be assigned to a management committee or an executive committee, or should it better remain the responsibility of the president or the chief executive officer? What kinds of issues can a single executive resolve that a group could not?

CASE 18 / Koch Electronics, Inc.

Shortly before the quarterly meeting that followed a reconstitution of the board of directors of Koch Electronics, Inc. (Exhibit 1), a group of directors wrote to the other members. Their letter (Exhibit 2) was in reaction to the agenda drawn up for the board's next meeting (Exhibit 3) and included a proposal that would considerably affect the activities of the directors.

Koch Electronics manufactured electrical communications equipment for sale to other industrial firms, to the federal government, and to the general public. Sales were approximately 50%-60% to industry, 30% to the government, and 10%-20% to retail customers. The industry's sales were on a rising trend and had some cyclical fluctuation but no seasonal pattern. Sales were generally steady from month to month.

The company was about forty years old and had been run by a stable management under the leadership of only two presidents. Within the past year, however, unsatisfactory financial results (see Exhibit 4) had brought pressure from the company's investment banker and a group of stockholders. This resulted in some resignations among the directors and the addition of others to the board.

Mr. John Walters, president and general manager, remarked: "I was sorry to lose those men. Mr. Husband was an outstanding electrical engineering consultant who had, at one time, headed his own firm. He helped us greatly with technical matters about which he and I or Mr. Sansone (engineering vice-president) conferred directly. Similarly, Mr. Pugh advised us on plant construction and location questions, and Mr. Bible helped with financial policy and bank relations. Nevertheless, I am looking forward to working with the new board members. We trust they will be able to provide advice to the management based on their special competence."

Stock ownership was diverse. No one stockholder, except Mr. Walters, held more than 2% of the outstanding shares. The stock was actively traded on one of the smaller stock exchanges (see Exhibit 5). Mr. Walters had built up his holdings of between 5% and 10% through the exercise of stock options awarded under various contracts. The present contract reserved 75,000 shares of the authorized but unissued stock for purchase by Mr. Walters over the next five years at the market price existing when the option agreement began (July of the previous year).

Required: (a) Do you agree with the letter from the three directors? Explain.

(b) What position would you, as a director, take toward the items on the agenda? Explain your reasoning.

Exhibit 1

Members of the Board of Directors of Koch Electronics, Inc.

Mr. Robert Smith, Chairman—President, Smith and Associates (investment counselors)
Mr. James A. Allen—Treasurer and Vice-President, Koch Electronics, Inc.
Mr. Hartley C. Ashford—President and Director, Middle State Insurance Co.
Mr. Robert Barlow—Vice-President and Sales Manager, Koch Electronics, Inc.
Mr. Hultgren Berg—Senior Partner, Chauncey, Gray and Berg (CPA's)
Mr. Weston R. Brown—President and Director, The Sales Advertising Co., Inc.
Mr. William F. Butcher—Wallace, Summers, Easton & Co.
Mr. John R. Saylor—Secretary, Koch Electronics, Inc.
Mr. Robert Sansone—Engineering Vice-President, Koch Electronics, Inc.
Mr. Leonard Smith—Production Vice-President, Koch Electronics, Inc.
Mr. John A. Baker—Five Persons Bank and Trust Company
Mr. John Walters—President, General Manager, and Director of Research, Koch Electronics, Inc.
Mr. Robert A. Weiss—Goldner Wax and Candle Company

Exhibit 2

The Board of Directors
Koch Electronics, Inc.

Gentlemen:

We are sending this letter to all of you—since we believe that these matters need more serious attention than they will receive at the next quarterly directors' meeting. Our observation is that the conduct of the meetings is such as to preclude major attention to items not already developed in detail on the agenda.

First, we propose that an executive committee of the board be established. It would meet monthly to review the course of operations under existing policy as approved by the board. It is our opinion that too little attention has been devoted in the past by the board to general matters of the direction of the company. Members of this committee should receive substantial compensation of about $1,000 per meeting plus expenses rather than the current payment for expenses only.

Second, we believe that the Development Investment Account now capitalized as an asset should no longer be so regarded, that the net amount remaining after amortization should be written off in a reasonably short period, and that no more charges should be made to this account. We recognize that patents that still have over ten years' remaining life have been secured from development work whose cost was charged to this account. However, we believe that the development work is mainly for product improvement and for maintenance of the firm's market position. Thus it is a current activity whose cost is properly a period charge.

We have requested that the secretary include these items on a revised agenda. Our letter is to acquaint you with our serious concern.

Very truly yours,

William F. Butcher, Wallace, Summers, Easton & Co.[1]
John A. Baker, Five Persons Bank and Trust Co.[2]
Robert A. Weiss, Goldner Wax and Candle Co.[3]

[1] A Chicago investment banking firm that had undertaken stock sales for Koch Electronics.
[2] A large Chicago bank.
[3] Mr. Weiss was president of this firm, which manufactured candles and paraffin waxes.

Exhibit 3

Agenda, Second Quarterly Meeting,
April 20, 1 to 5 p.m.

Koch Electronics, Inc.

Item One —Tour of the plant to view production changes and to inspect product modifications.

Item Two —Review of company operations and results—Mr. Walters. Review of industry and general economic conditions—Mr. Warren, consulting economist.

Item Three—Gift of shares to Midwest University and other organizations. For the past five years the company has issued a total of 1,000 shares each year to Midwest University and certain charitable organizations. The market value on date of issuance is deductible for tax purposes.
(Midwest University specialized in scientific and engineering education. Mr. Smith and Mr. Walters were alumni. Mr. Walters had been prominent in university and alumni affairs for some time.)

Item Four —Authorization of dividends on the common stock.

Item Five —Stock option agreements.

Item Six —Two executives resigned recently. It is proposed that the board authorize agreements with their replacements—Mr. Robert Sansone, engineering vice-president, and Mr. Leonard Smith, production vice-president—that 25,000 shares of unissued stock be made available for purchase by these executives at the present market price with a limit of five years to the agreements.

Exhibit 4

Selected Annual Financial Information
Koch Electronics, Inc.

First Quarter of Current Year and Ten Past Years
(All figures in thousands except dividends per share)

Sales	Net Profits After Tax	Dividends Total	Per Share	Retained Earnings Year End
$ 3,600 [1]	$ 70 est. [1]			
13,200 [2]	(600) [3]	$120	$ .40	$2,700
15,500	300	480	1.60	3,400 [4]
16,200	650	465	1.60	3,600
15,800	450	440	1.60	3,400
17,100	650	425	1.60	3,400
17,500	680	400	1.60	3,200
15,400	540	240	1.20	2,800
13,900	420	240	1.20	2,500
12,800	310	200	1.00	2,310
8,400	150	100	1.00	2,200

[1] First quarter, current year. [2] Last year. [3] Net loss. [4] Certain minor adjustments, in addition to dividends, affected the retained earnings.

Notes to the Last Annual Financial Statements

Note D—The accumulated cost to the Development Investment Account was $1,980,000. Amortization (based on patent life) amounted to $600,000. The balance was carried as an asset to the amount of $1,380,000. Current research and development costs of $262,000 were accumulated in the Development Investment Account.

Note E—Authorized capital stock consists of 800,000 shares of common stock. At the year end there were 300,000 shares outstanding leaving 500,000 of the authorized shares unissued. No stock options were exercised during the year.

Of the unissued shares, 75,000 were reserved in favor of Mr. Walters in accordance with a management contract between the company and Mr. Walters adopted by a resolution of the stockholders.

Exhibit 5

Stock Prices, Koch Electronics, Inc.

	High	Low	Average
Current Year	22⅛	21¼	
Preceding Year	42	25	32
" "	47	36	40
" "	52	38	44
" "	38	24	32
" "	30	26	27
" "	29	18	24
" "	27	15	18
" "	19	11	14
" "	16	10	12½
" "	16	8	12

EXECUTIVE PERSONNEL

Without suitable executive personnel in a company, sound strategy, effective policy, and a clear organization plan soon become unrealistic aspirations; with good executive personnel, they provide the guidance and the structure for purposeful enterprise.

Developing executive personnel

The development of a competent group of immediate subordinates is a duty that can never be fully delegated. Larger companies may have a service unit that provides assistance in dealing with executive personnel problems, but each executive still carries primary responsibility for having competent people in key positions under his or her direction.

The typical manager is concerned with only a relatively few executives and other key personnel. These are likely to be people he has worked with over a period of years; they may well include many of his best friends. As an executive he is expected to see that they perform today's tasks effectively and also develop so that they can assume the larger responsibilities of tomorrow. This development involves habits, attitudes, and skills that may take years. Except for filling unexpected vacancies arising from death or resignation, executive personnel is a long-run problem. Because of these *personal, intangible,* and *long-run* characteristics of executive personnel development, general policy is inadequate to deal with specific situations. In addition to using policy, the manager should give his personal attention to the delicate and highly personal situations in his company or his department.

Wide variation in company practice

Since executive personnel involves personal relationships, considerable difference occurs in the way executive selection and development is handled in various companies.

A president who evaded his responsibility. In one relatively small company with eight key executives, the president had been for many years the key figure in coordinating operations. Each subordinate was given considerable latitude within his own department, but he was expected to concentrate his attention in this area. The executives were very friendly with one another, and the president himself had a personal interest in and a deep loyalty to each of the members of the group. There was a general understanding that the sales manager would probably be the next president, and beyond that the matter of executive succession was given little thought.

The cold facts of the situation were that the sales manager was an excellent salesman but not an effective executive. He was indecisive and preferred not to assume administrative responsibility. As long as the president was active, these traits were not a serious handicap to the company. The sales representatives were experienced individuals who were glad to accept the kindly suggestions of the sales manager and who were able to proceed with a minimum of supervision.

When the president died and the sales manager succeeded him, the latter's lack of executive ability created an acute problem. Other executives found it difficult to get positive decisions from the new president, and in his effort to please everyone he was likely to reverse himself. Coordination, or lack of it, was largely a result of the voluntary contacts between the several executives. The new president could not adjust to his new responsibilities and suffered a nervous breakdown within three years. The person who was next appointed as president had considerably more ability but had been given virtually no training for the job as chief executive. Six to eight years elapsed before the company really recovered from the shock of the death of a president who failed to provide adequately for his replacement.

Note also that the president made no provision for change in the scope of company activities.

Looking back on this case, one wonders why a successful president for so many years failed to anticipate the difficulties upon his withdrawal from the company. Perhaps he never faced the question squarely. More likely, he recognized the limitations of the sales manager but could not bring himself to take the drastic action that would have been involved in the selection and training of another executive to be his successor. This would have created strain and upset personal friendship. Since no immediate action was necessary, he probably evaded the issue and hoped it would work out all right somehow. Had he taken the necessary action when he was still president, the company would certainly have been better off and the sales manager spared a nervous breakdown. This would have taken considerable courage, however, because there was no assurance that all the people concerned would have recognized the need for the action.

Informal development program. More thought is given executive development in many companies than appears on the surface. Frequently these concerns have no announced program or procedure but do give the matter of executive personnel regular attention. One company, for example, has a "little green seedbox'' that contains a card for each key person who is a present or potential manager of one of the concern's principal operations. Each year the work of these people is reviewed by a senior executive along with the individual's supervisor, and when a person is assigned to a new position his performance is watched closely. Then, as opportunities open, people are moved into positions of increasing executive importance. If it is decided, after watching a person for several years, that he has reached his maximum, his card will be removed from the file.

Wide variations exist in this type of approach. Typically, the cards or the pages in a loose-leaf notebook contain little information other than a record of the positions a person has held, his salary, and perhaps notations on his outside civic or educational work. If the president or a senior vice-president is the one who directs the activity and makes sure that each person's performance is reviewed at least once a year (though not necessarily in a formal review session), then it is likely that considerable executive development work will take place and that the selection of people for promotion will be based on a broad view of the person's experience.

Where the activity is treated more casually or where the reviews are sponsored by an individual who lacks prestige with other executives, the attention given to executive development will probably be substantially less. In any event, the kind of training on the job that occurs depends almost entirely upon the interest and the ability of the supervising executive. Given the proper company tradition, backed by the necessary inspiration and guidance of the chief executive, such informal plans for executive development have worked remarkably well in some companies.

Essential elements in a sound program

The informal approaches to executive development just illustrated have two basic weaknesses: (1) little thought is given to preparing for growth or major changes in strategy, and (2) executive development receives low priority in the plans of most executives. To overcome these limitations, highly formalized programs of executive appraisal and replacement schedules have been created, especially in multinational concerns where lack of qualified executives may be a major restraint on expansion.

Even though substantial disagreement exists on how formalized executive development should be, we can identify several basic elements that every manager should keep in mind when dealing with executive personnel problems. Whatever the forms and the procedures used, the manager's thinking should embrace the following steps:

1. A prediction of the types and number of executives his company (or department) will need for successful operations in the future.
2. A review, or inventory, of the executive talent now available.
3. A tentative promotion schedule, based on the two preceding steps, that provides for manning each of the positions in the anticipated organization and, insofar as possible, for a potential replacement for each of the key executives.

4. A plan for the individual development of each person slated for promotion, so that each may be fully qualified for the responsibilities.
5. Compensation arrangements that will attract and hold the executives covered in the foregoing program and provide incentives for them to put forth their best efforts.

The significance and the nature of each of these steps will be considered in the following sections. A detailed analysis of techniques, however, is beyond the scope of this book.

ANTICIPATING EXECUTIVE REQUIREMENTS

The basis for any long-range planning for executive personnel is a prediction of the kind of people that will be needed. Surprisingly, this obvious first step is sometimes overlooked. In one company, for example, the top administrator held the view that "we always have room for good people around here," and on several occasions he hired competent people with no clear-cut idea of what they were to do. These individuals either got bored waiting for a significant assignment or created friction by interfering with activities of other executives.

A more common failure is to assume that a title provides an adequate guide to the kind of person needed. A hard-driving, enthusiastic sales supervisor is quite a different individual than an analytical and imaginative planner of merchandising campaigns, and yet either of these persons might have the identical title of product sales manager. Before sound executive development can be done, a clear understanding is needed of (1) the jobs to be filled and (2) the characteristics of the persons needed for these jobs.

Jobs to be filled

A study of strategy and future organization, along the lines indicated earlier in this book, will result in a long-range organization plan with descriptions of each key position needed. These position descriptions are not necessarily put in writing, but there must be an understanding of the duties and the relationships of each executive position. If plans for the future administrative organization have not already been clarified, then organization analysis becomes a first step in the executive personnel program.[1]

Position descriptions prepared for organizational purposes differ in emphasis from those used in an executive development program. The more ticklish aspects of organization involve defining the borderline between the various units and spelling out interrelationships when activities must closely

---

[1] We clearly are recommending that organization design *precede* executive selection. Of course, in the short run a company must be managed by the executive talent available, and since the available executives may not fully match the ideal organization, the only practical action is to adjust the organization so that optimum results will be obtained. Executive development, however, should continue to be aimed toward the best future organization we can realistically expect to achieve.

coordinate. Such divisions of responsibility are not so important for executive development purposes. Here, interest centers on the major duties to be performed, the degree of decentralization and hence the judgment that must be exercised by people at different levels in the organization, the importance of initiative and enthusiasm, and similar matters. In other words, we need to sense the role the person in the executive position will play in the operation of the enterprise.

Characteristics of persons needed for these jobs

The second phase of this analysis of executive requirements is to translate the duties into *person specifications*, that is, the personal qualities an individual needs to fill a given position effectively. We can describe the duties of a football quarterback or a plant superintendent, but it is another matter to set up a list of qualifications that a person should have to fill such a position successfully.

These person specifications may be stated in terms of knowledge, supervisory skill, emotional stability, judgment, dependability, ability to deal with outsiders, social attitudes, and the like. Unfortunately, it is difficult to define requirements for positions in such terms because experience shows that people with quite different makeups may be successful in the same kind of a job. Another way to draw up person specifications is to list the principal things they will be expected to do, such as build customer goodwill, control expenses, plan for future expansion, or stimulate and develop their subordinates. This kind of a list is easier to prepare but is not entirely adequate when an individual is being selected for work that is quite different than he or she has already done. For instance, it is hard to appraise the ability of a crack salesman to be a sales supervisor because there has been no opportunity to observe him doing the kind of activity that is required of the sales supervisor.

In the establishment of person specifications, then, we find one of the first reasons why executive development cannot be reduced to fixed procedure. Specifications for the end product are not exact. Nevertheless, if there is to be any careful planning, it is necessary to build up reasonably accurate and useful descriptions of the kind of executives that will be needed to fill the organization.

One additional point should be emphasized. Much executive development work cannot be expected to show results in less than three to five years and some of it may take much longer. Consequently, the organization structure five years hence is more important than the present one.

The outlook and the strategy for the company must be studied to forecast the volume and the nature of activities. These will throw light on the organization structure that will be needed and hence on the requirements for executive personnel. Moreover, the existing organization may be far from ideal. A logical time to realign duties and to correct organizational weaknesses is when executive personnel is being shifted. If this is to be done, plans for executive development should, of course, be based on the new, rather than the old, organization structure.

INVENTORY OF EXECUTIVE TALENT

The second basic step in planning an executive personnel program is appraising the executives already in the organization. The organization and position analysis just discussed predicts what executive talent will be needed; the appraisal of executives, considered in this section, shows what talent is available to meet these requirements.

Generally an inventory of executive talent is taken to discover weak spots in the normal flow of executives through the promotion channel. It indicates where additional development work is needed to assure that satisfactory replacements are available when necessary.

A good inventory will also bring to light the competent executives who are not being used to their fullest capacity. For example, the president of a pharmaceutical company was shocked when his nephew resigned, along with two key salespeople, and established a competing firm. Evidence clearly indicated that these people had not been assigned to challenging positions and they considered their prospects for promotion so remote that they preferred to take the risk of establishing a new enterprise. A good plan of executive appraisal would have shown the president that these people were prepared for additional responsibilities. He should then have tried to find positions that would more fully utilize their ability, and if this was not possible, he should at least have openly examined the situation with each individual. In other words, an executive inventory would have been useful even though there was no immediate need for replacing key men.

Different uses of executive appraisals

Executive appraisals may be used in several different ways, and their value will be improved if these uses are recognized at the outset.

1. The primary purpose of executive review may be to *select* a person for an existing or anticipated vacancy. For this purpose an objective appraisal of the person's future potential is needed.
2. Executive appraisal may point to the need for development when abilities of executives are matched against the person specifications for a given position. Individual *development programs* can then be built around deficiencies. When the emphasis is on personal development, the appraiser can identify much more closely with the individual being reviewed and together they can seek out opportunities for improvement.
3. Executive appraisal may be used to establish bonuses and to pay increases or other forms of *compensation*. Here attention centers on past achievements rather than future potentials. Objectivity is needed here, as it is when considering individuals for promotion.

When a company uses its executive appraisal for several different purposes, as is usually true for those companies that have a well-rounded executive development program, it is important to maintain a balanced point of view. Objectivity is vital, while at the same time a sympathetic interest in the individual is needed for planning for individual growth.

Informal appraisal of executives

No systematic appraisal, or inventory taking, of executive ability is made in many companies. Nevertheless, considerable informal appraisal typically takes place. This was the method followed in a financial company, for example, that had 32 senior and junior officers and approximately 85 first-line supervisors and other key employees. The size of the company permitted each senior officer to know personally all of the executives as well as some of the outstanding operating persons.

The president and the senior vice-president made it a practice to "keep their eye on the staff." They asked questions and otherwise followed the work of the various executives closely enough to have a clear impression of what most of the people were doing. In addition, they occasionally talked with the individual officers about the people under their supervision and what might be done to assist in their development. The officers felt that more formal ways of inventorying executive talent were unnecessary in their situation.

Informal executive appraisal, such as that just described, is a natural and continuing process that should be used by everyone in a managerial position. The more formal appraisal techniques, discussed in the next paragraphs, supplement rather than substitute for this type of evaluation. The informal appraisal is done at convenient times, in connection with other work; consequently, it creates no special burden on executives.

Limitations of this method are: (1) some executives who are primarily interested in technical problems may fail to size up the persons with whom they come in contact; (2) the appraisals may be incomplete, with emphasis on past performance and little attention on future potential; and (3) in larger concerns where no one executive can know personally all of the present and potential managers, it is extremely difficult to compare candidates in one department with those in another and to exercise any measure of guidance and control over an executive development program.

Systematic evaluation of executives

To overcome the limitations of informal executive appraisals, several companies have definite procedures for executive personnel reviews. In their simplest form these evaluations consist of only an annual memorandum written by the supervisor of each executive outlining the person's outstanding accomplishments and weaknesses, the steps taken for development, and future potential.

At the other extreme are rather elaborate evaluation forms that record an overall appraisal of the person's work during the past year, a rating of personal qualities, promotion possibilities, and plans for individual development. The Armed Services use a similar technique; in fact, the file of fitness reports is the primary basis on which Navy officers are selected for promotion.

These formal evaluation plans build up a record covering each executive, which is very helpful when he or she is being considered for transfer or promotion. Usually several different people have submitted appraisals and the total record is not dominated by some single event, as may happen when sole reliance is placed upon informal appraisal. Moreover, the formal procedure tends to make the evaluation more thorough and consistent.

On the other hand, standard forms and procedures by no means insure that appraisals will be made carefully and honestly. Unless the executives making the appraisal believe that the whole process is worthwhile, they may fill in the form hastily and with answers that they think will lead to the promotions and transfers they would like to see made. Evaluation procedures do, of course, use time of busy executives, and they add a formality to highly personalized relations among executives.

In some manner suitable to the enterprise, a review or inventory of executive talent should be made. This knowledge of the capacity and the weaknesses of the executives is essential for building a sound executive development program. The formality of the approach depends on the size of the company, its rate of change, and traditions regarding attention to personnel matters.

PLANS FOR FILLING EXECUTIVE POSITIONS

Development of executive personnel, as already noted, is largely a long-run problem. Individuals need time to develop the knowledge, skills, and judgment required in most executive posts.

Need for planned executive progression

The treasurer of a medium-sized company recently told the president that he wished to retire within a year. In the discussion at the next meeting of the board of directors, two facts emerged: (1) the assistant to the treasurer, specially selected two years earlier, had displayed more energy than judgment and clearly was not qualified to replace the treasurer, and (2) there was wide misunderstanding about how vital a role the new treasurer should play in overall company operations (some board members wanted a senior executive, whereas the president thought in terms of a cashier). Two years elapsed before a satisfactory, strong person could be found.

Having the right person in the right position at the right time is of supreme importance, especially when expanding or shifting into a new field. Here is an area, then, where long-range planning is of vital importance—even though human behavior is hard to measure and to predict, and results may not turn out just as planned.

Staffing-plan approach

Transfer and promotion of executives is a normal occurrence in a typical business concern. Deaths, retirements, and resignations create vacancies. New positions, resulting from expansion, have a similar effect. If these positions are filled by promotions, additional vacancies are created in the lower ranks. In fact, one vacancy at the vice-president level may result in shifts of half a dozen people at lower levels. The problem is how a company can plan to meet such changes.

The staffing-plan approach rests on three ideas we have already discussed. The first is anticipating executive requirements in terms of positions to be filled and the person specifications of executives needed in such positions. The second is a policy of promotion from within. The third, assuming promotion from within, is the inventory of executive talent discussed in the preceding section, which provides the personnel data needed for concrete planning. Staffing tables are simply a device for weaving this information into a tentative plan.

Staffing plans, such as the one below, show for each executive position (and anticipated position) one or more persons who might be moved into that spot. The preparation of such plans requires that the person specifications for each position be used to select the best candidate available within the company. Some companies distinguish between candidates who are already qualified and those who need a year or more training before they would be prepared to take on the new duties. To be useful, such a chart should be realistic. Thus, if some

JOB NO.	JOB TITLE	JOB INCUMBENT	AGE	SENIOR CANDIDATE	JOB NO.	AGE	JUNIOR CANDIDATE	JOB NO.	AGE
	MANAGEMENT LEVEL GROUP "A"								
2C21	Service Manager	K. L. Foster	47				G. E. George C	5C64	38
							A. A. Day C+	3C23	35
2C52	Sales Engineer	B. C. Johnson	65	C. D. Dewey C	3C24	42	L. M. Mason D+	5A28	38
2C77	Const. Manager	E. E. Bryant	49	No Senior			E. F. Burnes C+	6B16	37
2C12	Accountant	F. G. Bray	55	No Senior			No Junior		
	"B" Office Managers								
3C22	Loc.	G. H. Miller	63	)			)E. D. Hill C	6F41	42
3C23	Loc.	A. A. Day	35	)G. E. George C	5C64	38	)M. N. Johns C+	7B18	35
3C24	Loc.	C. D. Dewey	42	)L. M. Mason D+	5A28	38	)W. X. Hobbs C	4A72	33
	Local Service Mgrs. "A" & "B" Offices								
5C31	"A" Office	R. R. Colby	62	)					
5C64	Loc.	G. E. George	38	)M. N. Johns C+	7F21	35	X. Y. Bell C+	6A57	37
5C65	Loc.	R. S. Williams	41	)W. X. Hobbs C	4A72	33	E. D. Hill C	6F41	42
5C66	Loc.	S. T. Fuller	57	)					
4C12	Zone Maint. Prom.	T. U. Webster	51				R. S. Williams D+	5C65	41
							X. Y. Bell C+	6A57	37
9C31	Zone Modern. Prom.	"Vacancy"		No Senior			T. V. Dodge D+	7D41	32
9C46	Zone Maint. Super.	V. W. Gary	58	F. E. Hyde C+	7F46	39	No Junior		
9C18	Zone Field Eng.	P. T. Monroe	39				T. U. Olson D+	7A81	48
							U. V. Larsen C	4B29	41

Staffing Plan

Sample sheet from staffing plan of Otis Elevator Company. "Senior candidates" are qualified to take over position without further training other than normal job indoctrination; "junior candidates" need one to five years more training. Letters after names tie in to annual executive appraisals. Note that some individuals, such as Hobbs and George, are listed as candidates for more than one position.

contemplated positions are now vacant, they should be shown in this way. If there are no real candidates for a given position, this too should be frankly revealed. Of course, one individual may be considered as a candidate for two or more positions.

Ideally, every senior post in the company should have one or more potential replacements listed. Some people contend that there should be a replacement for every executive throughout the organization. Such an ideal is often very difficult to achieve in practice, and there is serious question as to how much money and effort a company should spend training a replacement for a person who, in all probability, will stay in the present position for ten or more years. On the other hand, having replacements for executives who are likely to retire or to be promoted to other positions is highly important. Some staffing plans attempt to show this timing; but more often the likelihood of a shift, and consequently the need for a fully prepared replacement, is left to the judgment of the people reviewing the plan.

Such staffing plans are subject to frequent revision. Unexpected changes in company operations or in the personal lives of executives may shift requirements. Some people will develop faster and others slower than anticipated; in fact, as time progresses, some persons will be added and others will be dropped as candidates for particular positions. Not infrequently, an understudy is moved to still another position and a new understudy must be found. Nevertheless, preparation of staffing plans serves a very useful purpose in pointing up where available replacements or candidates for new positions are lacking. Moreover, it forces realistic review of the persons who are likely to be promoted; if they need further development, immediate steps may be taken to start the necessary training.

Staffing plans are, of course, confidential documents because they reflect highly tentative promotion plans that may have to be revised later. For this reason, some executives prefer never to put their ideas down in writing. For smaller companies or for a single department this may be satisfactory, *provided* the same basic thinking takes place. The chart is merely a device to help an executive think through a very "iffy" subject. It is the systematic analysis of executive placement, rather than the particular pieces of paper, that is important.

Methods of selection

Planned placement of executives modifies, but by no means eliminates, the need for wise selection of individuals to fill executive positions. Possible candidates must first be identified; later, one of these may be designated as an understudy; and when the vacancy occurs, the final selection must be made. This sifting process should improve the selection because judgments are made at different times, often several years apart, and this provides opportunity to reconsider earlier impressions. In addition, there will, of course, be unexpected vacancies for which final selections must be made quickly.

The use of periodic appraisals to provide data on individuals and the matching of such data against position descriptions and person specifications have already been recommended. The surprising thing is how often these basic steps in selection are disregarded. Many executives are inclined to substitute their intuitive likes and dislikes of individuals for the analytical approach suggested.

Selection will also be improved generally if *group judgment* is used. The appraisal of individuals involves so many intangibles and personal bias is so difficult to remove that the views of at least two or three people should be considered in making executive decisions. The final decision usually rests with the immediate supervisor, subject to approval by the boss. In addition, the views of other executives who have worked with the candidate, and of the central personnel advisor who has studied all available candidates, should be considered. Often the views of all these people will confirm the wisdom of the proposed selection. If there is a difference of opinion, then a warning has been raised and further observation on the points in question can be made. Probably in no other phase of business administration is group judgment more valuable than in executive selection.

When tentative selections of one or more candidates for a position are made several years before the actual vacancies occur, *trial on the job* may be possible. A candidate may pinch-hit in the job when the present incumbent is off on vacation or on special assignment. This is not an adequate test because usually the interval is too short for the candidate to exercise much initiative, but it may throw some light on that person's capabilities.

A more likely arrangement is to assign the candidates to work in a department or a branch where they can demonstrate ability to do certain phases of the work. Such assignments typically serve the purpose of both training and selection. If time permits, people may be tried out in several different positions. What people have done in the past is no definite assurance of what they will do in the future, but it is probably the best evidence we can obtain.

No mention has been made of psychological tests for selecting executives. When a quick selection has to be made from individuals outside the company, test data may be a useful supplement to other sources of information. However, when careful appraisals of people already in the company are possible and group judgment and trial on a series of different jobs can be utilized, psychological tests in their present state of development rarely add much that is useful.

DEVELOPMENT OF EXECUTIVE TALENT

Executive training cannot be accomplished well *en masse*. As already noted, executive training deals with a relatively few individuals each of whom is typically in a different stage of development and is preparing for a different job. Consequently, executive training should be approached on an individual basis.

Plans center on individuals

The planning for executive progression, already described, points to the areas where each individual needs further development. Any gap between the specifications for a position and the abilities already possessed by the candidate should receive attention in the development plan. Likewise, if a person's performance on the present job does not measure up to what is desired, these weaknesses should be corrected.

One company asks the following questions in designing a development program for each executive:[2]

Designing an Executive Development Program
1. WHAT IS THE PERSON? What are the candidate's executive qualifications, strengths, and weaknesses?
2. WHAT MAY THE PERSON BECOME? What are the candidate's possibilities and growth potential?
3. WHAT DOES THE PERSON NEED TO GET THERE? What experience does the candidate still need for the position aspired to?
4. WHAT PLANNED COURSE OF ACTION SHOULD BE TAKEN? What action is needed to fill the gaps in the candidate's experience?

One aspect of individual development plans deserves emphasis. Most of the initiative and the work must come from the individuals themselves. To be sure, the company has a vital stake in the matter and typically does a number of things to assist in the process. Nevertheless, good executives cannot be developed unless the persons do a large share of the work. Since in this chapter we are concerned with company action, our discussion necessarily focuses on what managers can do to guide and aid the process.

Training on the job

By far the most important and lasting training an executive receives is on-the-job training. In all types of work there is no adequate substitute for actually doing the operation; this applies to executive planning, direction, and control fully as much as it does to selling or operating a machine.

Supervisors or other executives close to operations can make work experience much more valuable if they will *coach* the people being trained. Just as athletic coaches make suggestions, watch performance, point out weaknesses, and encourage athletes to do better, so may executives help their subordinates to learn on the job. Good coaches need to understand the emotional as well as the intellectual makeup of their proteges and to use discretion in the time and the manner in which they make suggestions. They need to cultivate mutual respect and a desire for improvement. Conceived in this manner, the combination of work experience plus coaching can become a powerful tool for executive development.

---

[2] Formulated by George B. Corless, Standard Oil Company of New Jersey.

When an individual is a candidate for the position of an immediate boss, the *understudy* method may be employed. The younger person takes every available opportunity to put himself mentally in his boss's situation and to think through what action he would take if the responsibility were his. The senior, in turn, welcomes suggestions and wherever practical permits the understudy to participate in action or even to carry out particular projects on his own responsibility.

Often an executive cannot get all the needed training on a single job. For example, in preparing for the position of sales manager, the person may spend several years as a sales representative, two or three years in the sales promotion division, perhaps five years as a branch manager, and at least three or four years as an assistant sales manager. Many companies make a regular practice of such *job rotation* for purposes of executive training. The staffing plans described previously may provide for transfers that do not immediately put the best person available in each vacancy; instead they use some of these vacancies as training spots for individuals who are thought to have high executive potentials.

Job rotation for executive development normally assumes that a person will fill a given position for a few years and will show the ability to handle that job well before being moved on to the next position.

Training off the job

A variety of activities are useful supplements to training on the job. The following list, while by no means complete, indicates some of the possibilities.

Committees. Committees are rarely established solely for the purpose of training. Nevertheless, they often do provide fine opportunity to sense the viewpoints of other departments and to become acquainted with problems outside the normal scope of one's position. Consequently, people may be assigned to committees partly for the training they will get from participation.

Company conferences and courses. When a company undertakes a new activity or a new approach to some function, such as operations research or management-by-results, conferences or perhaps even a whole course on that subject may be desirable. The difficulty of finding a subject and a time when enough executives can attend such courses places a definite limit on how far this type of training can be carried.

Industry contacts. Literally thousands of trade associations hold meetings and make studies on various problems relating to their particular industries. Work with such trade associations, or with professional associations, provides a range of new ideas and an opportunity to explore problems with persons who are not indoctrinated with the same company approach. Trips to other offices or plants often have the same broadening effect.

University courses. Universities are giving increasing attention to executive education and often provide a variety of courses on business subjects. Many companies encourage their executives to take courses in areas where they have limited background. Also, several universities are offering intensive 4- to 12-week courses in top-management problems; these are particularly valuable for persons who are moving from departmental positions to jobs demanding wider perspective.

Individual reading. Few executives have the time or the energy, after a busy day, to study long and difficult books. They often do gain much information, however, from regular reading of trade periodicals and professional journals. Also, if they are assigned some special project, they may do considerable outside reading.

Adaptation of off-the-job training to individual needs is particularly important because the executive has only limited time to devote to such purposes. The executive has a major job to perform and, in trying to get the maximum benefit from on-the-job training, does not want to slight this major assignment. Consequently, the off-the-job training should have real significance for the individual to justify the additional effort it entails.

EXECUTIVE COMPENSATION

Plans for executive selection, promotion, and development will lead to limited success unless the executives believe that their compensation is reasonable. To round out the picture, then, we need to take a brief look at such issues as base salaries and pensions, executive bonuses, stock options, and nonfinancial compensation for executives.

Base salaries and pensions

The setting of executive salaries may be approached in the same way as was recommended for lower-level salaries in Chapter 12:

1. The different positions are compared with one another in order to establish a reasonable internal alignment. Usually salary grades are not necessary, but the several positions should be at least ranked and some means used to determine the approximate spread between the different positions.
2. Executive salaries are related to outside compensation. This is difficult, because comparable jobs in different companies are hard to find. Usually it is possible, however, to set the president's salary in some reasonable relationship to companies of similar size in the same industry. Also, salaries of junior executives frequently tie into, or overlap, those established under the employees' salary administration plan. With both ends of the "salary curve" established, a general curve for the entire group can be drawn.
3. Allowances for individual differences are made by establishing a range from starting salary to maximum for each position.

This approach to executive salaries is far from exact. The relative importance of positions is hard to measure and is likely to be colored by the efficiency or the inefficiency of the particular incumbent. Nevertheless, a decision as to salary has to be made, and this approach is as fair as anything yet devised.

Because of the uncertainty in evaluating individual positions, and also because there can be a wide difference in the individual performance of persons holding the same position, a wide salary range often with a 50% spread from the minimum to the maximum for a given job is customary. For example, it might be determined that the president should be paid somewhere between $50,000 and $75,000 per year, whereas the sales manager should be paid between $30,000 and $45,000 per year. This still leaves room for considerable judgment regarding the specific salaries, but there are at least some general guides from which to work.

Executive bonuses

Many companies use bonuses for their executives. In fact, one recent study shows that approximately 50% of all companies use this method of compensation in one form or another. Bonuses enable the company to vary executive compensation in good and bad times, and they serve as an important incentive.

The use of a bonus plan is illustrated by a lumbering concern that recently received stockholder approval for an executive bonus fund. A 6% return on the total stockholder investment is first set aside from net profit; then 20% of any profit in excess of this amount is put into the executive bonus fund. The division of the fund among the several executives is determined by the board of directors. Actually, percentage shares amounting to approximately three fourths of the total fund are assigned at the beginning of the year, at the same time that base pay for the executives is set. The remainder of the fund is kept in a "kitty" and is used to reward special performance during the year.

Variations on this general pattern can be made with respect to the size of the total fund and also the division of the fund among the several executives. But the general idea of a fund somehow related to profits is fairly common practice. Of course, many special bonus arrangements are designed to meet particular situations. For example, a sales manager may receive a bonus on total sales volume. Whenever such special arrangements are made, care must be taken to make sure the executive works as a member of the total management team, even though his bonus is determined by only one or two factors.

When executives have an opportunity to earn a large bonus, the size of their base salaries is usually cut. In general, the base salary plus the average bonus that will be earned over a period of years should about equal the total amount that would have to be paid a comparable executive earning salary alone.

Stock options

Executives may be given an opportunity to buy stock in their company for several reasons. Some people believe that stock ownership will significantly increase an executive's interest in company welfare. In other cases the company may not be able to pay executives a cash salary and bonus large enough to retain their services, and some form of stock bonus or stock option is used to supplement the cash compensation. By no means the least important reason for using stock options and similar schemes is an attempt to help executives meet their personal income tax problems.

Since income taxes rise sharply as the amount of the annual income increases, many executives find that a large portion of their bonus has to be paid to Uncle Sam. Consequently, executives would prefer to have their income relatively stable, rather than large in some years and small in others. Even better, they would like some arrangement to have their financial returns from the company classified as a capital gain on which the income tax is substantially less than on current income. Stock option plans, which give an employee the privilege of purchasing the company stock at some stipulated figure, may help an executive meet these personal income tax problems.

The laws and rulings on such matters are highly technical, but in general they provide that if executives buy stock below the current market value, they have to consider the difference between their purchase price and the market value as current income. Under special circumstances, they may be given an option to buy stock at close to the market price prevailing when the option is granted, then wait for the price rise before exercising the option, and still count their profit as capital gains. If executives hold their stock over a period of years and the market value rises in the meantime, they can, of course, sell the stock at the higher price and treat the rise in value as a capital gain. In general, then, stock options do not enable executives to avoid personal income tax. They may, however, give them more flexibility in adjusting the time when the income is considered to be earned, and possibly the income from a stock option may be treated as a capital gain.

Nonfinancial compensation

In thinking about executive compensation, we should recognize that virtually all managers are motivated by nonfinancial considerations as well as the cash payment for their services. In fact, after salaries enable them to live comfortably, the nonfinancial factors become increasingly important. For example, some persons respond to the urge for power, others desire social prestige, and some will sacrifice additional income for security. Improving the company's position in its industry or otherwise "winning the game" is often a strong spur, and the desire to create something and to render social service is a more common motive than is generally realized.

The ability of a company to provide such nonfinancial compensations usually is not a matter of deliberate decision by the board of directors; nevertheless, they are vital forces in enabling the company to attract and retain competent executives, and they should be recognized when decisions are being made regarding financial compensation.

SUMMARY

An able corps of executives is crucial for the execution of any strategy. The selection and the development of executive talent often is given inadequate attention, however, because problems are not diagnosed far enough in advance and because personal relationships may make an administrator reluctant to take the necessary action.

A systematic approach to building the needed corps of executives includes: (1) anticipating executive requirements through advance organization planning and forecasts of the positions to be filled along with specifications for persons needed to fill them; (2) taking an inventory of executive talent available within the company; (3) developing tentative plans for using the available talent to fill the anticipated positions, and noting needs for further training or additions; (4) developing individuals to meet their current and planned responsibilities through on-the-job and off-the-job training, and (5) providing compensation that will attract the quality of executives required and keep their morale high.

Larger companies may find printed forms and standardized procedures helpful, whereas the central managers in smaller firms may use the same method of attack with no formal paper work. In fact, there is always danger that the use of forms will become a substitute, rather than an aid, for the careful thought that development of good executive personnel demands.

Flexibility in the use of this systematic approach is necessary to adapt it to individuals. Developing executive talent is always a personalized matter, and no standard approach will fit all situations exactly. Application to a particular group of persons, or to a single department within a company, calls for ingenuity, especially in preparation for major changes.

QUESTIONS FOR CLASS DISCUSSION

1. How do executive personnel problems and the practical ways of dealing with such problems differ in Stage I, Stage II, Stage III, and Stage IV companies (described in Chapter 16)?

2. In family-controlled companies, the selection of presidents is often settled by birth, and everyone recognizes this. (a) What effect does such nepotism have on the total task of having qualified, well-motivated executives? (b) How should Junior be prepared for his eventual assignment? (c) Does nepotism generally result in a company's having less qualified executives than it would if no one had an "inside track to the top"?

3. (a) Company objectives differ for product lines in various phases of their growth as explained on pages 280-282. How will such differences in objectives affect executive personnel (1) requirements and (2) compensation and other incentives? (b) Companies now include socially responsible action among their objectives.

How can contributions toward these objectives be recognized as executive compensation and other incentives?

4. "The competition of company recruiters for the good college seniors is undesirable. Pay rates are bid up so high that the embryo executives are overpaid relative to other employees; this upsets morale, puts the new person in a tough spot, interferes with sound training, and makes salary increases during the first five years small. Also, the college seniors get such an inflated idea of their importance that they aren't worth much when you do hire them." Relate this statement to executive personnel practices described in this chapter. What should a company needing a reservoir of potential executives do about this kind of a situation?

5. How should the concept of "equal opportunity" be incorporated into the executive personnel practices examined in this chapter? Should preference in selection be given to any categories of candidates—such as blacks, women, native-born, mature, agnostic, etc.—which at present have disproportionately low representation in a tier or level of management jobs?

6. "The economic mission of some companies permits a lot of individual initiative and freedom of action, but many other firms such as public utilities and mass production operations require steady dependability to create the services people need. No organizational arrangement can change these basic requirements. Consequently, most of the younger generation that defies regulated behavior would be misfits in the latter type of business and should not be hired." Do you agree with this statement? Should organizations be modified to accommodate rebellious youth, and if so, how?

7. (a) When should executives be brought in from other companies? (b) How can this be done with the least disruption of morale to individuals already working for the company? (c) Does such action indicate a failure on someone's part in his executive development duties? (d) How does the concept of a dynamic strategy, emphasized earlier in this book, relate to the preceding questions?

8. Should two or more persons be kept in active competition for an executive position that will be vacated by retirement, or should a single "crown prince" be selected several years in advance? What are the advantages and the disadvantages of each system?

9. In Wardwell Vinyl Coatings, Inc., described on pages 268-274, the president would like to leave the company and enter politics. (a) What executive personnel difficulties would Mr. Beckley Wardwell's resignation at this time create? (b) How could these difficulties have been avoided? (c) If Mr. Wardwell agrees to stay with the company for two years, what actions should be taken in anticipation of his resignation at that time?

CASE 19 / Mercury Petroleum, Inc.

Shortly before he was about to be chosen for the job of Vice-President, Manufacturing, Mr. L. D. Shaw, a highly successful district manager, stated to a member of the board of directors that he would probably leave Mercury Petroleum in the near future. This disturbed the smooth and even course of the directors' deliberations. Their distaste for the interruption set some of them to thinking about other executive problems.

Mercury Petroleum, Inc. produces asphalt and tar products, which it sells to builders, contractors, government agencies, and large institutional buyers for their use on roads, roofs, and other building products. Although Mercury owns some producing oil wells in Wyoming, it does no refining. Rather, it sells its heavy crude oil to independent refineries and then purchases or repurchases the bottom ends from the refiners' distillation work for further processing in its own local plants.

Since the costs of transporting asphalt and tar products are high in relation to the sales value of the asphalts, the company builds local plants to serve its customers' needs. The plants are organized into seven districts, with the districts reporting to the Denver headquarters (see organization diagram on the following page).

The formal organization within each district is highly uniform since product, customers, and work to be done are stable and change little in their nature (although not in quantity) from year to year. Each plant superintendent is responsible for the activities of 1 or 2 local salesmen, 2 to 8 plant employees, and 1 or 2 office employees. Each district sales manager supervises salesmen in territories outside the plant cities and is also directly accountable for total district sales. He reports to the district manager, but commonly he spends a more significant portion of his time reporting to the Vice-President, Marketing. The district office superintendent reports to the district manager about all personnel and credit matters, but he is directly responsible to the Vice-President, Finance for all accounting and treasury procedures, for credit management policy, and for all cash transactions.

The district manager's major function is to ensure the profitability of his district as primarily measured by the return on investment in his district. In doing this he reports to both the Vice-President, Manufacturing and the Vice-President, Marketing. Matters relating to plant processes and equipment are determined by the Vice-President, Manufacturing except for questions about trucks used locally. These are the responsibility of the truck fleet manager.

In line with the district managers' responsibility for return on investment, their pay is partially salary and partially bonus. Each district manager receives a base salary of $25,000 and a bonus that varies as follows:

Return on Investment —Before Taxes on District Capitalization	Bonus as Percent of Base Salary
12%	0%
14	10
16	22
18	35
20	50
22	60
24	70
26	80
28	90
30	100
32 and above	100% plus 30% of district profits earned above the 32% return on investment rate.

Current Organization Diagram

Mercury Petroleum, Inc.

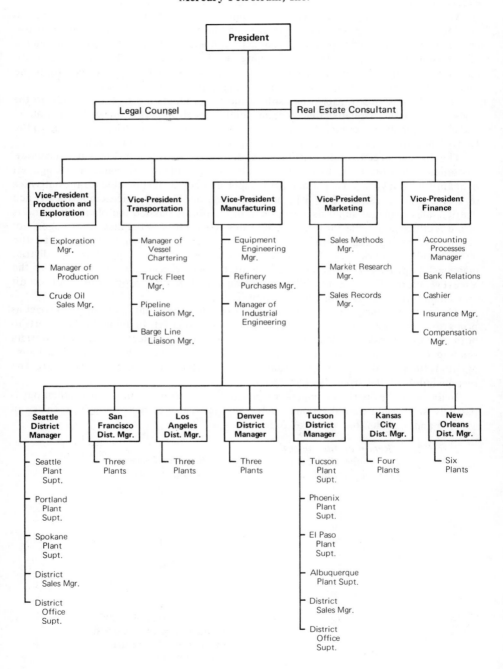

As is common amongst petroleum producing companies, Mercury has generous medical, group-life, and disability insurance plans; a pension plan to which each employee can contribute between 5% and 7½% of his salary (the company matches this, and the company's portion vests with the employee after 10 years' service); and a plan that allows each employee to allocate up to 10% of his salary toward the purchase of the company's common stock.

Since the nature of their work is reasonably stable and since they are not as directly responsible for profits of the company as are the district managers, local employees—including the superintendents—as well as department managers at headquarters are paid according to various salary scales that have beginning rates for each job and a range above this governed by location, seniority, and merit considerations.

The president and the vice-presidents share an executive bonus set each year in regard to total amount and who gets it by the Personnel Committee of the Board of Directors. The bonus is in addition to annual salaries of $50,000 for the vice-presidents and $75,000 for the president.

The following abstract from company personnel records shows ages, education, length of service, and salary ranges for selected managerial personnel; the abstract from company financial records shows comparative sales volume and return on investment for the various districts.

Abstract from Company Personnel Records

Manager	Age	Education or Degree Earned	Years with Company
Exploration	62	B.S. Geol.	40
Crude Oil Sales	44	M.B.A.	5
Truck Fleet	58	B.S.M.E.	31
Barge Line Liaison	63	B.S.B.A.	40
Refinery Purchases	60	B.S. Pet.E.	25
Accounting Processes	56	C.P.A.	26
Cashier	63	C.P.A.	42
Compensation	56	C.P.A.	33
San Francisco Dist.	42	M.B.A.	5
Los Angeles Dist.	44	B.S.B.A.	8
Kansas City Dist.	39	M.B.A.	2
Seattle Plant Supt.	64	Some High School	46
Spokane Plant Supt.	52	High School	22
Seattle Dist. Office Supt.	59	High School	30
Phoenix Plant Supt.	49	B.S.C.E.	27
Albuquerque Plant Supt.	52	High School	35
Tucson Dist. Office Supt.	48	B.S.C.E.	23
Transportation V.P.	60	B.S.B.A.	38
Marketing V.P.	59	A.B.	26
President	55	M.S. Geol.	3

Salary Ranges

Plant Superintendent	$15,000-$27,500
District Sales Manager	15,000- 27,500
District Office Superintendent	12,500- 22,500
Headquarters Managers	25,000- 50,000

Abstract from Company Financial Records

Index Number of Sales Volume (Present Year = 100)	Districts						
	Seattle	San Francisco	Los Angeles	Denver	Tucson	Kansas City	New Orleans
Current Year	100	100	100	100	100	100	100
Previous Years	96	94	93	98	95	93	95
" "	88	88	86	92	90	87	80
" "	80	82	79	88	86	82	70
" "	56	76	72	85	85	78	55
" "	46	70	65	82	84	74	50
Return on Investment, District Capitalization							
Current Year	n.a.	n.a.	n.a.	n.a.	n.a.	n.a.	n.a.
Previous Years	16%	12%	11%	24%	18%	14%	18%
" "	16	10	10	22	14	12	16%
" "	14	12	12	20	12	10	15%
" "	14	10	11	18	8	12	14%
" "	13	14	12	18	8	16	16%

Mr. G. B. Vance came to Mercury Petroleum 5 years ago from a subsidiary of the Humble Oil Company to be manager of the New Orleans District. During his tenure he has added 2 local plants and expanded sales from Louisiana and southern Mississippi to a marketing area covering Louisiana, Mississippi, Alabama, Arkansas, and western Tennessee. Mr. Vance is characterized by other managers as "belonging to the scientific school of management" and "ruling his district with an iron hand." His bonus percentages have been (in order) 22, 10, 18, 22, and 35. New Orleans employees say about him: ". . . sees that the job is done," and ". . . pays close attention to results."

Mr. G. C. Kurtz is now Tucson District Manager and has been there a year after 4 years in Seattle. He stepped into the Seattle District Manager's job from a sales supervisory position with the Chevron Oil Company. During his tenure in Seattle, sales doubled and a new plant was opened in Spokane. Mr. Kurtz took over a district with a poor performance record and a high turnover among office employees and converted it, through a great deal of work with the district's employees, into a satisfactory operation. When he left Seattle, the Seattle District Office Superintendent also requested a transfer to Tucson, but this was denied by the Vice-President, Finance.

Mr. Kurtz's bonus percentages at Seattle were 5, 10, and 22. Former Seattle employees have said: "You can walk into his office. and talk to him at any time." "Listens to your problems on and off the job and gives what advice he can." "Knows every employee."

Mr. L. D. Shaw now manages the Denver District. He came to Mercury Petroleum from the Union Oil Company for which he had been manager of a small refinery that Union Oil closed. Since taking over responsibility for the Denver District, Mr. Shaw has supervised the closing of one subsidiary plant in Clovis, New Mexico, and seen to the substantial re-equipment of 2 others. Sales have been relatively stable in the district and his bonus percentages have been 35, 60, and 70. Those who know him characterize Shaw as "energetic, competent, great drive." As part of his effort to make the Denver operation efficient, Mr. Shaw has insisted that the percent of salaries to sales for the district be cut 5%. This has been achieved through minimizing all wage increases and through hiring only at the base rate for any job.

Shaw, perhaps using his location as an advantage and after his initial success in closing out the Clovis operation, has been able to make his presentation for capital requests and price arrangements directly to committees of the Board of Directors and has uniformly gotten their approval. He incorporates in these presentations ideas from prior consultation with the Vice-President, Manufacturing.

Comments about Mr. Shaw from employees in the Denver District office are: "Demanding." "Wants to know what you are doing." "Leaves you alone as long as you tell him what your plans are." "Don't talk to a headquarters manager unless Shaw has cleared it first." "Don't recommend anything to anyone except Shaw."

The Vice-President, Manufacturing is about to retire and someone is needed to fill his job. The Personnel Committee of the Board of Directors considered none of the headquarters staff managers to have a broad enough experience to qualify, so they looked at the various district managers. Three are under consideration: Kurtz, Vance, and Shaw. But committee members were jolted when the Vice-President, Manufacturing told them: "I talked with Shaw recently about his future at Mercury Petroleum. He told me that he was about to leave for a job with another oil company as a refinery manager. That job may have a higher salary than his as a district manager but certainly not as much as he would get here as Vice-President, Manufacturing and it involves only one location. Shaw said he didn't like the 'administrative atmosphere' here—whatever that means. Certainly we haven't opposed him."

One committee member responded: "Perhaps we should look at all our district managers. I haven't liked going outside the firm to hire them, as we have had to do. And then a large number of them leave after being with us for only a few years. It's too bad we haven't been able to persuade more of the plant superintendents to try to move up. Maybe we should raise the district managers' base salary to $30,000 and cut down on the bonus percentages."

Another commented: "Our real problem is that no managers at headquarters seem to us qualified for promotion. They are good on their jobs and get all the chance at specialized training and at attending specialized conferences that they want. What else should we do?"

Required: (a) What should Mercury Petroleum, Inc. do to fill the Vice-President, Manufacturing vacancy?

(b) What changes, if any, should Mercury Petroleum make in its executive personnel practices?

INTEGRATING CASES / Strategy and Organization Structure

HOLDEN FARMS AND STORES PTY., LTD.[1]

The year that Grady Bratten, Managing Director of Holden Farms and Stores Pty., Ltd. of Bunbury, Western Australia, had allotted to gaining more experience with the retail grocery business and to becoming thoroughly acquainted with the members of his organization was now over. It was time, he knew, to see to it that the formal organization of his firm's three-part operation was rationalized and simplified and that the roles and responsibilities of the various executives were allocated so that the company could take advantage of the opportunities for growth that were surely before it. So he turned to his Assistant Managing Director, John White, for advice about reorganizing and for a plan to put any proposed changes into effect.

Two years ago Holden Farms and Stores, then located in Albany, a small city of about 15,000 inhabitants on the southern coast of Western Australia, purchased as an investment 80% of the common shares of Cooperative Groceterias, Ltd. The latter firm had originally been a wholesaler of dry groceries throughout the southwestern part of Western Australia. In recent years it had acquired some of its client retail stores and it now operates both as a wholesaler of dry groceries, frozen foods, and miscellaneous grocery products and as a chain of small-to-medium-sized grocery stores in towns and cities in the southwest but outside the Perth metropolitan area. Cooperative Groceterias also owns one store in Geraldton, a city on the Indian Ocean some 300 miles north of Perth.

The firm of Holden Farms and Stores had been owned for several generations by the Bratten family. From a small beginning as a dairy farm, the company had grown until it owned several dairy farms, a poultry farm, a sheep and wheat station,[2] and two retail grocery stores in Albany bought just prior to the acquisition of Cooperative Groceterias. (See Exhibits 1 and 2 for financial information.)

A year ago, following a second acquisition by Holden Farms and Stores of 85% of the common shares of Allied Supermarkets, Ltd., the headquarters of the firm was moved to Bunbury, a port city on the Indian Ocean about 110 miles south of Perth. Bunbury is more centrally located to serve the southwestern part of the state than is Albany. Exhibit 3 gives the location of Allied Supermarkets' stores.

Both Mr. Bratten and Mr. White agree that the present organization structure has to be simplified to increase effectiveness and to reduce overlapping responsibilities and

---

[1] A "limited company, proprietary" is—in Australia—a closely held corporation with less than twenty stockholders but with all the benefits of a limited company and some tax advantages.
[2] A "station" in Australia is a very large ranch.

Exhibit 1

Comparative Balance Sheets
(All figures in thousands of dollars, Australian)

	Allied Supermarkets		Cooperative Groceterias		Holden Farms and Stores	
Current Assets:						
Cash, Receivables	700		435		300	
Stock	1,560		1,026		286	
		2,260		1,461		586
Investments						6,900
Fixed Assets:						
Buildings, Equipment	5,478		3,390		2,600	
Less Depreciation Reserves .	2,559		1,470		1,200	
		2,919		1,920		1,400
Land		441		234		450
Livestock, etc.						580
		5,620		3,615		9,916
Current Liabilities:						
A/Cs Payable, Demand Loans		1,773		759		480
Mortgage Loans		1,827		1,362		2,050
Shareholders' Fund:						
Issued Capital	800		480		300	
Retained Earnings	1,220	2,020	1,014	1,494	7,086	7,386
		5,620		3,615		9,916
Contingent Liabilities:						
Leasehold Payments to 30.6.91		$7,500		$2,550		——

that the new organizational design should allow for the continued addition of new operating units since the directors of Holden Farms and Stores Pty., Ltd. expect to invest about $500,000[3] each year in the company's expansion. Mr. Bratten also believes that the purchasing activities of Allied Supermarkets should be made a part of the wholesaling operation of Cooperative Groceterias to increase the efficiency of purchasing.

After thinking about the question of executive roles, Mr. Bratten has concluded that he would be most comfortable in his own position if no more than three or four operating executives report to him in addition to the Director of Development (whose staff does much of the analytical work on new projects) and Mr. White, the Assistant Managing Director. John White ordinarily is responsible for special projects (such as the reorganization task) but also acts for Mr. Bratten during the latter's vacations and trips.

James Salmon, Managing Director of Cooperative Groceterias, claims that his wholesaling and retailing operations are now well-balanced. "Our own stores and other retail customers are not the typical supermarkets you find in Perth with its population of

---

[3] All monetary amounts are expressed in Australian dollars.

Exhibit 2

Other Financial Information

(All figures in thousands of dollars, Australian)

	Allied		Cooperative		Holden Farms	
	Sales[4]	*Net Income*[1]	*Sales*[2,4]	*Net Income*[1]	*Sales*	*Net Income*[1]
Current Year	21,500	580	14,481	160	17,700	882
Last Year	19,800	495	13,100	145	24,100	n.a.[3]
Previous Year	18,000	432	12,000	134	n.a.	n.a.
" "	15,200	350	10,800	130	——	——
" "	14,600	320	10,000	120	——	——
" "	13,800	275	9,500	140	——	——
" "	13,000	274	9,000	135	——	——
" "	12,200	256	8,600	130	——	——
" "	11,500	220	8,200	120	——	——
" "	10,800	206	7,800	104	——	——
Ten Years Ago ...	10,150	201	7,500	100	——	——

[1] Net income after tax. The current effective tax rate for limited proprietary companies was 42% of income.

[2] Sales of the wholesale division (which were purchases of the retail stores) were close to 47% of this total.

[3] Not available. Accounting practices for agricultural operations differed significantly in previous years from those of retail and industrial organizations.

[4] Purchases of bakery goods were about 6% of this total. One of the Allied Stores bought its bakery goods from Blackbird Bakery because the two managers were close friends.

750,000 people. We cater to local people who want their own tastes and attitudes recognized and who use the stores for social purposes as well as a location to buy food and then often have it delivered. Our store managers have to be carefully selected since they must know and cater to their particular groups of customers as well as handle adequately the usual tasks of controlling spoilage, training and managing clerks and cashiers, and liaison with the warehouse. With modern telephone and computer facilities, we control both the retail inventories and the deliveries from the warehouse to minimize costs and stock-outs. To tie in to our purchasing and warehousing facilities, a retail store has to be able to sell at slightly higher prices overall than the larger supermarkets—about 19% to 20% gross margin—because it will be ordering more frequently and in smaller lots. It will have less space than the typical Safeway or Allied Supermarkets store, and it will use different selling methods.

"It would be technically feasible for us to do some of the purchasing and warehousing for the Perth stores since they are only three hours by truck from Bunbury, but we would have to increase our investment in plant, equipment, and inventories by 25% to do so. My guess is that a detailed study would show that lower wage, building, and other costs in Bunbury would offset the trucking costs enough to justify expansion here rather than in new facilities in Perth. We would have to price the dry groceries, frozen foods, and miscellaneous household items—the lines that could most probably be handled from here—at costs to the Allied stores which would give us an after-tax profit of ½ of 1% of sales.

"This is a nice little operation we have going here now. There is still room for some cost reduction, and I can see a steady growth in sales ahead of us. The Brattens did well when they bought us."

Allied Supermarkets, Ltd. operates the six retail grocery stores indicated in Exhibit 3. In addition, the firm has an option to buy for $420,000 a site in a rapidly developing southern suburb of Perth. Mr. Whitten, Managing Director of Allied Supermarkets, and his staff had obtained the option and carried out the preliminary studies. They believe that the proposal is now ready for consideration by the directors of Allied Supermarkets, Ltd.[4]

Organization diagrams for Allied Supermarkets, Cooperative Groceterias, and Holden Farms and Stores are shown in Exhibits 4A, 4B, and 4C respectively on pages 448-450.

Allied Supermarkets, with headquarters in Perth, has full staff services there, as shown in Exhibit 4. Purchasing for the chain is Mr. Pullman's responsibility. Over the years as the chain grew, Mr. Pullman has changed his sources from wholesalers to buying direct from manufacturers and farmers. He buys produce to some extent at the central market but is moving more and more to annual contracts with some of the many truck farmers of Yugoslavian origin who grow vegetables through intensive-farming near Perth. Mr. Pullman explained: "For worthwhile price discounts from the manufacturers, we must order anywhere from a week to a month in advance.

Exhibit 3

Location of Stores

	Population	Distance from Perth	Distance from Bunbury	Allied Super-markets	Coopera-tive Gro-ceterias	Holden
Perth............	750,000	——		#1, #2, #3, #4		
Bunbury.........	20,000	110 mi.	——	#5	#1, #2	
Geraldton	20,000	300 "	410 mi.	#6	#3	
Busselton........	7,000	150 "	40 "		#4	
Margaret River ..	3,000	180 "	70 "		#9	
Manjimup	6,000	190 "	80 "		#5	
Collie	12,000	130 "	30 "		#6	
Mandurah	5,000	55 "	55 "		#7	
Midland	18,000	20 "	120 "		#8	
Albany	15,000	280 "	210 "			#1, #2

[4] Preliminary estimates indicated that a new retail building, with plentiful parking facilities, could be erected for $750,000, that equipment and fixtures would amount to $480,000, and that inventory would average $300,000—making a gross investment, including the land, of $1,950,000. However, the plan provided for a sale and lease-back of the land and building, with an annual rental of $140,000; and also rental of $300,000 of the equipment, at $43,000 per year. So the net investment would be $480,000. The firm expected its usual gross margin of 17% on predicted first year sales of $5,500,000. Wages were expected to be 9% of sales, miscellaneous expenses $30,000 per year, and depreciation on the owned equipment $18,000 per year. A study by an outside consultant indicated that several competing stores located with 3 miles of the new location would probably be opened during the next few years.

Exhibit 4A

ALLIED SUPERMARKETS
ORGANIZATION DIAGRAM

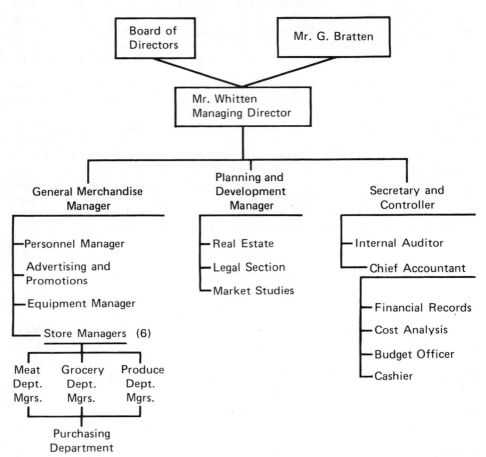

Our stores are large enough to receive drop shipments and to hold dry groceries, as necessary, in their own back rooms. Bakers generally have shelf-space allotted and control their own inventories. Through experience I have learned which farmers grow high-quality vegetables and which ones are open to new ideas, such as trickle-irrigation, to keep their costs down. Coordinating with the market gardeners demands much more scheduling and the time of two more buyers than would buying only at the produce market. But the higher quality of the produce is worth it. Take a look at our net profits and you will see what I mean. We are right up there with Safeway—the world's most efficient retail grocery chain—and we do better than the national chains such as Carter's and Coles New World Supermarkets."

George Forward, Director of Development for Holden Farms and Stores, currently has his staff analyzing the possibility of either acquiring an existing bakery or starting a

Exhibit 4B

COOPERATIVE GROCETERIAS
ORGANIZATION DIAGRAM

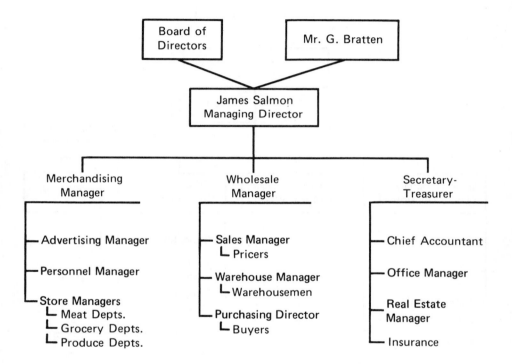

new one. A plant in either Perth or Bunbury could serve all the retail stores of the three operating companies except those in Geraldton. Mr. Bratten and the other directors of the firm had concluded some time ago that it might well be wise to extend the company's efforts into food processing since it was heavily committed at the farming and retail ends of the food industry but did no processing. Among the possibilities that occurred to them immediately were a poultry-processing plant that would utilize the eggs, hatchlings, and fryers now sold to others or an abbatoir to kill and cut the beef cattle now being raised extensively on the Linkletter, Wriston, and Rockefeller stations stretching east from Albany to Esperance. But a bakery has first priority for analysis.

Of the two alternatives available—purchasing an existing bakery or starting a new one to serve Holden's retail stores—Mr. Bratten prefers the former. In his view the capital equipment could be secured at a lower total cost, a new labor and executive force would not have to be trained, and key sales outlets would be available both from existing customers of the bakery and from Allied Supermarkets and Cooperative Groceterias units.

Exhibit 4C

HOLDEN FARMS AND STORES
ORGANIZATION DIAGRAM

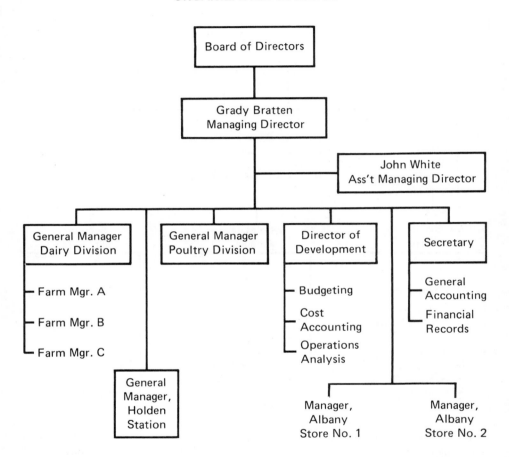

The development staff has completed a detailed and thorough survey of the bakery business in Australia, and a business broker has brought a potential purchase to Mr. Bratten's attention. Without repeating all the details or the extensive summary worked out by the staff, its conclusions can be stated briefly as:

1. The number of bakeries in Australia has declined 40% over the past twenty years.
2. Industry turnover[5] has risen 7% per year over the same period (with fluctuations around the average, of course.)
3. The number of production workers in bakeries is approximately the same as it was twenty years ago.
4. The average shopper spends 20% less of her shopping dollar on fresh bakery products now than she did twenty years ago.

---

[5] "Turnover" in Australia, as in Europe, is "sales" in the United States.

5. The real key to success in the bakery business is the control of stale returns. Stale returns are kept down by accurate forecasting of weekly sales by each customer.

Preliminary conversations with the Managing Director of Blackbird Bakery Pty., Ltd. (a family-owned concern located in Perth) indicate that the firm is for sale because none of his children wish to work for the bakery; he wants $500,000 in cash to diversify the family's investment; and he believes that he is now too old, at age 60, to effectively manage the company. (See Exhibit 5 for additional data.)

During conversations with various executives of the three firms about the question of establishing working relationships so as to make total operations both effective and efficient, John White has been struck by the firmness with which each man holds the idea that he should have either direct access to the Managing Director or, at the least, no less access than he now has. With that in mind, Mr. White began his task of recommending to Mr. Bratten a restructuring of the formal organization of the company.

Exhibit 5

Blackbird Bakery Pty., Ltd.

Current Balance Sheet

Cash and Receivables	$240,000	Current Liabilities	$200,000
Inventories	80,000	Mortgage Loan	100,000
Life Insurance—Cash		Net Worth	510,000
Surrender Value	50,000		
Buildings and Plant—			
Net after Deprecia-			
tion Reserve of			
$160,000	440,000	Total Liabilities	
Total Assets	$810,000	and Net Worth	$810,000

	Sales	Net Income After Tax
Current Year	$2,300,000	$43,000
Previous Year	2,200,000	44,000
" "	2,000,000	38,000
" "	1,700,000	30,000
" "	1,500,000	24,000

Note A–The firm has 23 production employees and a total of 38 employees. Executives responsible to the Managing Director (who is also the Sales Director) are the Plant Manager and the Secretary (who is responsible for accounting and office management).

QUESTIONS

1. If you were in Mr. White's position, what organization would you recommend to Mr. Bratten?
2. What provision have you made in your proposed organization for a bakery and/or a fifth Allied store? Do you believe the Blackbird Bakery should be acquired and the new Allied store built at this time?

THE HANCOCK COMPANY[1]

The Hancock Company is a chemical manufacturer making primarily drug chemicals such as vitamin preparations, sulfa drugs, antibiotics, hormones, and reagents. Its products are used by pharmaceutical and drug manufacturing concerns; veterinary products manufacturers; food and beverage manufacturing houses; educational, commercial, and industrial laboratories; industrial establishments; and ultimate consumers to whom they are dispensed by hospitals or physicians or on physician's prescription through retail drugstores.

Sales of the company have grown very rapidly, as shown by the following record:

Year	Sales	Year	Sales
25 years ago	$ 8,100,000	5 years ago	$ 81,100,000
20 years ago	8,370,000	3 years ago	93,200,000
15 years ago	15,660,000	2 years ago	108,500,000
10 years ago	37,350,000	Last year	111,700,000

Company profits have grown with sales, and its ratio of net profits to sales is about average for the large firms in the pharmaceutical industry.

No small part of this great expansion of sales has been the fruit of the extensive program of research that the company began in the early thirties and has continued to the present time. This department contains units specializing in organic and biochemical research, microbiological research, and physical and inorganic chemical research, plus a development unit specializing in chemical technology and production.

Since new products are frequently introduced into the line and the methods of use of the company products are constantly changing, the relative importance of different product groups in the sales pattern is constantly shifting. From time to time, new products or modifications of old products are introduced that do not fit exactly into existing product groups but that in either their research, production, or sales characteristics overlap almost any product grouping that may be set up.

For example, the table at the top of the following page shows the shifts in the percentage of total company sales volume experienced by a number of product groups, which for obvious reasons cannot be named specifically, during a period of 20 years.

These shifts in product line and sales volume naturally create planning and coordination problems, and this case is primarily concerned with the dynamic nature of the company's business. First the general organization will be briefly described; then measures taken to date for guiding individual products will be explained.

General organization

The general organization structure is indicated on the chart on the following page. Naturally the size and range of activities of each section varies, as is indicated in the following discussion.

---

[1] This case was written primarily by Professor Ralph S. Alexander for The Executive Program in Business Administration, Graduate School of Business, Columbia University. Reproduced by permission.

	Percent of Total Company Sales Volume		
Product group	25 years ago	15 years ago	5 years ago
A	11.3	10	5
B	9.6	8	5
C	7.7	2	—
D	7.3	5	1
E	7.0	12	0.5
F	6.9	3	2
G	3.9	4	3
H	3.9	2	0.3
I	3.8	4	1
J	—	15	27
K	—	7	6
L	—	—	15
M	—	—	12
N	—	—	9
Others	38.7	28	13.2

Production. Production is carried on in four plants, each of which has a manager, manufacturing manager, plant engineer, personnel manager, purchasing clerk, and financial services manager.

Plant	Location	Employees	Products
Main	Baltimore, Md.	4000	antibiotics, vitamin preparations, hormones, general drugs
Seneca	Oswego, N.Y.	1200	antibiotics, sulfa drugs, reagents, laboratory chemicals
Sawmill	Three Rivers, Mich.	1500	vitamins, hormones, antibiotics, general chemicals
Beacon	Beacon, N.Y.	550	specialty products for retail sale under Hancock label

In the Production Division there is a central Manufacturing Planning Department that (1) determines production requirements for all products and subdivisions consistent with production capacity, inventory levels, minimum costs, and related factors; (2) schedules all manufacturing, packaging, and quality testing operations; (3) establishes inventory levels for all goods and materials in accordance with established policies; (4) requisitions materials and containers; (5) maintains stock records for all types of goods and materials; and (6) collects and informs other divisions about production schedules, deliveries, inventories, batches, costs, charging rates, yields, raw material factors, and all other production matters.

Organization Chart—The Hancock Company

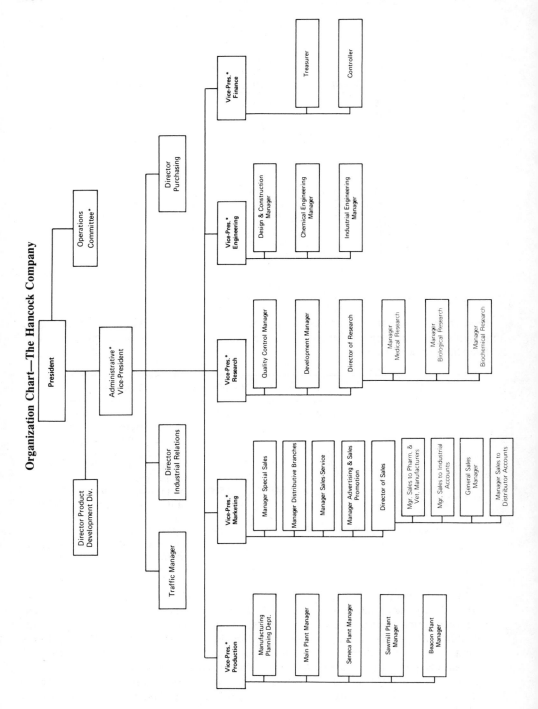

Marketing. The Manager of Special Sales handles all sales to competing or complementary firms and to all other house accounts. The Manager of Distributive Branches has charge of physical distribution of the products of the company through its four branch warehouses located at San Francisco, Chicago, St. Louis, and New York, and from the Baltimore plant. The Manager of Sales Service handles complaints and adjustments and plans and supervises the handling of the paperwork order routine. All advertising and sales promotion work is directed by the Manager of Advertising and Sales Promotion.

The General Sales Manager directs the activities of the field sales force through 20 district sales managers, each of whom has under his supervision about 10 sales representatives who call on wholesalers and pharmaceutical and veterinary manufacturers to make sales, on retailers to do missionary work, and on physicians and hospitals to do general promotional work. The Manager of Sales to Pharmaceutical and Veterinary Manufacturers and the Manager of Sales to Distributor Accounts develop policies, prepare plans, and generally supervise contact with the groups of customers they serve, working through the General Sales Manager in so doing. Neither of them has any direct official authority over sales representatives. The Manager of Sales to Industrial Accounts directs a force of 25 sales representatives; they have no necessary contact with the district sales offices beyond occasionally calling on those offices for desk space and secretarial service.

Research. All medical, biological, and biochemical research either is done in the laboratories in Baltimore or is closely administered from there. The Development Section, which assists in the development and improvement of production processes and in the solution of production problems in the various plants, has representatives stationed in each of the several factories.

Also in the Research Division is the important Quality Control Section, which is responsible for directing the establishment of quality standards and methods of testing. Purchased materials cannot be used in any plant until released by Quality Control; finished goods cannot be shipped until released by this section; and all wording on labels and advertising concerning quality must be approved.

Engineering. The Engineering Division is divided into three departments. The Design and Construction Department has charge of planning, construction, and installation of new equipment and facilities including buildings. The Industrial Engineering Department devotes its efforts to setting standards through time and motion studies and statistical analysis. It also studies operating methods and develops and plans improvements in equipment. The Chemical Engineering Department deals mainly with planning, development, and improvement of processes, including pilot plant operations on new products.

Records and finance. The activities of the Controller's Division and the Treasurer's Division are centralized in Baltimore, where a fairly complete battery of IBM machines is maintained. Customer billing is done there, and branch plant and warehouse payrolls are handled there. These divisions perform the normal accounting, tax, and financial functions, but they do not take an active part in the interpretation of financial data in terms of management problems.

Traffic. The Traffic Department handles all traffic operating procedures, selection of carriers, tariff work, schedules, and requests for rate revisions. Branch plants and sales branches comply with traffic instructions issued at Baltimore.

Purchasing. The work of the Purchasing Division is somewhat more decentralized. The purchasing clerks in each plant are authorized to write purchase orders up to $500 for any one order. In all other cases they requisition the central Purchasing Division in Baltimore.

Industrial relations. The Industrial Relations Division develops and administers employee relations programs to maintain high quality personnel and desirable employee attitudes. These programs include: personnel research, placement and education of employees, collective bargaining, wage and salary administration, employee services, security, health, and safety.

Special arrangements for products

The organization of The Hancock Company just described represents an expansion of the structure the company has had for many years. With the increase in dollar volume and number of products, however, a number of difficulties have arisen. To overcome these difficulties, a Product Development Division has been set up. The history of this division illustrates the character of the internal strains facing the company.

Product development. New products are typically discovered or at least developed in the Research Division. After a useful product has been found and the production processes have been worked out in the laboratory, it is then passed on to the Engineering Division for pilot-plant operation, planning of new equipment, and carrying through to the factory floor until the product is ready to be produced as a full-fledged member of the line.

Unfortunately, this arrangement for the technical aspects of new product work fails to solve all the problems connected with it. When a new article is ready for production and commercial use, it still has to be tested and released for distribution by the Food and Drug Administration and has to be worked into the sales line. If this work were left until the test-tube and pilot-plant stages were completed, the ultimate results from a profit standpoint might prove to be far from satisfactory. The commercial aspects of a new product need to be explored concurrently with its technical features. Stories are current in the industry of a firm that spent half a million dollars developing a new product only to find that its total possible sales were about $50,000 a year. The sales department was too heavily burdened with the day-to-day crises that attend the work of capturing and holding customers to do much with the task of exploring the market possibilities of a new product let alone that of appraising its probable effect on the cost and profit structure of the firm.

For many years top executives of The Hancock Company personally gave attention to this work, but as the company grew they had less and less time for it. After several make-shift arrangements, top management decided, five years ago, that a separate Product Development Department was needed. Mr. Paul Stanton was appointed head of this new unit, and he set out to explore the areas within which his unit might operate to the profit of the company.

Mr. Stanton soon felt himself handicapped by what seemed to him a lack of product policy on the part of the company. For example, there seemed to be no clear-cut determination as to the extent to which the company should sell products, such as insecticides, that were somewhat outside the drug field. There also seemed to be some confusion whether the company should develop a line of products to be sold over the retail drug counter under the Hancock label.

Exhibit A

(Statement for Organization Manual prepared by Mr. Stanton shortly after his appointment as Director of the newly created Product Development Department.)

Director, Product Development Department

Reports to: The President.

In carrying out his responsibilities he:

1. Correlates and directs all matters related to the establishment of new products by the company.
2. Surveys and analyzes the sales and market possibilities for present and new products in existing and new fields.
3. Determines sales potentials for products in development or suggested for development.
4. On the basis of market surveys and analyses, recommends development or production of new products.
5. Estimates actual sales of new products to guide the planning of necessary production and sales facilities.
6. Coordinates the company's efforts in developing new products, including the recommending of manufacturing capacity, sales programs, and distribution plans.
7. When necessary, carries out initial sales of new products prior to turning them over to the Marketing Division.
8. Studies and reports on the probable effects of the introduction of new products on the financial, cost, and profit structure of the company.

During the next three years, Mr. Stanton attempted to build up the organization of the Product Development Department and to expand its activities. (A statement of duties that Mr. Stanton prepared for inclusion in the company organization manual is given in Exhibit A.) In the process of doing so he engendered antagonism among several of the operating divisions to such a point that neither he nor his assistants were able to obtain the cooperation that was so vitally necessary to the proper performance of the department's functions. For example, he urged that the Product Development Department should employ a small force of specialty salesmen to conduct pilot marketing programs in the course of introducing new products to the market, and that most new products should not be turned over to the Marketing Division until the bugs had been worked out of the system of distributing them as well as producing them. This did not exactly endear his department to the members of the Marketing Division. Finally, Mr. Stanton made a connection elsewhere and left the company. His place was taken by Mr. John Boyle, a very able young man with excellent technical and business training, pleasing personality, and great vigor and drive, who previously had been an executive of a smaller company.

Marketing research. About this same time, at the suggestion of the Administrative Vice-President, careful study was given to the establishment of a Marketing Research Department. This step was finally decided upon when Mr. Boyle assumed direction of the Product Development Department (now elevated in the organization hierarchy to the status of a "division") and the new department was made a part of the enlarged division. Since Mr. Boyle was not able immediately to dissipate the lack of sympathy between his division and the sales groups and since the tasks of sales analysis and making sales estimates still remained in the Marketing Division, the work of the Marketing Research Department has been confined mainly to explorations of the market for new products and to economic studies for top management.

Product managers. The large number of products made by the company and their diversified nature caused other complications. Each product, or at least each group of them, possessed problems of its own with respect to its improvement, the control of its quality, its production, and its marketing. For example, the problems involved in handling narcotics are especially unique in the rigid control required because of government regulations and the socially dangerous nature of the products themselves. Several years ago the management decided that these problems required special attention. A product manager was appointed to devote all his attention to the narcotics line. Later, other persons were assigned to this type of work, each specializing in the problems of a separate group of products.

The responsibilities of a product manager are described in the organization manual of the company as follows:

> The product manager is responsible for assisting general management and operating executives in improving the profit contribution of the products assigned to him. Acting in a staff capacity, he is responsible for continuous analysis, evaluation, and coordination of all company activities affecting these products, including sales, production, scientific, purchasing, engineering, financial, and related matters. Serving as a focal point in the company for information about his products, he makes recommendations, after close collaboration with interested operating departments, on policies and programs designed to strengthen their competitive position and increase their profits. He is responsible for assisting in the management of contracts affecting the products and for maintaining outside contacts and relationships as assigned.

The results are not always happy. The operating executives sometimes complain that the product managers get in their way. For example, a product manager often feels the need of visiting members of customer trades in order to get a more realistic idea of the market conditions for his products than can be obtained from a desk in Baltimore. This is resented by the Marketing Division executives who feel that relations with a customer are a delicate matter and should not be disturbed by other representatives of the company whose questions might raise embarrassing doubts in the minds of the customers visited.

Likewise the sales executives are sometimes embarrassed by the estimate of sales possibilities issued by product managers. In estimating the sales of a product, the latter usually deal in terms of sales potentials, the volume that Hancock would get if it got all the sales of the product. When the sales executives submit their estimates of what they actually expect to sell during a coming budgetary period, general management sometimes fails to distinguish between the differing bases upon which the estimates are made, to the chagrin of the marketing group.

Initially, the product managers were to focus on *existing* products, serving as staff directly to the Operations Committee, whereas the Product Development Department was to concentrate on *new* products. However, the distinction between modification of existing products and new products was hard to draw in practice. Also, individuals who became familiar with a new product had a background that could be valuable in watching its market position, profits, changing costs, and other warnings of trouble ahead. For these reasons the product managers have been merged into the Product Development Division. The personnel picture (excluding secretarial help) under the merged setup is as follows:

Product or Activity Group	Personnel	Salaries
General Administration	1	$ 27,000
Miscellaneous Products	1	18,000
Industrial Products	1	15,000
Narcotics and Vitamins	3	34,000
Veterinary Products	1	16,000
Pharmaceutical Products	2	31,000
Specialties	1	10,000
Antibiotics	2	26,000
Laboratory Chemicals	1	15,000
Inorganic Chemicals	1	15,000
Total	14	$207,000

Examples of current issues

Typical of the problems that arise almost daily at The Hancock Company are the following:

Proposal A. At a recent meeting of the Pharmaceutical Manufacturers Association, Hancock's chief engineer picked up the information that Upjohn is about to patent a new process for the production of cortisone (used in the treatment of arthritis) that presumably will reduce the manufacturing costs to a tenth of present costs. Further, Upjohn is willing to license one or possibly two other manufacturers to use the new process. The license fee would be a flat sum to cover most of Upjohn's research cost on this project, plus a royalty on production of about 25% of the new manufacturing cost.

Hancock's Process Development Section has also been seeking a way to reduce cortisone costs. The research man in charge of the project says they have several interesting possibilities, any one of which might "break" in a few months. Of course, the output of any new process would have to be subjected to clinical tests, pilot plant operation, and FDA approval.

Proposal B. An assistant to the Manager of Sales to Pharmaceutical and Veterinary Manufacturers proposes that Hancock's product "L" be promoted to veterinary suppliers. "L" is a hormone product that under some circumstances aids human female fertility, and it has achieved a recognized position in the ethical drug field. Recently a veterinarian who works with fox farmers reported that "L" apparently had beneficial effects in breeding foxes. (Most foxes will breed only once in the spring of the year. If a female does not conceive, as often happens, she will have to be maintained for another year with no pups.)

The veterinary sales group in Hancock is always alert to possible animal use of drugs that have proven helpful to humans. The conversion of antibiotics to animal use, for example, has been a profitable development for Hancock. So, the Manager of Sales has forwarded the "L" proposal to the Veterinary Product Manager in the Product

Development Division with a note: "This looks like a good prospect. Can Manufacturing supply us with the large quantities needed for our market at reasonable prices?"

The Veterinary Product Manager has, to date, made two telephone calls. The Director of Medical Research said that the man who knew most about "L" was now deeply involved in "the new pill" project and should not be distracted because of the high priority potential of this project. The Sawmill Plant Manager, where "L" is now manufactured, said that any large increase in output would require new facilities; he further commented, "I'd prefer to keep veterinary production out of our plant. It upsets quality control. To get costs down you cut corners, and the men are likely to carry this attitude over to other products."

QUESTIONS

1. What changes in organization do you recommend to enable The Hancock Company to administer both existing and new products more effectively?
2. Are other changes, in addition to those you propose for the organization, needed?
3. Explain how Proposal A would be handled in your setup. Be specific about who will provide ideas, information, judgments, coordination, and binding decisions, and indicate the sequence and timing of decisions.
4. Do the same for Proposal B.

Part 4
GUIDING THE EXECUTION

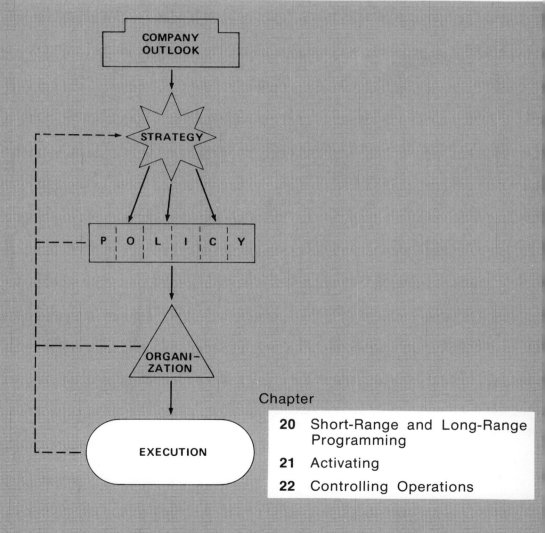

Chapter

Part 4
GUIDING THE EXECUTION

SHORT-RANGE AND LONG-RANGE PROGRAMMING

Establishing strategy and policy, building organization, and developing executives are all vital to the management of any enterprise. However, there is still another group of activities that requires executive attention if the company is to achieve its goals. Steps must be taken to "get things done." This group of managerial duties we shall call *execution,* and the term is used here to cover:

    I. *Short-range and long-range programming,* which deals with what actions are to be taken when.
   II. *Activating,* which is concerned with direction and motivation.
  III. *Controlling,* which seeks to assure that the results actually accomplished correspond with plans.

Steps in execution

A large part of the time of junior executives is devoted to execution, that is, detailed programming, motivating, coordinating, and controlling. Central managers also must give a significant portion of their energy to getting things done. Policy formulation and organization planning set the stage, but no services are rendered and no profits are earned until action by first-line operators actually takes place.

Again, a word of warning about these three steps in execution is appropriate. In practice, they are not watertight compartments that take place in just the order listed. Management is a continuing and complex activity in which the various phases are often mixed up. A program for putting a major policy change into effect may cut across minor policies, organization, and control procedures. Data developed in day-to-day control often are used in preparing short-range and long-range programs. Nevertheless, for purposes of understanding management, the division of execution into phases is essential, and the outline puts these various parts into logical relationship and perspective.

Nature of programming

Our preceding discussion of managerial tasks has put primary emphasis on *what* should be done and has given little attention to deciding *how much* and *when*. Programs add this element of sequencing and timing.

Once an objective or "mission" has been established, the executive making the program first decides what principal steps are necessary to accomplish the objective and then sets an approximate time for each. When an entirely new activity is involved, the program may also indicate who is to undertake each of the steps.

While central management can delegate most detailed scheduling work, it should take an active part in shaping broader programs. Key issues faced in this important task will be examined in terms of:

1. Short-range programming.
2. Critical path analysis.
3. Long-range programming.

SHORT-RANGE PROGRAMMING

Programs for special purposes

Numerous short-range programs are drawn up and carried out in each department of a company. These programs deal with activities ranging from launching a sales campaign to installing air-pollution control in a power plant. Normally, central management delegates this kind of programming to department executives. However, when several departments are involved, a large amount of capital is committed, or delicate external relations are at stake, central management takes an active part. Often for such situations the program is not neat and simple, as the following examples reveal.

Expansion program. The operators of the hotel facilities at the Grand Canyon wished to develop an expansion program that would enable them to give better service to the many people who want to visit this scenic spot. Investigation revealed that two types of changes were needed in the physical facilities—betterments that would improve the service in the existing plant and major expansion of room and restaurant facilities. Any significant addition to total capacity, however, would have required more water; additional water could be secured only by investing $1,500,000 to run a pipeline to a spring several miles up the canyon. Pumping water from the bottom of the canyon to the brim would require additional electric power. This would probably mean bringing in a new power line. Moreover, a new sewage line would have to be laid in a ditch blasted out of rock.

The investment in these new facilities would not have been justified if they were to be used only two or three months of the year. Consequently, serious attention had to be given to attracting visitors to the canyon in the spring and the fall when, in fact, the weather is more desirable than in the summer. There were additional factors involved, but enough have been listed to indicate the need for some kind of a program that would divide the total problem of expansion into logical *parts* and indicate a *sequence* in which these parts should be attacked.

In this case, a time schedule probably could be established only for the first two or three steps, but the program did indicate all the steps involved and a sequence for dealing with them. Thus the program laid out a systematic approach to a very complex problem. Since the desirability of expanding facilities depended so largely on extending the tourist season and building other off-season business, changes in facilities were restricted to betterments until the practicality of the promotion program was tested.

Tax revision program. The desirability of a special purpose program also became apparent to a company that sought to reduce the federal excise tax on its products. The company quickly recognized that the chances of success would be materially improved if the industry as a whole presented its case rather than each manufacturer operating independently. Clearly, the newly formed industry association should make contacts with all of the influential congressmen and senators. To be most effective, however, the pleas of the manufacturers needed to be backed up by significant pressure on the part of local constituents. This meant that the retailers, and to the extent possible the consumers, should be enlisted in the overall campaign.

If the efforts of all these people were to be most effective, there was need for a common program in which the role of each group could be clarified and some attention could be given to the timing of the several efforts. In a situation such as this, involving many independent enterprises and people, a detailed program and schedule covering an extended period probably would be of little value; but at least a general program was essential to get coordinated effort. Since the program was basically concerned with public opinion, there was great need for personal leadership and flexibility as the work proceeded.

Programs for special purposes, such as the two just discussed, are often difficult to project very far into the future. Forecasts of future needs and of operating conditions may be unreliable because the activity is so new and different. This unreliability of forecasts makes it hard to set dates and to estimate volume of work. Moreover, strategy in meeting competition or winning support of people often plays a key part in such programs, and it is difficult to decide on strategy very long in advance.

Basic steps in programming

The examples of programming given in preceding pages indicate that skill is needed in fitting the general concept to specific situations. Nevertheless, six elements or steps are found in the majority of instances. Managers will do a better job of programming if they are fully aware of the nature and the importance of each of these steps.

1. Divide the total operations necessary to achieve the objective into parts. The division of an operation into parts is useful for planning, organization, and control. Planning is improved because concentrated attention can be given to one part at a time. Organization is facilitated because these parts or projects can be assigned to separate individuals, if this will give speedier or more efficient action. Such division also aids control because the executive can watch each part and determine whether progress is satisfactory as the work is carried on without waiting for final results.

If the division into parts or projects is to be most effective, the purpose of each step should be clearly defined. The kind of work, the quality, and the quantity should all be indicated.

Often a single part of a large program is itself again subdivided; in fact, this process of subdivision may be continued for three or four stages. For example, an anniversary program of a department store may include as one of its parts a sale of men's suits. This sale in turn may be divided into buying, advertising, displaying, selling, etc. The advertising project may be divided up into selection of merchandise to be featured, writing the copy, preparing illustrations, scheduling the days and the newspapers in which the ad will appear, and integrating the suit sale ads with other advertisements of the store. Thus the concept of programming is applicable to situations ranging from large operations down to the work of a single individual.

2. Note the necessary sequence and the relationship between each of these parts. Usually the parts of a program are quite dependent on each other. The amount of work, the specifications, and the time of action of one step often affect the ease or the difficulty of performing the next step. Unless these relationships are recognized and watched closely, the very process of subdividing the work may cause more inefficiency than it corrects.

Any necessary sequences are particularly significant. For example, a motel chain had to complete refinancing its debt before embarking on a West Coast expansion. These necessary sequences have an important bearing upon scheduling. They tend to lengthen the overall time required for the operation, and since a shorter cycle gives a company more flexibility, the necessity of delaying one action until another is completed should be carefully checked.

3. Decide who is to be responsible for doing each part. If the operation being programmed is a normal activity for the company, the assignment of responsibility may already be covered by the existing organization. In an airline, for instance, the opening of a new route involves sales promotion, personnel, traffic, air operations, maintenance, and finance; but assignment of each of these activities is already set by the established structure. However, if the program covers a new operation, then careful attention should be given to the question of who is responsible for each part. These special assignments do not necessarily follow regular organization relationships and create only a temporary set of authorizations and obligations. In a very real sense, a special team is formed to carry out the program.

4. Decide how each part will be done and the resources that will be needed. The amount of attention that must be given to each step in setting up a program will depend upon the circumstances. Sometimes standing methods and standing procedures will cover almost all of the activities (as is true of military programming), and in other situations questions of "how" will be fully delegated to the persons responsible for each part. Nevertheless, the executive building the program must have enough understanding of how each part will be performed to appreciate the difficulties in the assignment and the obstacles that may be encountered. In particular, the executive needs some understanding of the *resources* that will be necessary to carry out each part of the program.

For realistic programming the need for (a) materials and supplies, (b) facilities, and (c) people must be recognized. Then the availability of these necessary resources should be appraised. If any one of them is not available, another project to obtain the resource should be set up; this may be treated either as an additional part of the original program or as a subdivision of the project needing the resource. For example, if necessary personnel are unavailable, then plans should be made for hiring and training new employees. Many programs break down because the executive preparing them does not have a practical understanding of how each part will be carried out and the resources that will be needed.

5. Estimate the time required for each part. This step is, of course, closely related with Steps 3 and 4 above and really involves two aspects: (a) the date or the hour when the part can begin, and (b) the time required to complete the operation once it is started. Possible starting time will depend upon the availability of the necessary resources. The time when key personnel can be transferred to a new assignment, the possibility of getting delivery of materials from suppliers, and the seasons when customers are normally in the market all have a bearing on when it is possible to begin any given part of a program.

The processing time once the activity is begun is typically estimated on the basis of past experience. For detailed scheduling of production operations, time-study data may permit a tight scheduling of activities. For a great many activities more time is consumed in conveying instructions and getting people actually to work than is required for the actual work itself. Unless this "nonproductive time" can be eliminated, however, it should be included as part of the estimated time.

6. Assign definite dates (hours) when each part is to take place. This overall schedule is, of course, based on the sequences as noted under Step 2 and the timing information assembled under Step 5. The resulting schedule should show both the starting dates and the completion dates for each part of the program.

Sometimes considerable adjustment and fitting is necessary to make the final schedule realistic. A useful procedure is to work backward and forward from some fixed date that is considered to be controlling. In promoting a new dress fabric, for example, the importance of the selling season may be so great that the retail season is taken as fixed and the schedule is extended back from these dates. In other situations the availability of materials or of facilities may be the controlling time around which the rest of the schedule is extended back from these dates. In other situations the availability of materials or of facilities may be the controlling time around which the rest of the schedule is adjusted. It is, of course, necessary to dovetail any given program with other commitments the company may have.

Another important qualification is to make some allowances for delay. It is not desirable as a general practice to have such allowances all along the line as this may tend to create inefficient performance, but there should be safety allowances at various stages so that an unavoidable delay at one place will not throw off the entire schedule.

Programs may have to be revised, of course, to take account of unexpected opportunities or difficulties. If each of the six steps just outlined has been well done, however, these revisions usually can be merely adjustments of the initial planning.

CRITICAL PATH ANALYSIS

Development of PERT

Critical path analysis is a special technique for studying and controlling complex programs. It was developed in its more elaborate form as an aid in the design and the production of Polaris missiles, and it has been used for virtually all subsequent space age projects. The particular technique applied to the Polaris program was called PERT (Program Evaluation and Review Technique); many variations of the basic ideas have been used before and since PERT received wide publicity. The technique is of interest to us here because the central concepts of critical path analysis can be helpful in many programming problems.

The design and the production of Polaris missiles involved a staggering number of steps. Specifications for thousands of minute parts had to be prepared, the parts had to be manufactured to exact tolerances, and then the entire system had to be assembled into a successful operating weapon. And, *time* was of the essence. The basic steps in programming, just discussed in the preceding pages, were applicable; but the complexity of the project (and the fact that many different subcontractors were involved) called for significant elaborations in the programs.

Major features of critical path analysis

The basic ideas involved in this refined programming technique are:

1. All steps and their necessary sequences are placed on a diagram (see the charts at the top of the following page) so that the total *network* is explicitly set forth.

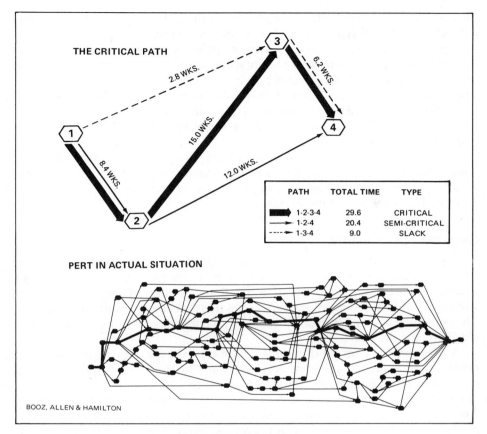

THE CRITICAL PATH

2.8 WKS.

6.2 WKS.

15.0 WKS.

8.4 WKS.

12.0 WKS.

PATH	TOTAL TIME	TYPE
1-2-3-4	29.6	CRITICAL
1-2-4	20.4	SEMI-CRITICAL
1-3-4	9.0	SLACK

PERT IN ACTUAL SITUATION

BOOZ, ALLEN & HAMILTON

Critical Path Analysis

The upper chart shows, for a very small segment of the total network, how the critical path is computed. The lower chart indicates how complex the networks may be.

2. The estimated *time* required to complete each step after the preceding step has been finished is recorded.
3. Then by adding the required times for each step in any necessary sequence—or path—the path having the longest time can be identified. This is the *critical path*.
4. If desired, the difference between the total required times of the critical path and other paths can also be computed. Such differences are *slack times* or margins in which delays would not hold up the final completion.

Now, having identified the critical path, management can focus its attention on either reducing the time of steps in this path or at least watching closely for any delays. Also, management knows from slack time data where high pressure to meet estimated processing times may be unwarranted.

The calculation of the critical path should, of course, be repeated as work progresses because some steps will be completed faster than anticipated and others will be delayed. These new data will certainly change slack time estimates, and a different critical path may arise.

With careful thought, the total network of steps and sequences can usually be prepared with reasonable reliability—at least for programs dealing with physical products. Time estimates prove to be less reliable, especially for new and unique activities. To deal with this uncertainty regarding time, often three estimates are obtained from the persons who will be doing the work: optimistic, most likely, and pessimistic. Then a weighted average of these three elapsed-time estimates is used.

In critical path analyses of complex programs, such as Polaris, computations are sufficiently involved to make use of an electronic computer very helpful. In simpler programming situations, such as building construction, a computer is by no means essential.

General applicability

The main features of critical path analysis have application to many programs that are not sufficiently complex to warrant the complete PERT treatment. Often just the preparation of a network chart of sequences of steps will clarify the interconnections between actions taken by various departments. The launching of an additional magazine by a publishing firm, for example, was aided by such a chart.

Moreover, the concept of a critical path can be used in many programming problems even though an entire network is not charted. In a company making nationally advertised men's shirts, for instance, the critical path runs from line-building through sales promotion to plant scheduling and on to order filling. Acquiring grey goods, training personnel, and similar steps have to be done, but they are not "critical" from a timing viewpoint because of the early leads necessary in sales promotion. Programming in other companies may be geared to erection of new facilities or perhaps training of personnel. In all these situations, a recognition of what steps are part of the critical path will direct management efforts in "getting things done" to the crucial spots.

A word of caution is in order. Critical path analysis focuses on time, and few companies have data that enable them also to fit costs into the same framework. We would like to know how much speeding up or slowing down each step will change costs. Usually such cost estimates—even rough ones—are prepared only after critical steps are identified and an executive is trying to decide whether to make a change in plans. Similarly, critical path analysis does not deal with alternative ways of reaching a goal. The network is presumed to be settled. Of course, if the analysis identifies a serious bottleneck, then management may resort to a different method and may establish a new network.

Nevertheless, for many programming problems, timing is the major consideration. And for such programming problems, critical path analysis can be a valuable refinement.

LONG-RANGE PROGRAMMING

Nature of long-range programming

Programming increases in difficulty as the time-span covered is extended, yet such extension is well worth the trouble in some circumstances. We have been discussing program cycles ranging from a few months to perhaps 2 years. Long-range programming seeks to extend the period covered to, say, 5 to 10 years.

Underlying any long-range program should be a well-defined strategy. The strategy establishes the basic directions and the criteria for which the program is developed. Policy, considered in Chapters 5 through 15, provides the guides and the limitations within which action is to fall. Establishing these is, of course, part of the total process of long-range planning. The *program* introduces a time schedule—the how much and when aspects—and thereby sets the intermediate objectives (which in turn become the targets for more specific and detailed short-range programs).

Applications

One of the classic examples of long-range programming is the conversion of the Bell System to dial telephones. Forecasts of telephone usage—based on propulation growth, higher gross national product (GNP), and telephoning habits—indicated that manual switching could not handle the load. Besides, automatic dialing would improve service and hopefully cut costs. So the goal was clear, but the magnitude of the task was tremendous. Design of equipment had to be refined for recording calls, relaying long-distance calls, tieing in with independent companies, and the like. Completely new exchanges had to be built, millions of dollars of switching equipment had to be manufactured, and millions of consumer units had to be produced. Before any of this physical equipment could be installed, people—engineers, installers, and operators—had to be trained. Incidentally, company policy dictated that the transition was to be made with only seconds of interruption in service and no layoffs of regular employees. The public had to be prepared for the switch and educated to use the new equipment; utility commissions had to be kept advised. And the multimillion dollar investment had to be financed.

This incomplete list suggests the range of elements in the program. Many of the preliminary steps were taken ten years before the conversion in that area was finished. And with new developments in technology and markets, the process is still going on.

The Bell System example is enlightening because (a) a whole series of interrelated steps were programmed years in advance, and (b) the programming was done in terms of several elements—markets, engineering, facilities, personnel, and finance—not for just a single element such as finance.

The magnitude and the predictability of the Bell System is unique, of course. Nevertheless, quite different companies can use a similar approach.

The Suburban Fuel Company, for instance, did long-range programming even though it was a small-town firm with net worth of only $100,000. For many years the family owning Suburban Fuel had been in the retail coal business. When fuel oil began replacing coal, the company also became a fuel oil distributor. Finally, when the grandson of the founder became president, he decided to withdraw from coal altogether and he set up a long-range program to do so. The program involved: (1) gradual disposition of coal facilities—no new equipment, sale of some trucks, and sale of the coal yard as a plant site in 5 years; (2) strengthening the fuel oil distributorship—adding trained burner servicemen, leasing more trucks, closer tie-in with sale of oil burners, and more systematic promotion of annual service contracts; and (3) withdrawal of most of the capital invested—the fuel oil distributorship to be "spun off" as a separate company, and liquidation of the original coal company at favorable tax rates. Initially a 5-year program, it actually was completed in 4½ years because a good opportunity to sell the coal yard turned up.

In this example, we again see (a) a series of interrelated steps extending over a period of years and (b) a plan that embraced several different elements. The timing of the various steps was subject to adjustment, as was also true in the telephone conversion, and no attempt was made to spell out detail several years in advance. But the master plan provided a definite guide for actions all along the way.

The preceding examples may be misleading because only a small portion of business firms actually prepare long-range programs in a clear-cut fashion. The main reason is simple. Most companies cannot, or do not, forecast the nature and the volume of their activities for 3, 4, or 5 years, let alone 10, years ahead. Perhaps they know the direction they would like to go (their objectives); but uncertainties about competition, technical developments, consumers' actions, political changes, economic changes, and the like make timing hard to nail down.

Because of the difficulty of precise long-term forecasting, we need to examine carefully the benefits the typical company can reasonably hope to obtain from long-range programming and problems that must be overcome if it undertakes this management device.

Major benefits of long-range programming

A central management that embarks on long-range programming usually seeks these advantages:

1. Long-cycle actions are started promptly. An automated plant takes at least 2 or 3 years to design, build, and get in operation. A bright idea for a new product often requires 3 to 5 years for research, development, testing, and process engineering before it is ready to be marketed. Recruiting and training sales-people for electronic computers takes several years—assuming they cannot be hired away from established competitors. Raising a new crop of timber for lumber may consume 25 years.

Long-term programming indicates when such actions should be started. Opportunities will be missed or crises in servicing customers may develop unless a company takes early action. To fail to act is equivalent to a decision to postpone entry into the contemplated operation. Even though predictions of need are uncertain, there may be no feasible alternative to starting down the road.

By preparing the best program that available knowledge will permit, a company increases the probability that it will be aware of when long-cycle actions should be initiated.

2. Executives are psychologically prepared for change. Many actions embraced in a long-range program need not, and should not, be taken immediately. They can await a year or more of actual experience, and by then some modification in the original plan may be desirable.

Nevertheless, even though the program is changed, the process of preparing it aids adjustment to new conditions. As a result of preparing the program, the idea that some kind of change in response to shifts in the environment must take place is already accepted. And, probably the nature of the adjustment will have been thought about—for example, transfers of personnel, refunding a bond issue, or local production in a foreign country. Then, when conditions are ripe, executives are prepared to move quickly. Good news or bad news may arrive unexpectedly, and the company response may differ from the program; but the ability to recognize the opportunity, to appreciate the range of actions that are necessary, and to get in motion has been sharpened by the mental exercise of preparing (and revising) a program.

The pace of technological and economic change is quickening. Product life cycles are shorter and competitors move into profit opportunities more quickly. Consequently, the ability of a company to adjust promptly to shifts in its environment is crucial to getting ahead and staying ahead in modern competition. So this psychological preparation for change that we have been discussing is more vital to central management today than it was a generation ago.

3. Actions having long-term impact are coordinated. Often an action taken to meet an immediate problem also significantly affects future operations of the company. For example, to get quick coverage of the West Coast territory, one firm gave exclusive distribution rights to an agent who also sold related products. The agent was successful in establishing itself as the local representative and the immediate problem was resolved. However, the firm soon expanded and diversified so that it needed a strong national sales organization of its own sales representatives; and the successful independent distributor on the West Coast proved to be very difficult to supplant.

The selection of executives for key posts, the licensing of a company patent, and acceptance of a government subsidy are further examples where short-run solutions may prove troublesome in the future.

Now, if a company has a long-range program, central managers will be able to sense more easily whether current decisions do, or do not, fit into a consistent pattern of long-term development.

Note that in this list of benefits of long-range planning we do not include "a blueprint for future action." Only rarely are prediction and control of conditions several years hence sufficiently accurate to permit close adherence to a 5-year plan. But such a program does help identify actions that should be initiated now, it lays a psychological base for prompt adjustment to opportunities in the future, and it provides a pattern so that action on today's problems can be compatible with long-range plans.

Problems involved in long-range programming

Preparation of a long-range program of the type we have been discussing needs guidance. Key problems are what topics and period to cover, how revisions will be made, and who will do the work of developing the plans.

Topics covered. Too often so-called "long-range programs" are merely financial estimates conjured up by a bright young analyst in the controller's office. Such estimates take the form of annual profit and loss budgets for perhaps the next 5 years.

For operating purposes, dollar sales estimates have little meaning unless someone has thought in terms of the products that will be sold, the customers who will buy them, the prices obtainable in face of competition, and the selling effort necessary to obtain the orders. Similarly, the projected volume of goods must be conceived in terms of the resources necessary to produce them: plant capacity, trained workers, flow of raw materials, engineering talent, etc.

Therefore, long-range programs should be stated in physical terms. But it is impractical to spell out such plans in full detail; instead, management should identify the crucial factors and build the program in these terms. One of the keys to successful programming is this identifying of topics to be used; omissions of vital factors will make the program unrealistic, whereas too many factors will make it unwieldy.

The long-range program should also be translated into dollar results: revenues, costs, profits, and capital requirements. Dollars are the best common denominator we have, and the financial results are an important aspect of any program. The point is that dollar figures alone are not enough.

Period covered. Five years is the most common period covered by long-range programs. There is no magic in this figure, however. Logically, long-range plans should be based on the necessary elapsed time for such important actions as product development, resources development, market development, or physical facility development. Three years may be long enough, or perhaps 10 years will be needed.

In fact, the necessary time varies. Resource development may have to be started 8 years before materials will become available, while 2 years may be adequate for market development. To deal with this variation, several companies (a) plan an action *in detail* only when a start is necessary, or (b) prepare a comprehensive program for 3 or 4 years ahead and then extend the period only for those areas requiring longer lead times.

Revisions. As results of first steps become known and new information about external conditions is learned, long-range programs need revision. The typical procedure is an annual review in which near-term actions are planned in greater detail, a new year is added on the end, and adjustments are made in plans for the interim period.

Under this scheme, programs are revised several times before the period to which they apply finally arrives. This provides flexibility in long-range programming. It also entails a lot of work, and executives may become cavalier about plans for 5 years hence since such plans will be revised over and over again. These disadvantages of several revisions are strong reasons for restricting the period covered and making sure the benefits listed on pages 472-474 are actually being obtained.

Who prepares long-range programs? Central managers will certainly participate in long-range programming, as noted in Chapter 18. Equally clear, however, is the fact that they cannot do the job alone. They will need help obtaining ideas and specific data. Moreover, if the programs are to guide current commitments and to have the desired psychological effect on executives throughout the company, all major executives should participate—research directors, plant managers, sales managers, and the like. Since these executives have other pressing duties, they probably will ask a staff assistant to help with long-range planning.

Altogether, then, central managers, operating executives, and their staffs probably will contribute ideas, data, judgment, or approval. A bit complicated, yes, yet necessary if the programs are to be carefully prepared and are to serve their intended purposes.

Long-range planning in small firms. Long-range planning in a small Stage I enterprise is necessarily more informal than in a large company. Executives lack the time to prepare detailed estimates; often basic historical data will never have been recorded. Nevertheless, the basic process as outlined above should be followed, for the small firm has as much to gain by anticipating opportunities as a large one.

One entrepreneur with only 16 employees has a loose-leaf notebook with alternative 5-year programs based on different key assumptions. Perhaps because of his engineering training, he has spelled out steps and resources for different rates of growth in either of three directions. The estimates are his personal, subjective guesses; but when he makes a major investment or signs a long-term contract, he has a clear idea of where the action is likely to lead him.

In addition to pressure on time, small business managers have difficulty thinking objectively about events several years away. Typically they are so immersed in day-to-day activities it is difficult to make a mental switch to a longer horizon. Preparing some estimates to present to a sympathetic board member can be a helpful discipline in this respect.

SUMMARY

Through programming, a manager formulates an integrated plan covering what, how much, when, and who.

Six basic steps should be taken: (1) divide the total operations necessary to achieve the objective into parts, (2) note the necessary sequences and relationships between each of these parts, (3) decide who is to be responsible for doing each part, (4) decide how each part will be done and the resources needed, (5) estimate the time required for each part, and (6) assign definite dates when each part will commence and end.

When faced with complex programming problems, a manager can use *critical path analysis* to identify those parts of the total activity that must be watched most closely if the final objective is to be met on time.

Long-range programming follows the same steps as any other programming. However, because of the great difficulty in forecasting accurately several years in advance, long-range programs have to be revised several times.

Long-range programming is part of the more inclusive process of long-range planning. Establishing strategy and setting policy are also parts; they set directions, criteria and limits. The *program* then introduces a time schedule—the how much and when—and breaks the broad plan into more specific steps.

While long-range programs must not be regarded as fixed, they do help flag actions with long lead times that should not be started immediately, prepare executives to act promptly when opportunities or difficulties do arise, and provide a basis for reconciling short-run solutions with long-term plans.

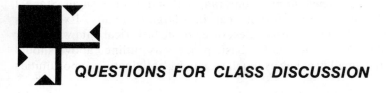

QUESTIONS FOR CLASS DISCUSSION

1. Jean Briggs and Dave Weiss want to set up a tutoring project for junior high students in a low-income urban area 5 miles from their college. Draw up a program for getting such a project launched.

2. The president of the Springfield National Bank has decided that the bank should increase its proportion of women employees from supervisor through officers. A conservative institution with 6 branches, the bank has 22 officers and 50 additional "exempt" personnel (supervisors, managers, etc.). Only 10 of these are now women, whereas the president believes the bank will be vulnerable to social and governmental pressures until the proportion reaches 20% to 33%. Turnover in the past has been low, 7% among officers and 10% among other exempt personnel. The proportion of women at the operating level is already high. (a) Outline a program for accomplishing the bank president's goal. (b) Explain whether the programming steps listed on pages 465-468 were relevant to your task in (a).

3. (a) Using your observations and general knowledge, work out a program for the construction of a new interchange and overpass of two major highways. What use did you make of the steps listed on pages 465-468 in preparing your program? (b) Do you recommend the use of PERT for the construction project dealt with in (a)? Explain the benefits and the drawbacks of the technique in this situation.

4. A U.S. auto equipment manufacturer has purchased a European patent for an antismog muffler. To make this new product, the following major steps must be completed:

A. Decision to add product.
B. Engineering work completed.
C. Financing arranged.
D. Material purchase orders placed.
E. Production started.
F. Sales campaign arranged.
G. Initial orders received.
H. Initial orders shipped.

Analysis indicates the following necessary sequences between the above events and the estimated time required to perform the work to advance from one event to the next. (Work cannot move forward until all necessary preceding work is completed.)

Necessary sequence	Estimated time	Necessary sequence	Estimated time
A to B	60 days	C to F	2 days
B to C	20 "	D to E	40 "
B to D	30 "	E to H	45 "
B to E	75 "	F to G	60 "
B to F	30 "	G to E	2 "
C to D	2 "	G to H	10 "

(a) Prepare a PERT diagram showing the network of the above events. (b) Determine the critical path. (c) Explain how your answer to (a) and (b) would be useful in launching the new product.

5. (a) Is there any need for long-range programming in an enterprise that lacks a clearly defined strategy and policy? (b) Will strategy and policy serve any useful purpose even though a company does not also do long-range programming?

6. The future rate of inflation is difficult to predict. Assume that you are the business manager for a local hospital and are preparing a program to be presented to your board of trustees for the construction of a new wing. How will the inflation rate affect this program? How do you propose to deal with this unknown?

7. Compare the length of period you would recommend for long-range programming of (a) a telephone company, (b) the college or university you are attending, (c) a

TV broadcasting station, and (d) a quiz show for TV. What are the reasons for differences in the period covered?

8. Many Stage III companies have created a position entitled "Director of Long-Range Planning" or just "Director of Planning." Often such staff people report to a central corporate executive and have counterparts at the division level. What should a director of long-range planning do? How will his work differ from that of his counterparts in the various divisions? To whom should each report?

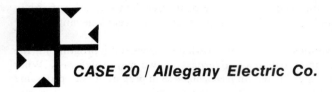

CASE 20 / Allegany Electric Co.

Allegany Electric Co., a privately owned utility company providing electricity to a variety of customers, faces a major expansion of its generating facilities. Mr. J. W. Harris, the newly elected chairman of the board, has requested a review of the expansion program for the next 8 years. "As a start, I want to see the broad outlines and identify the main points at which risk-judgments have to be made. This is to be a fresh review, using of course the best technical knowledge we have in the company." You have been asked to draw up the 8-year program and have obtained the following data from interviews with Allegany personnel.

An outside board member explained: "For years Allegany followed the policy of relying on tie-in lines with adjoining utilities for its reserve capacity. We sought to match our generating facilities only to our peak load requirements. Recently this strategy ran into serious trouble for two reasons. First, all of us underestimated the growth in demand, so in the entire area too little new construction was started. Since power can't be stored and it takes years to step up generating capacity, the whole situation became tight. Second, the real squeeze occurred when the 800,000 kilowatt nuclear plant that three companies including Allegany were building jointly fell two years behind its scheduled completion date. That led to brownouts and other interruptions in service, high costs to obtain temporary relief—and to a new chairman!"

The vice-president for customer service provided the following data on demand: "Here are the figures summarizing our estimates of future demand. During the last 10 years sales in kilowatt-hours (kwh) have grown at over 7% per year, and we anticipate a continuation of that trend. We can estimate demand rather closely for the next couple of years because we know our customers and their use habits. Of course, industrial users especially will be affected by general business conditions, but the only safe assumption is that the underlying growth trend will continue.

"These sales estimates do not provide for any large increase in home heating, which I'm sure we could get if we went after it. Peak demand has shifted from December to July, due to air-conditioning, so we could make money with a very low home-heating rate that would soak up idle capacity during the winter. As soon as we overcome our capacity difficulties, I'm going to push for a home-heating rate that will enable us to start developing that new source of revenue."

The manager of plant operations said: "We've been struggling with inadequate capacity for years. This year we finally are getting current from the nuclear joint venture, but we are still far below the capacity we should have. Don't be misled by

Sales Estimates
1,000,000's of kilowatt-hours—to Allegany customers

	Last Year Ac-tual	Pres-ent Year	2nd Year	3rd Year	4th Year	5th Year	6th Year	7th Year	8th Year
Residential	3,030	3,300	3,550	3,840					
Commercial	1,840	1,970	2,130	2,260					
Industrial	3,960	4,200	4,460	4,700					
Other	490	530	560	600					
Total	9,320	10,000	10,700	11,400	12,250	13,100	14,050	15,000	16,100
			Peak load in 1,000's of kilowatts						
Total	1,830	1,960	2,100	2,250	2,410	2,580	2,760	2,950	3,150

looking just at sales estimates of peak load. First, there are transmission losses; only 90% of the power coming off our generators shows up in the customers' meters. Then we need reserve for all sorts of contingencies—equipment repairs, breakdowns, and the like. The larger the generating units, the bigger the reserve we should have. We now have learned the hard way that we can no longer rely on others. Right now we have no reserve, and anyone in the industry who has any respect for customer service will tell you a 15% reserve is minimum. Of course, that reserve capacity costs money, but we in production aren't magicians; customers expect service whenever they flip the switch, and we can't provide it without adequate capacity. Presently we can just deliver peak requirements with everything running perfectly. To get the 15% reserve, we need 275,000 kilowatts more capacity today. Then add capacity for growth. The sales managers always seem to be low, but taking their 3-year estimate, it looks like this in 1,000's of kilowatts:

	This Year	2nd Year	3rd Year
New peak load	1,960	2,100	2,250
Previous peak load	1,830	1,960	2,100
Addition to peak	130	140	150
New generating capacity needed 125% (10% loss, 15% reserve)	162	175	187
Present deficit in reserve	275		

"In operations we only plan 3 years ahead; but if you can get a realistic forecast of demand, the magnitude of the future problem can be easily computed."

The power consultant to the company had firm opinions about ways to generate electricity: "Nuclear power is clearly the economical energy source of the future. We are approaching the limit on efficiency with fossil fuel (coal and oil), but we are just beginning with nuclear energy. Companies that don't go nuclear as fast as they can will find themselves with high costs, and that means rate problems."

The construction vice-president was less dogmatic. "I agree that nuclear energy is the answer for the year 2000, but we have some immediate problems that nuclear plants can't meet. The most obvious difficulty is lead time. We got into serious trouble once, and know that even the 6-year lead contractors now quote has some if's in it.

"Actually we have three basic alternatives for new power—four if you include buying it as we had to do the last couple of years. Each method has its advantages and drawbacks. Here's a summary:

	Minimum efficient capacity per plant	Construction lead time	Investment per kw capacity	Operating cost per kwh
Fossil fuel (coal or oil)	300,000 kw	4 years	$185	0.6¢
Nuclear fuel	600,000 kw	6 years	230	0.4¢ to 0.5
Gas turbines	25,000 kw	2 years	100	0.8¢
Purchased power	?	1 year	–0–	0.93

"The figures are our best estimates at present, but any of them can change, especially the investment costs and the operating costs of the nuclear plants. The capacity of either the nuclear or fossil fuel plants could be easily increased. The gas turbines are small, flexible units we could always use for peak requirements, but we know they have high operating costs.

"Let me qualify that table in one important respect. For very large plants we often seek a joint venture with another company—to lower the risk of a single failure affecting a high percentage of our power needs. Such joint ventures increase transmission costs somewhat, but more serious is that we have to add a year to the lead time for all the extra planning and negotiation.

"You know that we have under construction fossil fuel additions that will add 200,000 kw's this year, 200,000 kw's next year, and 100,000 kw's in the third year."

The treasurer contributed a different view. "A lot of misleading statements are made about reserves. We always have recognized the need for reserves, and we have had written agreements with other companies covering our emergency needs. This arrangement permitted us to keep our investment down and to use our plant at a higher percent of capacity. The slow completion of the nuclear plant is what squeezed all of us. But the amount we saved in the past should be considered as an offset to the power we had to buy at 9.3 mills per kwh for a couple of years. True, customers did not have 100% service, but I wonder how much idle equipment is justified in order to deliver power to everybody one hour on a hot afternoon.

"The future is a different story. Because of our past difficulties we are now in the spotlight. Even the security markets want to see reserve capacity—why I don't know, since we make more money without it, but we will have to pay an extra percent or more on our bonds if our projections don't look conservative. And on the quarter of a billion dollars new capital we will need, that's a lot of interest expense. I'm also concerned about roadblocks by the conservationists. My guess is that we're heading for delays and temporary shutdowns while the general public makes up its mind whether it wants modern living or fish and wild ducks. So maybe we ought to put the reserve in our calculations but then not be upset if we have to use it for temporary periods."

Required: Prepare a report, including an 8-year program, in response to Mr. Harris's request stated in the first paragraph.

ACTIVATING

21

The wisest strategy, policy, organization, and programs come to naught until they are put into action. This need to translate ideas into action has been a recurring theme throughout our discussion, but it warrants further recognition in a separate chapter. Central management plays an important role in activating an enterprise by:

1. Setting the *leadership tone*.
2. Fostering good *person-to-person communication*.
3. Providing an appropriate, viable *incentive structure*.
4. Bringing about major *changes* reflecting new strategy.

Controlling is also necessary in achieving results and will be explored in the next chapter.

LEADERSHIP TONE

Persons in central management positions cannot escape being public figures, at least throughout their organization. Their behavior is closely watched for cues. The vice-president who jokingly said, "Guess I'll walk through the office in my shirt sleeves just to start a rumor," was well aware that many people would try to infer meaning from even his casual actions.

Central managers influence the tone of an enterprise primarily by the way they deal with their immediate associates. These associates, in turn, have contacts with many more people, and the influence radiates on out.

Relations with immediate associates

Significant here is optimism (or pessimism) about the future, confidence that the company can achieve intermediate and long-range goals, aggressiveness in tackling tough problems, fairness in dealing with outsiders and insiders, and similar attitudes that affect morale. Senior executives convey their feelings on such matters partly by what they say, but even more by their decisions and actions. The people who work closely with them are naturally very sensitive about these attitudes because such viewpoints have a direct effect on their own futures.

No one has yet found a single formula that will generate good morale in all circumstances. The beliefs and ideals of one's associates as well as the demands of the current situation influence the effectiveness of a particular leadership pattern. The hard-driving, risk-taking leadership style of Henry J. Kaiser, for instance, would play havoc in a large New York bank. Within the limits of their own personal flexibility, individual managers must seek a leadership pattern that seems appropriate to the needs of the situation. In making this choice they should recognize that their behavior will be extended to some degree throughout the company.

Contacts throughout the company

A spirit of optimism, conviction, or caution and other aspects of company viewpoint are also conveyed through direct contacts of senior executives with various groups of employees. Such contacts are inevitably brief and often superficial. Nevertheless, employees like to see, and better to talk with, the individuals who make the major decisions in the company they work for. Political leaders know well the value of a personal handshake, and military commanders do not underestimate the need for personal visits to combat troops. Merely to have established some personal identification is valuable. If, in addition, senior executives can generate enthusiasm for company policy and programs, the effect may be substantial.

PERSON-TO-PERSON COMMUNICATION

A wholesome attitude and spirit—discussed above—helps activate plans, but it does not remove the elementary need to communicate such plans clearly. Here central management sets an example in dealing with immediate subordinates and promotes a general pattern for clear boss-subordinate communications throughout the enterprise. Important means toward this end are workable instructions, consultative direction, and goal-centered performance appraisals.

Workable instructions

Giving instructions appears to be so simple that it should not present a significant problem in activating plans. Experienced managers know, however, that faulty directions often do create trouble.

Example of inadequate instruction. The textile division of a large manufacturing company having several semi-independent operating divisions had experienced a rapid expansion in sales in one year and was preparing for even greater sales in the following year. Unfortunately, retail store buying slowed up and signs indicated that the industry was about to enter one of its frequent cyclical declines. At this time the company president and the division vice-president discussed the outlook and agreed that the division should trim its sails and inventory should be reduced rather than expanded. This agreement was in effect an order from the president to the vice-president.

Difficulty arose because the order really was not clear. The vice-president took immediate steps to cut off new orders for raw materials, to stop or reduce the size of production runs wherever this could be done without jeopardizing orders already on the books or leaving materials in a semifinished state, and to push the sale of finished goods by granting price reductions wherever this could be done without completely demoralizing the market. These steps undoubtedly cut the inventory below what it otherwise would have been, but the in-flow of materials already on order and in process resulted in continued receipts and manufacture considerably in excess of the sale of finished goods. Financial reports were not completed until two weeks following the close of a month and so it was six weeks before the president learned that inventories actually went up half a million dollars instead of down. He then called the vice-president to task for failing to follow instructions.

The vice-president explained that he was in the process of carrying out the instructions and that he assumed the president had in mind ''an orderly liquidation.'' Cancellation of orders from raw material suppliers would have created bad relations and probably claims for damages; forced sale of finished goods could have been made only at very substantial reductions inasmuch as retail stores did not want to increase their inventories. On the other hand, the president pointed out that the conditions in the industry had become steadily worse and that it would have been easier to get rid of the inventory six weeks ago than it was then. Again the president said, ''Inventories must go down.'' The vice-president proceeded to take what he considered to be drastic steps, but he naturally was concerned about keeping the operating loss at a minimum because he would be considered responsible for such losses by the board of directors. Many of his assistants argued that time was needed to work off the inventory and that cancellation of orders with suppliers would cause them trouble just at the time they needed help and consequently would injure the division's long-run reputation in the industry.

The president grew impatient with the time it was taking to carry out his instructions and finally resorted to putting the division under close cash control. Bills for wages and raw materials were paid only out of funds collected from customers of the division. This drastic action finally succeeded in getting inventories liquidated about seven months after the original decision to ''trim sails.'' In this instance there was no question as to the general intent of the directions given by the president. There was, however, considerable doubt as to how fast, how much, and at what expense the action should be taken.

Tests of a good instruction. The effectiveness of giving directions can be improved by making sure that the following simple tests of a good instruction are met:

    1. The instructions should be *complete*, indicating what is to be done, the quality of performance desired, and the time when the assignment is to be finished.

2. Compliance should be *reasonable,* that is, within the capacity of the person receiving the instructions under conditions prevailing at the time.
3. The instructions should be *clear,* that is, the executive giving the instruction should make sure that the ideas in his mind are actually transmitted to the person being directed.
4. Key points of all major instructions should be put *in writing*.

In the textile division example, the intent was clear but the instruction was incomplete with respect to time and cost. Also, had the president's order been complete, the vice-president probably would have questioned its reasonableness. If the president had consciously thought of the tests of a good instruction—or observed them out of habit—serious confusion involving hundreds of thousands of dollars would have been avoided.

In practice, wide differences exist in the extent to which orders are put in writing. It takes time and effort to reduce instructions to writing, and many executives feel that at least for simple instructions this work is unncessary. However, written instructions often add a certain definiteness to the direction and they reduce the occasions for argument when memories are faulty. As a general rule, instructions should be written when (1) several individuals are affected, (2) considerable time will pass before the work is completed, (3) complex and detailed information is involved, or (4) the matter is of such importance that special steps to avoid the possibility of misunderstanding are warranted.

On the other hand, routine instruction can be terse. For repetitive activities, often custom or standard procedures dictate how work is to be performed and the executive needs only to fill in the missing gaps. In other words, all the tests of a good instruction should be met, but some aspects are covered by previous orders and training.

One further qualification should be noted. The amount of detail in an instruction should be consistent with the delegation of authority to make decisions. For instance, if a president has given the chief accountant authority to establish the accounting system for the company, the president's instructions regarding, say, changes in salaries will not deal with recording such changes. Of course, the president and the chief accountant should have a mutual understanding about the results the accounting system is to achieve. In other words, delegations that are part of the established organization are like customary procedures noted in the preceding paragraph; they are part of the total behavior structure assumed when a new instruction is given. Obviously, if this assumed behavior structure is not understood by all people involved, the instruction will be ambiguous.

***Follow-up on instructions*.** After instructions—complete, reasonable, clear, and perhaps in writing—have been issued, sound practice requires that they be followed up. This is necessary not only to see that the particular instruction is carried out but also to cultivate the proper attitude toward instructions. Especially at the senior level, instructions should be followed up. Employees soon learn whether their executives "mean what they say." If instructions are issued but none followed up, employees tend to postpone work they find unpleasant. The executives will then never know whether they can count on performance, and they will have to spend more time finding out what really happened. On the other hand, if the executives are careful to see that all instructions are complied with, then any new assignments will be considered as something that must be done. There will be a sharpness and a positiveness about the administration in place of a casual, indifferent attitude.

This principle of follow-up of instructions imposes a burden on executives. They must be careful to issue only those instructions that they are sure they want to be carried out, for otherwise they will have their subordinates performing work that is not contributing the maximum to the broad objectives of the enterprise. The executives should distinguish between minimum standards of satisfactory performance and goals that are desirable but not necessarily essential to the successful operation of the rest of the company. Moreover, if for some reason the instructions are no longer applicable, the executives must be sure that they modify or withdraw them. Occasionally this may embarrass a president or a vice-president because it may appear that he made a mistake in issuing the instructions in the first place. However, employee attitudes and morale will probably be better if the instruction is revised than they would be if the instruction were disregarded or employees were made to perform what they probably would recognize as unnecessary work.

This suggestion that executives should always follow up on instructions they issue does not mean that they are autocrats in their administration. Subordinates may be given ample opportunity to participate in formulating the plans, and considerable authority may be delegated to them. Instead, it simply means that when instructions are issued they should be taken seriously.

Consultative direction

One of the most promising means of overcoming the difficulties of communication is called *consultative direction*. Under this technique the people responsible for executing an instruction are consulted about its workability and better ways of accomplishing the same result. Usually the senior executive will call in one or more subordinates and lay before them the facts of the situation that is being faced; then these people together will explore possible courses of action. The subordinates may have some additional information and often will have suggestions on what should be done. The various suggestions will be examined, and finally an agreement will be reached on what appears to be the wisest action to take.

Among the advantages of this method of giving instructions are the cooperation and the enthusiasm generated on the part of the people who have to carry out the instructions. Since they helped form the plan, they take a personal pride in carrying it out. The skillful executive will be quite willing to let his associates feel that they originated the solution, even though he, too, had thought of it, because of the added incentive they will then have to make it work.

The instructions resulting from consultative supervision may be more practical than the ideas that the executive would think of alone. Moreover, consultative direction provides an excellent occasion for developing executives through coaching, already discussed in Chapter 19.

Consultative direction is not without its drawbacks. Theoretically, the agreement reached in the discussion becomes the instruction from the senior executive, and as such it should meet all the tests of a good direction that are listed on pages 483-484. There is a risk that the discussion may terminate before the conclusions are fully crystallized and that associates will be left to make their own interpretation of what was agreed upon. The second drawback is that the subordinates may feel that it is within their province to modify the course of action inasmuch as they helped formulate the plan in the first place. Both of these risks, however, can be minimized if the senior executive insists that the conference conclude with a succinct summary of what is to be done and he then makes it clear that these instructions are to be carried out unless he personally approves of some modification. The third drawback is that consultative direction does take considerable time of several executives; consequently, its use should be reserved for problems that are of real significance to the company.

A recent study of joint consultation in British industry confirms American experience, and difficulties, with consultation. While this study dealt primarily with relations between an executive and a formally designated representative of the workers, the findings that are summarized in the accompanying table throw light on the entire supervisory process. The relationships range from deputation, in which the employees make a request of the executive, through negotiations, or bargaining, to consultation. This British report brings out again that the manner in which the plan is agreed upon has much to do with the attitude of the people who have to carry it out.

Effect of Relation with Executive on Employee Response

Meeting	Relation-ship	Method	Status and Authority	Sense of Responsi-bility	Decider
Deputation	Dominant-servile	Dictation	Rank	"His"	He decided
Negotiation	Competitive rivalry	Compromise	Strength	"No one's"	It was decided
Consultation	Collabora-tive	Integration	Function and quali-fications	"Ours"	We decided

From a report of the British National Institute of Industrial Psychology.

Consultation among the half dozen top central managers is relatively easy when they are located in nearby offices. To include a wider group, say the president and two supervisory levels plus key staff, becomes cumbersome if attempted on a total group basis. Occasional "staff meetings" primarily for the purpose of *personal* oral reports and answering questions builds morale, but effective planning sessions need to be much smaller groups of directly concerned executives.

Goal-centered performance appraisals

Our discussion of workable instructions and consultative direction has focused largely on communication regarding separate, unique operating problems. Often an executive performs a myriad of interrelated problems: the marketing vice-president, for instance, is concerned with advertising, pricing in specific markets, new products, sales training, and branch offices, just to mention a few subjects that might arise in a single week. To activate such work effectively, managers need a simple procedure to discuss plans and results with each of their subordinates. Goal-centered performance appraisal is such a technique.

The process begins with an employee (of any rank) agreeing with the manager about the results he or she is expected to achieve during an ensuing period—three months, six months, or perhaps a year. Such an agreement on results expected should be based on a mutual understanding about several things: (1) the sphere of activities the employee is concerned with, that is, the organization; (2) the desired goals for these activities, both long-run and short-run; (3) how achievement of these goals will be measured and the level of achievement expected by the end of the period planned; (4) the help the employee may expect from the manager and others; and (5) the freedom and the restraints on how the employee pursues the goal.

Then at the end of the period the senior manager and the subordinate again sit down to review what actually was accomplished, to determine why deviations—both good and bad—from goals occurred, and then to agree on a new set of goals for the next period.

At each review there is grist for a new discussion because a new set of results is available for appraisal and a new set of targets and priorities needs to be agreed upon. As the process proceeds, the manager has repeated opportunities for counseling the individual and for relating individual performance to company strategy, policy, organization, and programs. Hopefully, these discussions will be carried out objectively and frankly, as already suggested in connection with consultative direction. As a minimum, the subordinate should know what is expected of him and how his performance will be measured.

One of the advantages of goal-centered performance appraisals is that they set the stage for frequent interchange about goals and their achievement. In fact, when people work on distinct projects, the review may occur at the close of one project and the beginning of another. In other instances they become a part of programming discussed in the preceding chapter. If a person's total job and total performance are covered in such project or programming discussions, an additional period appraisal serves little purpose. Often, however, these discussions are sharply focused on a particular end result, and an annual examination of overall performance picks up loose ends and gives balanced direction. Whatever the timing, the important thing is that open communication take place between the key employees and their direct supervisors on the array of factors involved in setting goals and their achievement.

Such goal-centered performance appraisals are particularly well suited for activating managers of decentralized operating units and of units located some distance from the central office. Opportunities for casual contacts and informal coaching are fewer the greater the distance between the central office and the operating unit. Also when a shift in strategy has occurred, central managers need a mechanism that gives them a chance (1) to examine the interpretation of the new directions being made by subordinates and (2) to reinterpret their intent. Goal-centered performance appraisals do provide such opportunities to explore the implementation of new strategy.

INCENTIVE STRUCTURE

Important as leadership and communication are in activating a program, central management still has to create a situation in which key employees get deep personal satisfaction from achieving tough company goals. These key people—managers, top staff persons, and outstanding performers in engineering, sales, etc.—are a select group; they have ability and drive, as already indicated by the positions they hold. The challenge is to keep their vigorous efforts channeled toward the strategy that the company is pursuing.

Broadly speaking, central management can influence this eagerness to cooperate through:

1. Identifying factors that motivate these persons.
2. Recognizing the inherent limitations on management's capacity to use such incentives.
3. Applying incentives wisely to groups as well as to individuals.

Executive motivations

The influences that spur people to exert themselves are not obvious and clearcut. Also, individuals differ in their responses. Nevertheless, we can identify several factors that are likely to motivate the kind of persons who reach key positions.

Financial rewards. Overemphasized though it is, in our society money does matter. It is a crude symbol of success, and it is a means of achieving other ends such as security, living comforts, independence, and the like.

We have already discussed the setting of executive salary levels in Chapter 19. The desirability of keeping pay scales (1) in line with rates being paid by other companies and (2) in equitable internal alignment was stressed. Such a salary structure enables a company to attract and to retain competent executives. But note that the base pay tends to be stable and tied to other salaries. Central management is not free to jockey the pay up and down.

The variable pay elements are merit increases, bonuses, and perhaps stock options. These can be used as rewards for outstanding work toward achievement of a strategy.

Sense of achievement. Executives, like other people, take pride in the results of their efforts. Real satisfaction arises from knowing that telephone calls go through, homes are heated, news is timely, or test equipment improves quality. And there is satisfaction in being a good competitor in business just as there is in sports.

More subtle is an inner sense of achievement, of having a challenging assignment and doing it well. Here we are concerned with an important aspect of what the psychologists call "self-realization."

A sense of achievement is a personal matter; it depends on one's own aspirations and values. Central management cannot grant it. Instead, central management tries to create conditions in which key persons feel that they are achieving. Toward this end, winning a strong commitment to company strategy is a primary requirement. Then placing individuals in jobs matched to their abilities and aspirations is a second requirement. When both requisites are met, a strong drive toward company objectives arises.

Social status and recognition. Typical executives like recognition of their accomplishments. This can come partly from their supervisors and other respected individuals who are familiar with their work. In addition, the estimation of one's friends and the community at large carries considerable weight. Since people outside the company have no direct knowledge of what a person does, they rely on titles, nature of an office, and other perquisites—and spending patterns that presumably reflect salary. The "symbols of office," then, can provide strong motivation.

Part of our heritage is the idea that people can raise their social status. Most of our ancestors migrated poor and uneducated; the children and their children after them improved their station in society. Success in business has been one of the major ways of improving one's social status. The opportunity to do so is a strong incentive for many individuals who take on managerial responsibilities.

Power and influence. History records extreme cases of lust for power, but this motivation need not be pushed that far. There is a thrill that comes with making large purchases, watching a plant operate partly as a result of one's own guidance, seeing a new product that includes one's own choice of design, or supervising a pension plan that one piloted through to final adoption. This kind of exercise of power or influence is quite legitimate—in fact, essential. We observe it especially in government and charitable enterprises where the financial rewards are low. For some individuals it is a strong motivator.

Since power, status, achievement, and money are often all provided to some degree in a given job, we have difficulty discerning their relative influence. Also, individuals vary in the importance they attach to these and other motivators, so generalizations are dangerous. Nevertheless, executives can do a better job of winning enthusiastic support for a program if they can sense the weight each of their key people places on these various drives. (And they can also survive internal politics better if they recognize the drives of their peers and superiors.)

Restraints on use of motivators

Awareness of motivators is only a start. Using them requires insight and skill. For example, an action intended as an incentive usually has other effects too. Thus, W. J. McGill might respond favorably to more power, but the assignment of authority to McGill will involve an array of organization issues—scope of duties, decentralization, and the like. The same is true to a lesser extent for the use of titles to give McGill status. Perhaps maintaining a sound organization is more important than the incentive effect of a special concession to please McGill. So the use of most motivators has to be dovetailed with related considerations.

A second limitation, already alluded to, is that central managers do not directly control many of the "rewards." Social status must be won from the community—not the managers. The managers can *help* a person attain it, but their action is indirect. Similarly, bonuses based on sales or profits reflect external conditions as well as internal effort, and achievement also is greatly affected by factors outside the realm of central management. Of course, sophisticated executives recognize that limits exist on what managers are able to do for them, and the good intentions of central management are appreciated. Nevertheless, intentions alone wear thin if the personal satisfactions are not forthcoming fairly quickly.

Fairness and objectivity pose a third limitation. The feeling that any reward should be fairly won is very strong in the United States. A suspicion that favoritism or casualness has been involved in a promotion or a granting of power can cause a lot of hard feeling. Therefore, central managers try to have everyone who knows about a reward feel that it was fairly granted. This need for known reasons supporting a move cannot always be met, and central management then faces a dilemma of either withholding an incentive or antagonizing a number of people who will not understand why the action was taken. (A misunderstood reward can have far-reaching effects. If a belief arises among employees that promotions, bonuses, and the like are made on a capricious basis—and not for supporting official strategy—then a widespread attitude of "why bother to try" may develop.)

Individual versus group incentives

Also delicate is motivating particular individuals without upsetting group cooperation and morale. Incentives frequently single out one or two persons for distinctive treatment, and this inevitably creates disappointments if not hard feelings among those not so chosen. Clearly, when people are promoted or given more power, their status relative to their associates rises. When several individuals aspire to the same job, say vice-presidents hoping for the presidency, the disappointment of being passed by can be acute. Good people may resign, others may lose heart and stagnate. On the other hand, a sense of achievement can be as an individual within a group, and one person's satisfaction need not detract from that of others.

Bonuses and other financial incentives can be awarded either individually or on a group basis. If the entire executive group benefits from company achievement, cooperation and group adhesion is promoted. For this reason many executive bonus plans give everyone the same percentage of their base pay. The obvious disadvantage of such a practice is that the stronger people "carry" the weaker ones. To overcome this drawback, some plans provide for distribution of part of a bonus fund on a group basis and part according to individual contributions. But whatever the incentive plan, the more general problem of motivating individuals without doing too great damage to group cohesion is always present.

Demotion or discharge of an executive is hard to do because more often than not the person has been a personal friend for several years. Procrastination is expensive, however. The main cost of a weak executive is that his occupancy of a key position prevents a more able person from doing that work well. A baseball team cannot afford a rightfielder who bats only .100. If the person's weakness is recognized by other executives, failure to clean out "dead wood" from an organization tends to undermine the determination of other people to exert themselves. A wise and courageous practice is to remove an ineffective individual from a key post; if the company has an obligation to him, he can be given early retirement or a job better suited to his abilities.

Concluding this brief discussion of motivating—one aspect of the broader managerial function of activating—central managers have a never-ending task of sensing what impels their key people, trying within the limits of their powers and without undermining other aspects of administration to tie these motivations to company strategy, and all the while watching the impact of rewards going to one person on the whole executive group.

BRINGING ABOUT CHANGE

A new strategy or a major change in organization creates special problems in activating. Behavior previously endorsed now has to be modified. We are assuming that the redirection has been decided—the new product line selected, a merger with a captive raw material supplier completed, a shift to subcontracting research and development agreed upon, or a reorganization to decentralized product divisions set up—and that instructions regarding the new way of operating have been issued. The "make happen" stage remains. And as we all know, the momentum of a going concern is not redirected merely by giving an order. Central management can aid in the transition by:

1. Relieving anxiety promptly.
2. Identifying areas where modifications in individual and group behavior are needed.
3. Providing time to learn new behaviors.
4. Giving positive reinforcement to desired behavior.

Relieve anxiety promptly

Rumors about changes that might upset cherished relationships spread rapidly. Once the status quo is shattered, employees give attention to all sorts of idle speculation. For instance, just an announcement that the company has bought a new computer can generate stories about closing down an office, firing half the people in the accounting department, or transferring the engineering staff to San Diego. Anxiety builds up, each minor statement or action of central management is interpreted many ways, efficiency drops, and employees begin looking for other jobs.

Much of the anxiety comes from uncertainty—not knowing what is going to happen. To be sure, some anxiety also arises because people are unsure how well they will fit into a new position or under a new boss. Only actual experience in the new setup can remove the latter insecurity, but anxiety from the unknown can be reduced by management.

Prompt communication is vital. Even though specific answers of precisely what will happen often cannot be given because plans have not yet been developed in detail, full discussion of known facts is helpful. Publicly recognizing employee concern, presenting a positive feeling about the future, and scuttling a variety of mistaken rumors all relieve uneasiness. If decisions are not yet made, then a statement of when they will be made and how they will be communicated is much better than no news at all.

An especially sensitive period is when negotiations for, say, a merger are still in the confidential stage. Then the most that can be done is to check false rumors and to assure employees that they will be informed early of any action that will affect them. Confidence in management's credibility is important at this stage.

Identify behavior changes

Supplementing every formally planned organization are a host of customary though unspecified relations. Pat Lee knows whom to contact about payroll deductions, passes along advance information on big orders to the production scheduler, picks up hints on the boss's temper from his secretary, and in other ways fits into an intricate social structure. Now, when a major change in organization and activities occurs, the old social structure breaks down and for a time no one is sure (1) where to get and give bits of information, (2) who has influence in the revised power structure, and (3) whose "suggestions" to consider seriously. During this period of flux, work gets done very slowly.

By identifying the principal areas of disruption, central management can anticipate where trouble is likely to occur. Also, by supporting selected people in disputes, by feeding information through particular channels, and by weighing and if possible accepting recommendations coming from staff or line, central management helps shape the new social structure.

Individual values and habits have to be modified, as well as the social interaction just discussed. For example, for years Tom Novello has worked closely with six southern wholesalers; he knows their buyers personally, and their goodwill has been considered a real asset. Now a decision to sell direct makes these wholesalers insignificant customers. Novello has to stop giving them special attention; the priority goes elsewhere. Since in this instance, as is frequently the case, friendships are involved as well as personal skills or knowledge that gave the possessor a distinctive worth, the new policy is tough to accept. Because emotions and habits are involved, the implications of a major change may lead Novello to unconsciously reject the general idea even when he gives verbal acceptance to it.

Provide time to learn new behavior

Adjustments in behavior take time. When we first do any new task—riding a motorcycle or instructing a computer—we are clumsy and unsure how to interpret cues. The same is true of executive action. And when we *change* behavior, we may have to unlearn old habits and attitudes before picking up the new ones. Social interaction also has to be "learned"; here two or more people are involved, and they have to respond to each other as well as to their own motivations.

Management should recognize the need for this learning period. Even when employees have no reluctance to adopt the new objectives, the early operations will be hard and slow. Practice is needed, and minor adjustments often have to be made. Also, in the kind of strategy changes we have been discussing in this book, some jockeying for position by energetic executives is sure to occur. Time for a "shakedown cruise" is clearly necessary; the tough question of judgment is how long to allow.

Give positive reinforcement

Learning the new behaviors will occur faster if management notices new actions that are along desired lines and gives these strong encouragement. As just noted, usually the new behavior will require extra effort, and special recognition will help sustain that effort during the learning period.

Such recognition of desired behavior also helps relieve anxiety built up during the transition. People are unclear as to just what should be done in the new situation and they will welcome reassurance when they are on the right track. Some doubt is likely to exist about the feasibility of the new direction, so every opportunity to point out where it is succeeding should be used to build confidence in the plan.

Activating a new strategy or reorganization, then, calls for keen perception by central management of the modifications in customary behavior that will be necessary to make the revised plan succeed. By following closely the way people are responding, managers can spot the desired behavior and can encourage people to follow that course. Such positive management will reduce the learning time and will relieve anxiety.

SUMMARY

Central managers play a dual role in activating an enterprise, that is, "putting the show on the road." They must work with their immediate subordinates just as all other executives must initiate and stimulate action of people assigned to them. In addition, central managers strongly influence the activating process throughout the enterprise, partly by the examples they set and partly by establishing certain practices as standard procedures that all executives are expected to observe.

Important elements in this activating process are (1) leadership tone, (2) person-to-person communications, and (3) a viable incentive structure. Central managers in their daily contacts and in their "field" visits can do much to generate a spirit of optimism, confidence, aggressiveness, fairness, or other attitudes—often called leadership tone or climate.

Person-to-person communication between executives and subordinates will be aided by making sure that instructions are complete, reasonable, and clear; by resorting to consultative direction on major problems; and by regular use of goal-centered performance appraisals. The aim in following these methods is to increase mutual understanding and also to gain acceptance of assignments that are made.

Coupled with climate and communication must be a pattern of incentives that encourages cooperation with company plans. Status, sense of achievement, power, and financial rewards are among the motivators of executives. Central management, however, is limited in the extent it can influence these motivators, and it must maintain a careful balance between individual and group motivation.

New strategy, policy, or organization calls for special activating effort. When such major changes are introduced, central management should seek to relieve anxiety, identify where modifications in individual and group behavior are needed, provide time to learn new ways, and give positive reinforcement to desired behavior.

QUESTIONS FOR CLASS DISCUSSION

1. The Business School of Mid-Continent University has been coasting along for several years, with each professor pursuing his own academic interests. Most of the faculty felt dedicated to teaching and found Mid-Continent a pleasant place to work. Then a new dean was appointed. He stirred up a lot of discussion about school objectives, curriculum, admissions, promotion procedures, and the like—through an array of new committees—but no consensus emerged. At the end of his first year, notices of salary changes were mailed and half the faculty found that they were to receive no increase—not even a cost-of-living adjustment to which they were accustomed. The dean stated publicly that increases had been given only to those whom he thought would make significant contributions to building the school in the future. Howls of protest were heard in the University president's office. Morale was shaken. Faculty members started looking for new jobs. (a) What should the new dean have done to get a more constructive response to salary changes? (b) Assuming actions you recommend for (a) had been taken, would those actions have been enough to make Mid-Continent's Business School one of the leading schools in its area?
2. (a) The head of a new real estate firm set some very high volume goals for the company and announced these to his employees and to the public. The goals were achieved or exceeded each year for the first few years. Morale was high. What would have happened if results had been far below the goals? (b) For leadership purposes, how far above reasonable predictions should goals be set? Give examples. (c) How can such goals be tied to company programming discussed in the previous chapter? How can the company assure that optimism does not lead it to disaster?
3. (a) In the inventory liquidation problem described on pages 482-484, explain how consultative supervision might have reduced the losses that occurred. (b) In this situation the organization structure provided for a high degree of decentralization. What effect does the president's instruction to cut inventories have on the authority and the accountability of the vice-president? (c) Could this liquidation have been programmed? How far in advance?
4. Contrast the president's task of activating in a Stage I company and in a Stage II company—using the description of these two types of enterprises given in Chapter 16.
5. What part, if any, should a person with staff duties (as defined in Chapter 17) play in the different steps in activating? If you wish, in your answer assume that the staff person is concerned with sales promotion or with production scheduling and that we are interested in the activating of salesmen or of plant foremen.
6. General managers of foreign subsidiaries often come from the headquarters office. This simplifies relations between headquarters and the local general manager, but experience of foreigners in the U.S. and Yankees abroad indicates considerable difficulty in getting new programs running smoothly. (a) Why do you think general managers from abroad have difficulty activating a program?

(b) Are the same difficulties present when, say, a New Englander becomes a general manager of an operation in Mississippi? (c) What can be done to reduce these difficulties?

7. A management consultant says: "In my observations, senior.managers do a better job of communicating with and motivating their good subordinates than their weaker subordinates." What may account for this behavior, and what effect is it likely to have where it occurs?

8. Assume that you have a good job with a small but growing and successful competitor of Xerox. Your responsibilities have grown with the company; two years ago you transferred to the West Coast division and bought a house; the outlook is rosy. Two weeks ago the newspaper reported a rumor that your company was being acquired by Burroughs Corporation and would be fitted into their computer and office equipment department. Your boss says he knows nothing about the rumor; he did fly to headquarters for a two-day conference last week; he did ask you to update your three-year sales estimates. (a) How do you feel? (b) What do you say to the people working for you?

9. A major oil company has just decided to close down its Kentucky refinery two years hence; local crude oil is running out and the refinery does not have modern, efficient equipment. Many of the employees have 10 to 20 years of service in this refinery, which is on the Ohio River 20 miles from a minor industrial center. If you were in charge of the refinery, what steps would you take in anticipation of the closing?

CASE 21 / Southeast Textiles [1]

The Southeast Textiles company is a medium-sized manufacturer of heavy-duty clothing. Although 80% of its sales come from overalls, work pants and shirts, and work gloves, the company also sells semifinished heavy-duty fabric to other textile and manufacturing companies for conversion into industrial packaging material and for camping equipment. As a regional producer of a relatively specialized product line, Southeast has enjoyed more than 35 years of fairly stable profit and growth. In the past 5 years, however, increased competition both from larger domestic firms and from imports have shrunk Southeast's sales and profit margins, and last year the company suffered its first operating loss in two decades.

In an effort to increase efficiency in the company's major mill in Allison, North Carolina, where 90% of its products are produced, an intensive modernization program was undertaken. New equipment was purchased, new procedures were introduced, and the work force was cut from 800 to 690 hourly workers. A team of consultants was used to advise the company's management during the study that produced the program, and one member of the team, Norman Dean, was hired to become staff assistant to the plant manager, Roger Headrick.

Dean works closely with Headrick on the many problems associated with the modernization program and spends one to two days a week with the company's president, Oliver Hall, and the corporate treasurer, James Davis, advising them on the use of a newly acquired computer system. Hall had been the driving force behind the modernization and was the one who recommended that Headrick hire Dean. Headrick recognized that Dean had a fine background in industrial engineering and was a real "whiz" on computers and modern scientific management techniques. He had reservations, however, about taking him on as his assistant.

"Once we get the new methods and equipment functioning smoothly," Headrick said, "I'm not sure I'll know what to do with him. Despite all of his book knowledge, he still doesn't know many of the tricks of our business, and he has, on more than one occasion, rubbed my people the wrong way by trying to jam his ideas down their throats. Basically he is a pleasant young man, but he is trying hard to justify this program and the faith Hall has in him, and so he can be awfully pushy. But the president has quite a high opinion of him, and right now he is a big help in the transition."

Hall indeed does have a high opinion of Dean. "This is one of the brightest young men I have met," Hall said. "He knows his stuff and he won't be held back by any 'We have never done it that way' arguments. Rog Headrick is a first-rate man with a good solid background in the practical problems of our business. With Dean to keep him informed about more modern management techniques, we have a first-rate team in the mill.

"In addition, Dean is working with Jim Davis and me to get our overall management information-system modernized and to help us use that fancy new computer system we bought to do more than highly specialized clerical work. We had a tough time getting him away from his former firm and had to pay him a very fancy salary, but we think he will earn every penny of it."

One of the areas in which savings were expected from the modernization program was the production control department. James Rose, manager of production control, has been with the company for 12 years and in his present position for almost 5 years. He reports to Headrick and is responsible for scheduling the flow both of raw materials and of finished product as well as actual production planning. He works closely with the plant's purchasing agent and warehouse manager, Everett Sims, and the other members of Headrick's staff (see Exhibit 1).

Prior to the modernization program, Rose had 21 clerks, 3 expediters, and 4 supervisors in his department. With the completion of the plan for the new program, Dean recommended that Rose's department be reduced to 12 clerks, 2 expediters, and 2 supervisors. This was to be accomplished through new methods and through greater use of the company's computer located in the administrative offices adjacent to the Allison mill. The shift in production control required not only a reduction in work force but also a change in the nature of most of the scheduling clerks' jobs, requiring somewhat different and higher levels of skills. Rose, after studying the plan, recommended that the company implement it over a six-month period. This would allow him more time to reduce his work force by means of attrition and transfers and more time to retrain the clerks who would remain. Headrick was sympathetic to this approach but agreed with Dean that it would be too slow and costly. The transition was to take place in one month and on Davis' recommendation the existing work group was given three weeks' notice and the opportunity to begin retraining on their own.

Exhibit 1
PARTIAL ORGANIZATION CHART,
SOUTHEAST TEXTILES

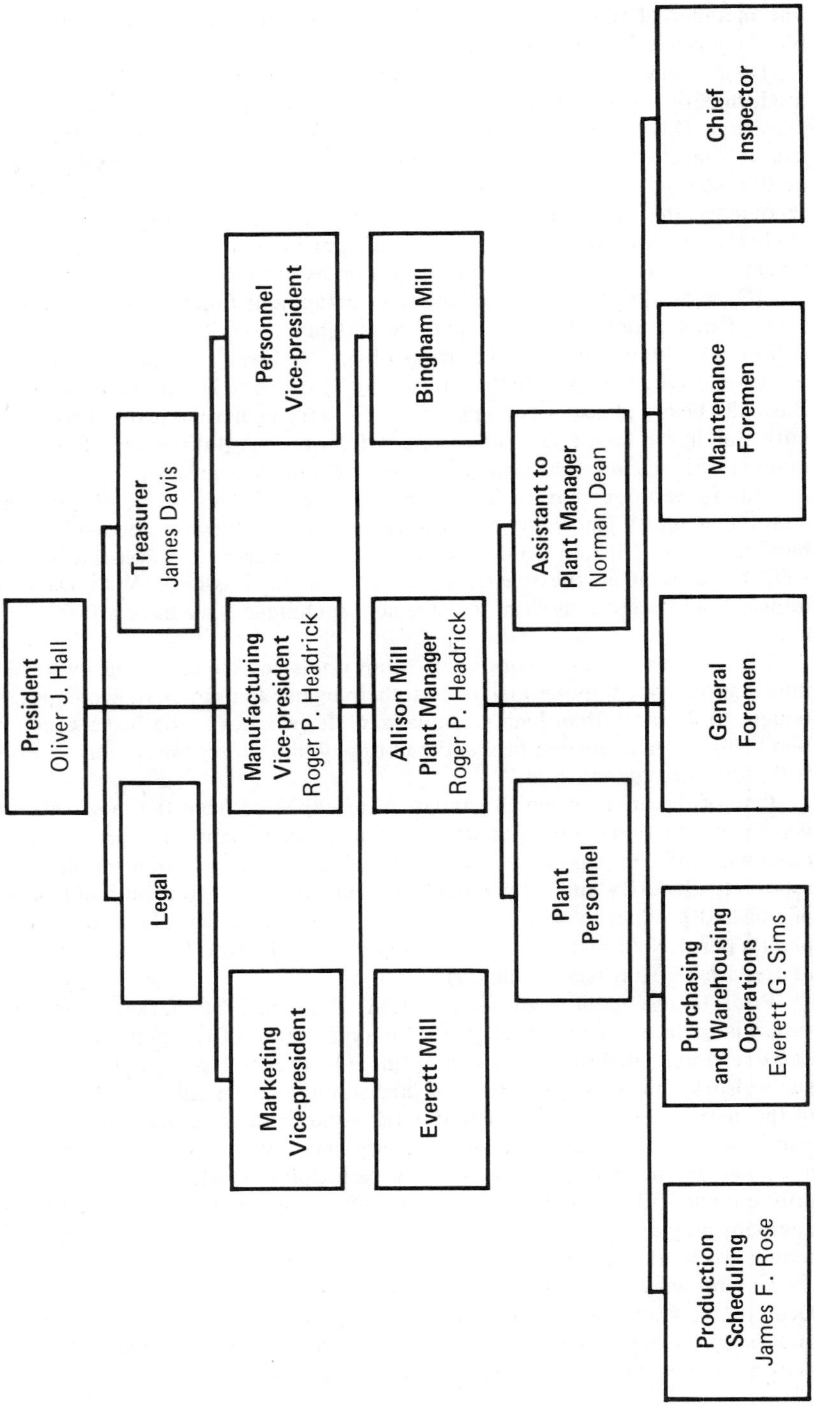

President
Oliver J. Hall

Treasurer
James Davis

Legal

Marketing
Vice-president

Manufacturing
Vice-president
Roger P. Headrick

Personnel
Vice-president

Everett Mill

Allison Mill
Plant Manager
Roger P. Headrick

Bingham Mill

Plant Personnel

Assistant to
Plant Manager
Norman Dean

Production
Scheduling
James F. Rose

Purchasing
and Warehousing
Operations
Everett G. Sims

General
Foremen

Maintenance
Foremen

Chief
Inspector

During this period, 8 of the original 21 clerks quit, and 4, at their own expense, had begun taking courses offered in a nearby technical institute. Three of the original group of clerks and 2 supervisors were transferred to other jobs. At the end of the month, 10 clerks, including one of the 4 attending classes, 1 expediter, and 2 supervisors were let go. Nine new clerks and 2 new supervisors were hired and the new system was formally introduced. Wage rates for the clerks were increased by 8%, and for the supervisors, by 10%.

The next eight weeks were extremely hectic ones throughout the mill where similar changes were taking place. In production scheduling, 2 clerks and 1 supervisor resigned and were replaced. During this period, Rose and Dean were almost constantly in conflict over how to resolve the numerous crises that arose. After several more months, things settled down, the work force stabilized, and it appeared that the program might at last begin to produce the savings that had been promised. At this point, costs are still running higher than Dean had originally estimated but lower than before the new program was instituted. Dean has worked long hours and has supplemented Rose's limited knowledge in certain aspects of the new system. He had at first recommended transferring Rose to another position and replacing him with someone more familiar with the new approach, but Headrick vetoed his proposal.

Because new equipment and layout costs throughout the mill had been high, the president was constantly checking with Headrick and Dean on when the economies would start to show up. Headrick was quick to admit that Rose had been of great help in curbing the president's desire to see more dramatic and more immediate cost reductions.

The three men who had been in Rose's department prior to the changeover seemed to adjust to the new system and to the newer employees, and the department's effectiveness increased. Headrick gave Rose much of the credit for the relatively smooth transition within the production control department because of Rose's skillful handling of his personnel. Many of the other departments had had a much rougher time maintaining morale in the face of the changes that took place. Rumors persist that production workers are being joined by many of the men and women doing technical, clerical, and low-level white-collar tasks in an attempt to bring in a union. So far, no formal request for representation elections have been made.

The president praised Headrick and Dean for their work, but warned them to keep an eye out for union trouble. Hall said: "We have too much invested in this new program to see it thwarted by having to work with a union. One of the reasons I moved the company down here in 1946 was to get away from the fetters a union can place on you. We may have to make a lot more changes before we are through and I don't want to have to bargain every change in wage-rates and work-rules with a union. So keep an eye out for trouble and try not to push your people any harder than you have to. Try to recognize and reward the good ones and get rid of the troublemakers."

Although operations continued more or less smoothly, a major problem arose in the production scheduling department on a certain Friday. As a result of a breakdown in the computer on Thursday afternoon, much of the data required for completion of production schedules for the next two weeks was not available. As a result, at 8:30 on Friday morning, Rose suggested to Headrick that they revert to procedures that were followed prior to the new program to complete the work which would be needed by Monday morning.

Headrick called Dean in and the three men discussed the problem. Dean listened to Rose's suggestion and said: "No good, Jim! If you go back to those methods with only

12 people, you'll never finish on time and we'll start the week in a real hole. Most of your men don't even know the old system. I think we had better just wait until they de-bug the "monster" [computer]. If they get it going by eleven o'clock, we can still finish up by giving your people a couple of hours of overtime."

Rose asked: "What happens if they don't get it fixed on time? If I start now, we can get the job finished with the old system even if we need a couple of hours tonight and a half-day on Saturday. The overtime costs will be a fraction of what it will cost us on downtime in the mill if we don't have the schedules by Monday morning."

Dean countered by saying he was sure they would get the computer problem traced in time to avoid the extra cost of bringing the men in on Saturday. "Besides, if worse comes to worst and they don't get us the data we need till this afternoon, then we can bring them in Saturday."

Headrick decided somewhat reluctantly to go along with Dean. By twelve o'clock on Friday the problem with the computer had been traced to the failure of a component in its central logic system. A replacement was promised by one o'clock. Work was at a standstill in his department and Rose again requested that he be authorized to get started on the old system. This time, both Dean and Headrick firmly agreed it was probably too late and that with the problem diagnosed they would get the data they needed by two o'clock. Rose was told to ask his people to put in 3 hours of overtime Friday night and a half-day on Saturday.

Unfortunately, the component needed in the computer was not delivered and installed until two o'clock, and when a test was run on the system, a more serious problem, hitherto undetected, was found. The computer servicemen indicated that now, even working through the night, they could not complete repair and testing in less than 24 hours. When Headrick was informed of the bad news by Dean, he called Rose and told him to get busy with the old system. Rose protested: "Look, Roger, it's almost three o'clock. It's just too late now. When I explained the situation to the boys earlier, I had a tough time getting some of them to agree to stay late tonight and an even tougher time getting them to agree to come in on Saturday if we needed them. Those with families want to get home, and the younger men have dates. I had to pull out all stops and virtually plead with several to come in tomorrow. All but one agreed to come if we needed them, but it was reluctantly. How can I go back now and tell them we do need them, when they'll find out, as the oldtimers know, the work simply can't be done even with a full day on Saturday?"

Dean's response was: "Plead? For heaven's sake, why should you have to plead? Don't those men have any loyalty to the company? Once in a rare while we really need to have them give a little extra and you have to plead? Perhaps if you didn't pamper them so, they would recognize that they have an obligation to the firm."

Rose answered angrily: "The firm has an obligation to them, too. If we keep 12 men late tonight and foul up their weekend plans, it should be for a darn good reason. If I get started now, we still won't finish until ten or eleven o'clock on Monday morning even if they work till eight o'clock tonight and all day Saturday. If we start fresh on Monday and I ask them to come in an hour earlier, we'll finish by noon if the computer is fixed this weekend. We are going to lose half a day in the mill on Monday any way we do it now and I don't see any point in making matters worse by asking my men to ruin their weekends."

Dean was equally adamant and insisted that Rose at least try to get the work done by Saturday. Headrick ended the discussion by saying: "Look, Jim, we've got a bad situation now no matter what we do. If I lose a half-day in the mill at this time of the year, it's not going to be good and the president won't listen to any excuses blaming the computer. He will want to know why we couldn't work around it. You know how touchy he is about his new brainchild. Get started right now, keep the men until eight o'clock tonight and as long tomorrow as necessary, but get those schedules done.''

When Rose left, Dean shook his head and commented: "I don't want to put all the blame on Jim, but if he knew more about the new system he would have been a day and a half earlier in requesting the data we need from the computer. The system was designed to protect against machine failure by giving us a day or so slack at the end of the month. I can't help but feel that this might have been avoided if we had a man in production control who was more familiar with the new system than Jim.''

After leaving, Rose announced the decision to his supervisors and then joined them to tell the scheduling clerks. They reluctantly agreed to stay, and the three who had worked under the old system were told to assist Rose in instructing the others.

One of the three, Ken King, asked to speak with Rose privately. He explained that he had planned on asking for the afternoon off so that he and his wife could get to the rehearsal for their son's wedding. The wedding was to be held in a town four hours' drive from their home. "When you asked us to stay late tonight, I almost died,'' he said. "If I have to stay, I will; but we'll miss the rehearsal and won't get in before midnight for the wedding tomorrow. No matter what you say about this afternoon, I can't come in tomorrow.''

Rose thought a moment and then advised King to tell the company nurse that he had a severe headache and wanted to go home immediately. "I'll okay it when she calls me,'' Rose said. "I'd like to give you the time, but under the kind of pressure we are facing, I can't.''

King thanked him, left, and did as he suggested. By eight o'clock, it was apparent to Rose that the department could not finish the work on Saturday and he called Headrick at home to ask what he should do. Headrick indicated that whether they finished or not, he wanted them to try and insisted that if they worked harder they might still make it. Nine of the 12 clerks reported for work on Saturday and worked until five o'clock, but the schedules were not completed until almost noon on Monday. Because King was one of the three who knew the old system, his absence had slowed things down, but Rose was certain they could not have finished much earlier even with King. He was surprised, in fact, that they had done as well as they had.

The mill worked on certain stock items Monday morning and did not get into the new schedules until almost two o'clock. As a result, a considerable increase over standard costs was anticipated.

On Monday morning, Dean learned informally of what had happened to Ken King. He confronted Headrick with what he had heard and suggested that the time had come to replace Rose.

Required: (a) If you were in Headrick's position on that Monday, what disciplinary action, if any, would you take with respect to Rose?

(b) What reaction up and down the organization would you anticipate to your action?

(c) What other actions do you recommend that Headrick and/or Hall take to establish a leadership tone that will aid in implementing changes in the company?

CONTROLLING OPERATIONS

Inspired strategy, wise policy, ingenious organization, and perceptive programming and activating all may fail to create an outstanding company unless the final phase in the management cycle—controlling—is also done well. Management control involves watching what is actually happening, evaluating this performance, taking corrective action if necessary, and developing a data base for the next round of planning. The primary aim of control is to assure, insofar as possible, that plans are actually carried out.

Numerous controls are used in every well-managed company. Central management obviously cannot, and should not, try to follow all these detailed measurements and evaluations that occur daily. Instead central management should focus on:

1. The design of the company control structure.
2. Exercising control of overall results and of unusually crucial activities.
3. Utilizing control data to help formulate new strategy, policy, and programs.

First we need to examine the nature and the variety of applications of the basic control process.

NATURE OF THE CONTROL PROCESS

Three elements will be found in every control system:

1. Standards of acceptable performance are established.
2. Actual performance is appraised in terms of these standards.
3. When actual results are found to be unsatisfactory, corrective action is initiated.

Many problems arise in the application of this simple sequence: what should be covered by the standards and how tough they should be; who will do the measuring of performance and how this information will get transmitted to the people who evaluate it; and what types of corrective action will lead to improved performance in the future. Let us look at a few illustrations.

Representative control systems

The three elements mentioned above are found in every control system, but the specific measures that make up a control system must be adapted to the particular activity being controlled. Representative applications are discussed in the following paragraphs.

Control of sales volume. For many years a chemical company had kept track of its sales in terms of dollars and physical units for each major line of products. Trends in these figures were the cause of rejoicing or dismay, but a new sales manager felt that they did not enable him to pinpoint difficulties and to take specific corrective action. Consequently, he expanded the sales control system in two ways. First, he kept track of sales results in much greater detail; all orders were analyzed in terms of sales representatives, type of customers, geographical areas, and products, and cross-classifications of each category were charted. Second, he tried to develop some criteria for what sales should be in each category. For this purpose, he developed an index of activity for types of customers (consumer industries), geographical regions, and long-term trends for products. From this information and data on past sales, he developed quotas for subdivisions of the sales analysis. These quotas were adjusted up or down as changes occurred in the market.

These two steps generated a mass of statistics. However, with the aid of a sales analyst, the sales manager could identify particular areas or industries where orders were falling behind quota. Often the sales representatives concerned had a good explanation for the deviation, but in other instances remedial action was obviously called for. The sales representatives grumbled about spending a great deal of their time with the new statistics. The sales manager, on the other hand, was convinced that the expanded controls brought to light difficulties that might have remained buried in the large totals formerly used. Experience also indicated that the sales representatives, who received the control data as soon as the sales manager, became more diligent about covering each part of their assigned territory.

This example raises the question of how detailed controls should be. The previous controls of the chemical company were too general to be useful for operating purposes. On the other hand, if the company had pursued the pattern of control to very small territories and fine industry divisions, the mass of statistics would have been overwhelming and the variations of doubtful significance.

Another notable feature of the system was a variable standard. If industrial activity in a particular territory was booming, the sales representative was expected to secure higher sales; but a decline in the market being served was also taken into account in appraising the sales representative's results. The assumption here is that the factors causing the expansion or the contraction in the market were beyond the sales representative's influence.

Inventory control. One way to achieve control in considerable detail and still not swamp executives with masses of information is to have measuring and corrective action taken by the people who are performing the operation—or perhaps done automatically. This possibility is illustrated by the inventory control system of a cash register manufacturer. This firm has to keep on hand 65,000 different parts so that finished machines can be assembled rapidly as customers' orders are received.

Briefly, the control system involves: (1) Establishing the minimum stock for each part (the *standard*). Whenever the supply on hand falls below this minimum, a standard order for additional stock is placed. (2) Maintaining a perpetual inventory record of each item and comparing this with the minimum standard. Formerly, this record and its examination (*appraisal*) was done by stockclerks on tags attached to the front of the bin containing each part. More recently, maintenance of the inventory record and comparison with the ordering point has been assigned to an electronic computer. (3) Whenever the stock on hand falls below the minimum standard, a requisition for additional materials is issued (*corrective action*). Of course, as demand and technology change, the standards have to be adjusted, and periodically a physical inventory is taken to make sure that the records are accurate.

This rather conventional inventory control system suggests two possibilities for many other controls. Once a clear-cut control is designed, it often can be operated by people close to the operation, perhaps the operators themselves. Upper management then can limit its attention to design of the system and checking to be sure that it is being properly utilized. And, in the extreme, when both the standards and the corrective action are clear-cut and current performance can be measured in quantitative terms, the entire control process can be automated.

Control of large capital expenditures. Typically, large capital expenditures must be approved by the board of directors before they can be advanced beyond the planning stage. Often all projects contemplated for a year are assembled together in a capital expenditures budget, as explained in Chapter 13, and specific approval is given for those projects the board considers most desirable. Once approved, the project description becomes the control standard, and subsequent steps are checked against this standard.

In terms of the basic control process, this procedure differs significantly from the two controls we just examined. In the previous examples, as in many controls, measurement takes place after action is completed. So these controls fall into the broad class of "post-action" controls. In contrast, the directors' review of capital expenditures occurs during the process—after the plan is completed but before commitments are made. This control, like many in-process quality controls, is a "yes-no" control. Action may not proceed until approval is given. The board of directors reserves the function of comparing specific proposals against its standards before any damage can be done. This holding a tight rein is in sharp contrast to a control system that operates routinely, if not automatically.

Executives maintain control over some activities by withholding permission to act until they give their approval to the specific acts. Appointment of key personnel, signing large contracts, selling fixed assets, and starting a sales campaign are often treated in this manner. Progress is slowed, but the executives feel the particular subjects are of such importance that they are unwilling to rely upon such standards as they can define with appraisal after the action is completed. Obviously only a limited number of activities may be treated in this slow manner in a large, vigorous enterprise.

Strategy control. In addition to post-action controls and yes-no controls, a third class is steering-controls. Control of a spacecraft headed for the moon, for instance, takes place days before the flight is finished. As soon as the craft leaves the earth, a forecast is made of where it is headed; corrective action is taken immediately based on the forecast. Post-action control, after the craft either hit or missed the moon, obviously would be too late.

Company strategy is like the flight of the spacecraft. We can't afford to wait for completed results before exercising control. Instead, we rely primarily on updated forecasts. (a) We monitor key assumptions about consumer tastes, governmental action, interest rates, competitors' actions, and the like. If new information indicates that operating conditions will differ from the original assumptions, corrective actions may be taken at once. (b) At major "milestones"—for instance, when market tests are completed or just before making a large investment—the entire strategy is reviewed, using all new information available, and a new forecast of results is made. The forecasted result is compared with company objectives, and a decision is made whether to continue on the present course or to modify it.

Steering-controls are far from precise, but they have the great advantage of prompting an adjustment while an array of possibilities are still open. Also, people being controlled feel that steering-controls are devices to help them reach objectives rather than a judgment of past success or failure.

Budgetary control. The best *comprehensive* control system is based on financial budgets. Here the already existing accounting structure is the base; the budgets are simply a prediction, or plan, of what various accounting figures should be at some future date. Income and expense accounts for, say, the next year are estimated and are summarized into a budgeted profit and loss statement. At the same time, changes in assets, liabilities, and equity are estimated and are summarized into a budgeted balance sheet for the end of the period.

For control purposes, the budgeted figures become the standards. Then when the normal accounting data come in, they are considered a measurement of actual performance and are easily compared with the budget standard. Of course this procedure can be followed for departments as well as the total company and for monthly, annual, or any other periods for which regular accounting figures are compiled.

Financial budgets have several outstanding advantages: (1) The measuring process is already well established and requires no additional expense. (2) All parts of the company are covered with the same comprehensiveness of official financial reports. (3) The use of dollars as a common language permits coordination and consolidation of plans for different parts of the business. (4) The control mechanism is directly related to one or more typical company objectives—for example, earnings per share, return on investment, or sales growth.

Being so closely tied to conventional accounting, financial budgets also have limitations: (1) Accounting figures do not promptly reflect intangibles such as customer goodwill, employee morale, executive development, research and product and process development, equipment maintenance, or market position. (2) The annual accounting period may not match the physical production or marketing cycle, so that expenses are hard to relate to resulting income and arguments arise over allocations. (3) Early warning of trouble is usually buried; also the accuracy desirable for financial reports delays budget comparisons. These drawbacks strongly suggest that budgetary control should be accompanied by other types of control in order to achieve a balanced control structure.

In actual operations the primary problem with financial budgets is how they are used by executives. If budgets are merely predictions by staff personnel or the central accounting office instead of carefully conceived plans by line managers, they will not be accepted as reasonable standards. And when the standard is not respected, the whole budgetary process is regarded as an annoying distraction. Also budgetary control has to be supported by central management—by its insistence that deviations be acted upon and by requesting revisions of budgets when changes in strategy and programs are made.

Control of executive development. The examples of control discussed thus far have all dealt primarily with objective data. Many important aspects of business operation are not so clear-cut. Nevertheless, control of these intangibles may be even more crucial to long-run success than things that are easily observed and measured. Executive development falls into this intangible category.

One well-managed company measures its progress in executive development in two ways. Annually, its key executives must report executive development activities undertaken by people in their departments. The reports cover special training assignments, appraisal reviews, training meetings, civic and trade association activities, and the like. The company recognizes that such reports omit perhaps the most important training that takes place on the job. It also recognizes that the activities reported may not have resulted in any significant executive development. However, the hope is that emphasis on training activities will encourage executives and operators alike to give attention to the basic process.

The second measure of executive development used by this company is the number of people considered to be ready for promotion. Data for this purpose are assembled from an executive inventory, such as the one described in Chapter 19. Again the unreliability of the data is recognized, but they are used simply as the best information available.

Two control techniques are illustrated in the case just cited. One is the use of activities rather than end results. This is done because the company cannot afford to wait until the end of the process (5, 10, or 20 years in the case of executive development). Moreover, actual measurement of progress is difficult if not impossible. Basic research, legal work, and public relations are further examples of business functions posing this sort of measurement problem.

The case also again illustrates the use of steering-control. If the number of people classified as promotable is inadequate to meet projected requirements, a danger signal has clearly appeared. In fact, more promotable people may be present than the inventory shows, or conversely, the estimates of employees' capacity to take on added responsibilities may be over-optimistic. Nevertheless, the warning is sufficiently serious so that more careful consideration and probably corrective action is called for. Every good control system makes wide use of steering-controls because they help to identify trouble in the early stages.

The attempts to control executive development just described also point to a danger. Executives can become so absorbed in making the measures look good—for example, lots of training meetings and high evaluations of subordinates—that they fail to accomplish the underlying objective. In other words, because the controls do not deal specifically with desired end-results, they may misdirect effort.

Standards of performance

The cases just discussed illustrate various kinds of controls. Now, let us turn to a more general review of the three basic steps in the control process—setting standards, appraising results, and corrective action.

Some standard or guide is essential in any form of control. Even informal control requires that executives have some plan or standard in mind by which to appraise the activities they are supervising. These standards should come directly from the strategy, policy, deadlines, specifications, and other goals established in earlier stages of the management cycle.

Satisfactory performance, of course, has many aspects, and it is impractical to set control standards for all of these points. Instead, *strategic control spots* are picked out for regular observation. Important considerations in picking these strategic points are: (1) catching important deviations in time to take corrective action; (2) practicality and economy in making observations; (3) providing some comprehensive controls that consolidate and summarize large blocks of detailed activities; and (4) securing a balance in control so that some aspects of the work, such as developing executives, will not be slighted because of close controls on other phases. What to watch is vital in every simple and effective control system.

"How good is good" is the next question. For each control point, an *acceptable level of performance* must be set. How many sales orders per month do we expect Jean Jones to obtain? What level of absenteeism is considered dangerous? Is a labor cost of $13.95 per unit satisfactory for our deluxe model? The answers to such questions become the accepted norms—the par for the course. One of the best ways of providing flexibility in a control system is to devise acceptable and prompt ways of adjusting these norms.

Appraising performance

Some comparison of actual performance with control standards may be done by a manager. A sales manager, for example, may occasionally travel with sales representatives to observe their performance and the attitudes of customers. Typically, however, *control observations* are made by someone other than the executive—an inspector, a cost analyst, a market research person, and the like. Also, some control data are derived as a by-product of other record keeping. Expense data, for instance, may come from payroll records and inventory records; sales data may be gleaned from a file of customers' orders.

Such separations of measuring performance from its evaluation and corrective action necessitates *control reports*. The information must be communicated from person to person, and this raises a host of questions: What form should be used? How much detail should they contain? To whom should they be sent? How often should they go? Can reports be simplified by dealing only with exceptions to standards?

The effectiveness of a control is usually increased by *prompt reporting*. If some undesirable practice is going on, it should be corrected quickly. Moreover, the cause of trouble can be learned better if people have not had several weeks to forget the circumstances. Also, employees, knowing that a prompt check on deviations from standards will be made, are more likely to be careful in their daily work. Consequently, the sooner a control report reaches a manager, the better the control will be.

Another practical issue in appraisal is whether *sampling* will provide adequate information. Perhaps refined statistical techniques, such as statistical quality control, can be used to decide the size of the sample and the inferences that can be drawn from it. In some operations—aircraft manufacturing, for example—100% observation is essential. And, we have already noted that for certain key actions—capital expenditures and executive appointments are typical—a manager may insist on giving personal approval before performance continues.

The engineering term "measuring and feedback" provides another way of describing this appraisal step in the control process.

Corrective action

Real control goes beyond checking on work performed. Unless corrective action is taken when standards are not met or when new opportunities appear, the process amounts to little more than a historical record.

As soon as a deviation from standard is detected, the causes of the variation should be investigated. If the deviation is unfavorable, perhaps the difficulty will be due to a lack of supplies, a breakdown of machinery, a strike in a customer's plant, or other hindrance in *operating conditions*. In such situations, the executive will take immediate steps to remove any obstructions he can.

At other times, the difficulty will be personal in nature. Perhaps there is a simple *misunderstanding,* a failure in human communication; this may be quickly corrected. More troublesome is *inadequate training* of persons assigned to do the work. As a rule in such cases, help is provided until the person has received the training needed. Of course, if investigation reveals that the person simply does not have the necessary *basic ability*—and never should have been selected for the job—transfer of the work or a replacement of the individual may be the only satisfactory remedy. All too often, the gap between performance and standard reflects a lack of effort. The person may be able to do the work and may understand what is wanted, the operating situation may be satisfactory, but the needed *incentive* is lacking. This, then, calls for additional motivation by the manager.

Corrective action sometimes leads to a *revision of plans*. The check on operating conditions and on selection, training, direction, and motivation of the operators may reveal that the standards themselves are unrealistic. If control is to have any meaning in the future, such standards should be revised. Also, the delay in work may have been so serious that schedules need to be rearranged, budgets revised, or customers notified. These changes in plans should give operators and executives a new set of standards that are reasonable criteria for future actions. Or the controls may have flagged results much better than predicted, and if such results can be expected to continue, new standards should be set.

CENTRAL MANAGEMENT CONTROL TASKS

What is central management's role in all this controlling activity indicated in the preceding discussion? The answer lies in three areas: (1) design of a balanced control structure for the total company, (2) actually exercising control at selected spots, and (3) using control data to help shape new strategy and programs.

Company control structure

The control structure of a company is more than the simple aggregate of the various controls used by different executives. These controls should be examined to be sure that no important considerations are missing; balance and emphasis should be checked to be sure they are in harmony with basic company objectives; and the compatibility of the controls with company planning, organization, and supervision should be assured.

Assuring adequate coverage. The table on the following page suggests a way to examine a company control structure. In the left-hand column should be listed all those result areas that central management believes should be controlled by someone in the enterprise. The areas listed in the table are merely suggestive. In practice, the management of any single company will undoubtedly want to be much more specific on some points and to omit others.

With the result areas identified, senior executives can discover a great deal about control in their company by filling in the rest of the table. Usually a company will have very good controls in some areas and only vague and informal systems in others. This may be due to historical custom or to the relative ease of obtaining certain kinds of data. As a result of the analysis, central management will know where to try to devise additional controls that will fill in the missing gaps.

Relation of controls to decentralization. In thinking about who should set specific norms, appraise current performance, and take corrective action, organization structure should be related to control structure. The greater the decentralization of authority to make decisions, the further down the hierarchy should be the short-run control activity. It is simply inconsistent to give a manager freedom to run a division or a department and then to have some outside person make frequent detailed checks of just what is being done and suggest corrective action. In fact, control of routine activities is often performed further down the line than decision-making.

On the other hand, the manager who makes a delegation needs some reassurance that the authorization is being wisely used. Consequently, summary reports of results are submitted monthly or quarterly to senior executives. Also, senior executives may wish to watch a limited number of "danger signals" both for control and as a basis for future planning.

In addition, senior executives may want to be sure that adequate controls are being used by their subordinates, even though none of the reports come to them. A simple example is insistence on tight controls on cash disbursements in a branch office with no further attention (except the annual financial audit) being given by the supervising executive. Quality controls and production controls are frequently handled on the same basis. In effect, a pattern of control is stipulated when the subordinate manger is appointed, but exercise of this control is a part of the delegation made to him.

Integrated data processing. A total view of the control structure for a company emphasizes the large number of control reports that must pass through the organization. Original data have to be compiled and then analyzed, and reports must be sent to the operator, the boss, and perhaps a staff group. In addition, summaries or reports of exceptions probably go to a senior executive. The total of these reports in a large company is staggering.

Electronic data processing equipment can speed up the analysis and the distribution of this control information—*if* it is in numerical form. Perhaps such

Approach to Company Control Structure					
System Design			Exercising Controls		
Result Area to be Controlled	Control Points	Form of Measurement (Indexes)	Set Specific Norms (Pars)	Appraise and Report	Take Corrective Action
General Management:					
Profitability	———	———	Who?	Who?	Who?
Market Position	———	———	"	"	"
Productivity	———	———	"	"	"
Technical Research	———	———	"	"	"
Personnel Dev.	———	———	"	"	"
Employee Relations	———	———	"	"	"
Public Attitudes	———	———	"	"	"
Sales:					
Output	———	———	"	"	"
———	———	———	"	"	"
———	———	———	"	"	"
Expenses	———	———	"	"	"
———	———	———	"	"	"
———	———	———	"	"	"
Resources used	———	———	"	"	"
———	———	———	"	"	"
———	———	———	"	"	"
Other	———	———	"	"	"
Production:					
Output	———	———	"	"	"
———	———	———	"	"	"
———	———	———	"	"	"
Expenses	———	———	"	"	"
———	———	———	"	"	"
———	———	———	"	"	"
Resources used	———	———	"	"	"
———	———	———	"	"	"
———	———	———	"	"	"
Other	———	———	"	"	"
Research & Eng.:					
Output	———	———	"	"	"
———	———	———	"	"	"
———	———	———	"	"	"
Expenses	———	———	"	"	"
———	———	———	"	"	"
———	———	———	"	"	"
Resources used	———	———	"	"	"
———	———	———	"	"	"
Other	———	———	"	"	"
All Other Divisions:					
———	———	———	"	"	"
———	———	———	"	"	"

equipment can also cut the expense of report preparation, though the usual result is a substantial increase in the number of reports (better control) for hopefully the same expense. However, to achieve this speedier, elaborated flow, the procedures for handling data have to be revised. Potentially, all original data will be fed into the computer, and there they become available for planning as well as control purposes. We then have integrated data processing.

This new speed and ready availability of data should be utilized in the company control structure. They may make certain controls in headquarters, *or* in the field, more feasible. At the same time, a danger should be recognized—a plethora of numerical reports will increase the tendency to overemphasize those factors that can be expressed numerically. Consequently, integrated data processing should be regarded as an aid and not as a determining factor in the design of a company control structure.

Relation of controls to other phases of managing. In stressing the desirability of having central management carefully shape the company control structure, we are not suggesting that a lot of controls be superimposed on other management activities. For example, the target dates set in programming of normal operations or elaborated in a PERT schedule automatically become norms in the control process; quality control standards are simply the logical extension of product policy dealing with quality; and so on. Controls are the means for assuring that such plans are fulfilled.

Similarly, goal-centered performance reviews include agreeing on personal goals for the next six months or a year and then comparing accomplishments with the goals at the end of the period. Many of the goals thus established will simply be norms for factors already included in the control structure, and control reports will be used in the discussion of results. Of course, additional unique goals may be agreed upon and a temporary control cycle set up. But if the company control structure deals with crucial areas, a factual basis will already exist for much of the performance appraisal discussion.

Controls exercised by central management

Design of an effective control structure is a major central management task. But even an ideal structure will not relieve central management from exercising some controls itself. Several attempts have been made to identify a limited number of key result areas that central management should watch. The most suggestive of these is a list used by the General Electric Company. According to this approach, the effectiveness of overall management can be appraised in terms of:

1. Profitability, in both percent of sales and return on investment.
2. Market position.
3. Productivity, which means improving costs as well as sales.
4. Leadership in technological research.
5. Development of future key people, both technical and managerial.

6. Employee attitudes and relations.
7. Public attitudes.
8. Balance of long- and short-range objectives.

Note that this list places considerable emphasis on strength for future growth as well as on current profitability.

In addition, the General Electric Company and others expect senior executives to single out crucial problems in their particular industry or function and to watch these closely. Incidentally, what is crucial shifts from time to time—union relations may be especially sensitive at one time, foreign competition at another. So, the attention of top management shifts, leaving for subordinates the task of continuing vigilance.

As emphasized in Chapter 18, central management has a particular responsibility to be alert to *new* developments that may create opportunities or obstacles. Consequently, much of the data examined by central management is not for routine control but a source of possible cues to future changes.

Using control data for future planning

Business provides a continuing flow of services. In the same day, managers are checking on final "delivery" to today's customers and also preparing for next year. Control contributes to this never-ending preparation for the future by feeding in appraisals of past successes and difficulties. For central management, inevitably removed from day-to-day action, this building for the future is certainly the most exciting facet of control.

The *replanning* that is prompted by control reports may be short-run. Often a program for raising capital or launching a new product has to be speeded up or slowed down because of success—or lack of it—in pilot plant tests. Or, a rise in production costs may precipitate a withdrawal from a marginal market or an adjustment in prices.

Likewise, control reports provide one of the main considerations in deciding what to aim for in the *next planning period*. The quality achieved, the rate of output, the expenses, and the consumer acceptance in the past period are guides to what may be expected in the next round. Care must be exercised in merely projecting the future on the basis of past experience, because conditions change and improvements are possible. Nevertheless, to disregard past performance is even greater folly. And it is control reports that provide the most readily available data on past performance.

Central management also uses control data in designing *new strategy*. Targets, we noted in Chapter 4, are one dimension of strategy; they identify the criteria by which success will be measured and indicate levels of achievement expected. So in considering strategy, one of the first steps management takes is to see how close to such targets actual performance has been. As with short-range planning, this past performance is a significant input in deciding where to set future targets.

More significant, however, are the reasons why targets have been exceeded or not achieved. Market potentials may have changed, international trade barriers may have been lowered, competitors may have exploited a new technology, or the company may have lost its distinctiveness in key personnel. Such factors as these may show that a new operational strategy is needed. We do not mean that control reports will be the only stimulus to revising strategy; environment and industry analyses, recommended in Chapters 2 and 3, should also flag future opportunities and problems. But in a going concern, the take-off point is a careful reading of how well we are doing relative to what we set out to do. In this manner, central management uses the control system as a springboard in deciding future strategy.

SUMMARY

Strategy, policy, and organization provide the broad guides and the framework for the activities of a company. Planning is then extended to detailed methods and procedures, and on to programs and schedules. The managers turn all this preparatory work into action as they issue operating instructions and motivate people to execute the plans. Even then, the task of managing is not complete; there remains the vital step of control.

Control is necessary to insure that actual performance conforms to plans. The specific measures for control should, of course, be adapted to the particular activity. Nevertheless, three basic steps must always be present: (1) Standards of satisfactory performance should be set up at strategic points—points that will provide timely, economical, comprehensive, and balanced checks—and, for each point, a norm or level of achievement should be agreed upon. (2) Actual performance should be compared with these standards by sampling, 100% inspection, or perhaps required confirmation, and appraisal reports should be sent to all persons directly involved. (3) When deficiencies are detected, corrective action is necessary—that is, adjusting operating conditions, improving competence of assigned operators, motivating, or perhaps modifying plans.

Central management becomes involved in controlling in three main ways: (1) It reviews the numerous controls that operate within the company to make sure that all key points are adequately covered and that the net emphasis of the controls is in harmony with company objectives. This is a matter of design of the total control structure. (2) Central management itself exercises control on overall company results and on a few selected activities that are especially crucial to long-run results. (3) Even more important, central management utilizes data from control reports to assess how well company strategy is being achieved. This analysis provides an important base for setting new targets and perhaps reshaping the operating strategy. Thus the controls serve as a feedback into company planning, and the management cycle of planning, organizing, activating, and controlling starts anew.

QUESTIONS FOR CLASS DISCUSSION

1. In an effort to reduce the cost of hospital care, the Riverdale Hospital is expanding its out-patient department. ("Out-patients" do not live in the hospital; instead, they come to the hospital, perhaps daily, only for the treatment.) Opinions differ as to the wisdom of this kind of arrangement. What can the hospital do (a) to assure that the quality of care in its out-patient department is good and (b) to keep the costs of such care within reasonable bounds?

2. Company strategy should include both operational concepts (services to be provided, etc.) and target results. Do you think controls are necessary for all phases of a strategy or will checking on results be adequate? Use either (a) an automobile dealership or (b) a tree surgeon and spraying company to illustrate.

3. What should the dean of a business school (within a university) try to control? How? Use this situation to illustrate (a) steering-control, (b) yes-no control, (c) post-action control, (d) control of an activity rather than results, (e) sampling, (f) adjustment of norms, and (g) corrective action.

4. The Cardiz Construction Company—builders of shopping centers, offices, schools, and churches—is concerned about its public relations. Complaints about noise, dirt, upsetting ecology, workers' disregard of community customs, etc. are becoming increasingly troublesome. "We talk to our people over and over," Mr. Cardiz says, "and they correct the specific complaint. But two weeks later a group of mothers are picketing around 'the old oak tree' or a town clerk wants us to sweep up some dust in front of the mayor's house." Like other construction firms, Cardiz gets its business through competitive bidding for contracts that normally have a fixed price and penalty clauses for late completions. Each project manager is measured on how well actual performance stacks up against contract provisions. His job is complicated by the use of subcontractors for many parts of the work. How do you recommend that Mr. Cardiz get better control of public relations?

5. In other parts of this book emphasis has been laid on sound forecasts, clear-cut organization, good executive personnel, and well-designed programs. In what ways will the presence of any one of these factors assist the management of a company to secure effective control?

6. Scientific management devotes much attention to motion and time study, production scheduling, selection and training of workers, preventive maintenance, materials specifications, and other features of shop management. What bearing, if any, does each of these facets of scientific management have on the job of a plant superintendent in controlling operations in the plant? Should the president be concerned about the use of such techniques in designing the company control structure?

7. Mr. Paul Ingram, owner-manager of a successful company making automatic scales and proportioning equipment for the feed, glass, rubber, coal, and other industries, is going to retire. For years he kept in close touch with all activities; but now, serving only as board chairman, he will need different controls. At

present the main formalized controls are: (a) a thorough final test and inspection of all outgoing equipment to assure quality; (b) job cost estimates coupled with actual job costs, used primarily to assure that prices used in bidding for new work are in line with actual costs; (c) a daily report on cash in the bank; (d) monthly profit and loss estimates; (e) semiannual balance sheet and income statement prepared by an outside auditor, who also prepares the income tax returns. Financial budgets have never been attempted; however, annual sales estimates are used to set quotas for the 6 regional sales representatives, and annual estimates of factory and administrative overhead are used to set overhead rates in the job costing system. Mr. Ingram says, "I know from talking with sales personnel about bids and orders what is happening in the market, and the number of people around (106 total, currently) determines most of the expenses. Our people know their jobs and do them well. But how to be sure that Walter Perez (the new general manager) is running a tight ship while I'm in Florida is another matter. Unfortunately, accounting reports don't tell whether your engineering is good enough to beat competitors on the new jobs that will keep the plant busy next year." What kind of a control structure should Mr. Ingram insist on, what reports should he receive personally, and what kinds of decisions should he reserve for his own yes-no control?

8. Many department stores that have opened suburban branches consider each branch simply as an additional opportunity to contact customers; the buying, advertising, credit, accounting, and most other activities are performed at one location by centralized divisions. In contrast, Race Brothers has branches in separate communities up to 150 miles from the state capital where its main store is located. Because of this dispersion, each branch is a fully integrated unit with its own buying, credit, accounting, delivery, etc. The main store does provide a variety of services for all branches, but each branch is expected to operate as an independent unit. Discuss the differences in control systems you would recommend for a company with suburban branches and for Race Brothers.

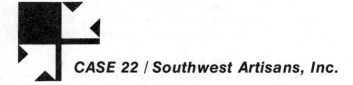

CASE 22 / Southwest Artisans, Inc.

Mr. Robert Balsher, president, stepped around his new desk (a company product) to gaze at the mountains through windows in the corner office of the just-completed building into which his firm had moved. "Well, it's quite an achievement," he said. "We've built our sales from $40,000 a year to an annual rate of $800,000 in just under four years. We've got a new building with twice the space of the older one. It looks good and it will be much more pleasant to work in."

Southwest Artisans, Inc. makes custom furniture and wooden television cabinets. Offices and plant are in a new 200-foot by 150-foot building that is a successful mixture of contemporary and territorial styling. It is an exciting setting for the pecan-wood and pecky-cypress paneled office walls, the modern and the Mediterranean furniture, and the Wilton carpeting. The building is as marked a change from the old cramped and bare quarters as is the change in production and sales volume.

"You remember that we had a tough time deciding last winter to make the switch. We knew physical conditions were poor. Fifty of us worked in 15,000 square feet, ventilation and lighting were poor, and we had those old-fashioned air-coolers in part of the building. The second-story location helped us to look like a second-rate outfit.

"I held back, though, because we weren't in the best of financial condition (see Exhibit 1), the move would cost something, our rent would triple, and we might produce inefficiently for a while. But sales volume was up and the backlog was climbing (see Exhibits 2 and 3).

Exhibit 1

Balance Sheets

	Current Date	Six Months Previous
Cash	$ 22,000	$ 80,000
Accounts Receivable	220,000	110,000
Inventories	140,000	116,000
Fixed Assets (Net)	96,000	90,000
Other Assets	2,000	4,000
Total	$480,000	$400,000
Accounts Payable	$125,000	$ 80,000
Notes Payable	87,000	60,000
Accruals	12,000	14,000
Long-Term Debt	116,000	96,000
Capital Stock	100,000	100,000
Retained Earnings	40,000	50,000
Total	$480,000	$400,000

Exhibit 2

Profit and Loss Statements

	Past 6 Months	Last Year
Net Sales	$400,000	$640,000
Labor and Materials Cost	274,000	375,000
Factory Overhead	81,000	135,000
Selling & Administrative Expense	55,000	85,000
Operating Profit	(10,000)	45,000
Taxes		16,250
Net Profit	$ (10,000)	$ 28,750

Exhibit 3

Order Backlog, End of Month

April	$ 80,000	July	$150,000
May	90,000	August	200,000
June	120,000	September	250,000

"The old landlord is trying to stick us with $5,000 for leasehold improvements that we caused in the old building and it looks as if the changes, construction expenses, and moving costs of coming in here will run $30,000 instead of the $10,000 we planned for. You know the construction people. There's still about two weeks' work to be done around the edges.

"Don't let me alarm you, though. We're in a good place to produce and we certainly are selling a lot of furniture."

Mr. Balsher and several silent partners purchased the company from its two original owners—both furniture designers. One original partner stayed on as a designer and production superintendent for six months, and then he left to work for a competing firm. Robert Balsher, a former product manager of Drexel Furniture Company, then purchased enough of the departing superintendent's stock to have a 35% ownership of the firm. The other directors own the balance of the stock, but they meet only as required by law and leave direction and management to Mr. Balsher.

To build a sales organization, Mr. Balsher hired manufacturer's representatives to call on decorators and selected furniture stores. Mr. Balsher thinks the representatives follow-up and service existing accounts well enough, but that they are not aggressive enough to get new customers. "If we had a sales manager, he could probably see to it that they did the job, but we can't afford one now. I take whatever time is necessary to do the selling, but that hasn't been much in the past year. We have been able to pick and choose as the orders fairly poured in. The market should continue to grow. The cities in which we sell are among the top five fastest-growing cities in the country and the people in them are getting wealthier all the time. Our rate of sales increase could easily be 30% per year. Sales to homeowners (about 35% of total volume), to businesses for custom office installations (30% of total volume), and to consumer electronics firms for television, record-player, and radio cabinets (the balance) should all increase." Although records are not kept by geographic area, Mr. Balsher estimates that 50% of sales occur within two cities about 150 miles apart.

Mr. Balsher continued: "Sales to the radio and television companies are new for us. We did well with an introductory order or two and now have as much volume as we can take. I like the size of the orders because we don't have to push hard for a lot of small orders as we do with decorators and stores.

"To succeed in the custom furniture business, what you have to have are the established contacts with decorators and store buyers so that they know that they can count on your quality and delivery. You also have to have good designers who can work in several styles. We have these, as anyone can tell from our rapid sales growth in four years. With the right contacts and the right designers, success is almost assured. The customers are wealthy, so they can pay."

Prices vary widely—from $8 for an individual piece of cabinetry to $30,000 for a complete custom installation. Mr. Balsher and the production control manager jointly set prices. They include these variables: time and cost estimates for each production operation, historical prices for similar items, the current competitive situation, an estimate of what the market will bear, and "intuitive judgment."

Efforts to collect costs by order are deemed impractical since many orders—especially repeat orders—are for one or a few items.

The employees' wage and benefit plan was revised recently to allow all rates to rise as area wages increased. The old plan had a learner's rate and a base rate ($.40 an hour higher) for each job. The learner's rate was paid for the first six months an employee was on the job. The new plan allows for increases every three months over a three-year period. The increases are not automatic but "are based primarily on job performance." Each step up requires a foreman's favorable recommendation. Finally, merit increases "for truly outstanding and exceptional performance" can be granted above the final step of the three-year progression. The wage spread over three years is $.50 per hour for assemblers, $.65 per hour for tenoner operators, and $.45 per hour for hand rubbers. Average hourly earnings are $.30 below the United States average and $.95 below the Pacific Coastal States average. The highest skilled workers are all in the machining and upholstery departments. Good men take time to find or three to four years to train.

The current organization chart for Southwest Artisans, Inc. is shown in Exhibit 4. There have been two major organizational changes in the last three years. Vaughan Nezelek, then production manager at age 55, became process engineer and cost estimator to get away from his former long hours. Greg Berdette, 36 and assistant

Exhibit 4

Organization Diagram

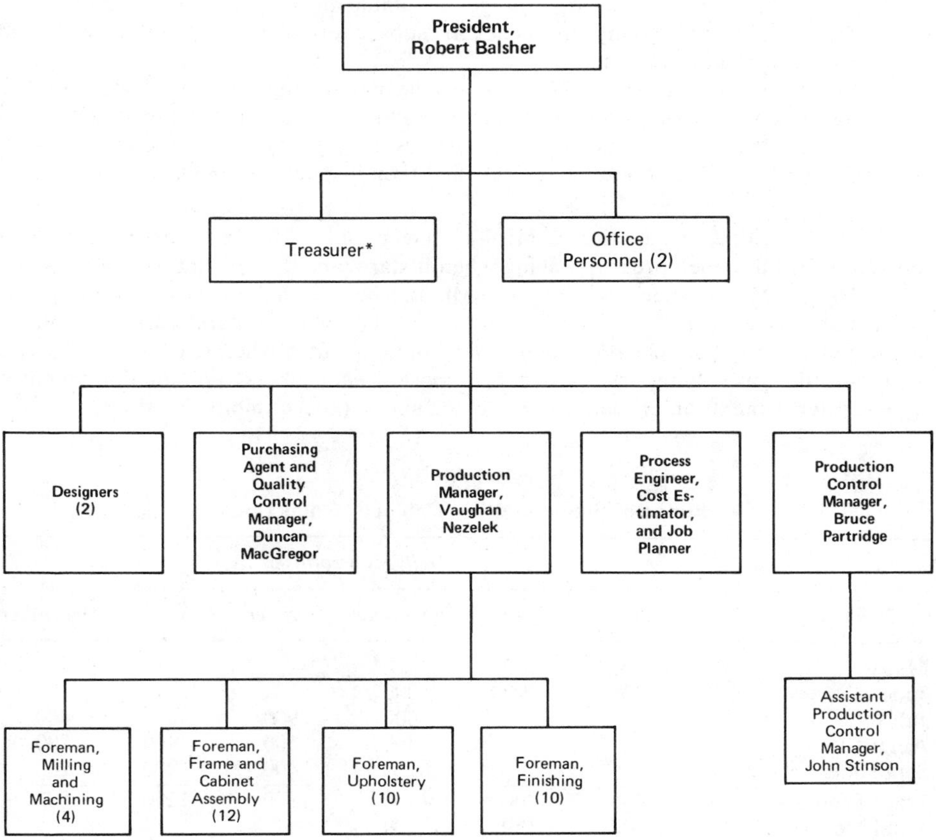

Numbers in parentheses are nonsupervisory personnel.

*The treasurer, a stockholder, worked one day a week without pay.

production manager of an electronics components firm, came in as production manager. He worked long hours to introduce more systematic production and production control procedures. Although he had impressed Vaughan Nezelek and was popular with the foremen, Mr. Balsher asked him to find another job after a year and a half because the company was losing money. Mr. Nezelek came back to the production manager's job. When new orders come in now, Mr. Balsher sets the sequence of operations—the work that Vaughan Nezelek had been doing. However, Mr. Nezelek has just resigned, effective in one month.

An order, when received, has with it a set of specifications established by a decorator for the customer or by one of the company's designers who has been working with a customer, or a set of blueprints sent in by the industrial buyer. The following major steps are usually required in sequence, although the subroutines and the time for each step varies:

1. Cut dried lumber to size, trim, mold, mortise, turn on a lathe, sand, bevel, and glue when necessary to make parts.
2. Assemble parts in working storage, assemble drawers, assemble cabinets or frames, glue and mount on a pallet for subsequent operations. Fit drawers and cabinets, then sand.
3. Finish by staining, shellacking, filling, drying, sealing, glazing, drying, sealing again, drying, lacquering, drying, and hand rubbing before final inspection.
4. Upholster by cutting the goods, sewing cushions, seats, skirts, backs, and arms, pad and join, insert and tie springs, and then inspect for quality control.

Bruce Partridge, production control manager and with the company for three months, schedules each order, planning when it starts and the amount to produce each week. He and Mr. Balsher consult before Mr. Balsher sets a delivery date on any new order. John Stinson, his assistant, starts jobs in the shop, confers with the foremen about materials and supplies for each order, and expedites when necessary. The two men issue three weekly reports: (1) a status report on each job, (2) a production schedule for each department, and (3) an order backlog sheet. (See Exhibits 5 and 6.)

Exhibit 5

Status of Stereo and TV Cabinets, Total Units

	Delivery Promised In					
Ordered In	*July*	*August*	*September*	*October*	*November*	*December*
May	200	200				
June	200	200	200			
July			800	900	600	400
August			400	600	400	200
September				400	200	200
Total Promised	400	400	1400	1900	1200	800
Total Delivered	400	350	700			
Rejects		40	47 (usually a 30-day delay in notification)			

Exhibit 6

Summary Sheet, Backlog by Departments

	July		August		September	
	Sales Value	*Number of Orders*	*Sales Value*	*Number of Orders*	*Sales Value*	*Number of Orders*
Machining	$ 40,000	12	$130,000	14	$170,000	14
Assembling	36,000	16	40,000	15	40,000	8
Upholstery	4,000	6	3,000	11	2,500	10
Finishing	70,000	22	27,000	14	37,500	8
Total	$150,000	56	$200,000	54	$250,000	40

Quality control is one of Duncan MacGregor's responsibilities. He has been on the job for six months after retiring from the Army Quartermaster Corps with a major's rank. In his view the firm's quality control problems are: "(1) Not enough time for inspection. We are always under pressure to ship. (2) No analysis of vendor capabilities. We buy from suppliers chosen by Mr. Balsher over the past four years. (3) No rewards for careful work in case and frame assembly. The men are really judged by how much they turn out. The new building should help if it provides more room for production operations. Industry data from the Furniture Manufacturers' Association show that the newer furniture plants in the South average 380 square feet of floor space per production worker, that the largest Drexel plant has 600 square feet per direct worker, and that the older plants in the North which utilize a hand technology much like ours may run up to 700 square feet per production worker. We still need other improvements, however." (A floor plan of the new building is shown in Exhibit 7.)

Daily operations are the responsibility of the foremen, all of whom have been with the company for over three years. Tom Cleveland, finishing foreman, believes that the new wage rates are being well received and that turnover is diminishing. "This is still a hard city in which to find a good job. It is high pressure for the supervisors. Our big quality problem is with staining and sealing. Sometimes we may not have just exactly the right product for the wood we are using or the men may make more than they should. Business is good and expanding, but 48 hours for the men often means 60 hours for the foremen."

A major reason for the pressure on production is the acceptance of several large orders for cabinets from a major consumer products manufacturer. The cabinets are similar in design and are not complex to make. They require minimal assembly and finishing work. However, delivery is behind schedule and some cabinets have been rejected. Mr. MacGregor attributes the rejects to "excess fussiness" by the buyer. "They are picking up nicks, scratches, and errors in mounting hole dimensions that no one has ever complained about before. Of course, we have never had orders of this quantity before either. We send a man to their plant to fix up the rejects since shipping back would be too costly. Also, we don't want an order canceled for delivery or quality reasons because the contract we signed has a clause hidden in the fine print that says that we will pay the extra costs if they have to buy at a higher price from someone else to meet their purchase schedules."

Exhibit 7

New Building, Floor Plan

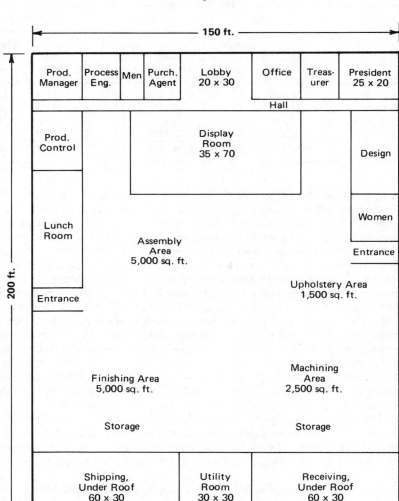

Required: (a) What measures is Mr. Balsher using to appraise his operation? What judgment has he come to from the indicators he uses? Do you agree with his conclusions?

(b) What are the company's major control problems? Explain.

(c) Design an overall control structure for this company. Explain why it will be useful in achieving the company's purposes.

(d) Looking at the firm from the standpoint of a director, what would you say are the important challenges and opportunities?

INTEGRATING CASES / Strategy and Execution

LOS RANCHOS DE PARAGUAY

"On the last Thursday in December, much to my surprise, I found myself on the plane from Brussels to Asunción reversing a journey I had made six months earlier when I came to Europe as an assistant to the managing director of La Société d'Aliment[1] to continue my year of executive training with this European manufacturer and distributor of food products. Although I had learned, during my four months at the meat-packing plant in Paraguay, that the sales and profit performance of Los Ranchos de Paraguay (a wholly-owned subsidiary of La Société d'Aliment) had been steadily deteriorating, neither I nor anyone else in the Brussels headquarters had suspected how bad the situation would become until the September floods resulted in the loss of about 10,000 head of cattle and the subsequent resignation of the managing director in Paraguay.

"On Tuesday, two days before my plane trip, the managing director in Brussels called me in to a meeting during which he and the other chief executives explained what they knew of the situation at Los Ranchos and then asked me if I would be willing to take over as managing director there.

"Since this would be my first central management assignment (at age 32), I told them, 'Provided you don't expect miracles, I'll give it a go.' We agreed then to have a formal review after I had been in Paraguay a year to see whether or not it would be worthwhile for me to continue my efforts there. Since Los Ranchos was the company's only cattle-raising and primary manufacturing operation, there had always been some question as to whether or not it was wise for La Société d'Aliment to be as fully integrated as to own a ranching and meat-packing company. La Société was diversifying steadily by adding new retail products sold in old and new geographical regions of Europe."

Malcolm Littleton, the teller of this tale, had grown up on a sheep station in New Zealand and had attended a technical institute to study animal husbandry. But then, after graduation, he had chosen to work for the Shell Oil Company. After ten years with Shell—most of which he spent in South America in various sales and personnel jobs—he left to join La Société d'Aliment.

"Our quick review and the briefing in Brussels showed me that the situation in Paraguay had rapidly worsened. Annual losses had mounted steadily over the past four years from $150,000 to $1,800,000. The effects of the disastrous flood had been increased enormously by a three-day delay in getting a fleet together for a rescue attempt while waiting in the hope that good news would come down the Rio Paraguay.

---

[1] Literally, in English, The Food Company.

In addition to the 8,000 cattle lost directly in the flood, about 4,000 others—cows in calf and some weakened by disease—died.

"The packing plant had operated for only three months in each of the two previous years, rather than the normal five months, and had slaughtered 46,000 head in contrast with a killing capacity of 100,000 head over a six- to eight-month season under the best conditions. As a trainee I had realized that morale was low. The work for the men on the killing floor had been cut back to a total of 50 days. They had an uninterested, surly way of working that differed markedly from their actions of shouting, whistling, and joking when things were going well. The men made up a unified gang. One was either in it or out because of the kind of work. A meat plant is a pretty bloody sort of a place with the animals hanging to be drained, the red and raw meat lying on tables, the gruesome-looking machines extruding fat and an unpleasant, dominant smell to the place. It took me at least four days to recognize that this was just a production process and that the people were rough, tough workers because of the kind of work.

"The plant workers seemed to walk off their jobs for nothing. In the warm climate of Paraguay it is pretty tough when 30 half-skinned carcasses are left on the line. All the managers then had to pitch to and work for six hours just to clear up the one line.

"I also remembered from my time as a trainee that the department heads had seemed careless about their responsibilities and that they argued and fought amongst themselves in a way I had never seen at Shell. Also, there appeared to be much friction between the ranchers and the plant management. Most of the ranchers thought of themselves as in the cattle-raising and cattle-tending business. They cared little or nothing about the beef potential of the cattle or the fat-to-lean ratio of the meat. Some of them remembered times when cattle were slaughtered for their hides and tallow and the carcasses were left to rot.

"Los Ranchos owned and leased 1,800,000 acres in various locations on both sides of the Rio Paraguay north of Concepción. On these it ran 90,000 head with an annual take-off of about 10%, that is, about 9,000 cattle were selected for slaughtering each year. Turnover[2] was $7,500,000 of canned, frozen, and processed meat from the packing plant. Most of the beef extract and corned beef was packed in our largest-sized cans for eventual sale to institutional buyers in Europe, Africa, and North America. The frozen beef was shipped in bulk to La Société d'Aliment plants in Europe for further processing.

"As on all the large ranches in Paraguay, our cattle count was never certain and the animals were mainly of poor quality. Low-yielding breeds, poor grass, and an unfavorable terrain and climate in the Gran Chaco contributed to this. Paraguayans seldom, if ever, got the 20% annual take-off that was common in Argentina.

"Local butchers bought up the best quality cattle from the Paraguayan ranches and left about 150,000 to 200,000 head to be slaughtered by the four packing plants that exported beef.

"The first task that I had to plunge into immediately upon arriving in Paraguay was to buy cattle forward for the slaughtering season that began in March. We had to make almost immediate purchases of cattle to be delivered later from April through August. The chief buyer was young and inexperienced and had just been appointed the year before. Never having done so, I did not know how to set up and organize a buying operation. We were going to learn through experience—a disproportionately time-consuming process. Also we did not understand at first that even the largest sellers

---

[2] "Turnover" is the European term for annual sales.

were ranchers and not economists. They were prepared to wait for a price they thought was just. They knew little of the procedures for maximum weight gain. My chief buyer did not clearly understand that the cheapest cattle did not result in the cheapest beef.

"That season we bought outside and brought in from our own ranches 76,000 head—the highest number processed since Los Ranchos had been purchased ten years before by La Société. When we found ourselves paying the highest prices at the end of the buying season for the wrong cattle with an insufficient yield analysis, we realized that purchasing would have to be planned by regions, that delivery deadlines would need to be set with the ranchers, and that the cost of walking, trucking, or barging the cattle to the plant would have to be balanced with the weight loss associated with the transportation.

"My two major objectives for the trial year were to reduce the loss by 50% and to increase plant volume substantially. Reducing the loss would mean, in part, tighter control on our own ranches to see that half of the 10,000 new head newly brought in from Argentina were not lost to rustlers—as had happened the year before. It also meant travel by small plane to the ranches to improve communications with the ranch managers who were often hard to find. (Small plane travel was dangerous because of terrain conditions, frequent storms, incomplete instrumentation, and understaffed weather advisory services). Increased plant volume was necessary to give our people work to see how the operating system responded under pressure, to cut overhead charges per pound of beef packed, and to provide employment in a country that badly needed jobs. About 1,500 men worked in the plant and 600 on the company-owned ranches, and there were 150 staff administrators.

"My first view of the managing director's job was that it was going to be a lonely kind of position. I could not get extensively involved with the people in the company for two reasons: (1) Doing so might well bias my opinions of them and my judgment as to whether or not the operation should be continued in the long run. (2) I could not forecast what I was going to find out about the managers during the first year. I even had to tell my wife to be careful about incurring social obligations to families or charitable groups.

"Three very early actions were intended to be symbolic. They affected the management only. We traded in the Buicks, Fords, and Chevrolets owned by Los Ranchos for Volkswagens and Fiats. We made the managers pay for milk. It was no longer free to their families. We reassigned the gardeners so that they no longer kept up the staff compounds around the plant. I would say that these actions were understood, although they were not liked.

"Two major administrators left. The administrative manager (age 56) had expected to move into the managing director's job. He quit when his gardeners were taken away. The controller, a 30-year-old Argentinian who was very dynamic, moved into the administrative job. Then the factory manager resigned at the end of the packing season. We went to three shifts for making cans for six months to build up stock and slaughtered 10 hours each day for five months. The factory manager told me this meant that his workload was 16 hours per day for the first four months of the season and that the work pace was too heavy for him.

"It was risky to build a stock of 2 million cans because they had to be made in advance of the selling season. If I guessed the wrong sizes, we could not move the product. If the cans were improperly made, the canned meat would go bad during the two months we held it at the plant and the cans would blow. Actually, we canned in two shifts for two months rather than by the former practice of one shift for as long as needed for the pack that year. By going to two shifts we packed in 7- to 12-oz. cans rather than in 4-lb. butcher cans. The meat then sold for a higher price per pound and gross revenues went up an extra 10%.

"During the first year we cut overhead from $1,650,000 to $1,200,000 and reduced our total loss to $911,000. Cutting overhead was not easy. We cut out the legal department entirely, cut teletype expenditures from $30,000 to $15,000, decreased our interest rates with the local banks from 13% to 10%, and reduced our compensating balances when I found that the banks were charging us standard commercial rates despite the fact that our loans were guaranteed from Brussels and Zurich. Since we were 1,500 miles up river from Buenos Aires, we had to carry a minimum two-month inventory of both supplies and meat; but we reduced to this from a four-month average. Also we cut our loans receivable from ranchers from $900,000 to $180,000. We could pre-finance them for their operations, but many of them were not rolling over the loan at the year's end. We tightened up on the promissory notes and made the ranchers agree to two signatures or a mortgage if they wanted pre-financing. Then also we insisted that the cattle being grazed for us would be stamped with our brand in advance of any financing.

"By the time these things were done, the end of the first year was approaching. I was eager to talk with the people in Brussels since I wanted them to give me help through advice and to recognize that there was no easy road ahead. Before the year's end they sent out an agricultural consultant for an independent view.

"I explained to him what had happened and then listed the following short- and long-range tasks that lay ahead without putting them in any order of priority:

"(1) Budgetary meetings have been pushed down to the plant department level for more participation, but each department budget still contains overhead and equipment account allocations. There is no direct-cost budget system as yet. Reports still come out 30 days after the month's end.

"(2) Benchmark controls such as daily cattle costs, the number of cattle processed per week, inventory investment before the packing season, and so on have not yet been introduced.

"(3) Each department (16 in total) is still run by a manager and an assistant manager when, in my opinion, only one is needed. What procedure can we introduce or use to be fair to the men who have to be let go? Some are Paraguayans, some European. The labor law requires two to three years' severance pay for long-service employees. How can we help in locating jobs?

"(4) I am about to hire an able young Argentinian as a replacement for the plant manager.

"(5) The tax per head slaughtered is renegotiated each year with the Paraguayan government. Would it be useful to work with the three other foreign-owned companies in tax negotiations?

"(6) The Swiss (Nestlé, Maggi, and Knorr) have formed a buying group and are successfully playing off the producers of meat extract one against the other to drive down prices. How can we best operate?

"(7) The ranching side of the business has no managerial accounting system. Can one be installed that would do more than report historical costs?

"(8) Although money was spent in the first year to repair fences, clean out water tanks, rebuild, repaint, and clean the men's sleeping huts, improve the dipping facilities, and sow some of the dry land in the Gran Chaco with Lehmann's lovegrass from South Africa and with blue gramma, there are still innumerable improvements possible on the ranching side.

"(9) I need some feedback from Brussels as to whether Paraguay is going to be an integral part of the supply situation in the future so that I shall not go ahead with putting up projects in the dark.

"(10) The company-owned ranches could be cut to 900,000 acres and still the stocking could be increased to 146,000 animal units.

"The consultant listened and left. One month later we met in Buenos Aires—the managing director from Brussels, the consultant, the director of production in France, the head of the legal staff, and I. I told them what I had told the consultant. They had the figures. The consultant said he had learned only one point that I had not covered—I was regarded by the management group in Paraguay as distant and cold, a little frightening to some, and there was a certain level of anxiety because they were not all getting to know me. He also had a recommendation. The company should sell off Los Ranchos de Paraguay. Even with the best efforts, it would not be more than a break-even operation.

"My view, as expressed, was that enough could be done to cut costs, raise prices, improve pasturage and cattle breeds, change the product mix, and improve the control system so that Los Ranchos would break even within another year and turn a handsome profit within two years. But profit and return on investment were not the question. Did operating a ranch and primary manufacturing facilities on a continent and in a country 7,000 miles from Brussels make any sense as part of a European secondary manufacturer and distributor of food products? What could Los Ranchos de Paraguay do for La Société that the market could not? Would I be shutting myself off from advancement in Europe by staying in Concepción to continue the turnaround of Los Ranchos? My assignment the year before had had all the earmarks of improvisation and I could see no point to continued improvisation in planning for Paraguay or for my future."

QUESTIONS

1. How would you answer Malcolm Littleton's questions in the preceding paragraph?
2. What programs appear to need to be planned for and with what priority if Los Ranchos is not sold?

MANAGEMENT OF CONVAIR [1]

The corporation

By 1960 General Dynamics had become one of the great corporations of the country. Its sales were around two billion dollars and it produced, profitably, some of the most complex equipment known to man. Its major operating divisions were:

Astronautic (Atlas missiles)
Electric Boat (submarines)
Fort Worth (B58 bombers)
General Atomic (nuclear development)
Liquid Carbonic (liquefied gas)

---

[1] For a fuller discussion of this period in General Dynamics history, see "How A Great Corporation Got Out of Control," by Richard Austin Smith in *Fortune,* January and February, 1962. The present case is composed of excerpts from these two articles. Reprinted by special permission; © 1962, by Time, Inc.

Electrodynamics (electric motors)
Pomona (electronics plus Terrier missiles)
Stromberg-Carlson (telephones, electronics)
General Aircraft (leases or sells planes traded-in for jets)
Canadair (aircraft)
Convair

This case focuses on one product of one division, but the issues raised are basic to the entire scope of General Dynamics and to many other companies. The division—Convair—was by far the largest component brought into General Dynamics (in 1954); and the product—the 880 and 990 passenger jets—rolled up the largest loss ever achieved by a nongovernment enterprise on a single venture, around $425 million.

General Dynamics was founded by John Jay Hopkins. Under his inspiration net earnings, $600,000 on sales of $31 million in 1947, rose to $56 million on sales of $1.7 billion in 1957, the year of Hopkins' death. Hopkins was a man of great energy who kept posted on each division of this expanding empire largely by direct and unannounced visits. In 1953 he did bring in Frank Pace as executive vice-president "to have someone in the office to answer the phone" and especially to maintain Washington's confidence in the company. Pace had served as Director of the Budget, and during the Korean crisis as Secretary of the Army.

Aside from golf, the law, and the high order of intelligence, Pace and Hopkins were complete opposites: Pace temperate in all things, oratorical, deliberate, anxious to be liked, a product of the federal staff system, prone to rely on his second-in-command in the making of decisions; Hopkins volatile, creative, earthy, intuitive, ingrown, willing to listen but unwilling to share the making of decisions with anybody, a loner more likely to give the world the back of his hand than to extend the palm of it. In 1957 cancer caught up with Hopkins. His hand-picked board of directors decided (over Hopkins' strong objections) that Pace should be president. Hopkins died three days later.

Pace described the task of managing the enterprise he inherited in these terms: "When you have a company, employing 106,000 people, made up of eleven different divisions, each a corporation really in its own right, most of which were separate enterprises before they joined the organization, and headed by men who were presidents of corporations, with their own separate legal staffs, financial staffs, etc., all of these highly competent men—the only way to succeed is to operate on a decentralized basis. Our total central office in New York City was something like 200 people, including stenographers. This group can only lay out broad policy. Your capacity to know specifically what is happening in each division just cannot exist. If you did try to know everything that was happening and controlled your men that tightly, they would leave or would lose the initiative that made them effective."

Convair's move into commercial jets

The Convair division was headed up in 1955 by General Joseph T. McNarney with John V. Naish as executive vice-president. Tough-minded Joe McNarney, ex-chief of U.S. forces in Europe, had always been pretty much of a law unto himself, while Jack Naish wore his fifteen years' experience in the airframe industry like Killarney green on St. Patrick's Day. The division had already pulled off a successful commercial-transport program; the propeller-driven 240's, 340's, and 440's were world-famous. But what prompted Convair to consider making the formidable move into jet transports was a suggestion by Howard Hughes.

Hughes wanted jets for TWA; but before Hughes and Convair could agree on a design, Boeing and Douglas came out with long-range jet transports (the 707 and the DC-8) which scooped the market. Still determined to get into jets, Convair turned to the medium-range market. For this plan, Hughes proposed to buy 30 planes. After considerable engineering work, the executive committee of General Dynamics' board, headed by Hopkins, unanimously approved McNarney's program based on the assumption it would make money after 68 planes were sold, that potential sales of 257 aircraft could be realized, and that the maximum possible loss was only $30 million to $50 million.

By this time three airlines—TWA, Delta, and KLM—had already taken options to buy the 880. Now the committee instructed Convair to go ahead and get letters of intent from them within the next fortnight. The committee laid down only three conditions in authorizing the program: first, that GE guarantee the 880's engine; second, that the ability of the airlines to pay for the jets be investigated by an *ad hoc* committee of Pace, Naish, and Financial Vice-President Lambert Gross; third, that management was not to go ahead without orders in hand for 60% of the estimated 68-plane breakeven point.

LACK OF POLICY

The last provision proved to be quite flexible. The breakeven point on the 880 had been understated: after closer figuring, Convair raised it to 74 planes in May, up 6 planes in two months. When KLM did not pick up its option, the executive committee indulgently dropped its 60% condition, allowing Convair to go ahead with only 50% of the breakeven point assured. The new figure was made to fit the fact that by now Convair had only 40 firm orders (10 from Delta and 30 from Hughes).

A Doubting Thomas

Both Convair assistant division manager, Allen Morgan, and B. F. Coggan, the division manager, had informed management back in 1956, at the time 30 planes were sold to Howard Hughes, that the 880 was underpriced. Their conclusions were ignored then because of the difficulty of substantiating their cost estimates at so early a date. But now a year had elapsed, the 880's design was frozen, and components had been ordered preparatory to starting up the production line. So the cost of the aircraft could be figured with precision; it was an amalgam of money that *had* been spent on research and development and money that *would* be spent on materials, fabrication, and assembly. Usually about 70% of the material costs of an aircraft is represented by items bought from outside suppliers—the engines, pods, stabilizers, ailerons, rudders, landing gear, autopilots, instruments, and so on—with only 30% of the total material costs being allocated to the airframe manufacturer himself. The 880 ratios followed this general pattern. But when an engineer in Convair's purchasing division began toting up the various subcontracted components, he came to a startling conclusion: outlays for the vendor-supplied components of each 880 totaled more than the plane was being sold for (average price: $4,250,000). He took his figures up the line, pointing out that when research and development costs of the aircraft (they totaled some $75 million) were added in, along with the 25 to 30% of the material costs allocated to Convair itself, nothing could be expected of the 880 program but steadily mounting losses. He recommended that Convair abandon the whole venture, even though the loss, according to his estimates, would be about $50 million.

NO INFO FLOW TO CEO *BAD PRICING*

Whether the engineer's recommendation and his supporting data ever reached New York headquarters is something of a mystery. In any event, when the engineer persisted with his analyses, Convair decided he was a crank and fired him—he was reinstated two years later after time had confirmed the accuracy of his judgments.

Target No. 1: United Air Lines

The sales problems that confronted Convair in 1957, however, were something that couldn't be sloughed off with the firing of a critic. At the start of the 880 program in March, 1956, the potential market had been estimated at 257 planes. By June of that year Convair had raised the figure to 342, but in September it was down to 150 after an on-the-spot appraisal had let the air out of the sales estimates for European airlines. These gyrations gave substance to an industry rumor that the division undertook a thoroughgoing market analysis only *after* commitment to the 880 program, but at least one point was clear about the "final" forecast of 150. The bulk of that number, as General Joseph McNarney, Convair's president, said at the time, had to be sold before July 1, 1957, or the 880's production line could not be economically maintained. The trouble was that an understanding with Howard Hughes had kept Convair from selling the 880 to anybody but TWA and Delta for a whole year. This had already caused the loss of customers who preferred a 707 or DC-8 in the hand to an 880 twelve months down the road. So in the spring of 1957, when Convair was at last free of the commitment, it had still sold no more than the forty 880's (to TWA and Delta) that started off the program. The success of that program, with only a few months to go before McNarney's July 1 deadline, now hinged on selling the remaining major airlines, American and United.

Convair's first target was United, which it had listed as a prospect for 30 aircraft. For a time things seemed to be going Convair's way in its pursuit of this critical $120-million sale. Boeing, Douglas, and Convair were all in competition for the United contract, but Convair had the edge with its 880, for it was then the only true medium-to-long-range jet aircraft being offered. All Boeing could offer was essentially the long-range 707, too big and, for its seating capacity, 50,000 pounds too heavy to suit United. The size could be reduced, of course, and some of the weight chopped out, but not 50,000 pounds unless Pratt & Whitney could substantially lighten the engines, the JT3C-6's used on the 707 aircraft. With Pratt & Whitney unwilling to make this effort, United's board decided in favor of the 880 on September 27, 1957, subject to a final going-over by United's engineers.

Soon thereafter, United's President William Patterson called General Dynamics' Executive Vice-President Earl Johnson, whom Pace had put in overall charge of the jet program, out of a board meeting to tell him Convair was "in." But perhaps the most consequential call was one Pratt & Whitney's Chairman H. Mansfield "Jack" Horner then made on Patterson himself. Spurred on by Boeing, Horner had been galvanized into action, and now he wanted to know whether something couldn't be done about getting Boeing back in the competition, if Pratt & Whitney could come up with a lighter engine. Patterson referred him to United's engineers, who made very encouraging noises. They themselves had been pushing Pratt & Whitney for just that. Both Boeing and Pratt & Whitney then went into a crash program, the former to scale down the 707.

Within a few weeks Boeing had come up with a new medium-range aircraft—the 720—45,000 pounds lighter than the 707. United then invited Boeing and Convair to cut their prices and both did, though Convair refused to cut below what Pace recently described as "the bare minimum." In November, United's chief engineer John Herlihy compared Convair's 880 and Boeing's 720 and then strongly recommended the latter. His reasoning: the commercial performance of the GE engine was an unknown quantity, while "we had the Pratt & Whitney engines in our other jets and wanted to regularize our engines if we could"; moreover, the narrower fuselage of the Convair 880 permitted only five-abreast seating, a shortcoming United had vigorously protested back in 1956 when Convair had first solicited its opinion of the 880 design; the Boeing 720, on the other hand, was wide enough for six-abreast seating, a difference of as many as 25 passengers at full load in the tourist section of a combination first-class/tourist airliner. This meant, in Herlihy's view, that the 720 with its lower operating costs per passenger-mile was a better buy than the 880 with a $200,000 cheaper price tag. On November 28, 1957, United's board approved purchase of 11 Boeing 720's, with options for 18 more.

"Merely a modification"

The loss of United meant a sharp reduction in the market potential of the 880, dropping it from 110 to 80 planes. Worse than this, Convair had a powerful new competitor in what had been its private preserve, the medium-range field. That competitor was now going to make it tough for Convair to sign up American Airlines just at the time when Convair expected to sell the airline 30 planes, nearly half of the 880's dwindling market potential. Discussions with American had been going on for some months, though pressure had naturally increased after United chose the Boeing 720 in November. But in January, 1958, American notified Johnson, who was in overall charge of the negotiations, that it too was going to pass up the 880 for twenty-five 720's.

In February, however, Convair was able to reopen discussions with American on the basis of a revolutionary new engine General Electric had just developed. Called a turbo fan-jet, it required 10 to 15% less fuel than a conventional jet to do the same job (under flight conditions) and provided 40% more power on take-off. The aircraft that Convair intended to use with these new engines, later designated the 990, was billed as "merely a modification" of the 880. It was a modification to end all modifications. The 990 had a bigger wing area than the 880 and a fuselage 10½ feet longer; weighed over 50,000 pounds more; required an enlarged empennage, a beefed-up landing gear, greater fuel capacity, and stronger structural members; and was supposed to go 20 mph faster.

Many of these changes were imposed by American's hard-bargaining C. R. Smith, whose talent for getting what he wanted out of an airframe manufacturer was already visible in the DC-7. But Smith hadn't stopped with just designing the 990; he designed the contract too, using all the leverage Convair's plight afforded him. In it he demanded that Convair guarantee a low noise level for the plane, finance the 990's inventory of spare parts until American actually used them, and accept, for America's $25-million down payment, twenty-five DC-7's that had been in service on American's routes. The DC-7 was then widely regarded as an uneconomical airplane, 12% less efficient to operate than the DC-6, and, as Convair discovered, it could not be sold for even $500,000 in the open market. When General Dynamics reluctantly accepted this down payment, worth only half its face value, American signed up for twenty-five 990's with an option for twenty-five more.

"We had to go ahead"

Looking back, director Alvord recently commented on the whole affair: "Earl Johnson brought back a contract written to American specifications with an American delivery date, but the plane was not even on paper. It was designed by American and sold to them at a fixed price. There was not even any competitive pricing." What is more, Alvord says, "the 990 was signed, sealed, and delivered without board approval.

It was just a *fait accompli.* An announcement was made to the board that there would be a slight modification of the 880.'' Pace himself believed at the time that the 990 was only a slight modification. He now says, ''If we had known at the outset that major changes would be needed, deeper consideration would have been given it.''

The decision to go ahead on the 990 was an important turning point in the fortunes of Convair and of General Dynamics itself. The reasoning behind it has been stated by Pace: ''When the Boeing 720 took away our sale to United, we found ourselves in competition with a plane just as good as ours. This is just what we wanted to avoid. The 880 seemed doomed. We had to go ahead with the 990 or get out of the jet business. American had not bought any medium-range jets . . . When the fan engine was developed, they told us, 'We will buy your plane if you produce a plane like the 990.' It was absolutely vital for us to follow American's wishes. We had to have another major transcontinental carrier. I thought I was taking less of a gamble then than I did entering the 880 program.''

But what this amounted to was that General Dynamics had now committed itself to a double-or-nothing policy, gambling that the success of the 990 (beginning with the American sale) would make up for the failures of the 880. The nature of this gamble is worth specifying, in view of the fiasco that eventuated:

The plane had been sold at a price of approximately $4,700,000. Yet nobody knew how much it would cost because its costs were figured on those of the 880, which were still on the rise and unpredictable.

The number of planes Convair must sell to put its jet-transport program in the black had gone up sharply. The breakeven point on the 880 had been 68 planes at the start (March, 1956), a figure that by 1958 should have seemed impossible of fulfillment. Nothing but dribs and drabs of sales to lesser airlines could be expected of the 880, for the ''majors'' (TWA, United, and American) had already been sold or refused to buy. Convair's commitment to the 990, which had a breakeven point of its own, meant the division must sell 200 of the 880's and 990's to keep out of the red.

The success of the 990 depended largely on its being the sole plane on the market with a fan-jet engine. When it built the plane around the GE engine, Convair was confident that Pratt & Whitney would not make a fan jet. Barred from making a *rear* fan jet—GE's licensing agreement prevented this—Pratt & Whitney simply built a *front* fan engine. Boeing used this for the 720B, which took away a good deal of the 990's potential market.

The 990 was to be built without a prototype, or advanced model. General Dynamics had ''lucked out,'' to use President Earl Johnson's phrase, on the 880 without testing a prototype. So now the company was again going to gamble that it could take a plane directly from the drawing board into production without any major hitches. Said Rhoades MacBride, by way of fuller explanation: ''Our time for debugging the 990 was severely compressed because we wanted to take advantage of being first with the fan-jet engine. If we had built a prototype and flown it, we would have minimized our advantage in having the fan engine before Pratt & Whitney had it. We realized that if everything went right, we would be way ahead. If the 990 didn't fly as stated, we would be in terrific trouble.''

"Our basic mistake"

Yet if ever a plane needed a prototype and plenty of time for testing, it was the 990. As Earl Johnson himself conceded recently: ''Our basic mistake in judgment was that we did not produce a prototype to fly to virtual perfection. From a management standpoint we should have said, 'If you haven't the time to build a prototype, then you shouldn't get into the program.'" The 990 was an extremely fast aircraft, with short-field characteristics and a brand-new engine. The decision to go it without a prototype meant that Convair had committed itself to attaining the very high speed demanded by C. R. Smith—635 mph—the first crack out of the box. As it turned out, a lag of only six minutes in the 990's flying time on a transcontinental run of 2,500 miles was to result in C. R. Smith's canceling his contract because American wouldn't be able to bill the 990 as the "fastest airliner in the world."

"The furnace treatment"

Just before Convair undertook the 990 program, General McNarney retired and the division got a new president, hard-driving John Naish. Naish's succession clearly indicated that Convair was still an empire within General Dynamics' empire and would likely remain so. Pace had wanted the Convair job for Earl Johnson, the old Army buddy he'd made his No. 2 man. McNarney wanted Naish; McNarney got Naish. And the new Convair chief had soon made plain his confidence he could handle anything that came along—if left strictly alone. As he said at the time: "The company has a great many people who like to solve their own problems. It believes in the furnace treatment—you throw people in the fire and you can separate the good metal from the dross very quickly."

Naish had already got a taste of the furnace treatment at Convair, for troubles were piling up on all sides. Total orders for the 990 were only 32, while those for the 880 were still stuck at 44. Overhead on the jet venture had risen as production of the Convair-made F-106 dwindled and the Atlas program, which also shared the San Diego facilities, had had to be moved to another plant on orders from the Pentagon. But these were just first-degree burns in comparison to the furnace treatment Convair's new head was about to get from Howard Hughes over the 880.

Hughes's vagaries had already caused Convair plenty of lost sales and missed opportunities. When the 880 got to the production stage, the Hughes group—TWA engineers and executives—had quietly set up shop in an abandoned lumberyard near Convair's San Diego headquarters and for a time Hughes caused more mystification than trouble. As 1959 wore on, however, it became increasingly difficult to get Hughes to commit himself on the final configuration (styling and arrangements) of his 880's and making it certain that overtime would have to be used to meet the tightly scheduled delivery dates of the 990's—they'd been promised to American for the spring of 1961—if their dates could be met at all. As a matter of fact, in September (1959) Sales Vice-President Zevely was already notifying the airlines the 990 would be late.

Convair let more precious months slip by trying to humor Hughes before it came to a shattering conclusion: all his stalling on the final configuration of his 880's had its roots in the fact that he hadn't the money to pay for them on delivery.

Convair chose to pull his 880's off the line and put them out on the field. What made this decision so fantastic was that 13 of the planes were in different stages of completion. Now the economics of an aircraft production line are geared to "a learning curve," which simply means that labor costs go down as each production-line worker becomes familiar with his particular phase of putting the plane together. On the first 880 the learning curve was at its peak with labor costs of roughly $500,000, on the fortieth or fiftieth plane labor costs were designed to drop below $200,000. Thus removing Hughes' thirteen 880's from the line in *different stages* of completion meant that the learning curve for them would have to be begun again at the top—to the cost of Convair, not of Hughes.

"It's not a baby any more"

This disastrous decision was made by Jack Naish, with an OK from Frank Pace and Earl Johnson. But even then New York was far from on top of the situation. Pace maintains he never knew the 880 was in serious trouble until after the Hughes decision: "We knew we had problems, but there were no major difficulties as far as we knew. The information that came to us fiscally, in a routine fashion, through Naish and substantiated by Naish, would not have led us to believe the extent of the losses that were occurring." Earl Johnson is not even sure just when he himself became alarmed over the jet program. "It's difficult to answer that. It's like living with a child—when do you notice it's not a baby any more?"

The sad truth was simply that General Dynamics was still being run as a holding company with no real control from the top. Its headquarters staff had been kept at 200, and this, in Pace's view, "automatically recognizes that it is impossible to police the operation of the divisions." But even if there had been a will, the means of policing seem slender indeed. Pace had established no reporting system that could tell him quickly when a division was in trouble; the key figures were buried in pages of divisional operating statements. General Dynamics' Financial Vice-President Richard Knight is still overhauling the system of auditing the divisional books so as to prevent any doctoring of the figures to make a divisional president look good. In short, millions of dollars of publicly owned money could be on its way down the drain at Convair before New York was aware of it.

In a letter of May 10, 1960, addressed to General Dynamics' stockholders, Pace reported jet-transport charges of $91 million (as of March 31, 1960) but added "[We] have every reason to believe [the program] will be one of our most successful ventures." By mid-August, however, Pace's springtime optimism began to show the signs of an early frost. It will be remembered that from the very beginning the 880 had been grossly underpriced in relation to its material costs; now Convair had virtually given up trying to keep those heavy costs within the budgeted amounts. For almost a year San Diego had been abuzz with rumor that losses on the 880, "the sweet bird of our economy" as local citizens called the 880, might reach $150 million. Some 880 components had overrun their original estimates by as much as 300%.

Four months later (January, 1961) Hughes got his financing and Convair was confronted with the problem of completing his aircraft. And some problem it was. Since no two planes were in exactly the same stage of completion, they couldn't be put back on the production line. They had to be hand-finished on the field, at costs many times those prevailing on the line. Moreover, engineering changes had to be made—some Convair's and some Hughes'.

A $40-million discovery

By February of 1961, General Dynamics was beginning to reap the economic consequences of the disastrous Hughes decision. New York "discovered" that Convair had not only failed to write off all jet losses the previous September but had incurred additional ones. These, amounting to $40 million, spelled the end for Jack Naish and for

August Esenwein, the executive vice-president Pace had put under Naish to try and control costs. "I felt," said Pace recently, "that if I couldn't get more accurate judgments from Naish than I had gotten, he ought to go." Then he added, "Whether these problems were passed on and not properly interpreted by Esenwein and Naish, I can't tell. There are conflicting points of view now that we go back into the problem. But we in New York didn't know the magnitude of the problem."

Regardless of whether New York knew then or not, the whole business community was shortly to learn how profound was Convair's trouble. The risky decision to build the 990 without a prototype began to bear some even more expensive fruit. Seventeen of American's twenty-five 990's had to be delivered during 1961, the first one in March. A flight test of this particular airplane in late January, 1961, four months later than the date scheduled in a previous announcement of Pace's, disclosed wing flutter and other problems that required rebuilding the landing flaps, the leading edge of the wings, and the outboard pylons. These were not too difficult to correct from an engineering point of view, but as a General Dynamics vice-president sadly remarked, "If you get into production with a plane whose design has to be changed, the magnitude of the troubles you then encounter becomes exponential." Moreover, these corrections now had to be made on overtime because of the tight delivery schedule to American. Ultimately this was to burden General Dynamics with an additional $116-million jet write-off.

The burning question, of course, is why New York *didn't* know the magnitude of the problem. Naish maintains he leaned over backward, because of his initial opposition to the jet program, to clear important decisions with either Johnson or Pace. Last fall a member of General Dynamics' executive committee, still puzzling over why New York had been so much in the dark for so long, pressed Pace on the point. He wanted to know why, even if Naish's information had been suspect, Convair's controller hadn't told Pace of the losses, or why he hadn't learned of them from MacBride, whom Pace had sent out early in 1961 to investigate, or from Earl Johnson, whom Pace had given overall responsibility for the jet program and sent to Convair in late 1958 and early 1959 when the division was plainly in trouble. Pace, at a loss to explain, wondered whether he ought to resign. No, said the director, and Pace needn't make any apologies. After all, he wasn't trained as a businessman. He (the director) made no apologies for not being able to walk into an operating room and perform like a surgeon. So Pace shouldn't feel badly about not being trained as a businessman.

The wages of sin

Unhappily for General Dynamics, the departures of Naish and Esenwein did little to lighten the corporation's load of trouble. Nor was Rhoades MacBride, General Dynamics' No. 3 man whom Pace put in as acting president of Convair, able to bring the division under control (after ten months he too was to be washed out of office). There had simply been too many sins of commission and omission to be cured by chopping off heads in San Diego.

General Dynamics ran into trouble with American over the 990. The gamble, mentioned earlier, that Convair's engineers could guess the jet power needed to meet the speed and fuel requirements in the American contract, had failed. In addition, the 990 was already six months late, so in September, 1961, Smith canceled his order. Now the General Dynamics board was confronted by two choices, both bleak. It could turn back the uneconomical DC-7's Smith had induced them to accept in lieu of a $25-million down payment, then with the $25-million cash reimbursement as a cushion, cut the price of the 990 and try to sell it to other carriers; or it could try to get a new contract from Smith. A few audacious directors, including Crown, were for trying choice No. 1, but the opinion of the majority, as epitomized by one member of the board, was: "Now let's not get C. R. mad. Earl Johnson knows him. Let's go and appeal to him."

The upshot was that Pace, Johnson, and Henry Crown paid a call on Smith. There Colonel Crown related a little story about his having let a construction company off the hook even though, legally, he had had every right to hold them to a disastrous contract. Smith made no comment but when Pace and Johnson pursued the same thought he finally said: "I understand your problem, but I have stockholders. You told me, Earl, that the plane would go a certain speed." A new contract was signed with American and it was a tough one. The airline cut its order from 25 to 15 planes, with an option to take 5 more if Convair could get the speed up to 621 mph. Upwards of $300,000 was knocked off the price of each aircraft. With wind-tunnel tests completed, chances are now good that Convair will be able to meet the 621-mph specification.

But even as this article goes to press in mid-January, the end of General Dynamics' jet travail is not in sight. Howard Hughes has just canceled his order for thirteen 990's, an order that, surprisingly enough, Convair had accepted during the period when Hughes couldn't even pay for his 880's. SAS and Swiss Air have cut their original order from nine 990's to seven. Moreover, the market is just about saturated insofar as additional jet sales are concerned, even for a fine plane like the 880. As for the 990, it too has missed its market. To date only sixty-six 880's and twenty-three 990's have been sold, which puts Convair well behind Boeing's 720 sales in the medium-range market. Small wonder that when somebody suggests selling off Convair, a General Dynamics vice-president ruefully remarks: "Would $5 be too much?"

"This has hurt us in Washington"

The failure of General Dynamics' management has had some serious collateral effects. As a member of the executive committee remarked: "The public has lost confidence in us. This has hurt us in Washington. We have to inject people of stature into the management." The company recently lost out on two of the three big defense contracts (the $400-million Apollo space-craft contract went to North American, Boeing got the $300-million Saturn S-1 booster system). Its executive committee has also failed to find a new chief executive officer, "a man forty years old with one hundred years of experience" as John McCone remarked in turning down the job, and this has further delayed General Dynamics' much-needed reorganization.

Though the great losses are now a matter of history, the subject of what went wrong with the company will no doubt be discussed for as long as there is a General Dynamics. "It's a grave question in my mind," said one of the company's senior vice-presidents, "as to whether General Dynamics had the right to risk this kind of money belonging to the stockholders for the potential profit you could get out of it. All management has to take a certain risk for big gains. But I don't think it's right to risk so much for so small a gain."

There are, however, larger questions of management's responsibility for the well-being of the corporation. That responsibility, in the jet age, is to keep management techniques developing at the same pace as the technologies they must control.

QUESTIONS

What should Frank Pace have done to get better control at General Dynamics?

Part 5
CONCLUSION: ACHIEVING BALANCE

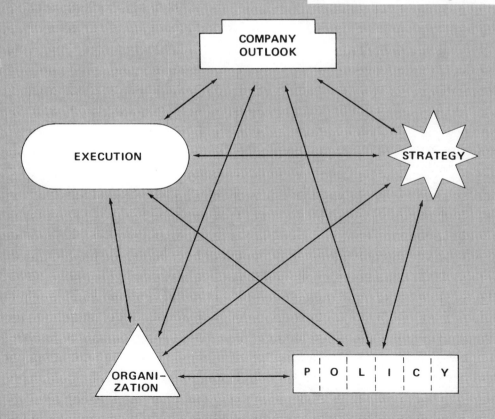

MANAGING MULTINATIONAL ENTERPRISES

The total task of managing

To think sharply about a complex subject like managing, we usually divided the subject into parts for separate analysis. Thus, in this book we have shifted our focus successively from selecting strategy to defining policy, on to designing organization, and finally to guiding execution. This separate treatment helps in analysis, but it also detracts from sensing the interconnection and the complexity of the total task of managing. Central managers necessarily give much attention to achieving a balance of the various actions they sponsor. They must build their company into an integrated whole.

In concluding, then, we want to put the parts back together again. We will do this in two ways, first by reviewing the overall task of managing a multinational company, and second by discussing the integrating role of central managers.

The attraction of multinational operations

"Go abroad, young man!" is the modern paraphrase of Horace Greeley's guide to opportunity. Companies, too, seek growth possibilities in foreign markets.

For years most U.S. firms were preoccupied with the vast free-trade area within our boundaries. In terms of time and communication, Los Angeles was then much farther from Chicago than Paris or Tokyo is today. But, as national markets became more competitive, exports took on added attractions. Also, oil, copper, steel, and other industries needed large supplies of raw materials from abroad. Those pressures led to substantial exports and imports.

Then as foreign markets grew and nationalistic controls hampered trade, business moved to the next and current phase of fully integrated operations—both manufacturing and selling—in offshore locations. For example, over one third of both sales and net income of Ford Motor, IBM, Colgate-Palmolive, National Cash Register, H. J. Heinz, and Pfizer arise outside the United States. Many other firms also are multinational in scope.

Such integrated operations abroad are growing rapidly—both for U.S. firms and for firms based in other countries. They create worldwide competition, with resources and know-how seeking opportunities in a highly adaptable fashion not confined to the country of origin. Most "multinational" companies start from a well established domestic operation but seek to optimize both the source and the allocation resources on a worldwide basis. They pose new challenges to our ability to manage.

This chapter deals with the *management* of companies that conduct manufacturing, selling, and related activities in several different countries. We will focus here on the issues that are particularly significant to multinational enterprises. Effective management of local operating units is assumed. This emphasis on "parent" operations serves two purposes: (1) it highlights the distinctive features of multinational companies, and (2) it illustrates the application of the basic analytical framework of the entire book to a different business.

STRATEGY OF MULTINATIONAL FIRMS

Multinational operation requires careful planning of overall strategy in terms of the international nature of the total business. Important issues in formulating multinational strategy are the synergistic benefits to be obtained, the selection of countries with the greatest long-run growth potential, and the timing of internal expansion.

Synergistic benefits sought

A firm embarking on a multinational course needs synergistic advantage to offset the inherent costs of operating in several different cultures. Many of the policy, organization, and control decisions that a firm adopts tie back to the fundamental question of "why we think we can do it better" than a local national company.

Important among possible rationales for operating abroad are the following:

1. *Technical know-how.* Manufacturing companies may go abroad to make use of the research and engineering already done for domestic operations. Clearly, one of the advantages Caterpillar Tractor has in its worldwide operations is its *engineering design* of heavy earth-moving equipment. *Processing know-how* is more likely a distinctive advantage for chemical and engineering companies. In some instances, as in pharmaceuticals, either the products or the processes are protected by worldwide patents, although even here the progressive updating of technology may be fully as important as the legal protection.

2. *Access to markets.* A worldwide company itself may provide an attractive market. Thus, large quantities of crude oil may be refined by companies that undertake worldwide exploration and production of their basic raw material. Or the company may have a widespread marketing organization and be able to dispose of much larger quantities than could any company in the country of origin—for example, Dole has a great advantage in disposing of Philippine pineapple. Perhaps a company has bigger access to markets simply because of its

superior marketing—a significant factor in Sears Roebuck's success in Latin America.

3. *Capital.* Especially in developing countries, the capital resources of a multinational company contribute to its relative strength. The ability to make large investments (coupled with technical know-how) has aided companies making everything from fertilizer to flashlights in India.

4. *Managerial skill.* Hard to determine and often overrated, the managerial skills provided by a multinational company often do provide it with a distinctive advantage. Philips' Gloeilampenfabrieken, the giant Netherlands electronics manufacturer, obviously owes part of its success to managerial ability; and the 57 varieties of H. J. Heinz are world-famous for a similar reason. The French writer, Servan-Schreiber, picks managerial ability as the basis for *the American challenge* to the entire European business community.

If a company bases its international strategy on any one or combination of the factors just discussed, it must be sure that it does in fact have an advantage that is both relevant and continuing. For example, mass marketing techniques that are geared to suburban shopping centers can cause disaster in foreign countries. Production processes based on high labor cost are not necessarily optimum in countries with a large labor supply. Some of the "know-how" advantages are fleeting; local competitors will catch up. So, if a long-run strategy rests upon a technological superiority, the multinational company must be reasonably confident that it can maintain its lead.

Defense rather than offense is sometimes the prime mover in multinational strategy. For years, a company making, say, radios or sewing machines may have exported to a South American or an African country. Then, local production or low-cost Japanese competition makes serious inroads. In this new environment, the company may have to choose between either establishing its own foreign plant or giving up a large segment of the market. But even if the strategy is initiated for defensive reasons, the company should have a clear advantage by which it hopes to keep a distinctive niche in each of the countries in which it operates.

Countries attractive for growth

Building a strong subsidiary in a country often takes years, and to obtain a significant industry position after other companies are entrenched is costly. Consequently, the multinational company needs some strategy regarding the kinds of countries that offer the greatest long-run potential. One metal container company, for instance, is setting up plants in developing countries—even though they may merely make bottle caps initially—in order to be established when real growth occurs. Other firms operate only where the per capita purchasing power is high. One rubber company, to cite a different criterion, will have nothing to do with countries affiliated with the Soviet bloc. Many other variations exist.

A useful approach to identifying countries attractive for growth is a careful appraisal of the following factors:

1. Estimate the potential demand for the major services the company expects to provide. This will be tied to industrial and economic development, living conditions, natural resources, population, education, consumption attitudes, and other social and economic influences.

2. Assess the importance in each country of the distinctive strengths of the company. These strengths will include the key synergistic factors the company hopes to exploit, which have been discussed in the previous section.

3. Predict the general environment and its associated risk. Important factors to consider in this connection are prospects for:
    Controls on foreign exchange
    Inflation
    Import and export restrictions
    Legislation against foreigners
    Expropriation and nationalization
    Onerous taxation
    Political upheaval
    War
    Deterioration of financial, utility, and other services

Analysis of this sort led a leading manufacturer of control equipment to concentrate its expansion in Western Europe, with secondary attention to Japan. All other parts of the world are to be served by exports from the United States or Europe. On the other hand, a large pharmaceutical manufacturer anticipates increasing pressure to manufacture at least the leading drugs locally. Consequently, it is setting up a large number of small local plants where much of the final fabrication and packaging is done. The company hopes that this localized activity will give it an edge in the importation of new and complex drugs (which carry wide gross profit margins) from the home country.

Timing of expansion

Timing also looms large. Five years often elapse between a decision to manufacture in a given country and the efficient operation of a new plant. Government permits, site acquisition, engineering design, building construction, import of specialized equipment, hiring and training of workers, establishing dependable sources of materials, overcoming start-up difficulties, and shaping a viable social structure all take time. For this reason, many U.S. companies entered the European Common Market early—before trade barriers had been significantly reduced. Not all of these plants proved to be wise investments, but some companies built a strong position because they were ready to produce quality goods when the market opened up.

Multinational service organizations face a similar question of when to enter additional countries. Thus, for years all but two U.S. banks relied on "correspondents" for most of their foreign activities. Then, the growth of the Eurodollar market precipitated a great scramble for offices at least in London. In this instance, as with advertising agencies, multinational service organizations have delayed expansion until worldwide marketing and manufacturing organizations were well established. Industrial engineering and public accounting firms, on the other hand, have built strong positions by being in the vanguard of economic development.

Political instability strongly affects timing strategy. Indonesia presents a classic problem of when multinational companies should enter a strife-torn area. Rich in human and natural resources, yet needing outside capital and know-how, Indonesia attracts investments of oil and other multinational companies. Nevertheless, serious losses have been incurred by companies that have entered the area under political regimes that were later overthrown. Comparable political difficulties have arisen in Central Africa. Here, companies anxious to get a foothold in the large potential market have often discovered that their early association with one political regime becomes a handicap at a later time.

What services to perform, in which countries, at what time are recurring issues in multinational strategy. Specific situations pose an array of additional angles, but these three issues give a sense of central management's strategy problems.

USE OF POLICY

The use of policy as a management tool is even more significant in multinational firms than in Stage III multidivision firms that operate within a single country. In both types of enterprise, the operating divisons have their own policies. However, the multinational enterprise must distinguish clearly between those facets of its activities in which it seeks synergistic benefits—and hence needs centralized policy and coordination—and those activities that should not be governed by central policy. Selectivity is crucial. Possible issues on which multinational guidance may be warranted are illustrated in the following paragraphs.

Standardization of products

The degree to which products will be the same in various countries calls for policy guidance. The most widely known product throughout the world is Coca-Cola. The Coca-Cola Company has a strict policy that its product is to be uniform, a standard that is difficult to achieve since bottling is done by numerous independent local distributors throughout the world. Product consistency and a worldwide reputation take priority over local tastes. In contrast, Unilever permits its operating companies to adapt their soap and food products to the particular tastes and needs of the countries in which they are operating. This flexibility permits local units to stress, say, margarine versus cooking oils in accordance with national dietary habits.

Equipment manufacturers find standardization among countries difficult to achieve. A U.S. food machinery manufacturer, for example, had to change all dimensions from inches to metric measurement, and to simplify shop operations also had to modify the specifications slightly. Electric motors, switches, compressors, and even bolts that were purchased had to be adjusted to what was locally available. Users of the machines wanted to be able to obtain repair parts quickly and they preferred designs with which local workers were familiar. Consequently, the policy of this company is to have separate specifications for Europe and for South America. IBM takes an opposite tack. The parts for its machines are the same throughout the world. Such a policy is feasible because IBM has long stressed providing its own service to customers, which includes assuming the burden of maintaining an inventory of repair parts.

The choice of a product standardization policy, then, is influenced by company size and its volume of sales in each country, the importance of adapting to local needs, and in particular the strategy the company has chosen to make its services distinctive.

Regional specialization of production

A multinational company has the possibility of concentrating production of each of its products in one plant and then trading. Theoretically, this permits sale of a full line in Country A, one product being made locally and the rest imported. The same situation prevails in Countries X, Y, and Z. The advantage, of course, is lower cost arising from making a large quantity of a single product in each plant instead of a variety of products only in the volume needed in the local market. In practice, the trades do not balance off neatly, but the central concept of regional specialization can be utilized. Singer Company, for example, partially concentrates production of its industrial, high-quality domestic, and low-quality domestic sewing machines in three different countries.

If the parts going into products are standardized, then regional specialization of parts manufacture is possible. IBM in Europe has made considerable progress in this direction.

Unfortunately, a regional specialization policy is difficult to apply. It relies on inexpensive and uninterrupted movement of goods across national boundaries; it assumes that product standardization and economies of scale are substantial; and it applies only when the production capabilities of the various countries are compatible. Note also that a high degree of central coordination is required.

Transfer prices

The prices at which raw materials, parts, or finished goods are transferred from one division of a company to another is always a troublesome problem. Transfers across national boundaries create additional difficulties. For instance, a high transfer price increases the profits earned in the exporting country and decreases the profits of the importer; this affects who gets income taxes and which local managements "look good." The transfer price may also influence the choice of long-term investment, selling prices, and local allocation of effort among products. Consequently, a multinational company must have some policy regarding the value attached to goods (and services) moving from one operating unit to another.

Mobil Oil Corporation, for instance, ships crude oil from Iran to a refinery in the Netherlands, and then ships the refined product from the Netherlands to Sweden for sale to consumers. The managers of Mobil's affiliates in each of the three countries and the respective national governments all naturally feel that their share of the final sales income should be higher. Where the profit shows up is not a matter of indifference to them.

Virtually all companies transfer at "market price" if such a figure exists for the product at the time and the place the transfer occurs. Beyond that, policies differ sharply. Some firms use a negotiated price—a figure that presumably approximates what a competitive price would be. Others use direct cost plus a markup percentage set up by headquarters. A few use total budgeted cost, including a "fair" return on local investment. In some circumstances, the starting point is a budgeted selling price from which distribution and processing costs are deducted to arrive at the value of the product received.

A guide for multinational managers among this array of possible policies, we suggest, is to focus on the incentive effect of transfer prices. Put the variability—the residual profits—in those units that have the greatest maneuverability to make or lose money. For divisions performing a standard function (for example, pipelines in an integrated petroleum operation), set transfer prices to cover full costs and depend on budgetary control rather than "profit margins" for incentives.

Proportion of local ownership

All multinational firms are holding companies. They are parent companies only, investing in local concerns that are organized in conformity with the requirements of the particular country in which they operate. A major policy question in this regard is what share, if any, of each operating company should be owned by local citizens. Billions of dollars of present and potential foreign investment are affected by this issue.

Referring to our discussion of partially owned subsidiaries in Chapter 15, the parent company gains many advantages from 100% ownership—flexibility in assigning functions, freedom in setting transfer prices, avoidance of arguments about fairness to minority interests, simpler decision-making, and by no means least carrying the full risk and receiving all the net profits.

Full ownership, of course, means higher investment. The chief drawback of 100% ownership is the loss of a potential incentive—stock ownership by local employees—but even this can be largely overcome by bonus plans and stock options in the parent company.

Multinational companies face an added dimension. *National pride* and *national economic independence* enter, often with heavy emotional and political overtones. The idea that a foreigner controls even a tiny part of the national gross product or the national employment can rally popular opposition. And if (1) a natural resource is involved and (2) a major sector of the economy is affected—as is true of copper in Chile and Zambia and oil in Libya—then governments can rise or fall on the ownership issue.

The alternative ownership arrangements are numerous. Simple variations start from full ownership by the parent, move to a minority local interest (the typical request of Canadians who want an opportunity to share in profits of local companies), and extend to 51% (controlling) local interest. Moreover, different kinds of shares with various voting rights can be introduced, and options or contracts to gain control at a later date can be added. The ownership right—itself a social device—can be circumscribed by contracts with individuals or governments.

From this array of possibilities, most multinational enterprises adopt a policy that gives them a consistent stand on this troublesome issue. Firms like IBM wish to use regional specialization and have a special reason for insisting on the flexibility that comes with 100% ownership. Also in this case rapid technological development makes avoidance of bickering over who deserves credit more significant.

In contrast, when the multinational company provides only technical know-how and the local firm carries complete responsibility for organizing production and marketing, a local ownership interest both is fair and generates incentive for local initiative that is essential for success. Who should eventually control the local operation depends on who will make the major *continuing* contribution—a matter hard to measure but at least shifting the discussion from power to a constructive issue.

Exploitation of natural resources generates the most emotion. Here, rising nationalism makes 100% foreign-owned companies politically untenable. An increasingly popular arrangement is to grant the multinational company control during the first twenty years and/or until it has recovered its investment plus, say, 20% profit per annum—and then to transfer majority ownership to local (perhaps governmental) interests.

These examples clearly indicate a close interdependence between a firm's strategy regarding products and countries and its policy on the sharing of ownership with local interests.

Optimizing exchange risks

Multinational firms inevitably face foreign exchange problems. Most transactions of each operating company will be in its local currency; but when goods are exported or imported and when dividends from local operations are returned to the parent company, the local money must be converted into foreign currency. Rates of exchange—the value of one currency in terms of another—do change, especially when a local inflation is creating balance-of-payments difficulties.

A common policy followed by smaller firms is to *ignore* exchange fluctuations. Under this approach, each local company seeks to maximize its profit, and transfers to the parent are made when surplus funds are available. Hopefully, exchange rates will be favorable, or at least average out over a period of time. The rationale for ignoring exchange fluctuations is that the firm will be more successful by concentrating on the business it knows than by dabbling where it is not an expert.

An alternative and more sophisticated policy is to *minimize exposure*. This can be done in several ways: (1) Borrow locally to finance local operations so that repayments never get involved in foreign exchange. The catch, of course, is that only part of the total needs of the local unit can be borrowed, and interest rates may be quite high. (2) Rent buildings and other assets, thereby reducing local investment. Again, availability and cost limit the extent to which this can be done. (3) Hedge in forward exchange markets by "selling" a foreign currency to offset fixed obligations (and perhaps investments in assets that will not depreciate) in that currency. For this, as for other methods, there is an expense involved in avoiding the risk.

In fact, firms adopt a policy of *minimizing interest costs,* even though doing so may add to foreign exchange risks. Money is borrowed where the interest rate is low and is transferred via foreign exchange to countries with high interest rates. When exchange controls hamper such direct movements, the same result can be achieved by either delaying or prepaying a settlement for goods that the multinational firm ships from one country to another. Since high interest rates frequently signal inflation and foreign exchange difficulties, such transfers of funds can increase exchange risks.

A still more daring policy is to deliberately *seek profits* from changes in exchange rates. Rarely will a multinational concern simply speculate in foreign exchange quite unrelated to its other business. However, it may feel that its intimate knowledge of some countries provides such a good basis for predicting rate changes that it is justified in shifting its holdings of these currencies in anticipation of future changes.[1]

The five policy issues discussed—standardization of products, regional specialization of production, transfer pricing, proportion of local ownership, and optimizing exchange risks—by no means exhaust the policy problems facing multinational enterprises. They do demonstrate that the concept of policy formulation can be helpful in dealing with the more unique aspects of multinational operations as well as with the more common problems facing national companies that were examined in Chapters 5 to 15.

ORGANIZING MULTINATIONAL OPERATIONS

Geographic dispersion of the multinational enterprise intensifies most of the organization problems faced by domestic firms. The variety of languages, laws, loyalties, and customs require more adaptation and complicate integrated action. Basically, the problems are the same; the difference is one of degree.

---

[1] Attempting to profit from changes in foreign exchange rates is similar to trying to outguess inflationary price changes. For policy restraint on such risk-taking see pages 209-211.

Worldwide departmentation

A multinational firm is a Stage III company (as defined in Chapter 16). The primary emphasis, of course, is on geographical divisions rather than product divisions. Normally, all activities in each country are placed under a single executive. Distance, national differences, and especially local political considerations accentuate the need for a coordinated, consistent posture in each country.

But the stress on national divisions leaves unsettled what activities should be performed in each country and how the national units tie into the overall organization.

For companies dealing with a single line of products that require large-scale operations, such as steel or copper, a basically *functional* structure works well. Each national unit is predominantly either marketing or production, so it can be assigned to an appropriate worldwide functional department. (Local sales in a producing country come under the country general manager but receive functional guidance from the sales department.)

In service industries where production plants are small, both marketing and at least the final stages of production can be performed economically within each country. So here, the *regional* type of structure remains dominant and the national units report to an overall regional or world office. However, a hybrid may be necessary with most operations in national and regional divisions just as indicated, but with engineering and basic production concentrated in two or three spots under a separate production division.

Of course, if the multinational company engages in two or more unrelated businesses—W. R. Grace & Company, for instance—then each business (*product*) normally should have its separate multinational organization. In other words, departmentation in multinational organizations is some combination of regional, functional, or product groupings common in domestic structures.

National or regional decentralization

Most multinational organizations are highly decentralized in some respects and centralized in others. Activities tied to consumers or operating employees—selling, granting credit, pricing, delivery, customer service, bookkeeping, warehousing, and the like—should be adapted to local conditions, and wide discretion in such matters should be exercised by managers of national units.

The benefits of synergy, on the other hand, usually come with centralized direction. For example, process and product know-how, worldwide quality reputation, and regional specialization of production can be fully utilized when they are centrally designed and controlled. Multinational firms whose strategies stress such concepts are committed to centralization on at least these key strategic weapons. Even a commitment to capitalize on managerial know-how implies that the techniques of planning, organizing, leading, and controlling will be stipulated by central headquarters.

The organizational task, then, is to sort out the kinds of decisions that need to be centralized and those that can be more expeditiously made in local units. And, having defined the dimensions of freedom at various levels, our multinational manager must make sure that the structure is understood by all executives—a substantial endeavor because of the diversity of backgrounds and expectations of the people involved.

Providing expert services where needed

A perpetual headache in multinational management is obtaining full advantage of the expertise that exists within the company. How can the know-how of executives in the domestic operating divisions and the wisdom of central staff be incorporated into decisions in operating companies dispersed throughout the world?

The difficulty arises from several causes. The experts are busy with their primary assignments, and they give low priority to a request for advice from Calcutta or Copenhagen. Even when they do spare time for foreign matters, they have difficulty in communicating. Language, background, and unfamiliarity with local conditions make it hard for them to perceive the local situation and give advice that is realistic. Moreover, the local executives often lack sufficient training to sift and adapt the ideas they receive.

The most common device for overcoming this barrier is a *liaison staff*, that is, people whose primary role is communicator of pertinent questions to the experts and translator of answers to operating personnel. Such a staff may be attached to the chief executive of international operations and/or to regional managers if they exist. Unfortunately, experience with a staff of this sort is not always favorable. Both General Electric Company and Ford Motor Company have created a large international staff, disbanded it, and recreated it. As with all staff, there is danger that persons far removed from the scene of action will become more bureaucratic than helpful.

An alternative is to try *lowering the communications barrier* itself. This may be done by increasing opportunities for travel, personal contact, and observation. Managers of domestic divisions may be given indirect or even direct "responsibility" for foreign activities similar to their domestic ones. Full-time task teams may be formed to study major problems. Cooperation may be explicitly added to performance appraisal factors. These and other devices are intended to create a "We're all in the same family" feeling.

Few multinational companies are happy with the spotty success they have achieved in getting good advice focused on local problems. Opportunities for improvement are high in this facet of organization.

Coordination between countries

Shipping products from one country to another requires careful coordination. The Singer Company, for example, ships sewing machines from

England to over thirty countries; the receiving countries want the right model at the right time, and the English plants want a balanced, stable production schedule. Multinational oil companies ship crude oil from half a dozen sources to several different refineries, which in turn ship finished products to a score of consuming nations. Or a company constructing a flour mill in South Africa imports specialized equipment that must fit the building erected on the spot. In each instance, activities in several countries must be closely synchronized.

This coordination task is complicated by its international dimensions. Usually a special organization unit is created to assure that misunderstandings are held to a minimum and that each country acts in a way that optimizes cost-income for the company as a whole. Oil companies often create a major Supply and Distribution Department devoted solely to this task. In other industries, a special scheduling unit is located at each plant, but it has a unique international status. The manager of one such unit observes: "The mechanics are easy once you understand the needs and cost factors of each location; I spend most of my time being an international diplomat."

Again we see—as with departmentation, decentralization, and specialized services—that multinational coordination has its particular difficulties and intensities, but it is basically the same kind of phenomenon faced by managers of domestic firms.

KEY PERSONNEL

Operating units in each country will have their own personnel policy suited to local needs. To realize the potential benefits of their multinational affiliation, however, key technical and executive personnel must somehow acquire the best knowledge and skills available in the total system. Capturing this benefit is crucial to a successful multinational enterprise.

Use of nationals as executives

IBM World Trade follows a practice of filling all executive positions in the hundred countries in which it operates with local citizens. Two ends are served by this local use of nationals (that is, citizens of the country in which they work). Executives in each country know intimately the language and the customs of their market and their workers. Moreover, nationalistic demands to give jobs to local citizens rather than foreigners are fully met.

But IBM is an exception. Virtually all companies agree that *most* local executives should be nationals, for the reasons just stated. Complete adherence, however, restricts promotion opportunities. Under the IBM World Trade system, the best person available *in the total company* cannot be shifted into a vacancy unless that person happens to be a national of the country in which the vacancy occurs.

An alternative is to give nationals preference, but when foreigners are clearly better qualified, to place them in the positions. Still another variation used by one large oil company that wishes to "internationalize" its general managers is a clearly stated policy that no nationals will be appointed general managers in any country (1) until they serve a tour of duty in a foreign country and (2) agree to accept a transfer at a later date out of their native land. Because this guide is consistently followed, executives seek foreign assignments since they know this is the path of advancement, and local employees resist less general managers who are foreigners because they are not regarded as obstacles to advancement of local people.

A final alternative we should mention is maximum use of nationals *except* in the top *financial* position; the presumption is that a non-national in this job will be freer of local loyalties and more objective in appraising operating results.

Developing multinational managers

If nationals are to fill most, if not all, of the key positions in each country, the need for executive training is obvious. In the newer countries, especially, competent and dependable executives are very scarce. And, a core of senior executives qualified to move from one country to another, or to top staff jobs, needs even broader training.

The special requirements for a multinational executive include: (1) language; (2) sensitivity and adaptability to differences in culture, especially with respect to communication and motivation; (3) background in international trade and finance and in the economic problems of the country where assigned; (4) grasp of company procedures, technology, and successful practices; and (5) unusual degree of patience and tact combined with perseverence.

The first three of these special qualifications can be developed off-the-job; the company can assist by making time available and paying expenses of outside courses. Knowledge about the company is normally acquired on-the-job in a series of assignments including work in company headquarters and in key departments. Tact and perseverance, insofar as they can be consciously developed, call for personal counseling. And so a whole array of executive development techniques should be carefully combined to foster the growth of multinational executives.

Compensation of executives in foreign assignments

Both the need to supplement local executive talent and the process of executive development call for assigning people outside their home country. Such working abroad complicates pay rates in two ways:

(1) Salary scales differ from country to country. For instance, using the official exchange rate, U.S. pay is about 250% of British pay for a similar job. So, when a Yankee works in England, should he be paid by U.S. or British standards? And what of a Britisher in the United States? Of course, living costs, taxes, government benefits, social requirements, and the like do differ substantially, but few executives agree on the extent to which such factors offset the differences in cash salary.

(2) People living abroad want some things that they enjoyed at home but that may be costly in a foreign country. Brazilians in the United States find that domestic servants must be paid what they consider executive salaries, whereas North Americans in Brazil find that frozen vegetables are exorbitant. Few executives—and their spouses—are adaptable enough to quickly give up all of the particular living comforts they are accustomed to.

One large multinational firm meets these pay pressures as follows: (1) Executives' base salaries and their retirement accumulations are tied to what the job they hold would pay in their home country. The assumption is that the executives relate their salaries to standards in their native land and that they plan to retire there. (2) In addition, they receive allowances for moving, extra living and housing cost, children's education, biennial trips home, and—if the location is unpleasant—"hardship."

This arrangement provides a consistent and "fair" pay in terms of a person's home base. However, two individuals from different countries might receive quite different total compensation for the same job, and this can become a source of irritation. (An American's base salary may be paid partly in local currency and partly in dollars in the U.S.A., so that his local scale of living will not conspicuously differ from that of his peers.) Also, if allowances are too liberal, the executives have trouble readjusting when they return home and receive only their base pay.

Whatever the particular system of allowances, clearly an executive away from home is a high-priced person. Possibly as international assignments become recognized as valuable steps on the way to the top, instead of an inconvenient way to save a few dollars, the premium paid to our mobile executives can be reduced.

CONTROLLING MULTINATIONAL ACTIVITIES

Distance and diversity of operating conditions also create problems of control within a multinational enterprise. The three dimensions of these control problems, discussed in the following paragraphs, illustrate the special burden a multinational firm undertakes in addition to the normal control tasks in each of the operating units.

Understanding the concept of constructive control

For cultural reasons, the control process is poorly understood in many countries. Often the significance of completing work on time and of maintaining quality is not accepted. Local life proceeds more casually; so when western control standards are imposed, the action appears to local workers as unwarranted and capricious.

Similarly, accounting records in many countries are scanty, inaccurate, and often manipulated to reduce taxes. Naturally, managers do not look to such records as aids to prompt coordination of activities.

In some cultures, business relationships are closely entwined with personal friendship, kinship, reciprocal favors, and *simpatico* feelings. In such situations objective appraisal and tough corrective action are too irritating to be tolerated.

A first step, then, for a multinational manager in securing control is to win acceptance of the concept. Executives in operating units must understand that survival in world business requires realistic objectives, performance standards based on these objectives, regular measurement of performance, prompt feedback of control data to people who can undertake corrective action, overall evaluation, updating of targets, and correlation of incentives with results. Without acceptance of this process, the best-designed control systems will achieve only moderate effects.

Operating controls that encourage optimum performance

Every multinational firm must have dependable, understandable accounting reports from each country. Due to local variations in bookkeeping practice, already mentioned, the establishment of a worldwide accounting system is no small task. But once in place, it does permit the introduction of annual and five-year budgets, measurement of growth in sales and profits, and other usual financial control devices.

Essential as such financial controls are, reliance on financial reports alone is especially dangerous in a multinational business. The opportunities and the difficulties in each country make necessary more complete and sensitive yardsticks. Criteria such as market share, government relations, quality maintenance, customer service, cultivation of new customers, physical productivity, employee training and turnover, plant maintenance, innovation and modernization, protection of assets from inflation, cooperation with other units of the company—all are control measures that the multinational headquarters should watch in each country in addition to financial reports.

Frequent evaluation is inappropriate. A thorough semiannual review plus prompt evaluation of major changes or deviations from plans serve most multinational companies better than monthly reporting, which is likely to become routine.

Periodic product stream evaluation

The controls just described help keep each operating unit "on course," but they do not check the continuing desirability of the course itself. This broader evaluation is difficult because most multinational firms sell the same product in different countries, ship materials or parts from one country to another, and in other ways seek synergistic benefits from joint activities. Separate controls in each country do not tell whether the desired overall benefits are being obtained.

Consequently, special studies that consolidate the incomes, costs, and investment from all countries dealing with a *product line* are needed. Since typically several lines are handled, at least when all countries are considered, a lot of unscrambling of assets and joint costs may be necessary. So the analysis becomes involved—too involved for routine periodic reports. Fortunately, a special appraisal, say every two years, is adequate because changes in product line or production strategy can only be made in relatively long time cycles.

With an analysis of how product lines are measuring up to original plans, a reappraisal also of markets, competition, technology, and other external factors is in order. This may lead to significant shifts in company strategy. And so we find outselves completing the full management cycle of strategy, implementing plans, execution, and control—which provides the basis for a revised strategy and a new cycle.

SUMMARY

Managers in multinational companies face a variety of issues arising from the international climate of the total operation. Balancing these issues calls for unusual skill. Company *strategy* seeks to extend strengths in one country to many other markets; it requires judicious selection of countries where these strengths will be most beneficial; and it lays out the timing of international expansion.

Among the *policy* issues created by worldwide operations are the extent to which products will be adapted to local needs, regionalization of production, allocation of profits to different countries via transfer prices, participation in ownership of operating units by local nationals, and speculating or avoiding foreign exchange risks.

Organization has to be adjusted to the strategy and the geographical dispersion. To capture full synergistic benefits of technological know-how, uniform quality, or reorganization of production, decision-making must be centralized—whereas national differences pull down decisions related to people. Special provision for communicating and coordinating is necessary to assure that the multinational advantages are attained.

Staffing with local nationals is desirable, but this creates a need for multinational training of executives. To provide such training, and in the senior levels to utilize exceptional talent, people must move across national boundaries. Whenever this is done, a prickly problem of salary and cost-of-living adjustments arises.

A multinational scope of operation increases both the need for and the difficulty of *control*. The underlying concept of constructive control has to be developed, reliable measures of tangible and intangible results must be created, and provision must be made for assessing integrated results as well as performance in each country.

Overshadowing these distinctive aspects of multinational management is the demonstration that the broad framework we have used throughout this book to analyze the central management tasks of national companies provides an equally effective means for thinking through the overall management framework of the most complex business enterprise man has yet conceived.

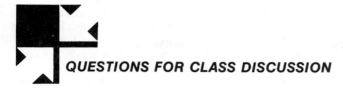

QUESTIONS FOR CLASS DISCUSSION

1. Most multinational enterprises deal with products or raw materials. Recently multinational advertising agencies have had a spurt of growth. (a) Recognizing that advertising must be run in local media, use the local language, and appeal to local viewpoints—what distinctive service does a multinational advertising agency provide? (b) What kinds of policies, organization, and control will a multinational advertising agency need to provide the distinctive service you identified in your answer to (a)?

2. Using the factors listed on page 542 as guides, compare Canada, Mexico, and Libya as potential areas for expansion of a U.S.-based multinational company engaged in (a) automobile manufacturing, (b) silver and gold jewelry production, and (c) frozen food processing and distribution. For each combination of country and industry that you consider has good potential, to what extent would you decentralize management to local nationals?

3. Give a specific example of each of the types of strategic synergies listed on pages 540 and 541—preferably by a company whose operations you know something about. For each of your examples explain how the desired synergy affects the nature, scope, and location of expert staff service the parent company should provide.

4. Multinational operations are faced with an additional array of uncertainties such as tariff charges, fluctuating foreign exchange rates and controls, different tax regulations, political upheavals, wars, varying growth rates, and additional sources of competition. Does the existence of these uncertainties mean that long-range programming (see Chapter 20) should not be attempted by multinational companies? If you do recommend use of long-range programming, explain how you would deal with these uncertainties.

5. Assume that you have a good job and a promising future with a bank, a manufacturing company, an advertising agency, or another kind of business that appeals to you. Your company has undertaken international expansion, and the president asks whether you would like a foreign assignment. (a) What inducements would you want before you accepted a 3-year assignment? a 20-year assignment? (b) What effect might the inducements you ask for have on your effectiveness in the foreign post? (c) Do you think nationals of other countries should receive the same kind of treatment that you request?

6. A major pineapple company decided to reduce its dependence on Hawaii as its sole source of supply and therefore established plantations and canning plants in the Philippines and in the West Indies. The president believes strongly in executive incentives based on profits earned by the operating unit in which the executive works. How will the corporation's policy on (a) transfer pricing, (b) use of local sources of capital, and (c) minority ownership in local companies by nationals of the country affect the applicability of the profit incentive concept?

7. Belmont Fashions sells a wide variety of men's dress shirts and sport shirts featuring some high-style brands and some low-cost brands. In addition to its

New York "contract" production, it runs its own plants in Texas and in Hong Kong. Compare the task of central management control of the Texas plant with control of the Hong Kong plant. In your answer consider (a) the criteria used, (b) who does the measuring and how often, (c) the interpretation of results, and (d) the types of corrective action that are likely to be effective.

8. One of the complications of multinational operations is the difference among countries in norms of ethical behavior and social responsibility. Both the formal standards (often expressed in law) and the strictness of their observance vary. (For example, wide differences exist with respect to bribery, tax evasion, treatment of workers, and agreements with competitors.) If you were working abroad for an English-based multinational company, which set of standards would you follow? What is the potential business impact of your ethical decisions?

9. A prominent Canadian says: "We believe the first loyalty of a Canadian company should be to Canada. That applies to foreign activities of a company as well as to its domestic affairs. My observation is that foreign companies operating in Canada act on the same principle—they put the interest of their own country first. Consequently our national policy, and the aim of Canadian companies, should be to encourage Canadian business by Canadians to the maximum extent possible." (a) How can you reconcile this view, and comparable ones held by citizens of other countries, with the concept of multinational business? (b) Do you endorse a comparable viewpoint for the United States? Why?

CASE 23 / Magna Electric Company (A)

Early in September, John Thorson, President of the International Group of Magna Electric Company, received plans for the coming year from two subsidiaries, Custom Cabinets (Pty.), Ltd. and Magna-Vaal Radio Co. (Pty.), Ltd., both of Johannesburg, South Africa. Since he saw fundamental differences in the two plans (summarized in Exhibits 1 and 2), Mr. Thorson immediately sent copies to Magna Electric Company's President, Eric Hausen, and called a meeting of the Plans Review Board to decide what to do.

Two days later members of the Board trooped into their sparkling meeting room fifty floors above Lake Michigan's shore. Some contemplated the views of the steel mills of South Chicago and the stockyards; others ruminated on what they knew about the South African subsidiaries and studied their copies of Exhibits 1 and 2, selected operating data (Exhibit 3), and comments on the economic outlook for South Africa (Exhibit 4).

Magna Electric Company had bought a 60% interest in the stock of each of the two companies from a South African investment company several years ago. Mr. Rosenberg, Managing Director of Magna-Vaal Radio Co. (Pty.), Ltd., and Mr. Jones, Managing Director of Custom Cabinets (Pty.), Ltd., each own 15% of the common shares of his local company. They have directed the firms for over a decade.

Exhibit 1

Plans Summary for the Coming Year
Custom Cabinets (Pty.), Ltd.

To: Plans Review Board

About: Your concurrence with our operating and capital plans for next year

1. Operations. We plan for sales revenue next year of $1,250,000 (U.S.)—a 10% increase over the present. This is justified by our forecasts of a 10% increase in radio sales in South Africa next year and a stable market share for our largest customer—Magna-Vaal Radio. No major changes are planned for the plant. Wage rates will increase 3% according to the union contract that will be in force throughout the entire year. Lumber prices will be stable through the year. Our plans for costs are: materials, $530,000; factory wages, $260,000; depreciation charges, $20,000; additional overhead, $200,000; factory profit, $240,000; selling, general, and administrative expense, $150,000.

2. Capital. We plan three items:

(a) Additions to woodlot and drying kiln, 5,000 square feet at $8 per square foot. This will alleviate an existing bottleneck and allow for an expansion 20% above next year's needs. Construction period, nine months including equipment order lead-time. Return on investment planned, 45%.

(b) A medium-size tenoner, $25,000 (U.S.). This will bring tenoning machine capacity into balance with moulding and gluing equipment. This fourth tenoner will fit into space currently available between the moulding and the sanding departments. Return on investment planned, 25%.

(c) Injection moulding machine for forming thermoplastics, $45,000 (U.S.) for an in-line reciprocating screw machine. This equipment is needed not for immediate production but for development and pilot work on plastics that will, we predict, eventually replace carved mouldings and other intricately machined wooden parts. Successful plastic mouldings promise to cut costs to 50% of the cost of carved wood. The savings will be both in materials and in the cost of hand labor.

Exhibit 2

Plans Summary for the Coming Year
Magna-Vaal Radio Co. (Pty.), Ltd.

To: Plans Review Board

About: Your concurrence with our operating and capital plans for next year

1. Operations. We plan sales revenue next year to be $3,675,000 (U.S.). This is 5% below the current year and reflects our expectation of a recession in the Republic of South Africa's economy. Our own prediction has been reinforced by that of our consulting economist. The recession is not expected to last more than fifteen to eighteen months. In line with this prediction we will shortly take steps to reduce the labour force and diminish stocks (primarily of finished goods). Our plans for costs are: cost of manufacturing, $2,950,000 (U.S.); selling, advertising, and administrative expense, $400,000; special employee benefits, $105,000; provision for depreciation, $57,500; income before taxes, $162,500.

2. Capital. No plans for any nonroutine projects.

Exhibit 3

**Selected Information on the Results of Operations of
Custom Cabinets (Pty.), Ltd. and
Magna-Vaal Radio Co. (Pty.), Ltd.**

	Custom Cabinets				Magna-Vaal Radio			
	Sales (in South African Rands)	Units Produced	Net Profits Before Income Tax (Rands)	Pre-Tax Return on Shareholders' Equity [1]	Sales (in South African Rands)	Units Produced	Net Profits Before Income Tax (Rands)	Pre-Tax Return on Shareholders' Equity [1]
Present Year (est.)	R810,000	125,000	R43,750	18%	R2,790,000	56,250	R150,000	18%
Previous	630,000	95,000	13,200	7%	2,500,000	53,750	150,000	20%
"	517,500	77,500	4,650	3%	2,365,000	52,500	156,000	22%
"	405,000	52,500	25,500	21%	2,260,000	52,500	102,000	15%
"	415,000	57,500	36,000	29%	2,465,000	57,500	178,000	24%

[1] The effective income tax rate for these companies in the Republic of South Africa is 40%. There is no restriction on the remittance of dividends to the United States.

Exhibit 4

**Comments by Vice-President for Economic and
Market Research of Magna Electric Co., Inc.**

1. This responds to your inquiry yesterday about the future course of the economy of the Republic of South Africa.

2. The consulting economist to Magna-Vaal Radio Co. (Ltd.), Dr. Jan Tinbergen, is a highly respected economist with an international reputation for his econometric and statistical studies. Of course, there are other economists who will differ with any particular forecast he may make.

3. A thorough study to enable us to make a reliable prediction about the future of the South African economy and its radio receiver market will require six months, hiring two consulting firms, and the attention of one of our staff. Given funds from the International Group's appropriation, we shall be glad to undertake the study.

Custom Cabinets (Pty.), Ltd., under the previous ownership, sold cabinets only to the radio manufacturing company. However, executives of Magna Electric Company encouraged Mr. Jones to seek other customers. In the past few years he has increased sales until the radio company now buys only 50% of the cabinet company's output. Mr. Jones believes that his previous problem of increasing sales of wooden cabinets for better radios was eased in the Republic of South Africa by the government's then existing ban on television.

The cabinet plant runs efficiently, uses the most modern machinery obtainable, and is staffed by highly trained European craftsmen who are organized into the European Labour Union. It, like the radio receiver plant, is located in a suburb about ten miles from the center of Johannesburg and similarly distant from low-priced housing.

The assembly department of the radio factory operates on a batch process. Demand for radio receivers is not large enough in the Republic of South Africa to set up an assembly line for each class of radio made. Therefore, while the shop has several lines, each line has to be shut down at times for minor adjustments to jigs and fixtures. Restarting requires a certain amount of training time for employees to adjust to the different parts and the slightly modified assembly procedure. Plant workers are mainly unskilled coloureds (persons of mixed blood) who learn on the job. Federal law forbids their joining unions.

An act of the South African Parliament requires that certain industries—radios, automobile assembly, etc.—incorporate from 55% to 90% of locally manufactured and assembled parts in the final product. Magna-Vaal Radio therefore has a components manufacturing department as well as an assembly department.

Magna-Vaal sells radio receivers in the medium- to high-priced segment of the South African market. It has a large share of the present receiver market.

One director said: "This orange smoke from the steel mills and the blue water remind me of homecoming at Urbana. But what shall we do about those outfits in South Africa? It looks to me as if it all adds up to whom we are going to believe."

Another director straightened his spine a fraction further and snorted: "When we run into problems like this, the whole thing is just not worthwhile. Look at the difficulties in South Africa. The Davis Cup. People picketing Engelhard Minerals and Eastman Kodak because they have plants there. Those wild-eyed militants pressuring banks on the West Coast not to invest in Johannesburg. I don't want any bleeding-hearts at our doors."

A third director said: "To get back to the issue—it's not whom we believe but whom will we trust? Which managing director do we want to put our money on?"

Required: What decisions should the Plans Review Board make?

Magna Electric Company (B)

The Plans Review Board decided to seek additional information before concurring with plans for the coming year presented by Custom Cabinets (Pty.), Ltd. and Magna-Vaal Radio Company (Pty.) Ltd. In two weeks Mr. Thorson flew to Johannesburg.

In their first conversation, Mr. Rosenberg said: "I've decided that we should lay off 25% of the assembly workers while keeping the testing crews, stockmen, office, and shipping and receiving crews intact. We will keep all the foremen. Costs will not go down as much as I would like, but it will be easier to resume high-level operations later.

"When I instructed Mr. Klaus, factory manager, to put through the reductions in force, he demurred, saying that business would not drop off, he thought, and that the staff would be needed for the orders on hand or about to come in. When I found, two weeks ago, that he still had not carried out my order, I appointed him as line foreman in charge of manufacturing components and promoted the head assembly factory foreman, Mr. van der Merwe, to be factory manager. He is now going through the factory personnel list and will shortly drop every fourth man.

"You will see that I was correct about the decrease in demand. Our production and shipments are already 10% below last year's rate for the past 10 days.

"When the labour force reaches the planned size and production drops, we can then undertake a rearrangement of the assembly department—knock out a few walls, that kind of thing—which will increase our efficiency. . . ."

Mr. Jones, Managing Director of Custom Cabinets (Pty.) Ltd., said to Mr. Thurston: "Mr. Smit, our factory manager, and I have decided not to lay off any workers. We do not believe in a recession in our economy—the sales rate is as good now as at any time in the past—and layoffs will probably result in wildcat strikes.

"One of the secrets of our profitability is a common trust between our craftsmen and management. I am not going to disrupt this by unwarranted firings. . . .

"If you talk to Klaus, over at the radio factory, you will find that receiver sales are holding up, too. There is a little trouble there with production. Van der Merwe is going to have his hands full. . . ."

Required: (a) Should Mr. Thorson give any instructions to Mr. Rosenberg or to Mr. Jones while in Johannesburg?

(b) On the basis of data you have, what recommendations do you think Mr. Thorson should make to the Plans Review Board when he returns to Chicago?

INTEGRATING ROLE OF CENTRAL MANAGERS

Each of the many managerial issues and tasks discussed in the preceding chapters deserves thoughtful attention. Sooner or later a central manager is likely to face all of them. Their full significance, however, lies in their contribution to a basic approach to managing a total enterprise. Each topic has been included because it fits into a framework for thinking about the challenge of overall, integrated management.

The following brief conclusion reemphasizes the central themes we have been unfolding. Individual chapters necessarily focus on separate facets. And there is always danger that we become so absorbed with these particular parts that the broader structure becomes blurred. To counteract this danger, we stress again the structure of the book as a whole. The selection of subjects and their sequence are significant; they present a mental framework—a way of thinking about a very complex phenomenon.

Three related themes deserve emphasis:

1. A way of moving from broad social-technological-political-economic developments to company programs tuned to these developments.
2. The design of balanced, integrated company programs in which (a) the several parts each contribute to a consistent central mission and (b) the magnitude and timing of effort is realistically related to company size and resources.
3. Recognition that such programs have long-run viability only when they include a practical reconciliation of diverse social pressures; and that, in fact, managers have a critical and unique role in devising bases for continuing cooperation that give realistic implementation to social reforms.

FRAMEWORK FOR STRATEGY AND PROGRAM FORMULATION

The managers of an enterprise are bombarded with data—from the daily press, television, customers, vendors, trade periodicals, their own people, government publications, their own observations, and many other sources. Some device is needed to screen out what is relevant to the enterprise, and these bits of information have to be related to practical action. Moreover, managers of going concerns are confronted with a host of "what do we do here" questions. And all these "inputs" appear in raw, unlabeled form. Clearly, a way of thinking is needed to bring some kind of order into the situation.

A framework for dealing with companywide problems has been presented in this book. It comes from a "general survey outline" used by a successful management consultant in several hundred companies, and it has also proved to be quite helpful to operating executives. Basically the framework identifies issues, puts them into a logical arrangement so that the normal interactions can be readily seen, and provides a flow of thought leading from external opportunities to concrete company actions. Although the framework is easier to describe as a sequence of steps, in practice we grasp ideas and information as they appear and use the framework more as a sorting and organizing device. Then when opportunities are spotted, the framework guides us to additional angles that should be investigated.

Select company strategy

The guiding thrust of all central management action is the company strategy. Strategy defines the mission. It provides the justification for the company's existence as an independent social unit. And being the top statement of purpose, it is the end result in terms of which many other subgoals and activities are weighed.

Viewed from another angle, strategy identifies the key bases for company survival. It should specify (a) the product/market niches the company seeks to serve, (b) the basic ways these services will be generated, (c) the sequence and timing of major moves necessary to provide the selected services in the selected manner, and (d) the criteria to be used in measuring accomplishments. No one of these elements alone is an adequate statement of strategy; each provides a necessary dimension to a meaningful, operational company objective.

To formulate strategy, we urge in Part 1 a two-pronged analysis. First, relevant factors in the whole dynamic environment can be brought into focus by concentrating on the outlook for the industry(s) in which the company functions. Careful review of the demand, supply, and competitive forces will yield a forecast of volume and profitability and will identify crucial factors for success in that industry. Second, an evaluation of the strengths and the weaknesses of the specific company will indicate its ability relative to competitors to take advantage of opportunities uncovered during the industry analysis. Then, in light of crucial factors for success and of company relative strengths and weaknesses, central management selects propitious market and/or supply niches as its field for social contribution.

Formulating strategy calls for keen judgment in selecting key factors that warrant emphasis. The strength of strategy is not an elaborate program. Instead its essence lies in singling out from numerous influences a few critical determinants. Companies will differ in the particular way each seeks distinctiveness. But unless a central management finds (and keeps up-to-date) some unique and attractive combination of the four dimensions listed above, its company will be unable to attract an inflow of resources essential for continued existence.

Use policy to elaborate strategy

While strategy is selective in its points of emphasis, policy provides more complete coverage. Through policy we assure that "all the bases are covered." There will be policy guiding relations of the firm with all its main resource groups.

A policy is a standing guide for making decisions on a given subject. Each time a question regarding, say, price discounts or employment of blacks arises, we turn to policy for the established answer. Policy provides consistency of action and greatly simplifies the process of management. By establishing policy in all major functions of a company, we can create reinforcing effort throughout the enterprise.

Policy offers an important means for correlating many facets of a business with strategy. The work of each division and department can be reviewed for its compatibility with a new strategy, and policy can be adjusted wherever opportunity is found for strong supporting action.

The array of policy issues, examined in Part 2 and relisted in the chart below, are likely to be affected by a change in strategy. So a good way to begin

---

USE POLICY REVIEW TO INTEGRATE COMPANY STRATEGY WITH OPERATIONS

Consider impact of strategy on policy for:

MARKETING:
  Product line and customer
  Pricing
  Marketing mix

HUMAN RESOURCES:
  Selection and training
  Compensation and benefits
  Industrial relations

CREATING GOODS AND SERVICES:
  Procurement
  Production
  Research and development

FINANCIAL RESOURCES:
  Sources of capital
  Allocation of capital
  Mergers and acquisitions

this reconciliation of strategy and policy is to check each of these issues. Not every one of the topics listed will be significant for a specific company, and others may need to be added to deal with unusual resource groups; but the topics do identify issues encountered by many, many enterprises—profit and nonprofit alike.

Such a policy review for consistency with strategy elaborates the strategy. Occasionally this spelling out of strategy implications will raise problems sufficiently serious to require a readjustment in the strategy itself. More often, it flags the need for updating a traditional pattern of behavior in one or more departments.

Build a supporting organization

Strategy and policy must have an organization to carry them out. Both historically and conceptually, organization is a vehicle to execute strategy. So essential is the organization, in fact, that a weak or unsuited structure can nullify the best of plans.

To assure a good linkage between strategy and structure, we propose in Part 3 that the operating activities implied by a strategy and its associated policy be laid out first, and then that an organization be designed which suits these activities. The conclusions of such an exercise must be tempered, however, by the size of company and the available personnel. Size forces us to consider typical stages in corporate growth, and key personnel is a moderating influence on the variety of auxiliary services fitted onto the underlying operating units.

Organization design directly affects the prestige, power, influence, and compensation of key individuals. It has a great impact on their motivation. So part of the skill in effective organization design is to arrange managerial and other positions so that these motivators encourage people to work for success of the strategy—and not for some divergent or bureaucratic ends.

Guide the execution

In one sense selecting strategy, formulating policy, and designing organization are all preparatory. The action we can observe objectively is the actual activity of shaping and exchanging products, services, and diverse satisfactions. It is the execution of plans that really counts.

Central managers devote a significant portion of their energies to execution—and first-line supervisors an even higher percentage. As outlined in Part 4, execution includes programming the action, communicatiing instructions, providing leadership and motivation, and controlling allocations and results. It is the "make happen" phase of managing.

Two aspects of a central manager's role in execution call for continuing self-discipline. (1) Since central managers personally can be active in only a small part of total transactions, they influence execution largely by setting patterns for others to follow. Through their own behavior they create a leadership tone; they foster control practices and check only occasionally to see that regular use is made of these control devices; and in resolving specific problems they are as much concerned with future precedent as with the case at hand. Every social group has its customary practices and values that govern its behavior. Central managers guide execution primarily by helping to shape the customs and the values followed within their company and in its relations with resource groups.

(2) The external calls on a central manager's time may be heavy. Sometimes the manager can't escape seeing an important customer, arbitrating a personnel dispute, appearing before a Congressional committee, meeting with a Consumers' Protective Committee, negotiating a new stock issue, and a host of other worthy activities. The danger is responding to so many external requests for time that the mission—the strategy—of the enterprise gets shunted aside. One of the main virtues of specific programs and well-designed controls is to keep primary attention focused on primary tasks to be accomplished each day. This means, of course, that we must see that the programs and the controls are regularly adjusted to match any changes in strategy.

Now, with this framework of strategy formulation, policy elaboration, organization, and execution—and the components of each—clearly in mind we can deal with the disorderly bombardment of data and problems noted at the beginning of this section. The numerous inputs can be quickly placed into a meaningful, operational way of thinking about a complex endeavor. The framework becomes a powerful tool for keeping perspective and making use of the wealth of information and ideas available to us.

NEED FOR INTEGRATED TREATMENT

Reconcile diverse changes

The strategy→policy→organization→execution framework has an appealing, logical flow. Unfortunately, management problems cannot always be treated in this convenient sequence. The managers of any dynamic enterprise always face a cluttered, mixed-up situation.

In a normal company several forces contribute to this jumble. (a) Pressure for change may originate anywhere—not just with an opportunity for improved strategy. Perhaps the Urban Redevelopment Corporation offers us a downtown plant, or a salesman has a great idea for advertising, or a control has failed to signal a shortage, or the government is challenging our fair employment practice, or we have an unexpected opportunity to hire an outstanding scientist. Such events may call for action anywhere in the total system.

(b) Diverse changes occur at the same time. With separate departments responding to their sector of the environment and pushing for their respective goals, one may be courting a foreign distributor while another is offering to increase local employment while a third is seeking a government subsidy.

(c) Moreover, a mixture of old and new often confounds the situation. This year's seniors must be taught while we are also designing new programs for entering freshmen; a new breed of systems analysts is working side by side with our traditional cost accountants.

This sort of bubbling, moving activity is fine *provided* changes in one place do not detract from efforts in another. Obviously, changes that reinforce each other, and thus yield synergistic benefits, are desired. Central management and other coordinating mechanisms have a never-ending task of reconciling the many changes that occur daily in a healthy organization.

One of the major contributions of a well-articulated strategy with its supporting policy, organization, and programs is to serve as the *basis for such reconciliation*. The diversity of the changes makes a central, preeminent rationale especially valuable. Proposed changes can be evaluated in terms of their contribution to the major mission. The very complexity of activities calls for such a synthesizing standard for coping with our environment.

Watch magnitude and timing of changes

In the short run, company resources are always limited. A progressive management sensing new opportunities must be careful not to strain these capacity limits.

Accounting reports and financial budgets typically provide a mechanism for living within the firm's financial ability. More difficult to measure and to predict is the capacity of personnel to handle external pressures and opportunities. Meeting a deadline on new pollution controls, launching a new product-line, and developing a matrix organization all at the same time may be so confusing that important actions are missed. A thinly staffed division may be able to keep a mature operation running as usual but lack capacity to switch production to foreign sources.

A related issue is timing of changes. Clearly an effort to increase the employment of blacks will not mix well with an economy drive and cutting of total personnel. A laboratory already running at capacity and considering a move is not ready for a new government contract.

The changes proposed in all these examples might be highly desirable when considered alone. But when they are combined with other changes, the total burden creates an overload. Here, again, the need for an integrated treatment is clear.

Several of the cases in this book, such as the Waukegan Wire Company and the Missouri-Ohio Barge Lines, Inc., give the reader some feel for the heterogenous array of issues confronting central management all at the same time. But even these cases contain only selected facts already sorted into categories; reality is much more messy. Central managers of business firms, because of the positions they occupy, face pesky, ambiguous, intractable pressures involving a variety of values not immediately reflected on company balance sheets. Great skill is needed to respond to the topsy-turvy world in ways that reinforce each other and that are within the capacities of the enterprise.

UNIQUE SOCIAL ROLE

A third dimension of the work of central managers, in addition to focusing on the strategy→policy→organization→execution approach and keeping the company moving in an integrated fashion, is contributing to social development. They do this—not as an extra duty on the side—but as an integral part of directing company responses to its changing environment.

In the process of finding workable bases for getting necessary resources, central managers make a unique and valuable contribution to social problems. They help shape many reform proposals and provide practical tests of their feasibility. Of course, many reforms do not directly affect business operations—court reform, integrated education, and urban government are examples. In such areas executives may be concerned citizens, but their positions in a corporation neither qualify them nor obligate them to be leaders. However, where a reform directly influences the conditions on which business is transacted—as in employment conditions, quality guarantees, and environmental protection—central managers and other executives make three kinds of contributions.

1. Managers help create the conditions on which cooperative endeavors take place. Each strategy conceives of a joint undertaking involving services, jobs, markets, taxes, etc. Each policy relating a company to its environment sets conditions on which exchanges will or will not be made. Each program lays out times and quantities when specific flows will occur. These interactions between a company and various interest groups are not incidental or charitable matters. They are necessary to performing a mission and to survival.[1]

As our discussion especially of policy indicated repeatedly, managers want a continuing flow of resource inputs and continuing outlets for services and satisfactions that the company generates. Consequently, they give close attention to maintaining markets, building reputations, assuring supply, obtaining permissions, and the like. This kind of concerned behavior lies at the very heart of successful business operations.

Now, if any interest group wants to alter the conditions on which transactions occur—either to satisfy its own aspirations or under outside pressure—thoughtful managers try to devise a way the new conditions can be met without jeopardizing the cooperative venture they direct. All sorts of adjustments in conditions of work, material utilized, information provided to investors, side effects on ecology, and the like are hammered out in the frequent negotiations that take place between providers of resources and a company. Necessity forces some of the changes, while others are invented to attract better resources. Whatever the motivation, clearly the managers benefit from helping to create workable reforms.

---

[1] For expansion of this point see the discussion of the "resource converter" model on pages 2-6.

Safety, shorter hours, paid vacations, company pensions, and air-conditioned offices illustrate improved working conditions featured by many firms to attract and retain workers. Product quality, often including guarantees, has long been a means of wooing customers. Stable earnings attract investors. These and many other business practices add to "the quality of life." Managers do not provide these conditions as a generous, emotional gesture. Rather, they try to put together a package of satisfactions that will assure a continuing flow of resources.

The tough, practical question is how much of what satisfaction it is possible for a business to offer. Managers are actual participants, along with the beneficiaries of a proposed added satisfaction, in creating specific answers to that question.

2. Managers serve as mediators for competing reforms. Worthy reforms often compete with each other. Consider the proposed goals for an electric power company as an example. Clean air, cool water, dependable and cheap electricity, low requirements for foreign exchange, beautiful countrysides, conservation of natural resources—are all commendable social objectives. But if we give unbridled priority to any one, several of the others will suffer. New technology may help, and power company managers have an obligation (and strong incentive, as noted above) to find improved ways to satisfy several of the listed objectives at once. Nevertheless, we know that a balance has to be struck in the degree to which the competing pressures will be met.

Central managers unavoidably serve as mediators in this balancing process. The firm as a resource converter—the power company in the preceding example—is the place where the competing pressures collide. For instance, environmentalists don't negotiate directly with consumers who are insisting on power for their refrigerators. Instead, each group puts pressure on the power company to serve its parochial desires. Managers of the power company would like to keep everybody satisfied, but they are caught in a squeeze. Consequently, the managers must try to negotiate an agreement with each group that will satisfy some of its desires but not be so burdensome that the company cannot also make peace with other pressure groups.[2]

When managers make proposals to a resource supplier and when they reject other requests, they are acting in effect as mediators.[3] They are exploring how far to go along with the desires of each competing group. This is a hard and unpopular assignment. But managers should accept the role because (a) they know best what impact concessions in one direction will have on the ability of their company to satisfy other pressures, and (b) they have a strong incentive to

---

[2] In this example several different quasi-judicial but nonetheless competing government agencies also get into the act. However, the main burden of initiating proposals for resolving the competing pressures rests with managers of the power company.

[3] This proposing and rejecting may take place in a formal bargaining process if the interest group is represented by an official body. Or, it may consist of testing the attractiveness of a "package of satisfaction" among customers, suppliers, or workers responding individually.

arrive at a workable understanding (their company shuts down if agreement cannot be reached).

3. Managers can serve as advisors on national priorities and institutional changes. Thus far we have pictured the manager as one who adjusts to new goals—not a person who sets the goals. We believe this emphasis is correct, but we do not intend to rule out a manager's participation in the debate that typically surrounds the establishment of a new social standard. Today setting new standards usually centers on some kind of legislation.

Federal and state governments are playing an increasing role in social change. They make laws that press the laggards into line—on minimum wages, food quality, plant safety, and the like. They also initiate reform in such areas as equal employment, air and water pollution, social security, and financial underwriting. And in spending 22% of our national income they support many causes.

In the arena where priorities get hammered out, business executives have a difficult and often conflicting role. As private citizens they are indeed entitled to voice their preferences on the directions national effort should take. And if their companies participate in filling a need, they will be more knowledgeable on that subject than the average citizen. A farmer, to pick another advocate, can speak from experience on the desirability of farm subsidies. However, a beneficiary such as a farmer can scarcely be expected to be impartial. So we rely on the legislative process to set priorities, and we look to interest groups for expert testimony and advocacy of their cause. The ethical problems involve the manner and the openness of pleading one's special interest.

A typical issue is society's decision as to the kind of environment it wants, with full recognition of the sacrifices necessary to achieve that end. Are consumers willing to pay more for poorer vegetables in a move to eliminate use of DDT? Should cities be built up rather than out so as to preserve the rural landscape? Do we want airports close to cities for the convenience of passengers or located far away to cut down noise for city dwellers? Resolution of such issues cannot, and should not, be made by business executives alone. They can provide expert testimony about feasibility and costs; but if they have an established position, they may also be admittedly biased advocates. Other interested parties should also be heard. And the social value decisions should be thrashed out in some legislative forum.

The very fact that business executives participate in setting values makes them a target for those who disagree with the guides that emerge. We do not suggest that business executives withdraw from the process of setting social values; they have practical knowledge to contribute to the forum, and they are entitled to advocate a course convenient to them just as other interested parties should advocate their preferences.[4] But it is a mistake to think that

---

[4] The concept of participating, but not dominating, in the establishment of social goals is vital. Much past criticism of business arose from unilateral, short-run decisions by business firms that were insensitive to the ramifications of their actions.

the primary social responsibility of business is sharing in the formulation of values—important though that may be.

The first responsibility of business is the generation of goods and services in harmony with the goals of society. When national priorities change, the business system must make a myriad of adjustments in the flow of goods and services. When growth and social attitudes bring particular aspects of our environment to a critical point, business must help fund revised methods of producing the services people want while keeping the environment healthy. As the economy becomes more affluent and people's personal desires shift, business must devise ways of providing more opportunities to achieve self-expression, security, and other aspirations. This kind of constructive adaptation is a cardinal task of central management.

From a pragmatic view, managers play a major role in social change. They are not preachers but doers. And this is a task they are uniquely well qualified to perform.

Permeating all three of the schemes we have been summarizing—strategy→execution→integration→social change—is a strong emphasis on the future and on adjusting and adapting to future needs and opportunities. This emphasis makes managing a creative, rewarding endeavor.

Part 6
COMPREHENSIVE CASES

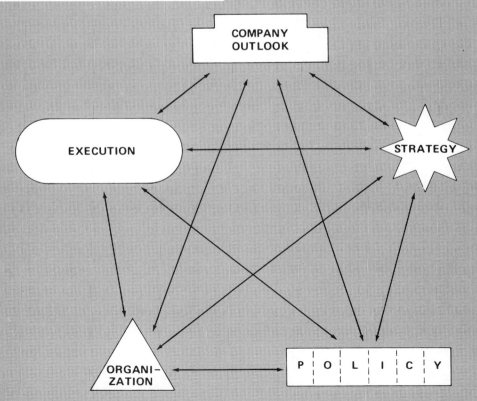

COMPREHENSIVE / Jodie's Ladies Wear
CASE 1 /

Yvonne and Craig Wakefield, proprietors, have enjoyed a considerable success during the two years in which they have owned and operated Jodie's Ladies Wear—a specialty shop that sells mainly ladies' outer wear.

The two young owners have been able to increase sales substantially by widening the lines and styles offered and by advertising effectively. During the same period they have learned and taught themselves much about the management of a retail store.

With sales volume now pressing the limits of the physical resources of their present operation, Yvonne and Craig are attempting to decide the future directions of Jodie's Ladies Wear. The choice of continued growth in the present and/or a new location is not easy or simple for it involves substantial financial and managerial problems.

BEGINNINGS

"Looking back, I think that it was a lapse in mental capacity that led us to buy out the previous owner and take over Jodie's Ladies Wear. It would have been more difficult to start a venture, but it might well have made more sense." So Craig Wakefield began his story about the acquisition and the early history of the store under his and his wife's (Yvonne's) management.

"We took over a store that sold clothes in misses' and women's sizes[1] to a 'mature clientele'—to use the previous owner's words. They were mature enough. We literally watched them die off. The median age was 65 years. If we held a layaway for three months and then sent a card as a reminder, the card was often returned with the notation that the buyer had died.

"We purchased $15,164 of inventory and retained two saleswomen (one full-time and one part-time) from the previous operation. The building had 950 square feet, of which 750 square feet made up the sales floor and the balance was the office, backroom, and bathroom. We negotiated a new, 3-year lease for a rent of about $240 per month plus

---

[1] Ladies dresses are made in six cuts or size ranges: (a) Junior Petite—sizes 1, 3, 5, 7, 9, 11, and 13; (b) Junior—sizes 5, 7, 9, 11, 13, and 15; (c) Junior Misses—sizes 4, 6, 8, 10, 12, and 14; (d) Misses—sizes 8, 10, 12, 14, 16, 18, and 20; (e) Half-sizes—12½, 14½, 16½, 18½, 20½, and 22½ (these are roughly Misses' sizes cut somewhat more fully); and (f) Women's—sizes 20, 22, 24, 26, etc. to 40. These are definitely for the larger women. Dresses are sold generally in two styles: (a) Contemporary (short dresses or "swinging" dresses) and (b) Mature, that is, more conservatively styled. No two manufacturers have identical cuts—even for a given size and size range. Each manufacturer has its own idea of the shape of a woman's body.

[2] Monterey Village is a small shopping center in the northeast sector of Tucson. It is located on the southwest corner of Speedway Boulevard and Wilmot Road. (See Exhibit 1, location A.)

$6.50 per month for maintenance plus ½ of 1% of gross sales as dues to the Monterey Village² Merchants' Association.

"The previous owner had claimed $65,000 in gross sales for the past year, but our later reconstruction from her partial records indicated a gross of $43,000. The inventory, when valued at the lower of cost or market, turned out to be worth $9,000. Much of the merchandise was old.

"There was no customer file. The only sales records available were for 40 charge-account customers. The clientele did fit the clothes well—most were in the Misses' size cut.

"To finance the inventory we signed a note for $14,000 payable to the former owner at $200 per month for 5 years with a lump sum due at the end of the period. We borrowed $2,500 from a bank to provide working capital, and we put up the balance of the equity ourselves.

"What was a merchant not yet 30 years old with a wife just turned 21 doing in a deal like this? It certainly required a far stretch of the imagination."

Craig Wakefield had, over the previous ten years, been a policeman, a rancher, a manufacturer and wholesaler of women's jewelry, a computer programmer, and a business systems analyst. He was carrying on the ranching, the jewelry wholesaling, and the systems analysis work for small companies simultaneously just before the purchase of Jodie's Ladies Wear.

"I was tired of school, I had learned all that I thought I could at the University. We had made some money in the stock market and had to do something with it quickly. The ranching showed a net loss, but not for long enough, so that soon the cash would be taxable.

"Neither of us had any background in retailing women's wear. Yvonne's contribution was a knowledge of fabrics and clothing construction, skill as a seamstress, and no fear of work. I also knew how to sew and looked on the new venture as a challenge to master and a field to find out something about.

"Our first major decision was to increase the total inventory and the selection available. We used all the increased investment to stock a younger style of merchandise in an attempt to satisfy younger walk-ins—although they were few and far between at first. Over eighteen months we gradually added $15,000 to the inventory, bringing it to a total of $30,000.

"We tried to eliminate all the things we did not like about the stores we used to shop in. Commission payments to employees created a pushy atmosphere—which we wish to avoid. So our employees are on straight salary. Refunds for cash create three problems: (1) banks charge us 5% for credit card use, which we lose if we give a full cash refund; (2) customers who pay by check get irate if they are asked to wait until the check clears, but a small percentage of them are known to get a cash refund and then stop payment on their checks; (3) a few persons will steal clothes and then ask for a cash refund while claiming they have lost the sales receipt. So no cash refunds and merchandise credits only.

"We want to allow the customers to browse and feel comfortable while having a chance to look around the store and find out what we carry. We also want to eliminate

---

² Monterey Village is a small shopping center in the northeast sector of Tucson. It is located on the southwest corner of Speedway Boulevard and Wilmot Road. (See location A on Exhibit 1, page 575.)

Exhibit 1

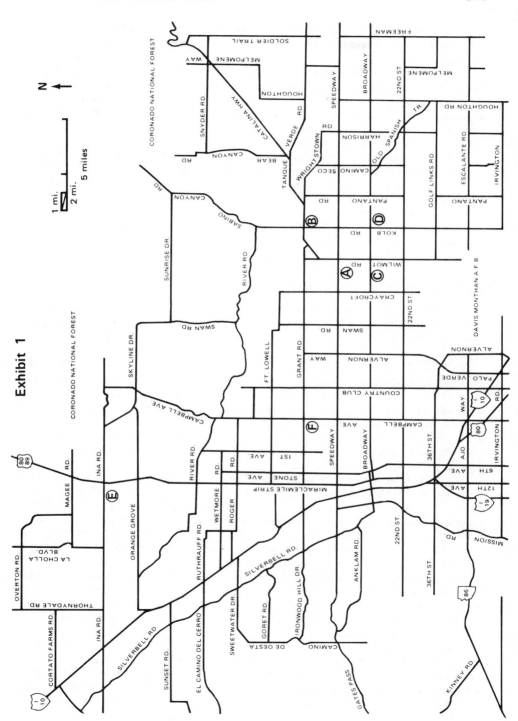

the feeling that, as a customer, you are always being watched and that the merchant does not trust you. There is a fine line between being ignored and being inspected that we want to walk.

"At first we hoped to alter and tailor clothes at no charge to the customer. We sell clothes in a medium-price range, but the clothes are not inexpensive to the customer. We soon found that many women wanted us to go beyond alterations that were necessary to fit the garment. They would say, 'Oh, it will only take you a minute to take the sleeves up ¼ of an inch here and to let out the upper back an inch while raising the hem.' Some expect a major remodeling for no charge.

"The inventory increase was designed not only to attract younger customers but also to offer a wider selection and a younger look to the original customers. We believed that they did not want to look as old as the clothes that were represented in the inventory that was originally in the store.

"Overall we wanted to make the store a pleasing place in which there was a soft atmosphere—not a hard or crass sell and not a place in which the customers felt that the merchandise was being pushed down their throats."

BUYING AND MERCHANDISING

The Wakefields purchased Jodie's Ladies Wear in early February. By that time orders had already been placed with manufacturers for the summer season to come. They cancelled no orders because they had no knowledge about where to buy nor experience in buying.

To buy for the fall season they decided to continue to purchase from the manufacturers whose lines were already represented in their store or from those whom the previous owner had recommended for a particular season. Some suppliers have especially good fall or holiday collections but not good selections for a Tucson summer. To show their fall lines, a group of salesmen set up displays in Del Webb's Town House in Phoenix. The Wakefields attended this so-called market, but they limited their buying to familiar lines and looked at new lines to learn rather than to purchase. Fall items are bought in May and delivered in July.

For the holiday season they looked for a market in which more complete collections were shown. For this they went to Los Angeles in July. There they concentrated their buying on younger sportswear, younger dresses, handbags (a new item for Jodie's), accessories such as scarves, gloves, shawls, and hosiery (also new items), and a change in the jewelry from big pins and brooches for the staid and proper country club set to less expensive jewelry in line with the times and what people were wearing (necklaces, bracelets, rings, and earrings). During the fall and holiday seasons, hosiery produced the maximum revenue per square foot of display space of any line in the store. Hosiery sales for these seasons amounted to $1,000 from a display area of 2 square feet. It should be noted that Jodie's is located next door to a lingerie and hosiery specialty shop. This experience proved to the Wakefields that they could do more with Jodie's than just sell ready-to-wear outer clothing.

A check of inventory just before the spring and summer buying season (November of the previous year for first orders and January for additional summer items and manufacturer's closeouts of spring items) showed that handbag and jewelry inventories were depleted as were the younger-styled items of clothing. The older styles still showed a substantial carryover. Craig Wakefield then decided to add shoes, all kinds of purses (casual and evening bags, cloth, good leather, and beaded bags), and a limited millinery selection.

"The question to date has not been how to decide what to purchase but who will sell to us. We can rely on suppliers who have been with the store for years, on hungry or brave new suppliers, and on those who are large enough to be willing to take a chance on a small order and give us credit. Credit is the problem. For example, the East Coast division of United Factors will deal with us, but the West Coast division will not.

"From manufacturers who will sell to us we look at style, fabrication, colors, price, and fabrics all together and attempt to judge what will interest our customers. For the first six months we had little choice. We had to buy from whomever came around. So we purchased the younger-looking items in the lines of our old suppliers. Buying in the first year was strictly good and bad luck. We are badly overstocked on sportswear by Koret of California. The salesman was experienced and we were not. Koret does not produce one line with coordinated items but 36 groups of sportswear per year. No two groups in any one year can be put together. Their items sell in great quantities, but, at the end of the season, we are stuck with lots of inventory. In a sense we are a warehouse for the manufacturer. It gets so that our customers, who are no dummies, wait for a sale. They come in often, check the racks, and then predict how long we can hold out before putting on a sale.

"We are, for some items, and hope to for all, changing to manufacturers whose entire line works together and who blend in one season's colors and fabrics with the next. It takes about three years to learn who does this successfully and then you have to be able to get to their salesman first so that he is not sold out and also hope that the firm will allow credit.

"We would like to carry Loubella Extendibles, for example. The entire line is blended. The separates (pants, blouses, sports tops, and sweaters) are all dyed to coordinate within their 8 or 9 combinations of body styles and fabrics. The line is carefully thought out so that one blouse can be worn with 5 or 6 different pairs of pants.

"Both Yvonne and I do the purchasing. We argue about the items and should argue more than we do. Then we would wind up with fewer markdowns. We work purchases down to those garments on which we both agree. If I like the print and she dislikes the style, the line or item is ruled out. We don't agree on very many things, and we find that if we do agree, there is a much better chance of selling those goods.

"Some days one of us feels incompetent, so we do no buying at all. Or one will screen the entire line to pick out favorites and the other will go through what has been picked. This is our way of buying only what we need.

"We look at the line of any manufacturer whose salesman comes around to the store. We do not pass up any chance to look at ladies' wear. It took us a while to learn how to say no, because there are some highly proficient sales people on the road.

"We now plan to attend markets in Denver, Phoenix, Los Angeles, and San Francisco (but not the two big ones—New York and Dallas) five times per year for the five seasons (spring, summer, transition, fall, and winter). At the markets we visit those manufacturers whom we definitely want to buy from and then use the rest of our time to look for a new resource to replace a line that is not performing well. Manufacturers change all the time. Bobbie Brooks and Gay Gibson are not now what they used to be.

"Purchasing takes constant attention. Anyone can buy, but few can know ahead how they are going to sell what they buy before they buy it. We now formulate ad ideas and promotions and combinations of wearing apparel and accessories before we buy. We look for bargains that will allow better than the full retail markup (customarily 50% of the selling price is markup). So we buy from an unknown manufacturer who sells at a relatively low price those items of a quality suitable for our customers. Before buying, you must know what your customers want. What are the fashion trends now or what are they going to be with our clientele? Should we take a chance on a new idea and possibly offend some of our existing clientele for the sake of bringing in new clients? For example, 18-to-25-year-olds buy 10% of the pants suits sold. To carry items for them makes the whole rack lean a bit toward being sexy and younger. Older clientele then get offended, although not outraged. Some will say directly, 'How could this be in my store? There must be some mistake.' We still carry what they want, as did the previous owner, but they are not happy to be in an atmosphere where the younger-looking things are.''

PROMOTION

The first promotion of Jodie's Ladies Wear, with the Wakefields as owners, was entirely by word of mouth. Old customers told their friends about the change—if they so desired; the Wakefields told their friends and new employees told their friends. Craig Wakefield quickly realized that this was insufficient promotion. He turned for help to officers of the Monterey Village Merchants' Association. They suggested the use of radio and newspapers. After trying these media (see Exhibit 2 for an early newspaper advertisement) Craig concluded that the cost per thousand readers of newspapers was excessive. He also learned from experience that radio was best for an immediate reaction and for sale announcements. Newspaper trials for one year demonstrated that a small, obscure, or unknown retail store could never afford to pay enough for space to compete with chain stores, department stores, and the already known large specialty shops of the city. The cost per thousand readers was considerably higher than the cost per thousand female viewers available on daytime television.

With some help from friends in the advertising business, Craig purchased early morning spots on the Today show, late evening spots on the Johnny Carson show, and sporadic spots throughout the day. The friends chose stations and shows that had the largest feminine audiences. They also prepared ads that were fair-to-middling as to their ideas, in the Wakefields' opinion. But when asked the age distribution of the feminine audience, his friends did not have data available. Also they made no story boards[3] so that the commercial could not be judged before it was presented.

By asking questions at the television stations, Craig Wakefield found that he could develop precise information about audiences. His friends could recommend, with no research, shows with a high percentage of women viewers, but they could not distinguish between 16- to 30-year-old viewers and 65- to 85-year-old viewers. The distinction is important to Jodie's. Further questioning of persons at the television stations and a close review of the Audit Research Bureau's data let Craig dig out the audience characteristics. This way he found out what was the best buy—the optimal combination of his prime audience and the cost of spots. By extensive searching he found out what kinds of audiences watched television in Tucson at what times of the day and on what channel. With this research completed, he was in a better position to purchase time suitable for Jodie's Ladies Wear than was the agency.

---

[3] A story board is a sequence of still photographs—each with a caption—pasted upon one piece of Bristol board (a stiff cardboard) to show the key action elements, the development of the story of the commercial, and the expression of the copy theme. It is made up before the commercial is filmed. Often several story boards are developed to allow the advertising manager a choice.

Exhibit 2

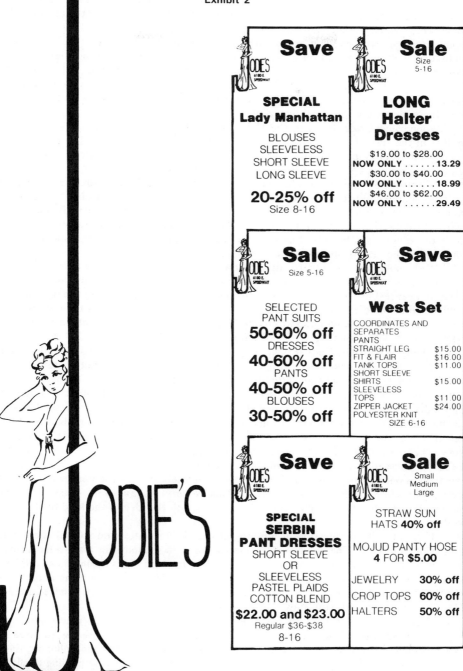

Save

SPECIAL
Lady Manhattan

BLOUSES
SLEEVELESS
SHORT SLEEVE
LONG SLEEVE

20-25% off
Size 8-16

Sale
Size 5-16

LONG Halter Dresses

$19.00 to $28.00
NOW ONLY 13.29
$30.00 to $40.00
NOW ONLY 18.99
$46.00 to $62.00
NOW ONLY 29.49

Sale
Size 5-16

SELECTED
PANT SUITS
50-60% off
DRESSES
40-60% off
PANTS
40-50% off
BLOUSES
30-50% off

Save

West Set

COORDINATES AND
SEPARATES
PANTS
STRAIGHT LEG $15.00
FIT & FLAIR $16.00
TANK TOPS $11.00
SHORT SLEEVE
SHIRTS $15.00
SLEEVELESS
TOPS $11.00
ZIPPER JACKET $24.00
POLYESTER KNIT
        SIZE 6-16

Save

SPECIAL
SERBIN
PANT DRESSES
SHORT SLEEVE
OR
SLEEVELESS
PASTEL PLAIDS
COTTON BLEND

$22.00 and $23.00
Regular $36-$38
8-16

Sale
Small
Medium
Large

STRAW SUN
HATS **40% off**

MOJUD PANTY HOSE
4 FOR $5.00

JEWELRY   **30% off**
CROP TOPS   **60% off**
HALTERS   **50% off**

To prepare commercials, Craig Wakefield took his own photographs and selected his own locations. His idea was to try to do something a little different—a little unorthodox. Both Wakefields worked hard at this until they were pleased with the results. One commercial showed evening gowns in a horse corral. Another had models in black, baby-doll nightwear posed on a patio at the Community Center during the day. This commercial was shot on a Sunday morning when few, if any, people were ordinarily around. But one father and his young son rode by on a bicycle. The boy said: "Daddy, look at the pretty ladies." The father turned his head to look, held the look, and rode into the pond below the small waterfall.

Yvonne and Craig drove to the Colorado Rockies to show swimsuits and shorts outfits in the snow-laced tundra above the timber line at 12,000 feet. The commercial went well when shown in Tucson in July. Another ad pictured a girl dressed in an elegant, crisp pants suit unloading garbage into a Dumpster.

"We strove for something a bit unusual to make viewers think—which most agencies believe people can't do. We are not trying to convince viewers that our stuff is better and cheaper than anyone else's. But we are trying to get their attention and then keep it with a visual style and with graphic effects. We do not talk a lot at the audience. We use little or no verbiage, because the more you talk, the more you and the audience forget the rest of the effects and the visual message.

"We began television advertising a year after we took over the store because no one seemed to be coming in as the result of the newspaper ads and, as far as we could tell, we could not get results from the radio advertisements. We dipped into our cash reserve and decided to allocate 25% of gross sales for advertising. We figured that the only way to get new people into the building was to let them know we existed and that we might have what they liked and that we were not too terrible to do business with.

"When I had studied advertising earlier, the best book that I read on influencing other persons' decisions convinced me that you cannot expect anyone to listen to your message unless you have their attention. This hit me over the head. In the world of advertising, where you are bombarded day after day with thousands of ad messages in all media every time you turn around, how many do you remember? Those that you dislike and those that are humorous and appeal to your sense of humor. Those that are out of place and those that are, esthetically, extremely pleasing. Analysis of various surveys convinced me that the most obnoxious soap commercial was the most effective because it stayed in the viewer's mind—consciously or unconsciously. But we did not want that kind of thing. The other route to getting attention was the hard sell. 'Mine is better and cheaper than anyone else's.' This is very old and very crass and very successful. But we did not like it and it did not fit with the idea of the kind of store we were trying to build.

"This still left the question of how to get the viewer's attention so that she would watch our message. The solution I developed for a 30-second spot was to have dead silence for the first twelve seconds—no audio at all; to show slides during those opening seconds. My reasoning was that if the viewer hears nothing at all when she knows it is the time for a commercial, she will look at the set to see what is wrong. Then we can say, 'Now we can talk with you, now that we have your attention.'

"Then we stated our copy theme: 'Jodie's has fashions that won't (pause) just hang in your closet.' How did we work out that theme? Well, there are two classes of women—married and single. Each class has two subclasses—happy and unhappy. Each group has associated with it a particular activity. The happy singles are playing the field, the unhappy singles are attempting to get married, the happily married are acting to keep their husbands happy, and the unhappily married are playing the field or trying to get their husbands reinterested in them. A good appearance is part, only a part, of the activities. That is why women buy new and stylish clothing—one of four reasons depending upon their situation. You can't say this in an ad because it is offensive. How then do you tell all four? We state that we have clothes that will not just be hanging in a closet. Then women can read any connotation they want into the statement and read the idea for themselves.

"For the first three months we spent 25% of gross sales on television advertising. After that we kept the dollar amount level. Our idea was and is that television advertising is in part a capital investment—getting our name and merchandising point of view embedded in the audience's long-term memory—and in part a period expense—showing our new fashions of the season.

"Some time later the station rates for spots were increased and I also decided to use less of the really off-hour times (1 a.m. and 7 a.m., for example). So we reduced the ads from 30 to 10 seconds. By then we had created a unique commercial—10 seconds in length, little said verbally, and it did not demand attention over any long span of time. I learned indirectly through trade sources that advertising courses at the University of Southern California were using Jodie's commercials as prime examples of how to use TV effectively for advertising. We have been widely copied in Tucson. Wigglesworth Volvo, for example, did an almost exact copy of our style. It is a super-soft sell, a complete reverse from the hard, harsh sell. Because it is a dramatic change in style, it is a success for us. We certainly created the image we wanted. I think that the major reason why it worked was that it was a new way in Tucson. The ads are not displeasing. That is a big plus for them.

"Our surveys showed that we created customers more from husbands sending in their wives to buy than from decisions by the women themselves. The evening ads had more results than the morning ads.

"Jodie's slogan became known—not a household word, but definitely by the other business people in town. Yvonne could shop in Steinfeld's (a major, locally owned, department store) and all the salesclerks there would recognize who she was and what Jodie's advertised.

"A year's experience with television advertising showed us that it is not a promotional expense. It can be best used to sell or create an image. To sell a specific product or a price or to maintain an image, newspapers are the most effective. Radio is used for fast results. If you do not get a response within 24 hours from a radio commercial, then change it.

"We have not really been successful in radio advertising. We have not found the key. The best that we have done with radio is to buy a cut-rate monthly package—X number of spots for the month—and then cram them all into one week to gain maximum exposure to that station's clientele. Then we either move to another station or try out a second idea at the first station to test any contrasts in response.

"In using television we expect and have found a 30- to 90-day delay before any results come from a particular idea. Since we are a small store we do not have lots of money to buy lots of space to sell a product now. The large department stores and chain stores (Levy's, Sears, Steinfeld's, Wards, Diamonds, Lerners, and Broadway) can do that.

"For our first fashion show, held at the Skyline Country Club, I wrote a letter to our manufacturers to explain this reason for the increase in the size of our order and to explain what had happened to our sales volume. Most of the manufacturers knew nothing about us and did not remember our history with them. Since I wanted our orders filled early on their first cutting, and also wanted dating[4] on them since early shipments and early payments would not fit our cash-flow schedule, I wrote a detailed letter. Somehow *Women's Wear Daily* picked up this letter and published an article based on it featuring Jodie's as 'The Small Retailer of the Year.'

"The show at the Skyline Country Club was shown on television news programs by the local stations—the first production of its kind. And at no expense to us.

"By now I do all the buying of time and space. I decide exactly what I want and when and where. I also control the production of the commercial and then have to sit at the television station to supervise the broadcast. Otherwise the station workers will inevitably foul up the commercial. I remember the panic one engineer went into when he got no audio—only video—on the first few seconds of an early commercial. He cut us right off the air.

"Tape has major advantages because it can be flowing and vivid and the station can't make errors with it. But we don't use video tape because it is too expensive. Instead, we use audio tape and slides. We have 200 slides so they can be changed readily. For each commercial I set a sequence: numbers 1, 11, 22, and 27 at 6 p.m. and numbers 8, 10, 23, and 27 at 9 p.m. Although the station has detailed information about the sequence, they cannot follow intricate scheduling. This takes my personal attention."

PERSONNEL

The two employees of the previous owner stayed with the Wakefields when they took over Jodie's. One lady who worked part-time is still with the store. Craig Wakefield characterized her as "a capable salesperson, a hard worker. She was once in business for herself so her outlook toward us differs from that of all our other employees." The other full-time employee, a lady aged 62 and an experienced seamstress, did not want to step onto the sales floor unless a customer whom she knew came in the door. "We eventually found that she would reluctantly do what I asked of her but would not take direction from Yvonne. She was determined not to let some young girl tell her how to work. It took us a while to recognize this and even more time to get up the determination to do something about it. We kept her 9 months—6 months longer than we should have.

"We tried to keep 2 employees in the store as well as Yvonne—who is there to manage. For the first 9 months we had a considerable amount of friction—a Donnybrook occasionally. There were disagreements over the day for pay, how often wages were to be paid, and how the business was going to be run.

"Our policy as to labor was to attempt to find reliable persons who could and would sell—persons who were looking for work, not just employment. So far we have found that we can only tell reliability and sales skills through experience—not through references or statements about past experience. Our initial employment practice was to hire people of various ethnic backgrounds. We took whoever walked in and applied for a job we happened to have open. We would hire them if they had the appearance and seemed to have the basic capability to do the work.

"In sequence we had a Mexican-American girl, a Jewish girl, another Chicano, and an Oriental. They all carried the idea of being a member of a minority group to an extreme. If we had any complaints, they each attributed this to racial prejudice on our part.

---

[4] "Dating" means shipping the goods but dating the invoices to be paid several months (usually up to six) after the shipment. The manufacturer gives credit to the retailer in this way.

"Then we turned to friends. This also turned out to be wrong. The first friend of Yvonne's worked well for a short time and then wanted the summer off. Summer is a bit slow and we agreed. Then her husband stopped traveling overseas when he changed jobs in the fall. So we lost her shortly after she returned to work. She was a good woman. Then another friend won a battle over custody of her son with her ex-husband. Since she really could not take care of herself, let alone her son, she had to move to California to be with relatives. Then we brought in a personal friend of mine who had good experience and was highly recommended by her previous employer. She turned out not to justify the recommendation. Then we hired another friend—an out-of-work school teacher who could not find work in District One (the large, local school district) because she had a Master's degree. The district has to pay a relatively high wage to teachers with advanced degrees, so such teachers are not hired. She really felt that she was doing us a favor by working for us. There were several problems.

"Had we been willing to pay an average wage plus commission, we might have gotten better help. But we are not willing to pay top dollar nor commissions. Turnover of employees to date has not been as rapid as it should have been. Also I may not yet have quite learned that my function with employees is not to be a counselor.

"We have just changed the system for disseminating information to employees. We do not now bring them into decision-making, but we do take the posture that they should have full knowledge of what we plan and why we plan it and that we want their opinion. If they think an item or a line is going to bomb, we want to know why they think so.

"For some reason our employees seem to feel that they should have or that they want to have loyalty to the proprietors more than to the business. I want them to be attracted to the work—their tasks—rather than to us and what they may regard as a psuedo or substitute family. In most cases loyalty is not enough. Incompetence can thrive when loyalty is rewarded. What I want to do is to create a good atmosphere, but only with employees who really are an asset to the firm.

"If you make an employee into a friend, it becomes difficult to let her go. It is hazardous to turn a friend into an employee. We have hired friends with long and successful experience in the apparel field. But they then expected us to make allowances for their personal problems. They brought problems with parents, with husbands, and with finances to work. At first we tried to help them work out the problems because we thought that they would be better employees if they felt freer on the job. They talked with us freely. We thought this would help them ease their minds. But those who came in having been friends prior to their employment expected to be able to dump their problems and disrupt the work-flow. We were to understand why they took three days off without notice and that they would tell us about it later.

"A big advantage of a very small operation is rapport. But supposed rapport can turn into a big disadvantage if it becomes assumptions about being understood.

"Either Yvonne or I can manage the store. But one of us needs to be there."

CUSTOMERS AND SALES

Located as it is in a small shopping center (Monterey Village) on the southwest corner of Speedway and Wilmot Road (see Exhibit 1), Jodie's draws most of its customers from sections of the city north of Speedway Boulevard and east, northeast, or northwest of the corner of Speedway Boulevard and Wilmot Road (location A on the map). The people who live in these sections are generally in the middle-income or upper-middle-income groups.

Expansion of Tucson takes place on the fringes. New housing developments—tract houses, town houses, and condominiums—are particularly common toward the northeast, east, and southeast. New apartments are built just north of Ft. Lowell road, and mobile home developments are most common toward the southwest. Some lower-priced tract developments are also found in the southern and southwestern parts of the urban area.

Monterey Village Shopping Center contains 28 stores in total. The largest are a Ben Franklin variety store and a Bayless Supermarket (one outlet of a local grocery chain). Other stores include a home furnishings shop, a franchised radio and phonograph equipment shop, a franchised ice cream parlor, another women's dress shop, a lingerie and hosiery specialty shop, and a hardware store. Services available include a movie theater, a real estate agent, a beauty salon, and a branch of one of the large commercial banks.

As stated before, Jodie's original group of customers was of an age range of 55 to 85 years. This range has been changed to 17 to 60 years. The store still carries clothes that the older clientele wear, but most of them do not seem to want to be in an atmosphere where contemporary clothes predominate. The customer list has increased from 40 to 8,000. Charge customers have been reduced from 40 to 28.

"Customers shop here for a mixture of reasons. All of the variables tend to apply to each shopper. They are attracted by our promotions, by the availability of goods in which they are interested, by the behavior of any one of our employees toward whom they may be attracted (some of those who work here have personal followings), and by our flexibility about alterations.

"We want our customers to get all the help they desire if they ask for it, but not to feel pushed. This feeling can be eliminated, but watching can't be. Shoplifting is always a possibility, and the salesperson has to be ready to give help and answer questions at the exact instant the customer wants aid or information.

"My experience as a policeman and in this dress selling business makes it necessary for me to assume that everyone who walks in our door is a thief. So we develop ways to achieve our objectives. We train our salespeople to continually straighten and re-size the clothes. The girls can be working and yet be within easy reach of a customer and alert to the customer. This awareness will tell them whether the customer wants help or information or needs to be watched.

"The salesgirls are doing small jobs to make sure that the store does not have a disheveled look. They are not bothering the browsers or the customers, but they are right there on the spot when they are needed.

"It is easy for a merchant to forget about goods on layaway. So we have a tickler file that warns us a month after the date of the layaway. If the customer makes no payment, we send her a postal card to let her know that the goods are still being held for her. After another 60 days, we remind her again. This friendly note asks her to pay within two weeks. We are making every effort to keep in contact.

"A very brief experience with free alterations and tailoring convinced us that such a policy is too generous. So we decided to limit alterations to those necessary to fit the garment and to charge a healthy fee for tailoring. We want from $2.50 for the simple hemming of a skirt to $15 or $20 to change the sleeves or do a major remodeling of a garment. These charges are substantial, so they are waived for a good, regular customer. Yvonne or I decide when to waive the charge.

"Some customers began to know the stock better than I did. They came in daily, looked at the sale rack and at the new merchandise we had brought in. They predicted how long we would keep a garment and waited for a sale to come along. So thus began musical garments.

"We moved racks from the right side of the store to the left side and from the back middle to the front middle. We then sold stuff that was five years old just because it was in a different place. Now we change the store randomly. We move items closer to the front window or farther away. We change the location of the fluorescent fixtures. We paint the walls a different color. We changed the sizing from right to left rather than left to right, but this became too confusing so we gave it up. Eventually we saw this practice recommended in trade journals after we began to read them, but we had had to stumble on it. A few trade journals have some very helpful display, layout, and merchandising ideas. We learned that Bonwit Teller, for example, constantly remodels its stores so that the interior decor, the coloration, the store design, the location of items, and the way they are displayed changes—but not on a predictable basis. One of our goals is to be able to spend $4,000 each year for remodeling the store. Doing so will easily increase annual sales by $16,000.''

NEW LOCATIONS

"About six months ago we decided that we had to think about expansion because we cannot maintain an inventory of $35,000 and, over the long run, make sales of more than $12 per square foot per month in the present shop. The limiting factors are how fast we can buy, how fast we can process the stuff that is bought, and the disruption of deliveries through the front door since we do not have a back entrance into our 900 square feet of space.

"Ideally, provided that we could manage it, we should add a second location with 1,100 square feet minimum to 1,600 square feet maximum and with a rear entrance for delivery. This would allow us to check purchases and to price the garments efficiently. With two stores we would not need to double our inventory but would increase it at most by 50%. With two stores we would also have the advantage of being able to move merchandise from one location to the other either to increase sales or to take advantage of slight differences in the buying habits and decision patterns of the different clientele. A second store would also allow us to have more than three dressing rooms here. Sometimes three is not enough.

"The developer of a new shopping center, El Capri, at 7000 East Tanque Verde Road (see location B on Exhibit 1) wants us to lease space at $10 per square foot on a yearly lease. He is, however, only renting a shell in a major new shopping center. We would have to invest $20,000 in leasehold improvements before moving in.

"Another deal is available at the Park Mall at 5870 East Broadway (location C on Exhibit 1). This center is still under construction, but Broadway Stores, Diamond's, and Sears all are operating major department stores there. The traffic patterns on Broadway, near Wilmot, are such that people who drive there tend to come in from the southeast and the west rather than from the northeast or the north. The developer will lease either 2,000 or 2,500 square feet of space in either a rectangular or a square configuration. The size would be ideal for a single operation, but we would have to pay $10 per square foot and pay for leasehold improvements. Also, we would lose customers if we moved.

"We could look for space in a minor shopping area, but that would mean pioneering a new location. There are one or two way out east on Broadway that I have considered. Space costs would be about half as much as at El Capri shopping center on Tanque Verde Road. But we would have to have a free-standing unit because there are no vacancies in any shopping centers. Well to the east there is considerable population growth, and the population density is increasing. Census statistics show that young-marrieds to middle-aged persons (our target population) of middle-level incomes live there. About 5 miles from our present location would certainly differentiate the two buying groups geographically. Despite our advertising, however, I doubt that we are well enough known to support a separate building on our own. I really want a shopping center location for the traffic it brings. One developer who plans to put in a center beyond Kolb Road (see location D on Exhibit 1) has offered a lease of $4.50 to $6.00 per square foot, depending upon our location in the center. But we would need $15,000 for leasehold improvements and we would be pioneering a new location. The developer wants to sign us to a firm lease and then use our balance sheet to help him get financing to build the complex.

"My ultimate goal is to earn $1,000 net profit per year per store if we have 50 stores or $2,000 if we have 25 stores.

"There are other locations in town we can consider. Two spots in the southwestern part of the city have stores available at the right size for a second location. Both have lots of traffic. But neither Yvonne nor I speak Spanish, so there would be a language barrier to some extent. The lease conditions are very favorable. Since the socio-economic pattern differs from the east side, we would be running essentially a completely new store. Our merchandising pattern would differ.

"On the northwest side, on Oracle Road near Ina (see location E on Exhibit 1), there is a shopping center with clientele and stores analogous to Monterey Village where we are now.The center has had three vacant buildings for over a year, but the landlord won't talk with us. I suspect that an existing store has threatened to move out if we move in. That store carries the same merchandise as we do, bought from the same manufacturers. But they put on their own labels and sell the clothes as exclusives.

"Our bank suggested a north central location on Campbell Avenue (see location F on Exhibit 1). Their branch in that area has the largest deposits per capita of all of its branches. We looked a bit further into who the depositors are. The bank figure is for savings deposits. Census tract data shows that the median age there is 20 years above the median for the city. The depositors are wealthy in bank cash holdings, but do they use the money for retirement funding or for consumer purchases? The one clothing store that has done well there in the 20 years of operation of the center is a budget store.

"The rental office here in Monterey Village has a location with 3,200 square feet available a few doors from where we are now. It can be rented for $900 per month plus another $144 per month for taxes, maintenance, and dues to the Merchants' Association. It is L-shaped, with the main entrance at the top of the L and windows all along the side of the L paralleling a walkway that goes to a mall at the rear of the store. The shape provides limited wall space.

"A round rack for dresses usually has a diameter of 5 feet. Straight racks require a minimum total horizontal distance of 5 feet to allow for space to hang the garments and a walkway of a minimum size along one side so that the garments can be looked at.

"Dressing rooms (how many should we have?) would need an aisle of at least 39 inches, and the rooms themselves should have interior dimensions of no less than 4 feet by 4 feet. And how could they be built so that a salesclerk or store manager could check or control the flow in and out of the rooms? An easy way to lose merchandise is to have a customer walk out wearing two or three costumes in the layered look.

It would be a difficult store to force traffic through and the size calls for either a vast, open operation or for increasing the inventory to $65,000 to fill the space. An inventory of that size, even if turned 3 times per year[5] at 50% markup, requires sales of $390,000 per year to support it. I don't really have the expertise to lay out such a store to utilize its shape effectively.

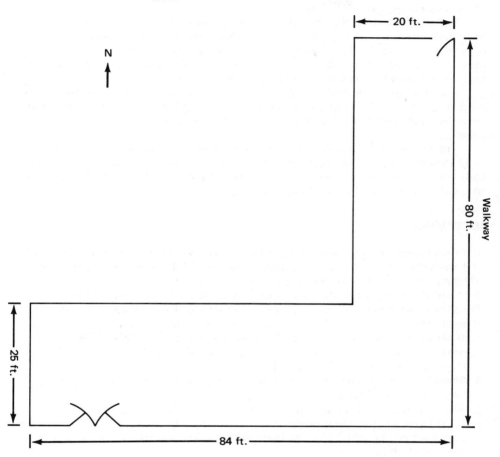

FINANCES

Craig Wakefield stated that the first accountant used by Jodie's Ladies Wear was of no help. "She had a good reputation as a general accountant, but she did nothing for us other than to relist our checks. Then I turned to a CPA firm. They would prepare a balance sheet and income statement but wanted me to keep the journals, make ledger entries, reconcile the bank statement, and be available to answer a lot of questions about their trial balance. Even with 8 years of accounting study and practice behind me, I couldn't do everything. There were too many operating and merchandising decisions that had to be made on the spot for me to spend time with bank reconciliations and ledger entries.

---

[5] Average inventory turnover for the industry is 2.7 times per year.

"So I let the CPA firm go and hired 2 part-time accountants—both students at the University. One of them also worked as an auditor for the city. He turned out to be an inept accountant and compounded our troubles by leaving town with 20% of our accounting records. He never returned.

"The other fellow has worked out well. His eagerness to learn and his common sense have made up for his lack of professional experience. He takes a low wage to get training in retail accounting. We have had to work our balance sheets backward from what we have now to reconstruct the past balance sheets. We have had to estimate and improvise. I would not call it the usual accounting practice.

"I do the tax work (both payroll and income) myself. There have been some complications with the farm and ranching business and with the wholesale jewelry operation in the past that made this necessary. Now we depend upon the store for our living.

"You can see from looking at the statements what our financial problems are."

(Exhibits 4, 5, and 6 on pages 589 and 590 are the financial statements for Jodie's Ladies Wear. Exhibits 7 and 8 on pages 590 and 591 give data about retail sales activity and competition in the Tucson area.)

QUESTIONS

1. In your judgment, what is the outlook for women's wear shops in Tucson, Arizona? Sales volume? Profits? Crucial factors for success? Will chain stores do better than singly-managed shops in any segments of the market?
2. What strengths and what weaknesses does Jodie's Ladies Wear have with its present ownership—relative to competitors? How do its strengths and weaknesses match the crucial factors for success that you singled out in answering Question 1?
3. What strategy do you recommend the Wakefields adopt for Jodie's Ladies Wear: (a) product/market scope? (b) sources of competitive advantage? (c) sequence of major steps? (d) key results to be sought in the next 2, 5, and 10 years?
4. Should Jodie's open one or more additional shops and/or move the present shop to larger quarters? If so, where?
5. Should existing policies and methods of sales promotion be altered?
6. (a) Do you have recommendations for improving purchasing? (b) For improving personnel practices? (c) How do these recommendations relate to your answer to Question 3 above?
7. (a) How do you propose that the expansion you recommend for Jodie's be financed? (b) Prepare a pro forma balance sheet reflecting the sources and allocation of funds that you believe are feasible and desirable 2 years hence and 10 years hence.
8. Should the Wakefields give any consideration to mergers? Who might gain what advantages from such a move?
9. What changes, if any, are desirable in the administrative organization of Jodie's Ladies Wear in order to carry out the program you recommend for this company?
10. (a) Do you think that the Wakefields are currently programming and controlling the operations of Jodie's as well as could be expected in the circumstances? (b) Will any changes in programming, activating, and controlling be necessary if the recommendations you have made in answering Questions 3 through 9 are adopted?
11. **Summary Question:** What answer would you give to the Wakefields if they asked your opinion about the feasibility and wisdom of adding a second shop in a new location to allow for continued expansion of sales volume for the firm?

Exhibit 4

Gross Sales by Month
Jodie's Ladies Wear

Month	Year 1	Year 2	Year 3
January	——	$ 3,992	$12,962
February	$ 1,630	9,559	12,762
March	4,044	6,828	
April	3,961	9,874	
May	4,041	10,317	
June	3,382	10,148	
July	4,607	10,021	
August	3,288	6,657	
September	3,055	6,313	
October	4,832	9,746	
November	4,969	12,127	
December	8,165	18,537	
Year's Total	$45,974	$114,119	

Exhibit 5

Balance Sheets
Jodie's Ladies Wear

	Opening	End of Year 1	End of Year 2
Cash	$ 4,526	$ 4,870	$ 3,333
Accounts Receivable	——	289	1,477
Inventory	15,164	26,351	35,000
Leasehold Improvements (net)	16,934	13,934	10,934
Total Assets	$36,624	$45,444	$50,744
Accounts Payable	——	$ 5,514	$10,985
Note Payable, Bank	$ 2,500	5,375	3,355
Note Payable (see Note A)	16,934	12,751	9,600
Proprietor's Equity	17,190	21,804	26,804
Total Liabilities and Net Worth	$36,624	$45,444	$50,744

Note A: Note payable to former proprietor to be paid at a minimum rate of $200 per month for 5 years. There is no penalty for prepayment. The balance is then to be paid in one lump sum.

Exhibit 6

Income Statements
Jodie's Ladies Wear

	Year 1 (11 months)	Year 2
Sales	$45,975	$114,119
Cost of Goods Sold	24,969	73,671
Gross Profit	$21,006	$ 40,448
Wages—Employees	$ 6,770	$ 7,015
Advertising	1,159	12,401
Rent	2,598	2,940
Utility Expense	1,106	944
Maintenance	73	78
Depreciation and Amortization of Leasehold Improvements	3,000	3,000
Dues—Merchant's Association	230	570
Total Expenses	$14,846	$ 26,948
Net Income Before Taxes	$ 6,160	$ 13,500

Exhibit 7

Index of Retail Sales
Tucson Standard Metropolitan Statistical Area

Month	Previous Year	Year 1	Year 2	Year 3
January	120	145	173	195
February	131	144	173	185
March	123	147	168	
April	129	145	171	
May	139	159	171	
June	139	153	185	
July	127	151	176	
August	127	145	167	
September	126	147	185	
October	145	157	174	
November	135	171	176	
December	149	182	233	

Note: Tucson, like almost all cities in the United States, undergoes changes in its general economic activity. The effect of the depressions of the 1960's and 1970's was somewhat lessened in Tucson because of the predominance of government as the major sector of the economy of the Tucson Standard Metropolitan Statistical Area.

Exhibit 8

**Number of Competitive Shops
City of Tucson**

	Year 1	Year 2	Year 3
Department Stores	10	11	13
Ladies Wear Specialty Shops	68	70	80

Envirometrics, Inc. is a new, growing company. It was established to serve new demands created by efforts to reduce air pollution. One source of air pollution is the burning of solid waste; consequently, many cities are placing sharp restrictions on the use of incinerators. This restriction has created a need for alternative equipment of the type made by Envirometrics.

Founded four years ago, the company has survived the difficulties of launching and early deficits. It is now making a profit, and a recent public stock issue provides financial strength that is unusual for a fledgling company. Comparative profit and loss statements and balance sheets are shown in Exhibits A and B on the following page.

Currently, the company faces a basic question of how to move into its next stage of activity. The outlook for environmental control equipment includes many uncertainties, and the widespread discussion of the field has attracted a lot of competitors. Several options for future development are outlined at the end of the case.

INDUSTRY OUTLOOK

Envirometrics manufactures and installs solid-waste compactors, primarily in large residential apartment buildings. A compactor receives all sorts of refuse, typically from a chute, and compresses the material to less than one quarter of its initial bulk; the compressed block is then dropped into a plastic bag for removal from the premises. This condensing and packaging step simplifies the handling of materials that otherwise are unruly, inflammable, and often smelly. The compacting equipment consists basically of a heavy steel chamber or box and a hydraulically driven plunger that squeezes anything in the box—including bottles and cans. Various kinds of gates, automatic controls, and safety devices are essential features of each machine. The "industry" that produces such compactors is a component in a much larger solid-waste-management industry that deals with the recycling and disposition of vast quantities of discarded materials.

Demand for compactors

Disposal of solid waste. The U.S. Council on Environmental Quality estimates that about 250 million tons of solid waste are generated each year in the United States in our homes, stores, public buildings, and industrial plants.[1] On a per capita basis, that is about 8 pounds per day, and the amount is increasing. Municipal waste (i.e., waste

---

[1] For more detailed information see the Council's *Annual Report on Environmental Quality,* available from the U.S. Government Printing Office.

Exhibit A
Envirometrics, Inc.
Comparative Profit and Loss Statement

	1st Year	2nd Year	3rd Year	4th Year
Sales	$ 26,000	$240,000	$1,684,000	$2,126,000
Cost of sales	$ 20,000	$269,000	$1,513,000	$1,676,000
Selling expenses	9,000	27,000	109,000	98,000
General and administrative expenses	3,000	10,000	71,000	123,000
Research and development	4,000	21,000	48,000	54,000
Total	$ 36,000	$327,000	$1,741,000	$1,951,000
Operating profit (or loss)	$(10,000)	$(87,000)	$ (57,000)	175,000
Income taxes	—	—	—	10,000*
Net profit (or loss)	$(10,000)	$ (87,000)	$ (57,000)	$ 165,000
Profit (or loss) per share	($.013)	($0.116)	($0.076)	$0.165

*Income taxes are low due to loss carryover from previous years.

Exhibit B
Envirometrics, Inc.
Comparative Balance Sheets
(in 1,000's)

Assets	Beginning current year	Beginning last year
Cash	$ 701	$ 49
Accounts receivable	806	350
Inventories	510	356
Prepaid expenses	22	2
Total current assets	$2,039	$757
Fixed assets, net	37	45
Other assets	6	8
Total assets	$2,082	$810
Liabilities and Equity		
Notes payable—bank	$ —	$ 75
Accounts payable—trade	186	225
Notes and accounts payable—affiliates	131	208
Accrued items, etc.	54	109
Total current liabilities	$ 371	$617
Term loan—bank	—	110
Total liabilities	$ 371	$727
Stockholders' equity:		
Common stock outstanding	$ 10	$ 8
Paid-in capital	1,690	229
Retained earnings (deficit)	11	(154)
Total stockholders' equity	$1,711	$ 83
Total liabilities and equity	$2,082	$810

collected from homes, stores, and factories) accounts for about 5 pounds per person per day. For example, in New York City alone 50,000 tons of solid waste must be handled and disposed of by the City each day.

> About 50 percent of municipal waste is paper; 12 percent, garbage; 15 percent, other combustible material; 8 percent, metal; 1 percent, plastics; and 7 percent, glass. The remaining 7 percent is unclassified. This sheer diversity of materials makes the recovery as well as the entire handling of municipal wastes difficult to accomplish because some types of disposal and some methods of recovery require that materials be separated into homogenous categories. The difficulty has been compounded by the gradual shift in composition from organic materials such as paper and garbage, which will decay or burn, to long-lived synthetic materials such as metals, glass, and plastics.[2]

The total costs of disposing of solid waste in the United States was about $3.2 billion in 1971 and is estimated to rise to $5.3 billion in 1981 (1972 dollars).

The age-old practice of disposing of solid waste in open dumps is rapidly passing. More recently, sanitary landfills and incinerators appeared to be satisfactory disposal methods. However, sanitary landfills and incinerators are encountering three serious objections, especially in metropolitan areas. (1) Suitable locations for landfills are disappearing, especially if we insist on retaining marshlands and tidal flats for ecological reasons. (2) Increasing scarcity of physical resources (relative to a growing demand) argues for fuller utilization of the resources we have extracted from the land.[3] (3) The typical incinerator adds to air pollution. It is this third consideration that has precipitated a sharp increase in the demand for compactors.

New restrictions on incinerators. Virtually all large apartment buildings constructed in the last couple of decades have incinerators to burn paper, garbage, and other combustible waste. This is a prompt method, greatly reducing the volume of solid waste that must be carted away. Incinerators are also often found in office buildings and industrial plants.

When air pollution became a critical problem in our cities, it was discovered that incinerators often contributed as much as 15% of the solid particles in the air. Consequently, agitation has been growing to either prohibit the use of incinerators or to insist that incinerators be equipped with devices (usually "scrubbers") which remove virtually all solid particles from the flue discharge. New York City pioneered in the control of this source of air pollution. A law was passed (a) prohibiting the installation of incinerators in *new* apartment construction and instead requiring the installation of compactors, and (b) requiring owners of *existing* apartment buildings either to convert their incinerators to compactors or to upgrade their incinerators with scrubbers. The anticipated effect of the latter requirement was that most existing incinerators would be replaced by compactors. Challenges to the new law in the courts delayed the start of enforcement for almost five years, and the deadline for full compliance set by the

---

[2] *More Effective Programs for a Cleaner Environment.* A Statement on National Policy by the Research and Policy Committee of the Committee for Economic Development, April 1974, p. 44.

[3] *Ibid.,* p. 45. "Despite growing enthusiasm for recycling, there is little evidence that it has increased the percentage of municipal solid waste reused in recent years. Some municipalities recycle cans and other metal items, but costs of separation and shipment to processors make this uneconomic in many areas. Rubber and plastic are hard to recycle, and negligible amounts are salvaged. Glass is easy to recycle, but the low price of raw materials limits the need to recycle. It has been estimated that about 20 percent of paper products are recycled."

enforcement agency is still four years off. So the process of conversion in New York City is now going on.

Other cities in the United States are considering legislation similar to that passed by New York. Detroit, Baltimore, Phoenix, Nashville, and Fort Worth actually have such legislation on the books; legislation is in progress in Los Angeles, Houston, Dallas, Cincinnati, Pittsburgh, Toledo, and Washington. Proponents of air pollution control believe that every major city in the United States will enact similar legislation within the next three to five years.

Potential markets for compactors. The legislative restraints on incinerators in New York City opened a large market for compactors. An indication of the size of this market is shown in the experience to date with either upgrading incinerators or replacing them with compactors. As the accompanying table shows, about a third of the 17,500 apartment buildings that had incinerators have already taken action to comply with the new law. Of the buildings that changed, about half installed compactors, with a somewhat higher percentage for the larger buildings. Most of the remaining buildings, over 11,000, are expected to take action within the next three years.

New York City Market for Compactors

Size of Building: Number of Families	Starting Number of Buildings with Incinerators	Changes to Date			
		Stopped Use of Incinerators– No Compactor	Installed Scrubber	Installed Compactor	Still to be Converted
20 or less	1,650	1,000	——	200	450
21 to 50	6,200	500	300	800	4,600
51 to 100	8,000	——	800	1,000	6,200
100 and over	1,650	——	500	1,000	150
Total	17,500	1,500	1,600	3,000	11,400

In the total United States there are an estimated 237,000 apartment buildings having 11 or more family units. About 85% of these buildings are concentrated in eight national metropolitan areas. The total number of incinerators, particularly in the smaller buildings, is unknown. Nevertheless, if the potential market for compactors is confined

Apartment Buildings in the U.S.

Size of Building: Number of Families	Number of Existing Buildings
11 to 20	163,000
21 to 50	56,000
51 and over	18,000
Total	237,000

to buildings with 21 or more families, there are 74,000 prospects. If the same ratio of these convert to compactors as has occurred to date in New York City, the total conversion market is 40,000 units. Assuming an average equipment cost of only $7,000 per unit, the prospective national market becomes $280 million.

The potential market for compactors in newly constructed apartment buildings is much smaller than that for existing buildings. The construction of buildings large enough to need either an upgraded incinerator or a compactor (20 or more family units) ranges between 6,000 and 10,000 per year, with the prime market (buildings for 50 or more families) being only 1,000 to 2,000 per year. Consequently, this new construction market—assuming present technology—will probably be less than 5,000 compactors per year for the entire country.

A large potential market for compactors exists in schools, hospitals, motels, hotels, offices, quick food service outlets, banks, and light industries. Prospects for legislation requiring compactors for these potential users is unlikely. Instead, this market will have to be sold on the basis of labor savings and good housekeeping. If a compactor could be designed that would pay for itself in two to four years, the market would be substantial. Production of compactors would probably have to be on a much larger scale than at present in order to get the costs down to a level that would tap this market.

Technological changes. The preceding analysis assumes that the technology for disposing of solid waste remains substantially unchanged. Actually, a lot of experimentation is going on, and several pilot plants are in operation. The main focus is on burning solid waste in electric generating plants. The hope is to deal with solid-waste disposal and energy shortages at the same time. Technical difficulties include the lack of uniformity in the fuel and the disposition of noncombustible items such as bottles and cans. However, as the cost of coal and oil—and also the cost of disposing of the solid waste—rises, the economic feasibility of such plants increases.

Another approach is to separate the various elements within the solid waste by chemical, electrical, or centrifugal processes (or a combination of these) and to produce an array of products such as fertilizer, road-building material, and the like. The adoption of any of these disposal methods might have a substantial effect on the way the solid waste is assembled and handled at the point of origin. Whether a compactor would fit into this scheme is by no means clear at present.

Increases in supply

The supply of compactors has risen quickly in response to the new demand. In fact, competition for the business is keen. This competition is due to ease of entry. The technology is simple and has been developed in Scandinavian countries. No significant patents exist that prevent almost any newcomer from adapting known designs. Moreover, the various components such as switches and pumps and cylinders can be purchased from existing suppliers, and the metal framework can be subcontracted. Consequently, no large investment is needed in fixed assets. In fact, many people have entered the business "on a shoestring." These newcomers have low overhead and offer sharp price competition.

The failure rate in the industry has also been high. The equipment must be approved by the Sanitation Department. Also, building owners are much concerned about reliability since a shutdown for even a day or two can cause a severe pileup of the neverending flow of solid waste. If a supplier overcomes these technical problems, it must have capital to finance inventories and accounts receivable. Experience at Envirometrics indicates that investment of about 65 cents in current assets is necessary for each dollar of annual sales, and the profit margin is not large enough to generate such capital from operations.

All of the competitors in the New York market started as small, independent ventures. There are still a dozen active competitors, four of which might be said to have an established position. The relative strength, in terms of estimated number of compactors installed, is shown in the following table.

Estimated Compactor Installations in New York City

	Number of Installations	Share of Market
Company A	800	27%
Company B	800	27
Envirometrics, Inc.	400	13
Company C	400	13
Company D	150	5
Company E	100	3
Company F	100	3
Five Others	250	9
	3,000	100%

Company A has achieved its strong position by aggressive marketing. Apparently it is now having some difficulty living up to its claims, and the man who did the marketing work has left the company. Consequently, it is less of a threat in the future. It is owned by a real estate firm.

Company B was the first in the industry and has a good position. Recently it was acquired by Carrier Corporation and is operated as a part of that corporation's solid-waste division. Carrier Corporation also owns Dempster-Dumpsters, so apparently it is gearing up to move into this field in a substantial way.

Company C had sales of only about $1,200,000 last year. It is now in a poor cash position (as was Envirometrics before the public offering), and there is doubt whether it can attract the capital necessary to maintain its market position. All the other firms are small, struggling enterprises.

In other cities where compactors are sold, small companies are springing up as they did in New York City. The three leading New York companies have occasional arrangements with manufacturers' representatives, but no one company has yet attempted to establish national distribution.

The AMF Company, a large conglomerate that is not shown in the above list, has a special unit designed for restaurants and similar institutions. This unit is stainless steel and of a size suitable for the restaurant industry. It is available through distributors on a national basis. AMF has not gone into the residential building field.

As the above information indicates, some of the large companies may attempt to enter the compactor field on a national basis. Except for the Carrier acquisition and the AMF effort, Envirometrics executives know of no other large companies that are now undertaking to enter the compactor industry on a broad basis. However, several large concerns are investing heavily in R&D directed toward reuse or recycling of solid waste.

If economically sound processes can be developed, the plants will probably be very large installations costing millions of dollars.

Since the New York City demand for compactors will undoubtedly drop off after conversion of existing incinerators is completed, each of the stronger companies now active in New York will have to search for new markets elsewhere.

ENVIROMETRICS' PRODUCT LINE

Present products

The original compactor made by Envirometrics was a hastily engineered copy of a Swedish compactor. Although it worked properly in the initial tests, it was not sturdy enough to hold up under operating conditions. Consequently, the company had to spend a lot of money servicing these products and eventually it replaced all of them. These early difficulties contributed significantly to the loss in the second year, and some of the replacement costs affected the operating expenses in the third year.

Once it was clear that the original product was unsatisfactory, the company stopped sales and production of that compactor and concentrated on designing a much more sturdy unit. This new unit is operating very well and has been the basis of the company's expanding sales.

The new unit is sold in three basic models: A-1, A-2, and A-3. Model A-1 is the simplest model consisting primarily of the compaction chamber. In a typical installation an operator must release the compressed block before the machine continues to operate. Model A-2 includes an arrangement for the automatic discharge of the first block into an awaiting plastic bag and continuing operation on the second block. Model A-3 has a rotary receiving platform that turns automatically and can accommodate up to 14 receptacles. Thus, the various models are designed for increasingly large installations, Model A-3 providing continuous operation capable of handling the needs of high-rise and large multiunit dwellings 24 hours a day. Each of these models can be equipped with different sized receptacles and with a varying array of automatic controls.

Three months ago, Envirometrics acquired the production rights for a smaller compactor that has more sophisticated design and controls. (It also acquired the services of the engineer who designed this machine, Kris Kinder, who is now Director of Product Development for Envirometrics.) This new machine will be lower in price and will enable Envirometrics to compete more effectively for installations where the heavy machine is unnecessary. Also, there are possibilities of adapting this new line for use in motels and fast-food restaurants.

Turnkey contracts

In New York City, Envirometrics rarely sells just its machine. Instead, it contracts to remove the incinerator and to install the compactor so that it can be operated by local personnel. Building operators are not qualified to make such an installation and they much prefer an arrangement for fully installed equipment.

In order to convert a building from an incinerator to a compactor, typically the incinerator is knocked out, hoppers and charging chutes are adjusted, electrical connections are made, plumbing connections are arranged so that the equipment and the surrounding area may be washed down, perhaps the fire sprinkler is rearranged, and the drains may need to be changed. Envirometrics arranges for local contractors—sheet-metal, electrical, plumbing, and masonry, as necessary—to do this installation work. To date, Envirometrics has considered these installation arrangements merely as necessary activities to sell its equipment. None of the local contractors knows enough about the installation of compactors to take the responsibility for proper installation. Normally, the contracting costs are simply added to the price of the equipment.

A different way of viewing this installation work is to separate machine manufacture from installation and think of the field organization as being in the contracting business. The company would then seek to earn a profit as a general contractor independently of the equipment manufacture and sale. This is the arrangement Envirometrics has with its distributors outside the New York area. A natural extension of the contracting activities would be selling and installing all sorts of equipment related to solid-waste handling. Envirometrics might even install scrubbing equipment on incinerators.

The expansion of turnkey activities would hopefully be profitable. Also, if the company could become a leading contractor, it would exercise better control over the sale of its equipment. Of course, if in the future independent solid-waste-management contractors develop, then Envirometrics might find itself in competition with some of its potential customers.

Envirometrics management has been so busy developing the sale of its equipment that no clear policy regarding turnkey activities has been formulated. Executives are aware that a variety of arrangements are used in the elevator and air-conditioning industries for serving large buildings.

Possible related equipment

Some consideration has been given to the sale of equipment frequently associated with the use of compactors. Concrete chutes for installation in new buildings, conveyors and special handling equipment for moving compacted waste to and from trucks, and peripheral equipment on the trucks themselves are all possibilities.

Also, Envirometrics might sell modernized incinerators that would meet the new air pollution abatement requirements. Equipment yet to be developed for the removal of metal and glass on the site is a future possibility.

Envirometrics would not necessarily manufacture this associated equipment. It could become a distributor for other manufacturers. It could then use its marketing efforts on customer contracts to sell a "full line."

The need for volume on its compactor line has been so pressing that Envirometrics executives have not had time to explore and negotiate possible product additions. Although no policy has been established, several members of management are thinking primarily of products that Envirometrics itself could manufacture.

MARKETING

Ninety percent of the company products have been sold in the New York City area where the company maintains its own selling and service organization. The remaining products have been sold by distributors, one in Boston and one in Philadelphia. Almost all sales are made to owners of existing buildings who are forced by law to upgrade their solid-waste facilities. For the customer, this is a one-time, unpopular purchase—a situation that makes Envirometrics' selling more difficult.

Marketing mix

The company has found it necessary to provide a combination of sales appeals in order to conclude a sale.

Product reputation. Through its prompt repair service and subsequent replacement of the original compactors, Envirometrics has overcome any stigma attached to its initial engineering problems. Products now on the market have withstood severe use in the field, and people acquainted with the machines regard them as reliable. Envirometrics equipment has been approved by the New York City Housing Authority, the Federal Housing Administration, and the New York State Division of Housing and Community Renewal.

Maintenance service. Dependable operation, day in and day out, is essential. As in the case of building elevators, compactor breakdowns are serious and must be repaired promptly.

Each unit manufactured by Envirometrics is tested before it is shipped, and the company gives to the purchaser a 1-year free service contract, a 1-year warranty on parts, and a 5-year warranty on the nonwearing metal parts of the unit. After a unit has been installed for a year, the company will provide maintenance service for an annual charge ranging from $150 for the smaller units to $360 for the large models. It is hoped that these charges will make the maintenance self-supporting, but not enough warranty periods have yet expired to know how many users will sign annual contracts. Nevertheless, the prospect of continued availability of maintenance service is an important factor in obtaining the initial sale of the equipment.

To provide this maintenance service, Envirometrics employs a service manager and 4 servicemen. Each serviceman is equipped with a radio van and with all necessary equipment and spare parts. The service department operates 12 hours a day, 7 days a week.

Competitive price. After a potential customer is assured of product quality and prompt maintenance service, price is an important consideration.

Because of variations in automatic controls and other features, precise comparisons of prices of competitive products are difficult. As a general policy, the Envirometrics company aims to keep its prices in line with its larger competitors. On the other hand, executives believe that list price must be double the manufacturing cost in order to cover engineering, selling, and administration costs and to provide a reasonable profit margin. A recent increase in the cost of purchase parts has caused an upward adjustment in list prices. As a result, the prices of Envirometrics' established line are probably about 15% higher than competitors' prices on comparable equipment. The actual list prices vary, of course, with the size and the complexity of the units sold and range from about $4,000 to $12,000. The average price received last year per machine (excluding installation cost) was $7,000.

Envirometrics' new line of smaller compactors is being priced 8% below competitive equipment, ranging from $2,500 to $4,000. Although the company believes this equipment is superior in design to its competition, the price is deliberately set at a low level in order to attract attention to this new entry in the market. At the present price, manufacturing costs are estimated at 60% of the list price.

Payment terms. The company seeks to meet competition but not be overly liberal in the extension of credit. Where an existing incinerator is being replaced, the company's sales contract normally provides that 10% of the contract price be paid on signing of the contract, 80% on completion of the installation, and the balance on the issuance of a certificate of compliance by municipal authorities. Collection of this final 10% may drag out for several months. (For new buildings there is no down payment and the final 10% is not due until a year after completion of the installation.) In practice, the company has had no bad debt losses but the collections are often slow. Several small competitors, however, have shut down at least partly because of difficulties in collecting receivables from customers who are annoyed by being forced to install compactors.

Selling effort. Sales leads are obtained primarily through direct-mail advertising, occasionally supplemented by newspaper ads. Most of the selling is done by personal calls and telephone contact. The Marketing Vice-President and two sales representatives devote almost all of their time to this personal selling in the New York City area.

Promotion of sales in new buildings follows a pattern similar to that for replacement of incinerators. However, the business originates with building contractors rather than owners. Another difference is that orders are typically placed a longer time ahead of delivery; and when construction is delayed, as it often is, Envirometrics must carry the finished inventory until installation is feasible. These delayed deliveries coupled with the difference in credit terms mean that more working capital is required for business with new construction than with existing buildings.

Use of distributors

Sales outside of the New York City area have been made through distributors. These distributors sell other equipment, including incinerators, but the Envirometrics line is the only compactor they sell. Each distributor is fully responsible for installing and servicing any equipment that it sells. Distributors get a discount of 20-10-2; that is, 20% as a trade discount, 10% if they buy in quantities of 3 or 4 units, and 2% for cash. The distributors are also entitled to a 90-day credit period before the net amount is due.

Until the recent employment of Jim Gruber as national sales manager, executives of the company have been too busy to give much attention to the activities of distributors. Orders received have been small, and there is a strong suspicion that distributors do not provide the kind of selling and service effort that has been necessary to develop the business in New York City. Distributors, it is believed, are glad to accept an order if a customer wants a compactor, but they do not aggressively seek such business. Jim Gruber was hired for the explicit purpose of developing business outside of New York City. One of his major responsibilities will be to help decide when and where distributors should be used.

PRODUCTION

The cost of goods sold includes both the installation expenses paid to contractors for on-site work and the cost of Envirometrics equipment. A breakdown of these costs for the most recent year is shown in the following table:

Cost of Goods Sold. 4th Year

Installation expenses paid to contractors		$ 655,000
Equipment costs:		
Direct costs:		
Purchased parts	$603,000	
Assembly, labor, and overhead	151,000	
Service allocations 1st year ($165 per unit)	35,000	
Total direct costs	$789,000	
Manufacturing overhead, including estimators, subcontract supervision, warehousing, and delivery	232,000	
Total equipment costs		1,021,000
Total cost of goods sold		$1,676,000

Low fixed expense

A striking feature of the production operations is the low fixed expense. The installation expenses and purchased parts, both of which vary with orders received, account for three-fourths of the cost of goods sold. Assembly, testing, and storage are the only physical operations performed in the company plant, and they entail direct expenses that are about one fourth the cost of purchased parts.

Purchase of parts. Company engineers determine the specifications of the specific equipment needed for each order. Purchase requisitions for the necessary parts are then sent to the company suppliers—except for some standard parts that are carried in inventory. All of the fabricated steel is manufactured to Envirometrics specifications by the Baruch Steel Works. The Baruch firm also does the pre-assembly of the steel parts. Electrical controls and hydraulic equipment are purchased from three or four companies whose products have proved to be reliable. This latter equipment is not specially made for Envirometrics and is bought at prevailing prices in the market.

All of this design and purchase activity is based on the company's standard line of products. Nevertheless, there are enough variations in sizes, gates, and optional control equipment so that each order must be matched up against variations in design which have already been worked out. On more complicated jobs the engineers visit the site and then prepare instructions for subcontractors as well as make sure of the specifications for Envirometrics equipment.

Assembly. At the company plant the hydraulic power equipment and control devices are attached to the pre-assembled steel structure. This is a relatively simple operation that is performed under the supervision of the foreman by recent high-school graduates. The equipment is then tested and placed in storage waiting for delivery release.

Company plant. Assembly operations and company offices are housed in a modern 8,500 square foot cinderblock building. The location is in Fairfield, Connecticut (one hour trucking time from New York City), which is fairly close to the Baruch Steel Works in West Bridgeport.

The building is rented under a 3-year lease, at $14,000 per year, which further reduces the company's investment in fixed assets. However, the company does have an option to buy the property during the period of the lease for $100,000.

If more production becomes necessary, the building could accommodate perhaps twice the present volume, and an addition could be built on the present site if this became desirable.

Reliance on one supplier

David Baruch was a cofounder of Envirometrics, Inc. and his company, Baruch Steel Works, provided a great deal of technical help in designing the original and present equipment of Envirometrics. During the early days, Envirometrics used space in the Baruch plant. Consequently, the relationship between the two companies is very close. The production people at the Baruch plant readily understand the specifications sent by the Envirometrics engineers, and they have assisted with rush orders when this was necessary. The feeling of the personnel in both companies is that they are working in affiliated businesses.

This cooperation with the Baruch Steel Works is important to Envirometrics because about 75% of its outlays for purchase parts are placed with Baruch. Because of the evolution of the relationship and the highly satisfactory service, no serious consideration has been given to looking for another supplier. Prices charged Envirometrics are based on "our cost plus the normal markup." Recently, when an increase in Baruch's charges led to a rise in Envirometrics' prices, Envirometrics' marketing vice-president raised a question of whether the production costs were as low as they should be. His question was reported to the board of directors, which decided not to press the matter.

FINANCING

It is possible to enter the compactor industry with relatively little capital, as the experience of Envirometrics indicates. Existing designs can be copied, so the original engineering costs can be low. Most of the parts of the equipment can be purchased from suppliers, thereby transferring the plant costs to them. And office and warehouse space can be rented. Nevertheless, a successful firm soon finds that working capital for inventory and accounts receivable is essential. Sales promotion and other start-up costs probably will not be recovered during the first year or two. Consequently, some capital is necessary to get started, and even more is needed if the company is successful. Envirometrics has successfully met these capital requirements, first by private investment and then by a public offering of stock.

Initial financing

Envirometrics, Inc. was founded by two men, Mike Morris and David Baruch. Mike Morris, who heads an electrical contracting firm, was keenly aware of public concern with protection of the environment, and when he saw a compactor in operation in Scandinavia he had the idea for a business. He went to his friend David Baruch, particularly for help in the manufacturing end. They started the business on a shoestring. Mike Morris and his brother, A. B. Morris, put up 60% of the capital and David Baruch 40%. As the business grew, additional investments became necessary and by the end of the third year they had paid in $237,000. In addition, both of the partners frequently endorsed notes to obtain loans from the bank, and accounts payable to the Baruch Steel Works rose to over $200,000.

During this growth, the capital account naturally went through several restatements. By the beginning of the third year 750,000 shares of common stock were outstanding. Mike Morris held 350,000, his brother 100,000, and David Baruch 300,000. At this time the two founders decided they needed additional executive talent to take full advantage of their new enterprise. Carl Curtis, a successful real estate developer, was added to the Board of Directors, and Pat Seymour was hired as director and Marketing Vice-President—the first full-time senior executive the company has had.[4] To attract these new directors, each was sold 125,000 shares of stock at $2 per share. This transaction did not provide any new capital to the company since the sales were made by the founders—150,000 by Mike Morris and 100,000 by David Baruch.[5]

New stock issue

As company sales expanded, pressure for additional working capital became acute. Fortunately, this need occurred at a time when public interest in all sorts of antipollution and environment protection activities was at a high pitch. Moreover, the stock market was rising. In these favorable circumstances, Carl Curtis was able to find an investment banking firm that would underwrite the sale of Envirometrics common stock to the public.

Envirometrics, Inc. common stock is a high-risk, speculative investment. The prospectus for the new stock (issued in May of the fourth year) pointed out that the company had shown losses in the first three years and that there was no assurance that the profits shown during the first quarter of the fourth year would continue. "Investors should therefore recognize that the offering valuation bears no relation to any recognized criteria of investment value and that, as a result, they may be exposed to a substantial risk in decline in the market price of the stock." Nevertheless, the underwriter did successfully sell 250,000 shares of stock at $7 a share. The net proceeds of the new issue and its effect on the capital structure of Envirometrics, Inc. are shown in the figures on the following page.

Actually, the market value of the common stock rose to $12 a share shortly after the new issue. Then the whole investment climate shifted, the stock market declined sharply, and investors' interest in speculative issues such as Envirometrics, Inc. dried up. Few of the shares are being traded and the current price appears to be between $2 and $2.50 per share.

The public financing greatly improved the financial condition of Envirometrics, Inc., as can be readily seen in the comparative balance sheet (Exhibit B). Almost a million and a half dollars of additional cash was received. Part of this cash has been used to reduce current liabilities and to pay off bank loans. In addition, over $600,000 has gone into increases in inventories and accounts receivable. Even after these changes, the company remains in a highly liquid position. The remaining cash from the new issue plus retained earnings enabled the company to show a cash balance at the beginning of the current year of over $700,000.

---

[4] Seymour receives a salary of $32,500 per year; none of the other directors has received any salary to date, even though Mike Morris serves as President and David Baruch as Vice-President.

[5] Only 20% of the purchase price has been paid, Mike Morris and David Baruch taking personal notes for the remaining 80%. When these notes have been paid off, Mike Morris and David Baruch will have recovered much more than their original investment in the company. Voting rights remain with the original owners of the shares until the notes are fully paid.

Proceeds of Public Stock Offering

Gross receipts—250,000 shares @ $7 per share		$1,750,000
Underwriting fee, 10%	$175,000	
Underwriters' costs	62,500	
Total underwriting expense, 95¢ per share	$237,500	
Company accounting, legal, printing expenses	49,000	286,500
Net cash received		$1,463,500

Change in Equity Accounts

	Before Financing	New Financing	After Financing
Common stock outstanding, @ 1¢ per share	$ 7,500	$ 2,500	$ 10,000
Paid-in capital	229,000	1,461,000	1,690,000
Deficit at beginning of year	−153,500		−153,500
Total	$ 83,000	$1,463,500	$1,546,500
Book value per share of common stock	$0.11	$5.85	$1.55

Most of the company's liquid balance is temporarily invested in short-term securities. Although these investments return some interest income, they obviously do not provide the growth prospects that investors sought when they bought the company's stock. Management of the company is in the enviable position of having financial resources available for investment in growth. There are a wide array of possibilities—product diversification, market expansion, plant investment to reduce costs, acquisition of another small company, and the like. On the other hand, prevailing conditions in the financial market are such that an additional financial issue would be difficult. Consequently, company management must select any new investments with care since it is uncertain when and under what conditions additional capital can be obtained.

ORGANIZATION AND KEY PERSONNEL

With only a small number of employees, the organization of Envirometrics is quite informal. All members know each other and communications are direct, face-to-face, as called for by the work. No one has ever bothered to write job descriptions or draw an organization chart. Nevertheless, there is a well-recognized pattern of work, with division of labor in natural functional groupings. If a chart were drawn, it would look much like the one on the next page.

The following brief comments on each executive give some feel for day-to-day operations of the company.

Mike Morris (58)[6], *President,* devotes his regular business day to his electric contracting business—an old, well-established firm with about 100 employees. At four

---

[6] Number in parentheses indicates age.

ENVIROMETRICS, INC.

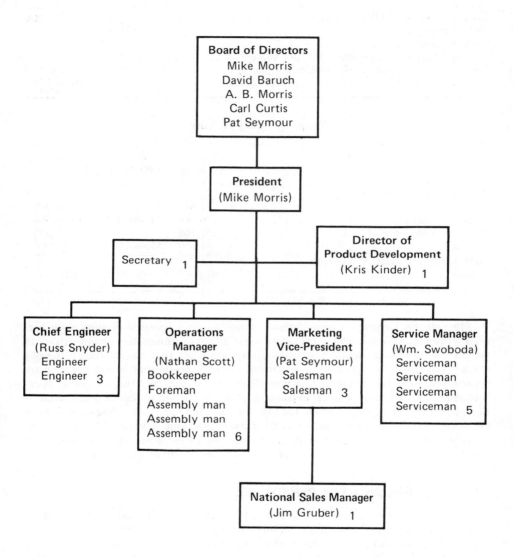

Number in box indicates full-time employees.

o'clock each afternoon he comes to Envirometrics where he discusses any new problems with the persons concerned and sees that work is progressing. He is a decisive man and has been the leader since the company was established.

David Baruch (60), Vice-President, is an active member of the Board of Directors but has never taken part in the day-to-day affairs of Envirometrics. He is busy running the Baruch Steel Works and his other business and public affairs.

A. B. Morris (52) is a passive stockholder, rarely comes to Board meetings, and relies on his brother to represent him. (This investment in A. B. Morris' name is a convenience to keep the Morris family finances in balance.)

Carl Curtis (45), Director, was invited to join the Board over a year ago "to help with finances." He is a vigorous Board member but never gets involved in daily affairs.

Pat Seymour (43), Marketing Vice-President, started his career selling commercial air-conditioning and subsequently was a sales supervisor for three building products concerns. Before joining Envirometrics almost two years ago, he was marketing director for a firm distributing TV antenna nationally. He joined Envirometrics for "the opportunity to share in the ownership and help build the company from scratch." Seymour likes personal selling and relishes "closing a deal." With Envirometrics he has devoted his entire time to building sales in the New York City area, gladly leaving the production and operation activities to other executives. "What this company needs is volume, and it's my job to provide it."

Jim Gruber (34), National Sales Manager, worked as a salesman and on the sales promotion staff of the furnace division of American-Standard, and in this capacity acquired a knowledge of the distribution of plumbing and heating equipment. He joined Envirometrics to get into an industry with more growth potential.

Russ Snyder (48), Chief Engineer, was Envirometrics' first employee. He is one of those resourceful persons who can make anything work; he likes to change engines in his cars, build an addition to his house, tinker with antique clocks. And the job gets done—maybe not on schedule, but it is never abandoned. Without formal training as an engineer, he thoroughly understands what is necessary for a compactor to function under a variety of circumstances.

Nathan Scott (39), Operations Manager, has also been with Envirometrics since its early days. He is a methodical, completely reliable individual who keeps track of all sorts of paperwork, orders, etc. He serves as Mike Morris' man-on-the-grounds, getting information and carrying out instructions, and his internal knowledge of the business is valuable to everyone. Rarely does he make decisions or take initiative other than calling a problem to Mike Morris' attention.

William Swoboda (28), Service Manager, worked for an electric appliance service organization in Manhattan before joining Envirometrics. He strongly believes that fast, dependable service is a prime way to build customer goodwill, and his enthusiasm has helped his company build an excellent reputation for keeping its machines moving. His men are well-trained and help with new installations as well as maintaining existing equipment. He is well-liked and works with a minimum of supervision.

Kris Kinder (37), Director of Product Development, is a trained mechanical engineer with several patents in his name. He has worked extensively with air-conditioning as well as solid waste. The new line of smaller compactors were designed by Kinder, and their acquisition by Envirometrics included an attractive consulting arrangement for Kinder to design still other equipment.

OPINIONS REGARDING FUTURE DEVELOPMENT

During the study of Envirometrics, each of the key officials was asked by the consultant (a college professor and friend of one of the executives) what the company should do to assure its continuing growth. Here in condensed form are their replies.

Pat Seymour, Marketing Vice-President, is enthusiastic about national distribution. "We now have a proven product line and know how to sell it, so we're ready to go national. I'm personally tied very closely to a lot of potential business in New York City. That's the reason we hired Jim Gruber who has instructions to work 100% of his time in new markets that we do not yet cover.

"My plan is to have our own branches in eight or ten of the big cities—Chicago, Los Angeles, and the like—where there is a big market like New York. To be strong in those markets we need our own sales personnel and service organization. The potential is there and you can't expect a distributor to give our line his individual attention. And we've got to be in there pushing as the market opens up. Three years late and we'll never get in.

"Then in the smaller cities where the market can't support a full-time organization, and to reach the thousands of motels, factories, and hospitals spread throughout the country, we'll use distributors. The branches come first because they will provide the inventory and the technical backup that the distributors will need. And the branch managers will know enough about the local situation to keep the distributors on their toes.

"Of course, just where we go first depends on legislation. Maybe we can help that along a bit. Outlawing incinerators in large, new buildings is coming very fast, everywhere. Requiring conversions as New York did is tougher and will take place in the big cities first, and that's where we want branches.

"Competition will be tough—little garage-type operators and big firms, too. We can meet that competition with good products and especially low costs. Building operators won't, and can't, pay Cadillac prices for equipment in the basement. For national distribution it's essential that we go into each market with very competitive prices that will discourage a lot of new entrants who become price chiselers before they finally toss in the sponge. With the right product at the right price, we can blanket the country."

Kris Kinder, Director of Product Development, sees a lot of technological change in the disposition of solid waste. "Recycling, energy generation, and giant landfills will all be tried. Also, apartment construction will change, and packaging will change. Each of these developments will call for a modification in our compactors.

"Actually, frequent changes are a good thing for a company like Envirometrics, because they provide an opportunity to keep ahead of the parade. By being a leader in design, we can overcome cutthroat price competition. Our products do not require any unique know-how to manufacture; and patents still obtainable relate to minor features and can be circumvented. Consequently, within two or three years after we—or any other company with real engineering competence—come out with an improved product, the little shops with low overhead will copy it. And they will knock down the price. When this happens we should be ready with an even better product.

"I see Envirometrics coming out with an improved product at least every couple of years. Some of these will be designed for a particular type of customer, say a motel, so the entire line won't change that often. But in this industry the way to grow is to keep the product line alive to new needs and new opportunities.

"The conversion market created by New York City law is a one-time affair. The new law created an instant demand. In the future, replacements and new demand will grow out of technology, not legislation. By flexibility and alertness, and a continuing investment in R&D, we can build a distinctive place in a rapidly growing industry."

David Baruch, Vice-President, believes the company "can do better what it is already doing. Last year's profit sure looked good after years of pumping money into losing operations. But it's only a start. If we get the margins we should, the profits would double. I know Pat Seymour faced an uphill fight with a lot of rough competition, and

I'm full of admiration for the job he is doing. Now that we have enough volume to cover the overhead, we should keep our prices firm even if we lose an occasional order. It's okay to trade dollars on contract work *provided* our equipment goes into the deal at list.

"As for reaching out, Mike Morris is the man to talk to. He's the one who came up with the idea for this business and kept pushing. Oh, we helped out with design, production, and money—he couldn't have done it alone. If Mike thinks we should go national, I have no objections. That is, it's fine with me if we can keep the margin up.

"There is one idea I think we should explore. Why not do our own contract work? Envirometrics sells a job, say for $10,000. Maybe $3,000 goes to contractors who have their profit figured in. Why shouldn't we make that profit? It's the same reason I was interested in Envirometrics in the first place. That $10,000 order has an Envirometrics machine in it worth $7,000, and my company sold $2,000 worth of parts to make that machine. My profit on those parts is small, but by investing in Envirometrics I get a piece of the action—the $7,000—downstream. The same way, if Envirometrics does its own contracting, it performs more work to earn a profit on. I'd like to be earning a profit on the full $10,000, not just $2,000. And so would all the other Envirometrics stockholders."

Carl Curtis, Director, has an outsider's point of view. "If you want my opinion, be ready for a surprise. Someone has to do more imaginative thinking than anything I've heard yet. As you may know, I spearheaded the public sale of stock, and that should be regarded as just a beginning. It's a good thing we got that injection of capital when we did because now when venture capital is scarce we have something to work with.

"First let me point out the dark side. Let's assume we use all the $700,000 cash now in the till to finance new business. Using present ratios of inventory and receivables to sales, that cash would finance roughly another million dollars of sales. At last year's profit rate, the operating profit on $3,125,000 of sales would be $257,000. Okay, you say the margin was low, so let's make the very optimistic assumption that the profit rate jumps from 8% to 13%—then the operating profit would become about $400,000. That is $200,000 after income tax, or only 20¢ per share of stock. A lot of stockholders who paid $7 a share are going to be very unhappy if we conclude that 20¢, or by some magic 30¢, is the best we can do for them.

"The basic error in the reasoning I just outlined is the failure to use leverage. In my business—real estate—if you don't use leverage, you find yourself working as janitor in a little building you own lock, stock, and barrel. No, someone in Envirometrics has to do some creative thinking. I don't know the industry well enough yet to understand all the angles. Ideas from other industries include leasing equipment like IBM, franchising like Country Fried Chicken, merging like ITT, buying up companies close to bankruptcy to acquire their customer list like *Saturday Review/World,* taking a systems approach to the entire process of solid-waste disposal—from the trash can to the sale of recycled raw materials—and you name it.

"What we need is some creative thinking of where to go from here."

Mike Morris, President, believes in what he calls a "feeling your way" approach. "We should keep pushing in several directions—with good men in key assignments—and see what develops. Of course, when you do uncover a good opportunity, as we did four years ago, you have to take some risks. Fortunately, it now looks like David Baruch and I will get back the money we already risked. Frankly, the amount was more than seed money to me before we turned the corner.

"Now we are in a good position to feel out other markets and look for new products without running a deficit. In fact, I hope Envirometrics can earn steady profits so that it can stand on its own strengths without endorsements from major stockholders, as were necessary in the early years.

"There is every reason to believe that environmental protection is a growing industry. From a small beginning we now have a niche in that industry. To guess what the industry will be like five years hence and risk all our capital on the accuracy of that five-year forecast would not be prudent management. Instead, I prefer to give good men considerable freedom to explore. As they develop good proposals, we'll try to find the resources to back them. I think we do have good men, and we are also in a strong financial position—so I think the outlook is bright."

QUESTIONS

1. What is the outlook for the "compactor" industry as of the time of this case? Include your forecast of the volume, profitability, and key factors for success in the industry.
2. (a) Should Envirometrics, Inc. try to expand its sales beyond the New York City market? If so, what kind of a distribution network do you recommend—company branches, distributors, franchises? (b) Should Envirometrics, Inc. try to sell its compactors to other types of users in addition to apartment buildings? If so, how do you recommend that it reach these customers? (c) Should Envirometrics, Inc. diversify its product line?
3. Mr. Seymour stresses the importance of competitive prices. Do you have suggestions for cutting costs and thereby placing the company in a stronger competitive position?
4. Do you think Envirometrics, Inc. has the key personnel that would be necessary to launch an expansion program? If not, where are the weak spots and what steps do you recommend for correcting these?
5. What should Envirometrics, Inc. do over the next few years with its $700,000 in cash?
6. Evaluate the various proposals for the future development recorded on pages 607 to 610. Should the company follow any or all of them?
7. What do you sense are the personal motives, insofar as Envirometrics, Inc. is concerned, of each of the individuals identified on the organization chart on page 606? How will these motivations affect individual endorsement or resistance to conclusions you reached in answer to Question 6 above? Does this individual response matter?
8. (a) Is Envirometrics, Inc. performing a useful service for society generally? (b) Have all the persons—executives, directors, and stockholders—who have made significant contributions to Envirometrics, Inc. been treated equitably? If not, who has gained at whose expense?
9. **Summary Question:** Considering the total situation, what strategy do you recommend that Envirometrics, Inc. adopt? Include in your recommendation the basic elements of strategy listed on page 64 of the textbook.

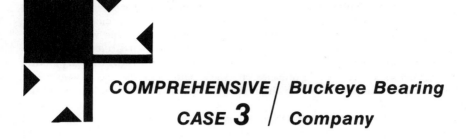

COMPREHENSIVE / Buckeye Bearing
CASE 3 / Company

Buckeye Bearing Company is in the process of transition. The transition involves both new executive personnel and new methods of operation. Almost three years ago the company founder, Mr. Andrew Quinn, died a millionaire as a result of his guidance of the firm. The stock of the company was acquired by Clyde Investment Fund, and this case describes the experience of the Fund in placing the company on a new and modern basis. The process is proving to be more difficult than anticipated; Mr. George Van Houten, president of Clyde Investment Fund, has directed his assistant to make a study of the situation. The following information has been collected.

NATURE AND BACKGROUND OF COMPANY

Andy Quinn and a partner ran a machine shop in a suburb of Cleveland, Ohio, in the 1920's. They learned how to make good quality roller bearings, and with increasing demand from machinery manufacturers this product soon received their major attention. Then came the depression and bankruptcy. Out of the ruins, Andy Quinn personally founded the present company. His recognized knowledge of roller bearings was an important factor in getting the company back on its feet.

For years Andy Quinn and the Buckeye Bearing Company were considered almost the same thing by members of the industry. He had a personal acquaintance among all the oldtimers, and he relished discussing technical problems with both customers and competitors. His opinions were respected because he had detailed knowledge of bearing uses and production.

Internally, the distinction between Andy Quinn and the company was also hard to draw. One of his younger associates reports: "Mr. Quinn was president, general manager, treasurer, credit manager, and sales manager—all in one. He worked six or seven days a week, long hours, and set an example for the rest of us. We typically spent a couple of evenings each week in 'scheduling meetings,' working on the production schedule for each order. We had no 'staff,' that is, no separate men for industrial engineering, production scheduling, quality control, and the like; when something had to be done, we did it ourselves. That was the only way we could keep alive."

Andy Quinn kept up this pace to the day of his death, at the age of 69. From his hospital bed, he conferred with the production manager on detailed schedules for two hours one Friday afternoon. The following morning he had an assistant bring over the accounts receivable records and he dictated credit letters. That night he died. Basically he never changed his work habits from the time he founded the company over thirty years earlier.

For years, especially after World War II, Andy Quinn never spent a nickel that he could avoid on new equipment. Many of the machines were fully depreciated. The plant layout was crowded and no clear workflow existed; machines were put wherever they might fit, often with ingenious arrangements for overhead belt drives. The office reflected a similar stability and parsimony. A well-worn railing was the only separation of incoming visitors from the entire office force. Andy Quinn used the one private office, and about the only status symbols for the rest of the workers were a couple of rolltop desks.

Once convinced of the desirability for a change, however, Andy Quinn was prepared to act. For instance, in a back room he had a fully modern IBM installation—used primarily to process the highly detailed job cost records. Also, at the age of 69, he laid out a "five-year plan" to modernize the plant. Almost $250,000 was invested in new equipment prior to his death. Before this time the company had never incurred long-term debt and rarely borrowed from the bank. "Mr. Quinn never quite forgot his harrowing experience during the depression." Nevertheless, he was prepared to borrow money to launch the modernization plan. Incidentally, the objective of the plan was to replace obsolete equipment; it involved no new direction, product, or strategy.

Also noteworthy is the fact that the company has never had a strike. Many of the workers feel that they are part of the company, and this group apparently dominates the local union. Relationships between the men and their foremen and executives have always been close. The men know that the company will adjust its wages to match the prevailing pattern in the area. Incidentally, the company always has had some blacks and women among its employees. The highest-paid operator of automatic equipment and the highest-paid man in the heat-treating department are blacks, both with 20 to 25 years of service.

Mr. Van Houten states that he and his associates were well aware of Mr. Quinn's conservatism when they acquired Buckeye Bearing. "Our experience indicates that a company with a good reputation but somewhat behind the time in its practices has more potential for growth than a firm where improvements have already been made. We like to acquire ailing companies, turn them around, and then hold them as long-term investments. That was the reason we were interested in Buckeye Bearing. Occasionally, we do dispose of a company and take our capital gains, but that is unusual; we are not traders."

Wise strategy for Clyde Investment Fund to follow with respect to Buckeye Bearing depends, in part, on the nature of its industry and its competition. Background information on these points is summarized in the next section.

Anti-friction bearing industry

Ball and roller bearings are essential components of modern, high-speed machinery. They greatly reduce the friction of moving parts in equipment ranging from steel mills to outboard motors. Annual shipments exceed $1.25 billion. During recent years, total output has been closely correlated with durable goods production; it more than doubled between the latest available Census of Manufacturers in 1958 and 1967. Annual figures from the industry trade association for the last five years are shown in Exhibit 1.

The specialized nature of bearing manufacture is indicated by the fact that virtually all ball and roller bearings are made by 126 establishments that produce only bearings. Machining must be held to close tolerances, and heat-treating to harden the metal is important.

Exhibit 1
U.S. Shipments of Anti-Friction Bearings
(In $1,000,000's)

	Ball Bearings	Tapered Roller Bearings	Other Roller Bearings	Parts, Etc.	Total
Last Year	475	384	241	180	1,280
2nd Previous Year	514	421	242	183	1,360
3rd " "	447	396	216	164	1,223
4th " "	408	348	184	144	1,085
5th " "	388	293	152	128	961

Source: Anti-Friction Bearing Manufacturers Association.

Large companies such as S.K.F., Timken, and New Departure make millions of bearings for "original equipment" such as automobiles. These firms produce 80% of the total output. A second group of companies, of which Buckeye Bearing is one, have 100 to 500 employees and typically are a significant factor in one part of the industry but do not attempt to make all types of bearings or to get the mass production orders. Finally, the smaller shops serve an area of only a few states and often deal with needs of only a special industry such as paper making. These small owner-managed shops usually have a minimum of engineering and overhead services, in contrast to the large companies that maintain a corps of metallurgists and engineers and quickly adopt the latest production techniques.

No one or two companies dominate the industry, however; patents are not significant; technology is relatively stable; and competition is keen. Almost all bearings have a housing that keeps the balls or rollers in place, and these vary widely in size, shape, and design to suit the particular use.

As Exhibit 1 indicates, products fall into three broad types: ball bearings used for lighter loads, tapered roller bearings used where both thrust and load are present, and cylindrical roller bearings that can carry heavier loads for their size than ball bearings. This last type, on which Buckeye Bearing concentrates, has been growing somewhat faster than the other types. Buckeye has about 2% of this market.

CHANGES MADE BY CLYDE

As soon as Clyde Investment Fund bought the stock of Buckeye Bearing Company from Mr. Quinn's estate, Mr. Van Houten moved swiftly to modernize the operations.

Revamped organization

New personnel and new organization had to come first to fill the vacuum left by Andy Quinn's death. Bruce Feenstra was appointed president. Educated as a metallurgist, Mr. Feenstra had worked as an engineer for the Ford Motor Company, then shifted to product manager of one of Ford's parts suppliers, and was anxious to "get into the number one spot of a small firm where I can make full use of my experience and ambition."

To fill the void in marketing, Mr. Feenstra selected Maurice Lombardi—a top salesman in one of Buckeye's distributors with twenty years of experience in the bearing and related industries.

Three men were promoted from within. "Chris Prichard, the accountant, was made controller," explained Mr. Feenstra. "He knows the figures from way back, and already had worked with IBM equipment. I changed public accountants and had the new firm work with Chris in reclassifying the accounts. With that help Chris is doing fine.

"In production, Tony Biccum was obviously the key man. He had worked as second in command under Quinn—insofar as anyone could—so we appointed him vice-president of manufacturing. He has had years of experience producing bearings, knows the men and the machines thoroughly, and provides an essential bridge from the old to the new. We had an understanding from the start that an industrial engineer—Jack Zwick it turned out to be—would work under Tony in modernizing the shop. This has worked well; between my pushing from the top and Jack helping from below with lots of fresh ideas, there is plenty of action. Tony is the voice of experience, so we have quite a team.

"Finally, we took the wraps off Joe Stigler so he can really function as chief engineer. For a long time Joe took care of customer requests for special products, and in the process he learned a lot about product design and how customers use roller bearings. This is an important function in our business, and Joe can perform more effectively with a title and some elbow room. . . . Someday we should have a treasurer, but for the present I carry the title and rely on Chris Prichard to supervise the routine work. . . . Here is the present line-up." (See Exhibit 2 below.)

Exhibit 2

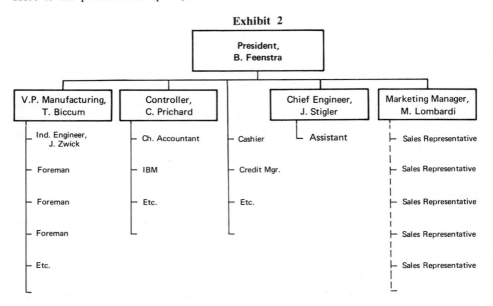

Plant modernization

Mr. Biccum confirmed the transformation in the plant. "You wouldn't know it is the same place. As new equipment came in, we got rid of the obsolete stuff—something Mr. Quinn would never do. And we put it where the new layout said. By now every machine in the place has been moved. The overhead drives are gone. Aisles are wider. Material moves are shorter, and we don't have semifinished lots sitting wherever there is an empty spot. Besides, we put in decent lights and used some paint. Also the new equipment runs faster, so we actually have fewer pieces of equipment. What a difference. Now, we're proud to have a customer see the plant; before we'd think up excuses to keep him out.

"And the offices. Within three months Bruce put up plywood paneling, new ceiling, and lights—also air-conditioning. It was a new world, and everyone in the organization knew it. That office bit cost only $2,500. What an investment in morale!

"Of course, the things you don't see are more important. We've gone to work on direct labor, because you can't save much on material. Between new equipment, better layout, reassigning work loads, improved scheduling, a central room for cutting tools, and better maintenance that reduces down-time, we have cut direct labor from 26% to 18% of total costs. And there was a wage hike absorbed in those figures, too. Jack Zwick is good on this; he keeps coming up with new ideas. He's working on inventory and quality control now. You may want to talk with him about that."

Inventory and quality as sales guides

"To properly comprehend industrial engineering," explained Mr. Zwick, "you must think in terms of all the complexities of the enterprise. In a formal sense we are part of manufacturing; but my men know, and Bruce Feenstra knows, we have a broader assignment. At first, getting costs down was essential to survival, so we focused on that. Now, while not relaxing on costs, we have to help raise plant through-put to take full advantage of the lower costs. This means shifting our focus to marketing.

"For Buckeye Bearing Company to thrive in the marketplace, we must give the customer prompt delivery of high quality merchandise. So we are devising an inventory model that will give optimum availability, reasonable stocks, and efficient production runs. Frankly, this is an unsavory undertaking because intuitively I know high inventories are inevitable. The real accomplishment will be improved customer service. In collaboration with marketing, we have selected some 308 items that will be "standards," that is, always kept in stock here at the plant. The trick then becomes better instructions to our schedulers regarding trade-offs between inventory size and production runs.

"Quality control should yield more observable improvements. Buckeye quality has always been good—with occasional slips, of course. Our task here is to be sure quality does not degenerate when volume rises and to achieve this end with a reasonable inspection cost. Two years ago we established a distinct inspection function, and now we are working on methods and instrumentation that will expedite the process. Automated inspection is impractical in a plant of this size with the many sizes and specifications, but we can design equipment that will lower the labor cost of performing the task."

Revitalized distribution

"Did you ever try to paddle a canoe with a broomstick? Well, that's the way I often feel," said Mr. Lombardi. "Here's the picture in a nutshell. Most of our sales are replacements. When the ultimate user—the fellow whose machine is being repaired—or the contractor he has hired to fix the machine wants to replace a bearing, he asks for one just like the original 99⁴⁴/₁₀₀% of the time—by name of maker. He normally buys the replacement from a bearing distributor—a local guy who is supposed to have a stock of bearings on hand for prompt delivery. Now, since very few Buckeye bearings are original equipment, nobody asks for our products.

"But let's assume the distributor has some of our bearings sitting on his shelf and he discovers that he is out of stock of the specific bearing asked for. Then maybe he will look at our sizes and specs, and if he has what is wanted, he'll tell the customer Buckeye is every bit as good and he can have it right now. You see what I mean by that broomstick. We don't have much leverage. We need to be where the current will pull us along.

"A little wider profit margin will help, but most distributors play it safe and give the customer what he asks for. A really high-grade distributor studies his customer's bearing needs in advance and makes an arrangement with the customer for carrying replacements. That kind of distributor knows his business well enough to be freer to make substitutions.

"If, over the years, a distributor finds that he can get good service and good quality from Buckeye, he is more likely to keep our bearings in stock and to recommend them more often. We use manufacturers' reps to contact the distributor. They are our salesmen although they are not on our payroll; they work on straight commission. Sometimes they are also distributors, in which case they get two profit margins on Buckeye bearings and are inclined to pick our products. Also the reps pick up leads on equipment manufacturers who might buy 'original equipment.' However, most of the reps are not good at this because they normally deal with the users of equipment, not the makers.

"After Mr. Quinn's death a lot of distributors and reps thought Buckeye would fold up. Our competitors probably encouraged the rumor. And our deliveries were erratic. My main job now is to overcome that setback.

"The thing that would help us most right now is a price rise. I wish I knew some legal way to get the big boys to be more realistic in pricing their replacements. They aren't set up for short runs like we are, so they must be losing money on most sizes. Unfortunately for us, overall they are making good profits and they are unwilling to have wide differences in prices of items that vary in volume. All we can do is keep our prices in line with theirs."

Financial results

Chris Prichard, the controller, is the only executive unimpressed with Buckeye's "progress." "The more we sell, the more we lose. I'll give you the statements and see if you can find anything to shout about. The comparative profit and loss statement (Exhibit 3) shows that our gross margin has dropped from 21% to 14% in five years. No company can take that kind of a beating. Lombardi says he can't raise prices, so that turns the spotlight onto cost of goods sold. Take a look at costs (Exhibit 4). The money that we are saving on direct labor is more than eaten up by the costs of staff supervision, added inspection, and inventory control in the storeroom. Check it out yourself. From a financial standpoint, we just are spinning our wheels.

"Maybe I'm guilty of negative thinking. That's what Mr. Feenstra thinks, even though he doesn't say so. The balance sheet is what really shakes me (Exhibit 5). Current assets have gone up with sales. We're putting a lot of money into new equipment—almost a million dollars in three years. All that is nice positive stuff. But

Exhibit 3
Buckeye Bearing Company
Five-Year Comparative Profit and Loss Statement
(Dollar figures in 1,000 s)

	Last Year		2nd Previous Year		3rd Previous Year		4th Previous Year		5th Previous Year	
Net Sales	$4,315	100.0%	$3,860	100.0%	$3,531	100.0%	$3,083	100.0%	$3,019	100.0%
Cost of Sales	3,711	86.0	3,221	83.4	2,841	80.5	2,441	79.2	2,385	79.0
Gross Profit	604	14.0	639	16.6	690	19.5	642	20.8	634	21.0
Selling Expense	302	7.0	293	7.6	234	6.6	230	7.5	225	7.5
Commissions	182	4.2	183	4.7	169	4.8	148	4.8	145	4.8
Administrative Expense	271	6.3	234	6.1	322	9.1	301	9.7	279	9.2
Interest, Discounts, Etc. (net)	55	1.3	30	.8	21	.6	16	.5	11	.4
Total Expenses	810	18.8	740	19.2	746	21.1	695	22.5	660	21.9
Net Operating Income (or Loss)	(206)	(4.8)	(101)	(2.6)	(56)	(1.6)	(53)	(1.7)	(26)	(.9)
Income Tax (or Tax Credit)	(89)	(2.1)	(48)	(1.2)	(18)	(.5)	(18)	(.6)	(10)	(.3)
Net Profit (or Loss)	(117)	(2.7)	(53)	(1.4)	(38)	(1.1)	(35)	(1.1)	(16)	(.6)

Exhibit 4

Buckeye Bearing Company

Cost of Sales—Five-Year Comparison

(Dollar figures in 1,000's)

	Last Year		2nd Previous Year		3rd Previous Year		4th Previous Year		5th Previous Year	
Materials	$1,261	31.0%	$1,082	31.3%	$975	32.1%	$833	31.1%	$804	32.2%
Direct Labor	734	18.0	692	20.0	789	26.0	645	24.0	651	26.1
Manufacturing Expense:										
Salary and Wages:										
Supervision	113		88		135		149		108	
Indirect Labor	178		189		154		173		121	
Overtime Premium	107		73		62		63		24	
Shift Premium	35		28		21		20		15	
Vacations and Holidays	116		87		79		69		56	
Total	549	13.5	465	13.5	451	14.8	474	17.7	324	13.0
Service Department Expense:										
Supervision	182		106		41		50		47	
Inspection	208		228		124		92		84	
Storeroom and Receiving	154		122		49		38		46	
Engineering and Drafting	49		30		21		19		25	
Building	188		138		87		82		101	
Total	781	19.2	624	18.0	322	10.6	281	10.5	303	12.1

	Amount	%	Amount	%	Amount	%	Amount	%	Amount	%
Supplies and Miscellaneous..	270	6.6	225	6.5	192	6.3	181	6.7	138	5.6
Power and Fuel..........	43	1.0	32	.9	34	1.1	33	1.2	24	1.0
Insurance (life, hospital, retirement, compensation).........	149	3.7	110	3.2	101	3.3	98	3.7	110	4.4
Social Security and Unemployment Tax.........	70	1.7	54	1.6	42	1.4	42	1.6	43	1.7
Repairs..........	89	2.2	66	1.9	50	1.6	37	1.4	45	1.8
Depreciation.........	125	3.1	102	3.0	84	2.8	57	2.1	53	2.1
Total Manufacturing Expense.........	2,076	51.0	1,678	48.7	1,276	41.9	1,203	44.9	1,040	41.7
Total Production Expense......	4,071	100.0%	3,452	100.0%	3,040	100.0%	2,681	100.0%	2,495	100.0%
Less Income in Inventories.....	360		231		199		240		110	
Cost of Sales.............	$3,711		$3,221		$2,841		$2,441		$2,385	

Exhibit 5

Buckeye Bearing Company
Balance Sheets, December 31
(Dollar figures in 1,000's)

	Last Year	2nd Previous Year	3rd Previous Year	4th Previous Year	5th Previous Year
Assets					
Cash	$ 222	$ 144	$ 109	$ 413	$ 451
Accounts Receivable, Net	539	497	466	384	382
Inventories:					
Raw Materials	241	264	268	222	157
Work in Process	790	648	1,045	860	689
Finished Goods	1,322	1,081	449	481	477
Total Inventories	2,353	1,993	1,762	1,563	1,323
Prepaid Expenses	21	24	30	32	29
Total Current Assets	3,135	2,658	2,367	2,392	2,185
Land	106	106	106	106	106
Buildings and Equipment	2,721	2,348	2,082	1,758	1,718
Reserve for Depreciation	1,816	1,667	1,544	1,421	1,332
Net Fixed Assets	1,011	787	644	443	492
Total Assets	$4,146	$3,445	$3,011	$2,835	$2,677
Liabilities and Equity					
Notes Payable	$1,400	$ 700	$ 300	$ —	$ —
Accounts Payable	286	241	173	211	74
Accrued Items	331	256	237	285	231
Total Current Liabilities	2,017	1,197	710	496	305
Common Stock	200	200	200	200	200
Capital Surplus	1,800	1,800	—	—	—
Retained Earnings	129	248	2,101	2,139	2,172
Total Equity	2,129	2,248	2,301	2,339	2,372
Total Liabilities and Equity	$4,146	$3,445	$3,011	$2,835	$2,677

when you combine those increases with operating losses, cash has to come from someplace. For us the source has been the banks, thanks to the endorsement of notes by the Clyde Investment Fund. The net result is that our current ratio is bad, our debt to equity ratio is bad, and our earnings on equity are negative!

"Don't get me wrong. All of us are working hard to turn this ship around. The plant is modern; the finished goods inventory does permit better deliveries; the quality is under better control; and the reduction in direct labor is much larger than I thought possible. We use the IBM to give us costs on each production lot, and if any lot is out of line from previous costs Biccum, Zwick, and I, and often Mr. Feenstra, dig in to find out why. And because those cost sessions often come two or three months after the lot was started, we have weekly reviews of actual output against schedule. Periodically Zwick puts one of his boys on analyzing machine down-time. Et cetera. The improvements you see are the result of hard work. Incidentally, the drop in administrative expenses two years back might be misleading. Most of that is Mr. Quinn's $65,000 salary, and also transfer of some expenses from administrative to selling.

"Last year we assumed the loss was due to extra expenses of changing our way of doing business. That's okay for one year. But how long and how deep do we have to go?"

FUTURE OPPORTUNITIES

During the examination of the company, a variety of suggestions were made for future development. For obvious reasons, several of these ideas had not been aired within the company itself, but they all could be appraised by Mr. Van Houten.

Mr. Feenstra stresses volume. "There's nothing wrong with this company that some additional sales won't cure. We have put the house in order and are prepared to give the trade the service it desires. We gained 12% last year and I'm hoping we can double that growth this year. It just takes a long while to rebuild confidence of distributors and to get a change in their buying habits. Maurice Lombardi is working hard in that direction, and so is Joe Stigler. We only need, say, 1% more of the industry total to make this place hum.

"To speed up growth, I've been looking for a smaller company that we might take over. Most of the smaller firms can't afford the staff services we have. They are usually one-man affairs. If we could find such a firm with a strong reputation in a geographical region or for a special type of bearing, we could put the production in our shop and simply maintain a warehouse and sales office in the other city. There are at least twenty companies in the country that fit my specifications, and certainly the owner of one of them is ready to toss in the sponge if we can locate him and approach him right."

Sales to original equipment manufacturers (o.e.m.) is a related approach. Mr. Stigler believes: "To build a sustained volume of sales we must have Buckeye bearings in a lot of original equipment. Then we will get requests for our bearings as replacements, just as the major companies now do. Those requests are valuable in their own right, and they encourage a distributor to stock other Buckeye bearings along with those that have a pre-established demand.

"The big companies have a lot of high-powered o.e.m. engineers who work closely with automobile manufacturers and other large users. That's not our game. We couldn't handle the business if we got it. However, there are hundreds of manufacturers whose use of bearings is too small for the big boys to go after. Actually, these firms need help in selecting the correct bearings for their particular purposes even more than large manufacturers do because their engineering staff is too small to have a bearing expert. That is where the opportunity for Buckeye lies.

"Let me give you an example. Snowmobiles offer us a unique market. A dozen companies want to get into the act. Probably not a single one understands bearings. The load isn't heavy, but bearing lubrication in the low temperatures and rough usage is very tricky. I'm working with a Canadian company on that now. If Buckeye can become known in this field, we can build an attractive original equipment and replacement volume. Actually at one time Buckeye was well established with outboard motors. Andy Quinn did the original selling. But then he lost interest and the business got away from us. Another example is some work we are doing with a printing press manufacturer. We do have competition from Torrington on that one, but they won't give it the same close attention we will and I hope to land the business.

"No one knows better than I that o.e.m. sales are slow in materializing. You may work with a company for a couple of years, send samples, make calls, and answer questions before you get a single order. But if you do get in, the o.e.m. and the replacement business should last for twenty years.

"Buckeye should build a reputation for providing engineering help on small-volume problems. That is where our production strength lies. We should match up customer engineering with our production strength and establish a distinctive place in the industry for Buckeye. We need two or three more engineers and better support from the management to do the job right."

Mr. Van Houten reported a recent converstation he had with Mr. Feenstra following a board meeting. "I was impressed with all of the merger announcements appearing in *The Wall Street Journal*. So, I asked Bruce Feenstra whether Buckeye should be thinking in terms of merger. Bruce was obviously upset and responded, 'Boy, let's not let that idea get circulating! If the men knew we were talking about selling out, the morale we've been trying so hard to build would go down the drain in a hurry. Everybody would start looking for another job and we'd have half a dozen resignations before the end of the year.' I tried to explain that a merger does not necessarily mean selling out. It could mean a real partnership with one or two other companies in related lines of business, or perhaps Buckeye could take the initiative in bringing together several other small bearing companies with complementary lines. The discussion then turned to the possible advantages of being associated with a ball bearing company, a miniature bearing firm, and someone making tapered roller bearings. The conversation ended with, "If we are going to get into that, we'd better get our own house in order first.'

"I haven't raised the question of merger with Bruce again, but I did make the following notes for my own file:

Merger Possibilities for Buckeye

1. Get taken over as an investment by a conglomerate. Buckeye to continue as independent organization. To be attractive, Buckeye would have to be profitable and have prospects for growth and earnings, same as present company objectives.
2. Develop some outstanding asset that would be attractive to a large bearing company.
   a. Strong position with group of o.e.m. customers.
   b. Unusual product, protected by patents.
   c. Low cost production capability. For us, probably low cost for short runs of odd sizes.
   d. Antitrust trouble unlikely because of small size of Buckeye.

3. Consolidation with another bearing company. Plant, equipment, inventories, engineering, and office all combined together. Economies would have to be developed. Buckeye now in poor bargaining position.''

Mr. Prichard viewed the total situation quite differently. ''You ask what we should do. I don't claim to have all the answers, but this break-even chart is one way to analyze the problem. (See Exhibit 6.) I figure that expenses were 60% variable and 40% fixed last year. Materials, direct labor, employment taxes, supplies and about two thirds of what we classify as 'salaries and wages' vary directly with volume of plant activity. And those items make up 65% of cost of sales. You can argue about a few dollars here and there, and still come out with that figure. Now 65% of cost of sales is 56% of the sales dollar; add to that 4% sales commission and you get 60% variable expenses.

''If 60% of the \$4,315,000 we took in last year went for variable expenses, the rest were fixed. In other words, recognizing our pre-tax deficit: \$4,315,000 × .40 + \$206,000 = \$1,932,000 fixed expense. With these figures we can draw up the breakeven chart.

Exhibit 6

Break-Even Chart

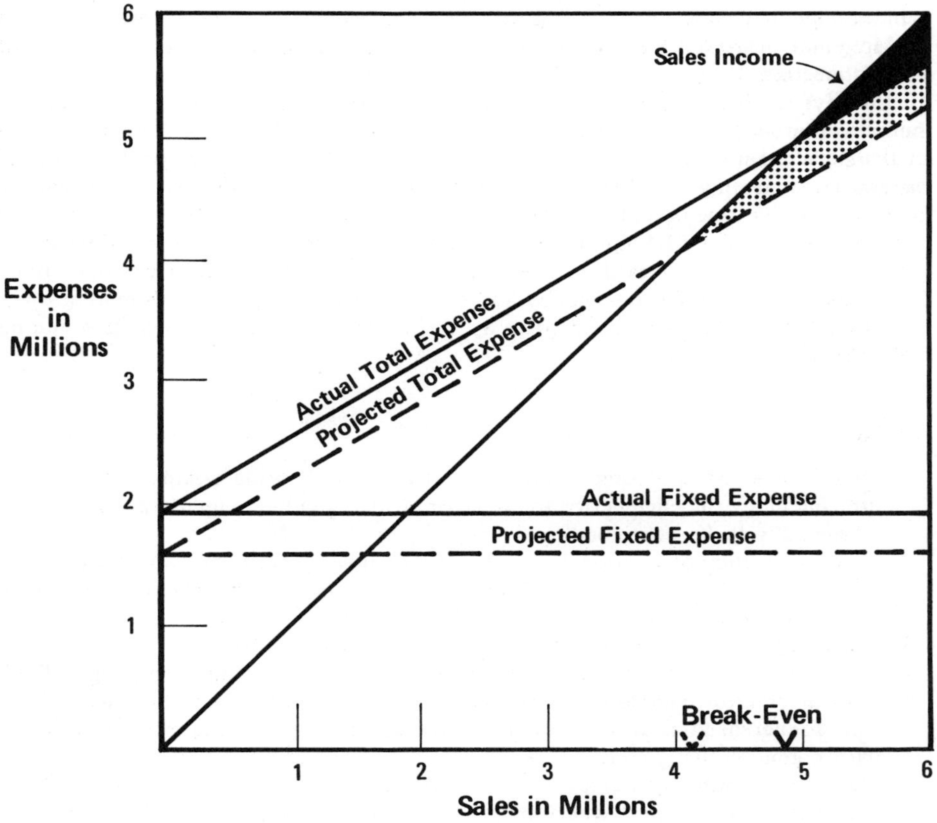

Sales in Millions

"Now that chart shows some interesting facts. First, following last year's pattern, our sales have to hit $4,800,000 before we just break even. Second, suppose by hard work but no increase in fixed expenditure we reach the rosy sales peak of $5,500,000, the profit before tax is only $268,000—or $134,000 after tax (Clyde's tax rate is 50%). That profit is just over 6% return on equity; it is not enough to pay off our debt in ten years. Third, even if by some miracle we got sales up to capacity, which is around $6,000,000—to go beyond that would require a third shift and a new jump in fixed expenses—the after-tax profit would be only $234,000. The obvious conclusion is that we can't go along the way we are and ever expect to make a decent profit.

"Okay, so what? I can't avoid the unsavory conclusion that we are living too rich. The fixed expenses have to be cut. True, you had to spend money to make all the improvements we now have. But now the house is in order we should pull our overhead back down. Return the management job to the line men and trim the staff. In two years the Service Department expense has gone up almost half a million dollars. We can never lop off all that, but look what would happen if we could save $250,000 in overhead.

"The dotted lines on the chart tell the story: break-even at $4,190,000, which is less than last year's sales. A $518,000 pre-tax profit at $5,500,000 volume, and $718,000 at $6,000,000. Maybe it is pie-in-the-sky, but at least it is large enough to strive for.

"Excuse my bluntness; I've been stewing about this for some time. There's not an executive in the place—with the possible exception of Tony Biccum—who wouldn't skin me alive if I made such a suggestion in a management meeting. It would be like damning motherhood. I have shown Mr. Feenstra the actual break-even chart but not the dotted lines."

Buckeye's board of directors consists of Mr. Van Houten, (chairman), Mr. Feenstra, the treasurer and the controller of Clyde Investment Fund, and a lawyer. Clyde's treasurer, William Hance, has never played an active role in Buckeye affairs. "I attend the quarterly meeting and that is about it. My impression from the sideline is that we made a bum investment, and the sooner we pull out the better. The bank loan is really our credit, so we have $3.5 million tied up in a venture with a dismal record. If we could sell for less than a $1 million loss—and the assets certainly are worth over $3,000,000—we could put our money and time into something else with more growth potential. Maybe your report will come up with something I have missed. It would be welcome news if it did."

QUESTIONS

1. Do you believe the present management of Buckeye Bearing Company was wise in utilizing industrial engineering to cut labor costs? Should the industrial engineering of Jack Zwick be continued?
2. Has the injection of additional capital by Clyde Investment Fund, via a loan guarantee, significantly aided Buckeye Bearing? What might the company have done without this source of capital?
3. What suggestions do you have for increasing sales volume?
4. Should the company attempt to improve profits by changing its pricing policy?
5. How much effort should the company devote to obtaining o.e.m. business? If you want to increase this effort, how should the company locate and maintain contacts with potential customers?
6. Should the company mount a research and development program of, say, $50,000 per year? If so, toward what objectives should the program be directed?

7. One director has suggested that Buckeye consider entering the automotive replacement parts business—parts such as universal joints or spindle bearings that require machining and heat-treating. What strengths would the company bring to such a business? Would these strengths provide a distinctive advantage over firms already in the automotive parts business? Is there any other product line that you recommend Buckeye take on?

8. Should Mr. Prichard's suggestion of cutting overhead by a quarter of a million dollars annually be adopted? On the basis of information available, where should the cuts be made?

9. Considering the poor record of Buckeye Bearing, should Mr. Feenstra be immediately replaced as president? Would you replace him with a person within the company or go outside? What inducements would you offer to an outsider?

10. Another medium-sized bearing company has just offered Clyde Investment Fund $2,200,000 cash for all the stock of Buckeye Bearing Company; Buckeye would have to pay off the notes payable from this sum. Assume that this is the best offer the other company will make, and if turned down the company will increase its capacity through other means. No other potential buyers have appeared. Should the offer be accepted?

11. **Summary Question:** Prepare a report to Mr. Van Houten giving your recommendation for what should be done at Buckeye Bearing Company.

COMPREHENSIVE / Saturday Review
CASE 4 /

At the time of this case, both the management of *World* magazine and prospective investors in *World* faced a question of future strategy for the magazine. *World* has an opportunity to buy back its erstwhile parent, *Saturday Review*, which has just come to the end of an experiment with profit maximizing.

The industry outlook is far from clear. Within the recent past, three giants—*Saturday Evening Post, Look,* and *Life*—have encountered such staggering deficits that they ceased publication, to the dismay of millions of readers (and advertisers) throughout the nation. Meanwhile, other magazines including *Reader's Digest* and *Playboy* flourish.

To understand the issues involved, an analysis of the distinctive characteristics of the magazine publishing industry and a review of the events leading to *World's* present status are necessary.

OUTLOOK FOR MAGAZINE INDUSTRY

Magazines' role in mass communication

Today the school child in Kyoto, Japan, and the retiree in Red Wing, Minnesota, can watch with only a split-second delay the marriage of a British princess. The technological advances in transportation, telecommunications, and printing have opened up communications—oral, printed, and pictorial—to all corners of the world. At the same time, the volume of new information pyramids. We know vastly more about many things—from heart palpitations to political candidates in an Israeli election. So, more facts and ideas are communicated to literally billions of people.

Magazines play a distinctive part in this whole communication process. Supplementing up-to-the-minute news, they can convey more background and analysis. Also they can be designed to deliver a particular character of message to a select audience. In contrast to books, magazines build up a continuing relationship—from every week to at least every three months—with their clientele. Each year about 5.6 billion copies of magazines go to 63 million U.S. homes and to millions of offices. Readership is rising steadily and is linked to rising incomes and to higher educational attainments.

The size and the growth of the magazine industry are shown in the census data on the following page. The Department of Commerce estimates that industry receipts will continue to grow approximately 6% per year in real terms, with the value of receipts reaching over five billion dollars by 1980.

A second way to view magazines is as an advertising medium. This viewpoint is significant because a majority of magazines that are published could not exist without

Periodicals in the U.S.

	Number of Companies	Value of Shipments (in millions)
1972	n.a.	$3,460
1967	2,430	3,096
1963	2,562	2,296
1958	2,245	1,651
1954	2,012	1,441
1947	2,106	1,060

Source: Census of Manufacturers.

the income they derive from advertising. (Newspapers, radio, and television also depend heavily on advertising.) While academic and religious journals often carry no advertising, many trade publications obtain all their income from advertisers; other magazines fall between these two extremes. For the industry as a whole, advertising provides 62% of total revenues, whereas readers contribute 38% through subscriptions or purchase of individual copies.

Magazines face strong competition for the advertising dollar. As indicated in the following table, only 6% of total advertising expenditures flows to magazines. Newspapers, television, direct mail, and radio each take a larger slice.

Advertising Expenditures

	1972 % Total Advertising	% Gross National Product
Newspapers	30	0.60
Magazines	6	0.13
Radio	7	0.14
TV	18	0.36
Outdoor	1	0.02
Direct Mail	15	0.29
Other	23	0.46
Total	100	2.00

Moreover, magazines are falling behind. During the decade 1963 through 1972 advertising revenues for magazines rose 43%, but total advertising grew 76% and GNP 95%. Only television maintained a pace equal to the national economy as a whole. (See table on the next page.)

The lackluster performance of advertising revenue for magazines is serious on two counts: (1) It leads to a serious profit squeeze, since costs are rising while incomes flatten. (2) It suggests that readers are spending less time with magazines. Advertisers want their messages where they will receive attention. If magazines cease to capture the interest and the time of their readers, they also cease to be good advertising media. Pushed to its logical conclusion, this argument says that, in the judgment of people who place advertising, magazines generally are doing a poorer job of serving customer needs than other communication channels.

Advertising Expenditures and Gross National Product
U.S.A. 1963-1972
(Index 1967 = 100)

Year	Gross National Product ($ Billion)		Advertising Expenditures ($ million)															
			News-papers		Magazines		Radio		TV		Outdoor		Direct Mail		Other		Total	
	$	Index	$	Index	$	Index	$	Index	$	Index	$	Index	$	Index	$	Index	$	Index
1972	1,151.8	145	6,960	141	1,480	116	1,530	148	4,110	141	290	152	3,350	135	5,340	133	23,060	137
1971	1,050.4	132	6,250	126	1,399	109	1,440	140	3,590	123	261	137	3,050	123	4,850	121	20,840	124
1970	976.4	123	5,745	116	1,323	103	1,308	127	3,596	124	234	123	2,766	111	4,628	115	19,600	116
1969	930.3	117	5,753	116	1,376	108	1,264	122	3,585	123	213	112	2,670	107	4,621	115	19,482	116
1968	864.2	109	5,265	107	1,318	103	1,190	115	3,231	111	208	109	2,612	105	4,303	107	18,127	107
1967	793.9	100	4,942	100	1,280	100	1,032	100	2,909	100	191	100	2,488	100	4,024	100	16,866	100
1966	749.9	94	4,895	99	1,291	101	1,010	98	2,823	97	178	93	2,461	99	4,021	100	16,679	99
1965	684.6	86	4,457	90	1,199	94	917	89	2,515	86	180	94	2,324	93	3,663	91	15,255	90
1964	632.4	80	4,148	84	1,108	87	846	82	2,689	92	175	92	2,184	88	3,405	85	14,555	86
1963	590.5	74	3,804	77	1,034	81	789	76	2,032	70	171	90	2,088	84	3,189	79	13,107	78
Increase '63 to '73	95%		83%		43%		94%		102%		70%		60%		67%		76%	

Source: Department of Commerce & McCann-Erickson, Inc.

Rise and fall of individual magazines

Industry data inevitably cover up shifts that are occurring within the total. A diversity of trends is especially characteristic of the magazine industry where over 2,400 firms publish more than 9,000 magazines. This wide array can be classified into nine broad groups: homemaking, professional, farm, trade and industry, business, recreational, religious, juvenile (including comics), and general reader. To a large degree, what happens to one group is unrelated to the appeal of another group. Even within groups, performance varies greatly. For instance, within the professional group are the *Journal of the American Medical Association,* which carries more pages of advertising than any other magazine, and also the *Business History Journal,* which has no advertising and struggles for existence.

Since *World* and *Saturday Review* fall in the general reader category, we should look at what is happening there. Three conspicuous deaths highlight the problems facing general reader magazines. In a span of less than four years, three of the most widely read magazines in the nation—*Saturday Evening Post, Look,* and *Life*—were suffering such large losses that their publication was abruptly halted. (See the table on page 630 for the trend in circulation of these and other well-known magazines.)

The first big jolt was the demise of the *Saturday Evening Post* in 1969. For years the *Post* had been *the* leading magazine of the nation, a hallmark of middle-class gentility, a pioneer in marketing research, a very prestigious outlet for the leading short-story writers and novelists of the day, and the most expensive advertising medium per page available. It was as universally respected as Benjamin Franklin whose picture was incorporated into its masthead, and it enjoyed a circulation of over 6 million copies each week. To many of its readers, the collapse of the *Post* was inconceivable.

In fact, the *Post* had been ailing for several years. Basically people got tired of reading it. *Life* and *Look* offered livelier, easier reading material on current topics; television provided entertainment in one's easy chair; paperbacks made good novels readily available. Moreover, the *Post* belonged to an older generation. While the *Post's* circulation stabilized, *Playboy* grew dramatically by providing pornography, satire, and fashion advice for the modern young male. Because the *Post* no longer provided a unique way of contacting the large middle- and upper-class market, advertisers turned to other media. Meanwhile costs of publication rose unremittingly. The drop in advertising income, coupled with higher costs, spelled large deficits. After several frantic attempts to change the magazine's image, the *Post's* management was forced by financial pressures to call a halt.[1]

Look and *Life* were both launched in the latter 1930's to feature photojournalism—full-page, candid shots of dramatic events and pictorial analyses of social issues. Both were very successful. *Look,* a biweekly published by Cowles Communications in Des Moines, Iowa, was initially directed at a slightly lower income level than *Life* and undertook fewer erudite series on such subjects as "Religions of Mankind" and "History of the Middle Ages." *Look* struck a responsive audience, and circulation soared to over 7 million. In 1970 it carried more than $60 million in advertising! Yet its last issue appeared on October 19, 1971.

A magazine like *Look* is expensive to prepare, print, and circulate. And all these costs were rising to swallow up the millions of revenue dollars. Rising costs, however,

---

[1] Subsequently the name *Saturday Evening Post* was sold to another company, which is trying to find an editorial strategy that will make viable use of the great reputation.

Circulation of Selected Magazines
Circulation in 1,000's
(Index 1960 = 100)

Year	Saturday Review		Saturday Evening Post		Look		Life		Reader's Digest	
	#	Index	#	Index	#	Index	#	Index	#	Index
1973	751ᵃ	314	b	0	c	0	d	0	18,232	147
1970	615	257	b	0	7,837	126	8,527	127	17,829	144
1965	398	167	6,640	107	7,663	124	7,327	109	15,603	126
1960	239	100	6,226	100	6,202	100	6,727	100	12,369	100
1955	151	63	4,638	74	4,077	66	5,604	83	10,236	83
1950	101	42	4,069	65	3,200	52	5,364	80	6,045	49

Year	New Yorker		Atlantic		Harper's		TV Guide		Playboy	
	#	Index	#	Index	#	Index	#	Index	#	Index
1973	477	111	326	118	332	139	18,775	274	6,670	611
1970	456	106	326	118	379	159	15,339	224	5,290	485
1965	469	109	285	103	290	121	10,261	150	2,925	268
1960	431	100	277	100	239	100	6,863	100	1,091	100
1955	396	92	221	80	192	80	2,980	43	228	21
1950	332	77	176	64	159	67	161	2	e	0

(a) As of April, 1973, when *Saturday Review* filed for bankruptcy. (b) Discontinued publication February 8, 1969. (c) Discontinued publication October 19, 1971. (d) Discontinued publication December 29, 1972. (e) Started publication December, 1954.

Source: Ayers' Directory of Publications & Standard Rate and Data Service.

were only part of the story. Renewals of subscriptions fell sharply, as did newsstand sales. In 1970 newsstand sales at 50¢ a copy were only 3% of the total, and renewals at the basic subscription price of 17 cents to 19 cents per copy for 1 to 3 years fell below 30%. These facts indicated that readers no longer felt that *Look* was worth its price. To bolster circulation (and thereby keep advertising rates up), *Look* undertook heavy promotion for subscriptions at cut prices ranging from 10¢ to 15¢ per copy. Seventy percent of new subscriptions were obtained only by discounting the single copy price up to 80%.

The disenchantment of *Look's* readers became known to advertisers. In the first six months of 1971, ad pages were down 1.4% to 572 in spite of a 100% gain in cigarette ads (due to the newly imposed ban on use of TV). The combination of the drop in advertising and circulation revenue and the rise in costs led to an estimated loss of $4 million for the year. The following year looked even worse, so management dropped the curtain.

Many writers in the trade press speculated about steps that might have been taken to save *Look*. Essential to all these plans was some formula to increase the value of the magazine to its readers. Apparently, the improvements in television news coverage were sufficient to undermine *Look's* primary appeal. No one found an adequate substitute before the end came.

The withdrawal of the *Post* and *Look* with a combined circulation of almost 15 million left a lot of readers that *Life* (published by Time, Inc.) might have picked up. But trouble in the general reader magazine field proved to run deeper than just competition. Even though subscribers were paying only about 12 cents for a copy of *Life* that cost 41 cents to edit and print, many in 1970-1972 failed to renew. *Life*, unlike *Look*, chose to let circulation drop, hoping that soon only loyal readers who would pay full rates would be left. But the subscriptions kept going down, as did newsstand sales. In addition, advertisers departed when they discovered that television could deliver the same mass audience at lower cost.

Life Magazine

Year	Circulation Average Paid (in thousands)	Advertising Pages	Gross Revenue (in millions)
1937	1,195	2,224	$ 4.4
1950	5,340	3,816	80.4
1955	5,604	4,398	121.0
1960	6,746	3,360	138.8
1965	7,368	3,247	163.2
1970	8,518	2,043	132.4
1971	7,111	1,993	111.0
1972	5,637	2,025	91.2

During the last five years of its existence *Life* accumulated a deficit of $35 million. Relief was sought in various ways—trimming the size, using a lower quality of paper, cutting the staff. On the editorial side, special efforts were made to deal with stories that received scant attention in the daily press and newscasts. Nevertheless, the tide kept running out. A final blow was an increase in postal rates that added $13 million to *Life's* cost each year. Forecasts for 1973 and 1974 showed an additional $30 million loss with no convincing reason to assume a turnaround would then occur. Even for Time, Inc. the burden was too heavy, and publication ceased at the end of 1972.

Not all general reader magazines are ailing. The most conspicuous exception is the *Reader's Digest,* with clearly the largest circulation (over 18 million in 1973) and still growing. Its editorial policy aims at general interest, nonpictorial articles for all the family. About half are digests and half are original. Topics covered embrace self-improvement, psychology, ecology, government, community action, health, "unforgettable characters," campus, travel, etc., and a liberal sprinkling of jokes. *Reader's Digest* has not succumbed to the cynicism and naked realism of much modern writing. It gives the reader a feeling that American virtues still have validity.

Also alive and kicking, though not growing, are the venerable monthlies *Harper's* and *Atlantic.* They cater to an audience with intellectual curiosity and concern for national well-being. The *New Yorker* is a flourishing regional magazine, focusing on the trials and the exhilaration of metropolitan living. Its biographies of unusual people are exhaustive, rambling, and threaded through pages of advertising. With guides to plays, concerts, dining out, and art exhibits, it has won an enduring loyalty among sophisticated readers. And there are many other magazines that have found a particular scope or viewpoint that appeals to a segment of general readers.

The *TV Guide* has made a unique record in the entertainment field. Overlaying the basic television programs with not-too-weighty stories on stars and shows, it has an amazing combined circulation of over 18 million.

Commenting on the success and the failure of individual magazines, a leading trade analyst observed: "All successful magazines have one thing in common: They must provide a service to the reader. This service aspect, whether it is construed as entertainment, how-to, information, news, etc., is the underlying assumption of all media. The ability to meet this challenge determines whether a magazine lives or dies."[2]

In concluding its analysis of the publishing industry, Standard & Poor's state that in 1973 periodicals specializing in homemaking arts, outdoors and sports, and sex were among those posting the strongest gains.

Revenue and cost factors affecting survival

While service to readers is the vital core of a magazine, economic factors also determine its ability to survive. Magazines have several distinctive characteristics affecting their (a) revenue, (b) costs, and (c) cash flow.

(a) Revenue, as noted in the preceding discussion, typically comes from two main sources—magazine sales (subscriptions and newsstand sales), called circulation income, and advertising. Briefly:

Circulation income = f (product, price, promotion)
Advertising income = f (circulation, rates, selling effort)

Thus, management faces a dual pricing problem; for example, it can sacrifice circulation income as *Look* did and hope to recover the decrease on advertising income. Quite different approaches are being followed by other magazines. *Harper's* in a letter to its subscribers in the fall of 1973 stressed that it had not raised its subscription price

---

[2] *Media Information Newsletter,* December 14, 1972.

since 1965, whereas virtually all its competitors had. On the other hand, *Esquire* in a full-page ad in the *New York Times* makes a strong point of its raising the subscription price while keeping advertising rates constant.

(b) Cost fluctuations are affected by the almost universal practice in the industry of no vertical integration; paper is purchased, printing is subcontracted, and physical circulation is frequently handled by a contractor. This practice lowers capital investment (and ease of entry) while increasing the proportion of variable costs.

A significant part of most magazines' costs vary with the size of the circulation—postage, paper, distribution, and printing (after 100,000). This variability is especially important when the subscription price is low; some magazines literally lose money on every additional copy they print and sell—unless this loss is offset by higher advertising income.

The costs that are not affected much by ups and downs in circulation—at least in the shortrun—include editorial expense, promotion of new subscriptions, company overhead (rent, accounting, top salaries, and the like), and circulation record-keeping. A rise above, say, 10,000 in circulation will not cause these expenses to change. However, such expenses rarely remain "fixed" over any length of time. Typically, management decides to *invest* more, or less, in these inputs with an eye to long-run benefits. A major promotional drive, for example, is an investment this year (even though it appears as an expense on the profit and loss statement) aimed at a continuing higher circulation and at higher advertising income in subsequent years. The payout on such promotional outlays obviously depends on what it costs to get new subscribers and whether they will renew their subscriptions. Editorial outlays, for example a foreign correspondent or a new feature column, have the same investment, delayed response, and uncertainty characteristics.

(c) The cash flow, and therefore the capital requirements, of a magazine publisher are affected by the income and the cost fluctuations just mentioned. Sizable disbursements may be required to build a strong editorial product and to develop market acceptance for that product. The income, especially when the purchase price of a copy of the magazine does not cover the variable costs, is delayed until the pages of advertising and the advertising rates rise.[3]

A unique offset to this delayed advertising revenue is the advance payments for subscriptions. Subscribers *prepay* for as long as three years. This prepayment generates cash—and also a liability to deliver magazines in the future. The liability aspect arose, for example, when *Life* ceased publication in 1972; a reserve of $7 million was set up to settle prepaid subscriptions that could not be transferred to some other magazine. Conservative financial practice is to segregate advance cash payments (in an investment account) and to make the cash available for operations only as magazines are delivered.

In addition to the "economics" of magazine publishing just discussed, managers must deal with inflation. The most pressing current hurdle is the announced 145% increase in Class II postal rates (to be spread over five years) and a proposal for an additional 38%. The U.S. Postal Service is trying to institute a policy requiring its rates

---

[3] A classic example of lag in advertising rates is the outstanding success of *Life* when it was first published. Circulation soared to over a million in the first year, and so did the variable costs. However, the rates charged for advertising were pegged at introductory levels. Consequently, before the advertising rates could be moved up, the phenomenal success had a several million dollar loss, and the publisher, Time, Inc., was placed in a very severe cash squeeze. At the time, no one knew whether the popularity of *Life* was just a flash-in-the-pan.

to cover all costs, and magazines—which on a per pound basis have been subsidized for years—will be hard hit. Paper, another major cost, is in short supply. Its price has already gone up sharply and probably will go higher. Wage and salary rates are rising in the entire publishing industry at least as fast as in the general economy.

Importance of renewals

The *percentage of subscription renewals* is the most sensitive index of a magazine's health. It reflects the success of editorial policy in serving readers—disinterested readers don't renew. Also, cut-price and high-pressure subscription drives usually seduce a lot of subscribers who are far from avid readers—and when the subscription expires they do not renew. Typically, only about 20% of new subscribers who were attracted to a magazine by cut prices ever renew at the regular price. In contrast, 40% of those who subscribe at the full price do renew, and the percentage rises to 60% for readers who subscribe for a third time.

Advertisers are fully aware that renewal percentages indicate the attention subscribers actually give to a magazine and hence its value as an advertising medium. Moreover, advertisers prefer a magazine with a consistent type of reader with a predictable response to an advertising message. Even when a magazine succeeds through extra promotional efforts in finding new subscribers to replace those who fail to renew, the quality of this audience is uncertain. So a poor and declining renewal rate can be very serious indeed.

The "economics" of magazine publishing are a bit tricky, as the preceding discussion of circulation, advertising, variable expenses, cash flow, and renewals indicates. Even more delicate is a workable balance between economics and editorial mission. Creating a distinctive and popular service to readers requires empathy, imagination, and strong commitment to a particular way of aiding the selected audience. Subjective judgments about what is suitable are often made under severe time pressures. Understandably, the persons performing such work become emotionally involved. Meanwhile, business executives may have trouble keeping economic forces in line. Consequently, tensions between editorial staff and business executives are common.

The balancing of editorial goals and economic factors has been a recurring issue in the history of the *Saturday Review*.

GROWTH OF SATURDAY REVIEW, 1924-1971

The editorial mission

In 1924 Henry Seidel Canby, Professor of American Literature at Yale, along with Christopher Morley and a few other associates, launched a weekly *Saturday Review of Literature*. Its start coincided with the birth of *Time* under the guidance of Henry Luce, and for a brief period the two fledgling publications shared a single business office. The *Saturday Review* soon won respect for its literary criticism, but it appealed to only a narrow circle of subscribers. By 1940, when 25-year-old Norman Cousins joined the staff, it had a circulation of only 14,000.

From the start the *Saturday Review* was actively concerned with the current world of ideas. Its reviews of poetry, history, biography, novels, music, and the like were primarily concerned with how these new books expressed new thrusts. Instead of academic, scholarly criticism—looking backward—the editors were concerned with social values of the day. As the United States passed through periods of prosperity and deep depression, the prevailing outlook on life shifted and the *Saturday Review* became a forum where new directions of thought were identified and analyzed.

Within two years after joining the staff, Norman Cousins became the full-time editor of the *Saturday Review*; and for the next three decades he strongly influenced its scope and editorial mission. While continuing strong emphasis on book reviews, Cousins added weekly columnists and feature writers whose comments on the current world of ideas appealed to a growing group of sophisticated readers. Cousins, who is an articulate liberal, provided a series of editorials that related the magazine directly to current political affairs. For example, he pioneered in discussing the implications of atomic energy, possible bans on nuclear testing, cigarette advertising, and protection of the natural environment. Discussions of U.S. education and of new developments in science were singled out as recurring supplements. A continuing theme throughout the magazine was freedom of intellectual inquiry.

With such a broad coverage, the *Saturday Review* obviously appealed to readers who have general interests. They are sophisticated individuals who lack time to pursue in depth all of the subjects that intrigue them. And the *Saturday Review* helped them keep abreast of developments in science, politics, literature, performing arts, and social change. Some critics contend that the information was inevitably superficial, but no one challenges its sophistication. By 1971 the circulation of the magazine, almost all mail subscribers, had risen to 660,000. The magazine was clearly an influential force in literary and intellectual fields.

Throughout its history the *Saturday Review* was more interested in content than showmanship. It prided itself on clear exposition with meaty, forceful content rather than on sensational journalism or cluttered wording. In recent years the *Saturday Review* used a restrained touch of color and occasional cartoons, but it remained conventional in size and layout. Unlike *Life* and *Look* it did not try to substitute photographs for written copy—nor has it gone in for four-color reproductions. Only its covers and some color advertisements are printed on heavy slick paper. As a result, the *Media Industry Newsletter* commented in July, 1971, that "the publication needs a facelift. It's drab."

The editor

As with entrepreneurs in economic theory, editors of magazines and the enterprise they direct are often closely intertwined. This clearly applies to Norman Cousins and the *Saturday Review*.

Norman Cousins has spent all of his adult life in the magazine division of the publishing industry. Born in New Jersey in 1915, he was a frail child and spent his eleventh year in a sanitarium recovering from what was believed to be tuberculosis. However, as an adult he appears to have limitless energy and optimism. From 1935 to 1940 he was Literary and Managing Editor of the magazine *Current History,* and from there he went to the *Saturday Review*.

In addition to his work on the magazine, Cousins is author or editor of several books, including: *Dr. Schweitzer of Lambarene* and *Talks with Nehru*. He serves as honorary President of the United World Federalists and is Co-Chairman of the National Committee for a Sane Nuclear Policy.

Active in various political affairs, on one occasion Cousins personally negotiated with Khrushchev for the release of Cardinal Slipyj, Archbishop of the Ukranian Rite

Orthodox Church, who had been interned in a Soviet prison for 17 years. He was a close advisor to President John Kennedy, and a probable appointment to a government post was interrupted by Kennedy's assassination. He continues to be an active and respected advisor on public affairs.

For fourteen months during the period when McCall Corporation owned *Saturday Review,* Cousins served as a corporate vice-president. In addition to the *Saturday Review,* he was in charge of the ailing *McCall's* magazine. The difficulties of that magazine did not improve, however, and he returned to full-time editing of the *Saturday Review.* His only other major publishing venture has been with *World,* which is described later in the case.

Ownership and financial control

During its early years the *Saturday Review of Literature* was perpetually in financial trouble. It was kept alive only through the generosity of Thomas L. Lamont, Chairman of J. P. Morgan & Company, and of Harry Sherman, founder of the Book-of-the-Month Club. In the middle '30s ownership was acquired by the world-famous oil geologist, E. L. DeGolyer, who was an enthusiastic supporter and financial backer of the magazine for another 20 years.

Shortly before his death in 1956, DeGolyer turned over ownership of the magazine to Cousins. Cousins kept 51% of the stock and distributed the rest to key members of the staff. This made Cousins both editor and majority stockholder.

Although the magazine was growing in circulation, it was still struggling financially. To tap greater financial resources, Cousins and his associates sold out to the McCall Corporation in 1961. The transfer of ownership was accomplished by an exchange of stock, the *Saturday Review* group receiving McCall's stock then worth approximately $3 million.

The new owners were anxious to keep Cousins at the helm. They gave him a 10-year contract and complete editorial freedom. In most respects this appeared to be a wise decision because the *Saturday Review* more than doubled its circulation during the 1960's. With the increase in circulation to 660,000 in 1971, advertising revenues increased to $5½ million annually. The reasons for the increase in the *Saturday Review* circulation during a period when general readership of magazines was declining are complex. Possibly the *Saturday Review* picked up some of the cast-off readers of *Saturday Evening Post, Look,* and *Life,* although the nature of the magazines was quite different. More important, there was a growing sympathy toward the editorial viewpoint of the *Saturday Review* and a larger number of people wanting intellectual stimulation. In other words, the *Saturday Review* grew not only because it changed but more because its audience changed.

The shifts in ownership from DeGolyer to Cousins and associates to McCall Corporation had minor effect on the editorial policy of the *Saturday Review.* Throughout, Cousins was the man the owners relied upon to direct the destinies of the magazine.

An ownership change that occurred in 1971 did drastically affect the magazine. The merger boom of the 1960's led to the inclusion of McCall Corporation in the Norton Simon, Inc. conglomerate. And since this new grandparent found the modest profits of the *Saturday Review* unimpressive, it welcomed an opportunity to sell the magazine to a new company organized by Nicholas H. Charney and John J. Veronis. As explained in the next section, these gentlemen saw a great future for the *Saturday Review*—a future, however, that required substantial modification in the objectives and the policies that had prevailed for the preceding three decades.

SATURDAY REVIEW UNDER MODERN MANAGEMENT

The sale of the *Saturday Review* by McCall Corporation to a newly formed company called Saturday Review Industries signaled a major change in financial and editorial policies. To understand the new approach to the management of the *Saturday Review* we need a brief look at the background of the two active executives in Saturday Review Industries—Nicholas H. Charney and John J. Veronis.

Track record of new managers

Before Nick Charney finished his Ph.D. dissertation on "The Effect of Scopolamine on Rats"—at the University of Chicago—he had developed a concept for a popular magazine about psychology. Unable to interest major publishers in the new idea, Charney scraped together $40,000 from friends and relatives and launched the venture himself. Then 25 years of age and with no experience in editing or publishing anything, he moved boldly to attract subscribers. From his kitchen table he mailed a description of the yet-to-be-born magazine to 30,000 members of the American Psychological Association, offering them a 3-year charter subscription for $15. This mailing had a remarkable return of 19.2% and about $80,000 in cash. Using the advance payment from the first subscribers for further mailings, Charney had almost 50,000 subscribers for *Psychology Today* before the first issue went to press. The magazine made full use of the latest printing techniques with careful attention to modern graphics, color, and quality reproduction.

The initial success of *Psychology Today* naturally required additional inputs of working capital, and at this stage John Veronis joined Charney as a full partner. Veronis already had a remarkable record in magazine publishing. After selling advertising for several magazines, he became, at the age of 26, part of the management of *American Home*. During this period he was also studying for his MBA at New York University. *American Home* was acquired by Curtis Publishing Company and Veronis had a rapid rise through the prestigious but ailing Curtis Magazine Division. So rapid was his rise that veteran publishers whom he passed along the way nicknamed him "Hungry John." A management shake-up at Curtis left Veronis looking for a job, and he spent the next couple of years with another publisher developing ways to capitalize on the information revolution and futuristic concepts such as McLuhan's "The Media Is the Message."

Charney and Veronis immediately set about to take full advantage of *Psychology Today's* successful birth. They pursued two related paths: (1) They continued the aggressive promotion of subscriptions to the magazine, and (2) they organized the Psychology Today Book Club for the purpose of direct-mail sales. The Book Club offers its members college texts, laboratory kits, educational films, posters, games, and an array of other items related to psychology. The magazine's subscribers are a highly selected market for special-interest merchandise.

Both the magazine and the associated book club prospered. To provide for a substantial need for working capital, Charney and Veronis set up a corporation called Communications/Research/Machines, Inc. (CRM). In a 3-year period they obtained $6 million from private investors but kept more than half of the ownership for themselves and the inside managers.

About five years after Charney put out his first mailing for *Psychology Today*, CRM was sold to Boise Cascade Company, which was then busily converting itself from a lumber and paper concern into a conglomerate. By that time CRM had annual sales of about $10 million. Boise Cascade put up the equivalent of $21 million, $5 million cash for additional working capital and $16 million in an exchange of its stock for the CRM equity. Charney and Veronis went to Boise Cascade with the deal.

The CRM division of Boise Cascade not only pushed *Psychology Today* and its Book Club (by this time the magazine's circulation was 600,000), they also sought additional magazines on which to apply their success formula. *Intellectual Digest*, with a circulation of 25,000, was acquired, redesigned, and aggressively promoted with a prompt increase in circulation to 200,000. An earlier venture, *Careers Today,* misfired and accumulated a $2½ million dollar loss before being discontinued.

In their search for new prospects, Charney and Veronis discovered that *Saturday Review* could be purchased. They studied this possibility carefully; but before the acquisition could be completed, Boise Cascade ran into financial stringency. Charney and Veronis were so enthusiastic about the prospects of revitalizing *Saturday Review*, however, that they resigned from Boise Cascade to take advantage of the opportunity. They attracted several other private investors, organized Saturday Review Industries, and purchased *Saturday Review* for a reported $5½ million dollars in cash. The McCall Trade Book Company came with the purchase. And so while still very young, Charney (30) and Veronis (42) brought substantial experience in magazine publishing along with their newly acquired ownership control of the *Saturday Review*.

Plans for modernizing the Saturday Review

Application of the techniques Charney and Veronis had already successfully used with *Psychology Today* and *Intellectual Digest* promised a substantial change in the financial results of the *Saturday Review*. Opportunities for financial improvement were not hard to find. According to Veronis, the magazine was underpriced. Subscribers were paying only 11.6 cents per copy, whereas basic printing and distribution costs were about 15 cents a copy. Thus the distribution of over 34 million copies per year netted a circulation loss of an estimated $1,170,000. Veronis figured the total overhead (editorial, freelance and art fees, selling of advertising, office expense, etc.) at about $4 million per year. So the overhead and the circulation deficit almost wiped out the advertising income of $5½ million.

In such a situation, a "modest" program would have been to raise the subscription price to 15 cents per copy, give the magazine a face-lifting, and launch a million dollar promotion campaign that Veronis believed would easily raise the number of subscribers to 750,000 and, on the basis of this 14% increase in circulation, could increase the advertising revenue at least 9% to $6 million per year. Under this plan the million dollar promotional investment in the first year could be recouped in the second year while subscriptions at the old cheap rate were running out, and by the third year a $2 million operating profit would be realized from the magazine alone. To this would be added profits from a newly organized book club.

The new management, however, did not adopt the first acceptable alternative that presented itself. Within a few months Charney and Veronis had developed a much more imaginative program for the *Saturday Review*. It embodied four major thrusts.

First, the weekly magazine was changed to a family of four monthlies. In successive weeks the *Saturday Review* would deal with (a) arts, (b) education, (c) society, and (d) science. However, binding these four monthlies together would be a regular weekly supplement with columnists and other general features of the old *Saturday Review*. Charney, in his second editorial, described the new program for readers as follows:

* * *

I have mentioned that this evolution of the expanded special-interest supplements is a logical editorial extension of the direction in which *Saturday Review* was already going. In fact, I believe it is also a necessary change. As we human beings continue to stride forward into tomorrow, it is becoming impossible for a single, general-format magazine to keep up with all that is taking place around us. There is too much happening at once. There are too many areas of innovation, experimentation, discovery, and performance to keep abreast of.

By concentrating SR's efforts on four critical, separate, and discrete areas of social concern today, more in-depth reporting and reflective writing can be offered in each area. . . .

* * *

. . . in *Saturday Review of the Arts*, whatever one's particular pursuits within the broad range of the cultural field, a reader should be able easily to find what interests him or her most in regular departments devoted to *Art, Music, Film, Communications, Theater, Photography, Design,* and *Architecture.* While these departments will contain critical reviews, they will also explore the arts in whatever ways yield the most provocative insights and understanding. . . .

* * *

. . . Eventually, *Education,* in addition to its three or four major articles in the field of education, will regularly cover events, research, problems, ideas, and experiments in the areas of *Early Childhood, School-Age Children, Young Adults, Continuing Education, Educational Policy,* and *Educational Materials.*

In *Saturday Review of the Society,* present thinking is to consistently cover the broad areas of *National Politics, Cities and States, Law and the Courts, Government Agencies, Business, Labor,* and *Consumers.* In *Science,* departments will be devoted monthly to issues and developments in *Health and Medicine, Environment, Physical Science, Life Science, Social Science,* and *Applied Science.*

In all of the *Reviews,* the departments will be in addition to, not in the place of, several key articles in the supplement's field. And alongside the supplements themselves, most of those general features of SR that have long made the magazine entertaining and provocative reading will continue.

In the *Reviews* we will also endeavor to put our resources, our access to information, to work for our readers. A monthly feature, "Saturday Review Recommends" in the issue devoted to the arts, will present a guide to films, theater, books, art exhibits, and dance compiled by respected critics in each of the areas. *Saturday Review of Education* will eventually include a regular feature, "Guide to Schools," which will note key data on schools: private and special education schools, graduate schools, and daycare centers.

The *Saturday Review of Science* will carry a regular annotated bibliography that will augment the articles contained in each issue; *Saturday Review of the Society* will soon feature a column providing information on where and how to take effective action on issues raised in the magazine.

* * *

The second major change dealt with the subscription price. *Each* of the monthly *Reviews* was to have an annual subscription price of $12. However, during the introductory period the price was to be a special rate of $6 per annum. In other words, if subscribers elected to receive all four of the new *Reviews*—that is, a publication each week—they would pay $24 a year. This price compared with $6 a year that the old *Saturday Review* a short time before charged for its weekly publication. Actually, Charney and Veronis did not expect many subscribers to opt for all four *Reviews*; nevertheless, the new subscription cost per copy would be quadrupled. Veronis pointed out that many monthlies charged substantially more than the *Saturday Review* introductory rates and that a market test showed that readers were ready to support a magazine that served their needs.

The third major thrust involved large-scale mailings to build circulation. This promotional effort was based on extensive market research. Veronis has stated that "Predicting reader interest has reached the status of a science in magazine publishing." To guide its promotion effort, the new management selected a random sample of a million names out of a universe of 18 million. The total sample was then divided into a hundred groups of 10,000 names each. Then a different mail package was sent to each subgroup. Various combinations of names and content for each of the four magazines were tested.

The market test was not just a polling of attitudes; new orders were sought. Veronis noted that "The results are really predicted on orders received for these magazines, not merely an interest reaction to them."

Based on this extensive market test program, millions of direct-mail solicitations were made. A major effort at the end of the year involved a 17-million piece mailing that cost about $4½ million. The target for this massive effort was a return of 3% new subscriptions. This would have increased the number of subscribers for each of the four magazines by over 125,000.

A fourth major change introduced by Charney and Veronis, directly transplanted from their experience with *Psychology Today*, was the introduction of book clubs. "We don't consider the reader," Veronis explained, "as a twelve dollar a year subscriber to a magazine but as a potential hundred dollar a year customer in the magazine's field of interest for books, records, games, posters, video, cassettes, conferences, school courses, and other products and services." A separate club was established for each of the four magazines, but major effort to develop each of these was deferred until past subscribers to the *Saturday Review* could sort themselves out into the new fourfold-interest division and until new subscribers could be obtained. Profits from this side of the venture were projected as increasing sources of income in the third, fourth, and fifth years of the 5-year program.

The development of this fourfold program naturally produced some other changes. One, which Charney and Veronis would have preferred to avoid, was the resignation of Norman Cousins. They urged Cousins to accept a position as Chairman of the Editorial Board and as a writer for the different magazines. Cousins politely but firmly turned the offer down. In an editorial explaining his resignation, Cousins wrote:

* * *

The differences between us are not over the need for change. SR has been the product of change ever since it began as a book-review periodical almost half a century ago. The present differences are over the kind of change that is planned. John and Nick may be successful in what they intend to do. They may well be right in their basic premises. I can only say that I cannot be comfortable with those premises. Nor can I justify to myself or anyone else the use of my name to advance a program I cannot support.

* * *

. . . The one thing I have learned about editing over the years is that you have to edit and publish out of your own tastes, enthusiasms, and concerns, and not out of notions of guesswork about what other people might like to read. . . .

* * *

In particular, Cousins objected "strongly to the commercial use of the *Saturday Review* subscription list for purposes that have nothing to do with the magazine."

Charney, who replaced Cousins as Editor, felt that an East Coast provincialism might be avoided by moving out of New York City. So the entire editorial staff was transferred to a newly decorated building in San Francisco—at a cost of $500,000. Moreover, to give the four magazines the kind of editorial effort that the new program implied and to provide backup strength in the office operations, the size of the staff was doubled—a $4 million increase in annual expense.

All of this expansion should be viewed in light of the future that Charney and Veronis saw for Saturday Review Industries. While recognizing the uncertainties of any 5-year projection "especially when new products and a major business expansion are involved," the publicly stated target was $85 million gross revenues in the fifth year.

Too much, too soon

The results of this great effort to change the *Saturday Review* did not come up to expectations. New subscriptions received from the massive mailing were little more than 1% instead of the hoped-for 3%. This meant that the cost of each new subscription was about $25, and the cash inflow failed by a wide margin to cover the promotional expense. Renewals by old *Saturday Review* subscribers started to drop as the fanfare for the new look increased.

The trade press in trying to explain this poor showing commented on the difficulty of producing "specialized magazines for generalists and generalized magazines for specialists." The magazines were promoted before each had an opportunity to develop a clear-cut character. The National Editor of the *Village Voice* observed: "The new *Saturday Review* never quite lost the reek of packaging. And for all the charts and formulas, *Saturday Review* was not the scientific publishing operation it professed to be. . . . Despite the computer-era trappings, financial bungling was legion. *Saturday Review's* rate base was raised prematurely; the 17-million piece promotional mailing last December was an all-or-nothing gamble; the move West was a foolish extravagance. But ultimately, *Saturday Review* died because the public didn't buy it. The public wouldn't buy it because, as several frustrated editors remarked, it never found its editorial soul."[4]

Understandably for a magazine in transition, advertisers did not rush to buy space. During the first full year of the new program, advertising pages declined from 1,575 to 1,408. With a one-time black and white page rate of $5,600 and a color page rate of $7,000, this decline was serious.[5]

The book clubs were losing $10,000 per week, and by competing with some potential advertisers they were beginning to hurt advertising revenue.

---

[4] Bob Kuttner, *Folio,* July, 1973.

[5] These are the gross rates subject to 15% discount for advertising agencies and 2% discount for cash; also there is substantial variation for location in the magazine and for multiple insertions.

The strain of expansion and promotion was too much. Twice the managers of Saturday Review Industries had to return to their financial backers for more capital. A total of $16 million, including the original investment, had been used up—and the end was not in sight. Less than two years after the newly formed company bought *Saturday Review* from the McCall Corporation, it filed for bankruptcy.

COUSINS' NEW WORLD

Fresh start on a well-worn track

Seven months after Norman Cousins resigned from the *Saturday Review* he was back in the magazine business with a brand new publication called *World*. This remarkably short incubation period was possible only because of the contacts, traditions, and goodwill Cousins had built up over three decades as Editor of the *Saturday Review*. Whereas Charney and Veronis took their business experience with *Psychology Today* and applied it to a new editorial mission, Cousins took his editorial bent and applied it to a new business organization.

The editorial aim of *World* has been described by Cousins in the following letter sent to former subscribers of the *Saturday Review*:

> My colleagues and I are pleased to announce that we are starting a new magazine later this Spring. It will be called *World* and will be published every two weeks.
>
> Ever since I resigned from the *Saturday Review* several months ago, I have been thinking and dreaming about starting an independent journal devoted to ideas, books, the creative arts, and the human condition. The principal point of difference between this magazine and existing magazines is that we will attempt to report on a world level. For example, instead of writing about important books published just in the United States, we intend to write about important books published throughout the world. Naturally, we will attempt to be highly selective. We will make no effort at detailed coverage; such a task is already being done in various places. What we will attempt to do is to view the world as a composite creative arena.
>
> We will also give major attention to an emerging new concept—the concept of planetary planning. We will write about the human condition at a time when the ability of human intelligence to meet its problems is being tested as never before. Our hope is to see the world as the astronauts saw it—a beautiful wet blue ball possessing millions of delicately balanced factors that make life possible. Our dominant editorial concern, then, is the proper care of the human habitat—protecting it against war, environmental poisoning, overcrowding, or any of the things that indignify and humiliate human beings.
>
> In this connection, we are pleased to announce that U Thant, former Secretary-General of the United Nations, and Buckminster Fuller, architect, poet, and philosopher, are joining our staff.
>
> We will also give major attention to what we believe will be one of the most compelling issues in the years ahead—the waste of human resources, far more costly than the waste of physical resources.
>
> There is no point in talking about conservation of land unless we also talk about conservation of life.
>
> I think I have said enough to indicate that the new magazine will direct its central editorial energies both to the enjoyment of creative living and to the pursuit of vital ideas. It is an error, however, to try to say too much about a magazine in advance of publication. A magazine has to describe itself, issue by issue. . . .

* * *

Some specifics: We have decided against cut-rate subscriptions. Most of the ills of the magazine business, we believe, are traceable to the highly competitive practice of cut-rate subscriptions. On a new magazine, the subscription list generally consists almost entirely of cut-rate subscriptions. By thus starting out on an unsound level, new magazines find it difficult ever to get squared away on a healthy basis.

Our full-term rates are $12 for one year; $20 for two years; $25 for three years. The reason we are able to make such a sharp reduction in the three-year rate is that substantial savings can be effected in processing costs.

* * *

In inviting you to join us in what we hope will be an exciting adventure in ideas, we realize we are asking you to take a chance on us. We have high hopes of justifying that confidence.

Sincerely,

/s/ Norman Cousins

Other publicity used the caption "WORLD: A Review of Ideas, Creative Arts and the Human Condition." Thus, the subjects covered were similar to those treated under Cousins' direction in the old *Saturday Review*, but in the new publication the scope was worldwide. A moral tone was reintroduced—to wit: "The greatest event in our lifetime is that the whole of humanity is now compressed within a single arena. The central question in that arena is whether the world will become a community or a wasteland, a single habitat or a single battlefield. More and more, the choice for the world's people is between becoming world warriors or world citizens."

To launch *World,* Cousins achieved a remarkable editorial transplant, bringing over more than a dozen *Saturday Review* writers and editors to the new magazine and enlisting two of his favorite contributors, U Thant and Buckminster Fuller, to write regularly. These familiar names enabled Cousins to appeal to the loyalty of his previous readers.

While the editorial mission had a familiar cast, the subscription price reflected a new view on how much of the total cost subscribers might be willing to bear. Compared with 1970, the annual rate was doubled for half as many copies. Even those subscribers who opted for the 3-year bargain were paying 32 cents a copy—compared with 11.6 cents in 1970. This change is particularly important to a new venture since subscribers will be paying the full incremental costs as circulation expands.

Many of the initial subscribers to *World* were obtained by a telephone campaign. Originally intended to provide in-depth information about reactions to the proposed magazine, the response was so phenomenal that the technique was converted into a subscription drive. A tape-recorded telephone solicitation by Cousins himself is followed up by an operator who engages in two-way conversation. Of former *Saturday Review* subscribers who were reached, 37% agreed to take the new magazine. The response was not nearly so good for nonreaders, but this expensive form of solicitation did build up the advance subscription list.

In addition to the telephone campaign, newspaper ads and letters such as that reproduced above were used. The total result was about 100,000 paid subscriptions when the first issue came off the press. Also surprising was the fact that over two thirds of the subscribers to the yet-to-be-born magazine opted for the $25 three-year subscription. This was indeed an impressive showing in face of the industry trends for general reader magazines prevailing at the time.

Press reviews of the first issue of *World* were by no means unanimous in their praise. *Newsweek* said, "The overall tone is ponderous." Reacting to Cleveland Amory's attempt at breezy humor, *Newsweek* quotes Amory, "Starting a new column is never easy" and observes that Amory then proceeds to prove his point conclusively.

Time magazine said that "Volume One, Number One is dominated by wordy pieces that reflect the stodginess of the old *Saturday Review*. . . . Cleveland Amory and Goodman Ace grind out their stale *Saturday Review* humor." *Time* does find kind words to say about the critical sections on books, ballet, and music and warmly endorses several of the articles. "But these editorial assets seem outweighed by the clinkers."

Despite this lack of enthusiasm by fellow journalists, *World* found many readers who liked its editorial mission and perhaps its style. By the end of its first year, paid subscriptions had risen to 178,000. Advertisers were learning to respect the selective, high-income audience reached by *World* and were also impressed with the relatively low advertising rates—$1,700 for a one-time black and white page and $2,340 for a four-color page. Prospects for break-even operations by the end of the second year were good.

Should the Saturday Review be salvaged?

When financial quicksand made continuation of the Charney-Veronis program for the *Saturday Review* impossible, they set upon a search for someone who might buy their magazines. The search was continued by the Receiver after the company went into bankruptcy. No one wanted to buy the *Saturday Review* as a going concern. Only Norman Cousins showed any substantial interest, and he was naturally cautious and choosy about what he might buy.

After long discussions about the possibilities of merging *World* and Saturday Review Industries, no feasible solution was found. The total unpaid bills for printing, paper, back salaries, and the like was at least $5 million. In addition, the company had substantial future commitments for both printing and paper. As a consequence, the people representing *World* concluded that the only thing they should even consider buying were two assets—the name of the magazine and the subscription list.

Negotiation for the purchase of these two assets has been prolonged. At the time of this present case, it appears that *World* could purchase, if it chooses to do so, the name—*Saturday Review*—all editorial and art inventory, and the subscription list under the following terms:

(a) *World* to acquire name "*Saturday Review*."
(b) *World* to acquire subscription list (all subscription and circulation records, and exclusive right to solicit continuation) for all four of the new *Saturday Reviews*.
(c) *World* to pay Saturday Review Industries $500,000 for above.
(d) *World* agrees to send magazines to prepaid *Saturday Review* subscribers for the remainder of their contracts.
(e) *World* and Saturday Review Industries to split 50-50 all future cash receipts from existing *Saturday Review* subscription contracts.
(f) Except for (d) and (e) above, *World* to assume none of the *Saturday Review* obligations nor any of its claims on accounts receivable.

The value of such an arrangement to World is, of course, difficult to estimate. The remaining goodwill attached to the *Saturday Review* name is immeasurable. Moreover, Cousins has demonstrated considerable success in wooing his former *Saturday Review* customers and the discontinuance of the new *Saturday Review* magazine should make recovery of these subscribers easier.

Nevertheless, some rough estimates of the results that might arise if *World* takes over both the name and the subscription lists from *Saturday Review* are possible. Here is one calculation:

Purchase price .... $ 500,000

Cost of servicing *Saturday Review* contracts to their expiration;
converting present *Saturday Review* subscribers to *World* at
renewal time; and other absorption costs 1,500,000
        Total *additional* outlay $2,000,000

Prospective benefits:

Of 750,000 present *Saturday Review* subscribers, securing renewal from 350,000 (mostly carry-overs from earlier Cousins editorship). Assumes that 400,000 subscribers primarily interested in single-purpose magazine would not renew. This addition of 350,000 subscribers plus existing 180,000 *World* subscribers would create new base of 530,000 for advertising rates. This would justify 200% increase—from $1,700 to $5,100 for single-insertion black and white page, and from $2,340 to $7,000 for four-color page.

After readjustment, gross revenue might become:
Circulation (530,000 × average annual price of $9.25) .... = $5,000,000 ±
Advertising (equivalent of 30 black & white pages per issue;
  discounts equal 1/6 of $5,100; so, 30 × 25 × $4,250) . . . = 3,000,000 ±
      Possible total gross revenue $8,000,000

Expenses at present prices:
Printing & distribution @ 16¢ per copy $2,200,000
Editorial $1,000,000
Advertising 1,000,000
Promotion, general and administrative 2,000,000   4,000,000
                                          $6,200,000
      Profit before tax $1,800,000

These estimates are subject to all sorts of adjustments based on judgment. For instance, if only 180,000 instead of 350,000 *Saturday Review* subscribers can be retained, and the total circulation becomes 360,000—the resulting one-third cut in circulation and advertising revenue and in printing and distribution costs would produce a break-even situation. If, in addition, advertising is the equivalent of 20 pages instead of 30 pages per issue, a serious loss would arise. Inflation and other external forces are likely to increase expenses faster than revenue.

The proposed acquisition of *Saturday Review* assets has major implications for the financing of *World*. Now, Cousins and his management associates have over 50% of the stockholder votes. When *World* was launched, Cousins had to secure financial backing, but because of his experiences with outside owners he naturally wished to retain control of the new venture. This was accomplished by what in effect is participating preferred stock that enables investors to share in profits on the basis of their relative contributions of capital while concentrating the voting rights in a smaller class of common stock.

The purchase of the name and the subscriber lists from *Saturday Review* together with the costs of absorbing the subscribers (estimated at $2,000,000 in the above table) would approximately double the capital investment needed by *World*. Cousins has located private investors who are willing to put up the money, but the conditions surrounding the investment remain sticky. For instance, one prospective investor would be glad to leave Cousins with complete *editorial* control but wants to combine the business activities with those of two or three other publishing ventures. Two other potential investors hold the conventional view that votes should be proportionate to investment. One of these prospects has suggested ''the normal stockholder position coupled with a five-year contract assuring management the independence of action we all agree is desirable.'' The present investors are prepared to increase their holding of ''preferred stock'' by another half million provided the *Saturday Review* purchase is made and a satisfactory plan for the total capital needs is developed. Still other wealthy individuals have expressed interest in the venture, although specific arrangements have not been discussed with them.

Clearly, the potential *Saturday Review* purchase would require substantial realignment in the financial structure of *World*. Moreover, a reassessment of the manner and the direction of the business operations would be in order, and new investors might be concerned with the long-run viability of editorial policies.

SUMMARY QUESTIONS

1. Assuming that equity financing can be obtained if needed, what do you recommend that *World* do about acquiring assets of Saturday Review Industries? If you propose acquiring the name and/or subscription lists, outline a program for *World* to fully utilize these new assets.
2. Assuming that you are invited to join a new group of investors in *World*, under what conditions or stipulations would you put up your money for acquisition of Saturday Review Industries assets?

"In five years I look forward to a public offering of our stock. This should take place when total sales for the company have reached $40 million, and I expect that to occur after we have acquired another company with sales of about $8 million. The principal problem we have now in working toward this is shaking down the organization so that it functions effectively both in making decisions and in carrying out operations. Not too long ago we switched from a formal organization that was basically structured by plants and products to one organized by departments. It seems to me that we have traded an arrangement in which the plant groups competed with one another, would not refer business to one another and, too often, said 'to hell with those guys' to a setup in which the department managers won't make decisions, won't cooperate across department lines, and have lost a sense of the whole company. This doesn't mean that everything is wrong with the firm. We are selling wire, operating the plants, adding new equipment, developing products, and making a little money. We have a problem, not a crisis."

John B. Beacon, the president, thus describes the principal concerns that he has about his family-owned wire manufacturing company.

Waukegan Wire Company, with its headquarters and main plant in North Chicago, Illinois, sells wire drawn from copper rod (which it buys from Phelps Dodge Corporation, American Smelting & Refining Company, Rome Cable Company, Southwire, Inc., and other copper producers) to industrial buyers who use the wire in manufacturing computers, electric motors, aircraft ignition and power cable, electric blankets, musical instruments, and many other products.

The plants of Waukegan Wire are located in North Chicago, Illinois; Beacon, New York; and Piedmont, South Carolina. In addition, the company has warehouses in Boston and Los Angeles to support its sales effort in New England and on the Pacific Coast.

Current financial data about the company are presented in Exhibits 1, 2, and 3 on pages 648 and 649.

THE INDUSTRY

Data from the Bureau of the Census and the Business and Defense Services Administration of the U.S. Department of Commerce indicate that there are 290 plants engaged in the production of copper wire and cable (more than one plant may be owned by one company). Major producing areas are New England and the Middle Atlantic states. The total value of shipments for the year just ending is close to $3.5 billion, which is about 15% above the previous year. Annual growth rates over the past ten years have been: value of shipments, 9.5%; employment, 3%. Exports are 1.5% of total shipments and imports are 0.5%.

Exhibit 1

Waukegan Wire Company
Selected Financial Data
(000's omitted)

	Total Profits	Total Sales	Conductor Sales	Magnet Wire Sales	Alloy and Mechanical Wire Sales
Current Year	$ 58	$18,055	$ 7,300	$ 8,205	$2,550
Last Year	85	17,000	6,960	7,610	2,430
Preceding Year	680	22,900	6,450	14,170	2,280
			Waukegan Plant [1]	Beacon Plant [2]	Piedmont Plant [2]
" "	750	27,200	14,300	7,100	5,800
" "	720	22,000	11,530	5,800	4,670
					Boston Plant [3]
" "	400	16,150	6,980	5,100	4,070
" "	225	14,800	6,700	4,500	3,600
" "	150	13,500	6,700	3,920	2,880
" "	40	10,450	6,000	2,900	1,550
" "	120	11,800	5,830	3,850	2,120

[1] Conductors, alloy and mechanical wires, and some magnet wire.
[2] Magnet wires.
[3] Boston plant and equipment was sold.

Exhibit 2

Waukegan Wire Company
Profit and Loss Statement
Current Year (Twelve Months)

Net Sales Billed............................	$18,055,000
Transportation Out and Other Deductions......	255,000
Net Sales.................................	$17,800,000
Cost of Sales.............................	14,820,000
Gross Profit..............................	$ 2,980,000
Selling, General, and Administrative Expenses................................	$ 2,512,000
Interest Expenses.........................	338,000
Provision for Profit-Sharing and Bonus........	11,000
Total Expense..................	$ 2,861,000
Income Before Taxes.......................	$ 119,000
Estimated Taxes...........................	61,000
Net Income...............................	$ 58,000

Exhibit 3
Waukegan Wire Company
Balance Sheet

	Previous Year	Current Year
Assets		
Cash.........,	$ 650,000	$ 600,000
Net Receivables.	2,700,000	2,950,000
Net Inventory.	2,800,000	3,178,000
Other Current Assets.	38,000	42,000
Total.	$ 6,188,000	$ 6,770,000
Fixed Assets—Net.	6,403,000	5,933,000
Other Assets.	40,000	30,000
Total Assets.	$12,631,000	$12,733,000
Liabilities and Stockholders' Equity		
Notes Payable.	$ 1,546,000	$ 1,380,000
Accounts Payable.	750,000[1]	800,000
Customer Deposits.	390,000	410,000
Accrued Taxes.	54,000	200,000
Other Current Liabilities.	240,000	230,000
Total Current Liabilities.	$ 2,980,000	$ 3,020,000
Long-Term Debt.	1,951,000	2,013,000
Stockholders' Equity.	7,700,000	7,700,000[2]
Total Liabilities and Stockholders' Equity.	$12,631,000	$12,733,000

[1] Almost all purchases are made from the major copper and nonferrous metal producers. Their terms are net cash 10 days. Buyers who do not pay on time have their allocations reduced by the amount of the delinquent order.

[2] Dividends paid in first half of current year amounted to $58,000.

Value of shipments in recent years are shown in the table at the top of the following page.

Per capita use of new copper wire and cable has risen 50% in the past decade.

Communication and signal wire and cable transmits weak signals over long distances. Its most important physical characteristic is a highly developed protective insulation that shields wires against each other as well as from outside interference.

Magnet wire is used in winding coils for electrical motors. Insulation varies from enamel to silk and asbestos. The wire has critical dimensional tolerances since the magnetic effect depends on the physical configuration of the coil. It also has to tolerate vibration; thus drawing and annealing techniques are important in making the wire to impart the correct resistance to breaking.

Building wire carries electrical power to lighting fixtures and appliances. Price and weight are the important characteristics.

Power cables carry high voltage to supply the light and power needs of commercial buildings and plants. Secondary cables (up to 600 volts) are insulated. Primary cables (the usual high-tension line) are bare. Very high voltage cables are insulated with oil-impregnated paper for cooling.

Value of Shipments
(in millions of dollars)

	Ten Years Ago	Five Years Ago	Preceding Year	Last Year	Present Year
Bare Wire and Cable	190	356	385	390	450
Magnet Wire	239	381	420	430	475
Communication Wire and Cable	489	755	862	830	1,050
Appliance Wire and Cord	84	125	150	160	175
Power Wire and Cable	199	297	407	420	460
Other Insulated Wire and Cable[1]	463	537	726	770	840
Total	1,664	2,451	2,950	3,000	3,450

[1] Includes marine wire and cable, aircraft, missile and automotive wire, and cable not included in bare wire category.

Bare wire (in addition to bare cable used for utility power lines) is sold by wiredrawing companies to firms that specialize in adding high-temperature or other critical insulating materials.

Industry shipments next year are estimated to be equal in pounds to the current year and 4% higher in dollar amount—with a 5% increase in communication wire and cable prices and a 3% increase in appliance wire and cord prices. Higher raw material prices will be the principal cause of these price increases.

In general, industry analysts not connected with any copper or wire and cable company see a bright future for the total industry over the next five years. Expected rises in communication (including telephone and telegraph equipment and wire) are seen to offer a potentially limitless market. Competition among metals is expected to intensify as aluminum becomes more prominent in power cable and in housing wire. However, copper wire will hold its own through expansion into new uses and new developments as research and development activities increase. Principal technological improvements will be the copper cladding of other metals—aluminum and steel—and the expansion of continuous casting to make smaller sections, thus by-passing the bar-rolling and rod-drawing equipment stage.

Analysts connected with the industry, including the presidents of several large wire and cable companies, generally see the outlook as being dominated by a "profit squeeze of classic dimensions." The two factors are widespread overcapacity in the industry and higher costs—especially for copper—that cannot always be passed on to customers because of competitive conditions. Materials—especially copper—are a very large proportion (approximately 65%) of all costs. Copper prices have exhibited a relatively rapid long-term upward trend.

Although none of this group doubts the existence of capacity levels well above market requirements, reliable statistics on capacity are hard to find. Producers are alleged to be reluctant to close down high-cost facilities or unprofitable product lines.

The "economic inevitability" of the replacement of copper power cable by aluminum cable and, eventually, sodium cable is generally accepted. Some believe that higher copper prices will force manufacturers of copper magnet wire to look elsewhere for basic materials. Aluminum now provides about 10% of the chief raw material for both magnet wire and building wire and is expected to make very rapid inroads in the latter field.

Those markets with bright futures (growth rates of 5% to 10% per year) are seen as utility power cable, communications wire and cable, and building wire and cable for distributing power within buildings. The highest annual growth rate of all is predicted for computing equipment—17% annually over the long haul. Space, operating temperature, flexibility, and connector requirements combine to make high-quality copper wire the only foreseeable material in uses in which wire is needed.

Recent actions by semi-integrated producers of insulated wire and cable include: the development of a miniature digital computer using integrated circuits and only three electric wires to operate all electrical and electrical-power circuits in automobiles; the development of machinery to squeeze wire out of a die rather than to pull it through (this reduces power, equipment, labor, and breakage costs); new plastic insulations for transportation and building wire; expansion into wholesale distribution through building warehouses or acquiring distributors; and packaging designed to attract and aid the do-it-yourself retail buyer of electrical cord and wire.

Sales growth over the past decade has been characteristic of the twenty largest wire and cable producers who now share about two thirds of the market among them. The increase in their sales has been the result of: acquisitions of other wire and cable producers; growth in the use of electrical wire; increased emphasis on effectiveness of insulating materials; forward integration into wholesale distribution; and forward integration into the marketing of cords, wire sets, and wires with connectors that can be directly used by the ultimate consumer with no further processing.

The large number of smaller firms in the industry have gained much less in total sales and have a shrinking share of the total market. The number tends to stay constant as firms enter and leave the industry yearly.

Selected ratios for the industry are given in the following table:

Selected Ratios—Last Year's Results
Copper Wire and Cable Manufacturers
Total Assets ($10,000,000 to $49,999,999)

Return on Shareholder's Equity	15.2%
Net Income to Sales	4.8
Current Ratio	2.5
Quick Ratio	1.2
Interest Expense (as percent of sales)	0.6
Engineering Expense (as percent of sales)	2.0
Total Debt to Net Worth	0.7
Inventory to Current Assets	51.0

MARKETING

Waukegan Wire Company has three product lines. The *conductors* are bare or plated wires sold to aerospace and electronics manufacturers for uses in which high-temperature, limited space, and reliability needs put a premium on the quality of the conductor. Waukegan sells some wires insulated with Teflon, polyester, or polyimide or plated with silver, gold, or nickel. Sizes range from 20 (0.0320 inches in diameter) to 56 (0.00049 inches in diameter). These wires are sold in single thicknesses or stranded into conductors. Items in this line are made by a limited number of small firms.

The *magnet wire line* is comprised of both bare and insulated wires sold as single wires or in strands over the size range from 20 to 56. The insulating material can be enamel, formvar, or polyurethane for low-temperature uses in RF coils, small motors, and solenoids, or polyurethane and nylon for uses in portable tools and small household appliances. Magnet wires have wide application in all electrical uses and, as a result, are manufactured by a large number of small and giant enterprises ranging from Western Electric and General Electric to small wire-drawing enterprises.

The *alloy and mechanical wire* product line includes wires supplied for electrical and nonelectrical purposes, with the electrical wires specially processed for high strength as well as high conductivity. A typical alloy wire is a base of cadmium chromium copper that may be supplied to the user bare or coated with silver or nickel. Manufacturers of alloy wires include fabricating subsidiaries of all the large copper companies, divisions of large electrical goods manufacturers, and semi-integrated wire and cable manufacturers such as Belden Manufacturing Company, General Cable Corporation, and Essex International, Inc. Other wires in the mechanical group are brush wires and brake-lining wires.

According to Norman Cortlandt, the marketing vice-president, sales volume has been a big problem for the company until recently (see Exhibit 1), but profitability is now the major issue. "We had high sales and good profits until a few years ago. Then a decline in sales to aerospace and aircraft companies together with increasing copper costs and the constant upward trend in wage costs hit profits real hard. We also lost some magnet wire sales—mainly because of a delivery problem. The first part of the current year was a real problem. There was just no way to get volume. But in recent months we have sold at a rate of $2.0 million per month.

"When I saw this sales increase coming along six months ago, I recommended a price increase of 3% on all magnet wire. Since customer inventories had been worked down, they had no alternative but to buy wire. I was sure that our competitors would follow, since their costs rise just like ours and they need the profits also.

"But John B. Beacon wouldn't buy the increase. He checked around with some friends in the industry, and they gave him a song-and-dance about their costs not increasing, about their having excess capacity, and about their believing that customer inventories were still relatively high. If we don't have the profits we should now, it is because we are throwing them away in low prices.

"For the overall success of this company we should strive to be the most technically sophisticated company in this business. About half of our managers understand this. We held a meeting recently to discuss and analyze company goals, and half of the department managers and vice-presidents at that meeting didn't even list technical competence when they talked about what we should aim for.

"As far as profitability is concerned, the thing that bothers me is that we do not have the proper information to make decisions about return on investment. That is, we can't decide clearly whether or not to stay in or to get out of any one product. Conductor wire in total may produce a satisfactory profit, but No. 1934, 3% silver, stranded copper is sold at below a 15% gross margin. It is the largest single item in the conductor group. Back when we had one man in charge of all sales and production out of one plant, he could have his own cost accountants and engineers figure out the costs and the margins for any item and price it for a profit. But now our system is too complicated. All our data goes to the Finance Department, and all they come out with is overall results (see Exhibits 9 and 10).

"Some expense categories have been shifted. Controlling warehouse expense is a new item for us. It is now $530,000 and it used to be charged to manufacturing. The reason for the shift is so that Sales can follow up on delivery promises to our customers. We now control the operation of the warehouses and of finished goods inventories. With this, we are in a better position to see that deliveries are made as the customers want. We can sell out of the inventories we have on hand as well as those items scheduled to be in finished inventory within the next month."

In explaining the outlook for conductor wires, Robert Sullivan, the product manager for conductors, said: "Our predictions for the conductor line are really based on a 10% increase over what we have been doing in the last half of the current year. After reviewing our major ultimate customers—the aircraft and computer builders who make up 85% to 90% of our sales—we saw the strong probability of this kind of increase. The major reason we are doing so well now is that we saw a need for 34- to 40-gauge nickel and silver-plated stranded wire for which there was not sufficient capacity in the industry. End-user contacts revealed this. We are now tooled up to make the wire. All we have to do is deliver it and the profits will roll in.

"My responsibilities are to supervise the sales work, to coordinate advertising for my products with the agency, to analyze costs and prices so as to recommend prices to the vice-president, to make sales forecasts of standard items, to determine the proper inventory levels for standard products in the warehouse, and to do product development work along with customer engineers and our product engineering manager for this line.

"I have two direct salesmen and several manufacturers' representatives. We sell to 30 key accounts and to 45 to 50 total accounts. When we have time left over, we call on our customers to give them advice about new products.

"My real problems are not in selling—we have good products that are easy to move—but in getting the right material into the plant and the products out of the plant. It seems to me that we are constantly out of materials. I find this whenever I am about ready to quote a big job.

"This firm does not make the return on investment it should. I see people in other divisions giving away the store. For example, if the price sheet carries a list price of $1 per pound, they will let 10 pounds go out for $10. We can't get out of the red with that kind of action. In this product line we have a minimum order size of $50.

"Also the year-end accounting reports and financial statements are overall and not by product divisions.

"In this line we stay away from adding more than the most basic of insulation because we don't want to compete with our customers. What we really sell is quality wire. In my view the keys to our success are our long-established positions with three of the big copper producers that allow us to buy their special brands and alloys and our skill in drawing the wire to small diameters—once we get the stuff in the plant, that is."

According to Frank Ulster, the product manager for magnet wire: "This is a big business with lots of potential. Annual sales volume for all magnet wire is about $600 million, of which about half is supplied by captive fabricators (for example, Western Electric to the Bell System and Anaconda to General Motors). We cannot produce squares, rectangles, or large sizes of cable or wire. Our products sell to producers of hundreds of electrical items from motors to electric wristwatches. Magnet wire is a basic product in the electronic age. Sales fluctuate with the general economy.

"Competitors are all the major copper companies, all the large wire and cable producers—such as Belden, Essex, and Simplex—and about four hundred small to medium-size wire-drawers.

"Our competitive edge is in the ability to draw fine wire, in our special packaging that limits breakage on takeoff by customers, and in our quality specifications that are higher than those of the National Electrical Manufacturers Association.

"This is a business with wild slumps and booms. We had a big copper strike some years ago. Before that, large customers had built up as much as a two-year inventory. This led to a runaway boom before the strike and a severe depression in this business after. Competition is noted for overreacting in building plant capacity. Our South Carolina plant, which went on-stream several years ago, ran at 50% of capacity for a year after it was completed and then had to sit idle for nine months at one point.

"Competition does not hesitate to cut prices to dump the volume it has with excess capacity."

John Hastings, the product manager for alloy and mechanical wires, said: "This line has a history of 'cheap and dirty'—especially in pricing. We are budgeting for 1,960,000 pounds of wire, which contrasts with our biggest year of 2,560,000 pounds of brake-lining wire and zinc-coated wire. But on the brake-lining wire we barely broke even on 850,000 pounds a year. We will replace those pounds with specialty wires.

"Heating cable makes up half of our volume. It goes into radiant heating units which are getting more popular for high-rise apartments—although this kind of heating is fast disappearing in individual homes with the central air-conditioning trend.

"Blanket wire and carpet wire (20% of sales) are large sellers, and we do well in this with our ability to make fine sizes.

"Brush wires are a $100 million market in total. The wires we make constitute 2% of this, and we sell about 25% of that with half going to Army Ordnance.

"The balance of our line is made of wire for music strings and of cold-heading wire. We once had 95% of the music string market, but now we are down to one of five suppliers since we can't draw to the tolerances desired. Cold-heading wire is sold to hundreds of customers to make pins and leads for transistors and all kinds of electrical connectors.

"The main areas of competition for all our lines are price and delivery. Quality and product design don't count. Customers will not live with an eight-to-ten week backlog. Most want two-week delivery, but they will hold still for four weeks."

MANUFACTURING

There are three plants. One, in Piedmont, South Carolina, was built six years ago and produces nothing but magnet wire. The location was chosen after an extensive search for a site at which there would be an ample supply of workers who could be expected to be hard-working and at which labor rates would be relatively low. These expectations have been realized. The State of South Carolina paid for training costs for new employees, and the town of Piedmont assisted with the construction costs. Product quality is satisfactory, production costs are below those in other plants, and Townsend Kingston, the plant manager, runs both a taut and a happy ship.

The second plant, in Beacon, New York, also produces magnet wire. It has, in the past, produced conductors and mechanical wires as well. Charles Morris, the acting plant manager for the past year, came to Beacon from the Waukegan plant at which he had been doing industrial engineering work for the stranding section.

The third plant, in North Chicago, Illinois, is known as the "Waukegan plant" and contains offices for the company as well as producing facilities. Peter Haverstraw, the third plant manager in four years, formerly managed a small division of Anaconda Wire and Cable Company that was sold. He sees the problem of the Waukegan plant as "getting out the goods."

"An incident at our recent NEMA[1] convention illustrates this. Under a sign with the company name on it, someone wrote 'When are you going to deliver the wire?" and signed it. Then someone else wrote 'Six months later' and signed it. This just symbolizes our delivery reputation."

Production scheduling has three ways that items can be ordered into production. The first is by customer order. Individual orders with the material, due date, and processing required are released to the foremen by the scheduling manager who reports to each plant manager. The second is by "special order." This is a call from the Sales Department—either because finished goods under its control in the warehouses are low or because of a special customer request—to the plant manager to speed a particular order ahead of the sequence to which it would otherwise be assigned. The third is the "bulk loading system." Based upon forecasts by the Sales Department, the scheduling manager in the plant puts through a large enough run of that item to take care of four weeks' sales. The items are packed as they come off the line and are inventoried as finished goods.

Since no one customer ever orders exactly a four-week run of any one item, individual orders are filled from the packed units available. When necessary, the items are repacked into smaller or larger containers, or a "special order" is put through to fill out the customer's requirement.

Mr. J. Kingston, the manager of administrative systems, commented: "We ran a special study. Here are the facts on the delivery problem. We analyzed customer orders, delivery dates promised, and actual shipments over a nine-month period and found the following:

1. Percent of orders delinquent in delivery:
   Waukegan plant—50%
   Piedmont plant—15%
   Beacon plant—10%
2. Percent of total orders shipped from:
   Monthly bulk load list—70%
   Special orders from sales department—20%
   Customer job order for an unusual item—10%
3. Disposition of the monthly bulk load list:
   Items sold and shipped within the next 4 weeks—33%
   Items in inventory after 4 weeks and sold within the next 4 weeks—33%
   Items called for by the sales forecast but not produced or not delivered into final inventory during the relevant 4-week period—33%

"The salesman's position always is that he will promise the delivery that the customer wants. Sometimes he checks the plant manager and finds that this can be done. Everyone is happy. Sometimes he finds, on checking, that it can't be done. Then, of course, he pressures for a modification in the plant schedule. Sometimes he promises delivery without checking with the plant. Usually this happens on bulk order items that are supposed to be available as finished goods. But the bulk order may not have gone

---

[1] National Electrical Manufacturers Association.

through because the proper copper wire was not available in the first place. Or we did not have the right insulating material in stock in raw materials.

"I have heard it said that settling the sales promises—manufacturing-delivery disagreement—is a prime function of production scheduling. But I think that the conflict element is never revealed to the scheduler. It first shows up at the vice-presidential level and then may well go to the president."

Peter Haverstraw, the Waukegan plant manager, said: "I knew when I came here that this plant has its problems. In part they stem from company headquarters being here and in part from the facility's being at this location for about seventy years.

"Many men feel that they have positions that belong to them because it has always been this way. In shipping and receiving, for example, there are some 4-hour jobs that 'just naturally' can't be changed.

"If you have on a white shirt and go out on the production floor, any foreman will run 4% silver on your say-so. It's the white shirt that counts. By this I mean, of course, that we have production managers, product engineers, salesmen, product sales managers, and executives running out of our ears because headquarters is here. Any one of them may have a legitimate interest in an order.

"In this plant our basic skill is in wire-drawing and stranding at high speeds. We have the men with experience and the equipment to do it. Pulling the wire through the dies, laying it properly, and winding it without breaks are the real keys to cost control and profits in this business. We have been doing just this for a long time, and it looks as if we will continue this way. We have the proper machinery and there is no hesitation about replacing it when something new in drawing and winding equipment comes along.

"I plan to solve the so-called delivery problem by taking away the forecasting function for bulk orders from Sales. Bulk-loading depends now on forecasts by the Sales Department, but they consider customers only and not our equipment and labor resources. We have both the data and the techniques to do demand forecasting, and we have experience in weighting and smoothing techniques as well as trend analysis. So we know more about data analysis and manipulation than does Sales.

"Furthermore, we have command over the crucial models. Our scheduling manager is already acquainted with production order quantity equations and simulation models for intermittent systems analysis. I can introduce network planning methods, including crucial path scheduling.

"To get the proper results for inventory levels and the lowest cost operation, we will use three analytical procedures: (1) the Holt, Simon Linear-Decision Rule; (2) the Magee Optimum Reaction Rate Method; and (3) the Simplex Method of Linear Programming. A balance among these will lower costs and optimize inventories."

James Hastings, the materials manager, said: "My responsibility is for all the money we have tied up in copper, silver, gold, and nickel. At prices ranging from 60 cents per pound to $50 an ounce, the excess materials on hand cost us a lot. I am not concerned with delivery schedules, but I have noted several things that are relevant. First, there seems to be a large number of men in white shirts who talk directly to the foremen. You watch any one foreman and you will see him change a machine or move an operator right after that visit from the man in the white shirt. Second, there are a lot of things going on in the plant that my buddies in Production Scheduling don't seem to get the word about. Yesterday, for example, Ray Smith, who runs a winder for silver-plated copper, had a hangover and didn't show up. Today, one of his machines is down for repair. Also Dominic Ulster, who works a drawing machine, is not here today. You won't find this information getting back to the plant office.

William Kingston, the manufacturing vice-president, said: "One element in the problem of delivery is that actual orders differ from the forecasts and that there are changes in the product mix. We have not, and probably can't, adapt production schedules to daily order results. I would guess offhand that 10% of the customers order something different than the sales department thinks they will and that the items we include on the bulk loading forecast are different in 20% of the instances from orders that customers put in for these items.

"John B. Beacon and I develop the basic loading for the plants. We assign the kinds of wire to be produced and determine the order in which the plants will be filled up. Of course, we load the Piedmont plant to 100% of effective capacity first. Then, as orders develop, we assign large orders so that the sequence does not call for extensive machine changeovers or new setups.

"At Waukegan it may even be necessary for us to have Production Scheduling change its monthly schedule to take care of the needs of an especially important customer. This is not usual, however, and we rarely do anything other than review the monthly bulk-loading schedule to check the priorities implicit in it."

PERSONNEL

Mr. Louis Tappan, manager of administrative services and personnel, said: "I came here last year partly as the consequence of a consultant's study of some production problems. They investigated our employee turnover problem and stated what everyone knew—that turnover is a problem in Waukegan, especially among the younger employees in both the office and the plant. The consultants claim that there are five contributing factors: (1) Our screening and training in the past has been spotty when it did exist. Training is entirely on-the-job, and screening consists of the plant manager's talking to a prospective employee on a when-time-is-available basis. (2) The geographic area—the lakefront cities north of Chicago are turning more and more into affluent suburbs. We compete for the people available in a market with rapidly rising prices. (3) The work hours—7 A.M. to 3 P.M. and 3 P.M. to 11 P.M. for the plant and 8 A.M. to 5 P.M. for the office—are less and less 'right' for the newer people here. (4) Bus transportation from the west and north is inadequate. (5) The whole notion of a 'mill in a suburb' is out of keeping; people don't think of working here when they look for a job.

"I am supposed to do something about the amount of employee turnover. I have talked to some who left and didn't learn much. The work is not hard, it just takes patience and application and careful attention. Our benefits are satisfactory when compared to other plants in Waukegan or Racine. The working conditions are good for an industrial plant. The work is clean and not very heavy physically, although the plant is noisy. Those who work in the clean rooms drawing and winding ultra-fine wire and packing it in vapor-proof containers have better air and cleanliness conditions than they would on a yacht in the middle of the Lake. We can't afford to contaminate 56-gauge wire. We have few grievances, just a lot of turnover. I have heard it said that the work is just not glamorous enough. Almost all of it—except packing, which is on incentive—is machine-paced and no one is overworked. The operators have to watch the drawing equipment and the winding machines carefully and be quick about making minor adjustments, but this is not nerve-wracking once you know what you are doing.

"One idea I'll have to look into is that the foremen are discouraged. If so, they won't bring the new men along properly and won't encourage them to stay. Perhaps there are some things in our whole way of operating that put an extra burden on the foremen.

"Staffing the plant is no problem in South Carolina. It is in Waukegan that we had 150% turnover last year. One third were good people we hated to lose, one third were poor people we let go, and one third were good temporaries who come back and know the job but just seem to want the summers off.

"Beacon is a high-wage area so we can't possibly raise rates there. In that plant, turnover was 166% of the work force last year. I don't know why no one seems concerned about that statistic when everyone hops all over the results in Waukegan. Charley Morris seems to get out the products all right, though. In my view, labor is going to get tighter and tighter in Beacon as IBM expands all through that area and as more new plants move to northern Westchester.

"The turnover problem may boil down to who are you going to hire. There are a lot of blacks in Waukegan or they could commute in. We have a share of them in the plant—about 5% of the work force—as winders, packers, and machine tenders; but the percentage could be a lot higher—double or triple if we wanted to. The high school dropouts whom we have taken on are mostly white kids whom someone has called about—the city welfare department, a local minister, or the school counselor. Even they require a lot of tender care and encouragement, and half of them don't stay. Should I deliberately seek out blacks and some of the hard-core unemployed and try to build up their percentage to three times what it is? I haven't gotten any policy guidance on this.

"Many people here talk about organization problems. What I think they mean is that the sales, manufacturing, and engineering vice-presidents were all plant managers in the past and ran sales as well as production and personnel out of these plants. They want to return to this.

"My view of the organization problems is that we have too many managers. There are so many overlaps in duties—for example, the plant manager and the materials manager—that the organization structure does not lend itself to an easy definition of responsibilities.

"I have to relate to two groups to function effectively. Manufacturing needs assistance with employee turnover and the effectiveness of foremen. My boss insists that I develop manuals to explain company benefits and that I develop records to give us information on salary averages by department and operating group. But I have been squeezed into a room next to shipping. The offices are through the plant and upstairs. The data processing group is on the third floor. The employee entrance and dressing rooms are elsewhere. The main financial offices are on the second and third floors in a part of the building separated from data processing. We are squeezed for office space. The building can't expand because the lake is on one side and roads or plants are on the others. My cousin, Don Tappan, says we can't build up because the foundations won't take it. I do a lot of running around. It's a good thing I need the exercise."

Louis Tappan continued: "The Waukegan plant manager has recommended several times that we raise the pay rates for the less-skilled help and the newer trainees. He says that this will attract those boys who want to work hard for a buck and that it will let us hold onto the high school dropouts. They are usually so discouraged that they leave work just as readily as they drop out of school, but maybe if we raise their pay rates they will stick around because of the good money. Some 50 people make up the group with rapid turnover. They earn about $2.97 an hour to start. We couldn't jump them more than 5% without distorting the wage scale excessively—although it might be wise to talk it over with the foremen. Since we don't have a union, the foremen can tell us best about the reaction of the longer-service employees on whom we really depend. I certainly would hate to have those people in Piedmont find out what we have to pay new men in the Waukegan plant. I guess I have about concluded that the labor problem here will only get worse and can't be solved.''

ORGANIZATION

The present formal organization has four departmental vice-presidents—sales, manufacturing, engineering, and finance. They are responsible to the president. In addition, the treasurer and senior vice-president, like the president, is responsible to the board of directors and, specifically, to the chairman of the corporation. Reporting to each vice-president are a group of department managers (see Exhibit 4).

Mr. John B. Beacon, the president, comments: "As I see the question of formal organization structure, there are drawbacks with the old and the new. When we were organized by plants—with each plant responsible for a limited product line and with a general manager in charge—there was too much direct competition between them. They were not interested in each other's problems and would not even refer business or customers to one another! Now, it seems to me, the various department managers won't make decisions, won't cooperate extensively across departmental lines, and have lost any sense of the whole business. They buck all possible problems to the vice-presidents.

"The question really is—despite what some others may say—how can we make the present structure fully effective?

"Organization problems that I see that I would like worked on are five-fold: (1) a lack of communications across organizational levels; (2) a lack of strong feeling for the other guy's problems; (3) a tendency to funnel matters up to the highest possible level (just yesterday two vice-presidents came in to me with a disagreement over the delivery date on an order); (4) building the status of the department manager group in their own eyes as well as everyone else's; and (5) increasing their executive confidence—the willingness to work out problems on their own and to get operational issues resolved at the lowest managerial level possible."

Norman Cortlandt, the sales vice-president, had been a very effective plant manager and general manager of what was formerly a semiautonomous division of the company. It is no secret that he prefers a divisional organization structure—with three general managers reporting to the president—to the present functionally based formal organization structure. He believes: "Working with three other vice-presidents is no way to get things done. Give us each some responsibility for a total operation."

The engineering vice-president, Don Tappan, has spent recent years giving his full attention to finding a site for and overseeing the construction of the new plant in Piedmont, equipping that plant, changing the layout in the Waukegan plant, and solving some water pollution problems in the Beacon plant. With those projects behind him, he is turning his attention to product development problems and, more particularly, to the relationship of his department with the sales department. "We have many mutual interests, of course, in our customers' technical problems, and there is always a question as to who has jurisdiction over the work with the customer and responsibility for the outcome of the project. It is a question of sitting down with the other vice-presidents and the president and getting these matters straightened out."

John B. Beacon commented further: "Norm Cortlandt, Bill Kingston, and Don Tappan disagree too much. They seldom, if ever, come to me with problems resolved and an agreement reached. Rather, they look for a referee for their differences. Right now Norm wants a big order for 10,000 pounds of No. 1934, 3% silver, stranded copper inserted in the schedule to push up its delivery from 8 to 4 weeks. Kingston wants an

Exhibit 4
Formal Organization Diagram

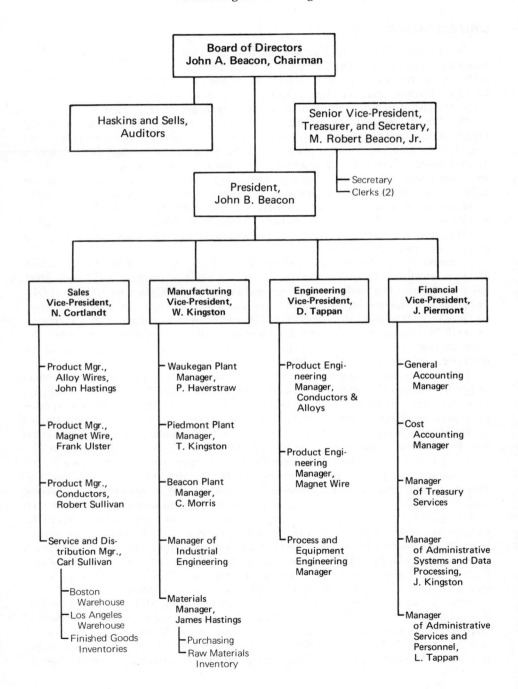

unchanged schedule, and Don wants to install a new strander and delay the whole thing another week. What should I say?

"This process among us is, for me, like being a fog sculptor. I can't knock a few heads and then see that things get done. I don't have a direct relation with customers and can't go to manufacturing to straighten out a big customer problem. I am not able to intervene directly in the negotiation between sales and manufacturing.

"Here's another organization problem. Carl Sullivan, the head of sales service and distribution, has come to me and said he can't handle the job. He also does not want to return to his old work in personnel and industrial relations in which he was very effective. Carl is an important kind of a guy to have around in an organization, for his personal manner is such that he eases a lot of tension just by talking with people and he can make almost anyone feel welcome. I know that he promotes after-hours social activities among some of the department managers just to get them calmed down. He seems to want to go out West. If he does so, we will part on good terms.

"Our public accounting firm suggests that we have a series of dinner meetings with scheduled speakers to work on this problem of communication and decision-making in the organization. I don't see as yet just how that might be effective; but whatever we do, I want to carry it on and not drop it. Who would speak and what would they say?

"Finally, I want to make sure that there is some means by which all executives know what we are aiming for. There is an underground current around here to the effect that our goals are not clear. I have often stated in conversations and in written statements that (1) we look for a return on investment equal to that of other firms of our size in our industry, and (2) we want to grow at a faster rate than the industry average."

FINANCE

When results for the final five months of the year just ending became available, John B. Beacon called a managers' meeting to review the information (see Exhibits 5, 6, 7, and 8).

His comments were: "I am satisfied with the control of selling, general, and administrative expenses. It is a very good performance. We have to keep constant pressure on our customers. A good customer is one who pays. I cannot emphasize enough the need to reduce inventories. Not all are out of line. There are two primary problems. Net income indicates an excellent performance—especially in relation to recent past years. Note that $174,000 of the pretax income is copper premium income. We buy at the U.S. producer price but charge our customers a price based on the industry average mixture of London Metal Exchange copper and U.S. producer copper."

The company has recently purchased a small computer in the IBM 360 series. John Kingston came in as data processing manager to convert the accounting and record-keeping systems from tabulating equipment to computer-processing and storage.

He said: "I was told, when hired, to 'bring this on-stream.' That's easy to do if you know what you are doing, but some characteristics of this industry make it difficult. Ideally, I should try to gear an IBM room for a limited range of volume. But which will it be—x volume of invoices or y? When sales fluctuate from $16 million to $27 million and then drop back toward $18 million, the direction is hard to know and the level is difficult to set.

"We are on-stream, all right, but now the problems are (a) in what order do you want this information, and (b) what is it you want from it? I can produce all the information we

Exhibit 5
Inventory Balances, Current

Raw Materials............................		$ 625,000
Work in Process...........................		2,010,000
Finished Goods...........................		1,750,000
Scrap Inventory...........................		92,000
Total Inventory........................		$4,477,000
Reserve for LIFO Revaluation.............	$1,214,000	
Reserve for Inventory Losses..............	68,000	
Reserve for Inventory Obsolescence........	17,000	
Reserve for FIFO Revaluation.............	—	1,299,000
Net Inventory...........................		$3,178,000

Exhibit 6

Schedule of Selling, General and Administrative
Expenses, Five Months to End of Year

	Actual	Percent	Budget	Percent
Selling...........................	$ 394,000	4.9%	$ 412,000	5.0%
Advertising and Sales				
Promotion....................	48,000	0.6	45,000	0.5
Corporate Engineering...........	128,000	1.6	176,000	2.1
Corporate Manufacturing........	57,000	0.7	54,000	0.6
Finance.......................	233,000	2.9	230,000	2.8
Executive Office................	160,000	2.0	146,000	1.8
Total..........................	$1,020,000	12.7%	$1,063,000	12.8%

Exhibit 7

Statement of Income
Current Year, Final Five Months

	Amount	Percent
Net Sales Billed..........................	$8,012,000	100.0
Deductions..............................	116,000	1.4
Net Sales.............................	$7,896,000	98.6
Cost of Sales.............................	6,120,000	76.4
Gross Profit..........................	$1,776,000	22.2
Selling, General, and Administrative		
Expense..............................	$1,020,000	12.8
Other Expense...........................	80,000	1.0
Provision for Profit-Sharing		
and Bonus............................	100,000	1.2
Total................................	$1,200,000	15.0
Income before Taxes......................	$ 576,000	7.2
Estimated Taxes..........................	296,000	3.7
Net Income..............................	$ 280,000	3.5

Exhibit 8

Cash Flow Statement, Final Five Months

	Actual	*Budget*
Cash Balance, Beginning of Period........	$ 610,000	$ 510,000
Funds Provided:		
Net Income.........................	$ 280,000	$ 270,000
Depreciation........................	196,000	190,000
Valuation Reserves..................	62,000	—
Decreases:		
Accounts Receivable................	—	—
Inventories......................	15,000	325,000
Fixed Assets.....................	—	—
Other Assets.....................	27,000	—
Increases:		
Accounts Payable..................	—	—
Tax Accruals.....................	243,000	—
Other Liabilities.................	315,000	162,000
Total Funds Provided............	$1,138,000	$ 947,000
Total Funds Available.................	$1,748,000	$1,457,000
Funds Expended:		
Increases:		
Accounts Receivable................	$ 710,000	$ 390,000
Inventories......................	—	—
Fixed Assets.....................	185,000	205,000
Other Assets.....................	—	3,000
Decreases:		
Accounts Payable..................	233,000	—
Tax Accruals.....................	—	—
Other Liabilities.................	—	—
Dividend Payments.................	—	16,000
Profit-Sharing and Bonus Payments.....	—	—
Tax Payments.....................	—	—
Total Funds Expended............	$1,128,000	$ 614,000
Net Funds Available..................	$ 620,000	$ 843,000
Financing:		
Borrowings........................	$ —	$ 270,000
Repayments........................	20,000	540,000
Cash Balance, End of Period...........	$ 600,000	$ 573,000

can use—and more. But I need to be told just what contribution the data processing room can make to the profits of the entire company.''

NEXT YEAR

Planning for the coming year includes the development of a budget and supporting schedules (see Exhibits 9 through 13), their explanation, and analysis at a managers' meeting.

Exhibit 9
Budget for the Coming Year
(000's omitted)

	Total		Con-	Magnet	A & M
	Amount	Percent	ductors	Wire	Wires
Net Sales Billed..............	$23,900	100.0	$10,750	$10,550	$2,600
Cash Disc. Allowed........	65		53		12
Transportation............	255		120	113	22
Net Sales..................	$23,580	98.7	$10,577	$10,437	$2,566
Cost of Sales...............	18,048	75.6	7,747	7,967	2,334
Gross Profit................	$ 5,532	23.1	$ 2,830	$ 2,470	$ 232
Selling, General and Adminis- trative Expense..........	$ 3,162	13.2	$ 1,642	$ 1,520	
Interest Expense.............	280				
Provision for Bonus and Profit Sharing...........	383				
Profit before Taxes...........	$ 1,707	7.1			
Provision for Taxes.........	901				
Net Income.................	$ 806	3.4			

Exhibit 10
Cost of Sales Budget for the Coming Year
(in thousands)

	Total	Con- ductors	Magnet Wire	A & M Wires
Cost of Sales at Standard..........	$16,219	$7,288	$7,053	$1,878
Manufacturing Variance...........	1,241	680	306	255
Price Variance on Material........	545	(249)	595	199
Provision for Inventory Loss.......	41	22	14	5
Gain or Loss on Sales of Scrap.....	(50)	(25)	(17)	(8)
Freight-In.......................	52	31	16	5
Total.........................	$18,048	$7,747	$7,967	$2,334
Gross Profit Percentage...........	32%	32%	33%	28%

Exhibit 11
Selling, General and Administrative Budget
(in thousands)

	Amount	Percent of Net Sales Billed
Sales.....................	$1,240	5.2%
Manufacturing.............	167	.7
Engineering...............	530	2.2
Finance...................	695	2.9
Corporate.................	530	2.2
Total.................	$3,162	13.2%

Exhibit 12
Pro Forma Balance Sheet, End of Coming Year
(000's omitted)

Assets		Liabilities and Stockholders' Equity	
Cash.................	$ 580	Notes Payable.............	$ 1,190
Net Receivables.......	3,420	Accounts Payable.........	778
Net Inventory.........	2,640	Customer Deposits........	406
Prepaid Expense.......	118	Accrued Taxes............	197
Fixed Assets (Net)[1]....	6,250	Other Current Liabilities....	230
Other Assets..........	44	Long-Term Debt[2].........	1,900
		Stockholders' Equity.......	8,351
Total............	$13,052	Total................	$13,052

[1] Depreciation for the year = $570,000.
[2] Payable at annual rate of $190,000.

Exhibit 13
Capital Expenditures Requirements for Coming Year

Classification	Category		Amount
Cost Reduction	Machinery and Equipment		$394,000
Increased Capacity	Machinery and Equipment	$388,000	
	Building	34,000	422,000
Quality Improvement	Engineering Equipment		13,800
Product Development	Research and Development		48,800
Replacement and Modernization	Furniture and Fixtures		8,500
Total			$887,100

Comments at the budget meeting

John B. Beacon, President: "This is the best budget we have ever had, but it can be met. We are going to stretch. We will have to stretch to attain it. We will have to pin each account to someone's chest and say 'You are going to do it.' What really makes our budget look ambitious is the change from the present year. If we do what we say we will, it *will* come out as planned."

William Kingston, Manufacturing Vice-President: "The manufacturing variance reflects certain inefficiencies. Also some of the standards are not quite right. This is a big, controllable cost element to hold down. The $1,240,000 amount (see Exhibit 10) gives us plenty of room to cut these predicted costs further next year.

"In scheduling, we are completely loading the Piedmont plant for three shifts, seven days per week. Then we have the Beacon plant loaded for two shifts, seven days per week, on heavy wire and for three shifts, six days per week, on fine wire. Each of these plants has expenses allocated according to the scheduled operating load and is then run as a cost center. Each department within the plant is also a cost center.

"The labor problem in Beacon is critical, that at Waukegan is very critical, and there is no problem at Piedmont.

"Waukegan is operating at 50% of three-shift capacity.

"Up-to-date standards are 7% above the published rates, so the 32% gross profit that you see in the budget will actually result in a 25% gross profit.

"Material costs and predicted inventory dollars are based on the six-month physical inventory taken by the manufacturing department. We don't use the perpetual inventory records in the financial statistics.

"As to equipment at Piedmont, we are looking for a rod machine to draw rod to No. 8 wire and are adding two Bridgeports to make heavy wire. In Waukegan we plan to add three Bartels, two Myhoffs, and a respooler."

Robert Sullivan, Sales Product Manager, Conductors: "We need 50% overrun capacity in any one month above the average forecast to take care of order fluctuations."

W. Kingston: "We can't possibly have people available for such a schedule."

R. Sullivan: "The people are only 15% to 20% of total cost, so that adding the flexibility will only increase costs by 5%. I gave you a quarterly forecast for 38-gauge wire at 20% above the market price, and we had to take one third of it out of the budget. So wire we could sell is not in the budget because the plant can't run."

W. Kingston: "We had to lay off last year, so these people are not available.

R. Sullivan: "Having six extra men is a lot cheaper than building inventory."

James Hastings, Materials Manager: "That may do it moneywise, but it kills the plant manager to have six people sitting around with nothing to do." He continued: "My forecast is easy. I analyze sales forecasts for the material content, add an average scrap allowance, and cost it out at the current metals prices. I don't use a forecast price since materials price changes can feed immediately into sales price changes."

John Piermont, Financial Vice-President: "This department is not as much overhead as everyone thinks. We contribute a service that is information so that everyone else can do their jobs better. The organization of this department is now complete, and enough positions have been established to do the job adequately. Although our cost system is complex, and some of you do not understand it, it is structured to be as up-to-date as any system in this region and is in thorough accordance with the latest financial and accounting thinking.

"We are working toward two goals. First, the investment possibility of getting more capital. Second, improving the accuracy of financial controls. We now have an absorption costing system that provides accurate costs by department. One of my thoughts is to move to a direct costing system that would provide accurate costs by product. We would not then report costs by department.

"We have an advanced computer ordered. The original delivery date is one month from now. IBM now tells us eight to eleven months more. I don't know where we will put it. There is no more office space here."

J. Hastings (to a group of other department heads): "That corporate financing budget and presentation was above reproach since I don't understand it." Most heads nodded in agreement.

Peter Haverstraw, Waukegan Plant Manager: "Statements come to me, but I have a hard time getting them explained. Piermont talked about profit goals for the company, but, as far as I can see, each department defines its own objectives and doesn't look at company goals to develop profits."

Don Tappan, Engineering Vice-President: "By way of background to explain the money we plan to spend, let me say this. Engineering has the following eight major responsibilities:

1. To develop products, manufacturing processes, and a small amount of work on new equipment. This is a little applied research but mainly development, and it takes one third of our time.
2. To lead the industry as to innovations and product modifications in conductor wires. Also to do some work on magnet wires. We are best known for this, but we have to depend on the copper companies for the basic metallurgy and alloying developments.
3. To investigate new facilities.
4. To provide technical service to customers—20% of our time.
5. To set standards for quality control.
6. To set product specifications.
7. To give assistance on manufacturing procedures when requested—25% of our time.
8. To undertake special projects and studies as these crop up.

"We plan the same level of staff and activities as last year. We develop projects to take up 50% of our time and submit them to Sales and Manufacturing for comment. The balance is left for unanticipated projects. Examples of approved projects are: improved equipment for nickel-plating; water-pollution control in Waukegan (we were ahead of state requirements and have throttled back to await state and federal standards); analyzing cost and quality differences in the Beacon and Piedmont plants; developing an antistatic wire for carpets; a comprehensive packaging study; improving magnet wire so that it can be used for hookup wire applications (this will lead to its direct competition with the existing cheaper grades of conductors).

"New work that our department has in mind includes: colored music strings; a scientific investigation of drawing lubricants (why is soapy water still the best?); the timing of a magnet wire plant expansion; and the future of the Waukegan plant—has it any future?"

John B. Beacon: "From what Don Tappan has just told us, we are beginning to see the payoff from an organizational change from separate engineering units in each plant to a distinct department as a full-time engineering responsibility. We could not have had our new layout and our 56-gauge facilities planned and carried through as a part-time task by someone running a magnet wire department. It is helpful to have someone to whom we can turn and know that he will have the time and the information available to do the job.

"Our long-term goal now is to have steady profits for several years so that we can bring out a public offering. This will go a long way toward solving our cash problems."

SUMMARY QUESTION

Assume that you are a newly appointed director of Waukegan Wire Company. To what key problems should central management give its primary attention? What do you recommend be done .vith respect to each of these problems?

COMPREHENSIVE / Digital Equipment
CASE 6 / Corporation[1]

Digital Equipment Corporation (DEC) is only 3% of IBM's size, but within its particular niche in the computer industry it is clearly the leader. And in recent years it has been growing faster than IBM. The board of directors of DEC at its next meeting will review management's plans for maintaining that leadership. Also DEC's president, Kenneth H. Olsen, must decide what attention—if any—to give to a challenging letter that an important stockholder sent to all members of the board.

The nature and the size of the total computer industry, the particular characteristics of DEC's niche—minicomputers—and DEC's strengths and present strategy all bear on what future plans should be. DEC has just reported record performance in its fiscal year ending June 30, 1973—gross income of $265 million and net income of $23½ million.

NATURE AND SIZE OF COMPUTER INDUSTRY

Growth of industry

The U.S. computer industry, insignificant twenty years ago, has grown from $45 million in 1952 to over $11 billion in revenues in 1972. Industry analysts estimate that the dollar value of the business will exceed $40 billion by 1980. If this prediction is accurate, the computer industry will rival the U.S. auto industry in size and economic contribution. With regard to international trade, it will likely exceed the contributions of the automotive industry to American export earnings.

Desk calculators, accounting machines, and IBM punched card tabulating machines all provided a base for modern computers. The first electronic computer, ENIAC, was developed for the Army at the University of Pennsylvania between 1944 and 1946 by J. Presper Eckert and John W. Mauchly. The 30-ton structure occupied 15,000 feet of floor space and contained over 18,000 vacuum tubes. Although it was difficult to run, the machine did produce results. Among the first problems given the computer was one in nuclear physics that would have required 100 man-years to solve. The ENIAC produced the answer in 2 hours.

Remington Rand (later Sperry-Rand) bought the company that produced this first machine and continued development with the Univac series. Meanwhile, IBM designed an electronic calculator, the prerunner of its 701 announced in 1953 for scientific use and its 702 in 1954 for commercial use. The race was on, with Univac in the early lead. However, IBM's market orientation, emphasis on customer service, and established

---

[1] This case is based on a series of cases on the computer industry written by Donald E. Shay, Jr., of Management Analysis Center, Inc.

relationships with tabulating machine customers helped this company move into a dominant position.

The 1950's were a period of intense competition. IBM and Sperry-Rand were joined by Burroughs, Honeywell, RCA, Philco, National Cash Register, General Electric, and Control Data. These manufacturers were known as mainframe producers because they produced the complete "hardware"—the actual machines that manipulate data—and "software"—the complex instructions necessary to tie the machines into a useful, applied system. In 1957 IBM sales passed the $1 billion mark; and by the end of the decade, IBM with 80% of the market led the industry towards the $2 billion mark.

As the 1960's progressed, computers found wider usage in a variety of fields. About a third were used by science and industry to perform lengthy calculations. A few were used as process control systems in electric power, petroleum, and chemical plants. The remainder were used to simplify the ever-increasing load of business record keeping. Banks, utilizing mark sense machines that could read magnetically encoded characters on checks, found computers almost a necessity in handling the billions of checks generated.

Technological change

Rapid technological change contributed to the growth and the competition during the 1960's. The first generation of computers, which used vacuum tubes, were bulky, costly, and consumed great amounts of power. Replacement of vacuum tubes with transistors in the second generation permitted sharp reduction in size and power requirements. Also speed and memory increased enormously. These improvements were quickly followed by introduction of integrated circuits on tiny chip transistors, enabling the third generation of computers to deal with access speeds of billionths-of-a-second—compared with thousandths-of-a-second for the first generation.

Prices relative to performance dropped with each new generation. Computer languages (FORTRAN and COBOL) and many high-speed input and output printing devices were necessary accompanying developments. With all the rapid changes, compatibility of one machine to another became crucial. To overcome such problems IBM devoted almost 4 years and the staggering cost of $5 billion to designing a whole new series of computers called the 360's. Currently great strides are being made in computer memories, with tiny one-eighth inch square silicon chips replacing magnetic cores that only 10 years earlier were heralded as a quantum advance.[2] And metal oxide chips will be even faster.

Types of companies

Many companies have entered the growing computer industry. Most of these are active in only one or two segments. A helpful division is by parts or types of computer systems.

The physical (hardware) parts of a computer consist of three types of units: the central processor, the memory, and so-called peripherals.

In addition, software programs that guide the use of the hardware for specific purposes are essential.

---

[2] Intel, a new company that successfully pioneered in making memory chips, grew in 5 years from 42 employees and sales of $2,672 to a multiplant company with 2,550 employees, annual sales of over $60 million, and annual profits of $7 million.

COMPONENTS OF A COMPUTER SYSTEM

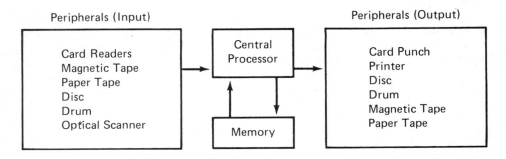

The primary industry is composed of mainframe manufacturers, those firms that supply the complete computer system, both software and hardware. These suppliers include Burroughs, Control Data, Honeywell, IBM, NCR, and Univac. Two smaller mainframe manufacturers are Digital Equipment Corporation and Xerox Data Systems.

Secondly, there are the independents such as Memorex, Intel, and Mohawk Data, who supply equipment and services aimed at supplanting and/or complementing mainframe equipment. For the most part, these independent firms market peripheral and core equipment to replace IBM hardware. These firms are able to compete by offering lower prices and/or better performance than IBM.

The third segment consists of software houses that produce specialized programs for various computers. Again, because of the ubiquitousness of IBM computers, a major portion of the software houses either write programs aimed for use on IBM computers or perfect and customize IBM-supported software.

There are also a number of miscellaneous subindustries serving the computer user, such as timesharing service bureaus, keypunching firms for data preparation, and used equipment brokers.

The "minicomputer" segment of the industry has experienced rapid growth in recent years. Minicomputers can be defined as computers with a word length of 8 to 18 bits, generally selling for under $25,000. Although minicomputers represent about 30% of all computers installed, they account for only 6% of the total value. On the other hand, large and very large computers represent 33% of the number installed yet account for about 75% of the installed value.

In total, at least 5,600 companies compete for business in the computer industry. About 700 make finished hardware, while another 1,500 produce supplies and components. There are more than 2,200 software and service firms. In addition, approximately 1,200 companies make computers in combination with measuring and control instruments.

Size of major subsectors

Because most large computers are leased to customers rather than sold, the dollar value of production in any one year differs from the revenue actually received. Minicomputers, however, are typically sold. So for a perspective on that sector, data on production ("new builds") is most relevant. The sum of all products sold or leased to date is called the "installed base."

An industry association—the American Federation of Information Processing Societies—compiled estimates of worldwide new builds and installed base for U.S. companies in 1971 and 1976. These figures are shown in the following table:

World Shipments of U.S. Firms and Year-End Installed Base for 1971 with Estimates for 1976

	1971 Consensus Estimate			Range of 1976 Estimates	
	New Builds $ (Million)	Installed Base # (Thousand)	Installed Base $ (Million)	New Builds $ (Million)	Installed Base $ (Million)
U.S.					
General Purpose Computer Systems	4,200	54.5	26,500	7,000- 7,750	33,000-48,000
Mini & Dedicated Application Computer Systems	250	33.5	1,600	600- 750	2,000- 3,500
Peripheral Equipment .	630	553.5	2,800	650- 1,200	5,000- 6,000
OVERSEAS[1]					
General Purpose Computer Systems	3,300	36.2	14,300	6,400	31,500
Mini & Dedicated Application Computer Systems	60	*	*	800- 900	*
Peripheral Equipment	*	*	*	550	*
WORLD TOTAL					
General Purpose Computer Systems ...	7,500	90.7	40,800	13,400-14,200	64,500-79,500
Mini & Dedicated Application Computer Systems ...	310	*	*	1,400- 1,700	*
Peripheral Equipment	*	*	*	1,200- 1,800	*

* No estimate available.
[1] Prices do not include customs and/or import taxes.
Source: Consensus of AFIPS July, 1972, Conference Workshop.

Shipments of computers grew explosively from 1955 until 1968. The 1969-70 recession and the maturing of the IBM 360 family created a temporary leveling. The 1970-73 figures indicate a resumption of growth, though not at such a dramatic rate. It is the consensus of experts in the field that although a strong demand remains for data processing equipment, the vacuum that urged on the high growth rate of the past decade and a half no longer exists. It is expected that future growth will come in three areas: the replacement market, communications, and minicomputers.

Leading computer manufacturers

Competition in the computer industry is so keen that even during a period of rapid growth many firms drop out of the race. The most noted withdrawals have been two industrial giants, RCA and General Electric.

RCA entered the computer business in the mid-50's but soon discovered its engineering skill in making television sets and other consumer goods was not easily transferred to computers. When IBM introduced its 360 series, RCA adopted a strategy of trying to woo away IBM users when they were shifting to the new equipment. By offering equipment similar to IBM's at a lower price, RCA did obtain annual shipments of over $200 million. However, expenses far exceeded income, and by 1971 RCA had accumulated losses in its computer operations of about $500 million. Its outlook was bleak and future capital requirements high. So it stopped production and sold its consumer base to Univac.

General Electric also struggled to get a significant share of the computer market with indifferent success. Its losses were smaller than RCA's, but in 1970 GE management decided its chances for future profits were too small to warrant further investment. So it sold the GE computer business to Honeywell, Inc. Honeywell absorbed GE's 27,000 employees, 7 plants, and 7,000 computers. The result has boosted Honeywell's market share from 5.5% (1971) previous to the merger to 8.4% (1972).

These two major withdrawals left seven primary producers. The relative size of these firms is indicated in the following table.

Value of Shipments and Installed Base—1972

	Shipments		Installed Base		
	In Millions	*% of Total*	*In Millions*	*% of Total*	*% Change over 1971*
IBM	$5,800	65.2%	$28,500	63.6%	6%
Honeywell	745+	8.4	4,500	10.0	14
Univac.................	485**	5.4	3,400	7.6	7
Burroughs	425	4.8	2,000	4.5	15
Control Data	255	2.9	1,800	4.0	15,
NCR	215	2.4	1,100	2.5	NA
DEC..................	195	2.2	690	1.5	46
All Others	780	8.7	2,800	6.3	29
Total	$8,900	100.0	$44,790	100.0	10% (avg.)

+ Includes GE operations.
** Includes RCA customer base for approximately one quarter.
NA-not available.

MINICOMPUTERS

Minicomputers, as the name implies, differ from their better-known counterparts mainly in size. They can process a smaller volume of "words" and have much smaller memories. And they have a much smaller price, ranging from $25,000 to as little as $1,000. Having less capacity, they usually are assigned fairly simple and specific tasks; or in the hands of sophisticated engineers they serve as components in other equipment.

Minicomputer applications

There are five major minicomputer application areas: industrial process control, scientific, data communications, business, and medical/scientific lab analysis. The percentage of total use of minicomputers in these areas and less important areas is shown in the following table.

Uses of Minicomputers—U.S.A.

	Percent of Total Use
Industrial Manufacturing Process Control	20.5
Scientific and Engineering Problem Solving	17.8
Data Communications	15.9
Business Data Processing	14.2
Medical/Scientific Lab Analysis	8.8
Military and Aerospace	7.2
Education and Computer-Aided Instruction	6.8
Time Sharing	6.3
Miscellaneous Applications	2.5
	100.0

Source: Modern Data Magazine.

Industrial process control is expected to grow from $15 million in sales in 1972 to $100 million in 1975. Two types of minis are included in this category. The first and more traditional application is in the area of inventory control. The other, direct process control (PC), is a stored program control system intended to perform the functions heretofore done by relay control panels. Typically, the mini is integrated into the manufacturing equipment. For instance, in metal working a mini is used to control the milling of a Wankel engine. Such process controls call for a simple computer—in terms of both cost and capability—and parts of this market are likely to be taken over by *micro*computers.

Scientific use includes laboratory applications where the mini is utilized to transform data from measuring instruments to recorded information. In most instances an analog-to-digital converter is used as an interface between the instrument and the mini. (DEC produces several types of these converters.) Other scientific applications include the performing of lengthy calculations and the monitoring and direction of experiments.

Data communications is predicted by some industry experts as the area with the greatest potential for growth, including such applications as message concentrators, switching systems and pre-processors for large computers. Here the minis serve as peripheral equipment for large computers and for long-distance communication systems.

Business use of the mini is a small but rapidly growing share of the mini market. It is expected that business use will increase rapidly as more businessmen become sophisticated in the use of the computer in general and as software and services for minis become more prolific. Much of this market is closely tied to accounting and other business machines.

Medical/scientific lab analysis includes pharmacy control, patient monitoring, medical history recording, menu control, laboratory reporting, and diagnosis. An annual growth rate of 17% is expected for this application area. The hospital and clinical laboratory information systems market is expected to exceed $980 million by 1980.

Mini future

The demand for minis is expected to continue to grow. The U.S. Department of Commerce in a report entitled "U.S. Industrial Outlook 1973 with Projections to 1980" predicted that:

Shipments of minicomputers in 1972 are estimated at around $200 million,[3] with sales in 1973 expected to go well over $250 million. Prices are expected to continue to decrease with growth in unit shipments rising, possibly to $500 million by 1975.

Minicomputers generally have been used in process control, numerical control, scientific problem solving, and data communications. Now more of them are being used for payroll and accounting purposes. Because of its relative low cost and flexibility, the minicomputer offers the businessman who cannot afford a large computer installation an efficient means of handling data processing and information needs. Its simplicity of operation also makes it easy to train personnel in its use.

Demand for minicomputers in France, Germany, and Japan is also good and is expected to grow at a greater rate than the market for larger computer systems. As domestic firms face greater competition in the U.S., they are expected to seek expansion in foreign markets.

Barron's reported in the November 6, 1972, issue that changes would occur in marketing. "The rules of the game are changing. Minimaking is shifting from a straight manufacturing to a service-oriented business. Buyers are demanding more customer support, and marketing expertise is becoming more important than technology." This is seen as a natural outgrowth of the increase in unsophisticated users who need and demand greater support.

The mini industry—suppliers

There are approximately 50 companies in the U.S. actively marketing minis. The industry can be subdivided into three segments. The first group consists of those that developed minis to complement and support their main product line. This category includes Hewlett-Packard and Varian, whose basic product lines consist of industrial, scientific, and medical instrumentation. Also included in this group are firms that found the mini to be a natural outgrowth of their traditional product line, such as Honeywell, Burroughs, and Texas Instruments. This segment accounts for about 20% of the mini market.

The second segment contains the greatest number of firms and consists of small- to medium-size companies such as Data General, Computer Automation, Interdata, and Modular Computer. Most of these firms were founded specifically in response to the growing demand for minis. Data General is noteworthy in that it was started by former DEC employees who left DEC when their proposal for a computer line was rejected by management. It has managed to double sales each year since its founding in 1969. In fiscal 1972, Data General made a profit of almost $4,000,000 on sales slightly over $30,000,000. Interdata, third in sales of minicomputers, was begun in 1966. This firm had sales of $13 million in fiscal 1972, up 49% from the previous year.

DEC, with over 45% of market volume, is the third segment of the mini industry.

---

[3] U.S. Department of Commerce figures include central processing units only; AFIPS figures include complete systems.

Future competition

The line separating minicomputers from other parts of the computer industry has always been fuzzy and may become more blurred in the future. Mini producers are likely to face pressure both from firms now focusing on larger equipment and from firms now concentrating on components.

On the upper side, companies such as Burroughs and NCR have extensive relationships with business data handling. Already involved with computerized systems, such companies might decide to extend their line to include minis for business applications. Xerox has a similar potential. In a comparable way, large companies working with communications, such as Western Union, Western Electric, ITT, and the mainframe manufacturers, are all looking at peripheral expansions of their product lines. All such companies have established contacts with potential customers and large selling and service organizations.

On the lower side, *micro*computers may take over segments of the market now served by minis. A micro consists basically of a number of tiny semiconductor integrated circuits mounted on a chip coupled with memory chips. The now common hand calculators are an example (the illuminated display of answers being an added feature). The micros have much less flexibility than the minis, since fixed programs are built into the product. But for some types of use, flexible programming is not required.

Business Week reported: "In most instances, the microcomputer is taking over the function of simpler logic circuits or electromechanical components, creating new products with expanded capabilities. In an automatic bottlefilling machine built by a conveyor specialties company, for example, the tiny computer replaces several racks of counters, timers, and relays. It tells the machine how to fill bottles of different sizes and when to perform each step."

The mini maker, of course, could choose to manufacture microcomponents; yet this route, too, has inherent problems. A company that wished to manufacture circuits would need a large initial capital investment and high volume to pay off. Since few of the start-ups have the wherewithal to sustain such an effort, a more likely answer would be a "closer relationship" with a component supplier, leading possibly to subsequent mergers. Ken Olsen, DEC's president, does not favor entering into the micro market. "They sell parts; we sell systems. They can make subcomponents (micros) and sell them for $10 to $20. It's not worth our getting into unless we don't trust their supply. They will get the parts business; we will get the systems business."

One response to the microcomputer was announced in May, 1973, when Computer Automation, Inc. introduced a mini produced on a card 15" × 15" × 1". Priced at $990 in lots of 200 or more, this mini came with basic programming and 4k of core. This was half the price of the cheapest mini then on sale.

Sol Zasloff, Computer Automation's marketing vice-president, remarked that, if micros continued to become faster and more powerful, "in the end, we'll (micros and minis) get more like each other, and then the battle will revolve strictly around marketing."

DIGITAL EQUIPMENT CORPORATION

Digital Equipment Corporation designs, manufactures, sells, and services electronic computers, associated computer accessory equipment, and computer subcomponents. The company's products are used in a wide variety of applications, including scientific research and computation, education, industrial process control, time-sharing systems, medical systems, instrumentation, and simulation. Currently, DEC occupies a dominant position in the minicomputer industry, accounting for 45% of "mini" market volume.

In fiscal 1972 (year ends June 30), DEC made a net profit of $15,300,000 on sales of $187,553,000. DEC stock was listed on the stock exchange in 1966. That year net income was $1,930,000 on sales of $22,776,000. By 1972 DEC employed 7,800 people worldwide in 10 manufacturing facilities and numerous service and sales offices.

DEC origins

DEC was founded in 1957 when two brothers, Ken and Stanley Olsen, along with Harlan Anderson, left MIT's Lincoln Labs to begin their own firm with the goal of building logic modules and test equipment. As a researcher, Ken Olsen had seen the need for a low-cost computer (the cheapest computer at that time cost about $1,000,000) for the laboratory and research fields. As he remarked later: "Digital was founded to develop real-time, interactive computing.[4] At that time, most computing was done in a batch way. People were pushed away from the computer's console. They were asked to drop their punched cards in a slot in the door and the next day they got the results—usually wrong. It was very commonly believed that one needed at least a whole day to digest the results, and this was good enough. Besides, computers were much too expensive and sensitive to allow users to get near them." DEC located in Maynard, Massachusetts, renting 8,500 square feet in an abandoned woolen mill.

DEC started out cautiously as a mail-order electronics manufacturer by producing logic modules (a computer subcomponent) for use by laboratories and engineers who built their own special purpose computers. With logic module sales growing well and the firm profitable, Olsen decided to begin development of a computer.

Morale among the 50 or so employees was high. DEC employees were close-knit and enjoyed a strong esprit de corps. Employees leaving at 5:00 p.m. were kidded about going home early.

In order to obtain financing necessary to support DEC during the early R&D effort, Olsen approached General Georges F. Doriot of American Research and Development (ARD), a venture capital concern. ARD was intrigued by Olsen's firm and invested $70,000, becoming DEC's largest stockholder. (This $70,000 investment is now worth $350,000,000, based on the price of shares on the stock market.) In addition to financial support, ARD provided counseling in finance and business matters.

Product line development

In late 1958 engineering work began on DEC's first computer, the PDP-1 (Programmable Digital Processor). Introduced in 1959 at a price of $120,000, the PDP-1 was a success; DEC sold outright to laboratories and sophisticated industrial users a total of 53 machines, many of which are still in use.

Ken Olsen believed that outright sale was best for both customer and DEC, since support required was minimal. DEC then lacked both the personnel and the software

---

[4] Real-time, interactive computing means that either a person or a device may interact directly with the computer without going through the steps of placing information on cards which at a later time are fed into the computer system.

necessary to provide strong support. As a result, customers were encouraged to be independent, and many customized their machines for their own particular applications.

A cheaper version of PDP-1, the PDP-4 (50 sold) was introduced in August, 1962. This computer was also aimed at the scientific market.

Olsen realized that, although DEC's first two computers had penetrated the scientific market well, there still existed an untapped market for still cheaper computers. At a price of $120,000, the PDP-1 was out of reach for many laboratories. To reduce costs, DEC turned to the use of a shorter word length. The minicomputer industry's beginnings can be traced to the introduction in 1963 of the PDP-5, a 12 bit-word length computer with lk of core (lk of core means that the computer has a memory with room for 1,024 characters of information). The PDP-5 was a scientific machine, designed to be attached to instrumentation for the purpose of collecting, interpreting, and analyzing data. Also, the PDP-5 could be used as a problem-solving computer, handling the lengthy calculations common to scientific work. As were its predecessors, the machine was directed at the scientific market where the end-user was not dependent on DEC for complete support.

The PDP-5 created, in effect, its own market. Priced at $27,000, it was within the reach of a whole new market of potential users. More than 100 PDP-5's were sold during the eighteen months it was actively marketed, leading DEC management to believe that there existed a market for even cheaper computers.

DEC's growth did not occur without problems. In 1964, a year in which DEC had net sales approaching the $11 million mark and employed just over 600 people, the firm set out to build a large-scale (36 bit-word) computer. The PDP-6 turned out to be a major setback for the company, and for a while it was rumored that the firm would go under.

Concurrently, efforts in the mini market were progressing well. DEC introduced an advanced version of the PDP-5, the PDP-8, in May, 1965, with the hope that its even lower price would open new markets. The mass-produced PDP-8 was four times faster and, at $18,000, about one-third cheaper than the popular PDP-5. Eight months after the introduction of the PDP-8, more than 200 had been sold. Initially, principal applications for the machine were found in aerospace, biomedical instrumentation, and physics. Later, minor adaptations and added software made it possible to produce a machine to be used by the publishing industry for automatic typesetting. The PDP-8 family grew rapidly through many additional models. There are over 13,000 PDP-8's installed worldwide with the least expensive, the PDP-8/F, selling for less than $4,000.

As DEC's product line developed, new applications were added to the software base. These new applications were created by coupling specialized software packages along with the basic PDP-8 and specialized peripherals, resulting in computer-based systems ready to perform very specialized tasks. Included among these systems are:

1. Manufacturing assembly line monitoring, quality control, and testing.
2. Communications systems that can concentrate up to 128 teleprinter lines into one or more medium-speed channels, drastically reducing the charges for telephone lines. The system can also receive messages, store them until the outgoing circuit is available, and then forward them to their destination.
3. A small computer-based, time-sharing system designed to accommodate up to 16 users. All users have immediate and direct contact with the computer.
4. A typesetting system for the publishing industry. It performs hyphenating, word spacing, and letter spacing to provide clean, justified lines of type—and can set copy at a rate of 12,000 lines per hour.

5. A complete range of pulse-height analyzers for nuclear research or industrial use. These turnkey systems feature complete proven software.
6. A radiation treatment planning system, which improves patient care while reducing the time required to plan effective radio-therapy by 90%.

DEC recently introduced (1970) a major miniproduct series, the PDP-11, which introduces a breakthrough in design with its Unibus feature. This feature allows networks of memories and peripherals to be used in virtually any combination by instituting a universal data channel. Orders for 150 of this machine were received within a week after its announcement.

DEC follows an evolutionary process in developing new models within a computer series. Every year or two, modified versions of the original model are introduced. These later models within a series are typically characterized by an increased price/performance capability. It is not uncommon for updated models to perform 2-5 times faster at half the cost than previous models. Coupled with the increased performance of each new model is an ever-widening base of software.

The company has also continued to update its original product, the logic module. They are solid-state, printed circuit devices that form the basic building blocks for both company products and outside manufacturers' products. Outside sale of modules now account for about 5% of DEC sales. It is likely that this line will slowly wither, as semiconductor manufacturers such as Intel and Texas Instruments produce cheaper computers—on a chip.

DEC began to integrate backwards in 1971 with the development of its own peripherals, such as a printer, disc system, and terminal. DEC had previously subcontracted out the production of these peripherals. It is hoped that in-house manufacture will reduce the costs of these peripherals to DEC, allowing DEC to reduce the cost of total systems to end-users. Generally, peripherals constitute 30-40% of the total cost of a system.

DEC is increasing its emphasis on the development of software. Although the specific split has not been calculated, one senior executive believes that the firm could well be spending more research money on software than it is on hardware at the present time. Another prediction is that, "Most projects underway at Digital Equipment Corporation point toward increased software development with only evolutionary changes on the hardware side of the firm's product line."

Pricing

DEC consistently follows a policy of decreasing prices for each consecutive model in a series. Also, it is not unusual for DEC to decrease the price for a particular model after it has been in production for some time. As Ken Olsen explained: "Prices are initially set high with a new machine and then lowered in response to decreasing costs." Decreasing costs are due to lowered production costs through economies of scale and to reductions in the cost of computer subcomponents through changes in technology. *Management Today* reported:

> Since 1965 the average value of integrated circuits in the U.S. has declined from $8.33 to $1.49. This in turn has permitted minicomputer manufacturers to lower their prices continually, in a price-elastic market. For example, a 1963 machine that sold for $28,000 would sell, after eight successive model changes, for around $4,000 today. However, unlike the manufacturers of semiconductors and integrated circuits, DEC has held its gross margins fairly constant; its margins are high even

when compared to those of the established and much larger mainframe manufacturers.

With respect to pricing, Ken Olsen remarked, "The overall goal in setting prices is to achieve a return of 20% before taxes on each system." He qualified this by continuing, "Of course, this varies along the product line; but an objective effort is made to aim for that 20% margin."

The mini market is price-elastic. The majority of minis are sold outright to sophisticated users who do not need total support. *Business Week* suggested the reason behind this in a January 30, 1971, article on the minicomputer industry:

> DEC's Nick Mazzarese, (former) vice-president for small computers, says the cuts are due primarily to the increased efficiencies of mass production and to the much lower cost of semiconductors. But the price competition is wide open because DEC and its rivals are not committed to protecting the value of a large asset-base of leased machines as is IBM in the field of big computers. Price was the most important consideration for the majority of sophisticated users. This emphasis on price was expected to change as minis were marketed to an ever-expanding market. Some industry experts predicted that with the development of software for minis and growth of support services needed to attract less sophisticated customers, the consideration given to price would decrease. Sophisticated customers, able to service their own machines, would still be very price conscious while new users would be more interested in service and reliability.

DEC traditionally responds to decreases in costs by reducing prices in order to widen the market for potential DEC users. For instance, DEC cut prices 15% to 37% on its DEC system-10 in October of 1972, citing a new lower cost memory system and increased production efficiencies. This action was consistent with Mazzarese's position that "Price cuts are healthy because they expand the market to companies that never thought they could afford a computer." DEC's competitors espouse another view, as voiced by David Methven, president of Computer Automation, Inc., who said, "We're in a price war, with DEC and Data General leading it." In January, 1971, *Business Week* noted that:

> The price war is spreading into the peripherals field, too. DEC announced a line of "miniperipherals" last fall. A $12,000 line printer, for example, was cut to $2,500 with comparable price cuts for DEC disc printers and magnetic tape units. The aim, says Mazzarese, was to open "major new markets in education and commercial fields" where users can accept low-cost peripherals that do less.
>
> This new focus on peripherals is part of a frantic effort by the minicomputer makers to carve out a few specialty application markets for themselves. Original equipment makers will remain important and will account for at least 40% of the business done even when the industry matures, according to one study. But most of the mini makers are trying now to make the difficult transition required for them to serve the end market because they can expand their profits by selling total systems to the end users. . . . To meet the demands of these new users, many makers of minicomputers will have to provide more services and must demonstrate stability.
>
> In this context, DEC seems well positioned to hold onto its market dominance in the years ahead because it has built a software and service operation from the start. The company has suffered from profit erosion, but it is still highly profitable despite its heavy spending to increase sales staff and plant capacity.

Sales and distribution

The company markets its products throughout the world, using its own sales engineers located in 82 sales offices in 28 states and 20 countries. The firm also maintains 130 field service offices worldwide. The primary function of the field service offices is to conduct maintenance, installation, and service at user sites. Many of 1,200 field service representatives also act as sales representatives.

The salesforce is partially segmented along market lines. Each market area has several sales specialists providing backup to the general salesforce. The DEC system-10 has its own salesforce.

The firm advertises on a limited basis (less than $4 million per year) in trade periodicals such as *Electronic News, Computerworld,* and *Scientific American.* Excessive demand caused Olsen to remark, half-seriously, that he saw little reason why DEC should advertise at all.

The company's products are sold principally to industrial users, educational institutions, hospitals, and various agencies of the U.S. government. Recently, approximately 5% of the company's total sales went to government agencies. No other single customer accounts for more than 3% of DEC's sales.

DEC's initial concentration on scientific and industrial markets provided for growth at minimum expense. As time passed, DEC broadened its marketing appeal and became less dependent on industrial and scientific applications. In 1967, 70% of DEC's sales were to laboratories and universities. By 1970 that figure had fallen to 20%. Industrial and manufacturing applications rose from 25% to 50% and communications increased from 5% to 30% in the same period.

Industrials users, such as Coca-Cola in Atlanta, Georgia, use DEC computers to direct and control the manufacturing of beverage bases. Previously, a relay-based system had been used; but when bids were received, the DEC mini system, at $120,000, was about half the average price of bids from the relay manufacturers. *Food Engineering* explains why:

> Schematics and specifications were developed for two control system concepts. A relay, or solid-state, system and a computer system. This was done for a true cost comparison and the documents were sent to various fabricators and equipment vendors for bidding. Quotes for relay, or solid-state, systems were from $200,000 to $300,000. However, the low bid for a minicomputer-based system was $120,000 including hardware, software, and consoles.
>
> How can that be? A computer system costing less than a relay system? Primarily, a relay system is designed and fabricated as a fixed dedicated control unit. Its programming is in its circuitry. Its physical size is directly proportional to its complexity and, therefore, its cost is likewise proportional to its complexity.
>
> On the other hand, a computer system is composed of two main parts—hardware and software. Hardware, like in a relay system, is the actual piece of equipment, e.g., the frame, circuits, wiring, etc. Software is a term for programming. The hardware for a computer is obviously more complex than any relay system. But it is not designed specifically for one particular control problem. From a single design, utilizing new multicircuit techniques, a minicomputer manufacturer builds thousands of the same machine. For this reason, minicomputer hardware can cost less than relay controls.

The company's general policy is to sell and not to lease its products. Customers who prefer to lease the company's equipment frequently make arrangements with third-party lessors.

Sales of the company to customers abroad amount to approximately 35% of total sales. This segment of the business is conducted principally through foreign subsidiaries, by direct sales, and, to a lesser extent, through various representative and distributorship arrangements.

Productive capacity

With regard to facilities, the 1972 Annual Report reported that:

Manufacturing, sales, service, and training facilities continued to expand. Work was begun on two buildings—a 400,000-square foot administrative building and a 40-classroom training center—to be located on a 100-acre tract within a mile of Digital's Maynard headquarters. Digital's principal offices will remain at their present Main Street location. The Westminister, Mass., facility was doubled in size to over a half million square feet, and in Western Massachusetts the first steps were taken to expand the manufacturing space of Digital's Springfield power supply and subassembly plant from 11,000 to 22,000 square feet.

The San German, Puerto Rico, facility doubled in size from 60,000 to 120,000 square feet. In San German, more than 800 employees work in the production of PDP-8 family computers and printed circuit boards for use in all Digital computers.

Construction was nearly complete at the close of Fiscal 1972 on the new Kanata (Ottawa) facility of Digital Equipment of Canada Ltd. Employees have already begun moving from the Carleton Place, Ontario, site to the 60,000-square foot Kanata plant, where manufacturing will be underway in Fiscal 1973 on PDP-11 computers, Computer-Lab teaching systems, and various other subassemblies.

The Galway Industrial Estate in Galway, Republic of Ireland, is continuing expansion. Here, more than 200 employees using 50,000 square feet of manufacturing space are expediting computer shipments throughout Europe—a prime factor contributing to this year's 46 percent increase in installed computers. Additionally, ground has been broken in Galway for a 130,000 square foot building.

When this construction is completed, DEC will have 2,700,000 square feet of production space in Massachusetts and additional facilities in Puerto Rico, Ireland, Canada, and Taiwan. The current expansion program will add $23 million, less $5 million depreciation, to the investment in fixed assets.

To staff these facilities, the company has embarked on a program to increase its employees within the next year from 8,000 to 13,000 persons. The company has always enjoyed good employee relations.

Because of the rapid technological changes in its industry, DEC regularly spends a substantial portion of its funds on research and engineering projects. Currently it is spending at the rate of $20 million per year for this purpose. The company has approximately 700 professional employees involved in research, engineering, and programming activities. Their primary emphasis is on applied research and engineering, which includes developing computers, peripheral equipment, and software, and expanding product applications.

Finance

The company's financial policies are reflected in the reports given on the next three pages. The financial summary on pages 682-683 shows a ten-year history of key items. The balance sheet and income statements on page 684 show the current position.

Financial Summary

OPERATING RESULTS

Fiscal Year	Net Sales*	Income Before Taxes*	Federal & Foreign Income Taxes*	Net Income*	Net Income Per Share
1972	$187,553	$25,100	$ 9,800	$15,300	$1.49
1971	146,849	18,000	7,400	10,600	1.06
1970	135,408	25,500	11,100	14,400	1.51
1969	91,244	17,300	7,900	9,400	1.04
1968	57,339	12,934	6,078	6,856	.78
1967	38,896	8,320	3,779	4,541	.52
1966	22,776	3,500	1,550	1,930	.24
1965	14,982	1,386	646	740	.10
1964	10,909	1,780	878	902	.35
1963	9,906	2,399	1,218	1,180	.47

FINANCIAL POSITION / GENERAL INFORMATION

At End of Fiscal	Working Capital*	Stockholders' Equity*	Research and Engineering Expenses*	Selling, General & Adminis. Expenses*	Employees at Year End
1972	$87,156	$144,807	$20,137	$44,301	7,800
1971	86,577	125,854	16,668	35,979	6,200
1970	56,058	76,344	13,269	29,213	5,800
1969	38,166	45,389	9,403	17,744	4,360
1968	19,756	22,691	6,367	9,232	2,600
1967	13,954	15,707	3,998	7,394	1,800
1966	N.A.	6,363	2,595	5,154	1,100
1965	N.A.	4,365	2,270	4,080	890
1964	N.A.	3,557	1,811	2,847	610
1963	N.A.	2,661	N.A.	N.A.	490

Fiscal Year	Return on Invested Capital	Return on Sales	Sales per Employee	Sales per Dollar of Invested Capital	Price Range per Share of Stock
1972	10.0+	8.1+	$24,045	1.29	$69½ to $103
1971	8.4	7.2	23,685	1.16	52½ to 85½
1970	18.8	10.6	23,346	1.77	48⅜ to 124
1969	20.7	10.3	20,927	2.01	46⅛ to 102¾
1968	30.2	12.0	21,794	2.53	31¾ to 59⅝
1967	28.9	11.6	21,600	2.47	9⅜ to 52
1966	30.6	8.5	20,700	3.57	5½ to 11¾
1965	16.9	4.9	16,833	3.43	N.A.
1964	25.3	8.2	17,883	3.06	N.A.
1963	44.3	11.9	20,216	3.72	N.A.

* In thousands of dollars.
+ % percentages.

Consolidated Balance Sheet
(000's omitted)

Assets		*Liabilities*	
Current assets:		Current liabilities:	
Cash	$ 3,392	Bank loans & commercial	
Accounts receivable (net) ..	68,367	paper	$ 14,416
Inventories................	62,117	Accounts payable	8,800
Prepaid expenses	889	Accrued taxes.............	12,209
Total current assets	$134,765	Accrued wages	5,310
		Customer advances	3,909
Investments in foreign		Other current liabilities	2,965
subsidiaries*	10,692	Total current liabilities ...	$ 47,609
Fixed assets:		*Equity*	
Land	$ 2,451	Common stock	
Buildings & improvements .	18,018	(10,342,771 shares out-	
Machinery & equipment ...	38,466	standing)................	$ 10,343
	$ 58,935	Additional paid-in capital.....	69,678
Less depreciation..........	11,976	Retained earnings	64,786
Net fixed assets	$ 46,959	Total equity...............	$144,807
Total assets	$192,416	Total liabilities & equity	$192,416

* Foreign subsidiaries' combined balance sheets showed:
　　Current assets, $30 million; plant and equipment, $4 million; total assets, $34 million.
　　Current liabilities, $15 million; intercompany obligations, $9 million; capital stock, $1
　　million; retained earnings (unremitted), $9 million; total liabilities and equity, $34
　　million.

Consolidated Statements of Income 1969-1972
(000's omitted)

	1972	*1971*	*1970*	*1969*
Net sales	$187,553	$146,849	$135,408	$91,244
Cost of sales...................	98,199	76,366	67,055	46,742
	$ 89,354	$ 70,483	$ 68,353	$44,502
Research and engineering				
expenses......................	$ 20,137	$ 16,668	$ 13,269	$ 9,403
Selling, general and adminis-				
trative expenses	44,117	35,815	28,828	17,744
Interest expense			756	55
Total expenses	$ 64,254	$ 52,483	$ 42,853	$27,202
Income before income taxes......	$ 25,100	$ 18,000	$ 25,500	$17,300
Federal and foreign income				
taxes*	9,800	7,400	11,100	7,900
Net income	$ 15,300	$ 10,600	$ 14,400	$ 9,400
Net income per common share,				
based on average number				
outstanding	$1.49	$1.06	$1.51	$1.04

　　* The decline in the rate of the provision for income taxes since 1969 is due principally to
increased operating income in Puerto Rico that is exempt from income taxes. The federal income
tax benefits attributable to the Puerto Rican operations in fiscal years 1972-1969 yielded a tax
benefit per common share of $.16, $.04, $.18, and $.03, respectively.

Growth has been financed partly by retention of earnings ($65 million) and partly by sale of additional shares of common stock ($69 million). Since the market price of a share of stock has often been more than fifty times earnings, selling stock is an attractive source of capital.

DEC follows a policy of retaining earnings rather than paying dividends. Win Hindle (Vice-President, Large Computers) explains this by commenting: "It has never really occurred to DEC to pay dividends. It seems more logical to grow from profits. There has never been any pressure to pay dividends. We have a stock plan that allows our employees to become owners of the company. We like to receive financial appreciation through a price rise in the stock rather than dividends."

Fiscal year 1971 was the first year since 1965 that DEC's profits had dropped. Profits have since recovered, but the 1971 squeeze is of interest in its indication of DEC's response to increased competition. Olsen reported why this drop occurred in the 1971 Annual Report:

> Despite the fact it was recognized early in the year that the recession would seriously affect our industry, several important steps were taken to prepare for the future.
> - We continued to invest in new development activities, thus permitting us to increase the breadth of our product line.
> - We expanded our sales, service, and marketing forces and programs, resulting in improved services and the development of new markets.
> - We increased our manufacturing facilities and developed new computerized production techniques to be in a better position to respond to market demands.

We are confident that our strategy has been sound and that, as a consequence, we are going into the new year in a stronger financial, product, and market position than in any previous year.

Management Today[5] expanded on Olsen's actions:

> In the 1971 financial year when the entire computer industry was in the doldrums—hit simultaneously by the cutback in government funded R&D and by the industrial recession—Olsen could have pulled in his oars, as did nearly every main competitor. Instead, he chose to pursue a policy of aggressive market-share expansion. Furthermore, he increased an R&D budget that is proportionately one of the highest in the entire computer industry. In consequence, net income dropped from $14.4 million the year before to $10.6 million.

> This show of strength was not lost on the opposition. Many small competitors in minicomputers, Olsen reckoned, would run for the hills. "I knew that investors were losing interest in small computer companies," he says. He knew also that a number of larger computer companies were thinking of going into the minicomputer field; a field in which, of the giants, only Honeywell is represented, and not too forcefully at that. Olsen figured that the combination of declining sales growth in the market plus DEC's flexing of its muscles would deter the giants.

> The strategy seems to have worked. "A lot of companies who were thinking of coming into our markets have dropped their plans," he says. Scores of small competitors were driven to the wall. "They made their competitors bleed to death," says an analyst. DEC was particularly aggressive in the 16-bit computer market. But a different security analyst suspects that this aggressive posture was after the fact and resulted from the company's miscalculation of market growth that year. Olsen denies this, saying, "It took a lot of bravery not to cut back."

---

[5] June 1972 issue.

Organization and management

A sense of informality and a distaste for a highly structured organization permeates DEC's management. This is due in part to the personal preference of most of DEC's managers, who are largely engineering oriented, and to the rapid rate at which DEC has expanded from 3 to 12,000 employees. *Management Today* characterized this feeling by reporting:

> At DEC there is greater managerial turbulence than in the typical corporation. The financial vice-president, in his previous job with a manufacturer of auto parts, spent a lot of management time predicting and refining the rates of return calculated on investment. At DEC this same calculation is done more casually and hastily. The turbulence and the frenzy build up in an atmosphere where the senior men all scurry about in their shirtsleeves, wearing plastic identification tags on their chests.

They strive to interact and interrelate free of hierarchies and excessive organizational structure. "We scoff a bit at structure," says Win Hindle. "And, we insist that if someone needs a job to be done he should go directly to the person who can help, though the bigger we get, the harder it is to keep that in force." He added that "Ken Olsen has insisted that we have open communications. Nobody does things in secret, off in a corner. There are no protected pieces of the company, everything is exposed and subject to being examined and questioned."

This desire for openness in communications is confirmed by Ken Olsen, who remarked: "We welcome proposals for projects from anyone in the company, ideally from the janitor on up." He noted one of the problems DEC has with this approach is instilling self-discipline in people whose projects have been accepted for development. Once resources are committed to a project, Ken Olsen feels that this randomness which invited the proposal in the first place has to be submerged to the demands of a formal development effort.

There is no long-range planning group within DEC. There is, however, an Operations Committee, comprised of the officers of the corporation,[6] which decides what projects will be undertaken.

An understanding exists among the employees that proposals are welcome. Proposals may include a new piece of hardware to be developed, a new marketing area to be investigated, or a new application or new software to be written. An emphasis is placed on randomness, on allowing individuals within the firm to develop and then propose projects that they may wish to manage.

Proposals are reviewed by the Operations Committee. If accepted, a project is funded and responsibility for its success is delegated to the person who initiated the proposal. Discussing the allocation of development monies, Ken Olsen states:

> We traditionally invest about 10% of our sales dollar in the development of new products. This investment will continue to increase in the future, but we expect the

---

[6] The Operations Committee consists of:
   Kenneth Olsen, President
   Gordon Bell, Vice-President, Engineering
   Al Bertocchi, Vice-President, Finance & Treasurer
   Winston Hindle, Vice-President, Group Manager, Large Computers
   Ted Johnson, Vice-President, Sales and Service
   Peter Kaufman, Vice-President, Manufacturing
   Andy Knowles, Vice-President, Group Manager, Small Computers
   Stan Olsen, Vice-President, Group Manager, Logic Modules

percentage of the sales dollar to be smaller as we standardize on a smaller number of product types that will be produced in larger numbers. Each year more emphasis has been placed on software development so that now about half of our development dollar is spent on software and the remainder on peripherals and central processors. The large library of software we have developed through the years is one of the significant advantages we enjoy.

Up to 1964 DEC relied primarily on a functional organization—engineering, manufacturing, sales, and finance. Rapid growth and frequent changes in products, however, called for more concentrated attention on each product line. So product line managers were added. By 1970 Ken Olsen states in the Annual Report: "We believe that a major source of Digital's vitality is its profit center structure. Each manager has total profit and loss responsibility for his product, including responsibility for design, development, and marketing. This system allows the maximum delegation of responsibility and helps foster individual enterpreneurship. Several new profit centers were established during the past year, and we have added more centers with the opening of the new fiscal year."

The main operations continue to be performed by the functional departments, each of which is headed by a vice-president. Fifteen product line managers (who report to three group vice-presidents) rely on people in these functional departments for the basic work of design, production, sales, etc. However, the product line manager is accountable for the success of his line. He analyzes competition; initiates product improvements; suggests pricing strategy; defines needs for software support, sales literature, customer service, and advertising; recommends distribution policy; makes sales estimates; and prepares an eighteen-month (quarterly) "business plan" showing projected income and product-line-related expenses.

In general, DEC has moved to a matrix organization. But, as already noted, a desire for informality and for quick adaptability overrides any uniform pattern. Normally, each product line manager submits his "business plan" (updated quarterly) to the Operations Committee. The sum of these product line plans becomes the company plan. Since the functional vice-presidents are members of the Operations Committee, they have an opportunity to review the general feasibility of the total projection. Much more significant for day-by-day operations is the coordination that occurs at lower levels. For instance, within the manufacturing department is a section for Advanced Manufacturing Engineering and Planning, and within the sales department are sections for Field Planning and Administration, Field Service and Customer Training, and Promotional Services. The product line managers (some of whom are vice-presidents) or their assistants work directly with such sections on developing and executing "business plans."

Management Today characterizes DEC as paternalistic:

> For instance, at Thanksgiving time Digital Equipment re-enacts a scene that industrialists liked to play a hundred years ago but have since given up in embarrassment: to wit, handing out turkeys to all employees. Next to the truck bringing the employee's turkeys, there is another truck parked in case any employee in turn should paternalistically give his turkey to the town's poor. Olsen despises unions, has little sympathy for failure (or for industries that fail and wither, as has happened to the New England shoe business), and keeps his personal family life sternly aloof from his business existence, a common enough trait in Britain but rare in the U.S.

Olsen strongly dislikes people who use their companies to build themselves as public figures; he scorns those industry leaders who make a hobby of issuing quotable forecasts and predictions. He wants a company that has a "withdrawn personality" and dreads the company's potential to build up stars.

The rules of the public relations game offend his practical, Puritan, engineering nature. He wants life plain, with the world of objects—what business is about, the commodities themselves—kept in the forefront of the company's collective sensibilities, by reducing symbol, image, and ritual to a minimum. There is no corporate dining room, "Because our customers come here to work. They'd rather eat sandwiches at lunch. They come here to see the equipment, work out the details, and then go home." "We aren't hung-up on having our names on spaces in the parking lot," says another executive. Instead, the ethic at DEC is one of craftsmanship and achievement; the elite are the engineering heroes who triumph in the world of things, who work on the frontiers of limitless growth potential and disdain the symbolic, the impalpable abstractions of management.

Olsen's views on DEC and growth

Ken Olsen expressed his thoughts on minicomputer development in a speech before the N.Y. Society of Security Analysts:

In the future we will see minicomputers in automobiles and other volume applications. These will probably be in the form of a whole computer on a single chip of silicon which needs little of the services we have to offer. These computers will be supplied by component manufacturers for $10 or $20 each.

We plan to continue to expand our advantages—high technical capability, software, peripherals, technical salesforce, software support, and a large service organization to serve that large part of the market that is dependent on these services.

In response to questions from the audience asking "If you look out three or four years, where do you see your company being in terms of volume? Do you see your company being a four hundred million dollar company?" he replied:

Oh, we never make predictions in the future. But, I'll tell you my philosophy. We set short-term goals, of a year or eighteen months. And, many of these we've got to make. Our general attitude on growth is, first, we want to do a quality job for our customers and our employees that we can be proud of and then growth comes automatically.

Although it sounds a little academic, it makes a big difference in how you operate the company on a day-to-day basis whether growth is the first goal, and quality comes second. Quality must come first. The only measure of quality I can think of without being too corny is . . . I hope I'm here the rest of my working days, and I want to be proud of what we've done each of these years. And then growth comes.

That's been our attitude from the start. And the growth comes easily then, but too many of our friends aren't with us anymore. They put growth first.

Now I always go back and tell our people, yes, but remember this next eighteen months we've got plans. We've got to meet them regardless. We're committed all the way.

Other questions asked were:

> At your annual meeting, I believe you mentioned that you were planning a 25% increase in employment. Based on your recent figures, you've already achieved that in the first six months of the fiscal year. We want to know whether you've set a new goal for year-end employment and what are the factors that have gone into raising this goal as I presume you have?

> Also, in the last years, Digital has been gearing its business more and more towards the end user and less and less towards the original equipment manufacturer (OEM). Do you believe that the profit margin potential of the end-user market is as great as the OEM market?

Olsen, referring to 1972, replied:

> During the first six months of the fiscal year, or the last six months of the calendar year, we had a large impulse of hiring we had to do. We're still hiring very significantly. But, we don't have any fixed number in mind.

> During the first six months, we increased employment about 30%. That's an ambitious program and no one can continue at that pace. I'm not sure that very many organizations have increased this fast when they've reached our size anywhere in history, except during the war, and yet made a profit. We're definitely not going to increase at 30% each six months.

> In answer to the second question, I'll address myself to a somewhat different area on the profit margin potential between the end-user and the OEM markets. The end-user, or turnkey business, was a relatively small part of our business. But, it is growing. In this as in other business areas requiring different approaches than those employed by other people, we naturally are very cautious. Our first concern is the customer.

> The difference between end-user and OEM sales is extremely difficult to break out; they all tend to be lumped together. Realistically, it doesn't make much difference to us if we sell 300 machines to somebody who sells to the telephone company. As far as we're concerned, it's the same thing. We make the same profit level on everything.

Later in the same speech, Olsen spoke as follows about the problems of rapid growth:

> We are now growing as fast as we can to fill the demand for our products. In the last six months of calendar 1972, we went from 7,800 people to 10,000 people, which is about a 30% increase in six months. We hired good people, and we have to turn down many good people because we just cannot absorb new employees any faster. This growth is expensive because new employees are often not effective for several months, and it takes the time of experienced people to train them. In some areas we could get more production for a while if we didn't hire new people.

> We made a conscious decision to incur expenditures for recruiting, relocating, and training new people, and this has had a material effect on our profitability. However, we are confident that these decisions are correct. We have to expand to meet the demand we have generated for minicomputers.

> We have also been building extensively. By the end of this spring, we will have completed 1,500,000 square feet in Massachusetts in addition to the old mill which

we still occupy. We have completed a 68,000 square foot building in Canada and a 73,000 square foot building in Taiwan where we have 500 employees assembling core memories, and a 158,000 square foot building in Puerto Rico where a thousand people produce modules and small computers, and a 130,000 square foot building in Galway, Ireland, where we now have 250 people.

There are costs associated with this rapid expansion, and there are also dangers. Assimilating new employees and maximizing their contribution quickly is a challenge. We have set up new organizations spread over larger areas, which means we can and sometimes do make mistakes. In addition, we are demanding a larger percentage of the production from our many suppliers. Failure on the part of any one of our suppliers for even a short period of time can very seriously affect our results for a quarter. And, any number of groups within the company can make mistakes with short-term consequences.

Management Today commented on DEC's rapid growth:

The successful management of growth, in DEC's circumstances, has required an enormous amount of restraint and self-discipline by Olsen and his top managers. The seemingly limitless growth potential stimulates a feverish atmosphere, in which there are continual claims on the company's finances and on top management's time; a continual barrage of conflicting market interpretations and new product development possibilities conceived by supercharged middle management. Through the years Olsen has faced an almost persistent criticism from some of his managers that he's too slow and cautious. "So many of the people who have been bold and aggressive aren't with us anymore. We've been quite conservative. It always looks to many in the company that we're growing too slowly. We've lost a lot of people because they felt we weren't growing fast enough.

"Some of our peripheral developments have been slower than some people would like them. The more intense pressures come from the technical people. If there is growth at 50% a year, that works out to only one new man hired every six months in a four-man department; and for some of these technical people that's not fast enough." Technical people want to realize their pet projects with maximum speed; they want their concepts to become fact, their dreams to turn into palpable, testable matter. For this reason, there is an almost permanent tendency for technical people to leave—either to start their own firms, or to join competing firms which are willing to invest greater resources in their area of speciality.

Ken Olsen has strong feelings about DEC and its place in the computer industry. He has little respect for firms that do not add concrete advancements in the marketplace. He is especially critical of firms that are dependent on others for their existence, such as those who offered substitute or replacement gear for IBM equipment. Olsen believes that firms derive a right to existence through their efforts at providing unique services and products to society. "DEC should not go after markets in which others are proficient, rather DEC should seek and develop new areas for computer applications."

Ken Olsen's foremost concern is the development and manufacture of good quality computers that meet society's needs. Growth is not viewed as necessary and is only the natural consequence of DEC's ability to manufacture a quality product for which there is a need. His concept of DEC corporate goals can be summed up as follows: "We want to do a good job, something we can be proud of. We want to make our customers happy."

Letter from a stockholder

An elderly DEC stockholder who has held a significant block of stock for over ten years has written the following letter to Ken Olsen. The letter arrived within the past week, and to date no reply has been made.

Mr. Kenneth H. Olsen, President
Digital Equipment Corporation
146 Main Street
Maynard, Massachusetts 01754

Dear Mr. Olsen:

At stockholders' meetings and other times in the past I have discussed with you the need for sound planning in a company like ours. I write you now, and am sending copies to other board members, because Digital Equipment Corporation is at a crossroads.

The fine record that the company has made in the past should not blind us to the following:

(a) Sales growth is slowing down.
(b) Competition will increase from other companies moving into our present market.
(c) Other companies are expanding capacity as we are, and as soon as capacity catches up with demand prices will fall.
(d) The drop in prices will hurt our earnings. When earnings fall, the price/earnings ratio of our stock will drop even faster. That means new capital will be hard to acquire.
(e) Also, a drop in dollar income will make the overhead of the enlarged plant hard to bear.

My question, Mr. Olsen, is whether the company is prepared to operate in a tough, narrow-margin, mature industry? You have publicly stated your preference for only short-range planning and for a loose organization. That kind of management may suit a rapidly growing industry but it does not fit the kind of future we now face.

I have seen many companies that became intoxicated with success and then fell on their face. We must guard against that danger, and the way to do it is through sound long-range planning.

As you know, I have a large personal stake in this matter. So I hope to arrange a meeting with you in the near future to discuss it more fully.

Sincerely yours,
/s/
Cyrus B. Old

SUMMARY QUESTIONS

1. Do you foresee any major hazards in DEC pursuing its present strategy? If so, what should DEC do to anticipate them?
2. Do you see any major opportunities that DEC is missing? If so, what should DEC do to grasp them?

COMPREHENSIVE CASE 7 / Missouri-Ohio Barge Lines, Inc.

This company, a regulated common carrier on the Mississippi River Inland Waterway System, has (together with its subsidiaries) pushed barges up and down the river from New Orleans to Chicago, Pittsburgh, Minneapolis, and Omaha for over half a century. The company is prosperous now. Within the scope of the opportunities available on the inland waterways, it can do many things. Some of these, its executives are now thinking about.

Missouri-Ohio has three main activities:

1. A barge line operating as a common carrier on the Mississippi, Ohio, Illinois, and Missouri rivers (see illustrations on page 693 and Exhibit 1).
2. A shipyard in St. Louis that builds barges used by the company's barge line or sold to other inland waterways operators.
3. A barge leasing company that owns barges and leases them on long-term contract either to industrial companies that have plants along the inland waterways system or to other barge line operating companies.

These three activities are closely related. The shipyard supplies capital equipment to the operating company and the leasing company, while they in turn provide demand for the barge-building operation. A high cash throw-off in some years from the operating company provides the funds for the leasing company's investment needs. Lessees who rent the barges may well buy new barges from the shipyard or work out operating interchange agreements with the barge line—thus increasing its revenues. Direct knowledge about barge users' needs as to size and design of equipment aids the design work done by the shipyard engineers and affects the yard's layout.

The firm's threefold strategy is a fairly recent development. Among the important considerations are: (a) the usefulness of this strategy for the economic opportunities in waterway transportation; (b) whether or not benefits are being realized; (c) the planning that may be needed to continue or modify the strategy; and (d) the provision of resources, an organization, and a control system to carry out the strategy.

THE LEGAL AND CORPORATE ORGANIZATION

Transportation operations are carried on through two legal subsidiaries—Missouri-Ohio Barge Lines, Inc. and Mississippi Line, Inc. Missouri-Ohio is regulated by the Interstate Commerce Commission and has operating rights on the Missouri, Lower Mississippi, Ohio, and Arkansas-Verdigris waterways. Through interconnections with other lines it serves Chicago via the Illinois Waterway and Minneapolis-St. Paul via the Upper Mississippi. Regulation by the Interstate Commerce

Inland waterways of the Central and Eastern United States. (Courtesy of American Waterways Operators, Inc., and Department of the Army, Corps of Engineers.)

Towboats and barges moving on the Mississippi River. (Courtesy of American Commercial Barge Line Company.)

Exhibit 1

Intercity Freight Carriers—Ton Miles and Revenues

(In millions of ton miles and millions of dollars)

Year	Railroads		Trucks		Pipe Lines		Inland Water		Air		Total	
	Ton-Miles	Revenue	Ton-Miles	Revenue [1]	Ton-Miles	Revenue	Ton-Miles	Revenue [1]	Ton-Miles	Revenue	Ton-Miles	Revenue
1954	557,000	$ 8,110	213,000	$ 4,737	179,000	$ 617	174,000	$282	400	$ 147	1,123,400	$13,893
1966	751,000	$ 9,751	381,000	$10,853	333,000	$ 941	280,000	$328	2,250	$ 503	1,747,250	$22,376
1980	1,026,000	$11,072	738,000	$23,545	710,000	$1,506	487,000	$385	18,000	$1,967	2,979,000	$38,475
Average Annual Percentage Increase, 1966–1980	2.7%	1.0%	5.0%	6.5%	5.5%	4.0%	4.5%	1.4%	17.0%	11.0%	3.9%	4.2%
Total Percentage Change, 1966–1980	37%	14%	94%	117%	113%	60%	74%	17%	706%	291%	70%	72%

[1] The revenue estimates are of federally regulated interstate carriers. Since a fairly large segment of interstate truck and water freight service is exempt from economic regulation, the estimates understate total revenues of truck lines and of interstate water carriers.

Source: American Trucking Association.

Commission means principally that Missouri-Ohio must accept all bargeload or greater traffic offered to it, that the rates for hauling traffic are made public and approved by the ICC, and that the line is restricted to certain territories.

If a carrier tows a maximum of three bulk commodities in any one tow, then this traffic can move exempt from ICC regulation. Bulk commodities mean freight that can be moved by shoveling or pouring. To take advantage of this bulk commodities exemption from ICC regulation, the Mississippi Line subsidiary provides a bill of lading for such bulk shipments. Those barges moving under the Mississippi Line bill of lading, provided they carry three or less bulk commodities, can be combined into one big tow with the Missouri-Ohio barges, despite the fact that other commodities are carried in the same tow under the Missouri-Ohio bill of lading.

Leasing operations are legally carried on through River Equipment Co., Inc. This firm was organized last year as a wholly-owned subsidiary of Missouri-Ohio Barge Lines, Inc. Its first act of consequence was to acquire eight small companies that had, individually, engaged in leasing barges.

In practice, Missouri-Ohio Barge Lines, Inc. has four main parts to its operating organization—which naturally differs from the legal organization. These are:

1. The barge operating division.
2. The shipbuilding division.
3. The sales division.
4. The finance division.

The rest of the case will take up these divisions one by one, describing their work and their individual contribution to the total strategy of the firm. From these descriptions will stem the conditions leading to possible modifications of company strategy or to changes in the plans, organization, resources, and control systems needed to carry out a successful strategy for Missouri-Ohio Barge Lines, Inc.

THE BARGE LINE

Providing and scheduling service

The transportation fleet now consists of 8 diesel-powered towboats with an aggregate of 29,640 hp and 263 barges of various sizes and types with an aggregate carrying capacity of 348,687 tons. The fleet includes 12 barges chartered from the company's Employees Pension Trust at an annual rental of $148,000 and 14 barges chartered from shippers on a month-to-month basis.

Scheduling uses the company's IBM 360 computer. Lists are compiled, with projections up to 60 days ahead, of the barges available at New Orleans to move north and at St. Louis to move south to New Orleans or north to Chicago. Information is constantly available from these projections as to the number of barges available at either point to make up a tow, and the date at which a tow is expected to leave from either point. Refinements of the computer projections due to weather or other unforeseeable delays in arrival time are initially added to the list clerically and are incorporated into the next day's predictions. The computer is also utilized to "build up" a suitable composition for a tow at either of the main assembly points, New Orleans or St. Louis. Once the tow of several barges has been made up, it is printed out on a specially prepared sheet and is constantly updated by hand as barges are either added or dropped en route.

In conjunction with a larger carrier, the company maintains a regular four-day service between St. Louis and Chicago. The two largest towboats are used on the St. Louis-to-New Orleans run because this is a stretch of fairly open, straight waterway with no locks. A third towboat is used on the St. Louis-to-Chicago run along the Illinois Waterway and a fourth on the Missouri River services. At present, no MOB towboats operate on the Arkansas or Upper Mississippi rivers (St. Louis to St. Paul), and any barges moving along these routes must be towed by other carriers. At present, MOB has very small volume on these routes. Owing to locks, the maximum number of barges that can make up a tow for either Chicago or St. Paul is 15.

MOB makes considerable use of towing from other companies, particularly to meet customer deadlines on arrival dates. It frequently happens that a tow must be delayed in order to obtain a better load, so barges that have an urgent deadline are then moved to another carrier. Cooperation so far has been both close and successful.

Revenue and competition

Exhibit 2 presents a listing of the company's share of total freight ton-miles on the Mississippi, Illinois, and Missouri rivers.

Exhibit 2
Total Waterborne Freight Ton-Miles on the
Mississippi, Illinois, and Missouri Rivers

Year	All Carriers (000)	Company (000)	% Company to All Carriers
Preceding Year	47,446,660	3,025,148	6.38%
Preceding Year	49,887,220	2,742,621	5.50%
Preceding Year	54,500,938	2,697,618	4.95%
Last Year	57,989,198	2,543,103	4.39%

Source: U.S. Army Corps of Engineers.

The decline of the company's freight ton-miles was due primarily to a reduction in the average length of haul for the company's equipment as a result of the elimination of certain long-haul routes that were not considered profitable. Furthermore, the company's total barge capacity decreased about 12%, primarily because of the retirement of older vessels. Starting last year, however, the additions of new barges to the company's barge fleet have exceeded the retirements of older vessels, with the result that the company increased its aggregate barge capacity by 19% this year. Next year the company expects to add approximately 55,000 net additional tons (an increase of 16%) of capacity to its barge fleet.

In addition to the economies inherent in water transportation, major factors accounting for the growth of inland water traffic include technological improvements in the equipment used and a substantial postwar migration of various industries to waterside sites. Modern diesel-powered and radar-equipped towboats are able to move large fleets of barges as single tows by pushing rather than pulling the barges. The largest towboats operated by MOB can move tows of up to 40 barges, with an aggregate carrying capacity equivalent to more than 1,000 conventional railway freight cars. Barge transportation has certain disadvantages, as compared with rail or truck transportation, that might be evaluated by shippers, such as slow transit time, larger minimum loadings, and irregular schedules.

MOB's operations on the Missouri River and the Upper Mississippi River between St. Louis and Minneapolis are generally limited, because of weather conditions, to the period between April and November of each year. Operations on the Illinois Waterway and on the Mississippi River between St. Louis and Cairo have, for the past five years, been affected between December and March by extremely cold weather and by low water levels between St. Louis and Cairo, with the result that operations have been curtailed or suspended for periods of from one to four weeks. In recent years the problem of low water and the question of whether the pattern of reduction in the water level of the Mississippi River between St. Louis and Cairo would have an adverse effect on future barge operations have received considerable attention by the barge transportation industry and shippers. The U.S. Army Corps of Engineers is studying what corrective measures, if any, should be taken.

The company's barge transportation operations are subject to vigorous competition, not only from for-hire water carriers, performing both regulated and exempt transportation, and from railroads, but also from the private carriage of shippers who transport their own freight by water. Because of the nature and the unit quantity of the freight, competition from motor carriers is negligible.

Railroads have published special "water-competitive" rates between water points that, in most instances, have been lower than their rates per mile for the same commodity between landlocked points. The company's transportation revenues have not been materially affected by such railroad rate competition.

Exhibit 3 lists competing barge lines, the tons of revenue freight carried by each, and their average number of employees.

Exhibit 3

Competing Barge Lines
Regulated Water Carriers Operating on the Mississippi River
System and Gulf Intracoastal Waterway

Name of Carrier	Revenue Freight, thousand tons	Average Number of Employees
American Commercial Lines, Inc.	5,739	159
Arrow Transportation Co.	2,485	104
Coyle Lines, Inc.	2,065	159
Dixie Carriers, Inc.	3,792	159
Federal Barge Lines, Inc., and Gulf-Canal Lines, Inc.	3,455	263
Igert	1,646	90
Ingram Corp.	2,428	88
Mechling, A. L., Barge Lines, Inc.	3,417	251
Midwest Towing Co., Inc.	2,400	81
Mississippi Valley Barge Line Co.	8,511	459
Ohio Barge Line	1,677	118
Ohio River Co.	19,070	731
Sioux City and New Orleans Barge Lines, Inc.	2,341	384
Union Barge Line Corp.	3,145	132
Warrior and Gulf Navigation Co.	2,537	192

MOB's barge freight revenues this year aggregated approximately $10,160,000, of which 30% was derived from shipment of iron and steel products including iron ore, 26% from grain, 12% from sugar, and 14% from aluminum ore. Other commodities included coal, fertilizer, lead, phosphate rock, rubber, and zinc. The ten largest customers accounted for approximately 65% of the total freight revenues; however, no customer accounted for more than 15%. About 27% of the aggregate barge transportation revenues of the company was handled under the bulk-exempt provisions of the Interstate Commerce Act.

MOB relies for a large part of its business on steady, repeat customers. About one third of its business is under contract. A major problem for the company is its lack of equipment, and as a result existing equipment is utilized pretty much to capacity. MOB was originally scheduled to receive 80 new barges this year from the St. Louis shipyard. However, this has now been cut back to 40. The sales manager feels that the new equipment needs of MOB are subordinate to gaining outside sales for the shipyard.

The sternest competition for freight tonnage is in northbound traffic. Southbound traffic on the Mississippi is normally pretty fully laden. Strongest competition for northbound freight comes from the previously owned barges of large companies such as Cargill, who have moved their freight down to New Orleans. They are prepared to pick up any bulk exempt cargo at very low rates (for example, salt or coal) to gain marginal revenue. Although MOB is unable to meet the rock-bottom costs of some of these private carriers, it can offer better, more reliable, and more dependable service. This is its major strength in combating this competition.

The sales manager sees good future prospects for MOB. He believes that river traffic will continue to grow and that the railroads will never be able to compete effectively on certain commodities. Furthermore, he believes that in an economic downturn, barge lines definitely tend to benefit from the desire of industry to cut back on costs. MOB's great asset in selling its services is its reputation for good, reliable service.

For five years the company has been providing special service for the temporary requirements of one customer, which accounted for revenues of $1,386,000 last year and was the company's largest customer in terms of freight revenue in that year. The customer, a large sulfur company, is expected to reduce substantially its use of the company's special freight service after next year. The company is unable to predict the reduction in freight revenue that may result.

Mr. McDonald, the Operations Division vice-president and head of barge operations, is not certain as to the termination date of the contract with the sulfur company to barge sulfur on the Lower Mississippi. In carrying out the contract, 35 barges ranging in age from 20 to 33 years and 4 towboats are used.

Equipment

In ten years, the company has spent about $17,571,000 to modernize its barge transportation fleet. Equipment disposed of during this period as being obsolete or not efficient had a depreciated cost of $2,816,000. The company plans to continue a program of expansion and replacement of the barge fleet and is contemplating adding 50 barges to the present fleet next year at an expenditure of about $4,100,000. Such an expenditure will be made from working capital to the extent available, supplemented by short-term borrowings if necessary, but without incurring additional long-term indebtedness.

Mr. McDonald states that his department spends considerable time in working out costs of operations with the sales department. These costs are worked out from historical data and are frequently updated. Thus, a standard set of costs for towing a barge between any two major points in the system is at hand. On long-term contracts an escalation clause is usually inserted to allow for cost increases.

The maintenance superintendent works out each year a budget for regular maintenance work and a budget for emergency repair work, for example, work necessitated by accidents. Estimates are then worked out and compared with actual figures on a monthly basis.

Maintenance work on MOB equipment is not carried out at regularly scheduled points in the life of the equipment or after a certain number of miles moved, but whenever "it appears to be necessary." The fleet has been slowly rehabilitated and modernized. This is especially apparent in towboats. For instance, 2 new boats can now fulfill the work between St. Louis and New Orleans that originally required 4 smaller towboats. The barge fleet is still undergoing modernization—there is in particular a lack of barges for carrying specialized cargoes. Mr. McDonald foresees a continued expansion of the fleet, with additions of about 40 barges per year over the next few years. He feels that more capacity is required, particularly for such areas as the Upper Mississippi where present services are thin. Mr. McDonald believes that his department has sufficient management personnel to handle a considerably larger operation.

The marine operations department is responsible for all running of boats, loading, unloading, docking, etc. Budgetary control is reasonably simple, wage rates are fixed by union contract, and fuel and supplies for the boats remain roughly constant and are easily calculable from historical records.

Rates for towing

A regulated rate must be filed with the ICC 30 days before it can become applicable. Common carriers on the waterways are allowed by law to agree on rates. Normally a consensus is reached by a group of carriers before any one member files a new rate with the ICC. A new rate must remain in operation for 30 days.

Competition on rates on regulated cargoes has been practically eliminated. Most rate changes are made to meet competition from railroads, or for other factors *outside* the industry.

On nonregulated cargoes, MOB usually adheres to regulated rates unless threatened by competition. In bidding for work against competitors, MOB will drop to a floor of about 120% of the cost of towing a single barge. The only occasion that MOB will drop below such a rate is when empty barges are returning from, for instance, New Orleans or Pittsburgh. Under these circumstances, a lower price may be charged to gain marginal revenue.

Employees and labor relations

At present, the company employs 930 persons, 660 in the shipyards and 270 in transportation operations. Approximately 800 of these employees belong to five labor unions. The relations of the company with its employees have generally been satisfactory. The company has six agreements with the five labor unions, two of which expire this year, two next year, and two in three years.

One of the advantages of the modern, high-power towboat is that it drastically reduces boat labor costs per ton-mile of cargo. As few as 17 men can now handle the larger towboats. Smaller towboats usually require at least as many men. Wages, food, and fringe benefits may run as high as $17,000 per year for a deckhand.

Attempts to reduce the number of men per vessel have met strong union opposition. However, the advent on the river of many nonunion ships that began to undercut the unionized ships because of lower wage rates helped to soften the union approach, and it is now possible to come to agreements with the labor unions to reduce the number of crew. Fairly good working conditions and pay as well as the fact that large groups of towboat workers can rarely be covered in one place have made organizing a very difficult task for the unions, and the number of jobs carried out under union contracts has seen a decline in recent years.

Mr. McDonald states that MOB would like to reduce the towboat crews still further, and that he will pressure towards this in labor contract negotiations. Since the crews carry out some maintenance work on the boats while they are actually in operation, he does not wish to reduce the crews to as few as 12 men, as certain operators are doing. Mr. McDonald has not worked out exactly what number of men MOB would regard as optimum.

Exhibit 4 presents a summary of direct operating expenses for waterline barge operations.

Exhibit 4

**Waterline Direct Operating
Expense Statement Summary
Barge Line Operations, Current Year
(In thousands)**

Crew Wages	$ 556
Accrued Time Off	315
Compensation and Liability Insurance	207
Taxes on Wages	37
Welfare and Pension	48
Crew Travel	13
Fuel	509
Lubrication	73
Food	66
Charter Rents	105
Per Diem on Barges, Dr.	93
Damage Repairs	169
Maintenance	884
Operating Supplies	157
Outside Towing	1,844
Equipment Rentals	722

	Preceding Year	Preceding Year	Preceding Year	Last Year	Current Year
Maintenance Expense	$968	$616	$651	$791	$884
Damage Repairs	564	189	347	314	169

SHIPYARD OPERATIONS AND SALES

The Shipyard Division of MOB is headed up by Mr. Edwards, a vice-president. His responsibility is both for building new barges and for repairing or refurbishing old ones.

The shipyard does work for the barge lines and the leasing divisions of MOB as well as for outside customers.

New barge sales depend upon general business conditions as well as competitors' actions; thus sales fluctuate from year to year. Vessel repair business volume is more stable. The market for new barge and repair sales includes most of the operators on the inland waterways. No one customer, however, accounted for more than 8% of aggregate construction and repair sales during the past three years.

Vessel construction and repair

The company is one of the leading designers and largest builders of barges of various types and of specialized equipment such as caissons, dry docks, and dredges. It has designed and built vessels for inland waterway carriers and for many leading corporations in the petroleum, steel, chemical, and other industries operating their own equipment on the waterways. In the barge construction field the company has developed a reputation as a designer and builder of dry cargo barges.

The vessel construction facilities are operated on an assembly line basis. At normal operating capacity, the shipyard is presently able to complete 8 standard 195 feet by 35 feet dry cargo barges per month. By adding new facilities at an estimated cost of $250,000 (to be expended from working capital) and changing assembly line operations, the company expects to increase such capacity to 10 barges per month. Construction of specialized barges and other equipment requires varying periods of time depending upon the size of the hulls and the complexity of the design. The level of construction has ranged from a low of $2,500,000 to a high of $5,000,000, including construction for the company at cost. The company has a backlog of new construction of $1,900,000, not including construction to be performed at cost for the company amounting to $3,070,000.

The company's shipyard is strategically located to service its repair customers. The St. Louis shipyard on the Mississippi River is only a few miles from the mouth of the Missouri and Illinois waterways.

The company's engineering successes are both in products and in production methods. Apart from the general reputation for turning out a good high-quality product, the firm has frequently been an industry leader in innovative characteristics. An early success in the manufacture of vessels was the all-welded barge. This gave the company an early good start. It was also the first to introduce the "assembly line" concept of vessel production, whereby the vessel is moved on rollers along an assembly line as each stage is completed. This allows specialized men and equipment to be kept in one place in the yard. Covered hopper barges and "easy-roll" covers were other innovations.

Competition

A number of shipyards compete in various aspects of the river shipyard industry. Seven other inland river shipyards are major competitors. Only a few competitors have dry dock facilities like those of MOB for repairs below waterline.

The price of a new barge depends on the type. The standard all-purpose barges at present under construction in the yard sell for about $95,000. There is considerable price warfare on barges, which are fairly standard equipment.

Sales

Mr. Drew, the present chairman of the board, originally headed the sales work. Later the job passed to Captain Rand, the president, and then, as the company grew, to Mr. Robbins, the Engineering Department manager in the Shipyard Division. With further expansion, Mr. Hastings became the barge sales manager in the Sales Division.

Since many of the common carriers have their own boatyards, most sales are made to contract carriers, Mr. Hastings views the major problem to be that of selling potential customers on the benefits of paying a premium price. Most contacts are with nontechnical people; thus engineering criteria alone are insufficient to clinch the sale. Another problem is that the higher-priced, higher-quality barge is harder to sell to the larger buyers. In this case, the purchaser, whoever he may be in the company, will have to sell his arguments for a higher-priced vessel to his own supervisors. With the smaller companies, Mr. Hastings is better able to sell direct to the highest level of management and thus clinch the sale at the outset.

Once a sale has been made, Mr. Hastings has little more to do with it, apart from acting as liaison man between the customer and the Engineering Department if necessary.

All the executive officers of MOB take any possible opportunity to press home a potential sale. Mr. Hastings' comment is that the engineering and production people are sometimes too production-oriented. They are overeager to sell what they regard as the best product, rather than what the customer asks for.

Mr. Hastings does not set prices. This is normally done by Captain Rand after he receives cost estimates from the Engineering Department. The method of pricing is flexible to allow for general business conditions, the need of the customer, the history of relations with that customer, and any knowledge of competitive bids. Attempting to obtain such knowledge is also part of Mr. Hastings' job. Under certain circumstances a boat may be sold at cost—if, for instance, the company is trying to build up relations with a new customer.

Mr. Hastings sums up his job as consisting in large part of maintaining personal contacts with appropriate people, either by attending trade conferences, boat christenings, and similar events at which people from the industry tend to congregate or by personal calls. Recently he has found that he is unable to make all the personal calls he would like to make. He does not believe that he needs an assistant, however, for the yard has an 18 months' backlog and more orders could not be accepted. His activity keeps the yard full.

Resources

Mr. Edwards, the Shipyard Division vice-president, has been with MOB for 38 years. He states his responsibility as covering all production of barges. Mr. Edwards has great admiration for Mr. Drew and believes that most of the company's engineering and production successes are due to Mr. Drew's foresight and willingness to accept good new ideas.

Organization in the shipyard is largely along functional lines. There is a yard superintendent, and there are superintendents for each of the following areas: steel yard, welding, electrical, machine pipe, and painting.

Mr. Edwards states that most of the equipment in the shipyard is fairly old. He believes that little equipment has been produced in recent years that is substantially more efficient than that which he is already using. The problem is not obsolete methods but high maintenance costs. High maintenance time tends to slow down operations. No big program of capital expenditure is contemplated for the shipyard, but the company is trying to improve the efficiency of existing equipment by making modifications in the yard.

One of the problems of barge production is that certain types of barges require special tools. MOB is never sure how many barges of a particular type will eventually be produced. Thus, although the company never refuses orders for barges, prices frequently are raised on a small number of specialized barges to cover retooling costs. Mr. Edwards states that there are no written work-flow procedures.

Mr. Edwards says that Mr. Drew takes considerable interest in the shipbuilding part of the operations.

Mr. Edwards believes that he can always produce people to fill responsible positions from within the yard, although this has given him some headaches. He states that outside people have never been brought into the production side; promotion is always from within. He believes that he has significant good people in charge in the yard at the moment, and he feels that he often cannot count on an outsider in a responsible position.

The yard has been unionized since 1945. In labor contract negotiations, Mr. Edwards carries out the negotiations along with the labor relations officer, Mr. Manning, and a labor relations lawyer. Mr. Edwards confers with Mr. Drew before undertaking labor negotiations. Mr. Manning handles all labor disputes in the yard.

Mr. Edwards believes that the difficulties in obtaining skilled shipworkers, welders, and fitters are locational. St. Louis is not a big shipbuilding center; thus, there is not a reservoir of people with these talents. To try to solve this problem, the shipyard has increasingly tried to attract young people out of vocational school. It spends 4 to 6 years training them. Mr. Edwards has found that his foremen are often poor teachers and that he has to carefully select the foremen to whom he sends the new recruits for training. The turnover rate of these people is particularly high; about 90% quit. Mr. Edwards puts this down to the hard and unpleasant work of the shipyard, plus the fact that he feels that the degeneration of American society results in its producing people who do not have the drive and determination to get ahead. Government welfare practices contribute to this, he feels.

Captain Rand feels that the equipment in the yard is fairly satisfactory. The policy is to spend money for new equipment only if it saves time in the building operation, that is, if it would be a superior piece of equipment for the operation. There are no plans for any large-scale capital outlays on shipyard equipment. Although barge-building costs are generally believed to be higher than they should be, Captain Rand feels that existing equipment and methods are as good as any available in the industry at present. Each superintendent makes requisitions for new equipment or machines for his area of operation. These then have to be approved by Captain Rand. He believes that a roof over the yard would be advantageous, but that the advantages will not justify the cost.

Mr. Edwards, the Shipyard Division vice-president, states that the sales manager tends to promise things that the Engineering Department might not be able to deliver or can deliver only at a high cost. This, in Mr. Edwards' view, is a major contributor to barge-building costs. He respects Mr. Hastings, the barge sales manager, as a fine salesman for the nontechnical, contact-type work. However, before anything definite can be accomplished, he must take an engineer along (frequently Mr. Robbins) to get exact specifications and engineering details of what is required. Mr. Hastings, of course, cannot quote prices, although he can and does give potential customers an idea of price.

LEASING EQUIPMENT

One of the two subsidiaries, River Equipment Company, leases barges for private transportation by shippers of their own cargo. This is not subject to regulation by the ICC.

River Equipment Company also leases barges to other transportation firms, which are generally contract carriers that tow a limited number of bulk commodities for one or a few shippers.

Arrangements have been made with a bank for River Equipment Company to borrow the money required to finance the company's barge customers by utilizing the credit of River Equipment Company and its subsidiary financing companies. Next year, the financing companies will purchase approximately $2,000,000 of equipment, which will be financed under such arrangements. Under such contracts the equipment is purchased by River Equipment Company or its subsidiaries and is leased to the operators with options to purchase.

River Equipment Company now has long-term charter-purchase contracts with customers for 2 towboats and 18 barges. In addition, charter-purchase contracts have been obtained from customers covering 22 barges on a long-term basis and 10 barges on a year-to-year basis. These 32 barges are scheduled for delivery next year.

Executives view the rental business as both necessary and desirable. The company is in the unique position of being able to construct the rented equipment, and then, if payments are defaulted, to take it back and use it for MOB.

ORGANIZATION AND PERSONNEL

Exhibit 5 on the opposite page presents an organization diagram for Missouri-Ohio Barge Lines, Inc. showing the line of command, the divisions, and the personnel.

Sales Division

This division is responsible for sales of barging transportation, repairs, and new barges, and for setting rates for commodities hauled.

The field sales force solicits new business and maintains personal contact with existing customers. Its size has been reduced greatly in recent years as the line increased its minimum quantity from carload to bargeload. Salesmen are paid a salary and a year-end bonus when the chairman, Mr. Drew, determines that the line has "done well."

At the moment, a rate war is going on in the towing business. However, Mr. Calender, the Sales Division general manager, is confident that the more powerful and more economical towboats of MOB will enable it to eventually win out over small carriers. MOB is required to publish towage charges with the ICC since it is a common carrier. Small exempt carriers are not certificated common carriers. Until now, they have been able to undercut MOB.

Mr. Calender has spent 40 years with MOB, all of it in the Sales Division. He believes that there is an adequate group of people in his division to handle present traffic plus some expansion. He notes that one or two recent high school graduates are now being given jobs in different departments in rotation and believes that this is a sound development toward solving any future executive problems.

Exhibit 5

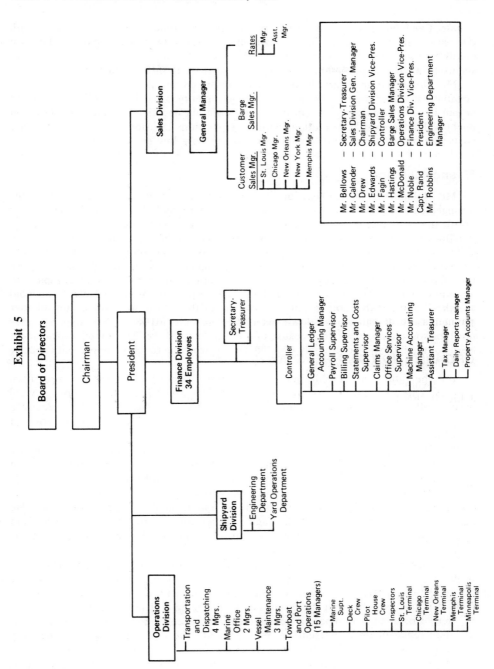

Mr. Bellows — Secretary-Treasurer
Mr. Calender — Sales Division Gen. Manager
Mr. Drew — Chairman
Mr. Edwards — Shipyard Division Vice-Pres.
Mr. Fagin — Controller
Mr. Hastings — Barge Sales Manager
Mr. McDonald — Operations Division Vice-Pres.
Mr. Noble — Finance Div. Vice-Pres.
Capt. Rand — President
Mr. Robbins — Engineering Department Manager

Mr. Calender spends a considerable amount of his time on personal contacts with company representatives to insure maintenance of goodwill. He personally keeps a monthly record of freight shipped by MOB for each company served. Any company that seems to have dropped off its use of MOB services is then contacted.

Mr. Drew, the chairman, is kept closely informed and actually participates in the negotiations of the largest contracts. Mr. Drew sometimes decides what final bid should be put in for a large contract. On the largest contract negotiations, the Sales Division might well have close consultations with the Operations Division to determine whether costs can be cut lower and to ascertain exactly how low a bid can be made.

Finance Division

Mr. Noble, the Finance Division vice-president, has responsibility for the financing arrangements of MOB and all its legal subsidiaries. Originally the accounting systems of MOB, the shipyard, and the leasing company were kept separate. Mr. Noble believes that one of the more pressing problems of the company is lack of management personnel and lack of young talent. He hopes that some sort of training program will be started to encourage promising young people to enter the company. He has already encouraged a program to bring high school students into temporary summer jobs in the company to attempt to build up an interest in it. He feels that the present managers have "grown old together" with, at the moment, little provision for the future. Mr. Noble sees another problem as the shortage of shipyard space. The present yard is unable to expand either north or south along the river because of other industry there. The annual replacement needs of the industry are roughly 600-700 barges, which is roughly the present capacity of the barge-building industry.

For the future, Mr. Noble believes that more barges are needed for specialized cargoes. One example is molten sulfur, for which MOB has manufactured several barges. MOB is not now operating any sulfur-carrying vessels since they require a separate tow. Mr. Noble believes that the margins are too low for separate tows at present.

Mr. Bellows, the secretary-treasurer, joined MOB in 1958 from Price Waterhouse & Co. He has been primarily concerned with the barge construction operations, but he did negotiate a $1 million loan for MOB for insurance companies.

Mr. Bellows' responsibilities are to find sources and provide funds, to keep an historical record of the company's progress, and to analyze and check costs. He believes that he, Mr. Noble, and Mr. Fagin, the controller, form a team with fairly fluid responsibilities in the financial operations of the company. Mr. Bellows also acts as liaison in certain legal and insurance problems.

Mr. Bellows believes that the company is financially strong at present. The major problem that he foresees is pressure for capital expenditures for new equipment in the future. Although Mr. Bellows believes that this can be met through retained earnings, he feels it is just possible that increased equity financing will be needed.

Bell, Brace, and Kemper, a consulting firm, recently completed a study of the eventual replacement of present top management. The consultants were particularly concerned with a successor to the chairman.

Mr. Bellows believes that the lack of good younger people in middle management is more pronounced in some areas of the company than in others. As an intermediate-sized company, MOB may have fallen between two stools—big highly-organized companies on the one hand and the small intimate companies on the other. Possibly insufficient attention has been given in the past to delegation of authority and responsibility. At present the company has many good people at the top and efficient workers at the lower end of the scale, but it tends to lack sufficient talent in the middle, in Mr. Bellows' opinion.

Captain Rand, President

Captain Rand spends a large amount of his time on industry affairs and has been instrumental in gaining support from various business firms—including competitive barge lines, railroads, and trucking companies—to lobby with Congress over transportation matters. During his period as president of MOB, Captain Rand has been concerned decreasingly with day-to-day operations and more and more with MOB's relations with the "outside world." His main concerns are dealings with the Interstate Commerce Commission, lobbying activities in Washington, contacts with the Corps of Army Engineers, and the Common Carrier Conference of Inland Waterway Carriers, of which latter body he is chairman. That body has conducted considerable lobbying and similar operations and is attempting to build up a favorable public image of the inland water carrier industry. It has 29 member companies. In this way, Captain Rand attempts to protect the interests of MOB by working for those of the industry as a whole.

Recently Captain Rand has been campaigning to improve the channel between St. Louis and Cairo, where the Ohio River joins the Mississippi.

Mr. Drew, Chairman of the Board

Mr. Drew graduated from college as a civil engineer. He began his work with a company in Pittsburgh, and later he moved to a St. Louis firm. Mr. Drew now controls a substantial plurality of the outstanding shares of MOB. Of the remainder, two thirds is held by the public and one third by company employees.

Mr. Drew believes that the company's success is basically due to its engineering talent. His policy has always been to shop around for good engineers who are about 35 years of age, already in fairly good positions, and stable, and to encourage them to work for MOB. It is much less common to hire a younger man and to develop him through the company. Mr. Drew feels that the company is too small to be able to lure college graduates to a first job. He believes that most professional men hired by the company tend to stay a considerable time.

Now in his 72d year, Mr. Drew is active in the company, spends about three fourths of each working day on its affairs, and has no plans to retire from active participation.

FINANCIAL DATA
Current data

Exhibit 6 is a consolidated statement of income showing revenue, expense, and income data for five years. Exhibit 7 is a consolidated balance sheet showing current assets, liabilities, and stockholders' equity.

Recently an engineering consulting company put into operation a system of allocation of man-hours to particular phases of the barge construction program. Previously man-hours had been allocated only to complete jobs, not to particular functions. These changes have already brought about cost reductions in barge construction.

Exhibit 6
Missouri-Ohio Barge Lines, Inc.
Consolidated Statement of Income
(In thousands)

	Preceding Year	Preceding Year	Preceding Year	Last Year	Current Year
Sales:					
Barge and Repair Sales...	$ 4,500	$ 4,300	$ 4,450	$ 5,050	$ 5,400
Transportation Revenues.............	12,880	11,535	11,400	10,913	11,645
Rental-Financing........	179	208	232	141	187
Total...............	$17,559	$16,043	$16,082	$16,104	$17,232
Costs and Expenses:					
Vessel and Repair.......	$ 4,015	$ 3,856	$ 3,875	$ 4,562	$ 4,650
Transportation..........	10,691	9,005	8,820	8,130	8,326
Rental-Financing (except interest)..............	74	94	96	57	72
Selling and Administrative................	1,664	1,470	1,452	1,420	1,511
Interest and Debt Expense..............	785	775	691	585	535
Total...............	$17,229	$15,200	$14,934	$14,754	$15,094
Income Before Taxes.......	$ 330	$ 843	$ 1,148	$ 1,350	$ 2,138
Estimated Taxes..........	140	327	415	450	895
Net Income...............	$ 190	$ 516	$ 733	$ 900	$ 1,243
Depreciation Included in Costs and Expenses......	$ 1,481	$ 1,457	$ 1,463	$ 1,338	$ 1,385
Cost of Barge Construction and Repairs for Own Account (not included in revenues above).......	$ 1,460	$ 260	$ 1,065	$ 600	$ 1,576
Net Income from Shipyard Operations..............	$ 82	$ (10)	$ 15	$ 200	$ 277

MOB operations are constantly surveyed by a daily expenditure sheet—the equivalent of a daily profit and loss statement. These reports are made up in the evening and are sent to Mr. McDonald (the Operations Division vice-president), to all officers of the company, and to Mr. Drew (the chairman). Comparisons are made with the same day's operations of the previous year. Formerly, a budget of expenditures was also worked out and compared with these figures. This is no longer done. Month-to-month running costs of the towboats are also carefully watched, as are crew costs.

The company has a high rate of cash flow, brought about by high depreciation rates on floating equipment. The depreciable life of a barge for tax purposes is 18 years. Since much old equipment still remains on the books, the average depreciable life of MOB's present equipment is about 9 years.

Long-term dividend policy is to pay out about 50% of earnings. Capital expenditures on new barges and on the newly acquired rental companies may limit dividend payments

Exhibit 7

Missouri-Ohio Barge Lines, Inc.
Consolidated Balance Sheet
Current Year
(In thousands)

Assets

Current Assets:

Cash...	$ 1,420
Accounts Receivable.......................................	1,507
Notes Receivable, Trade..................................	797
Expenditures on Construction Contracts...................	1,145
Materials and Supplies...................................	1,612
Prepaid Expenses..	78
Total Current Assets.................................	$ 6,559

Investments and Other Assets:

Capital Stock of Nonsubsidiary Companies (at cost)..........		232
Notes Receivable (vessel sales)............................		241
Other..		142
Land..	$ 420	
Floating Equipment...............................	22,312	
Buildings..	1,214	
Machinery...	3,156	
	$27,102	
Less Accumulated Depreciation.................	9,872	17,230
Total Assets.......................................		$24,404

Liabilities and Stockholders' Equity

Current Liabilities:

Current Maturity, Long-Term Debt.........................	$	406
Accounts Payable..		1,486
Accrued Wages and Benefits..............................		334
Accrued Taxes...		750
Other..		120
Total Current Liabilities...............................		$ 3,096
Long-Term Debt...		7,643
Unearned Transportation Revenues...........................		240
Deferred Federal Income Taxes.............................		1,407

Stockholders' Equity:

Preferred Stock, 7½, $10 par, 150,000 shares authorized and issued......................................	1,500
Common Stock, $1 par, 2,000,000 shares authorized..........	822
Retained Earnings..	9,696
Total Liabilities and Stockholders' Equity...............	$24,404

Note: The amount of deferred taxes represents the reduction in current federal income taxes payable due to the difference between depreciation deductible for tax purposes and that recorded on the books.

over the next 10 years. At present several new barges have been or are being constructed for the rental companies. A final objective is to add about 40 new barges to the River Equipment Company fleet.

The debt/equity ratio is now less than 1:1 and is not high for the transportation industry. More debt could be raised if necessary. However, limitations from indentures are such that any new debt must be accompanied by at least one-third equity financing. Mr. Noble does not expect that any debt will have to be raised for at least five years.

Projected data

Five-year projections of financial data for MOB are given in Exhibits 8 and 9. Exhibit 10 is a memorandum from Mr. Noble concerning the projected income statement.

Mr. Drew sees future expansion of the company as being mostly through the barge lines. He is now engaged in negotiations for the purchase of another shipyard. This has been precipitated by lack of new building capacity at the present shipyard. The potential new shipyard is located somewhere to the south of St. Louis. If the new shipyard is purchased from another company, it will probably be purchased outright for about $4,000,000 in cash. Mr. Drew is of the opinion that the high depreciation levels of MOB have generated large enough cash flows in recent years so that the company is in a position to pay cash. If a new shipyard is contructed by MOB in one of the Southern states (the alternative possibility to a purchase), it would probably be financed by tax-exempt bonds (available to encourage industry in certain Southern states).

Future of the inland waterway industry

Mr. Drew foresees a bright future for the inland waterway industry. He bases his forecast on the ability of cheap transportation to open up whole areas of the country to industry. Although industry moving to new areas may not initially use water transportation, it will still enjoy below-average rail rates forced by the river carriers' competition. His view is that this is an irreversible process. Furthermore, it is being encouraged by state and local governments, particularly in the South, to bring about development. In time of economic downturn, the water carriers may benefit as industry turns to low-cost transportation to cut costs.

Appendix A, which follows, presents a condensation of a government study of inland waterway transportation and throws additional light on the future of the inland waterway industry and possible future company action.

APPENDIX A

Transportation on the inland waterways [1]

Barge traffic on the nation's inland waterways over the past 15 years has been increasing at a rate much faster than intercity freight traffic by all modes, largely due to

---

[1] Information in this appendix is an abstract and condensation of the excellent study by Frank B. Fulkerson (Economist, Bartlesville Office of Mineral Resources, Bureau of Mines, Bartlesville, Oklahoma) entitled *Transportation of Mineral Commodities on the Inland Waterways of the South-Central States* (Washington: U.S. Department of the Interior, Bureau of Mines Information Circular 8431).

Exhibit 8

Missouri-Ohio Barge Lines, Inc.
Estimated Projected Income
(In thousands)

	Actual Current Year	Next Year	Year Following	Year Following	Year Following	Five Years Ahead
Sales and Revenues:						
Shipyards	$ 5,400	$ 5,500	$ 7,740	$ 7,740	$ 7,740	$ 7,740
Transportation	11,645	13,195	14,049	15,253	16,438	17,420
Rental Finance	187	600	700	700	700	700
Total Sales and Revenues	$17,232	$19,295	$22,489	$23,693	$24,878	$25,860
Memo—Own Vessel Construction	1,576	6,520	2,046	2,640	2,706	1,980
Total Volume	$18,808	$25,815	$24,535	$26,333	$27,584	$27,840
Income Before Taxes:						
Shipyards	$ 277	$ 660	$ 1,071	$ 1,071	$ 1,071	$ 1,071
Transportation	1,752	2,347	2,372	2,673	2,970	3,215
Rental Finance	109	265	320	350	380	400
Total	$ 2,138	$ 3,272	$ 3,763	$ 4,094	$ 4,421	$ 4,686

Exhibit 9

Missouri-Ohio Barge Lines, Inc.
Consolidated Summary of Projected Cash Items

	Next Year	Year Following	Year Following	Year Following	Five Years Ahead
Net Income After Taxes	$1,900	$2,180	$2,370	$2,560	$2,710
Depreciation	1,690	1,918	1,975	2,043	2,125
Cash Collections Long-Term Notes	628	—	—	—	—
Financing Companies' Loans—New Barges	$2,600	—	—	—	—
Cash Used For:					
New Equipment—Own Construction—Barges	$6,520	$2,046	$2,640	$2,706	$1,980
Shipyard Facilities	250	—	—	—	—
Debt Payments:					
Barge Line Loan	400	400	400	400	1,000
Finance Company Loans	280	448	448	448	448
	$7,450	$2,894	$3,488	$3,554	$3,428

Exhibit 10

Memorandum on Projected Income Statement
(From Stanley C. Noble, Finance Division Vice-President)

The projected income statements for the next five-year period have been prepared using this year's and last year's figures as a base.

The shipyard figures reflect results based upon orders received currently and an estimate of repair sales based upon past experience. The sales for the subsequent five years are based upon new construction of $7,500,000 in barges and $3,725,000 of repair sales. It is believed that these estimates are conservative and that they do not represent operating the yard at full capacity in each of the years.

The owned vessel construction next year represents 40 barges for the financing companies and 60 barges to be built at St. Louis for use in Missouri-Ohio's fleet. The owned construction in the next 4 years, consisting of 31 barges, 40 barges, 41 barges, and 30 barges, respectively, is for barges to be added to Missouri-Ohio's fleet that will be financed out of working capital.

Transportation revenues have been increased each year for the net increase in fleet capacity on the basis of revenue per barge now being realized by barges similar to the new barges being constructed. The projections include retirement of barges next year and later years so that in 5 years the barge fleet will not include any equipment built prior to 1958 other than the 26 units presently being used for the sulfur company contract. It is expected that this contract will be completed in 2 years or substantially reduced in operations. The projections assume that the contract will be completed, and the revenues estimated for this equipment have been calculated at 50% of the average revenue realized in the general transportation operations of Missouri-Ohio and Mississippi. As soon as more definite termination dates can be established for this equipment, we will seek to obtain long-term bulk contracts. However, the equipment can be used in operations on the Mississippi River Division.

The increase in transportation revenues will be realized from business that is presently being refused because of a lack of barge capacity. The increase in the subsequent years will require added sales effort to be realized, but with the continued growth of river transportation generally we expect that we shall be able to develop the increased revenues.

As previously mentioned, construction of new barges for the transportation fleet will be financed out of working capital. The company will increase its payments on long-term debt for debt to insurance companies.

The rental revenues from the financing companies are based upon presently signed agreements, and projections do not include any increase for the next 4 years. However, it is expected that these companies can secure rental contracts for 10 to 20 barges each year during the next 7 years.

It is apparent that there is ample coverage for maintaining the present dividend rate of 80¢ per share annually even after all common shares are eligible for dividends. This is further pointed out by the summary statement attached to the projected income statement.

Stanley C. Noble
Finance Division
Vice-President

the growing consumption of mineral commodities, development of more powerful towboats and larger and more specialized barges, improvements to loading and unloading facilities, and competition among barge lines for contract shipment of bulk commodities.

The Mississippi River and the Gulf Intracoastal Waterway, which together carry over half the nation's barge traffic, are major carriers of coal, crude petroleum, steel, marine shells, sulfur, salt, cement, and alumina. Greater quantities of these products will be transported by barge; however, oil pipelines and unit trains for coal are expected to limit increased barge traffic of these two commodities. Although congestion at certain locks is a current problem, the Mississippi River below St. Louis and other open-river stretches have the capacity to handle the increasing number of barges for the foreseeable future.

Pertinent data on island waterborne freight tonnage, carriers, and vessels are given in Tables 1, 2, and 3.

Table 1

Percentage Distribution of Ton-Miles of Internal Waterborne Freight by regulated, exempt, and Private Services, 1962–65[1]

Year	Million Ton-Miles	Percent Carried			
		Total	Regulated	Exempt	Private
1961	84,294	100	([2])	([2])	([2])
1962	89,613	100	20.4	59.1	20.4
1963	94,438	100	18.9	60.8	20.3
1964	101,924	100	17.9	62.1	20.0
1965	109,701	100	17.8	62.5	19.7

[1] Excludes coastwise, lakewise, and local ton-miles. [2] Not available.

Table 2

Vessels Operating on the Mississippi River System and the Gulf Intracoastal Waterway, 1966

Type of carrier	Companies		Vessels	
	Number	Percent	Number	Percent
Common[1]	45	5.0	4,109	26.1
Exempt	852	94.2	11,574	73.6
Private	7	.8	52	.3
Total	904	100.0	15,735	100.0

[1] Regulated by Interstate Commerce Commission.

Table 3

Inland Freight Tonnage
(Millions of tons)

Miles	Run	Tonnage	
		Downstream	Upstream
650	Minneapolis-St. Louis	4.0	5.0
250	Omaha-Kansas City	2.0	.3
400	Kansas City-St. Louis	3.0	1.5
200	Chicago-Peoria	3.0	15.0
150	Peoria-St. Louis	5.0	8.0
580	Pittsburgh-Louisville	8.0	15.0
400	Louisville-Cairo	8.0	23.0
200	St. Louis-Cairo	17.0	12.5
750	Cairo-Baton Rouge	21.0	21.0
120	Baton Rouge-New Orleans	17.0	10.0

Trends and factors affecting barge traffic

Towboats are becoming larger and higher-powered. The average towboat had about 500 hp 20 years ago. Today the average is about 3,000 hp, and several towboats operate with more than 5,000 hp. The use of more powerful towboats is feasible only on broad stretches of rivers, such as the lower Mississippi from Cairo to New Orleans.

Barges are also becoming larger and more specialized. The standard barge for dry cargo is about 195 feet long by 35 feet wide and transports 1,400 tons; the liquid cargo barge is about 295 feet long by 50 feet wide and carries 3,000 tons. Barges have been designed to carry such cargoes as molten sulfur, asphalt, cement, chemicals, liquefied petroleum gases, anhydrous ammonia, and cattle. Dehumidified barges have been developed by means of which moisture is pumped away from cargoes of steel. This equipment permits steel to be transported without costly moisture-proofing at the mill.

Ultimately, the rate at which larger barges and more powerful towboats can be utilized depends on development of channels and increased size of locks. There is no technical obstacle to developing larger towboats or using larger barges and tows.

A Corps of Engineers preliminary report has indicated the possibility in future years, beyond 1990, of supertows consisting of 36 to 72 barges, 110 to 150 feet in width, and 2,400 to 3,600 feet in length, on the upper Mississippi River system. Additional navigation depths in excess of the 12 feet now being projected should be considered in current planning, the report stated.[2]

Another development is the operation of giant ocean-going barge carriers. Lykes Brothers Steamship Co. expected to start operation in 1970 of three such carriers, each of which can transport 36 to 38 barges loaded with products such as molten sulfur, paper and paperboard, or unitized containers and general cargo.[3] Manufactured products may

---

[2] "River Problems Aired at Navigation Meeting," *Waterways Journal*, Vol. 81, No. 44 (January 27, 1968), p. 4.

[3] *Chemical Week,* Vol. 100, No. 11 (March 18, 1967), p. 46.

also be shipped by barge down the Mississippi River from inland points destined for export, using barge carriers for the ocean portion of the trip.

Completion of the Arkansas River project has added substantially to Mississippi River barge traffic. Mineral commodities such as petroleum, petrochemicals, primary steel products, coal, cement, and fertilizers are shipped to and from industries in the Arkansas Basin.

Mixed trends are apparent in the type of barge service used by mineral industry companies. Some firms operate their own equipment; others utilize barge line service. Peabody Coal Co. contracts for shipments of coal on the Ohio River and has subsidiary barge companies that operate on the Mississippi River and the Gulf of Mexico. Ormet Corporation ships alumina by Nilo Barge Co., Inc.; both companies are affiliated with Olin Mathieson Chemical Corporation. Cement companies generally hire towing services and ship cement in their own barges. Sulfur is moved by barge line under contract with producing companies. Cargill, Inc., an important factor in the salt and grain trade, has a subsidiary that operates towboats and barges. Other salt companies ship by barge line under contract. Some petroleum firms ship crude petroleum and refined products under contract and others have their own towboats and barges.

Data on the expected use of various types of carriers over the next five years are presented in Table 4.

Table 4

Tabulated Results of
Expected Use of the Various Carrier Types Over the Next Five Years
Total of All Industry Groups

	Number of Respondents (Base)		Expect That Over The Next Five Years There Will Be:			Carrier Not Currently and Not Expected to be Used
			An Increase	A Decrease	No Change	
Type of Carrier	Number	Percent	Percent	Percent	Percent	Percent
Railroads	(250)	100.0%	34.4%	10.0%	40.8%	14.8%
Truck Carriers	(250)	100.0	36.4	13.2	49.2	1.2
Air Carriers	(250)	100.0	20.4	1.2	45.2	33.2
Domestic Water Carriers	(250)	100.0	8.8	2.0	30.0	59.2
Express Companies	(250)	100.0	19.2	5.2	49.2	26.4
Freight Forwarders	(250)	100.0%	6.0%	8.0%	49.6%	36.4%

Domestic Water Carriers

Expect That Over The Next Five Years Usage Will:	Total	Food	Textiles	Wood, Paper	Chemicals	Metals	Machinery	Non-Mfg.
Increase	8.8%	20.0%	8.7%	—	6.1%	15.4%	12.5%	5.4%
Decrease	2.0	—	4.4	—	—	7.7	—	2.7
Remain the Same	30.0	28.0	30.4	34.5%	33.3	38.5	17.5	31.1
Not Currently and Not Expected to be Used	59.2	52.0	56.5	65.5	60.6	38.4	70.0	60.8
Total	100.0%	100.0%	100.0%	100.0%	100.0%	100.0%	100.0%	100.0%
Number of Respondents (Base)	(250)	(25)	(23)	(29)	(33)	(26)	(40)	(74)

Source: Clark Equipment Company.

Regulation and government spending

Competition between the various modes of transportation has received considerable attention by the transportation industry and government agencies. The late President Kennedy's transportation message to the 88th Congress included a recommendation that the present exemption from rate regulation by the ICC of transportation of bulk commodities by water carriers and of agricultural commodities by motor carriers be extended to all carriers. This would have eliminated minimum-rate regulation on about 70% of railroad traffic. Bills were introduced in the Congress but never voted upon. President Johnson recommended the imposition of a tax of 2 cents per gallon on all fuel used in transportation on the inland waterways. President Nixon submitted the same proposal (an original charge of 2 cents per gallon increasing to 10 cents per gallon in five years). Future legislation has consequences for the transportation industry.

The present mixed system of public and private investment in transportation in the United States is subject to three forces, as once stated by the Honorable Alan S. Boyd, the Secretary of Transportation.

1. *The importance we attach to freedom of movement—personal mobility.* This is a political right as well as a social value, and it supports the reality of a mass market over a vast territory, free of the Old World barriers to travel and commerce.

2. *Our system of private ownership and competitive free enterprise.* This very profound and pervasive approach in our society reinforces our dominant moral and ethical concepts. Though somewhat blurred in the operations of the carrier themselves, it is powerfully displayed by the great users, the shippers, as well as transport equipment manufacturers.

3. *The intervening authority of government—any level of government.* The classic partnership that exists between public and private investment may be viewed as a form of subsidy. But the power to give or withhold a franchise or license, and the power to set operating rules and standards, is a far more fundamental role. Here government is an instrument for the protection of the community's total interests.

*   *   *

We do not have a very good understanding of the social effects of transportation. Most refinements in transport technology have long-lasting consequences which, for our future happiness and perhaps even survival, we had best learn to anticipate. We have hardly begun to sound the depths of the human implications of our transport decisions.

*   *   *

What kind of a community do we want, and what kind are we willing to settle for? We must set our own standards in this matter, dealing with transportation as a servant rather than a master.

If we are not able to anticipate all of the ultimate results of our transport investment decisions, that should not be used as an excuse for not making any decisions at all.

Spending for transport facilities by state and local governments increased from $3 billion in 1947 to $15.1 billion in 1970. The total for all levels of government in 1970, as summarized in the following table, is $22.6 billion, or nearly 6½ times the 1947 total of $3.5 billion.

Table 5

**Summary of 1970 Government Spending for
Intercity Transport Systems and Facilities ***
(In millions)

	Federal	State and Local	Total
Airways, etc....................	$1,238	$ —	$ 1,238
Airports....................	89	530	619
Airline cash subsidy..........	41	—	41
Highways....................	5,741	14,124	19,865
Waterways..................	400	420	820
High-speed ground transportation (including rail).............	22	—	22
Total..................	$7,531	$15,074	$22,605

* Amounts for 1970, partly estimated in the sources shown, are for a fiscal year in some instances and for the calendar year in others.
Source: Association of American Railroads.

SUMMARY QUESTION

Assume that you are a newly appointed director of Missouri-Ohio Barge Lines, Inc. To what key problems should central management give its primary attention? What do you recommend be done with respect to each of these problems?

SELECTED BIBLIOGRAPHY

Chapter 1 ■ Social Responsibility and Central Management

ANDREWS, K.R. *The Concept of Corporate Strategy.* Homewood: Dow Jones-Irwin, Inc., 1971, Ch. 5.

ANSHEN, M. (ed.). *Managing the Socially Responsible Corporation.* New York: Macmillan Publishing Co. Inc., 1974.

KATZ, R.L. *Cases and Concepts in Corporate Strategy.* Englewood Cliffs: Prentice-Hall, Inc., 1970, pp. 13-21, 97-108, 195-205.

Social Responsibilities of Business Corporations. New York: Committee for Economic Development, 1971.

Chapter 2 ■ Predicting the Dynamic Environment

Achieving Energy Independence. New York: Committee for Economic Development, 1974.

BAUGHMAN, J.P., G.C. LODGE, and H.W. PIFER. *Environmental Analysis for Management.* Homewood: Richard D. Irwin, Inc., 1974.

JOLSON, M.A. "New Product Planning in an Age of Future Consciousness," *California Management Review.* (Fall, 1973.)

ROSOW, J.M. (ed.). *The Worker and the Job: Coping with Change.* Englewood Cliffs: Prentice-Hall, Inc., 1974.

U.S. DEPARTMENT OF COMMERCE. *U.S. Industrial Outlook 1975, with Projections to 1980.* Washington: U.S. Government Printing Office, see new annual editions.

Chapter 3 ■ Assessing Company's Future Strengths

ANSOFF, H.I. (ed.). *Business Strategy: Selected Readings.* Baltimore: Penguin Books Inc., 1970, Parts Two and Three.

CHAMBERS, J.C., S.K. MULLICK, and D.D. SMITH. "How to Choose the Right Forecasting Techniques," *Harvard Business Review.* (July, 1971.)

KATZ, R.L. *Cases and Concepts in Corporate Strategy.* Englewood Cliffs: Prentice-Hall, Inc., 1970, pp. 209-220 and 268-278.

Chapter 4 ■ Selecting Company Strategy

ANDREWS, K.R. *The Concept of Corporate Strategy.* Homewood: Dow Jones-Irwin, Inc., 1971, Ch. 1-4.

ANSOFF, H.I. *Corporate Strategy.* New York: McGraw-Hill Book Company, 1965.

GILMORE, F.F. "Formulating Strategy in Smaller Companies," *Harvard Business Review*. (May, 1971.)

KATZ, R.L. *Cases and Concepts in Corporate Strategy*. Englewood Cliffs: Prentice-Hall, Inc., 1970, pp. 345-366.

Chapter 5 ■ *Marketing Policy—Product Line and Customers*

HESKETT, J.L. "Sweeping Changes in Distribution," *Harvard Business Review*. (March, 1973.)

PHELPS, D.M. (ed.). *Product Management*. Homewood: Richard D. Irwin, Inc., 1970.

PRESTON, L.E. *Markets and Marketing: An Orientation*. Glenview: Scott, Foresman and Company, 1970.

STURDIVANT, F.D., et al. *Managerial Analysis in Marketing*. Glenview: Scott, Foresman and Company, 1970, Ch. 7.

Chapter 6 ■ *Marketing Policy—Pricing.*

DARDEN, W.R., and R.P. LAMONE. *Marketing Management and the Decision Sciences*. Boston: Allyn and Bacon, Inc., 1971, Ch. 6.

MULVIHILL, D.F., and S. PARANHA (eds.). *Price Policy and Practices*. New York: John Wiley & Sons, 1967.

Perspectives on Experience. Boston: The Boston Consulting Group, 1972.

STAUDT, T.A., and D.A. TAYLOR. *A Managerial Introduction to Marketing,* 2nd ed. Englewood Cliffs: Prentice-Hall, Inc., 1970, Ch. 27-29.

Chapter 7 ■ *Marketing Mix Policy*

BORDEN, NEIL H. "The Concept of the Marketing Mix" in P.M. Holmes, *Market Research: Principles and Readings,* 2d ed. Cincinnati: South-Western Publishing Co., 1966, pp. 27-34.

DARDEN, W.R., and R.P. LAMONE. *Marketing. Management and the Decision Sciences*. Boston: Allyn and Bacon, Inc., 1971, Ch. 7.

PRESTON, L.E. *Markets and Marketing*. Glenview: Scott, Foresman and Conípany, 1970, Ch. 9-12.

SCHOEFFLER, S., R.D. BUZZELL, and D.F. HEANY. "Impact of Strategic Planning on Profit Performance," *Harvard Business Review*. (March, 1974.)

STAUDT, T.A., and D.A. TAYLOR. *A Managerial Approach to Marketing,* 2nd ed. Englewood Cliffs: Prentice-Hall, Inc., 1970, Ch. 23 and 24.

Chapter 8 ■ *Research and Development Policy*

LANFORD, H.W. *Technological Forecasting Methodologies*. New York: American Management Associations, 1972.

LESLEY, K. L. "Subcontracting New-Product Development," *Management Review*, (March, 1973.)

MOORE, F.G. *Production Management,* 6th ed. Homewood: Richard D. Irwin, Inc., 1973, Ch. 11 and 12.

ROMAN, D.D. *Research & Development Management*. New York: Appleton-Century-Crofts, 1968.

Chapter 9 ■ *Production Policy*

BUFFA, E.S. *Modern Production Management,* 4th ed. New York: John Wiley & Sons, 1973.

MOORE, F.G. *Production Management,* 6th ed. Homewood: Richard D. Irwin, Inc., 1973, Ch. 3-10.

SKINNER, W. "The Focused Factory," *Harvard Business Review.* (May, 1974.)

STARR, M.K. *Production Management: Systems and Synthesis.* Englewood Cliffs: Prentice-Hall, Inc., 1972.

Chapter 10 ■ *Procurement Policy*

HEINRITZ, S.F., and P.V. FARRELL. *Purchasing Principles and Applications,* 5th ed. Englewood Cliffs: Prentice-Hall, Inc., 1971.

LEFF, N.H. "International Sourcing Strategy," *Columbia Journal of World Business.* (Fall, 1974.)

MEITZ, A.A., and B.B. CASTEMAN. "How to Cope with Supply Shortages," *Harvard Business Review.* (January, 1975).

PRATTEN, C.F. *Economies of Scale in Manufacturing Industry.* Cambridge: Cambridge University Press, 1972.

Chapter 11 ■ *Personnel and Industrial Relations Policy*

PIGORS, P., and C.A. MYERS. *Personnel Administration,* 7th ed. New York: McGraw-Hill Book Company, 1973, Ch. 14-17.

PURCELL, T.V., and G.F. CAVANAGH. *Blacks in the Industrial World.* New York: The Free Press, 1972.

STRAUSS, G., and L.R. SAYLES. *Personnel: The Human Problems of Management,* 3rd ed. Englewood Cliffs: Prentice-Hall, Inc., 1972, Ch. 18-20.

YODER, D., and H.G. HENEMAN. *Staffing Polices and Strategies.* Washington: The Bureau of National Affairs, 1974.

Chapter 12 ■ *Personnel and Industrial Relations Policy (Concluded)*

FRENCH, W.L. *The Personnel Management Process,* 3rd ed. Boston: Houghton Mifflin Company, 1975.

MYERS, M.S. "Overcoming Union Opposition to Job Enrichment," *Harvard Business Review.* (May, 1971.)

PIGORS, P., and C.A. MYERS. *Personnel Administration,* 7th ed. New York: McGraw-Hill Book Company, 1973, Ch. 8 and 20-22.

STRAUSS, G., and L.R. SAYLES. *Personnel: The Human Problems of Management,* 3rd ed. Englewood Cliffs: Prentice-Hall, Inc., 1972, Ch. 5.

Chapter 13 ■ *Financial Policy—Allocating Capital*

BIERMAN, H., and S. SMIDT. *The Capital Budgeting Decision,* 3rd ed. New York: The Macmillan Company, 1971.

BOWER, J.L. *Managing the Resource Allocation Process.* Boston: Harvard Business School, 1970.

PHILAPPATOS, G.C. *Financial Management: Theory and Techniques.* San Francisco: Holden-Day, 1973, Ch. 4.

VAN HORNE, J.C. *Financial Management and Policy,* 3rd ed. Englewood Cliffs: Prentice-Hall, Inc., 1974, Ch. 4.

Chapter 14 ■ Financial Policy—Sources of Capital

HELFERT, E.A. *Techniques of Financial Management.* Homewood: Richard D. Irwin, Inc., 1972.

PHILAPPATOS, G.C. *Financial Management: Theory and Techniques.* San Francisco: Holden-Day, 1973, Ch. 11.

VAN HORNE, J.C. *Financial Management and Policy,* 3rd ed. Englewood Cliffs: Prentice-Hall, Inc., 1974, Ch. 13-15 and 20-23.

Chapter 15 ■ Mergers and Acquisitions

BEMAN, L. "What We Learned from the Great Merger Frenzy," *Fortune.* April, 1973.

HERVEY, J.L., and A. NEWGARDEN. *Management Guides to Mergers and Acquisitions.* New York: John Wiley & Sons, 1969.

HOWELL, R. "Plan to Integrate Your Acquisitions," *Harvard Business Review.* (November, 1970.)

VAN HORNE, J.C. *Financial Management and Policy,* 3rd ed. Englewood Cliffs: Prentice-Hall, Inc., 1973, Ch. 24.

Chapter 16 ■ Matching Organization with Strategy

COREY, E.D., and S.H. STAR. *Organization Strategy: A Marketing Approach.* Boston: Harvard Business School, 1971.

KATZ, R.L. *Cases and Concepts in Corporate Strategy.* Englewood Cliffs: Prentice-Hall, Inc., 1970, pp. 501-516.

NEWMAN, W.H. *Administrative Action,* 2nd ed. Englewood Cliffs: Prentice-Hall, Inc., 1963, Ch. 9-10 and 14-17.

RUMELT, R.P. *Strategy, Structure and Economic Performance.* Boston: Harvard Business School, 1974.

Chapter 17 ■ Building an Integrated Structure

DUBIN, R. *Human Relations in Administration,* 4th ed. Englewood Cliffs: Prentice-Hall, Inc., 1974, Ch. 3 and 10.

HAMPTON, D.R., C.E. SUMMER, and R.A. WEBBER. *Organizational Behavior and the Practice of Management,* rev. ed. Glenview: Scott, Foresman and Company, 1973, Ch. 7.

LAZARUS, H., E.K. WARREN, and J.E. SCHNEE. *The Progress of Management,* 2nd ed. Englewood Cliffs: Prentice-Hall, Inc., 1972, Parts One and Two.

RICHARDS, M.D., and W.A. NIELANDER. *Readings in Management,* 4th ed. Cincinnati: South-Western Publishing Co., 1971, Ch. 17.

Chapter 18 ■ Board of Directors and Central Management Organization

LEWIS, R.F. "Choosing and Using Outside Directors," *Harvard Business Review.* (July, 1974.)

MACE, M.L. *Directors: Myth and Reality.* Boston: Harvard Business School, 1971.

MUELLER, R.K. *Board Life: Realities of Being a Corporate Director.* New York: AMACOM, 1974.

STIEGLITZ, H. *The Chief Executive–and his Job.* New York: National Industrial Conference Board, Personnel Policy Study No. 214, 1969.

Chapter 19 ■ Executive Personnel

GRANICK, D. *Managerial Comparisons of Four Developed Countries.* Cambridge: The MIT Press, 1972.

KELLOGG, M. *Career Management.* New York: American Management Associations, 1972.

NEWMAN, W.H., C.E. SUMMER, and E.K. WARREN. *The Process of Management,* 3rd ed. Englewood Cliffs: Prentice-Hall, Inc., 1972, Ch. 10.

RICHARDS, M.D., and W.A. NIELANDER. *Readings in Management,* 4th ed. Cincinnati: South-Western Publishing Co., 1974, Ch. 19 and 20.

SALTER, M.S. "Tailor Incentive Compensation to Strategy." *Harvard Business Review.* (March, 1973.)

Chapter 20 ■ Short-Range and Long-Range Programming

CLELAND, D.I., and W.R. KING (eds.). *Systems, Organizations, Analysis, Management.* New York: McGraw-Hill Book Company, 1969, Sec. 3, 4, and 8.

DENNING, B.W. (ed.). *Corporate Planning.* London: McGraw-Hill Book Company, Ltd., 1971.

SCHODERBEK, P.P. (ed.). *Management Systems,* 2nd ed. New York: John Wiley & Sons, 1971, pp. 443-482.

WARREN, E.K. *Long-Range Planning: The Executive Viewpoint.* Englewood Cliffs: Prentice-Hall, Inc., 1966.

Chapter 21 ■ Activating

CARROLL, S.J., and H.L. TOSI. *Management by Objectives.* New York: The Macmillan Company, 1973.

DUBIN, R. *Human Relations in Administration,* 4th ed. Englewood Cliffs: Prentice-Hall, Inc., 1974.

DUBRIN, A.J. *Fundamentals of Organization Behavior.* New York: Pergamon Press, Inc., 1974, Ch. 12 and 13.

LAZARUS, H., E.K. WARREN, and J.E. SCHNEE. *The Progress of Management,* 2nd ed. Englewood Cliffs: Prentice-Hall, Inc., 1972, Part Five.

SCHLEH, E.C. *The Management Tactician.* New York: McGraw-Hill Book Company, 1974.

Chapter 22 ■ *Controlling Operations*

BACON, J. *Managing the Budget Function*. New York: National Industrial Conference Board, 1970.

MOCKLER, R.J. *The Management Control Process*. New York: Appleton-Century-Crofts, 1972.

NEWMAN, W.H. *Constructive Control: Design and Use of Control Systems*. Englewood Cliffs: Prentice-Hall, Inc., 1975.

VANCIL, R.C. "What Kind of Management Control Do You Need?" *Harvard Business Review*. (March, 1973.)

Chapter 23 ■ *Managing Multinational Enterprises*

DYMSZA, W.A. *Multinational Business Strategy*. New York: McGraw-Hill Book Company, 1972.

NEWMAN, W.H. "Is Management Exportable?" *Columbia Journal of World Business*. (January, 1970.)

ROBOCK, S.H., and K. SIMMONDS. *International Business and Multinational Enterprises*. Homewood: Richard D. Irwin, Inc., 1973.

STOPFORD, J.M., and L.T. WELLS. *Managing the Multinational Enterprise*. New York: Basic Books Inc., 1972.

Chapter 24 ■ *Integrating Role of Central Managers*

BOWER, M. *The Will to Manage*. New York: McGraw-Hill Book Company, 1966.

PAINE, F.T., and W. NAUMES. *Strategy and Policy Formation: An Integrated Approach*. Philadelphia: W. B. Saunders Company, 1974, Ch. 1, 4, and 5.

INDEX

T

U

V